HP ATP FlexNetwork Solutions
OFFICIAL CERTIFICATION STUDY GUIDE
(Exams HP0-Y46, HP2-Z25, and HP2-Z26)

First Edition

Richard Deal
HP ASE Network Infrastructure

HP Press
660 4th Street, #802
San Francisco, CA 94107

HP ATP FlexNetwork Solutions
Official Certification Study Guide
(Exams HP0-Y46, HP2-Z25, and HP2-Z26)
Richard Deal

Published by:

HP Press
660 4th Street, #802
San Francisco, CA 94107

ISBN: 978-1-937826-58-1

Printed in Mexico

WARNING AND DISCLAIMER
This book provides information about the topics covered in the Implementing HP Network Technologies (HP0-Y46) certification exam. Every effort has been made to make this book as complete and as accurate as possible, but no warranty or fitness is implied.

The information is provided on an "as is" basis. The author, HP Press, and Hewlett-Packard Development Company, L.P., shall have neither liability nor responsibility to any person or entity with respect to any loss or damages arising from the information contained in this book or from the use of the discs or programs that may accompany it.

The opinions expressed in this book belong to the author and are not necessarily those of Hewlett-Packard Development Company, L.P.

TRADEMARK ACKNOWLEDGEMENTS
All terms mentioned in this book that are known to be trademarks or service marks have been appropriately capitalized. HP Press or Hewlett-Packard Inc. cannot attest to the accuracy of this information. Use of a term in this book should not be regarded as affecting the validity of any trademark or service mark.

GOVERNMENT AND EDUCATION SALES
This publisher offers discounts on this book when ordered in quantity for bulk purchases, which may include electronic versions. For more information, please contact U.S. Government and Education Sales 1-855-4HPBOOK (1-855-447-2665) or email sales@hppressbooks.com.

Feedback Information

At HP Press, our goal is to create in-depth reference books of the best quality and value. Each book is crafted with care and precision, undergoing rigorous development that involves the expertise of members from the professional technical community.

Readers' feedback is a continuation of the process. If you have any comments regarding how we could improve the quality of this book, or otherwise alter it to better suit your needs, you can contact us through email at feedback@hppressbooks.com. Please make sure to include the book title and ISBN in your message.

We appreciate your feedback.

Publisher: HP Press

Contributors and Reviewers: Wim Groeneveld, Kevin Richter

HP Press Program Manager: Michael Bishop

HP Headquarters

Hewlett-Packard Company
3000 Hanover Street
Palo Alto, CA
94304-1185
USA

Phone: (+1) 650-857-1501
Fax: (+1) 650-857-5518

About the Author

Richard Deal is an HP instructor who holds the following certifications: HP AIS Network Infrastructure, HP ASE Network Infrastructure, Cisco Certified Network Professional (CCNP), Cisco Certified Security Professional (CCSP), and Cisco Certified Systems Instructor (CCSI). Richard has worked as a network engineer, consultant, systems engineer, HP networking instructor, Cisco instructor (CCSI), and course developer.

Richard is a 25-year veteran of the network industry. He was the developer for the HP ATP Network Implementer Course and the lead lab guide developer for the *Migrating to HP Networking A-Series Products* course. He has also published several books, including *Cisco PIX Firewalls*, *Cisco ASA Configuration*, *The Complete Cisco VPN Configuration Guide*, *Cisco Router Security*, and *CCNA Security Study Guides*.

Introduction

This book helps you study for the Implementing HP Network Technologies (HP0-Y46) certification exam, the HP2-Z25 delta exam and the HP2-Z26 fast track exam. You can benefit from this guide whether you are attempting to expand your existing HP certifications or you have a former H3C, Juniper or Cisco background and want to become certified with HP. This guide is also a useful reference tool to describe, position, recommend, select, and architect an HP network based on customer needs in small-to-medium business (SMB) environments.

To pass the HP0-Y46 certification exam, you will need to demonstrate that you understand switching and wireless technologies and can implement a variety of switching solutions using HP switches and deploy diverse wireless solutions using HP MSM wireless access points (APs). For example, you should be able to install, configure, tune, and troubleshoot HP switches and access points (APs).

Note: In addition to helping prepare you for the HP0-Y46 exam, this book is recommended for the HP2-Z25 online exam for those who are upgrading from the HP AIS – Network Infrastructure [2011] certification. This guide can also be used for HP2-Z26, the online exam used for Fast Tracks from Juniper and the Cisco CCNA and CCDA certifications. The guide does not cover the server and storage technologies and cloud solutions that are briefly introduced and tested in each exam. To cover this content, HP recommends you take the *HP innovations for today's IT infrastructure* self-paced training.

HP ExpertOne Certification

HP ExpertOne is the industry's first end-to-end learning and expertise program. It delivers the comprehensive knowledge and hands-on experience you need to architect, design, and integrate multi-vendor and multi-service converged infrastructure and cloud solutions.

The ExpertOne program takes into account your current certifications and experience providing the relevant courses and study materials you need to pass the certification exams. As an ExpertOne certified member, you belong to a growing technical and professional network of more than 500,000 members. You can network with this unique global community using social media applications and tools to access professional guidance, expertise, problem solving, and best practices.

To learn more about HP ExpertOne certifications, including storage, servers, networking, converged infrastructure, cloud, and more, please visit: www.hp.com/ExpertOne.

Audience

Anyone can take the Implementing HP Network Technologies (HP0-Y46) exam, but most successful candidates have real-world experience implementing wired and wireless technologies using HP products and have also prepared for the test in a variety of ways. This study guide describes some of these methods and indicates where you can obtain further resources to prepare for the HP ATP – FlexNetwork Solutions certification.

Typical candidates are IT professionals who manage small to midrange solutions based on HP technologies including HP Reseller Systems Engineers, Customer IT Staff, HP Systems Engineers, HP Services Field and Call Center Support Engineers.

Minimum Qualifications

To pass this exam you should have at least one year experience in designing small and medium-sized networks with intermediate switching, basic routing and wireless technologies. Exams are based on an assumed level of industry standard knowledge that may be gained from training, hands-on experience, or other prerequisites.

Relevant Certifications

Once you pass these exams, your achievement may be applicable toward more than one certification. To determine which certifications can be credited with this achievement, login to The Learning Center and view the certifications listed on the exam's More Details tab. You might be on your way to achieving additional HP certifications.

Exam Details

The following are details about the exam:

- **Exam ID:** HP0-Y46
- **Number of items**: 68
- **Item types**: multiple choice (single-response), multiple choice (multiple-response), and pull down
- **Exam time**: 115 minutes
- **Passing score**: 66%
- **Reference material**: No online or hard copy reference material will be allowed at the testing site.

Preparing for the Exam HP0-Y46

This self-study guide does not guarantee you will have all the knowledge you need to pass the exam. It is expected that you will also draw on real-world experience and would benefit from completing the hands-on lab activities provided in the instructor-led training.

Preparing for the Delta Exam (HP2-Z25)

For those upgrading from the current HP AIS – Network Infrastructure [2011] certification, the five new networking skill areas that will be tested in the HP2-Z25 delta exam are covered in the following chapters:

- Chapter 2: HP Converged Infrastructure
- Chapter 12: OSPF Operation and Configuration
- Chapter 13: HP Intelligent Resilient Framework
- Chapter 15: HP Intelligent Management Center
- Chapter 16: Basic Network Design Concepts

Recommended HP Training

Recommended training to prepare for each exam is accessible from the exam's page in The Learning Center. To cover the server and storage technologies and solutions that are tested in the exams, HP recommends you take the *HP innovations for today's IT infrastructure* web-based training. See the exam attachment, supporting courses, to view and register for this course.

Obtain Hands-on Experience

You are not required to take the recommended, supporting courses and completion of training does not assure that you will pass the exams. HP strongly recommends a combination of training, thorough review of courseware and additional study references, and sufficient on-the-job experience prior to taking the exam.

Exam Registration

To register for each exam, go to www.hp.com/certification/learn_more_about_exams.html.

CONTENTS

1 Introduction

Overview of the Study Guide

The first goal of this book is to provide you with an introduction to the HP ProVision and HP Comware networking products, focusing on the ProVision switches, wireless HP Multi-Service Mobility (MSM) access points (APs), and the Comware switches. The second goal is to prepare you for common networking configuration tasks that you will be exposed to in small-to-medium-sized (SMB) businesses. And the third goal of this book is to help prepare you for the certification exam to obtain the HP Accredited Technical Professional (ATP) – FlexNetwork Solutions V1 certification.

Each chapter begins with specific Exam Objectives to help you focus on the topics required to pass the exam. The Assumed Knowledge section describes any prerequisite knowledge you should have before studying the chapter. At the end of each chapter is a Learning Check to test your comprehension of the chapter's topic. At the end of the guide, you will find a practice test to help you prepare for the exam, along with a glossary and an index to help you navigate the covered topics.

The following is a description of each chapter:

- **Chapter 1: Introduction**—Provides the reader with an outline of the book and details about what to expect.
- **Chapter 2: HP Converged Infrastructure**—Introduces the HP FlexNetwork architecture and HP Networking products.
- **Chapter 3: Basic Setup**—Introduces the command-line interface (CLI) of the ProVision and Comware switches.
- **Chapter 4: Protecting Management Access**—Explores password protection and the concept of restricting local and remote access.
- **Chapter 5: Managing Software and Configurations**—Discusses the bootup process, HP Networking device upgrades, and saving and restoring switch configuration files.
- **Chapter 6: VLANs**—Introduces VLANs, their creation and use, and the various VLAN implementations on ports: tagged, untagged, access, hybrid, and trunk connections.
- **Chapter 7: IP Services**—Reviews Dynamic Host Configuration Protocol (DHCP) server and relay implementation, the Network Time Protocol (NTP), and logging (including syslog).
- **Chapter 8: Introducing Spanning Tree**—Introduces Spanning Tree Protocols (STPs), including 802.1D, Rapid STP (RSTP), Per-VLAN Spanning Tree (PVST), and Multiple STP (MSTP).

- **Chapter 9: MSTP Configuration**—Explores MSTP configuration with load-sharing.
- **Chapter 10: Link Aggregation**—Reviews aggregated link implementation and load-sharing with link aggregation.
- **Chapter 11: IP Routing Overview**—Introduces routing components, static route implementation, and the Routing Information Protocol (RIP).
- **Chapter 12: OSPF Operation and Configuration**—Discusses Open Shortest Path First (OSPF) implementation, configuration, and operation.
- **Chapter 13: HP Intelligent Resilient Framework**—Reviews the HP Intelligent Resilient Framework (IRF) technology and goes over a simple IRF topology implementation.
- **Chapter 14: Mobility and Wireless**—Explores wireless communications and MSM AP configuration.
- **Chapter 15: HP Intelligent Management Center**—Introduces the HP Intelligent Management Center (IMC) network management product, how to access it, and the basics of using it.
- **Chapter 16: Basic Network Design Concepts**—Reviews basic switching designs, the technologies covered in this book, and how to apply them.

Note

This book is based on the HP official five-day course entitled "HP ATP – Building SMB Networks with HP Technologies Solutions V1." One advantage of taking the five-day course from an official HP Learning Partner is that you receive hands-on experience with the ProVision and Comware switches and with the MSM access points by implementing the technologies in a lab environment.

Prerequisites

This book is not an introduction to networking: you must meet specific requirements and have certain networking knowledge and expertise to get the most benefit from it.

Before reading this book, you should meet the prerequisites. These include two web-based trainings (WBTs):

- Getting Started with HP Switching and Routing (Course ID 00731204)
- Getting Started with HP Wireless Networks (Course ID 00731293)

The WBTs can be viewed in The Learning Center. Log in at www.hp.com/certification.

You should also have a solid understanding of and experience working with TCP/IP and its services. Assumed knowledge includes, but is not limited to:

- IP addressing and subnetting.
- Variable length subnet masking.
- Classless interdomain routing.
- IP services, including Telnet, SSH, TFTP, FTP, syslog, Simple Network Management Protocol (SNMP), and others.
- Exposure to command-line interfaces.
- VLANs.

For additional help, you can view HP Networking Fundamentals videos on the following topics:

- Binary numbering
- Open Systems Interconnection (OSI) model
- IP addressing
- IP subnetting
- Spanning Tree
- Routing
- Data flows
- TCP/UDP
- VLANs

These videos can be found in the My ExpertOne portal on the HP Certification website: www.hp.com/certification.

ExpertOne HP Networking Certifications

HP Networking solutions are built to deliver predictable performance, high availability, and security, using products and technologies that offer scalability, cutting-edge features, energy efficiency, and reduced complexity.

The HP ExpertOne program offers a full range of networking curricula, from beginning-level courses to Master Engineer classes. You will also find fast-track programs that let you leverage your current industry certifications from Cisco and other companies, building on the investment you have already made in networking education.

As a participant in the HP ExpertOne networking training and certification program, you gain:

- Access to robust courseware.
- Rapid professional cross-certification.
- Proven practices for networking interoperability.
- Differentiation in the job market.

You can benefit from this guide, whether you are attempting to expand your existing HP certification or you have a former H3C or a Cisco background and want to get certified with HP. The ExpertOne program takes into account your current certifications and experience, providing the relevant courses and study materials you need to pass the certification exams. As an ExpertOne certified member, you belong to a growing technical and professional network of more than 500,000 members. You can network with this unique global community using social media applications and tools to access professional guidance, expertise, problem-solving tips, and best practices.

Certification Exams

The HP ATP – FlexNetwork Solutions V1 certification is based on passing one of three certification exams:

- HP0-Y46
- HP2-Z26
- HP2-Z25

The HP0-Y46 exam is primarily aimed at administrators who are new to HP Networking products, and the HP2-Z26 exam is aimed at administrators who have networking certifications from other vendors, like the Cisco Certified Network Associate (CCNA) certification. The HP2-Z25 exam is a delta exam that will allow individuals who currently hold the HP AIS – Network Infrastructure [2011] certification to upgrade it to the HP ATP – FlexNetwork Solutions V1 certification.

To learn more about HP ExpertOne certifications, including storage, servers, networking, Converged Infrastructure, cloud, and more, please visit www.hp.com/ExpertOne.

To register for an exam, go to www.hp.com/certification/learn_more_about_exams.html.

Preparing for the HP0-Y46, HP2-Z25, and HP2-Z26 Exams

This self-study guide does not guarantee that you will have all of the knowledge that you need to pass the exam. It is expected that you will also draw on real-world experience and would benefit from completing the hands-on lab activities provided in the actual instructor-led training. The exams test the knowledge and skills necessary for an individual to gain HP ATP – FlexNetwork Solutions V1 certification. The exam questions are complex and demanding, reflecting the challenging nature of the tasks that the ATP candidate often faces in real-world HP network implementations.

You are not required to take the supporting course, although it is recommended, and completion of training does not assure that you will pass the exams. HP strongly recommends a combination of training, thorough review of courseware and additional study references, and sufficient on-the-job experience prior to taking the exam.

2 HP Converged Infrastructure

EXAM OBJECTIVES

In this chapter, you learn to:

- ✓ Identify components and elements of the HP Networking solutions (data center, campus LAN, and branch) and explain their roles.
- ✓ Identify and explain products and features in the HP Networking product line.
- ✓ Compare and contrast HP Networking solutions and features.
- ✓ Compare and contrast data center, campus LAN, and branch environments.
- ✓ Identify which HP Networking products should be positioned, given various customer environments and infrastructure needs.
- ✓ Identify and describe available tool sets for managing HP Networking products.

ASSUMED KNOWLEDGE

This chapter assumes that you have some familiarity with HP Networking product solutions, including the HP ProVision switches and HP Comware switches and routers. Knowledge of the configuration of these devices is not required, since this book focuses on that task.

INTRODUCTION

After completing this chapter, you should be able to understand the components of a converged infrastructure using HP's FlexNetwork architecture framework, which includes the following components:

- HP FlexFabric
- HP FlexCampus
- HP FlexBranch
- HP FlexManagement
- Software-defined networking (SDN)

An introduction to HP Networking products is also included. However, for details on the capabilities of the products, you should visit HP's website (www.hp.com/networking).

Note

A lot of technologies are introduced or mentioned in this chapter but are not covered in depth because this is an introduction to converged infrastructure. To understand how these technologies are used in a converged infrastructure in large enterprise networks, investigate technologies like Border Gateway Protocol (BGP), Transparent Interconnection of Lots of Links (TRILL), Rapid Ring Protection Protocol (RRPP), and Virtual Ethernet Port Aggregator (VEPA), to name a few.

HP FlexNetwork Architecture

The FlexNetwork Architecture is the basis for HP Networking's strategy for networks of all sizes—from global enterprise networks to small-to-medium-sized business (SMB) networks. The following is an overview of the FlexNetwork architecture.

A new dawn of technology innovation is driving unprecedented change. Mobility, virtualization, high-definition video, rich-media collaboration tools, and cloud computing are reinventing how businesses—and people—work.

Enterprises that can understand and successfully implement these innovations have new tools to drive business advantage and to build new opportunities in the global marketplace. When legacy networks are pushed to the limit, they become fragile, difficult to manage, vulnerable, and expensive to operate. Businesses with networks at this breaking point risk missing the next wave of opportunity.

Application-driven, service-oriented architectures (SOA) and virtualization have made the client/server model from the data center somewhat obsolete. Cloud computing also makes heavy use of server virtualization, which reshapes data center traffic flows and increases bandwidth demands at the server edge. According to the HP FlexNetwork architecture website, by 2014 network planners should expect more than 80 percent of traffic in the data center's LAN to be between servers.[1]

Efforts at flexibility can be hampered by legacy data center networks. They cannot provide high enough bandwidth and low enough latency between server connections to support highly mobile virtual workloads.

As business volumes rise, traffic levels are exploding. Virtualization has taken root across businesses of all sizes. Today, roughly 50 percent of all workloads are virtualized and Gartner expects[2] this to hit 75 percent by 2015 and to continue to grow beyond this level. Traffic within the server rack is expected to grow by 25 times. Immersed in technology at home, business workers have quickly acclimated to a rich-media experience and are using video and interactive collaboration tools. Soon, more than 25 percent of the documents that workers see in a day will be dominated by pictures, video, and audio. New video applications will push network capacity needs by four to ten times above current average levels.

Legacy networks, with their decade-old architectures, are likely to be overwhelmed by the steady growth of applications, virtualization, and rich media. Conventional three-tier data center networks cannot meet the security, agility, and performance requirements of virtualized cloud computing environments. The legacy three-tier network architecture is constrained by oversubscription, low bandwidth, and high latency—the exact opposite of what video collaboration requires. Mobility has quickly become a right, not a privilege. Soon, the combined installed base of smartphones and browser-equipped smartphones will exceed 1.82 billion units.[3]

The preferred way to connect will be through wireless LAN (WLAN) rather than through lower speed 3G or 4G networks. Workers need to access applications and content from anywhere to stay productive, and that means applications must be delivered flawlessly from a virtual data center to a virtual workplace.

Yet many enterprises have experienced disappointing results with their existing WLAN deployments because of a poor user experience and a network that does not scale to meet the increasing demand of mobile users. The embrace of smartphones and tablets at work will also break the traditional models for identity management and security that allow access based on a network port rather than on a user's identity. This is especially true for users that bring their own devices (BYOD).

Today's networks must be designed to meet the unique requirements of the data center, corporate campus, and branch office. By segmenting their networks, enterprises can more easily align business initiatives with the underlying network requirements. Companies can create functional building blocks to meet the requirements of the specific application or business service.

With this segmentation of functional building blocks, businesses can choose best-in-class solutions that fit their needs rather than being locked into a one-size-fits-all solution. By using standard protocols at the network boundaries, businesses can enable interoperability among the network segments and gain both agility and scale.

The FlexNetwork architecture and its functional building blocks (Figure 2-1) are key components of the HP Converged Infrastructure. Enterprises can align their networks with their business needs—even as they change—by segmenting their networks into four interrelated modular building blocks that make up the HP FlexNetwork architecture: FlexFabric, FlexCampus, FlexBranch, and FlexManagement.

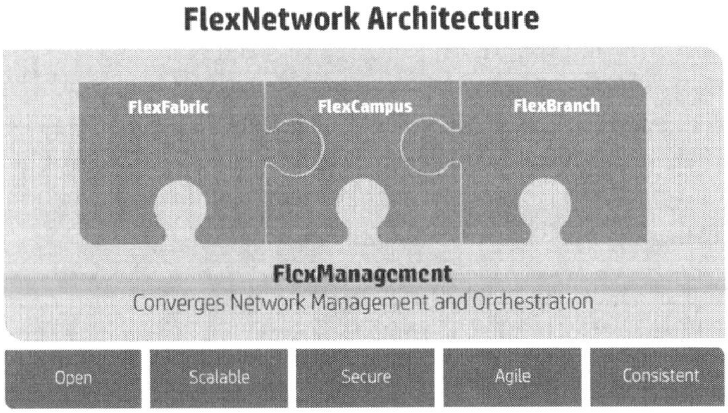

Figure 2-1. FlexNetwork architecture: Converged Infrastructure

FlexNetwork Benefits

FlexManagement unifies network management and orchestration. FlexFabric converges and secures the data center network with compute and storage. FlexCampus unifies wired and wireless networks to deliver media-optimized, secure, identity-based access. And FlexBranch unifies network functionality and services for simplicity in the branch office.

The HP FlexNetwork architecture is designed to allow IT to manage these different network segments through a single pane-of-glass management application, HP Intelligent Management Center (IMC). Since the FlexNetwork architecture is based on open standards, companies have the freedom to choose the best-in-class solution for their businesses. Figure 2-2 explains the benefits of this architecture.

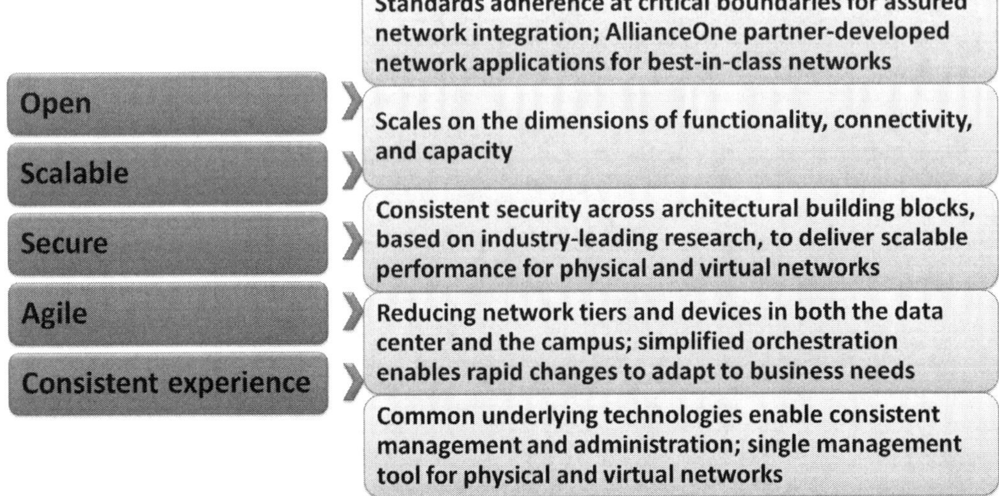

Figure 2–2. FlexNetwork benefits

Even with the shift to the cloud, the HP FlexNetwork architecture is ideal for supporting cloud networks. Enterprises deploying private clouds must implement simpler data center networks to support the bandwidth-intensive, delay-sensitive, server-to-server virtual machine and workload traffic flows that are associated with cloud computing. They must also be able to administer and secure virtual resources and to orchestrate on-demand services. HP FlexNetwork helps enterprises to securely deploy and centrally orchestrate video, cloud, and mobile-optimized architectures that scale from the data center to the network edge.

Trend 1: Data Center Consolidation and Cloud Computing

In the past, a campus had most of its applications running on local servers. Today, the trend is to consolidate all servers and services in a single, centralized data center or to locate the services in a private cloud. See Figure 2-3 for an illustration of this change.

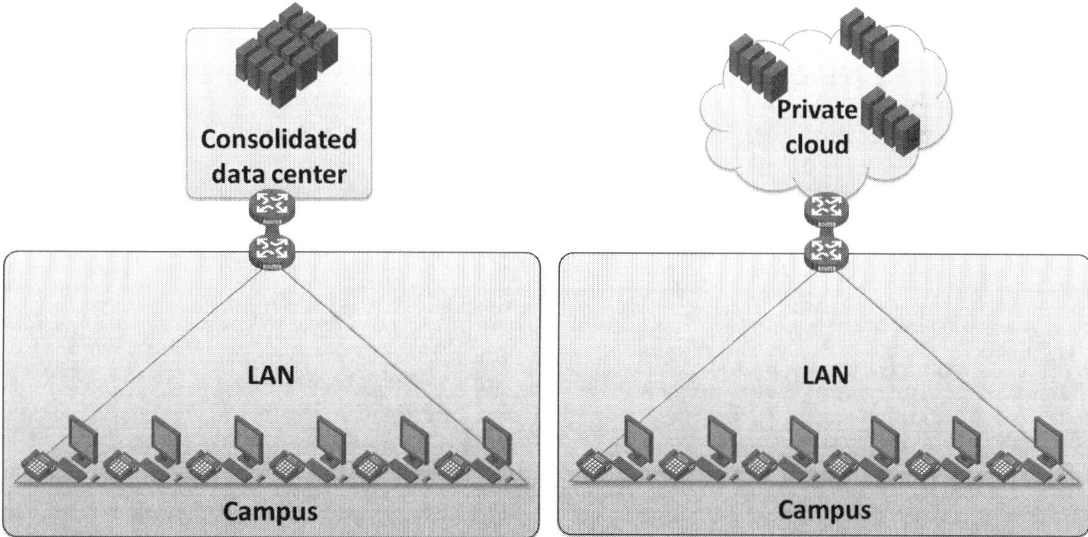

Figure 2-3. Trend 1: Data center consolidation and cloud computing

There are several reasons for this trend:

- **Operational**—It is easier to maintain (install, monitor, update, and troubleshoot) the systems if they are all located in the same place.
- **Resources**—There is no need to duplicate application servers, storage, backup resources, or even expert human assets.

In any of these cases, applications are accessed remotely via a WAN or a VPN and the total bandwidth available for the applications is limited by these links.

Note

The National Institute of Standards and Technology (NIST) defines a private cloud as follows: "The cloud infrastructure is provisioned for exclusive use by a single organization comprising multiple consumers (e.g., business units). It may be owned, managed, and operated by the organization, a third party, or some combination of them, and it may exist on or off premises." See www.nist.gov/itl/csd/cloud-102511.cfm for more information.

Trend 2: Application Architecture and Virtual Clients

In the past, typical business applications were based on the client/server model (see the left side of Figure 2-4). Different implementations of the client/server model would have differing functions at the client and at the server side, requiring varying levels of traffic between the client and the server. For example, some table lookups would be implemented directly in the server, and, in others, whole tables would have to be transferred to the client for the search.

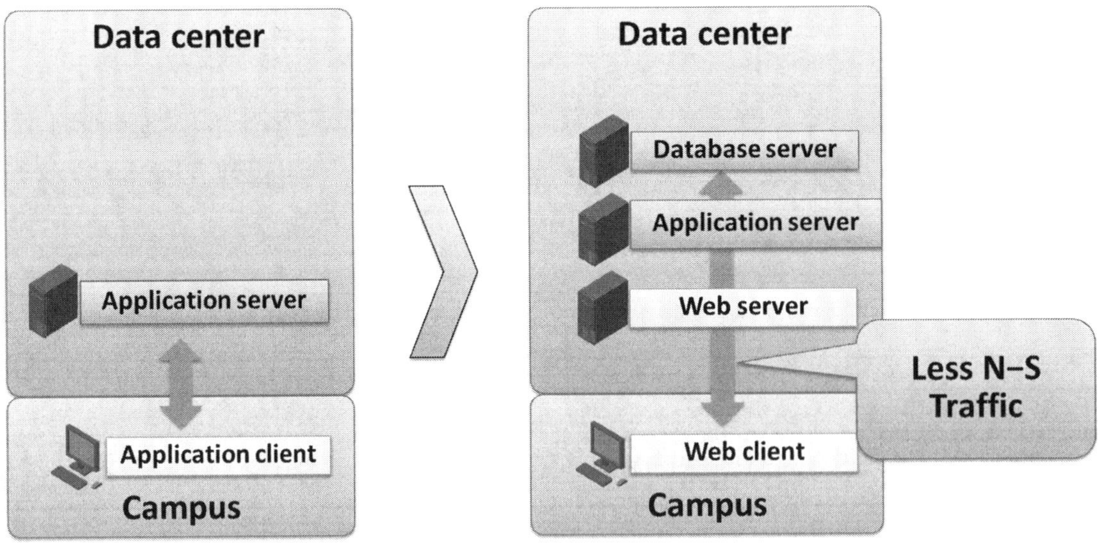

Figure 2-4. Trend 2: Application architecture and virtual clients

Today's business applications tend to be completely server-based with a web interface as the client. In other words, the client is virtualized in the server and controlled remotely via a web-based interface. The server side is no longer a single massive application. It is now a structured server set with a generic database server and storage system in the back end, an application server running the specific application logic in the middle, and a web server in the front to which the client connects.

In this scheme, the traffic between the user's station and the server system is minimal, except possibly when printing. This works well in the remote data center/cloud environment because it makes the best use of WAN/virtual private network (VPN) links possible. See the right side of Figure 2-4 for an illustration of this change.

Trend 3: UC&C: East–West Traffic

The dynamics of today's work environment make it almost impossible for people to meet face to face every time they need to collaborate. Yet the need for unified communication and collaboration (UC&C) is stronger than ever. Collaboration now requires multimedia applications that include voice, video, chat, and desktop/application sharing.

Traditional applications require traffic to flow between a client and server, and collaboration tools require traffic to flow between clients. Client-to-server traffic is called *north–south* (N–S) traffic, and client-to-client traffic is called *east–west* (E–W) traffic (see Figure 2-5).

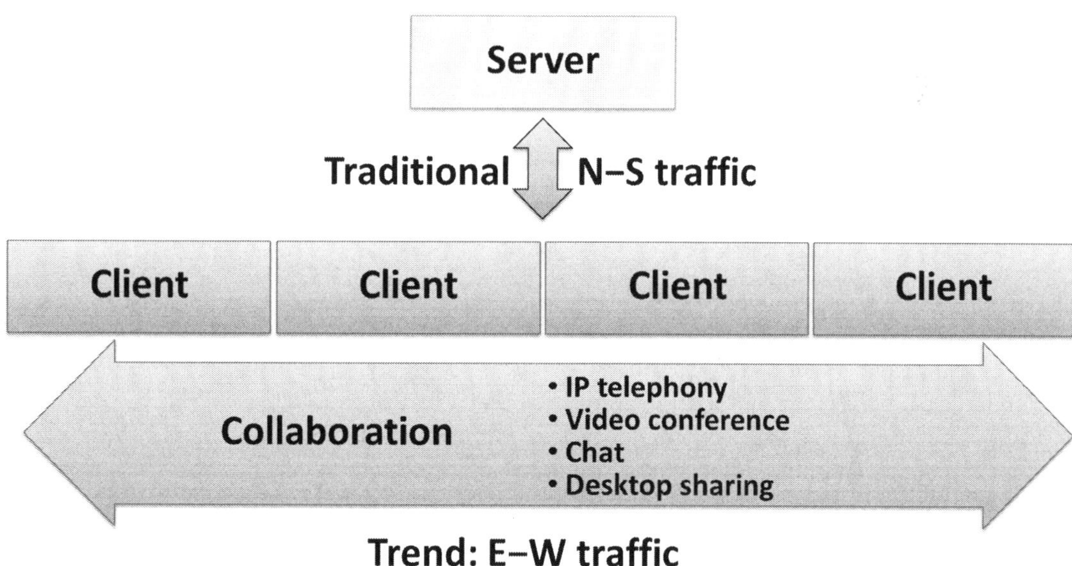

Figure 2–5. Trend 3: UC&C: East–west traffic

Even when three-tier database applications and remote data centers reduce the demand for bandwidth in the campus, collaboration applications re-establish that demand, adding the need for flatter LANs (less tiers), whenever possible. E–W collaboration traffic has different Quality of Service (QoS) requirements than traditional N–S traffic. E–W traffic requires low jitter and low delay and is intolerant toward packet loss.

HP FlexFabric

HP provides data center networking solutions that improve service levels, ensure business continuity, enable service agility, and reduce capital and operating costs. They are built from the ground up to meet the demanding needs of today's highly virtualized, large-scale application environments.

The FlexFabric Network architecture is a blueprint for interconnected, integrated, and aligned servers, storage, software, and power and management in an end-to-end Converged Infrastructure in data center networks. HP data center networking solutions are built to empower IT to deliver better business outcomes.

A *storage area network* (SAN) is a dedicated network that provides access to consolidated, block-level data storage. SANs are primarily used to make storage devices, such as disk arrays and tape libraries, accessible to servers so that the devices appear like locally attached devices to the operating system. A SAN typically has its own network of storage devices that are generally not accessible through the LAN by other devices.

Sharing storage simplifies storage administration and adds flexibility, since cables and storage devices do not have to be physically moved to shift storage from one server to another. Other benefits include the ability to allow servers to boot from the SAN itself. This allows for a quick and easy replacement of faulty servers, since the SAN can support a replacement server using the identity of the faulty server.

The way in which the applications access their data in SANs depends on the location of the storage within the SANs:

- **Fibre Channel (FC)**—A high-speed network technology (commonly running at 2-, 4-, 8-, and 16-gigabit speeds) primarily used for storage networking. Fibre Channel is standardized in the T11 Technical Committee of the International Committee for Information Technology Standards (INCITS), an American National Standards Institute–accredited (ANSI-accredited) standards committee. Basically, Fibre Channel is running Small Computer System Interface (SCSI), a bus standard for connecting computers and their peripherals. FC runs SCSI directly between the server hardware and the SAN.
- **Fibre Channel over Ethernet (FCoE)**—An encapsulation of FC frames over Ethernet networks. This allows FC to use 10 Gigabit Ethernet networks (or higher speeds) while preserving the FC protocol. Many data centers use Ethernet for TCP/IP networks and use FC for SANs. With FCoE, Fibre Channel becomes another network protocol running on Ethernet, alongside traditional IP traffic. The main limitation of FCoE is that the devices must be in the same Layer 2 network (broadcast domain or VLAN).

- **Internet Small Computer System Interface (iSCSI)**—Uses TCP, allowing two hosts to negotiate and then exchange SCSI commands using IP networks across different subnets (routed links). By doing this, iSCSI takes a popular high-performance local storage bus and emulates it over different networks, creating a SAN. Unlike some SAN protocols, iSCSI requires no dedicated cabling; it can be run over existing IP infrastructure. As a result, iSCSI is often seen as a low-cost alternative to FC, which requires dedicated infrastructure except in its FCoE form. However, the performance of an iSCSI SAN deployment can be severely degraded if not operated on a dedicated network or subnet (LAN or VLAN).

FlexFabric: Architecture

The HP FlexFabric architecture combines advanced, standards-based platforms and advanced networking technologies to optimize performance and to reduce latency in virtualized server environments. This approach reduces complexity, enables rapid businesses-aligned network provisioning, and lowers total cost of ownership.

HP FlexFabric connects servers to a virtualized, high-performance, low-latency network that consolidates multiple protocols into a single fabric to significantly lower network complexity and cost. This unique, wire-once approach enables businesses to combine Ethernet and storage networks onto one converged fabric that can easily flex with changing workloads.

FlexFabric is HP's vision for a next-generation, highly scalable data center network. This architecture radically streamlines deployment and management and drives end-to-end data center agility through advanced technology, simplified network designs, and tightly integrated management.. Combining intelligence at the server edge with advanced FlexFabric management tools, FlexFabric enables virtualization-aware networking, predictable performance, and rapid, secure, business-enabling provisioning of data center resources.

Along with a line of virtualization-optimized HP BladeSystem integrated network connectivity devices (Virtual Connect, Virtual Connect Flex-10, and Virtual Connect FlexFabric), HP offers a complete portfolio of data center networking products, including FCoE-capable, top-of-rack (ToR) server edge and high-performance, highly scalable aggregation layer and core switch platforms. With high-performance security and advanced network provisioning tools to securely and efficiently manage the networks, FlexFabric networks may be deployed today, providing a foundation for future growth.

FlexFabric: Data Center Products

The HP 12500 Switch Series is a family of powerful, next-generation routing switches with outstanding capacity for the network core or data center. Besides having innovative HP Intelligent Resilient Framework (IRF) technology that provides unprecedented levels of performance and high availability, the HP 12500 Switch Series incorporates Open Application Architecture (OAA) modules, which enable flexible deployment options for new services. These switches also have energy-efficiency features that drive down operational expenses and are ideal for organizations contemplating large-scale data center consolidations, business continuity and disaster recovery sites, metropolitan area network deployments, and other applications requiring a robust, high-performance switching platform.

Traditional switch architectures utilizing a cross-bar fabric will not scale to high densities of 40GbE and 100GbE connectivity. Switches with a CLOS architecture (10500 and 12500 Switch Series, as of the publication of this book) provide a high density on non-blocking 10GbE connections and can scale to 40GbE and 100GbE environments. Choose these switches for large-network customers who want a scalable, non-blocking solution. You also need to consider the switch fabric and connectivity modules, which must provide orthogonal connections between ports and the fabric to take advantage of the CLOS architecture:

- Advanced architecture: mid-plane, CLOS
- 13.32 terabit (Tb) switching capacity
- High-density 10GbE with 288 1:1, 576 4:1 ports
- 40/100 GbE ready
- Redundant switching fabric, power supply, fan tray

Note

The term *CLOS* is not an acronym but rather a reference to a *Clos network*, which is a type of circuit-switching network that was first formalized by Charles Clos.

The HP 5920 Switch Series is made up of high-density 10GbE ports, ultra-deep packet buffering and ToR switches. These switches are part of the HP FlexFabric solution module of the HP FlexNetwork architecture and are ideally suited for deployments at the server access layer of large enterprise data centers. The HP 5920 Switch Series is also designed for content delivery networks, especially when used to reduce network congestion at the I/O that is associated with the heavy use of server virtualization, in addition to multimedia, storage applications, and other critical services that often happen in bursts. With the increase in virtualized applications and server-to-server traffic, there is now a requirement for ToR switch innovations to meet the need for higher-performance server connectivity, convergence of Ethernet and storage traffic, the capability of handling virtual environments, and ultra-deep packet buffering—all in a single device:

- Ultra-deep packet buffering
- HP IRF for virtualization and two-tier architecture
- High 10GbE port density
- IPv6 support in ToR with full Layer 2/Layer 3 features
- TRILL and VEPA readiness for virtualized networks

The HP 5900 Switch Series is a family of high-density, ultra-low latency, ToR switches. It is part of the HP FlexFabric solution of the HP FlexNetwork architecture. Ideally suited for deployment at the server access layer of large enterprise data centers, the HP 5900 Switch Series is also designed for deployment at the data center core layer of medium-sized enterprises. With the increase in virtualized applications and server-to-server traffic, customers now require ToR switch innovations that meet their needs for higher-performance server connectivity, convergence of Ethernet and storage traffic, the capability of handling virtual environments, and ultra-low latency—all in a single device:

- Cut-through switching, low-latency, and large buffer options
- HP IRF for virtualization/two-tier architecture
- High 1/10 GbE port density with 40GbE uplink
- IPv6 support in ToR with full Layer 2/Layer 3 features
- Convergence ready with DCB (Data Center Bridging) and FCoE

The HP 5830AF Switch Series is a family of high-density, 1GbE, ToR data center and campus switches that are a part of the HP FlexNetwork architecture's HP FlexFabric solution module. The two models, the HP 5830AF-48G and HP 5830AF-96G switches, are ideally suited for deployments at the server access layer in medium-sized and large enterprise data centers and campus networks. The HP 5830AF-48G Switch delivers 48 1GbE ports and up to four 10GbE ports in a space-saving 1-RU (rack unit) package, and the HP 5830AF-96G Switch provides an industry-leading 96 1GbE ports and up to 10 10GbE uplink ports in a 2-RU form factor:

- Stackable, high port density for high scalability
- HP IRF technology for simpler two-tier networks
- Ultra-deep (1 GB and 3 GB) packet buffers
- Full Layer 2/Layer 3 features, IPv4/IPv6 dual stack
- Lower operating expenses and greener data centers

The HP 5820 Switch Series supports advanced features that deliver a unique combination of unmatched 10GbE, FCoE connectivity, high-availability architecture, full Layer 2/Layer 3 dual-stack IPv4/IPv6, and line-rate, low-latency performance on all ports. Extensible embedded application capabilities enable these switches to integrate services into the network, consolidating devices and appliances to simplify deployment and to reduce power consumption and rack space. Extremely versatile, the switches can be used in high-performance, high-density building or department cores as part of a consolidated network, for data center ToR server access, or as high-performance Layer 3, 10GbE aggregation switches in campus and data center networks:

- For enterprise edge or distribution/data center
- Up to 24 ports of 10GbE per unit/194 per stack
- Flex chassis—Modular resiliency (can include additional application modules)
- Cut-through switching for very low latency
- Hot-swappable I/O, power supplies, and fans

HP 5800 Switch Series offers an unmatched combination of Gigabit and 10-Gigabit Ethernet port density, high-availability architecture, and full Layer 2 and Layer 3 dual-stack IPv4 and IPv6 capabilities. In addition to wire-speed line-rate performance on all ports, the switches include patented IRF technology and RRPP, which allow local or geographically distributed HP 5800 switches to be interconnected for higher resiliency and performance. Available in Power over Ethernet (PoE) and non-PoE models, in addition to 1-RU and 2-RU flex chassis configurations, HP 5800 switches are built on open standards and include an OAA module slot that enables flexible deployment options for new services. These versatile switches are ideal for use in the network core of buildings or departments or as high-performance switches in the convergence layer or network edge of enterprise campus networks:

- For enterprise core, distribution, data center
- Flex chassis with modular resiliency
- Support for up to 84 ports
- OAA module for flexible deployment
- Redundant, hot-swappable power supplies, fans

Designed for the HP BladeSystem c-Class enclosure, the HP 6120G/XG and HP 6125G/XG blade switches provides 16 1GbE downlinks, four 1GbE copper uplinks, two 1GbE SFP (small form-factor pluggable transceiver) uplinks, plus three 10GbE uplinks and a single 10GbE cross-connect. A robust set of industry-standard Layer 2 switching functions, QoS metering, security, and high-availability features round out this extremely capable blade switch. The HP 6120G/XG blade switch is perfectly suited for data centers in transition, where a mix of 1GbE and 10GbE network connections is required. The HP 6120G/XG blade switch provides consistency and interoperability throughout existing network investments to help reduce the complexity of network management through resilient core-to-edge connectivity and automated provisioning technologies. With a variety of connection interfaces, the HP 6120G/XG blade switch offers excellent investment protection, flexibility, and scalability, in addition to ease of deployment and reduced operational expense:

- Layer 2 blade switch for BladeSystem c-Class
- Flexible Gigabit and 10-Gb connectivity
- Enterprise-class security, resiliency, management
- Lifetime warranty

Traditionally, there were only two ways to connect server blades to outside networks and storage—pass-thru modules or switches. The pass-thru approach is simple, but it leaves a company with countless cables and the associated cabling cost, reliability concerns, and risk of human errors. Blade switches reduce the number of cables needed but lead to more switches and their management. And, with either approach, it is hard to separate server management from network and storage management. HP Virtual Connect (VC) technology changes all of this. It is the next step in virtualization—helping IT fully realize the benefits of a converged infrastructure. It extends the benefit of virtualization beyond the server to the rest of your IT infrastructure. HP VC simplifies a company's IT infrastructure by virtualizing server-to-network connections. HP Virtual Connect is the industry-leading converged networking solution for bladed servers. Designed for the HP BladeSystem c-Class, Virtual Connect enables deployment of access layer solutions, including FCoE, in a simple and extremely flexible way to connect blade servers to IP LANs and FC SANs. HP offers the Virtual Connect FlexFabric 10 GbE/24-port module and three FlexFabric adapters. The HP VC FlexFabric modules and FlexFabric adapters extend Flex-10 technology to include FCoE and accelerated iSCSI. HP continues to advance simpler network infrastructure and server connection management with HP VC FlexFabric modules and FlexFabric adapters. A company can apply industry-standard convergence technology to address issues of network sprawl without disrupting LAN and SAN setup.

Figure 2-6 shows a simple example of how VC can leverage Comware switches by using distributed link aggregation, (Comware refers to this as bridge aggregation), from the VC module to the two Comware switches, like 5900s implementing IRF.

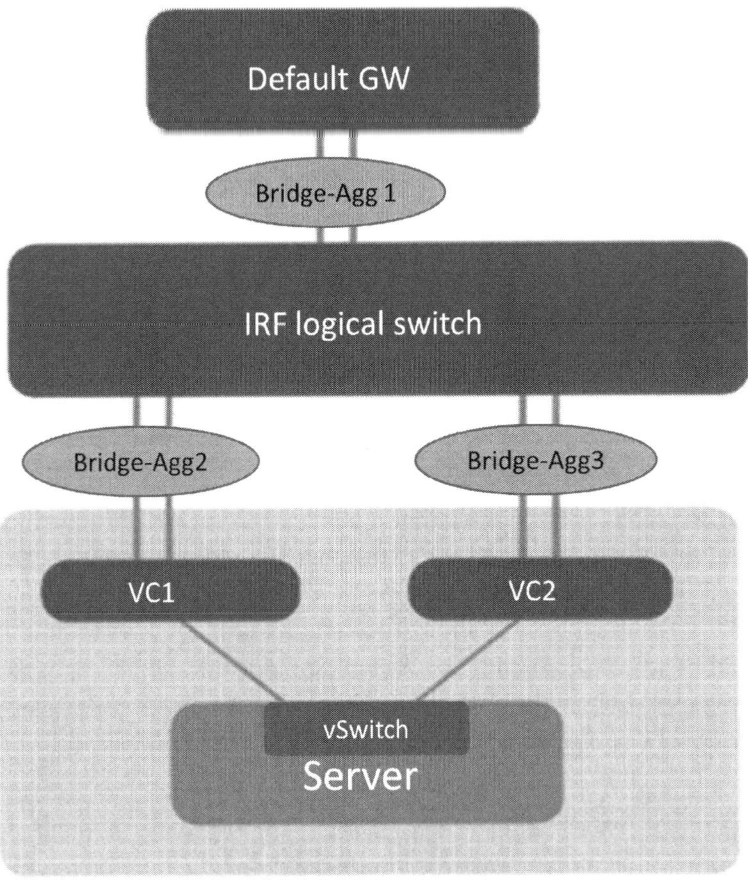

Figure 2–6. Virtual Connect overview

The HP 8800 Router Series provides wire-speed 10GbE forwarding, along with carrier-class services, security, and availability to meet the robust demands of service and application providers:

- Distributed architecture
- High-performance routing, with switching capacity of up to 1,440 Gbps and forwarding performance up to 864 Mpps
- Flexible chassis selection: 12 I/O-slot chassis, 8 I/O-slot chassis, 5 I/O-slot chassis
- High-density WAN and LAN (Ethernet, 10GbE, OC-3~192)
- Carrier-class reliability
- Advanced routing, switching, and security features

The HP HSR6800 Router Series is a portfolio of high-performance WAN services routers that are ideal for large-scale data center and campus WAN networks.

These routers are built with a multicore distributed processing architecture that scales up to 420 Mpps forwarding and up to two Tbps switch capacity. They deliver robust routing (Multi-Protocol Label Switching [MPLS], IPv4, IPv6, dynamic routing, and nested QoS), security (stateful firewall, IPSec/Dynamic VPN, denial of service [DoS] protection, and network address translation [NAT]), full Layer 2 switching, traffic analysis capabilities, and high-density 10GbE (and 40/100 GbE-ready) WAN interface options—all integrated in a single high-performance routing platform.

- **High-performance services**—With up to 420 Mpps forwarding and two Tbps switching capacity.
- **Multiple WAN interfaces**—Support Fast Ethernet/Gigabit Ethernet/10GbE ports, OC3-OC48 POS/CPOS, and ATM ports.
- **Flexible port selection**—Provides a combination of fiber/copper interface modules, 100/1000BASE-X auto-speed selection, and 10/100/1000BASE-T auto-speed detection, plus auto duplex and MDI/MDI-X; is speed adaptable between 155 Mb POS/622 Mb POS/ Gigabit Ethernet.
- **Loopback**—Supports internal loopback testing for maintenance purposes and an increase in availability; loopback detection protects against incorrect cabling or network configurations and can be enabled on a per-port or per-VLAN basis for added flexibility.
- **Separate data and control planes**—Provide greater flexibility and enable continual services.
- **Hot-swappable modules**—Facilitate the replacement of hardware interface modules without impacting the traffic flow through the system.
- **Optional redundant power supply**—Provides uninterrupted power; allows hot-swapping of one of the two supplies when installed.
- **Hitless software upgrades**—Allow patches to be installed without restarting the device, increasing network uptime and simplifying maintenance.
- **IP Fast Reroute Framework (FRR)**—Nodes are configured with backup ports and routes; local implementation requires no cooperation of adjacent devices, simplifying the deployment; solves the traditional convergence faults in IP forwarding; and achieves restoration within 50 milliseconds (ms), with the restoration time independent of the number of routes and fast link switchovers without route convergence.

The HP 6600 Router Series dramatically enhances service processing capacity with the HP FlexNetwork architecture. Distributed processing architecture, isolated routing and service engines, in addition to isolated control and service panels, provide higher reliability and continual services. Different software service engines can individually handle various services, such as NAT, QoS, IPsec, and NetStream, with no services modules needed. HP 6600 routers feature a modular design, embedded hardware encryption, and flexible deployment configurations, including High-speed Interface Modules (HIMs), Multi-function Interface Modules (MIMs), and OAA-enabled modules that provide network customization and investment protection. These routers provide carrier-class reliability at network, device, link, and service layers:

- Multicore CPU and distributed processing
- Carrier-class reliability and aggregation
- OAA platform
- Embedded hardware encryption
- Fully redundant and hot-swappable hardware
- Up to 252 Mpps (industry leading) forwarding performance
- Flexible chassis selection: 16 HIM-slot chassis, 8 HIM-slot chassis, 4 HIM-slot chassis, and 2 HIM-slot chassis
- Scalable system design (backplane designed for smooth bandwidth upgrade)

HP FlexCampus

FlexCampus, the HP end-to-end campus LAN solution, is a complete, secure networking infrastructure that connects users to mission-critical services across multibuilding campuses. By seamlessly connecting servers, storage, applications, and end users across a high-performance network with a single-pane-of-glass management platform, this solution provides simplified architecture, improved security, agile service delivery, and reduced IT costs.

FlexCampus Overview

The FlexCampus network, a modular building block of the FlexNetwork architecture, allows enterprises to converge and secure wired and wireless LANs to deliver consistent, video-optimized, and identity-based network access. New video applications can push network capacity needs by four to 10 times above current average levels.

FlexCampus is based on an advanced two- or three-tier architecture that improves the performance of media-rich collaboration applications by reducing latency and accelerating network throughput as a whole. As with the data center network segment, simplifying the campus network by eliminating the distribution layer improves performance, simplifies the network, and cuts costs. Building legacy three-tier architectures requires the use of many ports to interconnect a variety of switches. This, coupled with the necessity to use protocols, such as Spanning Tree, is likely to impact network performance and availability. Simplifying the network can reduce the number of discrete network elements to purchase, deploy, power, cool, and manage by up to 85 percent (www.hp.com/networking).

With the HP FlexNetwork architecture, organizations are free to build their campus networks. They can support user requirements for flexibility and mobility, and they can design their data center network and access network to meet those unique requirements. HP uses industry-standard protocols and protocol implementations at the boundaries of these network segments, enabling interoperability with the freedom to customize the network to specific functional requirements.

FlexCampus: Campus Products

The HP 10500 Switch Series sets a new benchmark for performance, reliability, and scalability with next-generation CLOS architecture. Designed for enterprise campus core networks, the HP 10500 Switch Series enables a cloud-connected and media-rich-capable infrastructure. The series provides industry-leading 10GbE/40 GbE port density, three-microsecond latency, and very low energy consumption. With HP IRF technology, the scalability and resiliency of the HP 10500 Switch Series can be extended and virtualized across up to four chassis with a single management interface, enabling flatter, more agile networks. The HP 10500 Switch Series, along with the entire HP FlexNetwork architecture, can be seamlessly managed through single-pane-of-glass management with HP IMC and offers:

- High-speed fully distributed architecture—Up to 11.52 Tbps switching capacity with current line cards and up to 13.72 Tbps switching fabric capacity with newer fabric modules provides non-blocking wire-speed 10GbE/40 GbE performance and future 100 GbE expansion capability:
  - With four fabrics, the switch delivers up to 8.571 billion packets-per-second (pps) throughput.
  - All switching and routing is performed in the I/O modules.
  - It meets the demand of bandwidth-intensive applications today and in the future.
- Scalable system design—Backplane is designed for bandwidth increases, and it provides investment protection to support future technologies and higher-speed connectivity.
- Flexible chassis selection—The chassis selection enables the tailoring of product selections to a budget with a choice of four chassis: 10504 switch (four open module slots), 10508 switch (eight open module slots), 10508-V switch (eight vertical open module slots), and 10512 switch (12 open module slots).
- Supports the advanced next-generation CLOS architecture.
- Rich features, including IPv6 and MPLS functionality.
- HP IRF technology, which virtualizes up to four chassis.
- Ultra-high 1/10/40 GbE density; 100 GbE ready.

The HP 7500 Switch Series is made up of modular multilayer chassis switches. These switches meet the evolving needs of integrated services networks and can be deployed in multiple network environments, including the enterprise LAN core, aggregation layer, and wiring closet edge. They offer 40GbE connectivity and cost-effective wire-speed 10 GbE ports to safeguard the throughput and bandwidth necessary for mission-critical data and high-speed communications. A passive backplane, support for load-sharing, and redundant management and fabrics help the HP 7500 Switch Series offer high availability. Moreover, these switches deliver wire-speed Layer 2 and Layer 3 routing services for the most demanding applications with hardware-based IPv4 and IPv6 support, providing:

- High-speed fully distributed architecture:
  - 2.4 Tbps backplane supports maximum 1152 Gbps switching capacity, offering enhanced performance and future expansion capability; with dual fabrics, the switch delivers up to 714 Mpps throughput.
  - All switching and routing is performed in the I/O modules.
  - It meets current and future demand of an enterprise's bandwidth-intensive applications.
- Scalable system design—Backplane is designed for bandwidth increases; provides investment protection to support future technologies and higher-speed connectivity.
- Flexible chassis selection—This enables customers to tailor their product selection to their budget with a choice of six chassis, ranging from a 10-slot to a 2-slot chassis.

The HP 8200 zl Switch Series offers high performance, scalability, and a wide range of features in a high-availability platform that dramatically reduces complexity and provides reduced cost of ownership. As part of a unified wired and wireless network infrastructure solution, the 8200 zl Switch Series provides platform technology, system software, system management, application integration, wired and wireless integration, network security, and support, common across HP modular and fixed-port switches. Together, they deliver an agile, cost-effective, high-availability network solution. With key technologies to provide solution longevity, the 8200 zl Switch Series is built to deliver long-term investment protection without added complexity for network core, aggregation, and high-availability access layer deployments. It provides these capabilities while bringing to market the industry's first highly available switch with a lifetime warranty, offering:

- Core, distribution, mission-critical access layer.
- Advanced, high-availability AllianceOne integration.
- Layer 2 to Layer 4 and intelligent edge feature set.
- Enterprise-class performance and security.
- High-speed, high-capacity architecture—The 1.12 Tbps crossbar switching fabric provides intra-module and inter-module switching with 739.2 million pps throughput on the purpose-built ProVision ASICs.
- Scalable 10/100/1000 and 10GbE connectivity.

The HP 5400 zl Switch Series consists of advanced intelligent switches in the HP modular chassis product line, which includes 6-slot and 12-slot chassis and associated zl modules and bundles. The foundation for the switch series is a purpose-built, programmable ProVision ASIC that allows the most demanding networking features, such as QoS and security, to be implemented in a scalable yet granular fashion. With 10/100, Gigabit Ethernet, and 10GbE interfaces, choice of Power over Ethernet Plus (PoE+) and non-PoE, integrated Layer 3 features, and HP AllianceOne solutions, the HP 5400 zl Switch Series offers excellent investment protection, flexibility, and scalability, along with ease of deployment, operation, and maintenance.

The HP 5400 zl Switch Series provides:

- Advanced access layer, distribution, and core.
- Integrated Layer 2 to Layer 4 intelligent edge feature set.
- High-speed, high-capacity architecture—One Tbps crossbar switching fabric provides intra-module and inter-module switching with 585.6 million pps throughput on the purpose-built ProVision ASICs.
- Enterprise-class performance and security.
- HP AllianceOne integrated.
- Scalable 10/100/1000 and 10 GbE connectivity.

The HP 5500 HI Switch Series comprises Gigabit Ethernet switches that deliver outstanding resiliency, security, and multiservice support capabilities at the edge layer of data center, large campus, and metro Ethernet networks. The switches can also be used in the core layer of SMB networks.With Intelligent Resilient Fabric (IRF) support and available dual power supplies, the HP 5500 HI Switch Series can deliver the highest levels of resiliency and manageability. In addition, the PoE+ models provide up to 1,440 W of PoE+ power with the dual power supply configuration. Designed with two fixed 10GbE ports and extension module flexibility, these switches can provide up to six 10GbE uplink or 70 GbE ports. With complete IPv4/IPv6 and MPLS/VPLS features, the series provides investment protection with an easy transition from IPv4 to IPv6 networks. Features of the HP5500 HI Switch Series include:

- High expandability for investment protection
- Premium resiliency and integrated management
- Enhanced MPLS/VPLS support
- Full-featured IPv4/IPv6 dual stack
- 1440 W of PoE+ power using dual power supplies for high resiliency

The HP 5500 EI Switch Series is made up of Layer 2/Layer 3 Gigabit Ethernet switches that can accommodate the most demanding applications and can provide resilient and secure connectivity, in addition to the latest traffic prioritization technologies to enhance applications on convergent networks. With complete IPv4/IPv6 dual-stack support, the series provides a migration path from IPv4 to IPv6 and has hardware support for IPv6. Designed for increased flexibility, these switches are available with 24 or 48 Gigabit Ethernet ports. PoE and non-PoE models are available with optional 1 GbE and 10 GbE expansion capabilities. The all-fiber model with dual power supplies is ideal for applications that require the highest availability. The HP 5500 EI Switch Series provides:

- Non-blocking architecture—Up to 192 Gbps non-blocking switching fabric provides wire-speed switching with up to 143 million pps throughput.
- High expandability for investment protection.
- Premium security and integrated management.
- Multilayer reliability.
- Convergence-ready support.
- Outstanding QoS.

The HP 3800 Switch Series is a family of nine fully managed Gigabit Ethernet switches available in 24-port and 48-port models, with or without PoE+ and with either SFP+ or 10GBASE-T uplinks. The HP 3800 Switch Series utilizes the latest ProVision ASIC technology and advances in hardware engineering to deliver one of the most resilient and energy-efficient switches in the industry. Meshed stacking technology is implemented in the HP 3800 Switch Series to deliver chassis-like resiliency in a flexible, stackable form factor, providing:

- Meshed stacking technology:
  - High-performance stacking—Provides up to 336 Gbps of stacking throughput; each four-port stacking module can support up to 42 Gbps in each direction per stacking port.
  - Ring, chain, and mesh topologies—Support up to a 10-member ring or chain and five-member fully meshed stacks; meshed topologies offer increased resiliency versus a standard ring.
  - Virtualized switching—When stacked, switches appear as a single chassis, providing simplified management. (This can eliminate the need for spanning tree in a switched network and reduce the number of routers in a routed network.)
- Fully managed Layer 3 stackable switch series.
- Low-latency, highly resilient architecture.
- SFP+, 10GBASE-T, PoE+, modular stacking.
- Highly resilient meshed stacking technology.
- Industry-leading lifetime warranty.

The HP 3600 EI Switch Series delivers premium levels of intelligent and resilient performance, security, and reliability for robust switching at the enterprise network edge. The series consists of Layer 3 Fast Ethernet and PoE/PoE+ switches, with advanced features that can accommodate the most demanding applications. Secure, resilient connectivity and the latest traffic-prioritization technologies enhance converged networks. Designed for increased flexibility and scalability, the HP 3600 EI Switch Series comes with 24 or eight 10/100 ports, four active SFP-based Gigabit Ethernet ports for stacking and uplinks, and a 24-port 100BASE-FX switch with two or four Gigabit Ethernet SFP slots. The HP 3600 EI Switch Series provides:

- Robust switching at the enterprise network edge.
- Advanced Layer 3 and multicast routing.
- IRF-automated stack and switching fabric setup.
- Integrated and distributed security enforcement.
- Enterprise-level non-blocking performance—Up to 17.6 Gbps non-blocking switching fabric provides wire-speed switching with up to 13.1 million pps throughput.

The HP 3500 Switch Series consists of advanced intelligent-edge switches, available in 24-port and 48-port fixed-port models. The foundation for these switches is a purpose-built, programmable ProVision ASIC that allows the most demanding networking features, such as QoS and security, to be implemented in a scalable yet granular fashion. With a variety of Gigabit Ethernet and 10/100 interfaces, integrated PoE+, PoE, and non-PoE options, and versatile 10GbE connectivity (CX4, X2, and SFP+) on Gigabit Ethernet switches, the HP 3500 Switch Series offers excellent investment protection, flexibility, and scalability, along with ease of deployment, operation, and maintenance. The HP 3500 Switch Series provides:

- High-speed/capacity architecture—Up to 153.6 Gbps crossbar switching fabric provides intra- and inter-module switching with up to 111.5 million pps throughput on the purpose-built ProVision ASICs.
- Advanced access layer and small distribution.
- Enterprise-class performance and security.
- Intelligent edge feature set with Layer 2 to Layer 4 support.
- Scalable 10/100/1000 PoE+ and 10/100 PoE.
- Unified core-to-edge ProVision software.

The HP 5120 EI Switch Series is made up of Gigabit Ethernet switches that support static Layer 3 routing, diversified services, and IPv6 forwarding, and it provides up to four 10GbE extended interfaces. Unique IRF technology creates a virtual fabric by managing several switches as one logical device, increasing network resilience, performance, and availability, while reducing operational complexity. These switches provide Gigabit Ethernet access and can be used at the edge of a network or to connect server clusters in data centers. High scalability provides investment protection with two expansion slots, each of which can support two-port 10GbE expansion modules. High availability, simplified management, and comprehensive security control policies are among the key features that distinguish this series. The HP 5120 EI Switch Series provides:

- High scalability for investment protection—Up to 192 Gbps non-blocking switching fabric provides wire-speed switching with up to 143 million pps throughput.
- Support for multiple services.
- Comprehensive security control policies.
- Diversified QoS policies.
- Excellent manageability.

The HP 2920 Switch Series consists of four switches: the HP 2920-24G and 2920-24G-PoE+ Switches with 24 10/100/1000 ports, and the HP 2920-48G and 2920-48G-PoE+ Switches with 48 10/100/1000 ports. Each switch has four dual-personality ports for 10/100/1000 or SFP connectivity.

In addition, the HP 2920 Switch Series supports up to four optional 10 Gigabit Ethernet (SFP+ and/or 10GBASE-T) ports, plus a two-port stacking module. These options provide flexible and easy-to-deploy uplinks and stacking.

Together with static and Routing Information Protocol (RIP) routing, robust security and management, enterprise-class features, free lifetime warranty, and free software updates, the HP 2920 Switch Series is a cost-effective, scalable solution for customers who are building high-performance networks. These switches can be deployed at the enterprise edge, in remote branch offices, and in converged networks, offering:

- High-performance Gigabit Ethernet access switch.
- Four optional 10GbE (SFP+ and/or 10GBASE-T) ports.
- Stacking capability with a total of four switches.
- Layer 2 and Layer 3, plus static and RIP routing, and PoE and PoE+ support.
- Lifetime warranty, sFlow, access control lists (ACLs), OpenFlow, and rate limiting.

The HP 2915-8G-PoE Switch is a fully managed eight-port 10/100/1000 switch with two additional dual-personality Gigabit Ethernet ports for copper or SFP connectivity. Together with static and RIP IPv4 routing, robust security and management, enterprise-class features, a free lifetime warranty, and free software updates, the HP 2915-8G-PoE Switch is a cost-effective solution. The switch is fanless, providing quiet operation and making it ideal for deployments in open spaces. In addition, its compact form factor allows for flexible deployments, including wall, surface, or rack mounting. These switches can be deployed at enterprise edge and remote branch offices or in converged networks. The HP 2915-8G-PoE Switch Series provides:

- Scalable 10/100/1000 connectivity.
- Layer 2 and 3 switching capabilities.
- sFlow, ACLs, and rate limiting.
- Energy-efficient design and quiet operation.
- Rack-mountable, compact form factor.

The HP 2620 Switch Series consists of five switches with 10/100 connectivity. The HP 2620-24 Switch is a fanless switch, providing quiet operation and making it ideal for deployments in open spaces. The HP 2620-24-PPoE+ Switch, HP 2620-24-PoE+ Switch, and HP 2620-48-PoE+ Switch are IEEE 802.3af- and IEEE 802.3at-compliant switches and provide up to 30 watts (W) per powered port. The HP 2620-48 Switch has variable speed fans for quiet operation. The HP 2620 Switch Series includes two 10/100/1000BASE-T ports and two SFP slots for Gigabit Ethernet uplink connectivity. An optional redundant external power supply is also available to provide redundancy in the event of a power supply failure. With IPv4/IPv6 static and RIP routing, robust security and management features, free lifetime warranty, and free software updates, the HP 2620 Switch Series is a cost-effective solution for customers who are building converged enterprise edge networks. The HP 2620 Switch Series provides:

- Cost-effective access layer switches.
- Lite Layer 3 IPv4/IPv6 static and RIP routing.
- 30 W PoE+ support on PoE models.
- Gigabit fiber uplinks.
- Enterprise-class features.

The HP 2615-8-PoE Switch is a fully managed eight-port 10/100 switch with two additional dual-personality Gigabit Ethernet ports for copper or SFP connectivity. Together with static and RIP IPv4 routing, robust security and management, enterprise-class features, a free lifetime warranty, and free software updates, the HP 2615-8-PoE Switch is a cost-effective solution. For details, please refer to http://h17007.www1.hp.com/us/en/support/warranty/index.aspx. The HP 2615-8-PoE Switch is fanless, providing quiet operation and making it ideal for deployments in open spaces. In addition, the compact form factor allows for flexible deployments, including wall, surface, or rack mounting. These switches can be deployed at enterprise edge and remote branch offices or in converged networks. The HP 2615-8-PoE Switch Series provides:

- Scalable 10/100 connectivity.
- Layer 2 and 3 switching capabilities.
- sFlow, ACLs, and rate limiting.
- Energy-efficient design and quiet operation.
- Rack-mountable, compact form factor.

The HP 2530 Switch Series consists of four fully managed Layer 2 edge switches, delivering cost-effective, reliable, and secure connectivity for business networks. Designed for entry-level to midsized enterprise networks, these Gigabit Ethernet switches deliver full Layer 2 capabilities with enhanced access security, traffic prioritization, IPv6 host support, and optional PoE+ and they include a product lifetime warranty. For details, see http://h17007.www1.hp.com/us/en/support/warranty/index.aspx.

Each HP 2530 switch has 24 or 48 RJ-45 10/100/1000 ports and four small form-factor pluggable (SFP) slots for fiber connectivity. For customers implementing PoE for voice, video, or wireless deployments, the HP 2530-24G-PoE+ and the HP 2530-48G-PoE+ Switches are IEEE 802.3af- and IEEE 802.3at-compliant with up to 30 W per port.

The HP 2530 Switch Series is easy to use, deploy, and manage via Simple Network Management Protocol (SNMP), command-line interface (CLI), and web graphical user interface (GUI). The series offers flexible wall, table, and rack mounting, quiet operation, and improved power savings, with features such as IEEE 802.3az (Energy Efficient Ethernet). These switches include a lifetime warranty and all software releases and technical phone support. The HP 2530 Switch Series provides:

- Cost-effective, fully managed Layer 2 switches.
- 24 or 48 Gigabit ports and four SFP uplink ports.
- PoE+ models for voice, video, and wireless.
- Weighted deficit round robin (WDRR), ACLs, IPv4/IPv6 host support.
- Lifetime Warranty, all software releases, and technical phone support. For details, see http://h17007.www1.hp.com/us/en/support/warranty/index.aspx.

The HP 2520 Switch Series is ideally suited for small and medium-sized businesses looking to deploy voice, video, or wireless solutions that require PoE connectivity. The series consists of four switches: the HP 2520-8-PoE, the HP 2520-24-PoE, the HP 2520-8G-PoE, and the HP 2520-24G-PoE switches. The four models offer a choice of either Fast Ethernet or Gigabit Ethernet connectivity. All models also include support for dual-personality Gigabit Ethernet ports that can be used for either copper or fiber connectivity. All products are fully managed via SNMP, CLI, and GUI and offer a Layer 2 feature set. In addition, the products provide deployment flexibility with compact, quiet, and energy-efficient designs. Th HP 2520 Switch Series provides:

- Fully managed Layer 2 switching in eight or 24 ports.
- Choice of 10/100 or Gigabit PoE models.
- Power over Ethernet for voice, video, and wireless.
- Energy-efficient design and quiet operation.
- Rack-mountable and compact form factors.

Working in unison with HP Multi-Service Mobility (MSM) access points, the HP MSM Controller Series delivers high-performance networking solutions. The enhanced architecture scales to 802.11n without requiring controller replacement. Robust identity- and roles-based user account profiles, in addition to Virtual Service Communities (VSCs) with independently configurable QoS, authentication, encryption, and VLAN support, deliver intelligence to the network edge. Scalable from small to larger deployments, the MSM wireless controllers support a fast-roaming capability. Wireless security is comprehensive with support for internal and external authentication, authorization, and accounting (AAA) servers, built-in stateful firewall, per-user VLAN mapping, and authentication. HP MSM Controllers provide:

- Ease of use, scalability, and redundancy.
- Enhanced architecture for flexible network design.
- IEEE 802.11a/b/g/n access point and access device support.
- Comprehensive WLAN security.
- Appliance and blade form factors.

The MSM 802.11n dual-radio access points (APs) are the highest-performance family of HP access points. HP is the first in the industry to offer three-spatial-stream multiple input multiple output (MIMO) technology to enterprise businesses. This brings IEEE 802.11n near Gigabit Ethernet performance to a theoretical maximum of 450 Mbps and enhances coverage areas with beam-forming technology. These APs deliver the highest performance in 802.11n access point technology, with outstanding price and performance. Each dual radio 802.11n access point operates in the 2.4 GHz and 5 GHz bands, providing backward compatibility for IEEE 802.11a/b/g legacy client devices. These APs can operate with or without a wireless controller and support all of the same enterprise features as the prior HP MSM wireless products, in addition to new features, such as beam-forming, band-steering, and concurrent 5 GHz operation. The MSM466 and MSM466-R access points also support a range of MIMO antennas, and the MSM466-R access point is in an outdoor enclosure and is designed to work under adverse conditions. MSM 460/466/466-R access points offer:

- The first three-spatial-stream MIMO AP in the industry.
- Up to 450 Mbps per radio on MSM460 and MSM466/466-R.
- Support for range of antennas on MSM466/466-R AP
- MSM430 AP is two-stream, price/performance leader.
- All APs use standard IEEE 802.3af PoE power.

HP FlexBranch

The branch office plays an important role in an organization's ability to attract, service, and retain customers and increase revenue. Branch office employees—the face of the corporation—can significantly impact customer satisfaction and loyalty. This is particularly true when they are supported by safe, dependable, and fast access to the corporate knowledge base (people, resources, and information) and to the productivity-enhancing tools in which the organization has invested. In addition, with today's increasing security vulnerabilities, branch office networks must be protected by comprehensive security policies and enforcement to help ensure business continuity.

Despite the critical nature of the branch office, legacy infrastructures often hinder customer service with slow, unreliable access to information and applications. Poor WAN performance can prompt employees to store data locally, preventing it from being backed up and putting the business and regulatory compliance at risk if a local device fails. The high cost of running a branch also prevents most organizations from maintaining a local IT staff, so branch office employees must manage and troubleshoot systems, decreasing productivity and taking the focus off the customer.

Many branch offices were built in isolation and may lack the interoperability needed to cost-effectively support business activities and growth. They are further restricted by a complex mixture of legacy network infrastructures that are expensive to expand and maintain. At a time when competing requirements include the implementation of new services, such as mobility and unified communications—along with rapid access with enhanced security to applications and services—businesses struggle to efficiently scale, manage, and secure their networks. The trend to data center consolidation and remote employee access to hosted applications is forcing employees to compete for resources across the WAN and is compelling organizations to rethink their strategic approach to the branch office.

Employees in a small branch office require email, file-sharing, local printing, and Internet access, in addition to secure access to the corporate network. The branch has a firewall and a site-to-site VPN over a broadband connection for encrypted access to the headquarters' network. Email is usually hosted in the corporate data center.

Challenges include inefficient WAN speed that affects productivity, slows access to main office file shares, and causes intermittent login problems. Frequent local network issues and a lack of reliable backups jeopardize the security of important customer data. Unreliable printing forces frequent reboots to clear the queue. Often, there is no IT staff on site.

FlexBranch: Solution

The HP branch office networking solution converges infrastructure and network applications to significantly improve performance, simplify deployments, centralize management, and reduce IT costs. The branch solution is a component in the HP end-to-end enterprise network infrastructure, which optimizes the network for secure, reliable, high-performance application delivery and a foundation for converged infrastructure for the extended enterprise.

When using a converged infrastructure, if most of the employees' resources are at the corporate office network, you should consider the following for FlexBranch-to-FlexCampus connectivity:

- Redundancy (not just in redundant connections, but possibly redundant edge connection devices, like routers, at the FlexBranch).
- Reliability of the service.

FlexBranch: Branch Products

The HP MSR50 Series routers are components of the HP FlexBranch solution, which is part of the HP FlexNetwork architecture. HP MSR50 Series routers are designed for large branch offices, regional offices, and enterprise deployments that require high-performance converged routing, switching, wireless, security, and voice services with modular, high-density WAN and LAN interface options in a single platform. HP MSR50 Series routers deliver full-featured routing, including IPv6, dynamic routing, QoS, MPLS, security, switching, wireless, and voice services with optional embedded hardware-based encryption and voice processing to deliver superior performance forwarding up to 1.28 Mpps. HP MSR50 Series routers provide:

- High-performance, modular LAN/WAN router.
- Converged routing, switching, voice, security.
- Embedded encryption, firewall, security features.
- High reliability, dual PSU, hot-swappable modules.
- Single-pane-of-glass management.

The HP MSR30 Series routers are components of the HP FlexBranch solution, which is part of the HP FlexNetwork architecture. HP MSR30 Series routers are ideal for medium-to-large enterprise branch and regional offices. They provide unmatched performance, integrated routing, switching, security, wireless, and voice services with a rich set of modular WAN/LAN connectivity options in a single device to reduce operating and capital costs and to simplify complexity. HP MSR30 Series routers are purpose-built routing platforms that deliver embedded applications, enhanced security, and performance acceleration and that support a wide range of flexible LAN, WAN, and voice interface options to enable remote users in branch locations to securely and reliably access enterprise applications and corporate resources. HP MSR30 Series routers provide:

- Converged routing, switching, voice, security.
- Excellent forwarding performance—Provides forwarding performance from 220 Kpps to 360 Kpps, meets current and future bandwidth-intensive application demands of enterprise businesses.
- Embedded encryption, firewall, security features.
- OAA with converged IP telephony solution.
- Unified wired and wireless WAN/LAN.
- Support for AC/DC power and PoE.

The HP MSR20 Series routers are components of the FlexBranch architecture. It features a modular design that delivers unmatched flexibility for small branch offices and for small-to-medium-sized businesses while reducing complexity, simplifying management, and increasing control. The HP MSR20 Series routers provide a full-featured, resilient routing platform, including IPv6 and MPLS, up to 180 Kpps forwarding capacity and 100 Mbps encryption. These products offer lasting investment protection and help reduce capital and operating expenses. These routers provide an agile, flexible network infrastructure that offers the ability to quickly adapt to changing business requirements while delivering integrated, concurrent services on a single, easy-to-manage platform. HP MSR20 Series routers provide:

- Converged routing, switching, voice, security.
- Embedded encryption, firewall, security features.
- Modular WAN/LAN interface options.
- Unified wired and wireless.
- Single-pane-of-glass management.

The HP MSR20-1x Series routers are components of the HP FlexBranch solution, which is part of the HP FlexNetwork architecture. HP MSR20-1x Series routers are full-featured, economical routers designed for converged wired and wireless WAN and LAN environments at small remote branch offices and small-to-medium-sized businesses. HP MSR20-1x Series routers deliver high-performance integrated routing, switching, security, wireless, and voice services while reducing complexity, simplifying management, and increasing control. These routers enable an agile and flexible network infrastructure that can quickly adapt to changing business requirements while delivering integrated services on a single, easy-to-manage platform. HP MSR20-1x Series routers features include:

- Routing, switching, security, wireless, and voice.
- Forwarding performance up to 160 Kpps; meets current and future bandwidth-intensive application demands of enterprise businesses.
- Compact design for both desktop and rack mounting.
- Fixed-port and modular WAN/LAN interface options.
- Embedded encryption, firewall, security features.
- Single-pane-of-glass management.

The HP MSR900 Series routers are components of the HP FlexBranch module of the HP FlexNetwork architecture. HP MSR900 Series routers deliver integrated routing, switching, security, and 802.11b/g wireless LAN in a single box for secure, reliable, small branch connectivity. These routers are perfect "branch-in-a-box" appliances that deliver converged network solutions, including data, voice and video, IPv6 support, and robust QoS, and that help ensure that they can handle both current enterprise networking applications and the future connectivity and capacity demands of an HP FlexNetwork architecture. Additionally, a standards-based design provides complete interoperability in multivendor environments. HP MSR900 Series routers are perfect for small office/home office:

- Converged routing, switching, security, and WLAN.
- Excellent forwarding performance—Provides forwarding performance up to 100 Kpps; meets current and future bandwidth-intensive application demands for enterprise businesses.
- Embedded encryption—Supports up to 100 VPN tunnels and 8 Mbps encryption throughput.
- Integrated two Fast Ethernet WAN ports and either a four-port or eight-port LAN on board.
- Unified 802.11b/g wireless LAN and 3G wireless WAN.
- Embedded encryption, firewall, security features.
- A unified management platform.

HP FlexManagement

If you are a network or IT administrator, you know the problems: you are dealing with a growing wave of enterprise video content, and your network is struggling to keep pace with exponential traffic increases and the shift toward mobile access. You are trying to address the escalating demands of the virtualized and cloud-ready data center. And you have seen how difficult—make that, nearly impossible—it is for network IT to secure and orchestrate services in the virtual cloud and the virtualized workplace.

At the same time, your users' expectations are higher. Today's enterprise users demand constant and immediate connectivity across wired and wireless links. They want instant-on access to business applications from their fixed and mobile workstations. Users expect to switch seamlessly and transparently from traditional IT to private and public clouds and back.

Keeping pace with these requirements is a tall order for the IT manager. As a result, many organizations find that IT staff time and budget is overwhelmingly devoted to ongoing operations and maintenance instead of developing new initiatives and projects or expanding capacity to support business growth. In fact, more than 70 percent of any IT budget is spent just keeping the lights on, leaving less than 30 percent to deliver business-critical innovation.

Solving such seemingly intractable problems calls for a new type of network management, one that combines a capability for single-pane-of-glass multivendor management with automated virtual machine orchestration and automatic synchronization of network connectivity information. HP calls this FlexManagement. And it is available today in the HP Intelligent Management Center (IMC).

IMC is a unified, single-point network management solution that provides visibility across entire networks, enabling complete management of resources, services, and users. Unifying wired, wireless, and user management leads to increased performance, enhanced security, and reduced infrastructure complexity and costs.

Note

IMC is SNMP-based but has support for other vendor products that do not primarily rely on SNMP, like Cisco.

IMC is a scalable solution that comes in two versions: Enterprise and Standard, managing up to 10,000 nodes with a modular design which enables comprehensive monitoring and management capabilities. Standard Edition is the next-generation management software and supports up to 100 managed devices. Additional node licenses can be purchased to extend the node limit of IMC. Enterprise platform allows for management of 200 nodes and includes the Network Traffic

Analyzer (NTA) module. It also enables hierarchical management of other IMC deployments within an organization. In addition to NTA, a couple of other plug-ins to IMC worthy of consideration are:

- **Endpoint Admission Defense (EAD)**—Can be used to analyze a network endpoint's security status to locate security threats, detect security events, and carry out protective measures to reduce network vulnerabilities. EAD can determine endpoint patch level, ARP attack, abnormal traffic, and the installation and operation of illegal software. Administrators can choose enforcement policies and remediation options that are appropriate to particular endpoints.
- **User Access Manager (UAM)**—With the addition of this module, the system implements unified and centralized access management, supporting access through authentications, such as LAN, WAN, WLAN, and VPN. It supports strong authentication using smart card, certificate, and more, and it supports various methods for endpoint access control and identity-based network services that efficiently integrate the management of user resources and services.
- **Wireless Services Manager (WSM)**—The WSM software provides unified management of wired and wireless networks, adding network management functions into existing wired network management systems. WSM software offers WLAN device configuration, topology, performance monitoring, radio frequency (RF) heat-mapping, and WLAN service reports.

Note
ProCurve Manager (PCM) has been replaced by IMC, which is covered in "Chapter 15: HP Intelligent Management Center."

Software-Defined Networks

Many enterprises are unable to create business innovation because of aging networking environments. Network design and architectures have remained largely unchanged for more than a decade. Although applications and systems have evolved to meet the demands of a world where real time rules, the underlying network infrastructure has not kept pace.

Software-defined networking (SDN) redefines the way we think about the network and removes the barriers to innovation by giving cloud providers and enterprises complete programmatic control of a dynamic, abstracted view of the network. With SDN technologies, IT can become more agile by orchestrating network services and automatically controlling the network according to high-level policies rather than low-level network device configurations. This section gives an overview of software-defined networking and how HP is leveraging SDN to deliver the Virtual Application Networks strategy.

SDN represents a new architecture that separates the network control plane from the forwarding hardware, allowing a centralized controller (or set of controllers) to define forwarding behavior through high-level policy. HP believes that SDN is defined by the ability to apply business logic to network behavior in a dynamic fashion. This is achieved in three steps:

1. An open standards–based mechanism must exist to access the infrastructure.
2. The control plane and data plane functions of a device should be separated. Network control is centralized; forwarding remains distributed.
3. The centralized control (or controller) should deliver open programmable interfaces to allow the orchestration of applications and automation of network functions.

To better understand SDN, you first have to understand what it is not:

- SDN is neither just OpenFlow nor just OpenStack. OpenFlow is a protocol, and OpenStack is an orchestration tool. These may be used to deliver SDN elements, but they are not synonymous with SDN.
- SDN is not just a software implementation of a network device. HP chooses not to define software routers or virtualized appliances as SDN.
- SDN is not just providing proprietary programmatic Application Programming Interfaces (APIs). It is more than exposing device configuration APIs and automation.
- SDN is definitely not the end of hardware innovation. HP will continue to drive hardware innovation in support of SDN.

Legacy Implementation Versus SDN

Networks are increasing in complexity: they are bigger and faster, and applications and services are deployed more dynamically. Both users and applications require security, resiliency, privacy, traffic separation, end-to-end virtualization, and priority treatment. In a legacy network, there is a 1:1 relationship between servers and switch ports. With the adoption of server virtualization, network demand has increased dramatically by enabling as many as 50 servers behind a single port, each requiring their own network and security policies. The network cannot change or adapt fast enough today without deploying complicated and fragile programmatic network management systems or employing vast teams of network administrators to make thousands of changes per day.

As you can see from Figure 2-7, legacy networks are difficult to automate as the control plane intelligence is distributed. SDN promises an easier, more dynamic interaction with the network through the use of a "clean" interface obtained through abstraction of the control plane. This reduces the complexity of managing, provisioning, and changing the network.

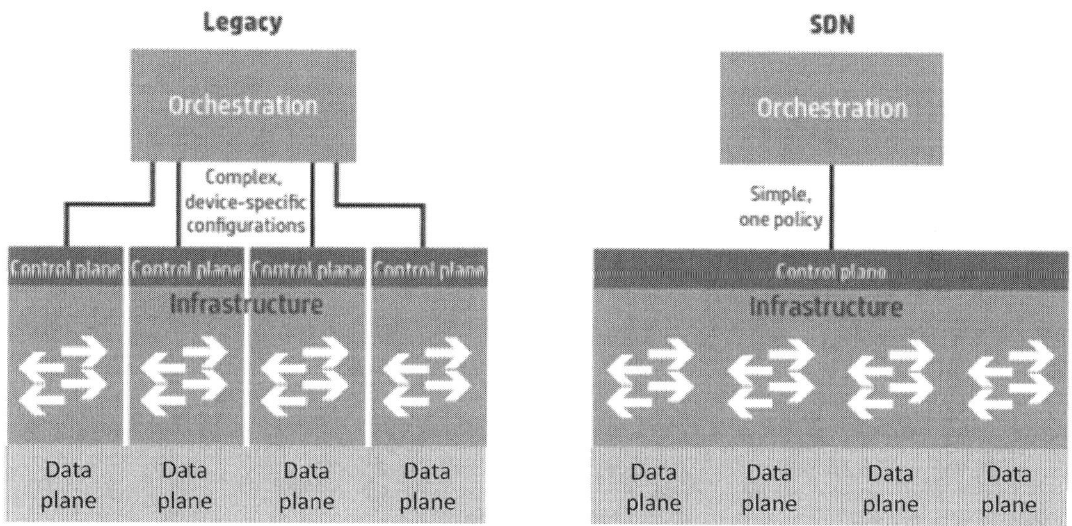

Figure 2-7. Legacy implementation versus SDN

Traditional networks have also struggled to bridge the gap between the systems they support and the services they deliver. Attempts to bridge this gap in the past resulted in complex network configuration aimed at enabling network devices to monitor application traffic, inferring application status and need, and then responding according to configured policy.

By separating the control plane and the dynamic state it contains, away from the data or forwarding plane, SDN makes it possible for the network's status and capabilities to be exposed directly to the business service layer, allowing business systems to request services from the network directly rather than trusting the network to guess successfully.

By exposing the control plane of the network via open interfaces, SDN levels the playing field for network innovation, lowering the barriers that have previously kept new entrants from bringing fresh and interesting capabilities to the market, and allowing businesses to unleash the true power of the network.

Components of Building an SDN

There are three critical components to a building an SDN (see Figure 2-8):

- Infrastructure layer
- Control layer
- Application layer

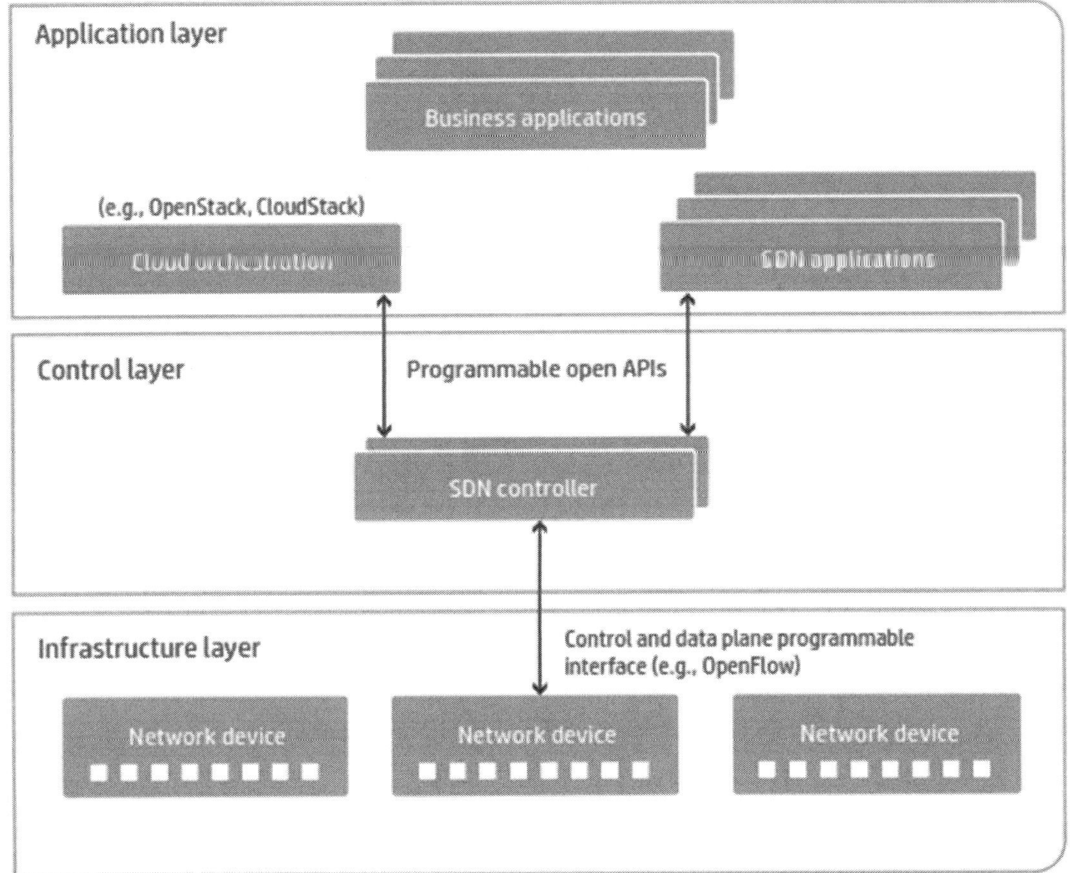

Figure 2-8. Components of building an SDN

The infrastructure includes the underlying ports and forwarding hardware that move data across your network. It is important in an SDN environment that the infrastructure supports a means of programmatic access to its data and control plane.

The control element of an SDN resides in a central controller. This control presents an abstracted view of the infrastructure, allowing the network administrator to apply one or more policies across the network. The controller's job is to enforce these policies. A controller needs to communicate with the infrastructure but must also be able to communicate with applications.

Applications in an SDN environment could be compared to the protocols that ran our legacy networks for the past 20 years. The key difference is that SDN applications are presented with a view of the entire network, allowing them to focus on optimizing business applications and providing a true end-to-end service level agreement (SLA) comprising performance, quality of service, and security. SDN applications are responsible for tasks such as path computation, loop avoidance, and routing—but there is more. The promise of SDN is that applications can easily be developed to accommodate virtually any use case. As applications communicate with the control layer using open, standards-based APIs, SDN means that applications can be developed in-house.

The APIs used to communicate between the layers of the SDN stack are grouped based on their function in an SDN architecture (see Figure 2-9):

- **Northbound APIs**—Communicate between controllers and applications.
- **Southbound APIs**—Communicate between controllers and infrastructure.
- **Eastbound/Westbound APIs**—Communicate between groups or federations of controllers to synchronize state for high availability.

Since SDN technologies are still maturing, there will initially be very few pure SDN deployments outside of massive provider networks that require SDN to solve their scaling problems. Within the enterprise, we will see the deployment of hybrid networks that continue to operate in a traditional fashion but leverage SDN to provide additional features and functionality.

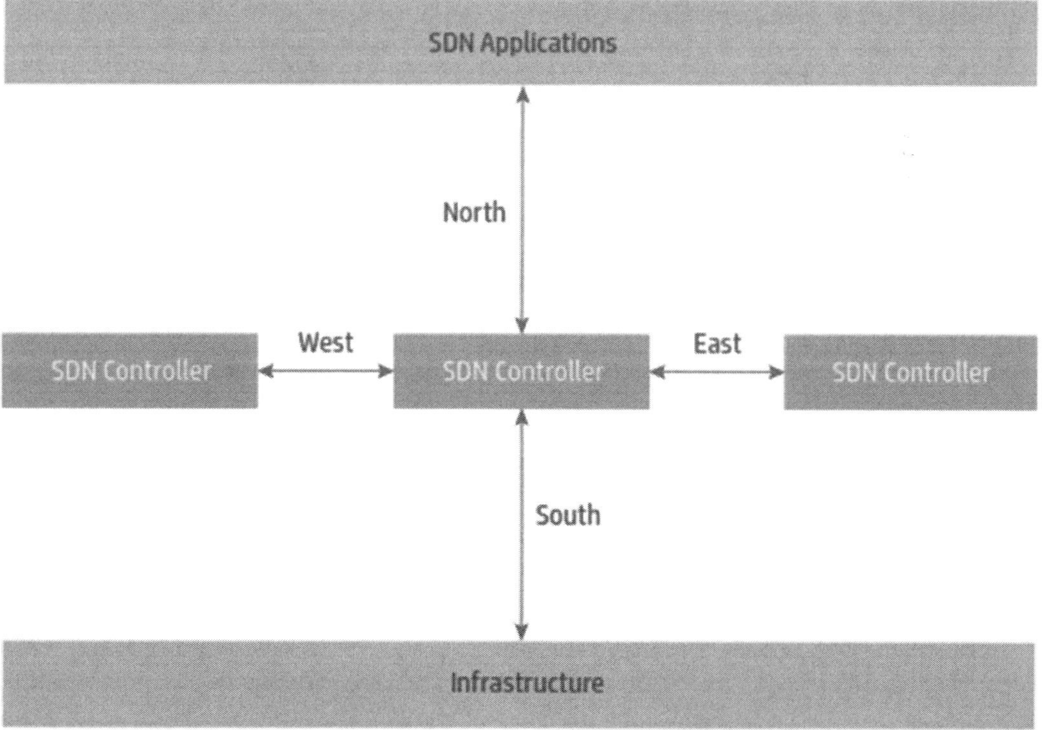

Figure 2-9. API directionality in SDN

HP Virtual Application Network Strategy

The HP Virtual Application Networks strategy embraces software-defined networks to deliver on its three key principles:

- **Application characterization**—Gaining intelligence and characterizing applications and traffic on the network, which are essential to consistently, reliably, and repeatedly automating network configuration for delivering specific applications.
- **Network abstraction**—Enabling multitenant networks with on-demand topologies that are device independent.
- **Automated orchestration**—Automating how the network is configured in response to the policy-driven decisions built into network applications. HP FlexNetwork architecture forms the foundation of the HP strategy and delivers an open and standards-based infrastructure with scalability on three dimensions: security, agility, and consistency.

HP delivered on the promise of application characterization at the network edge through the release of the HP Virtual Application Networks Manager plug-in for the HP IMC. To deliver on the goals of network abstraction and automated orchestration, HP has developed an HP Virtual Application Networks SDN Controller. This controller is the platform for a number of SDN applications that deliver Virtual Application Networks.

Centralized Network Control and Automation

The HP Virtual Application Networks SDN Controller, available as software or as an appliance, is the centralized control platform for the software-defined network. It interfaces with the network infrastructure using open-standard interfaces and control protocols (or southbound APIs), such as OpenFlow, to expose an abstracted and centralized control plane to network applications. These network applications have been built and integrated into the controller to provide network services, such as network virtualization, security, and traffic engineering.

The controller is further extended with robust authentication and authorization mechanisms which, in part, allow HP to expose varying levels of control and access to SDN applications residing within or interfacing with the controller. This mechanism and others work together, allowing customers to reap the benefits of increased network flexibility through SDN while preserving the integrity of the network by preventing unauthorized applications from negatively impacting network stability or performance.

The HP Virtual Application Networks SDN Controller is ready for the cloud and will be integrated with OpenStack and CloudStack to provide elastic provisioning of the network alongside storage and compute. Finally, the controller provides a RESTful northbound API, which is intended to expose network features and functionality naturally to off-controller SDN applications, orchestration and management systems, and business applications.

The controller has been architected to provide enterprises and service providers with a scalable, extensible, and stable solution through which they bridge the gap between the services on which the business depends and the infrastructure over which those services run. The Virtual Application Networks SDN Controller provides the platform for a number of network applications that leverage SDN to deliver the promise of Virtual Application Networks and to increase business agility.

HP Virtual Cloud Network

The HP Virtual Cloud Network (VCN) application delivers Virtual Application Networks elements, leveraging HP Virtual Application Networks SDN Controller and OpenFlow-compliant virtual switches, to automatically create overlay virtual networks.

The HP VCN allows cloud service providers to deliver secure multitenant public clouds at the scale necessary to compete in their markets. Enterprises can leverage HP VCN to gain the advantages of automation within their private clouds, while enabling secure integration of public cloud environments into their private estate. HP VCN provides the network abstraction necessary for service providers and enterprises to take maximum advantage of the public and the private cloud. The HP Virtual Cloud Network application enables public cloud providers and enterprises to overcome the challenges facing them today.

Public cloud providers require massive scale to meet the price points that allow them to compete in their marketplace. Yet existing network automation and virtualization solutions have difficulty scaling to the levels a public cloud provider requires.

The HP VCN solution enables public cloud providers to scale and reduces their risk. First, the HP VCN overlay allows providers to scale beyond the constraints of current solutions. Second, the HP solution focuses network changes at the edge, reducing the risk of each change and making automation at scale a reality.

Enterprises are challenged to interconnect their private environments with their public cloud presences without compromising the integrity of their existing networks. The HP VCN enables the enterprise to securely connect to the cloud and to apply its own "identity" to its cloud environment.

Since the Virtual Cloud Network solution is already integrated with OpenStack, public cloud providers can deliver an automated self-service solution to their tenants and enterprises can securely connect their private estates to public cloud environments.

Sentinel Security

HP's latest innovation in security is the Sentinel security application for HP Virtual Application Networks SDN Controller. Sentinel is able to stop threats before they reach your network. Sentinel security can be deployed across a campus or data center network to protect you from more than 700,000 malicious malware, spyware, and botnet threats.

One possible use case for Sentinel is the redirection of Domain Name System (DNS) queries from user machines to the Sentinel application running on the HP Virtual Application Networks SDN controller. Take, for example, a corporate user who clicks a link in an email message:

- First, the user's DNS query is sent to the local OpenFlow-enabled HP access switch.
- Then, the switch forwards the traffic to the HP Virtual Application Networks SDN controller via an OpenFlow rule implemented by the Sentinel application targeting DNS queries.
- After the SDN controller receives the query, the Sentinel application jumps into action by checking the hostname against the HP TippingPoint Digital Vaccine Labs (DVLabs) Reputation Digital Vaccine (RepDV) database of known threats.
- Finally, if Sentinel determines that the site is legitimate, the query is forwarded across the access layer switch. If Sentinel detects a threat, an unresolvable response is sent back to the client, the action is logged with HP ArcSight, and the user is prevented from accessing the threat.

Sentinel can be used in any network environment where security is a concern, including data center and cloud computing environments. HP envisions a network where Sentinel security can be implemented for unprecedented network visibility, event correlation accuracy, and security control.

OpenFlow

OpenFlow is an emerging open standard protocol that has been a key enabling technology for HP Virtual Application Networks. OpenFlow development started in 2007 and was led by Stanford University and the University of California at Berkeley. In 2011, the protocol standardization was taken over by the Open Networking Foundation (ONF).

OpenFlow allows applications or SDN controllers to access the data plane of the network device. This enhanced level of access allows administrators to dynamically change the way traffic flows through the network. The OpenFlow protocol uses a standardized instruction set, which means that any OpenFlow-enabled controller can send a common set of instructions to any OpenFlow-enabled switch, regardless of vendor.

HP demonstrated the first commercial, hardware-based switch implementation of OpenFlow at ACM SIGCOMM in 2008. HP also participated in a public demonstration of OpenFlow at InteropNet Lab in May 2011. HP has been an active contributor to the OpenFlow standards effort and is a founding member of the Open Networking Foundation. HP continues to work closely with partners, such as Indiana Center for Network Transactional Research and Education (InCNTRE), to drive research in SDN and to ensure multivendor interoperability for OpenFlow-enabled solutions.

Most modern network devices have flow tables that run at line-rate for implementing firewalls, NAT, QoS, and collecting statistics. The OpenFlow protocol provides a means of programming these flow tables from a centralized controller through a Secure Sockets Layer (SSL) channel.

OpenFlow uses a well-defined set of matching rules to classify network traffic into flows (see Figure 2-10). It also defines a set of actions that the network architect can use to instruct OpenFlow-enabled network devices to manage those flows. The devices may include routers, switches, virtual switches, or wireless access points. Traffic moves across paths that are predefined by characteristics such as speed, fewest hops, or lowest latency, giving network managers the ability to tailor network services to meet the needs of different types of applications and data.

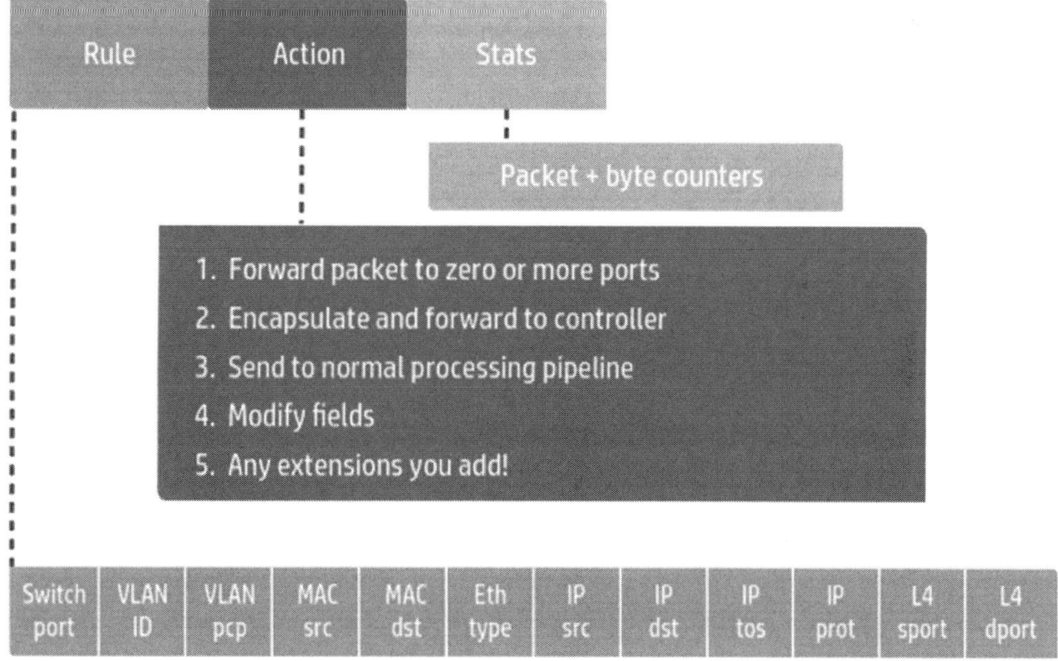

Figure 2-10. OpenFlow flow table entry

The OpenFlow switch flow table is used to give network managers both coarse- and fine-grained control over data flows. Network managers can use OpenFlow's match rule attributes, such as ingress port, MAC or IP source and destination address, or VLAN ID, to take forwarding actions. These actions could be forwarding packets to switch ports or the controller, flooding along Spanning Tree, dropping packets, or pushing the packets through the device's normal packet pipeline.

HP has extended the OpenFlow protocol with vendor-specific attributes to allow for the enforcement of QoS actions, such as placing into a specific queue or rate-limiting using a specified meter. OpenFlow can also modify traffic flows, such as changing a VLAN setup or VLAN priority, or setting the source and destination address for MAC, IP, or TCP/UDP. The OpenFlow controller maintains all of the network rules and distributes the appropriate instructions to the network devices. The controller essentially centralizes the network intelligence, and the network maintains a distributed forwarding plane through OpenFlow-enabled switches and routers.

OpenStack

OpenStack is a collection of open source software projects that enterprises/service providers can use to set up and run their cloud compute and storage infrastructure (see Figure 2-11). Rackspace and NASA were the key initial contributors to the project, but since the project's inception, the OpenStack foundation has managed to attract more than 150 members, with HP being one of the key contributors.

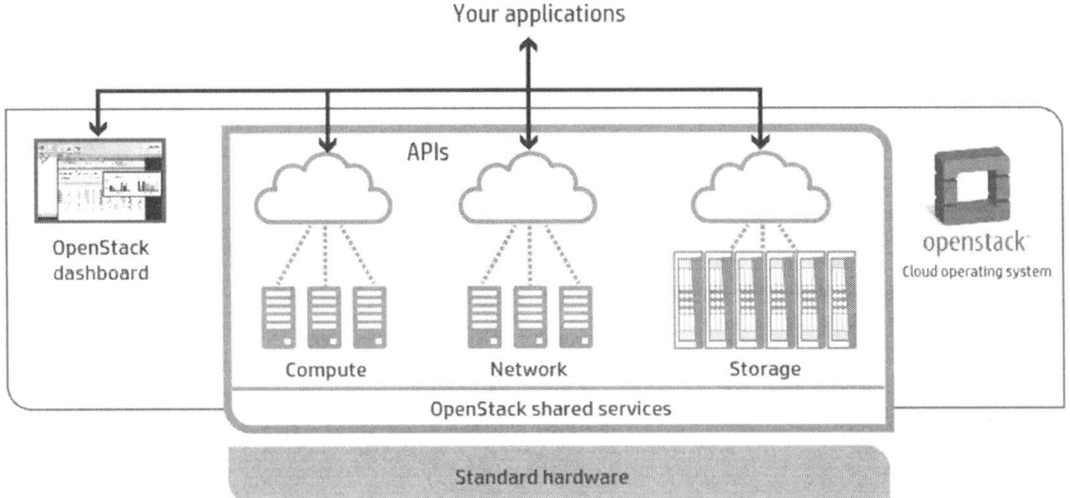

Figure 2-11. OpenStack example

OpenStack provides an open framework for interacting with pools of compute, networking, and storage resources and for provisioning them on demand. Corporations, service providers, value-added resellers (VARs), SMBs, researchers, and global data centers are implementing OpenStack today for large-scale private or public cloud deployments.

HP is a platinum member of the OpenStack Foundation and is committed to furthering the development of OpenStack and to providing OpenStack support across our network portfolio.

Learning Check

The following questions help you measure your understanding of the material presented in this chapter. Read all of the choices carefully, since there may be more than one correct answer. Choose all correct answers for each question.

Questions

1. List the four components of FlexNetwork architecture.
2. Which of the following is not a benefit of the FlexNetwork architecture?
   a. Open standards
   b. Scalability
   c. Reliability and redundancy
   d. Number of users and devices supported
3. In today's data center networks, does most traffic flow north–south or east–west?
4. Which of the following allows for speeds over 10 Gbps for SAN access?
   a. Only FC
   b. Only FCoE
   c. Only iSCSI
   d. Only FCoE and iSCSI
   e. FC, FCoE, and iSCSI

Answers

1. ☑ The components of the FlexNetwork architecture are **FlexFabric**, **FlexCampus**, **FlexBranch**, and **FlexManagement.**

2. ☑ **D** is correct. The number of users and devices supported is not a benefit of the FlexNetwork architecture.

   ☒ **A**, **B**, and **C** are incorrect because they are benefits of the FlexNetwork architecture.

3. ☑ Most traffic flows **east–west** in data centers today.

4. ☑ **E** is correct. FC, FCoE, and iSCSI all support speeds over 10 Gbps.

   ☒ **A**, **B**, **C**, and **D** are incorrect because they do not contain all possible options.

References

1. Gartner, Inc., "Your Data Center Network Is Heading for Traffic Chaos," Bjarne Munch, 27 April 2011.
2. Gartner, Inc., "Emerging Technology Analysis: How Virtual Switches Are Solving Virtualization Issues in the Data Center," Severine Real, 16 November 2010.
3. Ibid.

3 Basic Setup

EXAM OBJECTIVES

In this chapter, you learn to:

✓ Identify, describe, and explain Virtual Local Area Networks (VLANs).

✓ Identify and explain products and features in the HP Networking product line.

✓ Compare and contrast HP Networking solutions and features.

✓ Prepare equipment for installation.

✓ Perform installation and configuration of devices.

✓ Validate the installed solution.

✓ Troubleshoot wireless, switched, and routed networks.

✓ Use general troubleshooting tools.

✓ Verify network performance and parameters.

ASSUMED KNOWLEDGE

This chapter assumes that you are familiar with the following concepts:

- Basic Ethernet concepts, including framing and operation
- Basic switching operations, including learning and forwarding
- Basic VLAN concepts
- IP addressing and subnetting
- ARP

INTRODUCTION

After completing this chapter, you should be able to access the console of the HP ProVision and HP Comware switches. Using the command-line interface (CLI), you should be able to establish a very basic configuration, including the setup of interfaces and the verification of your configuration. Additional topics, like password protecting the switches, Spanning Tree Protocol (STP),

VLANs, and more, are covered in other chapters.

Here are the topics covered in this chapter:

- Accessing HP networking products
- Exploring levels of access and privilege
- Introducing CLI
- Learning basic configuration
- Configuring the interface
- Troubleshooting

HP Switch Components

This section covers the components of HP's switches. The main focus is on console access to the CLI and on the nomenclature of interfaces.

HP ProVision Switch Components

This section focuses on the console access to the HP ProVision switches and on the nomenclature used to identify the interfaces of the switch from the CLI.

ProVision 8212 zl Switch

The HP 8212 zl modular switch, shown in Figure 3-1, features high-performance, high-availability features required by small and midsized businesses (SMBs) that rely on their network to provide core business services. It can be deployed at the core, distribution, or access layer in campus environments.

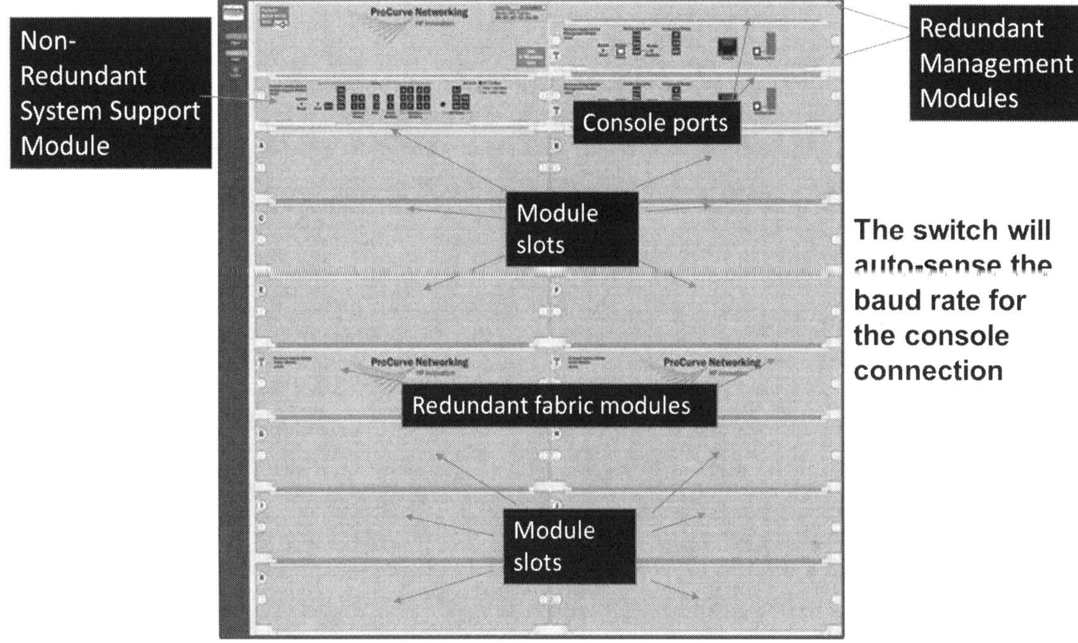

Figure 3-1. ProVision 8212 zl switch

Key features include support for redundant management modules, fabric modules, and power supplies. The switch's 12 module slots support a substantial array of port options, enabling customized configurations for gigabit and 10GbE connectivity over copper or fiber. The HP 8212 zl switch supports advanced routing features, including:

- **Open Shortest Path First (OSPF)**—A dynamic routing protocol that allows the switch to exchange routing information with other network switches.
- **Protocol Independent Multicast (PIM)**—Allows hosts, such as streaming video servers, to send messages to multiple hosts simultaneously. Hosts join multicast host groups to be become eligible to receive specific multicasts.
- **Virtual Router Redundancy Protocol (VRRP)**—Provides routing redundancy.
- **Border Gateway Protocol (BGP)**—Allows connectivity to an external Autonomous System (AS), such as an Internet Service Provider (ISP).

These and other advanced features allow the HP 8212 zl switch to support all of the demanding applications and complex topologies in a contemporary LAN. HP also offers the 8206 zl switch, a six-module model that offers high performance and redundancy to SMBs that do not require the port densities supported by the HP 8212 zl switch.

You can access the CLI in two ways:

- In-band
- Out-of-band

With *in-band* management, your management communications run over network connections with user traffic. You require IP connectivity to the networking device through a direct or indirect Ethernet connection. To open an in-band management session to access the network device's CLI, you must use terminal emulation software, such as PuTTY, that supports either Telnet or SSH. With Telnet, data is transmitted in clear text, whereas SSH encrypts the data you exchange with the switch.

To manage these products through in-band (networked) access, you should configure the product with an IP address and subnet mask compatible with your network. Also, you should configure the appropriate password or passwords to control access privileges from the console and in-band remote management. After an IP address has been configured on the product, these features can be accessed more conveniently through a remote Telnet or SSH CLI session, through the product's web browser interface, or from a Simple Network Management Protocol (SNMP) station running a network management program, such as HP Intelligent Management Center (IMC).

Out-of-band management is the most secure form of managing a networking product. With this method, you connect your management station to the switch's console port with a serial cable. This connection is dedicated to your management session, which you open using terminal emulation software, such as TeraTerm, HyperTerminal, or PuTTY. (These similar software products are generally shareware and can be downloaded for free.) Out-of-band management connections can also include network connections, like SNMP, telnet, or SSH, but these connections must traverse dedicated links or management connections separate from user traffic.

Note

Out-of-band management is the most secure form of managing a networking product.

This section focuses on the initial console access (using a serial connection) to your networking device, and later sections discuss the initial configuration of the ProVision and Comware switches and routers.

To access the CLI of a ProVision switch for the first time, you have two choices. You can create an out-of-band connection with a serial cable. Alternatively, you can allow the switch to receive a dynamic IP address on VLAN 1 (which is configured, by default, to accept a Dynamic Host Configuration Protocol [DHCP] address). You can then determine the IP address that the DHCP server leased to the switch and access the switch using another type of management session, such as Telnet. The console method is the preferred approach.

ProVision switches and Comware switches and routers come with a default console (serial) port configuration. If you want to operate the console using a different configuration, make sure that you change the settings on the terminal and the switch so that they are compatible. First, change the switch settings and save your changes. Then, change the terminal settings, reboot the switch, and reestablish the console session.

After you establish console access to your ProVision switch and the switch has booted up, press `Enter` two or three times. You now see the copyright page and the message, "Press any key to continue." Press a key, and the switch CLI prompt displays. For example:

```
Switch #
```

The ProVision switches have a full-featured, easy-to-use console interface for performing switch management tasks, such as:

- Monitoring switch and port status and observing network activity statistics.
- Modifying the switch's configuration to optimize switch performance, enhance network traffic control, and improve network security.
- Reading the event log and accessing diagnostic tools to help in troubleshooting.
- Downloading new software to the switch.
- Adding passwords to control access to the switch from the console, web browser interface, and network management stations.

ProVision 5406 zl Switch

The ProVision 5406 zl is a six-module switch, shown in Figure 3-2, designed to support up to 144 10/100/1000 Base-T ports. The ProVision 5400 zl switch is also available in a 12-module version, the 5412 zl switch, which supports up to 288 ports. Both models support an array of accessory modules, including eight-port 10GbE modules and specialized modules to support mobility solutions.

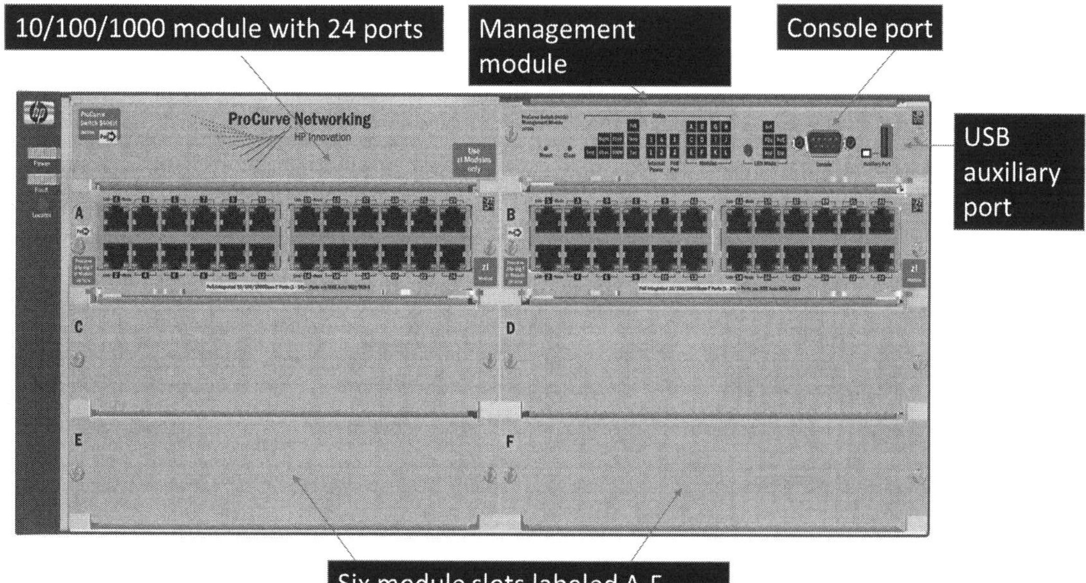

Figure 3-2. ProVision 5400 zl switch

All ProVision 5400 zl 10/100/1000 models support Power over Ethernet (PoE) or PoE+ and advanced routing features, such as OSPF and PIM.

ProVision Port Nomenclature

Each port on your ProVision switch is given an identifier. The model of the switch—modular or fixed-chassis—determines which type of nomenclature you use. Examine Figure 3-3, which displays a module for a ProVision modular switch.

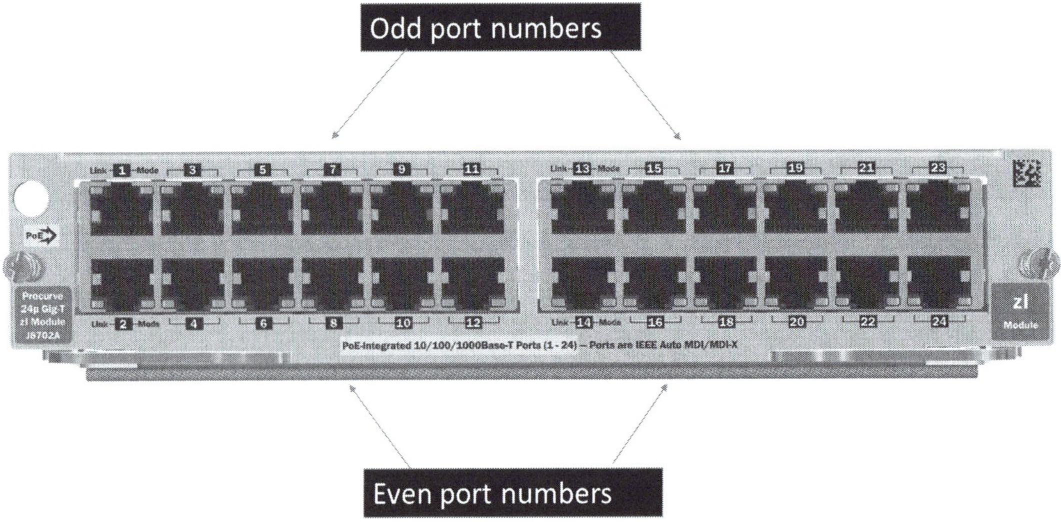

Figure 3-3. Port nomenclature for a modular switch

On ProVision modular switches, such as the 8200 zl and 5400 zl switches, a port is identified by a module letter followed by the number of the port in the module. For instance, if module A is populated with a 24-port 10/100/1000 module, the ports would be named a1 to a24. On the 5406 zl and 8206 zl switches, the modules are identified by letters A through F. Module A is in the upper-left corner of the switch. Module B is immediately to the right of module A. The second module row contains modules C and D. The final row includes modules E and F. Modules on the 8212 zl and 5412 zl are lettered A through L. On each 24-port module, the ports are divided into two sections, with ports 1–12 on the left and 13–24 on the right. The odd-numbered ports are on the top of the module, and the even-numbered ports on the bottom.

Here is a summary of the ProVision port nomenclature process for modular switches and their modular line cards:

- Port names include slot name and port number. For instance, port 1 in the A module is port a1 or A1.
- Odd-numbered ports are in the top row; even-numbered ports are in the bottom row.
- Ports 1–12 are in the left group; ports 13–24 are in the right group.

For the fixed-port chassis or stackable switches, the ports are numbered 1, 2, 3, and so on. Examine the ProVision 3800 stackable switch in Figure 3-4. The fixed ports in this image are numbered 1–24, where the odd-numbered ports are in the top row and the even-numbered ports are in the bottom row.

Note
Letters are not used to identify ports on the fixed-chasses ProVision switches.

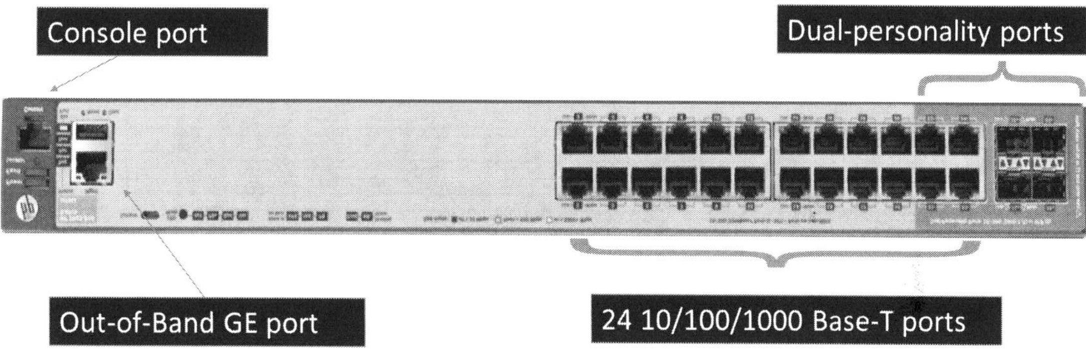

Figure 3-4. Fixed-port switch example

Here is a summary of the nomenclature of interfaces (ports) on fixed-port switches:

- Fixed ports are numbered 1–24.
- Odd-numbered ports are in the top row; even-numbered ports are in the bottom row.
- Dual-personality ports support 10/100/1000 or mini-small form-factor pluggable (SFP)/SFP+ transceivers.

Note
The dual-personality ports are *not* additional ports—you can use either the port with the RJ-45 connector *or* install an SFP/SFP+ transceiver. If you use the RJ-45 dual-personality port, the corresponding SFP/SFP+ transceiver port is not usable, but you can use a mixture of these ports, where, perhaps, two RJ-45s are used and two SFPs are used, but not with the same port numbers.

HP Comware Switch Components

This section focuses on the console access to the HP Comware switches and on the nomenclature used to identify the interfaces of the switch from the CLI.

One unusual quirk between the Comware switches and routers is the default port that they use for initial console access. Comware switches use the auxiliary (aux) port for their default CLI (console) access. Comware routers use the console (con) port for their default console access, but most of the Comware routers also support an additional auxiliary port for a secondary CLI access. This could optionally be used for dial-in access. Unlike Comware switches, ProVision switches only have a console port.

Both ProVision and Comware switches support remote management:

- Telnet
- SSH
- Web browser
- SNMP

On most Comware switches and routers, most management protocols must be explicitly enabled, like SSH, SNMP, and web-based SSL access. ProVision switches, on the other hand, have Telnet, SSH, and HTTP enabled by default. Remote access protocols are discussed in "Chapter 4: Protecting Management Access," along with how to secure the different methods of access.

Console Cable

Initially, the console port must be used to configure the Comware switches and routers; there is no other way to connect to them. The console cable is a rollover cable, shown in Figure 3-5, included with the Comware switch or router. (ProVision switches also use a rollover cable.) It is the same type of cable that most Cisco networking devices employ. With a rollover cable, pin 1 on one side connects to pin 8 on the other side, pin 2 to pin 7, pin 3 to pin 6, and so on. In other words, the pin-out of the remote side of the cable is reversed (rolled).

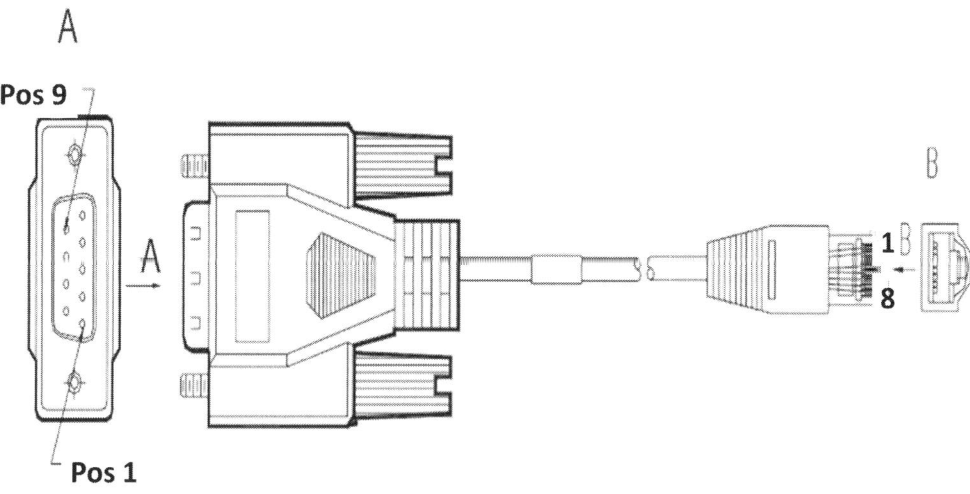

Figure 3-5. Comware rollover console cable

Comware *con* and *aux* Ports

Figure 3-6 shows the console and auxiliary ports of a Comware MSR router. The console terminal can be a standard ASCII terminal with an RS-232 serial interface or, more commonly, a PC. On a PC, you need to use terminal emulation software, like HyperTerminal, TeraTerm, or PuTTY. You need to set your terminal emulation software settings to:

- 9600 bps
- 8 data bits
- No parity
- 1 stop bit
- No flow control

Comware devices use relatively common settings for asynchronous serial (console) connections. There is no restriction on the terminal emulation program you can use, as long as the above settings are set for the local PC COM port.

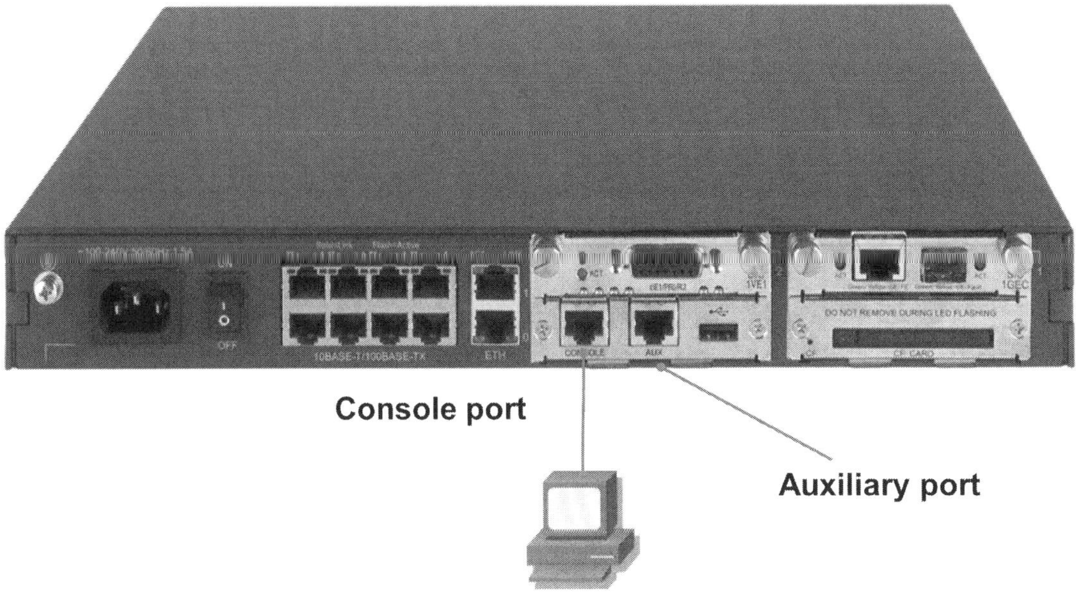

Figure 3-6. Console and auxiliary ports on Comware MSR router

Comware Interface Nomenclature

The nomenclature of interfaces on the Comware switches and routers uses the following structure: `interface-type A[/B]/C`. The interface type is the data link layer type, like `GigabitEthernet` for Gigabit Ethernet. Interface types can be abbreviated, for example, `GigabitEthernet` can be represented as `g`. `A` represents the module, where `0` are the fixed interfaces; `B` represents the sub-slot number; and `C` represents the port number. On the switches, port numbers start at 1; on the routers, port numbers start at 0. For example, on a router, `g0/0` indicates the first fixed Gigabit Ethernet port. On a switch, interface `g1/0/1` indicates port 1 on module 1.

Switches only support Ethernet interfaces; routers support interfaces of many different types. However, this book only focuses on the configuration of Ethernet interfaces.

Here is a quick summary of the interface nomenclature of Comware routers:

- **Fixed slots**—The slot number is 0.
- **Modular slots**—Slot numbers start at 1.
- **Ports**—These always start at 0.
- **Example for an MSR router**—`serial 2/0`.

Here is a quick summary of the interface nomenclature of Comware switches:

- **Fixed and modular ports**—Slot number begins at 1.
- **Ports**—These always start at 1.
- **Example for a HP Comware 5800 switch**—`gigabitethernet 1/0/1`.

Access and Privilege Levels

This section looks at the initial access to ProVision and Comware switches, focusing on the levels of access, or what Comware refers to as *views* or *contexts*.

Note

The ProVision and Comware switches run different operating systems, and, therefore, there are a lot of differences between them. This is apparent when you go through the rest of this chapter.

ProVision Initial Access

In most cases, initial configuration of a ProVision switch is performed through a console connection. Three options are available:

- CLI interface—Enter commands directly.
- Access **menu** interface—Offers fewer configuration options than the CLI, via a character-based menu interface (see Figure 3-7).
- Access switch **setup** screen—Offers limited options for initial configuration (enables you to configure a VLAN 1 IP address so that the switch can be accessed remotely).

```
ProVision Switch 5406zl                          13-Jul-2009  16:19:03
======================- CONSOLE - MANAGER MODE -====================
                                    Main Menu
   1. Status and Counters...
   2. Switch Configuration...
   3. Console Passwords...
   4. Event Log
   5. Command Line (CLI)
   6. Reboot Switch
   7. Download OS
   8. Run Setup
   0. Logout



To select menu item, press item number, or highlight item and press <Enter>.
```

Figure 3-7. ProVision menu-driven interface

The menu interface provides quick, easy management access to a menu-driven subset of switch configuration and performance features:

- IP addressing
- System information
- VLANs
- Local passwords
- Port security
- SNMP communities
- Port and Static Trunk Group
- Time protocols
- Spanning Tree

The menu interface also provides access for:

- Setup screen.
- Switch and port statistic and counter displays.
- Event Log display (discussed in more depth in "Chapter 7: IP Services").
- Reboots.
- Switch and port status displays.
- Software downloads.

The CLI is the most comprehensive management tool, enabling access to all switch configuration options. Consequently, it is emphasized in this book. You can also use the CLI to access the menu and to set up interfaces, using the `menu` and `setup` commands, respectively.

Note

You almost always access the CLI to begin the initial configuration of the ProVision switch. This is typically done via the console port; however, the switches have the DHCP client enabled for VLAN 1, and, if they can obtain an IP address, you can then telnet into the switch, since no password methods are configured. SSH will also work since ProVision switches generate an RSA key-pair when they first boot up (tuning this is covered in more depth in "Chapter 4: Protecting Management Access." Most administrators will use the console for the initial configuration.

After you have access to the CLI, students can go to the menu interface to perform the configuration, or they can use the `setup` option in the menu interface to perform the configuration; however, this book focuses on using commands from the CLI.

ProVision Privilege Levels

You can access the CLI of a ProVision switch as one of the following user types (shown in Figure 3-8):

- **Operator**—This allows read-only access. You can only view statistics and configuration information.
- **Manager**—This allows read/write access. As a manager, you can make configuration changes and view information.

You can protect access to the switch by configuring passwords for each user.

Warning

At factory default settings on ProVision and Comware, there are no passwords. Password configuration is discussed in "Chapter 4: Protecting Management Access."

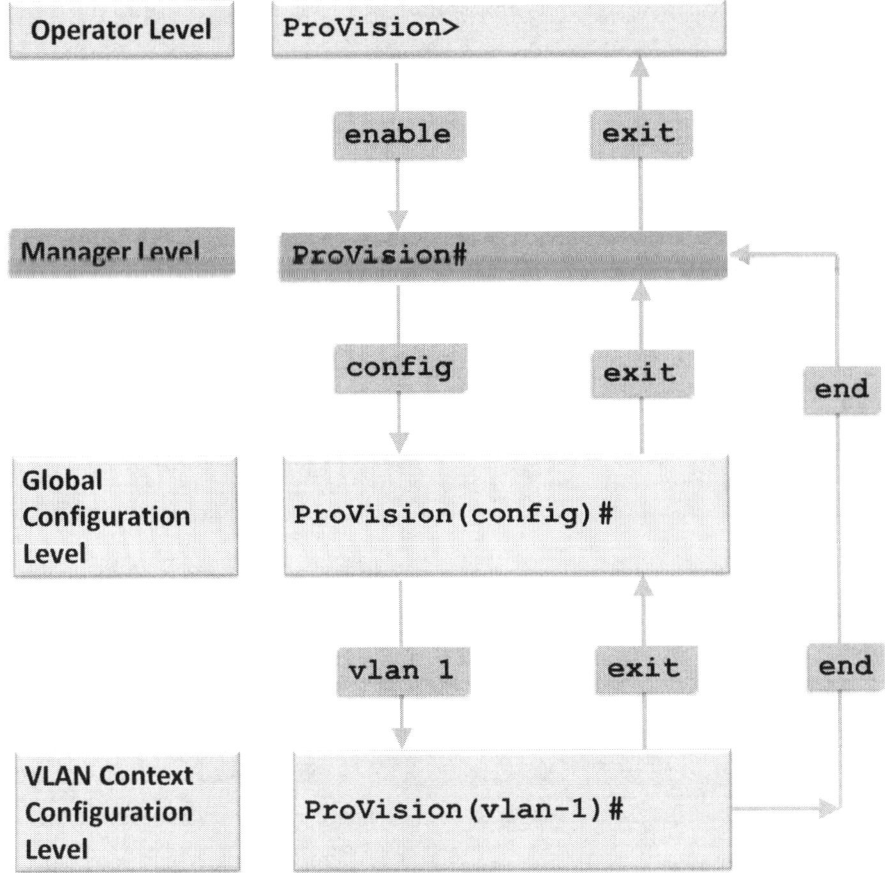

Figure 3-8. ProVision levels of access

The ProVision switch CLI is organized into different levels or *contexts*. You can tell which level you are at by the current switch prompt. Table 3-1 shows an example of the access levels and the commands used to navigate the levels. The `enable` command is used to move from the Operator to the Manager level. The `config` command is used to move from the Manager level to the Global configuration level. The `exit` command takes you back one level. When used in a configuration level (Global or Context), the `end` command takes you back to the Manager level. The `logout` command logs you out of the switch from either Manager or Operator level.

Table 3-1. Access levels on the ProVision switches

Access Level	CLI Prompt	Description
Operator	`Switch>`	View statistics and configure information.
Manager	`Switch#`	Begin switch configuration, such as updating system software.
Global Configuration	`Switch(config)#`	Make configuration changes to the system's software features.

Context Configuration	`Switch(<content>)#`
	Examples:
	`Switch(vlan-1)#`
		Make configuration changes within a specific context, such as to a VLAN, one or more ports, or routing protocols.

Note

If you are familiar with configuring Cisco IOS devices, using the CLI of the ProVision switches will be easy: the ProVision CLI heavily borrows the IOS's semantics and command structure.

Comware Views (Contexts)

Access to the Comware switches' or routers' CLI can be done out-of-band or in-band via user interfaces. User interfaces on Comware switches control the settings for each type of access. For example, the user interface dictates how you authenticate and log in to the switch.

Out-of-band access is slightly different between the two sets of products. The routers support a console (designated as `con 0`) and auxiliary user interface (`aux 0`). The console interface is what you use for the initial access, and the auxiliary interface is used as a backup. The switches support one auxiliary interface, which is used for console access.

In-band (Telnet or SSH) access is accomplished by using virtual user interfaces—one interface for each virtual access connection. The virtual interfaces are designated as `vty 0` to `vty N`, where `N` varies, depending on the Comware product.

The Comware switch CLI is divided into views, each of which contains a set of related commands. Figure 3-9 illustrates a breakdown of Comware's views. In addition to having the privilege to enter a particular command, you must be in the correct view.

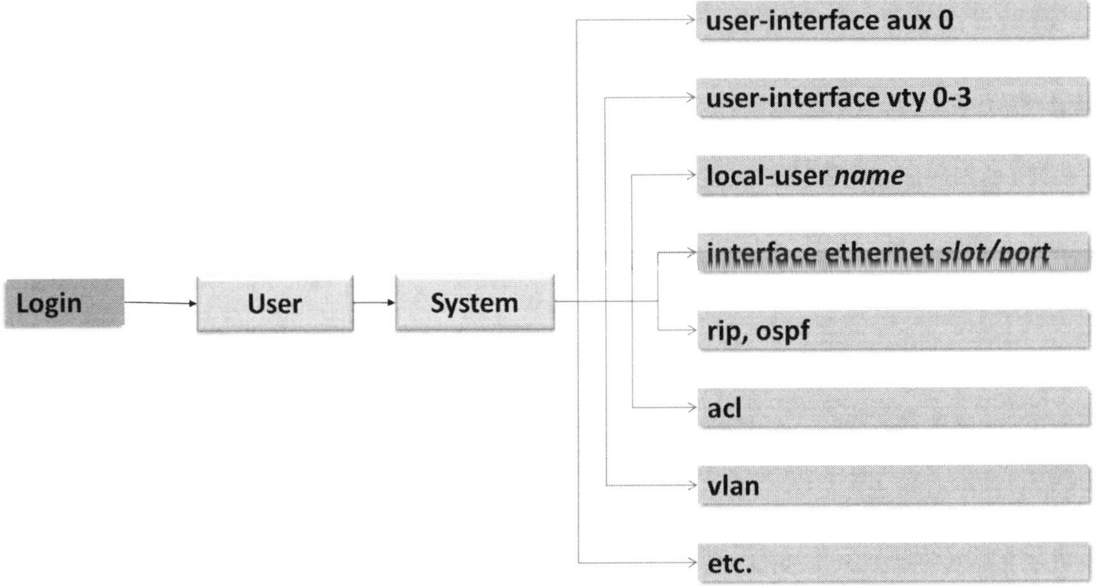

Figure 3-9. Comware views: User and System

If the Comware router or switch has not yet started, turn on the device's power supply to see the starting process. After the startup is complete, press `ENTER` to see the User View of the router:

```
<DeviceName>
```

The *DeviceName* value is the device name of the product. Levels of access can be given to users, according to access method (console or Telnet, for example) and according to user. The types of commands that you can enter depend on your privilege level, which the Comware switch assigns to you when you log in. (You learn about configuring these in "Chapter 4: Protecting Management Access.")

There are two basic views, as described in Table 3-2. Your initial CLI connection gives you access to User View, designated by the following prompt:

```
<Comware>
```

User View is mostly used for operations on the flash file system: list, rename and delete files, save and delete working configurations, and execute `debug` commands.

Table 3-2. Comware CLI Views

View Name	Prompt	Description
User View	`<DeviceName>`	View settings, perform troubleshooting (`debug` command), clear tables (`reset` command), and manage configurations and files. Move to the System View by entering `system-view`.
System View	`[DeviceName]`	Make changes to the switch's configuration. Also access other command views. Move to the User View by entering `quit`.
System Sub-View	`[DeviceName-<view>]`	Configure settings for specific physical or virtual interfaces, user interfaces, or other features. Move back a view by entering `quit`. Move to the User View by entering `return` or by pressing `Crtl+Z`.

System View is needed for most other configuration commands and is presented by the following prompt:

```
[Comware]
```

Available commands depend on the access level of the user (discussed in the next section). To move from User View to System View, use the system-view command:

```
<Comware> system-view
[Comware]
```

Other views (commonly referred to as *Sub-Views*) within the System View are shown by the prompt text:

```
[Comware-GigabitEthernet0/0]
```

Sub-Views are used to configure a particular feature of the Comware device, like an interface, VLAN, or routing protocol, to name a few. The above example is an Interface View and would be accessed by the following System View command:

```
[Comware] interface GigabitEthernet0/0
[Comware-GigabitEthernet0/0]
```

Typing **`quit`** in a Sub-View moves one branch up the tree. Here is an example:

```
[Comware-GigabitEthernet0/0] quit
[Comware]
```

CLI Introduction

This section introduces some basics for working with the CLI of both the ProVision and Comware switches. These basics include:

- Context-sensitive help.
- Command auto-completion.
- Command recall and shortcuts

Context-Sensitive Help

The ProVision and Comware switches offer help features to assist you in navigating the CLI and in entering commands. This feature is commonly referred to as *context-sensitive help*. Table 3-3 shows the conventions for using the context-sensitive help feature. To obtain help, enter **?** at the prompt.

Table 3-3. Context-sensitive help feature

CLI	Description
`?` or `help`	See brief description of all available commands at your context or view.
`<string>?`	See commands that start with certain letters.
`<string>[Tab]`	Auto-complete a command: Type as many characters as necessary to identify the command uniquely, and press `Tab`. Note that you do not have to complete the command—you can just enter the unique characters.

The use of the `help` command or the question mark (?) is used to employ this feature, as shown in the command example below from a ProVision switch:

```
ProVision# ?
Exec commands:
  <1-99>            Session number to resume
  access-enable     Create a temporary Access-List entry
  access-profile   Apply user-profile to interface
<-output omitted->
  copy              Copy from one file to another
  debug             Debugging functions (see also 'undebug')
  delete            Delete a file
  dir               List files on a filesystem
 --More--
```

If there is more information than will fit in one screen, you will see the "--More--" prompt at the bottom of the screen: using the spacebar will display one screen at a time; using the `<ENTER>` key will display one line at a time. Enter the letter "`q`" or `CTRL+C` to break out of the display.

You can also use the context-sensitive help to list commands or parameters that begin with a certain letter or string of characters:

```
ProVision# c?
call    ccm-manager  cd          clear
clock   cns          configure   connect
copy
```

In the above example, the context-sensitive help lists all of the commands that begin with the letter "c."

You can even use the context-sensitive help to list parameters for commands, like this:

```
ProVision# copy ?
  /erase          Erase destination file system.
  /noverify       Disable automatic image verification after copy
  cns:            Copy from cns: file system
  flash:          Copy from flash: file system
  ftp:            Copy from ftp: file system
  null:           Copy from null: file system
  nvram:          Copy from nvram: file system
  pram:           Copy from pram: file system
  rcp:            Copy from rcp: file system
  running-config  Copy from current system configuration
<-output omitted->
```

Here is a quick summary of the context-sensitive help feature:

- It can list the commands supported at a particular level.
- It can list parameters supported by a command.
- You can immediately follow a character or part of a command or parameter with a question mark to get a list of commands or parameters that begin with that letter or those letters.

Command Auto-Completion

When entering commands, you do not need to type in the full command. You can type in enough unique characters so that the CLI understands the command, or you can type in part of the command, press the <TAB> key, and the CLI auto-completes the command for you, as shown below:

```
Switch# conf<TAB>
Switch# configure
```

You need to type as many characters as necessary to identify the command uniquely and then press <TAB>.

With Comware devices, if you do not type in enough characters to make the command or parameter unique, the CLI parser displays the most common command or parameter. When pressing the <TAB> key a second time, the next matching command or parameter is displayed. Using the <TAB> key repeatedly will cycle through all the matching commands or parameters, eventually taking you back to the first command or parameter.

Let us examine the use of Comware's command auto-completion using the <TAB> key. You can do this from either view. Here is an example of showing all of the `display` command parameters that begin with the letter "`a.`"

```
[Comware] display a?
   acfp
   acl
   acsei
   archive
   arp
   arp-snooping
[Comware] display a
```

Notice that there are many parameters that begin with the letter "`a.`" Also notice that, when executed, `display a` remains on the command line, which is a feature of the context-sensitive help. The following example illustrates what happens when you press the <TAB> key after the letter "`a`" and then continue to press the <TAB> key.

```
[Comware] display a<TAB>
[Comware] display arp<TAB>
[Comware] display arp-snooping<TAB>
[Comware] display acl<TAB>
[Comware] display archive<TAB>
[Comware] display acfp<TAB>
```

```
[Comware] display acsei<TAB>
[Comware] display arp
```

Note

The <TAB> key in Comware works a little differently from what you see on ProVision switches. With ProVision switches, the <TAB> key only auto-completes unique commands and/or parameters: if the command or parameter is not unique, nothing happens on the CLI.

Command Recall and Shortcuts

This section introduces ProVision and Comware command recall and shortcuts.

ProVision Command Recall and Shortcuts

Table 3-4 lists the shortcut keys you can use to maneuver the ProVision CLI.

Table 3-4. ProVision CLI shortcut keystrokes

Shortcut	Description
Ctrl+A	Jumps to the first character of the command line.
CTRL+B or <LEFT ARROW>	Moves the cursor back one character.
CTRL+C	Terminates a task and displays the command prompt.
CTRL+D	Deletes the character at the cursor.
CTRL+E	Jumps to the end of the current command line.
CTRL+F or <RIGHT ARROW>	Moves the cursor forward one character.
CTRL+K	Deletes from the cursor to the end of the command line.
CTRL+L or CTRL+R	Repeats current command line on a new line.
CTRL+N or <DOWN ARROW>	Enters the next command line in the history buffer.
CTRL+P or <UP ARROW>	Enters the previous command line in the history buffer.
CTRL+U or CTRL+X	Deletes from the cursor to the beginning of the command line.
CTRL+W	Deletes the last word typed.
ESC+B	Moves the cursor backward one word.
ESC+D	Deletes from the cursor to the end of the word.
ESC+F	Moves the cursor forward one word.
<BACKSPACE>	Deletes the first character to the left of the cursor in the command line.

To view commands you have previously executed, use the `show history` command:

```
ProVision# show history
6        sh vers
5        sh hardware
4        display hotkey
3        exit
2        enable
1        show interfaces
```

Note the number to the left of each entry in the history. You can repeat any command in the history by entering `repeat`, followed by the index number of the command:

```
ProVision(config)# repeat <index-number> [count <number-of-repeats>]
```

If you do not specify a count, the command continually repeats. Press any key to stop the command from repeating. For example, the following command repeats the `show interfaces` command twice:

```
ProVision# repeat 1 count 2
```

Comware Command Recall and Shortcuts

The Comware products support hotkeys to do common CLI tasks using shortcut control sequences. Table 3-5 lists the Comware hotkeys. You can use the `display hotkey` command from the CLI to view the hotkeys. Note that you cannot create your own hotkeys.

Note

You can copy text from the CLI, and you can paste text into the ProVision and Comware CLI.

Table 3-5. Comware hotkey shortcuts

Hot Key	Description
Ctrl+A	Moves the cursor to the beginning of the current line.
Ctrl+B	Moves the cursor one character to the left.
Ctrl+C	Stops performing a command.
Ctrl+D	Deletes the character at the current cursor position.
Ctrl+E	Moves the cursor to the end of the current line.
Ctrl+F	Moves the cursor one character to the right.
Ctrl+G	Displays the current running configuration.
Ctrl+H	Deletes the character to the left of the cursor.
Ctrl+K	Terminates an outgoing connection.
Ctrl+L	Displays the IP routing table.
Ctrl+N	Displays the next command in the history command buffer.
Ctrl+O	Disables debugging when in User View.
Ctrl+P	Displays the previous command in the history command buffer.
Ctrl+R	Redisplays the current line information.
Ctrl+V	Pastes the content in the clipboard.
Ctrl+W	Deletes all the characters in a continuous string to the left of the cursor.
Ctrl+X	Deletes all the characters to the left of the cursor.
Ctrl+Y	Deletes all the characters to the right of the cursor.
Ctrl+Z	Exits from System View to User View.
Ctrl+]	Terminates an incoming connection or a redirect connection.
Esc+B	Moves the cursor to the leading character of the continuous string to the left.
Esc+D	Deletes all the characters of the continuous string at the current cursor position and to the right of the cursor.
Esc+F	Moves the cursor to the front of the next continuous string to the right.
Esc+N	Moves the cursor down by one line (available before you press Enter).
Esc+P	Moves the cursor up by one line (available before you press Enter).
Esc+<	Specifies the cursor as the beginning of the clipboard.
Esc+>	Specifies the cursor as the ending of the clipboard.

The CLI automatically saves recently used commands in the history command buffer. You can access and execute these commands again. Use the `display history` command to display the previously executed commands. Then, use your UP ARROW (or Ctrl+P) key to recall older commands and the DOWN ARROW (or Ctrl+N) key to recall more recent commands. Likewise, the LEFT ARROW key moves you to the left in the CLI, and the RIGHT ARROW key moves you to the right.

By default, the CLI can save up to 10 commands for each user. To set the capacity of the history command buffer for the current user interface, use this command:

```
<Comware> history-command maxsize <number-of-commands>
```

If a command contains syntax errors, the CLI reports error information. Table 3-6 lists common command line errors (similar to ProVision switches).

Table 3-6. Common command line errors

Error Information	Cause
`% Unrecognized command found at '^' position`	Command not found
`% Incomplete command found at '^' position`	Incomplete command
`% Ambiguous command found at '^' position`	Ambiguous command
`Too many parameters`	Too many parameters
`% Wrong parameter found at '^' position`	Wrong parameters

Basic Configuration

This section provides an introduction to the configuration of the Comware and ProVision switches.

VLAN Activity

Throughout this book, you will participate in review activities, which are designed to help clarify your understanding of key concepts introduced in the pre-reading web-based training for the ATP certification and in the free HP web-based videos discussed in "Chapter 1: Introduction." These items can be freely downloaded from HP's website. The review activities also allow you to explore any areas you may have overlooked during your independent study, and they reinforce important concepts. Please note that VLANs are covered in depth in "Chapter 6: VLANs." This section provides a quick review based on the default VLAN configuration of the switches.

VLAN Questions

Taka few moments to answer these questions:

1. What is a VLAN?
2. Why are VLANs used?
3. What must be different between VLANs at Layer 3?
4. What must be enabled to move traffic between VLANs?

VLAN Answers

1. A VLAN is a broadcast domain, a Layer 3 subnet, a logical Layer 2 grouping of computing devices, and more.
2. VLANs are used to segment the network and for security, reducing broadcast/multicast traffic's impact on devices in a network, quality of service (QoS), separate job functions, and more.
3. The network number assigned to the VLAN must be different for each VLAN at Layer 3 of the Open Systems Interconnection (OSI) Reference Model.
4. Routing must be enabled on the network device for traffic to move between VLANs.

ProVision Basic Configuration

This section covers placing a basic configuration on a ProVision switch. Here is a sample configuration:

```
Switch> enable
Switch# config
Switch(config)# hostname myswitch
myswitch(config)# vlan 1
myswitch(vlan-1)# ip address 192.168.1.1/24
myswitch(vlan-1)# exit
myswitch(config)# ip default-gateway 192.168.1.254
myswitch(config)#
myswitch(config)# write memory
myswitch(config)# show running-config
Running configuration:
; J9470A Configuration Editor; Created on release #K.15.03.0007
hostname "myswitch"
module 1 type J94ddA
<-output omitted->
```

The following sections discuss these commands in more depth.

Assigning a Hostname to a ProVision Switch

To define the name of your switch, use the following syntax:

```
ProVision# config
ProVision(config)# hostname <switch-name>
```

The prompt immediately changes to display your new hostname, like this:

```
ProVision(config)# hostname myswitch
myswitch(config)#
```

Assigning IP Addressing Information to a ProVision Switch

By default, one VLAN exists on the switch: VLAN 1. All ports belong to this VLAN. You can assign an IP address to the switch in this VLAN by using the following configuration:

```
ProVision(config)# vlan 1
ProVision(vlan-1)# ip address <ip-address>/<subnet-mask>
```

Here is a simple example:

```
ProVision(config)# vlan 1
ProVision(vlan-1)# ip address 192.168.1.254/24
```

If your switch is a Layer 3 switch, it can have multiple IP addresses—one for each VLAN—where the switch is the default gateway for each VLAN. (VLANs are discussed more in "Chapter 6: VLANs.")

Note
Prefacing a command with the `no` parameter negates the command. For example, `no ip address` would remove a configured IP address on the switch.

When the switch is a Layer 2 switch, you can assign a default gateway address that the switch should use when accessing subnets not directly connected to the switch:

```
ProVision(config)# ip default-gateway <ip-address>
```

Note
Layer 3 routing is disabled, by default, on ProVision switches.

Basic Management Commands for ProVision Switches

Configuration changes can be made to the configuration file in RAM. To view this file, use the following command:

```
ProVision# show running-config
```

Here is an example:

```
ProVision# show running-config
<-output omitted->
hostname "ProVision-1"
interface 22
   disable
exit
interface 23
   disable
exit
vlan 1
   name "DEFAULT_VLAN"
   untagged 1-24
   ip address dhcp-bootp
   exit
snmp-server community "public" unrestricted
```

To save your changes so that they are used when the switch is rebooted, use the following command:

```
ProVision(vlan-1)# write memory
```

This command saves the configuration to non-volatile RAM: flash memory.

Note

`wr mem` and `wr m` are shortcuts for write memory.

To return the switch's configuration back to its factory default settings, use the following command:

```
ProVision# erase startup-config
```

When you are prompted to confirm that you want to reboot the switch, press y. The switch will be rebooted.

Note
The HP switches do *not* automatically save their configurations—you must do this with the write memory command on ProVision switches! On Comware devices, use the save command to perform the same action.

Comware Basic Configuration

This section covers placing a basic configuration on a Comware switch. Here is a sample configuration:

```
<HP> system-view
[HP] sysname myswitch
[myswitch] interface vlan 1
[myswitch-vlan1] ip address 192.168.1.1 24
[myswitch-vlan1] quit
[myswitch] ip route-static 0.0.0.0 0.0.0.0 192.168.1.254
[myswitch] save force
[myswitch] display current-configuration
```

The following sections discuss these commands in more depth.

Basic Host Settings for Comware

The Comware device name is used to identify a device in a network. In the system, the device name is the same as the prompt of the CLI. For example, if the device name is "Sysname," the prompt of the User View is:

```
<Sysname>
```

To change the device name, use the sysname command:

```
[Comware] sysname <sysname>
```

The device name is "H3C" or "HP," by default, depending on the software version of the Comware devices. Here is an example of changing a switch's name to "myswitch":

```
[H3C] sysname myswitch
[myswitch]
```

Notice that the device name in the CLI prompt changed to "myswitch."

The system clock, displayed by system time stamp, is determined by the configured relative time, time zone, and daylight saving time. To view the system clock, use the `display clock` command.

Note

The `display` commands are the equivalent of the `show` commands on the ProVision switches. The `display` commands can be executed from either User View or System View.

Use these steps to configure the system clock:

```
[Comware] clock datetime <HH:MM:SS> {<YYYY/MM/DD> | <MM/DD/YYYY>}

[Comware] clock timezone <zone-name> {add | minus} <HH:MM:SS>
```

To set the time and date, use the `clock datetime` command. To set the time zone, use the `clock timezone` command. The default time zone is Universal Time Coordinated (UTC).

Note

To negate a command, preface it with the `undo` parameter. This is the equivalent of the `no` parameter on the ProVision switches.

Assigning IP Addresses to Comware Layer 3 Interfaces

IP addresses are assigned to Layer 3 interfaces on the Comware products. On the Comware routers, this is to a physical interface, like g0/0. On a switch, by default, this is to a VLAN interface (or an interface where the port mode was changed to routed). The `ip address` command is used to assign the address. Here is the basic configuration:

```
[Comware] interface <interface-type> <interface-ID>

[Comware-<int-view>] ip address <ip-address> <subnet-mask-bits>
```

Here is an example of the configuration of a Comware router interface's IP address:

```
[Router] interface GigabitEthernet 0/0

[Router-GigabitGigabitEthernet0/0] ip address 10.1.1.1 24
```

Here is the configuration of an IP address for VLAN 1 on a Comware switch:

```
[Switch] interface vlan-interface 1

[Switch-Vlan-interface1] ip address 10.10.1.1 24
```

VLANs are discussed in more depth in "Chapter 6: VLANs."

Static Route Configuration for Comware

Comware devices (switches and routers) automatically have routing enabled. Therefore, static routes are configured to define remote destinations, including a default gateway. Static routes are added manually to the device by the network administrator—they are not added or learned by any routing protocol. In a small network, static routes are commonly used.

Static routes are added to the Comware products by using the following syntax:

```
[Comware] ip route-static <destination-network> <mask>
            <next-hop-ip-address> [preference <preference>]
            [description <description>]
```

When creating a static route, you must enter the destination network, the destination subnet mask, and the next-hop IP address or gateway. You can also change the preference or assign a description to the static route. (Preferences are discussed in "Chapter 11: IP Routing Overview.")

Note

IP routing is enabled, by default, on the Comware products. No special command needs to be entered to enable it.

Here is a configuration example using static routes:

```
[RouterB] ip route-static 0.0.0.0 0.0.0.0 10.1.6.2
```

In the above example, static route is a default route with a gateway address of 10.1.6.2. The last static route has a description associated with it. To examine the routing table of a Comware device, use the `display ip routing-table` command. Static routing is discussed in more depth in "Chapter 11: IP Routing Overview."

Viewing the Active Configuration

Here is a partial display of the currently running configuration of a Comware switch:

```
<Comware> display current-configuration
 version 5.20, Release 2202
 sysname Comware-Switch
#
 irf mac-address persistent timer
 irf auto-update enable
 undo irf link-delay
#
```

```
 domain default enable system
 telnet server enable
 undo ip ttl-expires
#
vlan 1
<-output omitted->
```

Note

You can also use the `Ctrl+G` hotkey to display the current running configuration.

The `save` command saves the active configuration to flash. You are prompted if you want to save the file, and, if it already exists in flash, you are also prompted if you want to overwrite it. You can use the `save force` command, which performs the save operation but disables the prompting.

Interface Configuration

The following two sections introduce you to the basics of configuring interfaces on the ProVision and Comware switches.

ProVision Interface Configuration

Here are the default interface (sometimes referred to as a *port*) configurations for ProVision switches:

- Interfaces are enabled.
- Speed, duplex, and MDI are set to auto.
- All interfaces belong to VLAN 1.

Here is a sample configuration:

```
ProVision(config)# interface c7
ProVision(eth-c7>)# disable
ProVision(config)# interface c1-c3,c6 enable
ProVision(config)# interface c7 enable
ProVision(config)# interface c7 speed-duplex 1000-full
ProVision(config)# interface c7 mdix-mode mdix
ProVision(config)# interface c7 name 2008-Server
```

The following sections discuss the configuration of these commands.

Identifying and Enabling Interfaces

The `interface` command is used to configure the switch's interfaces. The CLI is flexible in the interface configuration in that you can configure an interface's (or multiple interfaces') parameters globally or within the interface context, as follows:

```
ProVision(config)# interface <port-list> <interface-command>
```

Or like this:

```
ProVision(config)# interface <port-list>
ProVision(eth-<port-id>)# <interface-command>
```

Either approach is appropriate. Note that, in the above syntax, you can substitute `int` for `interface`, as in: `int <port-list>`.

Disabling and Enabling Ports

All ports are enabled, by default. To disable or enable them, use the `disable` or `enable` commands, respectively:

```
ProVision(config)# interface <port-list> [disable | enable]
```

Or:

```
ProVision(config)# interface <port-list>
ProVision(eth-<port-id>)# {disable | enable}
```

Here is an example of disabling a single interface:

```
ProVision(config)# interface c3 disable
```

Or:

```
ProVision(config)# interface c3
ProVision(eth-<port-id>)# disable
```

Here is an example of disabling a handful of interfaces:

```
ProVision(config)# int c1-c3,c6 disable
```

The command disables interfaces c1 through c3, in addition to c6. The hyphen between ports acts like range, and the comma starts the next port(s).

Note

Do *not* use the `no` form of the command to disable or enable a port.

Setting the Speed and Duplexing for Interfaces

By default, all ports on ProVision switches auto-negotiate speed and duplex settings. However, administrators can define settings using this command:

```
ProVision(config)# interface <port-list> speed-duplex <setting>
```

The speed/duplex setting parameters can be different for interfaces, depending on their maximum speed. For example, a Gigabit Ethernet port supports the following settings: `auto-10`, `10-full`, `10-half`, `100-full`, `100-half`, `auto`, `auto100`, and `1000-full`.

Configuring MDI-X for Interfaces

Copper ports on the switch can automatically detect the type of cable configuration (medium dependent interface [MDI] or medium dependent interface crossover [MDI-X]) on a connected device and adjust to operate appropriately. This means that you can use a "straight-through" twisted-pair cable or a "crossover" twisted-pair cable for any of the connections—the port makes the necessary adjustments to accommodate either one for correct operation. ProVision Auto-MDIX was developed for auto-negotiating devices and was shared with the Institute of Electrical and Electronics Engineers (IEEE) for the development of the IEEE 802.3ab standard. ProVision Auto-MDIX and the IEEE 802.3ab Auto MDI/MID-X feature are completely compatible. Additionally, ProVision Auto-MDIX supports operation in forced-speed and duplex modes.

The following port types on your switch support the IEEE 802.3ab standard, which includes the Auto MDI/MDI-X feature:

- 10/100-TX xl module ports
- 100/1000-T xl module ports
- 10/100/1000-T xl module ports

Using the above ports:

- If you connect a copper port using a straight-through cable on a switch to a port on another switch or hub that uses MDI-X ports, the switch port automatically operates as an MDI port.
- If you connect a copper port using a straight-through cable on a switch to a port on an end node, such as a server or PC, that uses MDI ports, the switch port automatically operates as an MDI-X port.

If you require control over the MDI/MDI-X feature, you can set the mode with the following command:

```
ProVision(config)# interface <port-list>
                         mdix-mode <auto-mdix | mdi | mdix>
```

Here is an explanation of this command's parameters:

- **Manual MDI**—`mdi` is the manual mode setting that configures the port for connecting to either a PC or other MDI device with a crossover cable or to a switch, hub, or other MDI-X device with a straight-through cable.
- **Manual MDI-X**—`mdix` is the manual mode setting that configures the port for connecting to either a switch, hub, or other MDI-X device with a crossover cable or to a PC or other MDI device with a straight-through cable.
- **Auto MDI-X**—`auto-mdix` is the default and allows the switch port to auto-sense the MDI type to use.

Assigning Names to Interfaces

The `name` command option enables you to set a *friendly name* for each port, which can make it easier to identify a port in the CLI and in other management interfaces. To configure a friendly port name for the interface on your switch connected to a device or devices, use the following command:

```
ProVision(config)# interface <port-list> name <port-name-string>
```

Each port can have a unique name, or the same name can be applied to multiple ports. You can display friendly port name data in the following combinations:

- `show name`—Displays a listing of port numbers with their corresponding friendly port names and quickly shows you which ports do not have friendly name assignments.
- `show interface <port-number>`—Displays the friendly port name, if any, along with the traffic statistics for that port.
- `show running-config`—Includes friendly port names in the per-port data of the resulting configuration listing.

Here is an example of displaying the port names:

```
ProVision# show name

 Port Names

  Port   Type      Name

  ------ --------- ----------------------
```

```
  1       10/100TX  Finance Server
  2       10/100TX  HR Server
  3       10/100TX  HR VLAN
  4       10/100TX  HR VLAN
  5       10/100TX  Finance VLAN
  6       10/100TX  Finance VLAN
<-output omitted->
```

Interface Verification

To view the status and statistics (counters) for a port, use this command:

```
ProVision> show interface [<port-id>]
```

You can page through all of the interfaces or examine the statistics for a specific interface. Here is an example of the use of this command:

```
ProVision> show interface a1
 Status and Counters - Port Counters for port A1
  Name  :
  MAC Address      : 001871-b934ff
  Link Status      : Up
  Totals (Since boot or last clear) :
   Bytes Rx        : 521,841            Bytes Tx    .   : 67,315
   Unicast Rx      : 130                Unicast Tx      : 112
   Bcast/Mcast Rx  : 2339               Bcast/Mcast Tx  : 569
  Errors (Since boot or last clear) :
   FCS Rx          : 0                  Drops Tx        : 0
   Alignment Rx    : 0                  Collisions Tx   : 0
   Runts Rx        : 0                  Late Colln Tx   : 0
   Giants Rx       : 0                  Excessive Colln : 0
   Total Rx Errors : 0                  Deferred Tx     : 0
  Others (Since boot or last clear) :
   Discard Rx      : 0                  Out Queue Len   : 0
   Unknown Protos  : 0
  <-output omitted->
```

If the Link Status is `Up`, the port has a data link layer connection to a connected device.

To examine the assigned or defaults names of the interfaces, use this command:

```
ProVision> show name
```

Here is an example of the use of this command:

```
Switch# show name
 Port Names
  Port   Type      Name
  ------ --------- -----------------------------------
  1      10/100TX  Finance Server
  2      10/100TX  HR Server
  3      10/100TX  HR VLAN
  4      10/100TX  HR VLAN
  5      10/100TX  Finance VLAN
  6      10/100TX  Finance VLAN
<-output omitted->
```

To examine a summary status of all ports on your switch, enter this command:

```
ProVision> show interface brief
```

Here is an example:

```
ProVision> show interface brief
 Status and Counters - Port Status
                   | Intrusion                          MDI  Flow Bcast
  Port  Type       | Alert    Enabled Status Mode       Mode Ctrl Limit
  ----- --------- + -------- ------- ----- ------- ---- ---- -----
  1     10/100TX  | No       Yes     Up     100FDx     MDI  off  0
  2     10/100TX  | No       Yes     Down   10FDx      Auto off  0
  3     10/100TX  | No       Yes     Down   10FDx      Auto off  0
  4     10/100TX  | No       Yes     Down   10FDx      Auto off  0
```

Comware Interface Configuration

Here are the default configurations for Comware interfaces:

- Layer 2 interfaces are enabled, by default.
- Layer 3 interfaces are disabled, by default.
- Speed, duplex, and MDI are set to auto.
- All interfaces belong to VLAN 1.

The following sections discuss the configuration and verification of Comware interfaces.

Interface Configuration

To configure the properties of an interface, you have to enter the Interface Sub-View in System View. Here are some common commands to configure your interface properties:

```
[Comware] interface <interface-type> <interface-ID>
[Comware-<int-view>] description <description-text>
[Comware-<int-view>] [undo] shutdown
[Comware-<int-view>] mdi {normal | across | auto}
[Comware-<int-view>] duplex {auto | full | half}
[Comware-<int-view>] speed {10 | 100 | 1000 | 10000 | auto}
[Comware-<int-view>] [undo] jumboframe enable
[Comware-<int-view>] port link-mode {bridge | route}
[Comware-<int-view>] display this
```

Use the `interface` command to enter Interface View. Switch interfaces are enabled, by default, and router interfaces are disabled, by default. Use the `shutdown` command to disable an interface and the `undo shutdown` command to activate an interface. The `mdi` command defines the cable type attached to the interface. By default, it is set to auto. The speed and duplexing of a port also default to auto.

Ethernet frames longer than the standard Ethernet frame size (1,536 bytes) are called *jumbo frames*, and are typical of file transfer. Jumbo frames are supported on Gigabit Ethernet ports and faster. If you set an Ethernet interface to accept jumbo frames, it allows frames up to 9,216 bytes to pass through. If you disable an Ethernet interface to accept jumbo frames, it allows frames up to 1,536 bytes to pass through. This configuration is controlled by the `jumboframe` command.

Note

The default for Ethernet frames is a payload size of 1,500 bytes, with an 18-byte header. When performing 802.1Q tagging (discussed in "Chapter 6: VLANs"), an additional 4 bytes are added (1,522 bytes).

An Ethernet interface operates in either Layer 2 (bridge) or Layer 3 (route) mode. To meet networking requirements, you can use a command to set the operating mode of an Ethernet interface to bridge or route. By default, Ethernet interfaces operate in bridge mode on the Comware switches and in route mode on the Comware routers. Use the `port link-mode` command to change the interface's operation mode.

The `display this` command is very useful because it displays the configuration of the current Sub-View that you are currently within.

Here is an example configuration of a Comware router interface:

```
[Comware] interface GigabitEthernet0/0
[Comware-int-GigabitEthernet0/0] undo shutdown
[Comware-int-GigabitEthernet0/0] duplex full
[Comware-int-GigabitEthernet0/0] speed 100
[Comware-int-GigabitEthernet0/0] undo jumboframe enable
[Comware-int-GigabitEthernet0/0] display this
interface GigabitEthernet0/0
 undo shutdown
 duplex full
 speed 100
 undo jumboframe enable
```

Port Groups

Some interfaces on your switch may use the same set of settings. To configure these interfaces in bulk rather than one by one, you can assign them to a port group. You create port groups manually. All settings made for a port group apply to all of the member ports of the group. For example, you can configure a VLAN for multiple interfaces in bulk by assigning these interfaces to a port group. Any configuration command you make for a port group is replicated and saved for all the interfaces within that group. Therefore, creating and using port groups reduces the number of commands you must configure if you have multiple interfaces that need to share the same properties.

To create a port and assign interfaces to it, use the following configuration:

```
[Comware] port-group manual <group-name>
[Comware-port-group-manual-<group-name>] port group <interface-list>
```

Here is an example of setting up a port group and assigning the same description:

```
[Comware] port-group manual vlangroup1
[Comware-port-group-manual-vlangroup1] port group g1/0/1 to g1/0/12
[Comware-port-group-manual-vlangroup1] description Members of VLAN1
```

Port group configurations are persistent; they remain in the configuration. The `interface range` command allows you to quickly apply a configuration to a range and/or list of ports.

Here is the syntax:

```
[Comware] interface range <interface-list>
[Comware-if-range]
```

Here is a configuration example:

```
[Comware] interface range GigabitEthernet 3/0/1 to GigabitEthernet
3/0/24 vlan-interface 2
[Comware-if-range] shutdown
```

In the above example, interfaces 1–24 on slot 3 and VLAN interface 2 are being disabled.

Note

The `range` parameter is a recently added feature in Comware—older versions of Comware were restricted to the use of port groups when applying a configuration simultaneously to multiple ports. Note that port group configurations, themselves, do not remain in a saved configuration; however, the configuration applied to their associated interfaces does remain. This also applies to the use of the `range` parameter

Interface Verification

To see a summary status of all the interfaces on a switch or router, use the `display brief interface` or, in more recent versions of software, the `display interface brief` command:

```
[Comware] display brief interface
 The brief information of interface(s) under route mode:
  Interface        Link      Protocol-link  Protocol type  Main IP
  NULL0            UP        UP(spoofing)   NULL           --
  Vlan1            UP        UP             ETHERNET       40.1.1.2
  The brief information of interface(s) under bridge mode:
  Interface        Link      Speed          Duplex    Link-type  PVID
  GE1/0/1          UP        1G(a)          full(a)   trunk      1
  GE1/0/2          DOWN      auto           auto      access     1
  GE1/0/3          ADM DOWN  auto           auto      access     1
<-output omitted->
```

This command has two sections. The top section displays the Layer 3 interfaces and their status. The bottom section displays the Layer 2 interfaces and their status.

Note

The *port VLAN identifier* (PVID) is the VLAN assigned to the port. VLANs are discussed in more depth in "Chapter 6: VLANs."

One handy feature on the switch is that, with certain `display` commands, you can use regular expressions and only display certain lines of the output display. Let us look at some examples:

```
[Comware] display brief interface | include UP
[Comware] display brief interface | include trunk
[Comware] display brief interface | exclude auto
[Comware] display brief interface | begin 2/0/1
```

The first command displays only lines that have the word "`UP`" in them. The second command displays only lines that have the word "`trunk`" in them. The third command displays all lines that do not have the word "`auto`" in them. The last command begins the display with the first line that has "`2/0/1`" in it. Please note that the strings you use for your filtering are case-sensitive. When you search for a particular word, the word is case-sensitive and the CLI parser is looking for an exact match. So, for example, if you look for the word "`up`," but the display output has "`UP`," this is *not* considered a match.

Note

The "|" symbol also works with ProVision `show` commands.

The `display interface` command is used to verify the status of an interface. If you do not qualify which interface, all of the interfaces are displayed. Here is an example of a Layer 2 switch port:

```
<Comware> display interface GigabitEthernet 1/0/1
GigabitEthernet1/0/1 current state: DOWN
Line protocol current state: DOWN
Description: GigabitEthernet1/0/1 Interface
The Maximum Transmit Unit is 1500, Hold timer is 10(sec)
Link delay is 0(sec)
Internet protocol processing : disabled
IP Packet Frame Type: PKTFMT_ETHNT_2, Hardware Address: 0023-8927-affe
IPv6 Packet Frame Type: PKTFMT_ETHNT_2, Hardware Address: 0023-8927-affe
Media type is twisted pair
 Port hardware type is 1000_BASE_T
 Port priority: 0
 Unknown-speed mode, unknown-duplex mode
 Link speed type is autonegotiation, link duplex type is autonegotiation
 Flow-control is not enabled
 The Maximum Frame Length is 9216
 Peak value of input: 0 bytes/sec, at 2000-04-26 17:18:22
 Peak value of output: 0 bytes/sec, at 2000-04-26 17:18:22
 Last 300 seconds input: 0 packets/sec 0 bytes/sec
 Last 300 seconds output: 0 packets/sec 0 bytes/sec
 Input (total): 0 packets, 0 bytes
    0 unicasts, 0 broadcasts, 0 multicasts, 0 pauses
 Input (normal): 0 packets, - bytes
    0 unicasts, 0 broadcasts, 0 multicasts, 0 pauses
```

```
Input: 0 input errors, 0 runts, 0 giants, 0 throttles
   0 CRC, 0 frame, - overruns, 0 aborts
   - ignored, - parity errors
Output (total): 0 packets, 0 bytes
   0 unicasts, 0 broadcasts, 0 multicasts, 0 pauses
Output (normal): 0 packets, - bytes
   0 unicasts, 0 broadcasts, 0 multicasts, 0 pauses
Output: 0 output errors, - underruns, - buffer failures
   0 aborts, 0 deferred, 0 collisions, 0 late collisions
   0 lost carrier, - no carrier
```

The current state of an interface refers to the physical and data link layer statuses of an interface and can be one of the following:

- `DOWN (Administratively)`—The Ethernet interface was shut down with the `shutdown` command, so the interface is administratively down.
- `DOWN (link aggregation interface down)`—The Ethernet interface is physically down because the aggregate interface corresponding to the aggregation group that the Ethernet interface belongs to was shut down with the `shutdown` command.
- `DOWN`—The Ethernet interface is administratively up but physically down (possibly because no physical link is present or because the link has failed).
- `UP`—The Ethernet interface is both administratively and physically up.

Note

Line protocol current state indicates if a Layer 3 address, like an IP address, is assigned. For a Layer 2 interface, this will always be DOWN.

Troubleshooting Basics

The following two sections include an introduction to some basic troubleshooting commands and the link layer detection protocol (LLDP).

Basic Troubleshooting Commands

Table 3-7 contains some basic commands for simple troubleshooting. Logging is discussed in more depth in "Chapter 7: IP Services." Currently, the ProVision switches support some of the Comware commands, like `display`. For a detailed list that maps the corresponding commands between ProVision and Comware, download the HP CLI Reference Guide from HP's site.

Table 3-7. ProVision and Comware troubleshooting commands

Troubleshooting Task	ProVision Command	Comware Command
View technical support information	`show tech all`	`display diagnostic-information`
View the recently executed commands	`show history`	`display history`
View the active configuration	`show run`	`display current-configuration`
View the saved configuration	`show config`	`display saved-configuration`
Display locally saved logging information	`show logging`	`display info-center`
Save and reboot	`write memory` `reload`	`save` `reboot`
View software version information	`show version`	`display version`
View MAC address table	`show  mac-address`	`display mac-address`
View ARP table	`show arp`	`display arp`
Test Layer 3 connectivity	`ping`	`ping`
View Layer 3 hops between source and destination	`traceroute`	`traceroute`
View interactions of processes running on switch	`debug`	`debugging` and `terminal debugging`

The `show version` and `display version` commands are discussed in "Chapter 5: Managing Software and Configurations." The following sections discuss some of these commands in more depth.

MAC Address Table

One of the functions of the switch is to learn which MAC addresses are associated to which ports so that the switch can make intelligent forwarding decisions. To view the MAC addresses either dynamically learned or statically defined, use the ProVision `show mac-address` command. Here is an example:

```
ProVision> show mac-address

 Status and Counters - Port Address Table

  MAC Address   Port    VLAN

  ------------- ------- ----
```

```
  001517-f11740 Trk1    1
  0024a8-867421 Trk1    1
  68b599-154240 Trk1    1
  68b599-1563c0 Trk1    1
  68b599-1563fd Trk1    1
  68b599-1563ff Trk1    1
  c09134-e4bdc0 Trk1    1
  001517-f11740 1       10
<-output omitted->
```

Here is what the MAC address table on a Comware switch looks like:

```
<Comware> display mac-address
MAC ADDR        VLAN ID  STATE    PORT INDEX                 AGING TIME
000f-e201-0101  1        Learned  GigabitEthernet1/0/1
--- 1 mac address(es) found ---
```

ARP Table

To see the ARP table of a ProVision device, which resolves IP addresses to MAC addresses, use the `show arp` command. Here is an example:

```
ProVision> show arp
 IP ARP table
  IP Address       MAC Address       Type    Port
  ---------------  ----------------- ------- ----
  10.4.1.1         68b599-1563c0     dynamic Trk1
  10.4.1.3         c09134-e4bdc0     dynamic Trk1
```

Here is a Comware example using the `display arp` command:

```
<Comware> display arp
            Type: S-Static D-Dynamic
IP Address  MAC Address    VLAN ID  Interface              Aging Type
10.1.1.2    000f-e201-0101 1        GigabitEthernet1/0/1   D
```

Ping Testing

When you configure and manage networks, you can use the ping utility to verify Layer 3 connectivity between devices. The ping utility sends Internet Control Message Protocol (ICMP) echo packets to a destination device. If the destination device receives the packet, it sends return ICMP packets.

Here is an example of the use of the `ping` command:

```
ProVision# ping 10.1.10.10
10.1.10.10 is alive, time = 1ms
```

The ping utility shows the results of the ICMP, reporting successful receipt of a reply or a dropped packet.

Note

Some network devices, such as network security devices, do not send reply ICMP echo packets. This security precaution is designed to prevent malicious users from using the ping utility in a reconnaissance attack.

Here is the syntax of the Comware command:

```
<Comware> ping [<options>] <ip-address>
```

Table 3-8 lists some of the options you can use with the `ping` command.

Table 3-8. Commonly used ping options for Comware

Ping Option	Description
-a	Specify a different source IP address.
-c	Specify the number of echo requests to be sent.
-f	Specify packets not to be fragmented.
-h	Specify time-to-live (TTL) value for echo requests to be sent.
-m	Specify the interval in milliseconds to send packets.
-n	Numeric output only. No attempt will be made to look up host addresses for symbolic names.
-s	Specify the number of data bytes to be sent.
-t	Specify the time in milliseconds to wait for each reply.

debug Commands

You have attempted to use `display` commands to troubleshoot a problem, but you are not seeing enough information to solve the problem. Comware and ProVision products support the `debug` command for more detailed troubleshooting. There are two Comware commands used to enable and view debug information:

```
<Comware> debugging <process-name> [<debugging-option>]

<Comware> terminal debugging
```

The first command enables debugging of a particular process on a Comware device—some `debug` commands support options to restrict the output that is displayed. By default, you do not see the output of the `debug` commands unless you execute the second command: `terminal debugging`.

Note

Remember that, on Comware devices, you need the `terminal debugging` command in order to *see* the actual debug output on the CLI.

By default, ProVision devices send debug messages to the internal logging buffer (discussed in "Chapter 7: IP Services"). To see debug output on the console or Telnet/SSH session, use this command:

```
ProVision# debug destination {logging | session | buffer}
```

The `logging` parameter sends debug messages to a syslog server. The `session` parameter displays them at the CLI. The `buffer` parameter sends them to the switch's internal memory buffer with other logging messages.

Note

Because it is CPU-intensive, you should disable all debugging when you have completed troubleshooting your problem: `undo debug all`. You can also use the `Ctrl+O` hotkey to disable debug. For ProVision, use the `no debug all` command.

Link Layer Discovery Protocol (LLDP)

In a heterogeneous network, it is important that various types of network devices from different vendors can discover one another and can exchange configuration information for the sake of interoperability and management. Therefore, a standard configuration exchange platform was created. The Internet Engineering Task Force (IETF) drafted the LLDP in IEEE 802.1AB. The protocol operates on the data link layer to exchange device information between directly connected devices. With LLDP, a device sends local device information (including its major functions, management IP address, device ID, and port ID) as type, length, and value (TLV) triplets in LLDP data units (LLDPDUs) to the directly connected devices and, at the same time, stores the device information received in LLDPDUs sent from the LLDP neighbors in a standard management information base (MIB). It allows a network management system to fast detect Layer 2 network topology change and to identify what the change is.

All current ProVision switches and Comware switches and routers support LLDP, which provides a tool for learning about connected devices, such as switches and wireless access points, which also support the protocol. Described in IEEE 802.1AB, LLDP packets contain data about the transmitting switch and port. It is a data link layer protocol and does not require IP addressing to be configured on a device. LLDP packets survive only one hop. When a switch receives an LLDP packet, the switch places the information from the packet into an entry in an LLDP neighbors table in the MIB.

The information in LLDP packets includes details about routing and switching capabilities, switch model, IP address, and MAC address. LLDP has many uses, including:

- Troubleshoot Layer 2 connectivity problems.
- Share device information.
- Auto discovery functions, like the VLAN for voice, auto-QoS, and power requirements with PoE.

Note

Even though LLDP is sent out as a multicast, a connected device will *not* flood it. Therefore, you will only see directly connected neighbors via LLDP.

Here is a quick summary of using LLDP for troubleshooting:

- If you see LLDP messages, this indicates that Layer 2 is functioning between your device and the connected device.
- If you do not see LLDP messages, this indicates that LLDP is not enabled on this or the remote device, the remote device is sending Cisco Discovery Protocol (CDP) or Foundry Discovery Protocol (FDP) and not LLDP, there is a Layer 1 or Layer 2 problem between the two devices, or an interface is not enabled, among other possible issues.

ProVision: LLDP

By default, LLDP is enabled for all ports on ProVision switches but can be disabled per port by entering `lldp admin-status <port-id> disable` at the CLI. You can also disable or enable LLDP transmission or reception independently.

To view LLDP information about connected devices, use the following command:

```
ProVision> show lldp info remote-device [<port-id>]
```

Here is an example of the use of this command:

```
ProVision> show lldp info remote-device

 LLDP Remote Devices Information

  LocalPort | ChassisId                 PortId PortDescr SysName
  --------- + ------------------------- ------ --------- ---------
  20        | 68 b5 99 15 63 c0         3      3         Router_1
  21        | 68 b5 99 15 63 c0         1      1         Router_1
```

Here is an example looking at the LLDP information for a particular port:

```
ProVision> show lldp info remote-device 20

 LLDP Remote Device Information Detail

  Local Port   : 20
  ChassisType  : mac-address
  ChassisId    : 68 b5 99 15 63 c0
  PortType     : local
  PortId       : 3
  SysName      : Router_1
  System Descr : ProVision J9470A Switch 3500-24, revision K.15.03.0007, RO...
  PortDescr    : 3
  Pvid         : 1

  System Capabilities Supported  : bridge, router
  System Capabilities Enabled    : bridge, router

  Remote Management Address
     Type    : ipv4
     Address : 10.4.1.1
```

```
Poe Plus Information Detail
  Poe Device Type           : Type2 PSE
  Power Source              : Unknown
  Power Priority            : Unknown
  Requested Power Value     : 0 Watts
  Actual Power Value        : 0 Watts
```

Comware: LLDP

By default, LLDP is globally enabled on the Comware switches but globally disabled on Comware routers. You can enable or disable it globally or on a per-interface (or port group) basis:

```
[Comware] [undo] lldp enable
[Comware] interface <interface-type> <interface-ID>
[Comware-<int-view>] [undo] lldp enable
```

You should at least disable LLDP on interfaces where connected devices do not support it or are not trusted.

To view LLDP information, there are various `display lldp` commands you can use:

```
<Comware> display lldp status
Global status of LLDP: Enable
The current number of LLDP neighbors: 2
The current number of CDP neighbors: 0
LLDP neighbor information last changed time: 0 days, 0 hours, 4
minutes, 40 seconds
Transmit interval : 30s
Hold multiplier : 4
Reinit delay : 2s
Transmit delay : 2s
Trap interval : 5s
Fast start times : 3
```

```
Port 1 [GigabitEthernet1/0/1]:
Port status of LLDP : Enable
Admin status : Rx_Only
Trap flag : No
Polling interval : 0s

Number of neighbors : 1
Number of MED neighbors : 1
Number of CDP neighbors : 0
Number of sent optional TLV : 0
Number of received unknown TLV : 0

Port 2 [GigabitEthernet1/0/2]:
Port status of LLDP : Enable
Admin status : Rx_Only
Trap flag : No
Polling interval : 0s

Number of neighbors : 1
Number of MED neighbors : 0
Number of CDP neighbors : 0
Number of sent optional TLV : 0
Number of received unknown TLV : 3
<-output omitted->
```

As the sample output shows, GigabitEthernet 1/0/1 of Switch A connects to a Media Endpoint Discovery (MED) device, and GigabitEthernet 1/0/2 of Switch A connects to a non-MED device. Both ports operate in Rx mode—in other words, they only receive LLDP messages.

To display a summary of the neighbors connected to your Comware device, use the `display lldp neighbor-information list` command. Here is an example:

```
<Comware-1> display lldp neighbor-information list
System Name     Local Interface Chassis ID     Port ID
Comware-2       GE1/0/19        0023-89d9-c161 GigabitEthernet1/0/19
ProVision-1     GE1/0/21        e411-5bcc-cc40 43
```

Learning Check

The following questions help you measure your understanding of the material presented in this chapter. Read all of the choices carefully, since there may be more than one correct answer. Choose all correct answers for each question.

Questions

1. Which ProVision commands take you from Operator level to Manager level and then from Manager level to Configuration mode?
2. Which Comware command takes you from User View to System View?
3. Which character do you type to use the context-sensitive help?
4. What is the name of the feature on Comware which allows you to apply a command to multiple interfaces simultaneously?
5. Which ProVision and Comware commands display the currently active configuration file?
6. Of the following information, which cannot be seen in the LLDP table of a switch for neighboring devices?
   a. Major device functions
   b. Current users logged in
   c. Management IP address
   d. Device identifier
   e. Local port identifier

Answers

1. ☑ `enable` is the ProVision command which takes you from Operator level to Manager level, and `config` takes you from Manager level to Configuration mode.

2. ☑ `system-view` is the Comware command which takes you from User View to System View.

3. ☑ `?` is the character you type to use the context-sensitive help.

4. ☑ Port group is the name of the feature on Comware which allows you to apply a command to multiple interfaces simultaneously.

5. ☑ `show run` (ProVision) and `display current-config` (Comware) are the commands which display the currently active configuration file.

6. ☑ **B** is correct. Current users logged in cannot be viewed from LLDP .

   ☒ **A**, **C**, **D**, and **E** are incorrect. Major device functions, Management IP address, Device identifier, and Local port identifier can be viewed from LLDP information.

4 Protecting Management Access

EXAM OBJECTIVES

In this chapter, you learn to:

- ✓ Define and recognize the purpose and interaction of common TCP/UDP-based upper layer applications.
- ✓ Describe and explain basic network security.
- ✓ Describe network management.
- ✓ Install and configure management and administration solutions.
- ✓ Perform network management.
- ✓ Perform administrative tasks.

ASSUMED KNOWLEDGE

This chapter assumes that you are familiar with the following protocols:

- Telnet
- SSH
- Hypertext Transfer Protocol (HTTP) and Hypertext Transfer Protocol Secure (HTTPS)
- Simple Network Management Protocol (SNMP)

INTRODUCTION

This chapter introduces basic management access to the switches (local and remote). You will learn how to implement simple password protection and user name and password protection for command-line interface (CLI) access, whether it is in-band or out-of-band. You will learn how to enable Telnet, SSH, and SNMPv1, v2c, and v3 access on the switches, focusing on secure protocols and methods.

The topics covered in this chapter include:

- Implementing basic protection using local and remote authentication.
- Implementing remote management with Telnet, SSH, web, and SNMP access.

Basic Protection

In the factory default configuration, the HP switches have no Internet Protocol (IP) address, subnet mask, or passwords. In this state, they can be managed only through a direct console connection.

You can access the CLI in two ways:

- In-band
- Out-of-band

With in-band management, your management communications run over network connections with user traffic. You require IP connectivity to the networking device through a direct or indirect Ethernet connection. To open an in-band management session to access the network device's CLI, you must use terminal emulation software, such as PuTTY, that supports either Telnet or SSH. With Telnet, data is transmitted in clear text, whereas SSH encrypts the data you exchange with the switch.

To manage these products through in-band (networked) access, you must configure the product with an IP address and subnet mask compatible with your network. Also, you should configure the appropriate password or passwords to control access privileges from the console and in-band remote management. After an IP address has been configured on the product, these features can be accessed more conveniently through a remote Telnet or SSH CLI session, through the product's web browser interface, or from an SNMP station running a network management program, like IMC, for all HP and other vendor networking products.

Out-of-band management is the most secure form of managing a networking product. With this method, you connect your management station to the switch's console port with a serial cable with a serial cable or a dedicated links or a management VLAN. This connection is dedicated to your management session, which you open using terminal emulation software, such as TeraTerm, HyperTerminal, or PuTTY. (These similar software products are generally shareware and can be downloaded for free.)

Note

Out-of-band management is the most secure form of managing a networking product.

Local and Remote Restrictions

The following sections introduce the concepts of implementing local and remote access restrictions on HP switches. Authentication, authorization, and accounting (AAA) are also introduced; however, an in-depth discussion of AAA is beyond the scope of this book.

AAA Introduction

There are three components to AAA: authentication, authorization, and accounting. AAA provides a uniform framework for implementing network access management. It provides the following security functions:

- Authentication
  - Who?
  - Identifies users and determines whether a user is valid.
- Authorization
  - What?
  - Grants different users different rights and controls their access to resources and services. For example, a user who has successfully logged in to the device can be granted read and print permissions to the files on the device.
- Accounting
  - When?
  - Records all user network service usage information, including the service type, start time, and traffic. The accounting function not only provides the information required for charging but also allows for network security surveillance.

Location of AAA Credentials

AAA usually uses a client/server model. The client runs on the network access server (NAS), and the server maintains user information centrally. In an AAA network, a NAS is a server for users but a client for the AAA servers, as shown in Figure 4-1. If a network administrator attempts to access a switch and passwords are configured on the switch, the following occurs:

1. The switch prompts the administrator to enter a password (or user name and password, if a user name has been configured).
2. The administrator enters the password (or user name and password, if the switch is so configured).
3. The switch grants access if the administrator enters the correct credentials; the switch blocks access if the credentials are incorrect.

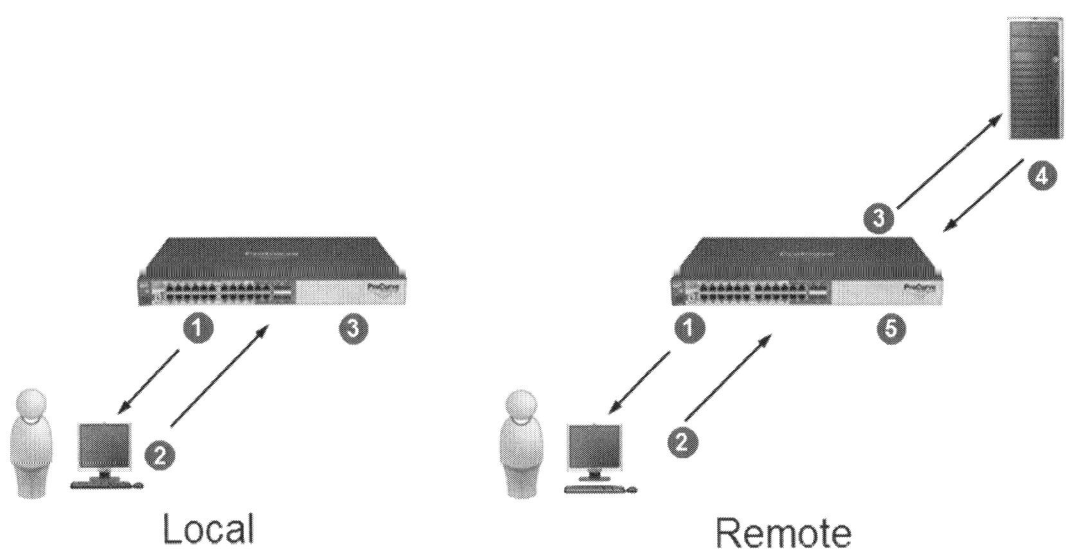

Figure 4-1. Location of AAA credentials

Authentication of access to the HP Networking products can be done via one of two methods: local or remote (commonly referred to as *AAA* or *centralized authentication*). Figure 4-1 illustrates this process. If a network administrator attempts to access a switch and remote authentication is configured, the following occurs:

1. The switch prompts the administrator to enter a password (or user name and password, if a user name has been configured).
2. The administrator enters the user name and password.
3. The switch forwards the login credentials to the Remote Authentication Dial-In User Service (RADIUS) or Terminal Access Controller Access-Control System Plus (TACACS+) server.
4. The server validates the login credentials against its database and notifies the switch if they match. It also notifies the switch which privilege level the administrator should be given.
5. The switch grants the appropriate access level.

Authentication is critical for controlling who accesses the networking devices and the tasks they can perform. The following two sections briefly introduce these topics as they relate to the two series of HP networking products.

There are three common protocols that networking devices might employ when interacting with an AAA server:

- RADIUS
- TACACS
- Lightweight Directory Access Protocol (LDAP) (Kerberos)

Of the three, RADIUS is the most common implementation with different vendors and their networking devices. HP primarily relies on the use of RADIUS.

RADIUS is a distributed client/server system that secures networks against unauthorized access. It is an open standards protocol that uses UDP to share information between the NAS and the security server. The only part that is encrypted between these two devices is the key (password)—all other information is sent in clear text, making this protocol susceptible to eavesdropping attacks. Another problem with RADIUS is that many additions have been made to the protocol by a lot of different vendors, and this typically creates incompatibility problems. Radius uses UDP, and its packet format and message transfer mechanism are based on UDP. It uses UDP port 1812 for authentication and port 1813 for accounting. RADIUS basically has one advantage over the other two protocols: it has a more robust accounting system and, therefore, is very common for user connections, like remote access virtual private networks (VPNs), 802.1X, dial-up, and more.

Note

HP Comware and HP ProVision also support TACACS through their HWTACACS protocol. The main problem with TACACS is that it started as an open standard (Internet Engineering Task Force [IETF] Request for Comments [RFC]), but, different vendors, like Cisco and HP, made their own proprietary changes to it, basically making it a closed protocol between different vendors' networking equipment. This book only covers RADIUS.

HP Comware Authentication

As you learned in "Chapter 3: Basic Setup," the HP Comware switches and routers have user interfaces, which control various forms of management access. The three most common types of interfaces are:

- **Console**—This is used on the Comware routers for console access (the Comware switches have a physical console port, but the Comware configuration refers to it as an *AUX* or *auxiliary* port, which can be confusing to administrators).
- **Auxiliary**—This is used on the Comware switches for console access; the Comware routers also have an auxiliary port, which is used as a secondary console port for out-of-band management.
- **Virtual terminal type (VTY)**—This is used for remote access to the CLI via Telnet or SSH management connections (the number of VTYs depends on the product).

On each interface, you can select one of the following forms of authentication:

- **None**—Not recommended.
- **Password**—All users who log in through the same interface use the same password and receive the same level of access.
- **AAA authentication scheme**—Users authenticate either to a local list of users or to an external RADIUS or TACACS server and, in either case, are authorized for the level of access associated with their accounts.

Password authentication is defined locally on the Comware device. AAA authentication supports *local authentication*, where the authentication and authorization credentials are defined locally on a device, or *remote authentication*, where the AAA credentials are stored on a server.

When using remote authentication, an AAA protocol must be configured to interact with the AAA server. RADIUS is the most common, because it is an open standard. Defining AAA policies on a single server or on multiple servers for redundancy purposes provides more flexibility and centralized management.

HP Provision Authentication

The HP ProVision and Comware products have slightly different methods for authenticating and authorizing users. ProVision switches can authenticate management users in two ways:

- **Local authentication**—All operators log in with a single operator account, and all managers log in with a single manager account. This solution can be implemented in one of two ways: there is a single operator and a single manager password; or you can have multiple operator and/or manager accounts, each with their own password.
- **Remote RADIUS authentication**—With remote authentication, you can separately control each access method (Telnet, SSH, console, or web browser interface) to the switch. Each management user has a unique user account, and, when a user logs in successfully, the authentication server (which is typically a RADIUS server) assigns each user an attribute for operator or manager access.

ProVision Management Access

You can access the CLI of a ProVision switch as one of the following user types:

- **Operator**—This allows read-only access. You can only view statistics and configuration information.
- **Manager**—This allows read/write access. As a manager, you can make configuration changes and view information.

You can protect access to the switch by configuring passwords for each user.

Warning

At the factory default settings, there are no passwords on ProVision switches.

Resetting Passwords

The ProVision switches have two recessed buttons on the front panel, *Reset* and *Clear*, shown in Figure 4-2. These buttons can be seen on the left side of the switch chassis. (Please note that the location of these buttons can change from switch to switch.)

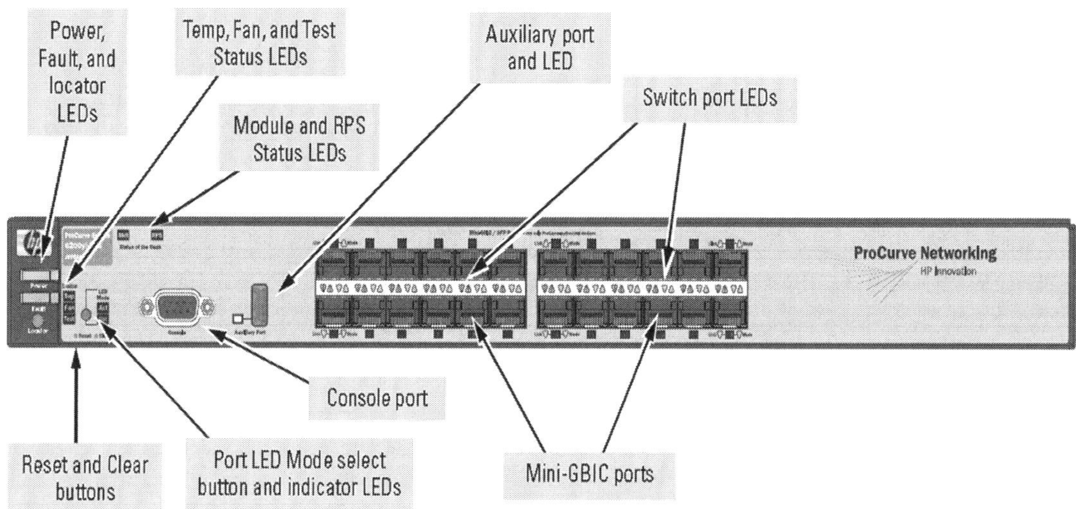

Figure 4-2. Reset and Clear buttons on the ProVision chassis

The Reset button is used to reset the switch while it is powered on. This action clears any temporary errors that may have occurred, and it executes the switch self-test.

The Clear button can be used for erasing passwords. When pressed by itself for at least one second, the button deletes any switch console access passwords that you may have configured. Use this feature if you have misplaced the password and need console access.

Warning

The Clear button is provided for your convenience, but its presence means that, if you are concerned with the security of the switch configuration and operation, you should make sure that the switch is installed in a secure location, such as a locked wiring closet. You can disable the use of the buttons on the front of the chassis. If they are disabled on the front of the chassis, and the administrator needs to do a clear function, he or she can do so from the console as the switch is booting up in the BootROM menu, discussed in "Chapter 5: Managing Software and Configurations."

You can also combine the use of the two buttons to erase the startup configuration on the switch, which causes the switch to boot from the factory default configuration. From the front panel, do the following:

1. Press the **Clear** button, and then press the **Reset** button.
2. Continue to press the **Clear** button while releasing the **Reset** button.
3. When the Self-Test LED begins to flash, release the **Clear** button.

Note

When the above steps are performed, any configuration changes you made through the switch console, the web browser interface, and SNMP management are removed, and the factory default configuration is restored to the switch. Therefore, remember to always back up your switch's configuration to a remote server before making any changes!

ProVision devices utilize the Reset and Clear buttons on the front panel to help users reset the switch configuration to factory default or to reset the console password. This capability creates a security risk anywhere that it is impossible to prevent physical access to the switch. ProVision makes it possible to disable this functionality to protect from malicious use of these features.

There are two components to front-panel security:

- Password clear
- Factory reset

Both must be disabled to fully secure the device. In the switch's default mode, a malicious user can utilize the front-panel Clear button to reset a console password stored locally on the switch. To disable this feature, issue the command:

```
ProVision(config)# no front-panel-security password-clear
```

The other capability built into ProVision switches is the ability to reset the switch configuration to the factory default mode:

```
ProVision(config)# [no] front-panel-security factory-reset
```

Executing this command prevents reset of the switch configuration by use of the front-panel Reset and Clear buttons.

It is critical to understand that disabling these features severely restricts administrator options if the password is lost or forgotten. Before making these changes, users are strongly encouraged to review all considerations outlined in the *Access and Security Guide* for your switch model.

Note

The front-panel security settings are stored in switch flash memory and do not appear in the configuration file.

If you erase the startup configuration and reboot the switch, the front-panel security settings are not restored to the default settings. That is, the front-panel security settings that you configured previously are retained.

Restricting Access

The default authentication on ProVision switches allows you to set a password for the operator and manager user types. Here are the commands to configure the passwords:

```
ProVision(config)# password operator
New password for manager: <password>
Please retype new password for manager: <password>
ProVision(config)# password manager
New password for manager: <password>
Please retype new password for manager: <password>
```

Passwords are automatically encrypted in the switch's configuration.

After you have set the passwords, you can test them by logging in to the switch, like this:

```
Password: <password>
ProVision> enable
Password: <password>
ProVision#
```

Warning

By default, no passwords are preconfigured on the ProVision switches, and Telnet is enabled. Therefore, if the switch has an IP address (via Dynamic Host Configuration Protocol [DHCP], for example), someone could telnet to it without any restrictions! Also, passwords are case-sensitive and can contain spaces, in addition to special haracters. Also, all password credential information is saved in a separate location in the ProVision flash memory from the rest of the configuration. This file is called mgrinfo.txt and is discussed in more depth in "Chapter 5: Managing Software and Configurations."

You can store and view the following security settings in internal flash memory by entering the `include-credentials` command:

- Local manager and operator passwords and (optional) user names that control access to a management session on the switch through the CLI, menu interface, or web browser interface
- SNMP security credentials used by network management stations to access a switch, including authentication and privacy passwords
- Port-access passwords and user names used as 802.1X authentication credentials for access to the switch
- TACACS encryption keys used to encrypt packets and secure authentication sessions with TACACS servers

- RADIUS shared secret (encryption) keys used to encrypt packets and secure authentication sessions with RADIUS servers
- SSH public keys used to authenticate SSH clients that try to connect to the switch

The benefits of including and saving security credentials are as follows:

- After making changes to security parameters in the running configuration, you can experiment with the new configuration and, if necessary, view the new security settings during the session. After verifying the configuration, you can then save it permanently by writing the settings to the startup-config file.
- By permanently saving a switch's security credentials in internal flash memory, you can upload the file to a Trivial File Transfer Protocol (TFTP) server and, later, download the file to the ProVision switches on which you want to use the same security settings without having to manually configure the settings (except for SNMPv3 user parameters) on each switch.
- By storing different security settings in different files, you can test various security configurations when you download a new software version (by changing the configuration file used when you reboot the switch).

To enable the security settings, enter the `include-credentials` command.

```
ProVision(config)# include-credentials
```

This command enables the inclusion and display of the currently configured manager and operator user names and passwords, RADIUS shared secret keys, SNMP and 802.1X authenticator (port-access) security credentials, and SSH client public keys in the running configuration. To view the currently configured security settings in the running configuration, enter one of the following commands:

- `show running-config`
- `write terminal`

AAA Authentication

To set up AAA authentication, use the following command:

```
ProVision(config)# aaa authentication [telnet | console | web | ssh]
                   [login | enable] [radius | tacacs | local |
                    radius local | tacacs local]
```

With this command, you can specify the method of access (Telnet, console, web browser, or SSH), the method of access (operator or manager), and where to find the user name and password. If you use the keyword `local`, you can define the local user names using the following command:

```
ProVision(config)# password [operator | manager] user-name <name>
```

User names can be created from the CLI or web browser interfaces but not from the menu interface.

If you are using RADIUS or TACACS, you must define how to access the external server. Here is the command to specify a RADIUS server:

```
ProVision(config)# radius-server host <ip-address> key <encryption-key>
```

Here is the command to specify a TACACS server:

```
ProVision(config)# tacacs-server host <ip-address> key <encryption-key>
```

The encryption key is used to encrypt password information sent to the RADIUS server.

Here is an example of setting up AAA authentication:

```
ProVision(config)# aaa authentication telnet login radius local
ProVision(config)# radius-server host 192.168.1.253 key mysecretkey
ProVision(config)# password manager user-name richard
New password for operator: <manager_password>
Please retype new password for operator: <manager_password>
```

In this example, Telnet access to the operator level is authenticated using an AAA RADIUS server. The backup is the local database, where the "richard" account has been defined.

Access Restrictions

By default, there is no restriction on who can access the switch remotely after an IP address has been assigned to it. If your switch has multiple Virtual Local Area Networks (VLANs), you can designate a specific VLAN that is your management VLAN—only users (or devices) from this VLAN can connect to the switch:

```
ProVision(config)# management-vlan <vlan-id>
```

Warning

The `management-vlan` command includes *all* IP traffic, not just Telnet or SSH. This includes SNMP traffic from your management station, for example, so use this command with care since it could lock out remote devices that are needed to manage the switch.

Also, the management VLAN is a local VLAN: as long as the remote management traffic is entering the switch from this VLAN, it is allowed—even if the remote device is in a different remote VLAN.

You can also limit remote access connections by specifying the IP address(es) that can establish connections by using the following configuration:

```
ProVision(config)# ip authorized-managers <ip-address>
255.255.255.255

ProVision(config)# ip authorized-managers <network> <subnet-mask>
```

Note

For the best security, you can use both the IP authorized managers and a management VLAN: they can complement each other.

Comware Management Access

Restricting access can be accomplished by using one of three access restrictions:

- **None**—The prompt appears immediately after connecting. This is the default.
- **Password**—Prompts for a common password for all users connecting to the associated user interface.
- **Scheme (with local or remote authentication)**—Requires the use of user names and passwords. For local authentication, a local user must be created. For RADIUS or TACACS authentication, an AAA server configuration must be completed.

By default, you have no password protection at access. Other options, shown above, must be configured by an administrator.

The following sections introduce securing access to the user interfaces of Comware devices and the implementation of privilege levels.

Authentication Modes

After the Comware switch or router boots up and you log into the console, you can access the command line. On Comware devices, each CLI command is associated with one of four levels. The level for each command is configurable, but most customers leave the commands at the default settings. Table 4-1 lists the command levels and basic functions associated with each, from the highest privilege level to the least privilege level.

Table 4-1. Comware switch command levels

Level Number	Level Name	Description
Level 3	Manager	System (file and user) management commands (read/write)
Level 2	System	Services configuration commands (read/write)
Level 1	Monitor	Basic read-only commands
Level 0	Visitor	Diagnosis commands, such as ping and trace route

All of the commands are categorized into four levels—Visitor, Monitor, System, and Manager—and are identified from low to high, respectively, by 0 through 3:

- **Level 0 (Visitor)** involves commands for network diagnosis and commands for accessing an external device. Configuration of commands at this level cannot survive a device restart. Upon device restart, the commands at this level are restored to the default settings. Commands at this level include `ping`, `tracert`, `telnet`, `ssh2`, and certain `display` commands.
- **Level 1 (Monitor)** involves commands for system maintenance and service fault diagnosis. Commands at this level are not allowed to be saved after being configured. After the switch is restarted, the commands at this level are restored to the default settings. Commands at this level include `debug`, `terminal`, `refresh`, `reset`, `send`, and certain `display` commands.
- **Level 2 (System)** provides service configuration commands, including routing configuration commands and commands for configuring services at different network levels. By default, commands at this level include all configuration commands except those at Manager level.
- **Level 3 (Manager)** involves commands that influence the basic operation of the system and commands for configuring system support modules. By default, commands at this level involve the configuration commands of file system, FTP, TFTP, Xmodem download, user management, level setting, and parameter settings within a system (which are not defined by any protocols or RFCs).

User Interfaces and Password Protection

A user interface (also called a *line*) allows you to manage and monitor sessions between the terminal and device when you log in to the device through the console port directly or through Telnet or SSH. One user interface corresponds to one user interface view where you can configure a set of parameters, such as whether to authenticate users at login, whether to redirect the requests to another device, and which user privilege level is assigned after login. When the user logs in through a user interface, the parameters set for the user interface apply.

Only one user at a time can use a user interface. The configuration made in a user interface view applies to any login user. For example, if user A uses the console port to log in, the configuration in the console port user interface view applies to user A; if user A logs in through VTY 1, the configuration in VTY 1 user interface view applies to user A. A device can be equipped with one AUX user interface and 16 VTY user interfaces. These user interfaces do not associate with specific users.

When a user initiates a connection request, the system automatically assigns an idle user interface with the smallest number to the user, based on the login method. During the login, the configuration in the user interface view takes effect.

At present, Comware supports the following three user interface types:

- **Console user interface**—Local configuration via the console port interfaces (referred to as `con 0`).
- **AUX user interface**—Used to manage and monitor users that log in via the console port. The type of console port is EIA/TIA-232 DTE (referred to as `aux 0`).
- **VTY user interface**—Used to manage and monitor users that log in via VTY. A VTY port is used for Telnet or SSH access (referred to as `vty` followed by a terminal number).

To avoid unauthorized access, the switch defines user privilege levels and command levels. User privilege levels correspond to command levels. When a user at a privilege level logs in, the user can use commands only at that level and at lower levels.

A user privilege level can be configured by using AAA authentication parameters or under a user interface with passwords. This section discusses the latter.

To set up a password for a user interface, you must specify the authentication mode and the password. Here's the syntax to configure these:

```
[Comware] user-interface <user-interface>
[Comware-ui-<user-int>] authentication-mode password
[Comware-ui-<user-int>] set authentication password
                         {simple | cipher} <password>
[Comware-ui-<user-int>] user privilege level <number>
```

The user-interface command takes you into the sub-view for the specified user interface. The authentication-mode command specifies the authentication mode to use to authenticate access to the user interface. The `set authentication password cipher` command specifies the password to use (based on mode of password) and that the password will be protected with encryption. The `simple` parameter stores the password in clear text. The `user privilege` command defines the default privilege level for the user interface:

- On the routers, con 0 has a default privilege level of 3.
- On the switches, aux 0 has a default privilege level of 3.
- All other user interfaces have a default privilege level of 0.

Here is an example of protecting the auxiliary (console) interface of a switch:

```
[Comware] user-interface aux0
[Comware-ui-aux0] authentication-mode password
[Comware-ui-aux0] set authentication password cipher mysecret34
```

Note

Under the User Interface context, configuring the `screen-length 0` command disables the prompting for display commands: once executed, the entire output is displayed without any interruption.

Restricting Access with Privilege Levels

The types of commands that you can enter depend on your privilege level, which the Comware switch assigns to you when you log in. Privilege levels equate to the CLI commands that you can execute, based on the privilege level to which you are currently equated. You can enter any command at your current privilege level or below. To move between levels, simply enter:

```
<Comware> super <level-number>
```

It is always possible to move to a lower level than your current level. To move to a higher level, you must enter the super password for that level. For example, to move to the manager level, enter:

```
<Comware> super 3

Password: <password>
```

Note

Console access has no user login and the highest access level (Level 3). Other access methods, like Telnet and SSH, require user login with an associated access level.

Users can switch to a user privilege level, temporarily, without logging out and terminating the current connection. After switching, users can continue to configure the switch without the need of re-login, but the commands that they can execute will change. For example, if the current user privilege level is 3, the user can configure system parameters. After switching to the user privilege Level 0, the user can only execute some simple commands, like `ping` and `tracert`, and only a few `display` commands. The switching operation is effective for the current login. After the user re-logs in, the user privilege is restored to the original level.

The privilege levels can be protected using passwords or user names and passwords. This is controlled with the following command:

```
[Comware] super authentication mode {local | scheme}
```

The default is local.

To assign passwords to the privilege levels, use the

```
[Comware] super password [level <user-level>]
                    {simple | cipher} < password>
```

If you do not define the user level, it defaults to Level 3 (Manager). If the authentication is scheme, you need to define the local user accounts as described in previous sections with the local-user command. Here is an example of defining a Manager password:

```
[Comware] super password level 3 cipher secret2
```

Switching between user privilege levels is done with the `super` command from user view.

User Interfaces and Local User Accounts

If the authentication mode of a user interface is scheme, the user will be prompted for a user name and password, where the user name can be defined locally or on an AAA server.

Follow these steps to configure the user privilege level by using schemes with local user accounts:

```
[Comware] user-interface <user-interface>
[Comware-ui-aux0] authentication-mode scheme
[Comware-ui-aux0] quit
[Comware] local-user <user-name>
[Comware-luser-<user>] password cipher <password>
[Comware-luser-<user>] service-type {terminal | telnet | ssh}
[Comware-luser-<user>] authorization-attribute level {0-3}
[Comware-luser-testuser] quit
```

The `cipher` parameter in the password command encrypts the administrator's password. The service-type command can be used to restrict the access services allowed. `terminal` refers to console or auxiliary port access. The authorization-attribute command assigns the privilege level to the user, from Level 0 (Visitor) to Level 3 (Manager).

Here is an example of defining a user called *testuser*, with a password of 12345678, that is used for access to the console of a switch:

```
[Comware] user-interface aux0
[Comware-ui-aux0] authentication-mode scheme
[Comware-ui-aux0] quit
[Comware] local-user testuser
[Comware-luser-testuser] password cipher 12345678
[Comware-luser-testuser] quit
```

Restricting Access with AAA

The RADIUS protocol is configured scheme by scheme. Therefore, before performing other RADIUS protocol configurations, you must create a RADIUS scheme and enter its view using the radius scheme command. In this sub-context, you define the server(s) used for authentication, authorization, and/or accounting, with the appropriate encryption keys to encrypt the messages between the Comware device and the AAA server.

After you have created the scheme, you must then reference it in a domain. When referencing it in a domain, you can specify a primary and secondary scheme, like RADIUS and local. With a dual scheme, the Comware device will initially try the first defined scheme, like RADIUS, and, if the AAA server or servers are not reachable, it will try the second scheme, like the local database on the Comware device.

Here is the syntax for setting up RADIUS to be used with AAA:

```
[Comware] radius scheme <scheme_name>
[Comware-radius-<scheme_name>] primary authentication <server_IP_addr>
[Comware-radius-<scheme_name>] secondary authentication <server_IP_addr>
[Comware-radius-<scheme_name>] key authentication <string>
[Comware-radius-<scheme_name>] primary accounting <server_IP_addr>
[Comware-radius-<scheme_name>] secondary accounting <server_IP_addr>
[Comware-radius-<scheme_name>] key accounting <string>
[Comware] domain <name>
{Comware-domain-<name>] scheme radius-scheme <scheme_name> [local]
```

Note

The configuration of AAA on a Comware device can be complicated, but with the complication comes a lot of flexibility in defining which servers are used, based on the method of access. The configuration is only introduced in this book; extended and advanced configurations of AAA are beyond the scope of this book.

Remote Management

The remainder of this chapter focuses on setting up remote access on ProVision and Comware switches: this includes Telnet, SSH, web, and SNMP access.

CLI Access: Telnet and SSH

This section introduces the configuration of Telnet and SSH access on the ProVision and Comware switches. Telnet and SSH offer an approach to log in to a remote device: Telnet provides clear-text access, and SSH provides secure access via encryption and strong authentication.

Warning

The use of Telnet is not recommended, since everything is sent in clear text, including any user name and password used to authenticate to a networking device. Secure access to the CLI should be done either using an out-of-band method, like direct console access, or using SSH.

Telnet and SSH Access for ProVision

The ProVision switches use Secure Shell version 1 or 2 (SSHv1 or SSHv2) to provide remote access to management functions on the switches via encrypted paths between the switch and management station clients capable of SSH operation. Like Telnet, SSH is enabled by default. Upon the first bootup of a ProVision switch, it will generate RSA keys if they do not exist in the switch's flash.

SSH provides Telnet-like functions but, unlike Telnet, SSH provides encrypted, authenticated transactions. The authentication types include:

- Client public-key authentication, like PuTTY, TeraTerm, or SecureCRT.
- Switch SSH and user password authentication.

This option uses one or more public keys (from clients) that must be stored on the switch. Only a client with a private key that matches a stored public key can gain access to the switch. (The same private key can be stored on one or more clients.)

Note

At a minimum, HP recommends that you always assign at least a Manager password to the switch. Otherwise, under some circumstances, anyone with Telnet, web, or serial port access could modify the switch's configuration.

Here are the necessary commands to restrict remote access to the CLI for SSH usage only:

```
ProVision(config)# crypto key generate ssh rsa bits <key-size>
ProVision(config)# ip ssh [version 2]
ProVision(config)# no telnet-server
```

You must have a public and private host key pair on the switch. The switch uses this key pair, along with a dynamically generated session key pair, to negotiate an encryption method and session with an SSH client trying to connect to the switch. The key sizes supported are 512, 768, and 1,024 bits in length. The switch will automatically generate a key pair when it boots; however, you can override this by manually creating a key pair.

The host key pair is stored in the switch's flash memory, and only the public key in this pair is readable. When you generate a host key pair on the switch, the switch places the key pair in flash memory (and not in the running-config file). Also, the switch maintains the key pair across reboots, including power cycles. You should consider this key pair to be *permanent*—that is, avoid regenerating the key pair without a compelling reason. Otherwise, you will have to re-introduce the switch's public key on all management stations you have set up for SSH access to the switch using the earlier pair.

Here is an example:

```
ProVision(config)# crypto key generate ssh rsa bits 1024
Installing new RSA key. If the key/entropy cache
is depleted, this could take up to a minute.
ProVision(config)# ip ssh version 2
ProVision(config)# no telnet-server
```

In this example, the 1,024-bit keys are generated, SSHv2 is enabled, and Telnet is disabled.

Removing (zeroing) the switch's public/private key pair renders the switch unable to engage in SSH operation and automatically disables IP SSH on the switch. (To verify whether SSH is enabled, execute `show ip ssh`.) However, any active SSH sessions will continue to run, unless explicitly terminated with the CLI `kill <session-number>` command (the session number is displayed in the output of the `show ip ssh` command).

The `ip ssh` command enables or disables SSH on the switch and modifies parameters that the switch uses for transactions with clients. After you enable SSH, the switch can authenticate itself to SSH clients. SSH is *enabled*, by default, on ProVision switches.

You can also set up SSH authentication using AAA:

```
ProVision(config)# aaa authentication ssh enable
                   {local | tacacs | radius> [local | none]
```

Warning

Remember to disable the use of Telnet after SSH has been configured. This is accomplished with the `no telnet-server` command. The RFC for SSH requires the prompting for passwords; however, on ProVision switches, even though you are prompted for usernames and passwords, if none are defined, pressing <ENTER> will give you access to the CLI. So always remember to define usernames and passwords when implementing SSH on ProVision switches.

Telnet and SSH Access for Comware

By default, SSH access is disabled. Depending on the version of software, telnet is disabled (older versions of Comware) or enabled (newer versions), by default. However, even in newer versions, you must set up authentication for telnet to function. The following example sets up Telnet access using a local scheme:

```
[Comware] telnet server enable
[Comware] local-user admin1
[Comware-luser-admin1] service-type telnet
[Comware-luser-admin1] password cipher mypassword
[Comware] user-interface vty 0 4
[Comware-ui-vty0-4] authentication-mode scheme
[Comware-ui-vty0-4] protocol inbound telnet
[Comware-ui-vty0-4] user privilege level 1
```

The `telnet server enable` command enables the use of Telnet on the VTYs. A local user account, called "admin1," is defined, which allows Telnet access (service-type telnet). Five VTYs (0-4) use a local authentication scheme where only Telnet access is allowed (protocol inbound telnet) and the default privilege level is Level 1 (Monitor). By default, both the Telnet and SSH protocols are allowed unless you restrict them.

With Comware, SSH requires the use of schemes—user names and passwords—for authentication. The configuration of SSH is similar to Telnet, with the exception of these commands:

```
[Comware] ssh server enable
[Comware] public-key local create {dsa | rsa}
```

The first command enables SSH (disabled by default). The second command creates a public/private key pair. The most common key pair implementation used is RSA (Ron Rivest, Adi Shamir and Leonard Adleman).

Here is an example configuration that enables SSH for access to a Comware device:

```
[Comware] ssh server enable
[Comware] public-key local create rsa
[Comware] local-user admin1
[Comware-luser-admin1] service-type ssh
[Comware-luser-admin1] password cipher Hp123
[Comware] user-interface vty 0 4
[Comware-ui-vty0-4] authentication-mode scheme
[Comware-ui-vty0-4] protocol inbound ssh
```

For the `protocol` command, the `inbound` parameter restricts connections coming into the Comware device. Optionally, the `outbound` parameter is used to restrict SSH client (or Telnet) connections to remote devices.

Warning

The use of telnet is not recommended since everything is sent in clear text, including any usernames and password used to authenticate to a networking device. Secure access to the CLI should be done either using an out-of-band method, like direct console access, or using SSH.

To view the users that are currently logged in, use the following command:

```
<Comware> display users
The user application information of the user interface(s):
  Idx UI      Delay    Type Userlevel
F 3   AUX 0   00:00:00      3
  29  VTY 0   00:01:42 SSH  3
```

Following are more details.

```
VTY 0   :
        User name: sradmin
        Location: 10.1.1.12
 +     : Current operation user.
 F     : Current operation user work in async mode.
```

In the above example, there is on user connected via SSH to VTY 0.

To disconnect a connected user, use the `free user-interface` command. Here's an example and a verification of the disconnect:

```
<Comware> free user-interface vty 0
Are you sure to free user-interface vty0? [Y/N]: y
 [OK]
<Comware> display users
```

```
The user application information of the user interface(s):
  Idx UI       Delay    Type Userlevel
F 3   AUX 0   00:00:00      3
 +    : Current operation user.
 F    : Current operation user work in async mode.
```

Web Access

HP ProVision switches use SSL version 3 (SSLv3) and support for Transport Layer Security (TLSv1) to provide remote web access to the switches via encrypted paths between the switch and management station clients capable of SSL/TLS operation. ProVision switches use SSL and TLS for all secure web transactions, and all references to SSL mean using one of these algorithms (unless otherwise noted).

SSL provides all the web functions, but, unlike standard web access, it also provides encrypted, authenticated transactions. The authentication type includes server certificate authentication with user password authentication. You can generate a self-signed certificate, or you can obtain a certificate from a certificate authority (CA); however, the configuration of this is beyond the scope of this book. Certificate authorities have their advantages and disadvantages:

- **Advantages**—CAs allow both the switch and the administrator PC to mutually authenticate each other (both must have certificates).
- **Disadvantages**—An device must obtain a root and identity certificate, and this slows down the setup process; must set up a CA or purchase certificates from a third party; and the device connecting to the HP device must also have a certificate.

Web-based access to ProVision switches is allowed by default; however, the interaction between your web browser and switch is clear text. If you want to use SSL (HTTPS), you need to create a public/private key pair, generate a self-signed certificate (or obtain a certificate from a CA), enable SSL, and optionally disable clear-text HTTP access by using the following commands:

```
ProVision(config)# crypto key generate cert rsa bits <512 | 768 | 1024>
ProVision(config)# crypto host-cert generate self-signed
ProVision(config)# web-management ssl
ProVision(config)# no web-management
```

Here is a configuration example of setting up web access for using SSL only on a ProVision switch:

```
ProVision(config)# crypto key generate cert rsa bits 1024
ProVision(config)# crypto host-cert generate self-signed
Validity start date [11/19/2012]: 11/19/2012
Validity end date [11/19/2013]: 11/19/2017
```

```
Common name [0.0.0.0]: myswitch
Organizational unit [Dept Name]: Human Resources
Organization [Company Name]: HP
City or location [City]: Roseville
State name [State]: CA
Country code [US]: US
ProVision(config)# web-management ssl
ProVision(config)# no web-management plaintext
```

Note

Comware also supports web access. However the use of the Comware web browser interface is beyond the scope of this book.

SNMP

Simple Network Management Protocol is an Internet-standard protocol for managing devices on IP networks. Devices that typically support SNMP include routers, switches, servers, workstations, printers, and more. It is used mostly in network management systems to monitor network-attached devices for conditions that warrant administrative attention. SNMP is a component of the Internet Protocol Suite as defined by the IETF.

An SNMP-managed network consists of three main components:

- **Managed device**—the device that is to be managed, like a switch or router
- **Agent**—Software which runs on managed devices and is responsible for the management information base (MIB)
- **Network management station (NMS)**—Software which runs on the manager

A *managed device* is a network node that implements an SNMP interface that allows unidirectional (read-only) or bidirectional (read/write) access to node-specific information. Managed devices exchange node-specific information with the NMSs. Sometimes called *network elements*, the managed devices can be any type of device, including, but not limited to, routers, switches, firewalls, VoIP phones, IP video cameras, computer hosts (PCs, laptops, and servers), and printers, to name a few.

An *agent* is a network-management software module that resides on a managed device. An agent has local knowledge of management information and translates that information to or from an SNMP specific form, called a *management information base*.

A *network management station* executes applications that monitor and control managed devices. NMSs provide the bulk of the processing and memory resources required for network management. One or more NMSs may exist on any managed network.

SNMP itself does not define which information (which variables) a managed system should offer. Rather, SNMP uses an extensible design, where the available information is defined by MIBs. You can manage the switch via SNMP from a network management station running an application such as IMC. For more on IMC, see "Chapter 15: HP Intelligent Management Center."

To implement SNMP management, the switch must have an IP address, configured either manually or dynamically (using DHCP or Bootstrap Protocol [Bootp]). If you use the switch's Authorized IP Managers and Management VLAN features, ensure that the SNMP management station and/or the switch port used for SNMP access to the switch is compatible with the access controls enforced by these features. Otherwise, SNMP access to the switch will be blocked. The following sections introduce the configuration of SNMP on the ProVision switches.

SNMP provides the following five basic operations:

- **Get operation**—The Get operation is a request sent by the NMS to the agent to retrieve one or more values from the agent.
- **GetNext operation**—The GetNext operation is a request sent by the NMS to retrieve the value of the next object identifier (OID) in the tree.
- **Set operation**—The Set operation is a request sent by the NMS to the agent to set one or more values of the agent.
- **Response operation**—The Response operation is a response sent by the agent to the NMS.
- **Trap operation**—The Trap operation is an unsolicited response sent by the agent to notify the NMS of an event that occurred.

The device sends the first four kinds of packets to UDP port 161, and the agent sends traps to UDP port 162. By using two different port numbers, a single device can simultaneously act as an agent and as an NMS.

Note

SNMP is HP's primary method of large-scale management of devices, whereas IMC, discussed in "Chapter 15: HP Intelligent Management Center," is the tool HP highly recommends for managing ProVision, Comware, and other vendors' devices.

SNMPv1 and SNMPv2c

SNMP version 1 (SNMPv1) is the initial implementation of the SNMP protocol. SNMPv1 operates over protocols, such as UDP and IP. Version 1 has been criticized for its poor security. Authentication of clients is performed only by a *community string*—in effect, a type of password which is transmitted in clear text.

SNMPv2c revises version 1 and includes improvements in the areas of performance, security, confidentiality, and manager-to-manager communications. However, the new party-based security system in SNMPv2c, viewed by many as too complex, was not widely accepted by networking vendors.

As presently specified, SNMPv2c is incompatible with SNMPv1 in two key areas: message formats and protocol operations. SNMPv2c messages use different header and protocol data unit (PDU) formats from SNMPv1 messages. SNMPv2c also uses two protocol operations that are not specified in SNMPv1.

ProVision Configuration

Configuration of SNMPv1 and v2c on ProVision switches is simple. To allow access to read (get operations) the MIB on the switch, use the following command:

```
ProVision(config)# snmp-server community <community-string>
                   operator restricted
```

The community string is the equivalent of a password—it must match what is configured on the management station.

To allow read/write access (set operations), use the following command:

```
ProVision(config)# snmp-server community <community-string>
                   manager unrestricted
```

To send trap notifications to a management station, you must define the SNMP management station's IP address and the community string defined on the server:

```
ProVision(config)# snmp-server host <ip-address> <community-name>
```

Comware Configuration

This section highlights several methods that can be used to secure the deployment of SNMP within Comware devices. It is critical that SNMP be properly secured to protect the confidentiality, integrity, and availability of both the network data and the network devices through which this data transits. SNMP provides you with a wealth of information on network device health. This information should be protected from malicious users who want to leverage it to perform attacks against the network.

SNMP Community Strings

Community strings are passwords that are applied to a Comware device to restrict access (both read-only and read/write access) to the SNMP data on the device. These community strings, as with all passwords, should be carefully chosen to ensure that they are not trivial. Community strings should be changed at regular intervals and in accordance with network security policies. For example, the strings should be changed when a network administrator moves to a different role or leaves the company.

The following commands set up SNMPv2c access:

```
[Comware] snmp-agent community read <community-string>
[Comware] snmp-agent community write <community-string>
[Comware] snmp-agent target-host trap address udp-domain <ip-address>
        params securityname <community-string> [v1 | v2c |
        v3 [authentication | privacy]]
```

The first command enables the set string, and the second command enables the get string.

These lines configure a read-only community string of READONLY and a read/write community string of READWRITE:

```
#
snmp-agent community read READONLY
snmp-agent community write READWRITE
#
```

Note that the preceding community string examples have been chosen to clearly explain the use of these strings. For production environments, community strings should be chosen with caution and should consist of a series of alphabetical, numerical, and non-alphanumeric symbols.

SNMP Traps

The SNMP agent sends traps to the NMS to inform it of critical and important events (such as reboot of a managed device). Two types of traps are available: *generic traps* and *vendor-specific traps*. Generic traps supported on the device include: authentication, coldstart, linkdown, linkup, and warmstart. The others are self-defined traps which are generated by different modules. Because traps that occupy large device memory affect device performance, it is recommended not to enable the trap function for all modules but only for specific modules, as needed.

With the trap function enabled on a module, the traps generated by the module will be sent to the information center. The information center has seven information output destinations. By default, traps of all modules are allowed to be output to the console, monitor terminal (monitor), loghost, and logfile; traps of all modules and with level equal to or higher than warnings are allowed to be output to the trapbuffer and SNMP module (snmpagent); and traps cannot be sent to the logbuffer. You can set parameters for the information center, based on the levels of the traps generated by each module, and thus decide the output rules of traps (that is, whether traps are allowed to be output and what the output destinations should be). For the configuration of the information center, see "Chapter 7: IP Services."

To enable an interface to send linkup/linkdown traps when its state changes, you need to enable the trap function of interface state changes on an interface and globally:

```
[Comware] snmp-agent trap enable [configuration | flash | standard
[authentication | coldstart | linkdown | linkup | warmstart] * | system]
[Comware] interface <interface-type> <interface-ID>
[Comware-<int-view>][undo] enable snmp trap updown
```

Use the `enable snmp trap updown` command to enable the trap function on an interface, and use the `snmp-agent trap enable [ standard [ linkdown | linkup ] * ]` command to enable this function globally.

SNMP System Information

System information includes the ID and the contact method of the administrator, the location of the switch, and the version of the SNMP. The ID and the contact method of the administrator is a character string describing the contact information used for the system maintenance. Through this information, the device maintenance staff can obtain the manufacturer information of the device so as to contact the manufacturer in case the device is in trouble. You can use the following command to set the contact information. The location information of the switch is a management variable of the system group in MIB, which represents the location of the managed device.

Perform the following configuration in system view:

```
[Comware] snmp-agent sys-info {contact <sysContact> |
              location <sysLocation> | version {{v1 | v2c | v3} *
              | all}
```

SNMPv1/v2c Sample Configuration

Here is a sample configuration. Note that comments begin with a hash (#):

```
# Configure the SNMP basic information, including the version and
community name.

[Sysname] snmp-agent sys-info version v1 v2c

[Sysname] snmp-agent community read public

[Sysname] snmp-agent community write private

# Configure the contact person and physical location information of
the switch.

[Sysname] snmp-agent sys-info contact Ms.Alina-Tel:3306

[Sysname] snmp-agent sys-info location telephone-closet,3rd-floor
```

```
# Enable the sending of traps to the NMS with an IP address of
1.1.1.2/24, using public as the community name.
[Sysname] snmp-agent trap enable
[Sysname] snmp-agent target-host trap address udp-domain 1.1.1.2
params securityname public v1
```

Ensure that the SNMP version specified in the `snmp-agent target-host` command is the same as that on the NMS. Otherwise, the NMS cannot receive any trap.

SNMPv3

By adopting User-based Security Model (USM) and View-based Access Control (VACM) technologies, SNMPv3 enhances security. USM offers authentication and privacy functions, and VACM controls users' access to specific MIBs. USM introduces the concepts of user name and group. You can set the authentication and privacy functions. Authentication is used to validate the sending end of the authentication packets, preventing access of illegal users; privacy is used to encrypt packets between the NMS and agent, preventing the packets from being intercepted. USM ensures a more secure communication between the SNMP NMS and the SNMP agent by using authentication with privacy. Authentication without privacy—or no authentication and no privacy—is less secure.

VACM defines the five elements: groups, security level, contexts, MIB views, and access policy. These five elements together control users' access to management information. Only a user with access rights can manage the objects. You can define different groups on the same SNMP entity; these groups are bound with MIB views. In addition, you can define multiple users in one group. When a user accesses the management information, that user can access only the objects defined by the corresponding MIB view.

In summary, a user defines the methods of protection:

- **Confidentiality**—Encryption algorithm and key (must be pre-shared)
- **Data integrity and authentication**— Hash-based Message Authentication Code (HMAC) function and key (must be pre-shared)

And the group defines the access restrictions:

- Which MIBs can be accessed
- Which access type (read-only or read/write)

HP Networking devices support SNMPv1, SNMPv2c, and SNMPv3. To make SNMPv1 and SNMPv2c compatible with SNMPv3, you can configure group, user, and view for these two versions. In this case, you only need to configure the parameter settings of the community name on the NMS as the user name configured on the device. You can enable multiple SNMP versions on the device at the same time, but you need to make them consistent with those on the NMS.

Note

An SNMPv3 group defines the kind of access, for example, which MIBs can be accessed and whether the access for the MIB is read-only or read/write. Users (the term does not really describe its correct definition) define the kind of protection for the information transported between the NMS and the networking device.

ProVision Configuration

To enable SMNPv3 operation on the ProVision switches, use the following command:

```
ProVision(config)# snmpv3 enable
```

You may (optionally) restrict access to only SNMPv3 agents by using this command:

```
ProVision(config)# snmpv3 only
```

To restrict write access to only SNMPv3 agents, use this command:

```
ProVision(config)# snmpv3 restricted-access
```

Note

Restricting access to only version 3 messages makes the community named "public" inaccessible to network management applications (such as auto-discovery, traffic monitoring, SNMP trap generation, and threshold setting).

The `show snmpv3 enable` command displays the operating status of SNMPv3, and the `show snmpv3 only` displays the status of message reception of non-SNMPv3 messages. The `show snmpv3 restricted-access` command displays the status of write messages of non-SNMPv3 messages.

Configure an SNMPv3 User Name and Password

SNMPv3 user names and passwords define the type of protection used for a particular management station's access. Here is the syntax of the command:

```
ProVision(config)# snmpv3 user <username> auth <md5 | sha>
                   <auth-pwd> priv <des | aes> <priv-pwd>]
```

Authorization and privacy (encryption) are optional, but, to use privacy, you must use authorization. When you delete a user, only the `<username>` is required. With authorization, you can set either MD5 (Message Digest 5) or SHA (secure hash algorithm) authentication. The authentication password `<auth-pass>` must be 6 to 32 characters in length and is mandatory when you configure authentication.

With privacy, the switch supports Data Encryption Standard (DES) (56-bit) and Advanced Encryption Standard (AES) (128-bit) encryption. The privacy password <priv-pwd> must be 6 to 32 characters in length and is mandatory when you configure privacy. If you do not configure privacy, it defaults to DES.

Here is a configuration example:

```
ProVision(config)# snmpv3 user Nika auth sha securepassword
                        priv aes securepassword
```

To display the management stations configured to access the switch with SNMPv3 and to view the authentication and privacy protocols that each station uses, enter the `show snmpv3 user` command.

Configure an SNMPv3 Group

An SNMPv3 group associates an SNMPv3 user to the SNMPv3 implementation it uses and to the restrictions applied to the user account. The syntax command is as follows:

```
ProVision(config)# snmpv3 group <group-name> user <username>
                        secmodel {ver1 | ver2c | ver3}
```

Group names for SNMPv3 users include:

- `managerpriv`
- `managerauth`
- `operatorauth`
- `operatornoauth`

The first two parameters allow read/write access, and the last two allow read-only access.

Other SNMPv3 Topics

SNMPv3 also supports notifications, commonly referred to as *traps*. This feature allows the switch to send a notification message to a management station when a particular event occurs. By default, the following notifications are enabled on a switch:

- Manager password changes
- SNMP authentication failure
- Link-change traps: when the link on a port changes from up to down (linkdown) or down to up (linkup)
- Port-security (web, MAC, or 802.1X) authentication failure
- Invalid password entered in a login attempt through a direct serial, Telnet, or SSH connection

- Inability to establish a connection with the RADIUS or TACACS+ authentication server
- DHCP snooping events
- ARP protection events

Other notification types can be enabled. The configuration of other SNMP notification types is beyond the scope of this book.

Comware Configuration

SNMPv3 uses an authentication and privacy security model. On the NMS, the user needs to specify the user name and security level, and, based on that level, configure the authentication mode, authentication password, privacy mode, and privacy password. In addition, the timeout time and the number of retries should be configured. The user can inquire and configure the device through the NMS.

The steps for configuring SNMPv3 on Comware are:

1. Set up an SNMPv3 group.
2. Set up an SNMPv3 user.

The following sections discuss the configuration of SNMPv3 on Comware devices.

Step 1. SNMPv3 Group Configuration

An SNMP group defines security model, access right, and other details. A user in an SNMP group has the same public properties. Use the `snmp-agent group` command to configure a new SNMP group and to specify its access right:

```
[Comware] snmp-agent group v3 <group-name> [authentication | privacy]
              [read-view <read-view>] [write-view <write-view>]
              [notify-view <notify-view>][acl <acl-list>]
```

Here are the parameters used with this command:

- `<group-name>`—Group name (a string of 1 to 32 characters).
- `authentication`—Specifies the security model of the SNMP group to be authentication only (without privacy): HMAC without encryption.
- `privacy`—Specifies the security model of the SNMP group to be authentication and privacy: HMAC and encryption.
- `read-view`—Read view (a string of 1 to 32 characters). The default read view is ViewDefault. Read view controls which MIB objects a group can view. By default, the group can view all MIB objects. Configuring read view is beyond the scope of this book.

- write-view—Write view (a string of 1 to 32 characters). By default, no write view is configured. The NMS cannot perform write operations to any MIB objects on the device. Configuring write view is beyond the scope of this book.
- notify-view—Notify view, for sending traps (a string of 1 to 32 characters). By default, no notify view is configured. The device does not send traps to the NMS. Configuring notify view is beyond the scope of this book.
- acl—Associates a basic access control list (ACL) with the group. <acl-number> is in the range 2000 to 2999. By using a basic ACL, you can restrict the source IP address of SNMP packets—that is, you can configure to allow or prohibit SNMP packets with a specific source IP address so as to restrict the intercommunication between the NMS and the agent.

By default, SNMP groups configured by the snmp-agent group v3 command use a no-authentication-no-privacy security model.

Step 2. SNMPv3 User Configuration

Use the snmp-agent usm-user v3 command to add a user to an SNMP group:

```
[Comware] snmp-agent usm-user v3 <user-name> <group-name> [cipher]
              [authentication-mode {md5 | sha} <auth-password>
              [privacy-mode {3des | aes128 | des56}
              <priv-password>]] [acl <acl-number>]
```

The user name configured by using this command is applicable to the SNMPv3 networking environments. If the agent and the NMS use SNMPv3 packets to communicate with each other, you need to create an SNMPv3 user.

Here is an explanation of the parameters for snmp-agent usm-user v3 command:

- <user-name>—User name (a string of 1 to 32 characters). It is case sensitive.
- <group-name>—Group name (a string of 1 to 32 characters). It is case sensitive.
- cipher—Specifies that auth-password and priv-password are cipher text passwords, which can be calculated by using the snmp-agent calculate-password command.
- authentication-mode—Specifies the security model to be authentication. MD5 is faster than SHA, but SHA provides a higher security than MD5.
    - md5—Specifies the authentication protocol as MD5.
    - sha—Specifies the authentication protocol as SHA-1.

- <auth-password>—Authentication password (HMAC key). If the cipher keyword is not specified, auth-password indicates a plain text password, which is a string of 1 to 64 visible characters. If the cipher keyword is specified, auth-password indicates a cipher text password of 32 or 40 hexadecimal characters.
  - If the md5 keyword is specified, auth-password is a string of 32 hexadecimal characters.
  - If the sha keyword is specified, auth-password is a string of 40 hexadecimal characters.
  - See additional notes that follow to determine the cipher text password.
- privacy-mode—Specifies the security model to be privacy. The three encryption algorithms, AES, 3DES, and DES, are in descending order in terms of security. Higher security means more complex implementation mechanism and lower speed. DES is enough to meet general requirements.
  - 3des—Specifies the privacy protocol as 3DES.
  - des56—Specifies the privacy protocol as DES.
  - aes128—Specifies the privacy protocol as AES.
  - <priv-password>—The privacy password (encryption key). If the cipher keyword is not specified, priv-password indicates a plain text password, which is a string of 1 to 64 characters; if the cipher keyword is specified, priv-password indicates a cipher text password of 40 or 80 hexadecimal characters.
  - If the 3des keyword is specified, priv-password is a string of 80 hexadecimal characters;
  - If the aes128 keyword is specified, priv-password is a string of 40 hexadecimal characters;
  - If the des56 keyword is specified, priv-password is a string of 40 hexadecimal characters.
  - See additional notes that follow to determine the cipher text password.
- acl—Associates a basic ACL with the user. acl-number is in the range 2000 to 2999. By using a basic ACL, you can restrict the source IP address of SNMP packets—that is, you can configure to allow or prohibit SNMP packets with a specific source IP address so as to allow or prohibit the specified NMS to access the agent by using this user name.

Additional Notes—SNMPv3 User Configuration

Here are some additional notes for the SNMPv3 configuration on Comware devices:

- Why to use the cipher keyword—If you do not use the cipher keyword, your SNMP authentication and privacy passwords will be transmitted in clear text.
- If you specify the cipher keyword—The system considers the arguments `auth-password` and `priv-password` as cipher text passwords. This means that you have to enter the passwords as a 32-, 40-, or 80-character cipher version of the password. Use the process described below to determine the cipher text password. If the SNMP engine IDs of two devices are the same, you can copy and paste the SNMPv3 configuration commands from the configuration file on device A to device B. The cipher text password and plain text password on the two devices will be the same.
- If you do not specify the cipher keyword, the system considers the arguments `auth-password` and `priv-password` as plain text passwords. In this case, the passwords will be transmitted in clear text.
- To determine the cipher text password—When using the SNMPv3 user configuration command with the `cipher` keyword, you can get the cipher of the plain text password using the command:
    - `snmp-agent calculate-password <passphrase> mode <privacy-mode> <engine id>`
    - When running this command, make sure to use the same:
        - Privacy mode as is used in the `snmp-agent usm-user v3 cipher` command.
        - Engine ID as is used on the device.
- A plain text password is required when the NMS accesses the device. Therefore, please remember the user name and the plain text password used to generate the cipher text.

SNMPv3 Configuration Example

Here is an example of an SNMPv3 configuration for Comware that only uses HMAC protection (no encryption):

```
[Sysname] snmp-agent group v3 testGroup authentication
[Sysname] snmp-agent usm-user v3 testUser testGroup
               authentication-mode md5 authkey
```

Here is an explanation of the configuration:

- Sets the SNMP version on the NMS to SNMPv3
- Defines the user name as "testUser"
- Sets the authentication protocol to MD5
- Sets the authentication password (HMAC key) to "authkey"

Here is an example SNMPv3 configuration for Comware that uses both encryption and HMAC protection:

```
[Sysname] snmp-agent group v3 testGroup privacy
[Sysname] snmp-agent usm-user v3 testUser testGroup
          authentication-mode md5 authkey privacy-mode des56 prikey
```

Here is an explanation to this configuration:

- Sets the SNMP version on the NMS to SNMPv3
- Defines the user name as "testUser"
- Sets the authentication protocol to MD5
- Sets the authentication password to "authkey"
- Sets the privacy (encryption) protocol to DES
- Sets the privacy password (encryption key) to "prikey"

Learning Check

The following questions help you measure your understanding of the material presented in this chapter. Read all of the choices carefully, since there may be more than one correct answer. Choose all correct answers for each question.

Questions

1. Which of the following is the most secure method of managing devices?
   a. SSH
   b. SSL
   c. SSH and SSL
   d. Telnet
   e. Telnet and SSH
   f. Out-of-band

2. Which of the following is not a method of supported authentication method for a Comware user interface?
   a. Asymmetric keys
   b. None
   c. Password
   d. Scheme

3. Which of the following are user types for ProVision switches? (Select two.)
   a. Monitor
   b. Manager
   c. Operator
   d. System
   e. Visitor

4. The Comware system level of access is equated to which privilege level number?

5. Which Comware command will change your privilege level?

6. Which of the following is true concerning ProVision and Comware switches?
   a. Telnet and SSH are disabled on both products.
   b. Telnet and SSH are enabled on ProVision but disabled on Comware.
   c. Telnet is enabled on both products, but SSH is disabled on both products.
   d. Telnet is enabled only on ProVision and disabled on Comware. SSH is disabled on both.
   e. Telnet and SSH are enabled on both products.

Answers

1. ☑ **F** is correct. Out-of-band is the most secure method of managing networking devices.

   ☒ **A** through **E** are incorrect because, even though some of these methods are encrypted, they could qualify for either in-band or out-of-band (for example, via a management VLAN).

2. ☑ **A** is correct. The Asymmetric keys method is not a supported authentication method for a Comware user interface.

   ☒ **B**, **C** and **D** are supported and, as such, are incorrect answers.

3. ☑ **B** and **C** are correct. Manager and Operator are the two levels of access on a ProVision switch.

   ☒ **A**, **D**, and **E** are incorrect because these refer to Comware levels of access.

4. ☑ The Comware system level of access is equated to privilege Level 3.

5. ☑ `super` is the Comware command that will change your privilege level.

6. ☑ **D** is correct. Telnet is enabled on Provision (but not on Comware), and SSH is disabled on both sets of switches.

   ☒ **A** is incorrect because Telnet is disabled on Comware and SSH is disabled on both. **B** is incorrect because SSH is disabled on ProVision. **C** is incorrect because Telnet is disabled on Comware. **E** is incorrect because Telnet is disabled on Comware and SSH is disabled on both.

5 Managing Software and Configurations

EXAM OBJECTIVES

- ✓ Define and recognize the purpose and interaction of common TCP/UDP-based upper layer applications.
- ✓ Identify and describe available tool sets for managing HP networking products.
- ✓ Prepare equipment for installation.
- ✓ Optimize small to medium-sized wireless, switched, and routed network infrastructure for small and midsized business (SMB) and commercial customers.
- ✓ Perform network management.
- ✓ Perform administrative tasks.

ASSUMED KNOWLEDGE

This chapter assumes that you are familiar with the management commands discussed in earlier chapters and that you have experience with the following protocols:

- TFTP
- FTP
- SFTP
- XMODEM

INTRODUCTION

This chapter introduces the management of the operating system software and configuration files used by the HP switches. The contents of these files are stored in flash on the HP switches; however, the ProVision and Comware products are managed differently. You will be introduced to the basics of upgrading and specifying the operating system version and configuration file used when the switch boots up. You will also be introduced to backing up and restoring configuration files.

Here is a quick summary of the topics covered in this chapter:

- Understanding the bootup process of the HP switches
- Understanding the use of the flash file system on the HP switches
- Upgrading the operating systems on the HP switches
- Managing configuration files on the HP switches

This chapter provides a basic introduction to upgrading the software and managing configuration files. Enterprise management software, like IMC, can also perform and automate this on a very large scale. IMC is covered in "Chapter 15: HP Intelligent Management Center."

Bootup Process

The bootup process is similar across the HP switches, where hardware diagnostics are performed, with the option of entering a boot read-only memory (ROM) menu to perform password recovery and emergency upgrades, the loading of the operating system, and the execution of a startup configuration file. This section introduces the bootup process of both switches, including access to their bootup/ROM utilities and performing the password recovery process.

ProVision Bootup Process

The bootup process of the ProVision and Comware operating systems are similar. During the bootup of both product families, you have the option of entering the Boot ROM to perform an emergency upgrade (in case you accidentally delete the operating system from the CLI), breaking into the switch (if you forget the manager password for ProVision or the Level 3 super password for Comware), and other management items. Entering the Boot ROM is not a common task.

Here is an example that displays the bootup process of a ProVision switch:

```
Build date:       Jun 28 2011
   Build time:       17:00:29
   Build version:    KA.15.05
   Build number:     47232


Boot Profiles:
0. Monitor ROM Console
1. Primary Software Image
2. Secondary Software Image
```

```
Select profile (primary):
Booting Primary Software Image...
Decompressing...done.
initializing. initialization done.
Waiting for Speed Sense.  Press <Enter> twice to continue.
```

Notice that the default boot profile option is "1" (Boot from the primary software image). You have approximately five seconds to choose an option. If you do not choose an option, the bootup process continues using the default option (a later section discusses how to change the default from the primary and secondary software images).

ProVision Monitor ROM Console

If you choose option "0" during the bootup process as the boot profile, you are taken into the Monitor ROM Console, as shown below:

```
HP 3800-48G-4SFP+ Switch (J9576A)
ROM Build Directory: /sw/rom/build/tamrom(ec_tamrom_transam_t5b)
        ROM Version: KA.15.05
     ROM Build Date: 17:00:29 Jun 28 2011
   ROM Build Number: 47232
   ROM Image Booted: Primary
    Initial Version: KA.15.05
Config File Version: 1.2
        SSC Version: 12000c
   SSC Image Booted: Primary
        MSI Version: 7
        CSI Version: 10
<-output omitted->

Enter h or ? for help.
=>
```

To list the commands, you can execute in the Monitor ROM Console, use the help command or the "?".

```
=> ?

LAN Monitor Commands

do(wnload) - Download via XMODEM
sp(eed) - Set a new baud rate
h(elp) - Display help screen
? - Display help screen
id(entify) - Print out identification string
jp(jump) - Jump to product code, optional 1-primary, 2-secondary
q(uit) - Exit the monitor
boot - Reboot the system
reset - Reset the system
v(ersion) - Display version information
lsdev - Display I/O device table
fsck - File system check
ls [path] - Terse directory listing
ll [path] - Detailed directory listing
format - Format storage device
blkdump - raw I/O
pwd - Print current working directory
cd - Change directory
mkdir - Make directory
MORE? (Ctl-C to abort)
rmdir - Remove directory
rm - Remove file
cp - Copy file
mv - Move file
```

```
cat - Dump file contents
attrib +- - Change the attributes on a file
(a)rchive, (h)idden, (s)ystem, (r)ead-only
=>
```

Note that the output displayed might vary depending on the ProVision switch model and code version you have. Also, some commands can be abbreviated.

If you press `V`, it displays version information of the primary image:

```
=> v
Directory: /sw/rom/build/bmrom(t2g)
Build Date: 23:33:11 Apr 24 2009
Version: K.12.20
Build #: 24648
=>
```

Typically, a switch will boot into Monitor ROM when it has a bad or corrupted flash or when the image is not compatible with the Boot ROM. The way to fix this is to put a different, compatible image on the switch. In ROM mode, do this by using XMODEM on the console port. Since the default serial console speed typically defaults to 9,600 baud (very slow), you should change the speed to the fastest: 115,200 baud:

```
=> speed 115200
```

To initiate the XMODEM transfer, type `do` for download:

```
=> do
```

You have invoked the console download utility.

```
Do you wish to continue? (Y/N)>
```

The switch will prompt for confirmation. Press **Y**, and then start the transfer from your terminal emulation program, like PuTTY or TeraTerm. It will take a while to transfer the file. After the file has been transferred, you can issue the command `boot` to reboot the switch.

Note

The ProVision switch OS is not loaded and the switch is not forwarding traffic when the switch is in the Monitor ROM Console mode. Also the commands executed here are basically Unix commands and are not the same as the commands used when the OS has successfully loaded on the switch.

Comware Bootup Process

Depending on the Comware switch model, what you see when the switch boots up might be slightly different. Here is the example output of a 5800 switch:

```
Starting......

*********************************************************************

* *

* HP 5800-56C BOOTROM, Version 007 *

* *

*********************************************************************

Copyright (c) 2010-2012 Hewlett-Packard Development Company, L.P.

Creation Date : Dec 2 2011,17:43:47

CPU Clock Speed : 750MHz

Memory Size : 512MB

Flash Size : 512MB

CPLD Version : 001

PCB Version : Ver.B

Mac Address : 000ef2005800

Press Ctrl-B to enter Extended Boot
```

The last line of the above output asks whether you want to enter the Boot ROM menu. The system waits five seconds for your response before continuing the boot process.

Note

According to HP, you have five seconds to press `CTRL-B`; however, from practical experience, the time period is typically much shorter. So you need to be quick with the control sequence to gain access to the Boot ROM menu.

Comware Extended Boot Menu

The Boot ROM menu is accessed with CTRL-B during the bootup process. This menu can also be used to recover lost local passwords. Here is an example of the main Boot ROM menu:

```
==========<EXTEND-BOOTROM MENU>=======
| <1> Boot From CF Card                  |
| <2> Enter Serial SubMenu               |
| <3> Enter Ethernet SubMenu             |
| <4> File Control                       |
| <5> Modify Bootrom Password            |
| <6> Ignore System Configuration       |
| <7> Boot Rom Operation Menu            |
| <8> Clear Super Password               |
| <9> Device Operation                   |
| <a> Reboot                             |
======================================
Enter your choice(1-a):
```

This boot ROM access gives you many more options than the ProVision switches. If you accidentally deleted the operating system file in the Comware switch's flash or if the OS has become corrupted, you can correct this from the Boot ROM menu using XMODEM via the console or across the network, using TFTP or FTP. To do an upgrade across the network using TFTP or FTP, follow the steps in the subsequent paragraphs.

Enter **3** for "Enter Ethernet SubMenu," which allows you to copy the application code from an external server to flash on the device. You will see the following menu:

```
===================<Enter Ethernet SubMenu>==============
|Note:the operating device is cfa0                      |
|<1> Download Application Program To SDRAM And Run      |
|<2> Update Main Application File                       |
|<3> Update Backup Application File                     |
|<4> Update Secure Application File                     |
|<5> Modify Ethernet Parameter                          |
|<0> Exit To Main Menu                                  |
|<Ensure The Parameter Be Modified Before Downloading!> |
```

```
=========================================================

Enter your choice(0-5):
```

Enter **5** to access the “Modify Ethernet Parameter” submenu:

```
========<ETHERNET PARAMETER SET>=========
|Note: '.' = Clear field.               |
|  '-' = Go to previous field.          |
| Ctrl+D = Quit.                         |
=========================================
Protocol (FTP or TFTP) :tftp ftp
Load File Name         : <src-file-name>
Target File Name       : <dest-file-name>
Server IP Address      : <server-ip-address>
Local IP Address       : <local-ip-address>
Gateway IP Address     : <default-gateway>
FTP User Name          : <user-name>
FTP User Password      : <password>
```

Enter a period (“.”), and press **Enter** to clear a field. Enter a hyphen (“-“), and press **Enter** to go to a previous field. Press **Enter** to go to the next field. After you are finished making changes, enter CTRL-D. Select the protocol you want to use for the download (FTP or TFTP). The load file name is the name of the source file, and the target file name is the name of the destination file. After you are finished, return to the main menu.

Enter **3** in the main Boot ROM menu to enter the Ethernet interface submenu. Then, enter **2** (Update Main Application File) to upgrade the main application program. Here is an example:

```
Loading..................................................................
.....................................................................
..........Done!
22165484 bytes downloaded!
Updating File cfa0:/update.bin
```

Enter **0** to return to the main Boot ROM menu.

Enter **4** for "File Control," to specify booting from the newly downloaded file. Here is the screen you are taken to:

```
=======================<File CONTROL>===================
|Note: the operating device is CF Card                  |
| <1> Display All File                                  |
| <2> Set Application File type                         |
| <3> Set Configuration File type                      |
| <4> Delete File                                       |
| <5> Exit To Main Menu                                 |
========================================================
Enter your choice(1-5):
```

Enter **2** for "Set Application File type." The file control submenu is displayed. Here you can display the type of application file saved in the storage device, modify the file name, or delete a file:

```
'M' = MAIN 'B' = BACKUP 'S' = SECURE 'N/A' = NOT ASSIGNED
====================================================================
|NO. Size(B) Time Type Name |
|1 22165484 Dec/20/2007 09:18:10 S cfa0:/update.bin |
|2 22165484 Dec/20/2007 09:42:28 M cfa0:/main.bin |
|0 Exit |
===================================================================
Enter file No:
```

Enter the number of the file name to be modified. In the above example, this would be "1." You will now modify the file attribute (which file to boot from):

```
====================================================================
|<1> +Main   |
|<2> -Main   |
|<3> +Backup |
|<4> -Backup |
|<0> Exit    |
====================================================================
Enter your choice(0-4):
```

Enter **1** to set the selected application program to the main application file or, in other words, the default boot file of the system.

Enter **0** to return to the main Boot ROM menu.

Enter **1** to boot the system.

This completes the process of upgrading the operating system from the Boot ROM menu.

Boot Menu Options

Table 5-1 compares the options in the Boot menus of the two switches. Notice that "Boot without password credentials" for ProVision only works if you have not configured the `include-credentials` command, discussed in "Chapter 4: Protecting Management Access." And, unlike with Comware, you cannot boot a ProVision switch by ignoring the existing configuration file: instead, you must delete it and then boot it. This process is explained in more detail in the next section.

Table 5-1. Boot menu options for ProVision and Comware switches

Option	ProVision	Comware
View directory structures	Y	Y
Copy, move, and delete files in flash	Y	Y
Created and delete directories in flash	Y	Y
Upgrade via XMODEM (console)	Y	Y
Upgrade across the network	N	Y
Password protect menu	N	Y
Boot without a configuration	N	Y
Boot without password credentials	Y	Y

Password Recovery Process

The next two sections contain the details of performing a password recovery on the ProVision and Comware switches.

ProVision Password Recovery

You can access a ProVision switch for emergency reasons using the Monitor ROM Console in ProVision. The term *password recovery* is somewhat misleading, since the process described here erases all operator and manager password information so that you can gain access to the switch. If you recall from "Chapter 4: Protecting Management Access," password information is not included in the startup configuration file, by default. The `include-credentials` command allows this but is not configured by default. If you have not configured this command, you can follow these steps to delete the password file:

1. Access the console port, and reboot the ProVision switch.
2. Use option 0 for Monitor ROM Console.
3. Execute `ll` for a directory listing.
4. Execute `cd cfa0/` to move to the default flash location.
5. Re-do the directory listing.
6. You should see a file called "mgrinfo.txt."
7. Execute `cat mgrinfo.txt` to look at the contents.
8. Execute `rm mgrinfo.txt` to delete the file.
9. Execute `boot` to boot the switch.

If you have included the credentials in the startup configuration file, you will need to delete this file (or you could rename it). This file will be called "config" underneath the "cfg" directory:

1. Access the console port, and reboot the ProVision switch.
2. Use option 0 for Monitor ROM Console.
3. Execute `ll` for a directory listing.
4. Execute `cd cfa0/` to move to the default flash location.
5. Change to the configuration directory by executing `cd cfg`.
6. Re-do the directory listing.
7. You should see a file called "`config`."
8. Execute `cat config` to look at the contents.
9. Execute `rm config` to delete the file.
10. Execute `boot` to boot the switch.

Warning

You should only do the latter steps in an emergency, since that approach erases the entire startup configuration file and causes the switch to boot up using the factory default configuration. Therefore, you should *always* back up your switch's configuration to a remote device whenever you make changes!

Comware Password Recovery

There are two options from the Boot ROM menu to break into the switch. Option 8 from the menu clears the super passwords configured, allowing you to gain access at Level 3 from the console. However, if AAA has been configured, you need to boot up the switch without a configuration, which is option 6. The advantage of this approach over ProVision is that, with ProVision, you must delete the startup configuration file to perform the recover; however, with Comware, option 6 boots up the switch without a configuration file (it ignores it). Upon booting with a default configuration (no passwords), you can then recover the ignored configuration file from flash by loading into memory (this is discussed in a later section in this chapter).

Note

Here is a quick summary of the password recovery process of the two switches. For ProVision, if the `include-credentials` command is not used, the administrator can delete the mgrinfo.txt file. If it is used, you have to delete the configuration file (hopefully you have it backed up).

For Comware, you can erase the super passwords and/or boot up, ignoring the currently saved configuration (unlike with ProVision, you can recover the saved configuration after the switch has booted up and you have gained Level 3 access).

Flash File System

The ProVision and Comware devices have flash on their motherboards: this is not a solid state drive (SSD) flash drive, but a simple flash component, and thus is greatly restricted in size and speed. The size varies based on the switch product. The use of flash on ProVision and Comware is different, and this is explored in the following sections.

ProVision Flash File System Management

This section introduces you to basic file management on the ProVision switches. You will learn how to manage and upgrade the operating system of the switches and how to manage the configuration files on the switch.

The ProVision switches feature two flash memory locations for storing switch software image files:

- **Primary flash**—The default storage for a switch software image
- **Secondary flash**—The additional storage for either a redundant or an alternate switch software image

With the primary and secondary flash options, you can test a new image in your system without having to replace a previously existing image. You can also use the image options for troubleshooting. For example, you can copy a problem image into secondary flash for later analysis and place another, proven image in primary flash to run your system. The switch can use only one image at a time.

Note

An administrator should have a backup operating system in flash in case the new one has problems. You can then easily boot from the old one without having to reinstall it. You can *only* have two operating systems in the flash of a ProVision switch. Also, after you upgrade the OS on a switch, you must reboot the switch for the image to become active.

Show Flash Command

If the flash image sizes in primary and secondary are the same, then, in almost every case, the primary and secondary images are identical. The `show flash` command provides a comparison of flash image sizes, plus the Boot ROM version and the flash image from which the switch booted. For example, in the following case, the images are different versions of the switch software, and the switch is running on the version stored in the primary flash image:

```
ProVision# show flash
Image               Size (bytes) Date     Version
-----------------   ------------ -------- --------------------
Primary Image     :     13540118 08/18/11 KA.15.03.3004
Secondary Image   :     13540118 08/18/11 KA.15.03.3004
Boot ROM Version  : KA.15.05
Default Boot      : Primary
```

Show Version Command

The `show version` command identifies the software version on which the switch is currently running and whether the active version was booted from the primary or secondary flash image. Here is an example:

```
ProVision# show version
Image stamp:    /sw/code/build/tam(KA_15_03)
                Aug 18 2011 15:34:19
                KA.15.03.3004
                49
Boot Image:     Primary
```

The `show version` command displays which software version the switch is currently running and whether that version booted from primary or secondary flash. Thus, if the switch booted from primary flash, you will see the version number of the software version stored in primary flash, and, if the switch booted from secondary flash, you will see the version number of the software version stored in secondary flash. Thus, by using `show version`, rebooting the switch from the other flash image, and then using show version again, you can determine the version(s) of switch software in both flash sources. In this example, the switch is using a software version of KA.15.03.3004 stored in primary flash.

Comware Flash File System Management

The flash file system is used to store application (operating system) and configuration files. Sometimes this is flash on the motherboard (`flash:`), like most of the switches, and sometimes it is a compact flash card (`cf:`), like most of the routers. If there is more than one compact flash slot, you would reference them as `cfa:`, `cfb:`, and so on. All the Comware products support USB drives via their USB port or ports. To reference this flash, use the `uf:` designator. The `dir` command displays the contents of the flash file system on the motherboard, by default. Here is an example of the use of this command:

```
<Comware> dir
Directory of flash:/
   0     -rw-      1624  Apr 26 2000 12:02:59   h3c.cfg
   1     -rw-  21624756  Apr 26 2000 12:02:19   s5800_5820x-cmw520-
r1109p01.bin
   2     -rw-      5148  Sep 24 2010 10:30:12   hpn01_ca.cer
   3     -rw-      1765  Sep 24 2010 10:30:30   hpn01_local.cer
   4     -rw-  21371636  Apr 26 2000 23:09:16   s5800_5820x-cmw520-
r1110p03.bin
   5     -rw-       151  May 02 2000 08:45:51   system.xml
   6     -rw-      1972  May 02 2000 08:45:53   config.cfg
   7     -rw-   3360764  Apr 26 2000 12:06:07   logfile.log
515712 KB total (465772 KB free)
```

Note
Unlike ProVision switches, Comware devices have no limits as to the numbers and types of files in flash, except for the flash size limit. In other words, you could have two, three, or even four application images in flash.

Version Information

To view the hardware installed on a switch, in addition to the software version it is running, use the `display version` command. Here is an example of a 5800 switch:

```
<Comware> display version
HP Comware Platform Software
Comware Software, Version 5.20, Release 1109P01
Copyright (c) 2010-2012 Hewlett-Packard Development Company, L.P.
HP 5800-32C uptime is 0 week, 0 day, 0 hour, 16 minutes

HP 5800-32C with 2 Processor
512M    bytes SDRAM
4M      bytes Nor Flash Memory
512M    bytes Nand Flash Memory
Config Register points to Nand Flash

Hardware Version is Ver.B
CPLD Version is 003
BootRom Version is 101
[SubSlot 0] 24GE+4SFP Plus Hardware Version is Ver.B
[SubSlot 1] No Module
```

Here is an example of a Comware 5500 switch:

```
<Comware> display version
HP Comware Platform Software
Comware Software, Version 5.20.99, Feature 2218P01-US
Copyright (c) 2010-2012 Hewlett-Packard Development Company, L.P.
HP 5500-24G-SFP EI Switch with 2 Interface Slots uptime is 0 week,
1 day, 4 hours, 41 minutes
```

```
HP 5500-24G-SFP EI Switch with 2 Interface Slots with 1 Processor
256M    bytes SDRAM
32768K  bytes Flash Memory

Hardware Version is REV.C
CPLD Version is 002
Bootrom Version is 509
[SubSlot 0] 24SFP+8GE Hardware Version is REV.C
[SubSlot 1] 2 CX4 Hardware Version is REV.A
```

In this example, the 5500-28C-EI switch is running version 5.20.99, Feature 2218P01-US.

Comware Flash File System Commands

Table 5-2 briefly reviews the commands to manage the files in the flash file system. These commands can only be executed from user view. (You will get an error message if you try to execute them from system view.)

Table 5-2. Commands to manage the Comware flash file system

Command	Description
`dir [/all] [<file-url>]`	Display directory information.
`Wd`	Display the current working directory.
`cd <directory>`	Change the current working directory.
`mkdir <directory>`	Create a directory.
`rmdir <directory>`	Remove a directory.
`undelete <file-url>`	Restore a file from the recycle bin.
`more <file-url>`	Display the contents of a file (currently only a text file can be displayed).
`rename <fileurl-source> <fileurl-dest>`	Rename a file.
`copy <fileurl-source> <fileurl-dest>`	Copy a file.
`move <fileurl-source> <fileurl-dest>`	Move a file.
`delete [/unreserved] <file-url>`	Delete a file (place it in the recycle bin or permanently delete it).
`reset recycle-bin`	Empty the recycle bin.

The `file-url` specifies the location of a file, which could be the flash file system or a USB drive. For files in the default flash, you do not need to preface them with `flash:` or with `cf:`, since these are the default locations for the switches and/or routers.

When removing a directory with the `rmdir` command, it must be empty; before you remove a directory, you must delete all the files and subdirectories in this directory. For file deletion, see the `delete` command.

The `delete /unreserved` command deletes a file permanently, and the action cannot be undone. When you delete a file, it is placed in the recycle bin, which works much the same way as in Windows on a PC. Files in the recycle bin still occupy storage space. To delete a file or files in the recycle bin, execute the `reset recycle-bin` command. HP recommends that you periodically empty the recycle bin to save storage space.

Note

The recycle bin, which is similar to that of many desktop operating systems, like Windows, is where files are placed when you execute the `delete` command (unless you use the `/unreserved` parameter). The files in the recycle bin use up space in flash until the recycle bin is emptied but allow you to quickly recover an accidentally deleted file. Just remember that you might have to empty the recycle bin with the `reset recycle-bin` command before loading a new operating system.

Upgrading and Managing Software

Before upgrading networking equipment, like switches, you should perform some important preparation tasks. These tasks ensure that the upgrade only causes minimal disruption to the network, and they provide a way of backing out of the upgrade in case something goes wrong. Some of these tasks include:

- Back up the current/running configuration file.
- Make sure that you have a copy of the old operating system.
- Schedule downtime.
- Check release notes for known issues, like documented changes in system defaults.
- Have a recovery plan in case the update does not go according to plan.
- Test the upgrade in a lab network or in a less important part of the network before rolling it out to many switches.

The following sections discuss how to upgrade the operating systems on the ProVision and Comware switches.

Upgrading ProVision Software

This section describes commands for updating the primary and secondary flash locations. When you copy the flash image from primary to secondary or the reverse, the switch overwrites the file in the destination location with a copy of the file from the source location. This means that you do not have to erase the current image at the destination location before copying in a new image.

There are basically three options you can use to upgrade the OS on your switch:

- A USB drive
- An external server (TFTP or SFTP)
- XMODEM (via a console connection)

Upgrading from a USB drive and an external server are discussed in the sections that follow.

Note
XMODEM upgrades are typically not performed, since the update process is very slow. The fastest clock rate of the console connection is 115K, so, for a very large image, an administrator has to wait for a long time for it to complete. The only time XMODEM should be used is when the switch doesn't have access to an external server to use TFTP/SFTP or when you are doing the upgrade remotely and do not have direct access to the USB port.

USB Drive Installation

The `dir` command displays the contents of the USB drive in the USB port. Here is an example:

```
ProVision# dir
Listing Directory /ufa0:
-rwxrwxrwx    1    10125499 Jun 30 15:26 KA.15.03.3004.SWI
```

The `copy` command enables you to copy software to either flash area. Here is the syntax:

```
ProVision# copy usb flash <image-name> {primary | secondary}
```

Here is an example of upgrading the OS image in the secondary flash location:

```
ProVision# copy usb flash KA.15.03.3004.swi secondary
The Secondary OS Image will be deleted, continue [y/n]?
```

Note
The syntax of the `copy` command specifies the *source* first (from) and the *destination* second (to). So, for example, `copy usb flash primary` would copy an image from the USB port to the primary flash location on a ProVision switch.

Remote Server Installation

You can also copy an image from a remote TFTP or SFTP server. Here is the syntax for copying the image from a server using TFTP:

```
ProVision# copy tftp flash <ip-addr> <remote-file-name>
     {primary | secondary}
```

For some situations, you may want to use a secure method to issue commands or to copy files to the switch. By opening a secure, encrypted SSH session and enabling SFTP, you can use a third-party software application to take advantage of Secure Copy (SCP) and Secure FTP. SCP and SFTP provide a secure alternative to TFTP for transferring information that may be sensitive (like switch configuration files) to and from the switch. Essentially, you are creating a secure SSH tunnel as a way to transfer files with SFTP and SCP channels.

As described earlier in this chapter, you can use a TFTP client on the administrator workstation to update software images. This is a plain-text mechanism, and it connects to a stand-alone TFTP server or to another ProVision switch acting as a TFTP server to obtain the software image file(s). Using SCP and SFTP allows you to maintain your switches with greater security. You can also roll out new software images with automated scripts that make it easier to upgrade multiple switches simultaneously and securely.

SFTP is unrelated to FTP, although there are some functional similarities. After you set up an SFTP session through an SSH tunnel, some of the commands are the same as FTP commands. Certain commands are not allowed by the SFTP server on the switch, such as those that create files or folders. If you try to issue commands, such as `create` or `remove`, using SFTP, the switch server returns an error message.

You can use SFTP just as you would TFTP to transfer files to and from the switch, but, with SFTP, your file transfers are encrypted and require authentication, so they are more secure than they would be using TFTP. SFTP works only with SSHv2.

SFTP is not enabled on the ProVision switches, by default. Instead, you need to enable SSHv2 (SSHv1 is not supported) and enable SFTP. Enabling SSH was discussed in the last chapter. To enable SFTP, use the following command:

```
ProVision(config)# ip ssh filetransfer
```

When you enable SFTP, TFTP is automatically disabled. Then, when executing the `copy` command, reference `sftp` instead of `tftp`.

Warning

Note that FTP and TFTP use dynamic ports for the actual transfer of data—not port 21 for FTP or port 69 for UDP. These latter ports are control ports. The data is transferred across additional connections, which may break through a filtering device, like a router or a firewall. You must plan for this accordingly, or file transfers will fail.

Testing the Flash Image

The `boot` command is used to control the bootup options of your ProVision switch. If you want to test the image you copied with an immediate reboot, use the following command:

```
ProVision(config)# boot system flash {primary | secondary}
```

Specifying the Default Flash File System

You can specify the default flash to boot from on the next boot by entering the `boot set-default flash` command:

```
ProVision# boot set-default flash {primary | secondary}
```

Here is an example:

```
ProVision# boot set-default flash secondary
ProVision# show flash
Image                Size(Bytes)  Date     Version  Build #
-----                ----------   -------- -------  ------
Primary Image     : 7476770       03/15/11 KA.15.03  64
Secondary Image : 7498720         03/15/11 KA.15.10  64
Boot Rom Version: KA.15.02
Default Boot      : Secondary
ProVision(config)# boot
This management module will now reboot from secondary and will
become the standby module! You will need to use the other
management module's console interface. Do you want to continue
[y/n]?
```

Rebooting the Switch

As you saw in the last example, the `boot` command, without any parameters, reboots the switch and runs the diagnostic tests as the switch is booting up. Another option is to use the `reload` command. The `reload` command reboots the switch from the current flash image (primary or secondary) or the flash image that was set either by the `boot set-default` command or by the last executed boot system flash `{primary | secondary}` command. Because `reload` bypasses some subsystem self-tests, the switch reboots faster than if you use either of the boot command options. If you are using redundant management and redundancy is enabled, the switch will failover to the other management module. Here is the syntax of this command:

```
ProVision# [no] reload [after <[dd:]hh:]mm> | at <hh:mm[:ss]>
                [<mm/dd[/[yy]yy]>]]
```

Note that you can schedule a reload. If you do not schedule it, the switch reboots immediately. Here is an example:

```
ProVision(config)# reload after 04:14:00

Reload scheduled in 4 days, 14 hours, 0 minutes. This command will
cause a switchover at the scheduled time to the other management
module which may not be running the same software image and
configurations. Do you want to continue [y/n]?
```

Note

When using redundant management, the `reload at/after` command causes a switchover at the scheduled time to the other management module, which may not be running the same software image or have the same configurations.

Upgrading Comware Software

Comware device software includes the Boot ROM program and the system boot file. After powering on, the device runs the Boot ROM program, initializes the hardware, and displays the hardware information. Then, the device runs the boot file. The boot file provides drivers and firmware for hardware and implements service features. The boot file is commonly referred to as an *application file*. The Boot ROM program and system boot file are required to start up and run a device.

Comware Application Code

Application code is specific to the Comware switch or router series, but version numbers indicate parity of feature sets. To obtain code, log on to HP's support site (www.hp.com/networking), where you can locate links to software versions for Comware (and ProVision) products. For Comware, there are two versions of application code that can be installed.

Common upgrade methods for Comware devices include:

- **USB flash drive**—Copy the application and configuration files from the USB drive using the command line.
- **TFTP/FTP**—Upload/download the application and configuration files on the TFTP/FTP server in the command-line mode.
- **Boot ROM menu**—Upgrade the application software on the TFTP/FTP server through an Ethernet interface in the Boot ROM menu.
- **XMODEM**—Upgrade the Boot ROM and application through the console interface over XMODEM.

The first two methods are the preferred approaches. The third option should be used only if the current operating system in flash is corrupt. The fourth option is the least desirable because the speed of the console port causes the upgrade to take a very long time.

Follow these steps to upgrade the application file:

1. Copy the application file to the root directory of the device's storage medium by using FTP or TFTP.
2. Specify the application file to be used at the next boot at the CLI.
3. Reboot the device to use the specified application file.

With the validity check function enabled, the device can strictly check the application file for correctness and the version configuration information to ensure a successful upgrade. Note that the steps are the same whether you are using the Boot ROM menu or the CLI.

Note
The new unified image upgrades both the bootrom and the application code at the same time.

You can use the `copy` command to copy an application file from a USB flash drive to the primary flash of the Comware device, or you can use TFTP or FTP to perform a remote copy. After you have copied the file to the flash file system, you have to specify it as the main application file and reboot the device to use the new code. The following sections will discuss each of these processes.

Copying the File

If you used a USB drive on an MSR-series router to copy your application code, where the destination was the first compact flash card slot, the resulting `user view` command would look like this:

```
<Comware> copy ufa:/update.bin cfa:/update.bin
```

If the application file was on a TFTP server, you would use the `tftp user view` command to copy the image to the default flash on your device. Here is an example for an MSR-series router:

```
<Comware> tftp 10.1.1.2 get update.bin
(10.1.1.2 is the tftp server)
File will be transferred in binary mode.
Downloading file from remote tftp server, please wait
.........................
TFTP: 11446188 bytes received in 63 second(s).
File downloaded successfully
```

If the application file was on an FTP server, you would use the `ftp user view` command to copy the image to the default flash on your device. Here is an example for an MSR-series router (note that you must set the file transfer to binary mode):

```
<Comware> ftp 10.1.1.1
Trying 10.1.1.1 ...
Connected to 10.1.1.1.
220 WFTPD 2.0 service (by Texas Imperial Software) ready for new user
User(10.1.1.1:(none)): myusername
331 Give me your password, please
Password: mypassword
230 Logged in successfully
[ftp] binary
200 Type set to I.
[ftp] get update.bin
```

As you can see from the above example, Comware products use an FTP client that is similar to other FTP clients in the market.

Specifying the Application File to Use

After the copy is complete, you must specify your newly copied file as the default operating system to use and you must reboot the device. Here are the commands to accomplish this:

```
<Comware> boot-loader file <url-file-name> {main | backup}
<Comware> reboot
Start to check configuration with next startup configuration file, please wait...
This command will reboot the device. Current configuration may be lost in next startup if you continue. Continue? [Y/N]: Y
```

The `display boot-loader` command specifies which files are the main and backup files being used.

Here is an example of specifying the boot image and rebooting the device:

```
<Comware> boot-loader file cfa:/update.bin main
<Comware> reboot
```

```
Start to check configuration with next startup configuration file,
please wait...
This command will reboot the device. Current configuration may be
lost in next startup if you continue. Continue? [Y/N]: Y
```

Note
You can also schedule a reboot with the `schedule reboot` command.

After the system reboots, use the `display version` command to verify the upgrade.

Managing Configuration Files

The ProVision and Comware switches have support for a different number of configuration files. However, the way that the configuration files are managed is different between the two switches. The following sections discuss the management of configuration files on the ProVision and Comware switches.

Managing ProVision Configuration Files

The ProVision switches maintain two configuration files:

- **Running-config**—Running configuration stored in RAM
- **Startup-config**—Startup configuration stored in flash memory

The running-config file exists in volatile memory and controls switch operation. If no configuration changes have been made in the CLI since the switch was last booted, the running-config file is identical to the startup-config file. The startup-config file exists in flash (non-volatile) memory and is used to preserve the most recently saved configuration as the permanent configuration. Booting the switch replaces the current running-config file with a new running-config file that is an exact copy of the current startup-config file.

Saving Configuration Changes

Making changes to the running-config file creates a new operating configuration. Saving a new configuration means overwriting (replacing) the current startup-config file with the current running-config file. This means that, if the switch subsequently reboots for any reason, it will resume operation using the new configuration instead of the configuration previously defined in the startup-config file. There are three ways to save a new configuration:

- **CLI**—Use the `write memory` command. This overwrites the current startup-config file with the contents of the current running-config file.
- **Menu interface**—Use the `Save` option. This overwrites both the running-config file and the startup-config file with the changes you have specified in the menu interface screen.

- **Web browser interface**—Use the Apply Changes button or other appropriate button. This overwrites both the running-config file and the startup-config file with the changes you have specified in the web browser interface window.

Managing Multiple Configuration Files

The switch allows up to three startup-config files with options for selecting which startup-config file to use for:

- A fixed reboot policy using a specific startup-config file for a particular boot path (primary or secondary flash).
- Overriding the current reboot policy on a per-instance basis.
- Specifying a particular file to use for a reboot policy or an individual reboot.

Choosing which configuration file to use for the startup-config at reboot provides the following flexible options:

- The switch can reboot with different configuration options without having to exchange one configuration file for another from a remote storage location.
- Transitions from one software release to another can be performed while maintaining a separate configuration for the different software release versions.
- By setting a reboot policy using a known, good configuration and then overriding the policy on a per-instance basis, you can test a new configuration with the provision that, if an unattended reboot occurs, the switch will come up with the known, good configuration instead of repeating a reboot with a misconfiguration.

The switch uses three memory slots, with identity (ID) numbers of 1, 2, and 3. A startup-config file stored in a memory slot has a unique, changeable file name. To view the configuration files, use the `show config files` command, shown here:

```
ProVision# show config files

Configuration files:

 id | act pri sec | name

 ---+-------------+------------------------------------------

  1 |          *  | config1

  2 |  *   *      | baseConfig

  3 |             |
```

With multiple configuration enabled, the switch can have up to three startup-config files. Because the `show config` command always displays the content of the currently active startup-config file, the command extension shown below is needed to view the contents of any other startup-config files stored in the switch:

```
ProVision# show config <filename>
```

This command displays the content of the specified startup-config file in the same way that the `show config` command displays the content of the default (currently active) startup-config file.

Changing the Reboot Configuration Policy

For a given reboot, the switch automatically reboots from the startup-config file assigned to the flash location (primary or secondary) being used for the current reboot. You can use the following command to change the current policy so that the switch automatically boots using a different startup-config file:

```
ProVision(config)# startup-default [primary | secondary]
                    config <filename>
```

This command specifies a boot configuration policy option: primary and secondary. If not configured, it applies to both (use this option when you want to automatically use the same startup-config file for all reboots, regardless of the flash source used).

For redundant management systems, this command affects both the active management module and the standby management module. The config file is copied immediately to the standby management module and becomes the default on that module when the next bootup occurs, unless redundancy is disabled or the standby module has failed self-test.

To override the current reboot configuration policy for a single reboot instance, use the `boot system flash` command:

```
ProVision# boot system flash {primary | secondary} config <filename>
```

This command provides a method to manually reboot with a specific startup-config file other than the file specified in the default reboot configuration policy. This command affects only the immediate boot instance and allows you to override the current reboot policy.

Renaming Configuration Files

The rename command changes the name of an existing startup-config file:

```
ProVision# rename config <current-filename> <new-name>
```

A file name can include up to 63 alphanumeric characters. Blanks are allowed in a file name enclosed in double (" ") or single (' ') quotes. File names are not case-sensitive. For redundant management systems, renaming a config file affects both the active management module and the standby management module, unless redundancy is disabled or the standby module failed self-test.

Copying Configuration Files

As mentioned earlier, the switch allows up to three startup-config files. You can create a new startup-config file if there is an empty memory slot or if you want to replace one startup-config file with another. This is accomplished with the `copy` command:

```
ProVision# copy config <source-filename> config <target-filename>
```

This command makes a local copy of an existing startup-config file by copying the contents of an existing startup-config file in one memory slot to a new startup-config file in another, empty memory slot. This enables you to use a separate configuration file to experiment with configuration changes while preserving the source file unchanged. It also simplifies a transition from one software version to another by allowing you to preserve the startup-config file for the earlier software version while creating a separate startup-config file for the later software version. With two such versions in place, you can easily reboot the switch with the correct startup-config file for either software version. If the destination startup-config file already exists, it is overwritten by the content of the source startup-config file. If the destination startup-config file does not already exist, it will be created in the first empty configuration memory slot on the switch. If the destination startup-config file does not already exist but there are no empty configuration memory slots on the switch, a new startup-config file is not created and, instead, the CLI displays the following error message:

```
Unable to copy configuration to "< target-filename >"
```

Backing Up and Restoring Configuration Files

Like OS upgrades, you can back up and restore configuration files from a USB drive or a remote server (TFTP or SFTP). In both cases, the copy command is used.

To back up the current startup-config file to a USB drive, use the following command:

```
ProVision# copy startup-config usb <filename>
```

To restore a startup-config file from a USB drive to flash, use the following command:

```
ProVision# copy usb startup-config <filename>
Device may be rebooted, do you want to continue [y/n]? y
Rebooting switch...
```

In addition to using USB, you can use TFTP or SFTP to back up and restore your configuration files. To back up your configuration file from flash to a TFTP server, use the following command:

```
ProVision# copy config <src-file> tftp <ip-addr> <remote-file>
           <pc | unix>
```

You need to specify the operating system type at the end of the command.

To restore a configuration from a TFTP server to the switch, use the following `copy` command:

```
ProVision# copy tftp config <dest-file> <ip-addr> <flash-file-name>
          <pc | unix>
```

Resetting the Switch Back to Factory Defaults

You can erase any of the startup-config files in the switch's memory slots. In some cases, erasing a file causes the switch to generate a new, default configuration file for the affected memory slot. In a redundant management system, this command erases the config or startup-config file on both the active and the standby management modules, as long as redundancy has not been disabled. If the standby management module is not in standby mode or has failed self-test, the config or startup-config file is not erased.

Note

When a file is assigned to either the primary or the secondary flash but is not the currently active startup-config file, erasing the file does not remove the flash assignment from the memory slot for that file. Thus, if the switch boots using a flash location that does not have an assigned startup-config, the switch creates a new, default startup-config file and uses this file in the reboot. (This new startup-config file contains only the default configuration for the software version used in the reboot.) Executing `write memory` after the reboot causes a switch-generated file name of configx to appear in the `show config` files display for the new file, where x corresponds to the memory slot number.

There are two ways of resetting a ProVision switch back to its factory default configuration:

- Use the CLI.
- Use buttons on the front of the chassis.

The `erase startup-config` command reboots the switch, replacing the contents of the current startup-config and running-config files with the factory default startup configuration. Here is an example:

```
ProVision# erase startup-config
Configuration will be deleted and device rebooted, continue [y/n]?
```

Press **y** to replace the current configuration with the factory default configuration and reboot the switch. Press **n** to retain the current configuration and prevent a reboot.

In a redundant management system, this command erases the startup-config file on both the active and the standby management modules as long as redundancy has not been disabled. If the standby management module is not in standby mode or has failed self-test, the startup-config file is not erased.

To reset a switch back to its factory default configuration from the front panel of the switch, perform the following steps:

1. Press the **Clear** button followed by the **Reset** button.
2. Continue to press the **Clear** button while releasing the **Reset** button.
3. When the Self-Test LED begins to flash, release the **Clear** button.

Managing Comware Configuration Files

A configuration file contains a set of commands. You can save the current configuration to the configuration file so that the configuration can take effect after device reboot. In addition, you can view the configuration information conveniently, or you can upload and download the configuration file to/from another device to configure devices in batches.

Like the ProVision switches, there are basically two configuration files used on the Comware products: *startup configuration file* and the *running configuration file*. The startup configuration is used for initialization when the device boots. If this file does not exist, the system boots using null configuration. *Null configuration* is the factory default configuration, which may differ from the default settings of commands. The factory default configuration may vary with device models.

You can view the startup configuration using either of the following methods:

- Use the `display startup` command to view the startup configuration file currently being used.
- Use the `more` command to view the content of the configuration file.

The current running configuration is the startup configuration and any commands that are modified or added during system operation. The current running configuration is stored in the temporary storage medium of the device and will be removed if not saved when the device reboots. You can use the `display current-configuration` command to view the current validated configuration of the device:

```
<Comware> display current-configuration
         [interface [<interface-type-and-id>]
         [ | {begin | exclude | include} <regular-expression> ]]
```

Saving the Current Running Configuration

To make configuration changes take effect at the next startup of the device, you can save the running configuration to the startup configuration file to be used at the next startup before the device reboots.

To save the current running configuration to the startup configuration, use the following command:

```
<Comware> save [safely] [backup | main]
```

The fast saving mode is used when you execute the `save` command without the `safely` keyword. This mode saves the file more quickly but can lose the existing configuration file if the device reboots or if the power fails during the process. The safe mode is used when you execute the `save` command with the `safely` keyword; this mode saves the file more slowly but can retain the configuration file in the device even if the device reboots or if the power fails during the process. The fast saving mode is suitable for environments where power supply is stable. The safe mode, however, is preferred in environments where uninterruptible power is unavailable or remote maintenance is involved.

You can have two startup configuration files by default: *main* and *backup*. When the device boots up, it uses the main file. If you do not specify which one in the `save` command, it defaults to main.

Note

Do not forget to save any changes you want to keep after the next reboot!

Specifying the Startup Configuration File

To specify a startup configuration file to be used at the next system startup, follow these guidelines:

- Use the `save` command. If you save the running configuration to the specified configuration file in the interactive mode, the system automatically sets the file as the startup configuration file to be used at the next system startup. (For a device supporting main/backup startup configuration file, the system sets the file as the main startup configuration file to be used at the next system startup.)
- Use the `startup saved-configuration` command to specify a startup configuration file to be used at the next startup.

Here is the syntax of the previous command:

```
<Comware> startup saved-configuration <config-file> [backup | main]
```

The configuration file must use ".cfg" as its extension name, and the startup configuration file must be saved in the root directory of the storage medium.

Note

Use the `display startup` command to check whether you have specified a startup configuration file to be used at the next startup. If the file is set as NULL or does not exist, the backup operation fails.

Also, the Comware fixed-port switches save their config file in flash as config.cfg, whereas the chassis switches and the routers save the config file in flash as startup.cfg.

Backing Up the Startup Configuration File

The backup function allows you to copy the startup configuration file to be used at the next startup from the device to a TFTP server. The backup operation backs up the main startup configuration file to a TFTP server for devices supporting main and backup startup configuration files.

Use this command to back up the startup configuration file:

```
<Comware> backup startup-configuration to <dest-ip-addr>
        [<dest-filename>]
```

Ensure that the server is reachable and enabled with TFTP service and that the client has read and write permission.

Restoring a Startup Configuration File

The restore function allows you to copy a configuration file from a TFTP server to the root directory of the storage media of all the member devices and to specify the file as the startup configuration file to be used at the next startup.

Use the following command to restore a startup configuration file:

```
<Comware> restore startup-configuration from <ip-addr> <filename>
```

After execution of the command, use the `display startup` command to verify that the file name of the configuration file to be used at the next system startup is the same as that specified by the file name argument.

Another option allows you to replace the running configuration with a file in flash, but you do not have to reboot! This is accomplished using the `config` command:

```
<Comware> config file replace <startup-config-file-name>
```

Note
The `config file replace` command does not merge a configuration file in flash with the one running in RAM—it completely replaces the configuration running in memory with the one you specify in flash.

Deleting a Startup Configuration File

You can delete a startup configuration file to be used at the next startup at the CLI. On a device that has main and backup startup configuration files, you can choose to delete the main, the backup, or both. If the device has only one startup configuration to be used at the next startup, the system sets only the startup configuration file to NULL. With startup configuration files deleted, the device uses null configuration at the next startup.

Use this command to delete a startup configuration file:

```
<Comware> reset saved-configuration [backup | main]
```

This command permanently deletes startup configuration files to be used at the next startup from all member devices. Therefore, use it with caution.

Learning Check

The following questions help you measure your understanding of the material presented in this chapter. Read all of the choices carefully, since there may be more than one correct answer. Choose all correct answers for each question.

Questions

1. What is the name of the ProVision file that you delete in Monitor ROM Console mode to remove the user credentials from the switch?
   a. mgrinfo.txt
   b. config
   c. users.txt
   d. user-config.txt

2. Which of the following can you do from the Boot ROM menu when performing the password recovery process on a Comware device? (Select two.)
   a. Delete the super passwords.
   b. Delete the saved configuration file.
   c. Ignore the saved configuration file.
   d. Reformat flash.

3. How many operating systems can you install in flash on a ProVision switch?
   a. One
   b. Two
   c. Three
   d. Unlimited

4. Which Comware command permanently removes all deleted files from the flash file system?

5. Which command name is used on the ProVision switch to specify the primary flash location as the default boot file?

6. Which Comware command erases the startup configuration file?

Answers

1. ☑ **A** is correct. Delete the mgrinfo.txt file to remove the user credentials from the switch.

   ☒ **B**, **C**, and **D** are incorrect because these files do not exist on the ProVision switches.

2. ☑ **A** and **C** are correct. From the Comware Boot ROM menu, you can delete the super passwords or ignore the saved configuration file when booting.

   ☒ **B** and **D** are incorrect because these are not options from the Comware Boot ROM menu.

3. ☑ **B** is correct. You can have, at most, two operating systems installed in flash on a ProVision switch.

   ☒ **A**, **C**, and **D** are incorrect because these are not the maximum allowed installed operating systems on ProVision switches.

4. ☑ `reset recycle-bin` is the Comware command that permanently removes all deleted files from the flash file system.

5. ☑ `boot set-default flash primary` is the command name used on the ProVision switch to specify the primary flash location as the default boot file.

6. ☑ `reset saved-configuration` is the Comware command that erases the startup configuration file.

6 VLANs

EXAM OBJECTIVES

In this chapter, you will learn to:

- ✓ Describe and contrast the most common Ethernet concepts.
- ✓ Explain Layer 3 routing concepts and apply Layer 3 protocols, with detailed focus on IPv4.
- ✓ Identify, describe, and explain VLANs.
- ✓ Perform installation and configuration of devices.
- ✓ Use general troubleshooting tools.
- ✓ Perform administrative tasks, including moves, adds, changes, deletions, and password resets.

ASSUMED KNOWLEDGE

This chapter assumes that you have read the web-based pre-reading material and therefore have a basic understanding of what VLANs are and how they are used. You should also be familiar with these concepts:

- Definition of a VLAN
- Broadcast domain
- Access port
- Trunk (multi-VLAN) port

INTRODUCTION

This chapter introduces VLANs. This chapter reviews the information found in the web-based pre-reading material and expands upon it. The content primarily focuses on the different VLAN types and the configuration and verification of VLANs, including the assignment of IP addressing information to VLANs on the HP switches.

Here are the topics covered in this chapter:

- Reviewing VLANs
- Understanding the different VLAN types
- Understanding the VLAN port types (access, trunk, hybrid, tagged, and untagged) and their configuration and verification
- Assigning IP addressing to VLANs
- Routing between VLANs

VLAN Review

VLANs enable you to group users by logical function instead of by physical location. This helps to control bandwidth usage within your network by allowing you to group high-bandwidth users on low-traffic segments and to organize users from different LAN segments according to their need for common resources and/or their use of individual protocols. You can also improve traffic control at the edge of your network by separating traffic of different protocol types. In addition, VLANs can enhance your network security by creating separate subnets to help control in-band access to specific network resources.

A group of networked ports assigned to a VLAN form a broadcast domain that is separate from other VLANs that may be configured on the switch. On a given switch, packets are bridged between source and destination ports that belong to the same VLAN. Therefore, all ports passing traffic for a particular subnet address should be configured to the same VLAN. Cross-domain broadcast traffic in the switch is eliminated, and bandwidth is saved by not allowing packets to flood out all ports.

Common definitions of VLANs include:

- Broadcast domain
- Layer 3 subnet (IP subnet)
- Different departments of a company
- Logical grouping of users

VLAN technology delivers the following benefits:

- **Confining broadcast traffic within individual VLANs.** This reduces bandwidth waste and improves network performance.
- **Improving LAN security.** By assigning user groups to different VLANs, you can isolate them at Layer 2. To enable communication between VLANs, routers or Layer 3 switches are required.
- **Flexible virtual workgroup creation.** Since users from the same workgroup can be assigned to the same VLAN—regardless of their physical locations—network construction and maintenance is much easier and more flexible.

To move traffic between VLANs, a routing process must occur. Basically, the router is moving the traffic between the VLANs (different subnets or networks). This increases security, since you can easily implement access control lists to restrict inter-VLAN traffic flows. Also, assigning IP addresses using an intelligent IP addressing scheme, based on your VLAN assignment, allows you to easily manage your network.

VLANs: Problems and Solutions

Main problems of large Layer 2 networks include:

- Broadcasts and multicasts affecting performance of devices.
- Identifying devices based on MAC addresses.

Using VLANs to segment a network creates many benefits for companies:

- Traffic within each VLAN is isolated from traffic in other VLANs. As a result, users on one VLAN do not have access to data in another VLAN, and this makes it more difficult for users to compromise security.
- Each VLAN is a separate broadcast domain. Broadcast packets sent in a VLAN will only be received by hosts that are members of that VLAN.

Solutions typically involve one of two kinds of devices: routers or switches. Other types of networking devices could be deployed (for example, firewalls), but this section focuses on routers and switches. When using routers, each segment or port is a separate broadcast domain. However, port density on routers is an issue, since router ports can be expensive when compared to switch ports. When using switches, many ports can be used to group devices into a VLAN, and these ports are much cheaper when compared to router ports. However, some type of tagging is needed to uniquely identify frames in different VLANs between linked switches. In addition to this, a switched solution requires Layer 3 switching or a router to route frames between different VLANs.

Switches and VLANs

Figure 6-1 shows an example of a physical topology with VLANs. Notice that VLAN 1 has nodes (PCs) spread across two different switches, making the nodes' locations independent of each other (obviously an advantage).

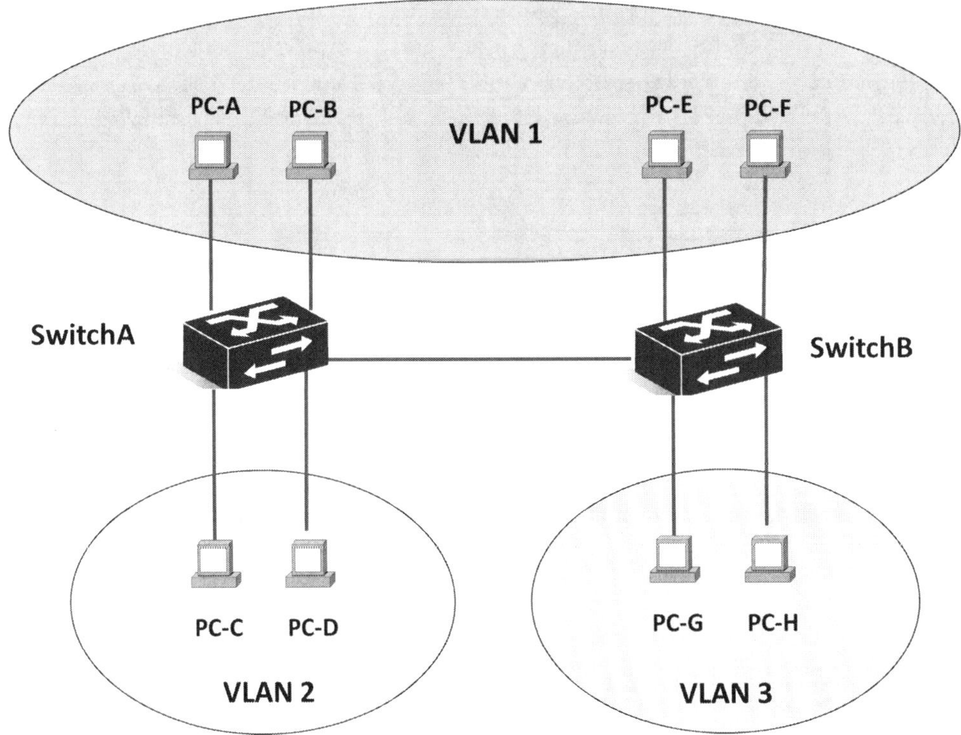

Figure 6-1. Physical topology view of VLANs

However, the two switches, SwitchA and SwitchB, must somehow be able to distinguish between the traffic for the different VLANs when it traverses between them. This is discussed later in the "Identifying VLANs" section of this chapter.

Figure 6-2 illustrates a *logical* picture, based on Figure 6-1, of what the users see in a network that implements VLANs. Notice that the VLANs are separated by a Layer 3 device, which could be a routing switch or a traditional router. In either case, the routing device prevents the VLAN broadcasts from crossing between VLANs and it provides subnet and routing boundaries.

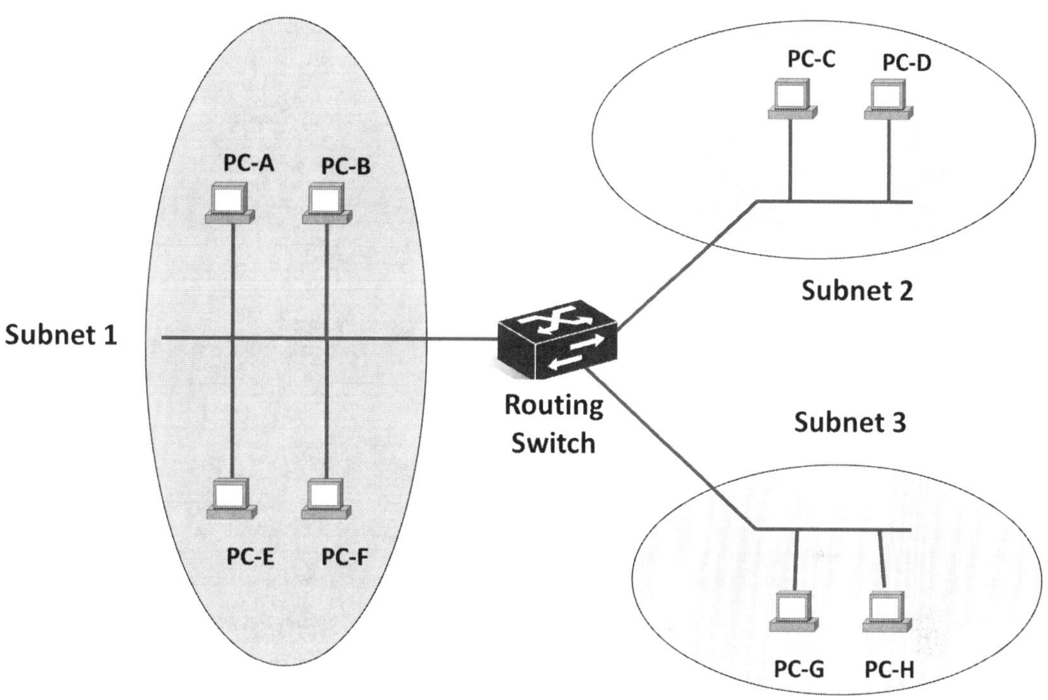

Figure 6-2. Logical topology view of VLANs

VLAN Types

A VLAN consists of multiple ports operating as members of the same subnet (*broadcast domain*). Ports on multiple devices can belong to the same VLAN, and traffic moving between ports in the same VLAN is bridged (or *switched*). (Remember that traffic moving between different VLANs must be routed.) A *static VLAN* is an 802.1Q-compliant VLAN configured with one or more ports that remain members, regardless of traffic usage. Static VLANs are configured with a name, VLAN ID (VID) number, and port members. A *dynamic VLAN* is an 802.1Q-compliant VLAN membership that the switch temporarily creates on a port to provide a link to another port in the same VLAN on another device.

Here are some common VLAN types:

- Port-based
- MAC address-based
- Protocol-based
- IP subnet-based
- Policy-based

The following section introduces different VLAN types; however, this book primarily focuses on port-based static VLANs.

Port-Based VLANs

Port-based VLANs group VLAN members by port. A port forwards traffic for a VLAN only after it is assigned to the VLAN—in other words, the port maintains the VLAN boundaries. For example, if a port was associated to VLAN 1, traffic for VLAN 2 would *not* be forwarded to the port. With port-based VLANs, the network administrator must manually map ports to their associated VLANs. This is the most common implementation of VLANs. Even though the other types of VLANs are introduced, this chapter only focuses on port-based VLAN implementations. Implementing the other VLAN types described below is beyond the scope of this chapter.

Note

The most common method of VLAN assignment is port-based, in which a VLAN is statically assigned to a port.

MAC Address-Based VLANs

The *MAC address-based VLAN* feature assigns hosts to VLANs based on their MAC addresses. This feature is used in conjunction with security technologies, such as 802.1X, to provide secure, flexible network access for edge devices, like PCs, laptops, IP phones, and more.

With the MAC-based VLAN configured, the device processes received frames and then looks up the list of MAC-to-VLAN mappings, based on the source MAC address of the frame, for a match. Matches can be defined manually from the CLI, where you specify which MAC addresses belong to which VLAN, or you can use an authentication server to associate MAC address-to-VLAN mappings. In either approach, you can specify that a range of MAC addresses, like those for a particular vendor's VoIP phone, are assigned to the same VLAN.

Note

The MAC address-based VLAN assignment method is very uncommon, since an administrator must build and maintain a table of MAC addresses and the VLANs to which they belong. This can be done on the switch or centralized on an AAA server, depending on the vendor's implementation.

Protocol-Based VLANs

Protocol-based VLAN configuration applies to hybrid ports only (discussed later in this chapter). Inbound frames are assigned to different VLANs based on their Ethernet protocol types and encapsulation formats. The protocols that can be used for VLAN assignment include IP, IPX, and AppleTalk. The encapsulation formats include Ethernet II, 802.3 raw, 802.2 Logical Link Control (LLC), and 802.2 Subnetwork Access Protocol (SNAP).

A protocol type and an encapsulation format make up a protocol template. You can create multiple protocol templates for a protocol-based VLAN, and different protocol templates are assigned separate protocol index values. A protocol template can be uniquely identified by a protocol-based VID and a protocol index, combined.

When using commands to associate protocol templates with ports, use the protocol-based VID and the protocol index to specify the protocol templates. An untagged frame reaching a port associated with protocol templates is processed as follows:

- If the protocol type and encapsulation format carried in the frame match a protocol template, the frame is tagged with the VLAN tag corresponding to the protocol template.
- If the frame matches no protocol templates, the frame is tagged with the default VLAN ID of the port.
- The port processes a tagged frame as it processes tagged frames of a port-based VLAN.

Note

Protocol-based VLANs are used sometimes in networks migrating from IPv4 to IPv6: this allows a company to separate the traffic of both protocols in the network. The HP Comware switches can easily implement this using hybrid ports (both VLANs are untagged), which is discussed later in the chapter.

IP Subnet-Based VLANs

In *IP subnet based VLANs*, frames are assigned to VLANs based on their source IP addresses and subnet masks. A port configured with IP subnet-based VLANs assigns a received untagged frame to a VLAN, based on the source IP address of the frame. This feature is used to assign frames from the specified network segment or IP address to a specific VLAN.

Policy-Based VLANs

Policy-based VLANs are sometimes referred to as *dynamic VLAN assignment*. Policy-based VLAN assignment is probably the second-most common method of VLAN assignment, and it is typically employed in networks using 802.1X. Based on something from the user, like MAC or IP address, or login credentials from 802.1X, the switch dynamically assigns the port to a particular VLAN. In the case of 802.1X, since AAA and an AAA server are used to authenticate the user, the AAA server passes back the VLAN number to assign to the port, based on the user's profile or the group profile to which the user belongs on the AAA server.

Note

Of the above types, HP ProVision does not support subnet-based VLANs. Comware, however, supports all the types. Other VLAN types supported include Super VLANs, Isolated User VLANs, and Voice VLANs. Super and Isolated User VLANs are used to implement private VLANs. The discussion of these types of VLANs is beyond the scope of this book. These VLAN types, however, are introduced in "Chapter 16: Basic Network Design Concepts," and are covered in much more depth in the Accredited Solutions Expert (ASE) certification track.

Identifying VLANs

IEEE 802.1Q is the networking standard that supports Virtual LANs on an Ethernet network. The standard defines a system of VLAN tagging for Ethernet frames for switches and other VLAN-aware devices in handling these frames. The standard also contains provisions for a quality of service (QoS) prioritization scheme commonly known as *IEEE 802.1p*.

Portions of the network which are VLAN-aware support the use of VLAN tags. Traffic on a VLAN-unaware portion of the network cannot contain VLAN tags. When a frame enters the VLAN-aware portion of the network, a tag is added to represent the VLAN membership of the frame's port or the port/protocol combination, depending on whether port-based or port-and-protocol-based VLAN classification is being used. Each frame must be distinguishable as being within exactly one VLAN. A frame in the VLAN-aware portion of the network that does not contain a VLAN tag is assumed to be flowing on the native (or default) VLAN. HP refers to this as the *Port VLAN Identifier* (PVID).

Note

HP uses two different terms to describe this tagging process, depending on the switch you are configuring. Comware refers to tagged frames sent across a link as a *trunk* port. However, ProVision refers to tagged frames sent across a link as a *tagged* port. The term "trunk" on ProVision switches refers to link aggregation covered in "Chapter 10: Link Aggregation," 802.1Q tagging.

VLANs are based on the IEEE 802.1Q standard, which defines a 4-byte field that can be inserted into an Ethernet frame after the MAC addressing fields. The 802.1Q field allows each Ethernet frame to be identified as part of a particular VLAN. The components of the 802.1Q field are defined as follows:

- The Tag Protocol ID (TPID) field identifies the frame as an 802.1Q frame.
- Three components make up the Tag Control Information (TCI) field, one of which identifies the frame's VLAN:
    - The Canonical Format Indicator (CFI) field indicates whether the information in the frame's MAC address is in canonical format.

- The VLAN ID field associates the frame with a specific VLAN.
- Called the 802.1p standard, the User Priority field allows devices to apply QoS to traffic. That is, 802.1p-compliant devices can classify and mark frames with a priority, in which: "7" is the highest and represents network management traffic, "6" represents voice, "5 represents video, "4" represents controlled load traffic, "3" represents excellent effort traffic, "2" is not used, "1" (the lowest) represents background traffic, and "0" represents normal traffic (best effort).

Note

802.1p is one way to ensure that delay-sensitive applications, such as VoIP, receive priority handling. QoS is covered in depth in HP's ASE-level certifications.

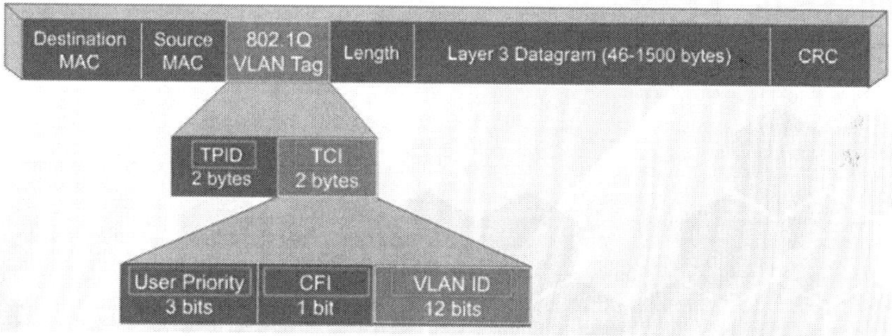

Figure 6-3. 802.1Q VLAN tagging

Devices that commonly support tagged VLAN frames include switches, routers, and file server network interface cards (NICs). Devices that do not support 802.1Q cannot insert or recognize the field. They may even consider a frame that contains the 802.1Q tag to be an illegal frame and therefore drop it, because such a frame is larger than the 1,518-byte Ethernet frame by 4 bytes (for a total of 1,522 bytes). These devices can still be part of a VLAN, however. You must configure their connected switch ports to be untagged members of a VLAN so that the devices can send and receive frames that do not contain the 802.1Q field.

Note

The default priority is 0 unless modified by the switch or another networking device. Also, VLAN numbers can span from 1 to 4,094 (0 and 4,095 are reserved).

Most user endpoints do not support VLANs (tagged frames). As you just learned, you must configure their connected switch ports to be untagged members of a VLAN so that the devices can send and receive frames that do not contain the 802.1Q field. Typically, you will configure switch ports that connect to endpoints to support only one VLAN. The 802.1Q field allows switches to support multiple VLANs, however, and ports that connect to other switches will usually need to forward traffic from more than one VLAN. You will configure these ports to support multiple VLANs.

Table 6-1 has some commonly used VLAN terms with which you should become familiar.

Table 6-1: VLAN terms

Term	Definition
Dynamic VLAN	An 802.1Q VLAN membership temporarily created on a port linked to another device, in which both devices are running Generic Attribute Registration Protocol (GARP) VLAN Registration Protocol (GVRP). (Discussion of GVRP is beyond the scope of this book.)
Static VLAN	A port-based or protocol-based VLAN configured in switch memory.
Tagged frame	A frame that carries an IEEE 802.1Q VID, which is a 2-byte extension that precedes the source MAC address field of an Ethernet frame. A VLAN tag is Layer 2 data and is transparent to higher layers.
Tagged VLAN	A VLAN that complies with the 802.1Q standard, including priority settings, and allows a port to join multiple VLANs.
Untagged frame	A frame that does not carry an IEEE 802.1Q VID.
Untagged VLAN	A VLAN that does not use or forward 802.1Q VLAN tagging, including priority settings. A port can be a member of only one untagged VLAN of a given type (port-based and the various protocol-based types).
VID	VID is the acronym for a VLAN Identification Number. Each 802.1Q-compliant VLAN must have its own unique VID number, and that VLAN must be given the same VID in every device in which it is configured.

Using VLAN Tags

On HP switches, all ports belong to the default VLAN (VLAN 1), and devices connected to these ports are in the same broadcast domain. Except for an IP address and subnet configured on the switch, no configuration steps are needed to accomplish this setup. The following sections discuss the movement of traffic in a network that contains switches.

Multiple Port-Based VLANs

In Figure 6-4, routing within SwitchA and SwitchB is disabled (the default for ProVision switches). This means that communication between any routable VLANs on the switch must go through the external router. In this case, the three VLANs can exchange traffic through the external routing switch. Note that VLAN 1, the default VLAN, is also present but not shown. (The default VLAN cannot be deleted from the HP switches. However, ports assigned to other VLANs can be removed from the default VLAN, if desired.) If internal (IP) routing is enabled on SwitchA and/or SwitchB, the external routing switch is not needed for traffic to move between different port-based VLANs.

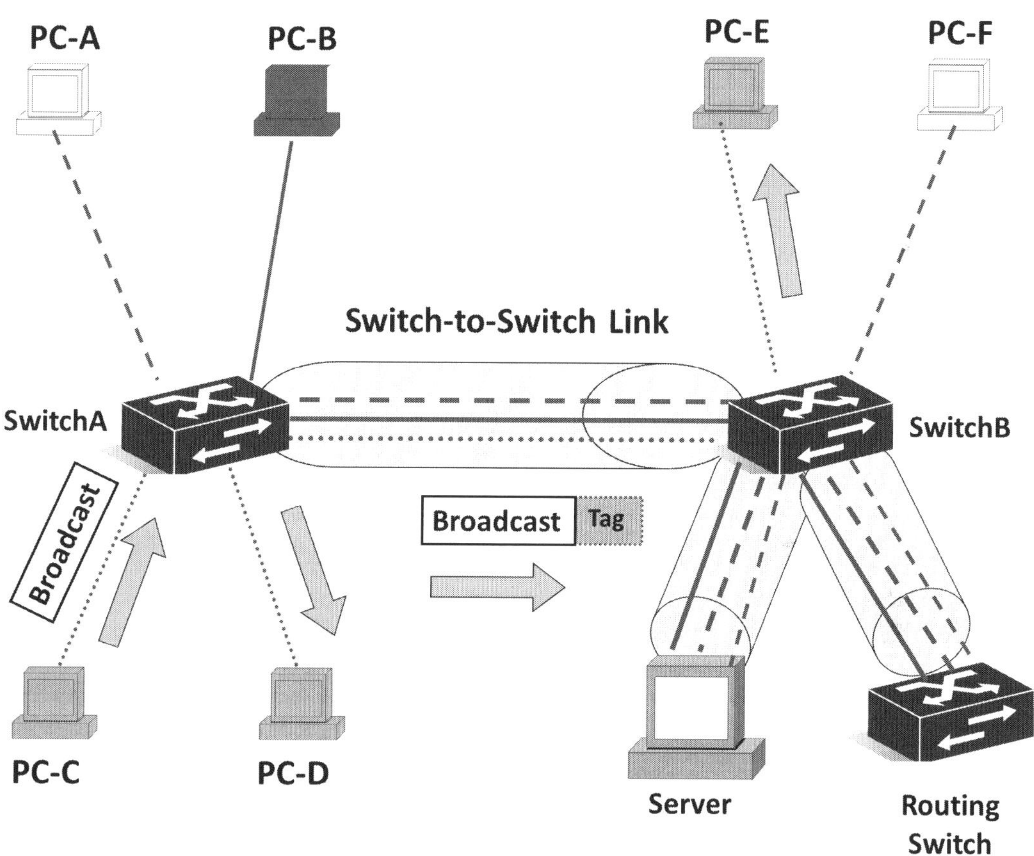

Figure 6-4. Using VLAN Tags

Tagged VLANs

A port can be a member of more than one VLAN of the same type if the device to which the port connects complies with the 802.1Q VLAN standard. For example, a port connected to a central server using a network interface card that complies with the 802.1Q standard can be a member of multiple VLANs, allowing members of multiple VLANs to use the server (see Figure 6-4). Although these VLANs cannot communicate with each other through the server, they can all access the server over the same connection from the switch. Where VLANs overlap in this way, VLAN *tags* are used in the individual packets to distinguish between traffic from different VLANs. A VLAN tag includes the particular VID, or number, of the VLAN on which the packet was generated.

Similarly, using 802.1Q-compliant switches, you can transport multiple VLANs through a single switch-to-switch link. SwitchA and SwitchB maintain the VLAN integrity between them. For example, if PC-C generates a broadcast, SwitchA sends it out to PC-D as an untagged frame but tags it and sends it to SwitchB. SwitchB strips off the tag when forwarding it to PC-E but retains the tag when forwarding it to the server and the routing switch. In this example, PC-A, PC-E, and PC-F do not see the broadcast because they are not in the same VLAN. This is not to say that the connections need to be between switches, but can be between any networking device that is 802.1Q-compliant, even a file server NIC, as shown in Figure 6-4. Comware refers to this as a *trunk connection*, whereas ProVision uses the term *tagged* or *multi-VLAN port*.

VLAN Operating Rules

You should follow these rules when implementing VLANs:

- If a tagged frame arrives on a port that is not a tagged member of the VLAN indicated by the frame's VID, the switch drops the frame. Similarly, the switch drops an inbound, tagged frame if the receiving port is an untagged member of the VLAN indicated by the frame's VID.
- To enable an inbound port to forward an untagged frame, the port must be an untagged member of a port-based VLAN. That is, when a port receives an incoming, untagged frame, it processes the frame according to the following ordered criteria:
    - If the port has no untagged VLAN memberships, the switch drops the packet.
    - If the port is a member of an untagged, port-based VLAN, the switch forwards the frame to that VLAN. Otherwise, the switch drops the frame.
- If a port is a tagged member for a VLAN, the frame can be forwarded out an egress port as a tagged frame if the VLAN of the frame is also associated with the egress port. For an egress port that has the same VLAN associated with it as an untagged member, the tag is removed from the inbound frame before forwarding it out the egress port (as untagged).

Forwarding Within a VLAN on HP Switches

A Layer 2 switch uses the Layer 2 (MAC address) destination address in each frame to make forwarding decisions. Traffic is confined to the source VLAN and is not forwarded to other VLANs. A Layer 3 switch (which is sometimes called a *routing switch*) can forward packets among different VLANs. Routing is discussed in "Chapter 11: IP Routing Overview," and "Chapter 12: OSPF Operation and Configuration."

To help illustrate the switching process, examine the network in Figure 6-5, which uses ProVision switches. When a host in VLAN 20 sends a frame, the switch submits the frame to the VLAN 20 forwarding table. The forwarding table indicates that the sender is connected to a port that is statically defined as a member of VLAN 20. Consequently, the only valid destination ports for frames entering from VLAN 20 ports are other ports in VLAN 20.

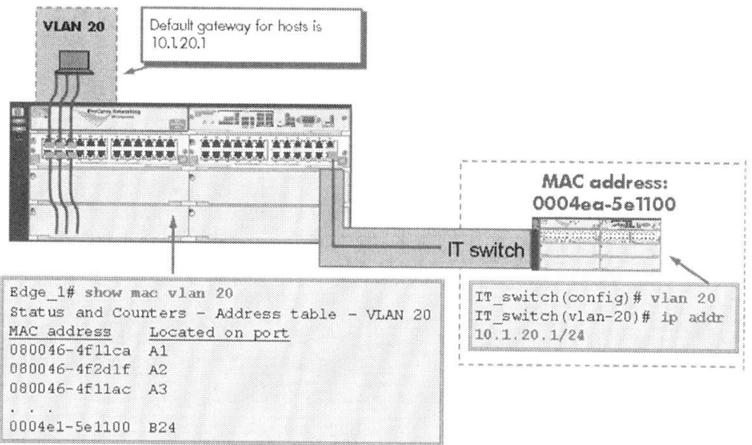

Figure 6-5. Forwarding traffic within a VLAN

In Figure 6-5, the uplink port on the Edge_1 switch that has several ports for VLAN 20 connects to a switch in an IT department. The IT switch has a logical interface for VLAN 20 with an address of 10.1.20.1/24 and acts as the default gateway for all VLAN 20 hosts. This configuration enables VLAN 20 hosts to access network services from the IT switch and its associated VLANs. The default gateway also enables VLAN 20 hosts to reach other destinations within the network and the Internet.

Step-by-Step: Layer 2 Forwarding Between Hosts in the Same VLAN

To have a better understanding of the forwarding process, examine Figure 6-6. This example illustrates Layer 2 forwarding when two hosts in the same VLAN communicate. Here, the hosts are in VLAN 30 and are spread among three floors of a building. This implies that the edge switches must be able to forward VLAN 30 traffic in addition to any other VLANs they support. In this scenario, a backup server on the second floor runs a scheduled backup task for the database on a server located on the third floor. Both of these servers are in the same VLAN but are connected to different switches.

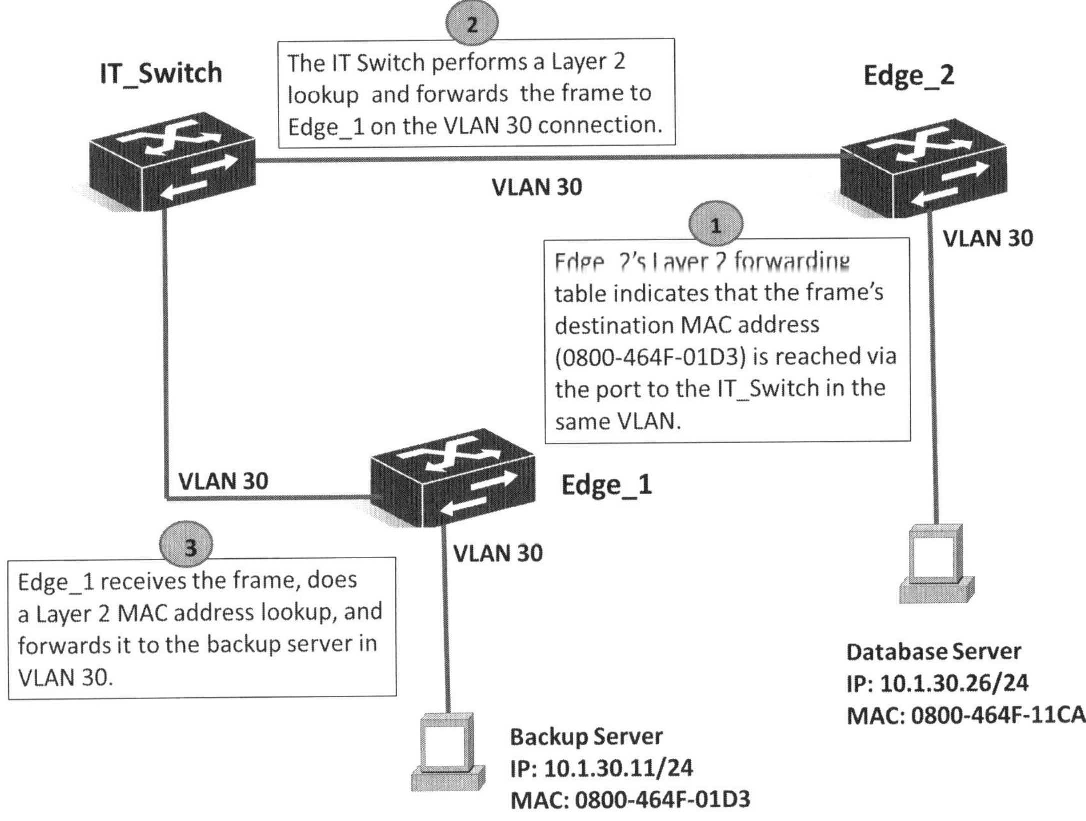

Figure 6-6. Forwarding between hosts in the same VLAN

The communication is initiated when the client backup program on the database server determines it must communicate with the backup server. The client's first step is determining whether the backup server is in the same network address range. In the example, the two servers are in the same network (10.1.30.0), which implies that the database server (10.1.30.26) should be able to resolve the MAC address of the backup server (10.1.30.11).

Here are the steps described in Figure 6-6:

1. If this is the first transmission between the two devices, the database server will send an ARP request to obtain the backup server's MAC address. If the database server has recently communicated with the backup server, the database server's ARP cache will already include the backup server's MAC address. In either case, the database server sends the frame with the backup server's MAC address as its destination. In this example, the switch named Edge_2 is configured to perform only Layer 2 forwarding. Edge_2 receives the frame from the database server, submits it for lookup in its forwarding table, and determines the backup server's MAC address (0800-464F-01D3) is reached through the port to IT_Switch.

2. The IT_Switch core switch uses the destination MAC address to determine whether to forward using Layer 2 or Layer 3. Since this frame has a destination MAC address other than its own, the IT switch uses Layer 2 information to forward the frame. It submits the destination MAC address to its Layer 2 forwarding table, determines that MAC address 0800-464F-01D3 is reached through the port to the Edge_1 switch, and forwards the frame accordingly.
3. Like Edge_2, switch Edge_1 is configured to perform only Layer 2 forwarding. Switch Edge_1 receives the frame from the IT_Switch, submits the frame to lookup in its forwarding table, and determines that the Backup_Server port leads to the destination MAC address 0800-464F-01D3. The switch forwards the frame out of this port to the backup server.

Step-by-Step: Tag Manipulation in Layer 2 Forwarding

Let us continue the example by examining the tag manipulation process occurring in Figure 6-7. Because the entire path between the database and backup servers is within the same VLAN, all of the switches involved in the transaction use Layer 2 forwarding. Figure 6-7 illustrates how switches add and remove IEEE 802.1Q tags to transport the traffic.

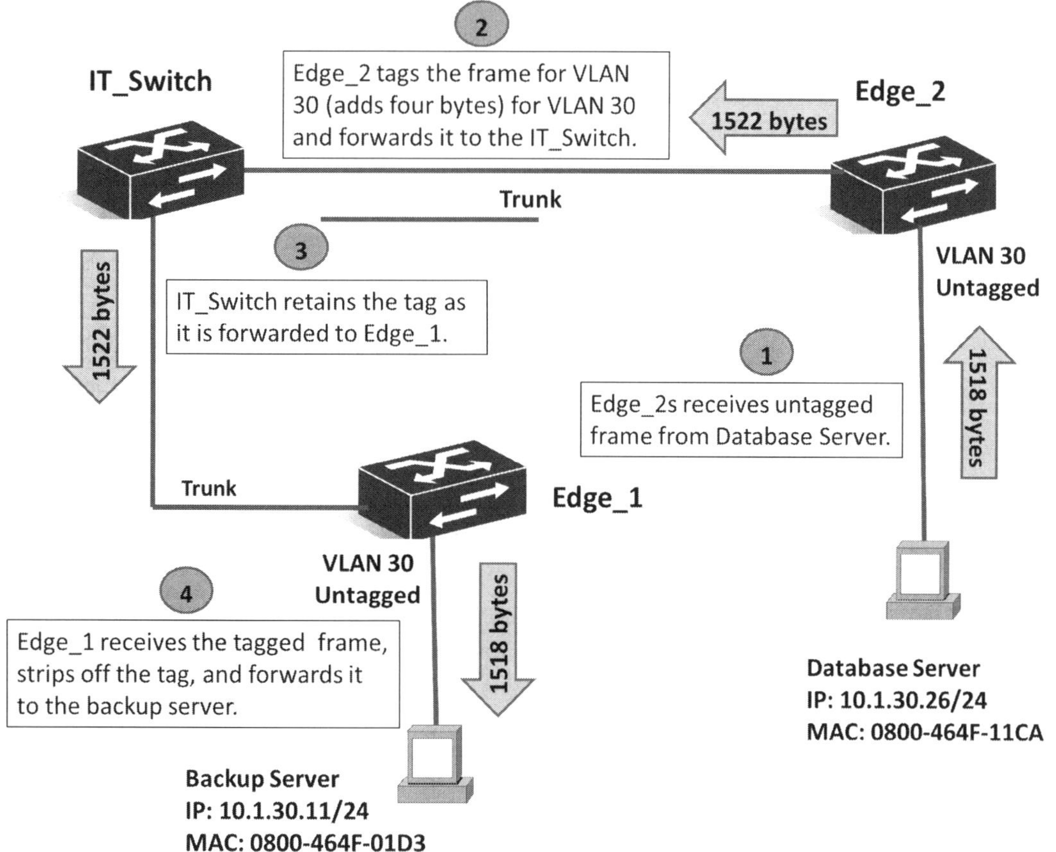

Figure 6-7. Tag manipulation in Layer 2 forwarding

Here is the continuation of the steps (see Figure 6-7) involved in transmitting the traffic:

1. The database server knows that the destination host (the backup server) is in the same subnet and sends frames directly to the backup server's MAC address.
2. The database server is not aware of VLAN designations, but the VLAN configuration of Edge_2 indicates that the database server is a member of VLAN 30. The switch performs a lookup and determines that the port connected to IT_Switch leads toward the backup server's MAC address. Because this port is a tagged member of VLAN 30, Edge_2 adds a tag that identifies VLAN 30.
3. The IT_Switch core switch receives the tagged frame and submits it to its VLAN 30 forwarding table. It determines that the port connected to the Edge_1 switch leads toward the backup server's MAC address. Since this is also a tagged member of VLAN 30, IT_Switch retains the tag and does not change it before forwarding the frame to the Edge_1 switch.
4. The Edge_1 switch receives the tagged frame and submits it to its VLAN 30 forwarding table. The outbound port is an untagged member of VLAN 30, so Edge_1 strips the tag before forwarding it through the port connected to the backup server.

VLAN Activity

Examine Figure 6-8. PC-A sends a frame to PC-B, and both devices are in VLAN 30. What would be true about whether a tag is needed on each of the four links? The PCs need to communicate with each other and there is a trunk connection between SwitchA and SwitchB but no trunk between SwitchB and SwitchC. Fill in the shaded text boxes on each link with the word **None** if no tag is necessary, or add the **VLAN number** if a tag is needed.

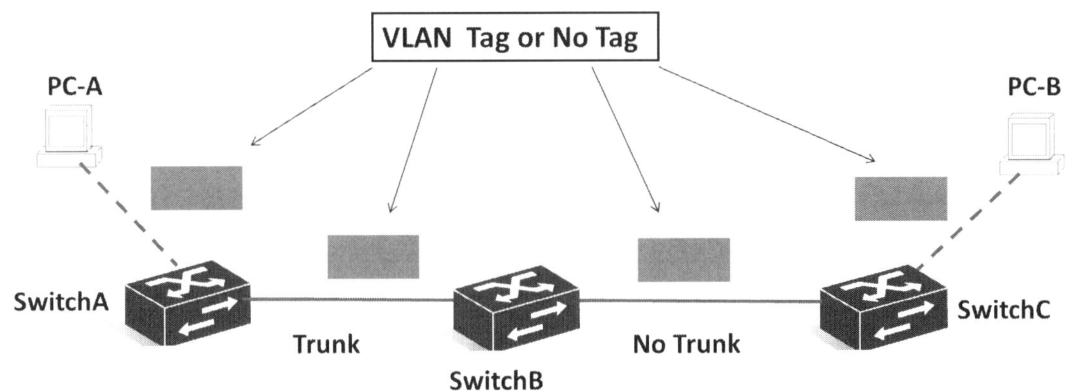

Figure 6-8. VLAN activity topology

VLAN Activity Answer

Typically links between users and their connected switches are not tagged. There is one trunk, between SwitchA and SwitchB; therefore, tagging of the VLAN is necessary. Notice that SwitchB and SwitchC do not have a trunk connection; therefore, no tagging takes place. This means that all the users connected to SwitchC will probably be associated to the same VLAN (30, in this example). Note, however, that if you were to add any additional VLANs to SwitchC, you would need to convert the link between SwitchB and SwitchC to a trunk. The answer is shown in Figure 6-9.

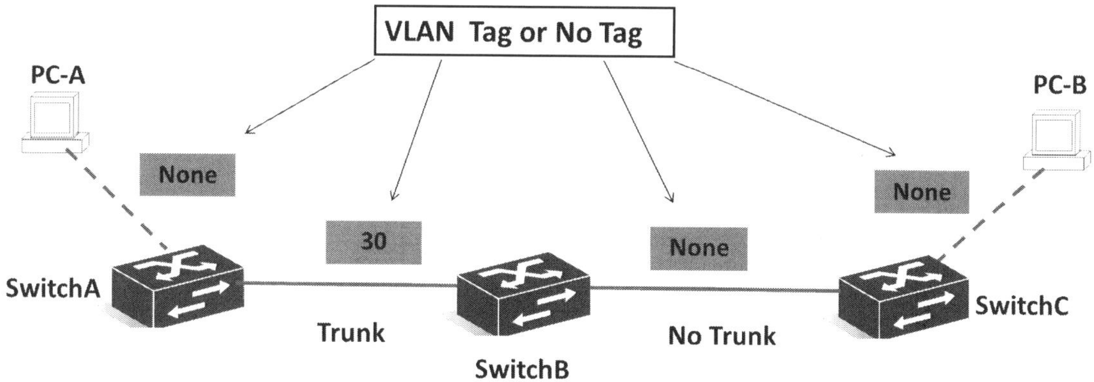

Figure 6-9. VLAN activity answer

VLAN Port Types

The following port types are discussed in this section:

- Untagged
- Tagged
- Access
- Hybrid
- Trunk

HP Terminology

When it comes to VLANs, Comware and ProVision switches use different terms that describe the state of the frame (tagged or untagged). The following two sections explain these differences in more depth.

HP Comware Terms

Port-based VLANs group VLAN members by port. A port forwards traffic for a VLAN only after it is assigned to the VLAN. By default, all the ports are assigned to VLAN 1 and therefore can communicate with each other. You can configure the link type of a port as *access*, *trunk*, or *hybrid* on a Comware switch:

- **Access port**—Belongs to one VLAN, and frames are untagged. An access port belongs to only one VLAN and sends traffic untagged. It is typically used to connect a terminal device unable to recognize VLAN tagged-frames or when there is no need to separate different VLAN members.
- **Trunk port**—Carries multiple VLANs on a single physical link; VLANs are 802.1Q tagged and the port VLAN identifier is untagged. The PVID, by default, is the default VLAN (VLAN 1). A trunk port can carry multiple VLANs to receive and send traffic for them. Except traffic of the default VLAN, traffic sent through a trunk port will be VLAN tagged. Usually, ports connecting network devices are configured as trunk ports.
- **Hybrid port**—Belongs to multiple VLANs where they can be untagged and tagged. This is typically used for VoIP phones that share a switch, two or more virtual machines (VMs) sharing an interface, or two or more protocols used by a PC or server (like IPv4 and IPv6). If there is more than one untagged VLAN on a hybrid port, some method is needed for the switch to correctly identify the VLAN that should be associated with the traffic. Dynamic methods include MAC addresses, IP addresses, protocol, 802.1X credentials, and Link Layer Discovery Protocol–Media Endpoint Discovery (LLDP-MED) (voice) information. Like a trunk port, a hybrid port can carry multiple VLANs to receive and send traffic for them. Unlike a trunk port, a hybrid port allows traffic of all VLANs to pass through VLAN untagged. Usually, hybrid ports are configured to connect those devices for which support of VLAN tagged frames is unclear.

HP ProVision Terms

Comware switches support all three port types discussed on the previous page: access, trunk and hybrid; however HP ProVision switches only support *untagged* (access) and *tagged* (trunk) ports. ProVision switches do not support hybrid ports; however, you can have multiple VLANs untagged on a ProVision port if you are using some type of dynamic VLAN assignment (like policy-based VLANs implemented with 802.1X).

Note

ProVision switches use the term *tagged* link or port when referring to VLAN-aware links, where multiple VLANs can traverse the same link. However, most vendors in the industry, including the Comware switches, use the term *trunk* to describe this kind of port. This can be confusing, since the ProVision switches do have a *trunk* port; however, a trunk port on a ProVision switch refers to an *aggregated* link (two or more physical connections between two devices that are treated as a *single* logical connection). Link aggregation is discussed in "Chapter 10: Link Aggregation." Except as noted, this chapter uses the term *trunk* when referring to a port link that tags multiple VLANs.

HP Port Types Example

Figure 6-10 shows an example network with different port types. Interface Gi1/0/2 on switch SW-A is an example of an access port. Interface Gi1/0/3 on the same switch is an example of a hybrid port in which VLAN 200 (for the phone) and VLAN 100 (for data PCs) are both untagged. Interface Gi1/0/1 on the same switch is a trunk in which all frames are tagged to the Distrib1 switch except for the PVID VLAN. The PVID, which is VLAN 1 by default, is used for management functions, like Spanning Tree Protocol bridge protocol data units (STP BPDUs) and LLDP.

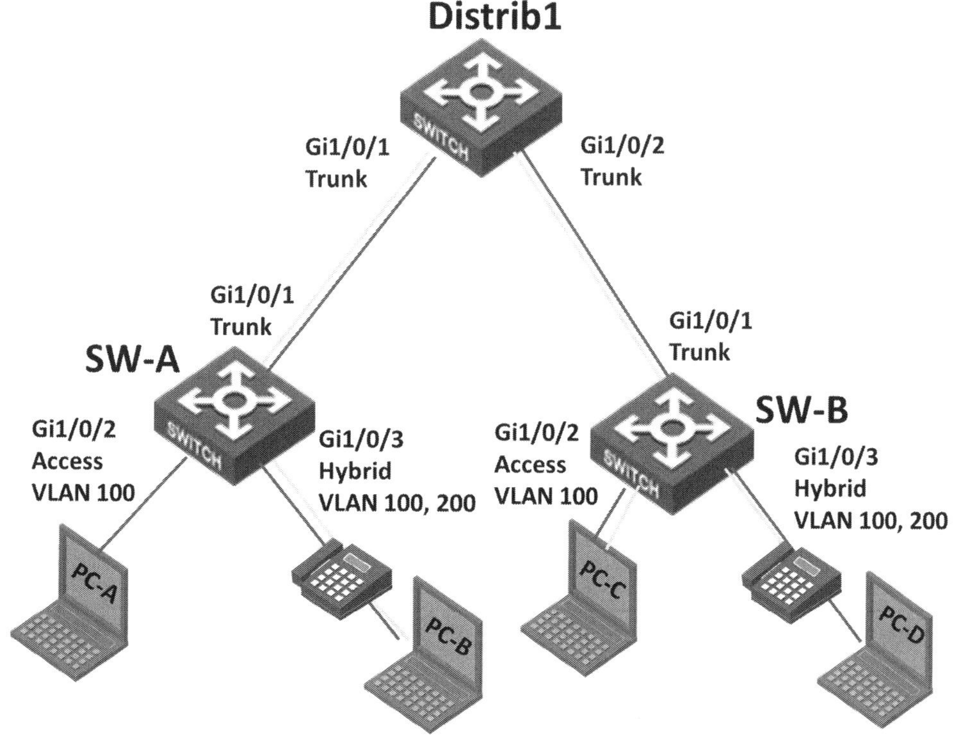

Figure 6-10. Example network, illustrating the three port types

Note

The main difference between a hybrid port and a trunk port is that, on a trunk port, there is one (and only) untagged VLAN. In Figure 6-10, the links to the PC/phone connections could be traditional trunks (if the VoIP phone understands 802.1Q tagging) or a hybrid port (if the VoIP phone only understands untagged frames). For the latter, the ports on the switches would have to use something to help them differentiate the traffic for the two VLANs, like the MAC addresses of the devices, to correctly correlate the traffic to their respective VLANs.

VLAN Configuration

Keep these rules when implementing VLANs on HP switches:

- A port must be a member of at least one VLAN. In the factory default configuration, all ports are assigned to the default VLAN. (This is named the DEFAULT_VLAN on ProVision switches. Both ProVision and Comware use VID = 1.)
- You can rename the default VLAN, but you cannot change its VID (1) or delete it from the switch. Any ports not specifically removed from the default VLAN remain in the DEFAULT_VLAN, regardless of other port assignments. Also, a port must always be a tagged or untagged member of at least one port-based VLAN.
- A port can be a member of one untagged, port-based VLAN. All other port-based VLAN assignments for that port must be tagged. (The "untagged" designation enables VLAN operation with non-802.1Q–compliant devices.)
- When deleting a VLAN, any ports in the deleted VLAN will automatically be placed into the default VLAN.
- Changing the number of VLANs supported on the ProVision switches requires a reboot. (From the CLI, you must perform a `write memory` command before rebooting.) Comware switches do not support the limiting of the number of VLANs defined on a switch.

The remainder of this chapter focuses on implementing VLANs on ProVision and Comware switches. This includes creating VLANs, assigning access ports to VLANs, creating trunks and hybrid ports, and assigning IP addresses to VLAN interfaces on the switches.

Note

The GVRP, which allows you to create a VLAN on one switch and have it propagated and dynamically created on other switches, is supported by both Comware and ProVision. However, this book does not cover GVRP, nor is it commonly used in the industry.

VLAN Configuration on ProVision Switches

In the factory default state, all ports on a ProVision switch belong to the (port-based) default VLAN, with a name of DEFAULT_VLAN and a VID of 1. The default VLAN is also the primary VLAN. At default settings, you can configure up to 255 additional static VLANs by adding new VLAN names and then assigning one or more ports to each VLAN. The ProVision switches accept a maximum of 2,048 VLANs with VIDs numbering up to 4094, including the default VLAN and any dynamic VLANs the switch creates if you enable GVRP. The `max-vlans` setting must be increased to support more than 256 VLANs. The following sections discuss how to create and delete VLANs.

Changing the Number of VLANs

In the default VLAN configuration, the switch allows a maximum of 256 VLANs. Depending on the switch model, this can extend up to 2,048 VLANs. You can expand this by using the following command:

```
ProVision(config)# max-vlans <number>
```

You can specify any value from 1 to 2,048. As part of adding additional VLANs, you must execute a `write memory` command (to save the new value to the startup-config file) and then reboot the switch.

Here is an example:

```
ProVision(config)# max-vlans 300
```

This command takes affect after saving configuration and reboot:

```
ProVision(config)# write memory

ProVision(config)# boot

Device will be rebooted, do you want to continue [y/n]? y
```

Creating a New Static VLAN

Creating a new VLAN is accomplished with the `vlan` command:

```
ProVision(config)# vlan <vid | vlan-name>

ProVision(vlan-id)#
```

The `vlan` command operates in the global configuration context to either configure a static VLAN and/or to take the CLI to the specified VLAN's context.

If the VLAN ID (<vid>) does not exist in the switch, this command creates a port-based VLAN with the specified VLAN number. If the command does not include options, the CLI moves to the newly created VLAN context. If you do not specify an optional name, the switch assigns a name in the default format: *VLANx* (where *x* is the VID assigned to the VLAN). If the VLAN already exists and you enter either the VID or the VLAN name, the CLI moves to the specified VLAN's context.

Note

You must use a VID when creating a VLAN; however, you can reference the VID or VLAN name to enter the VLAN context.

To assign a name to the VLAN, either use the `name` parameter:

```
ProVision(config)# vlan <vid> name <vlan-name>
```

Or the `name` command in the VLAN context:

```
ProVision(config)# vlan <vid | vlan-name>
ProVision(vlan-id)# name <vlan-name>
```

VLAN names cannot contain following characters: @, #, $, ^, &, *, (, or). To include a blank space in a VLAN name, enclose the name in single or double quotes (' ' or " "). Using spaces in VLAN names is not recommended.

Deleting a VLAN

The `no vlan` command deletes a VLAN:

```
ProVision(config)# no vlan <vlan-id>
```

If one or more ports belong only to the VLAN to be deleted, the CLI notifies you that these ports will be moved to the default VLAN and it prompts you to continue the deletion. For example, if ports B1–B5 belong to both VLAN 2 and VLAN 3, and ports B6–B10 belong to VLAN 3 only, deleting VLAN 3 causes the CLI to prompt you to approve moving ports B6–B10 to VLAN 1 (the default VLAN); ports B1–B5 are not moved because they still belong to another VLAN.

Here is the example syntax:

```
ProVision(config)# no vlan 3
The following ports will be moved to the default VLAN:B6-B10 Do you
want to continue? [y/n] y
```

Note

Before deleting a VLAN, it is recommended that ports first be moved to a different VLAN. On some switches, such as the 5400 zl Switch Series, if you do not explicitly reassign all untagged members to another VLAN, you are prompted to allow the untagged members to be moved to the default VLAN. On other switches, you must explicitly move the untagged port members to the default VLAN or to some other VLAN.

Defining the Secure Management VLAN

Configuring a secure management VLAN creates an isolated network for managing the ProVision switches that support this feature (discussed in "Chapter 4: Protecting Management Access"). If you configure a secure management VLAN, access to the VLAN and to the switch's management functions (menu, CLI, and WebAgent) is available only through ports configured as members of the secure management VLAN. Multiple ports on the switch can belong to the management VLAN. This allows connections for multiple management stations you want to have access to the management VLAN, while at the same time allowing management VLAN links between switches configured for the same management VLAN. Only traffic from the management VLAN can manage the switch, which means that only the workstations and PCs connected to ports belonging to the management VLAN can manage and reconfigure the switch.

By default, no management VLAN exists. Here is the configuration to designate an existing VLAN as the management VLAN:

```
ProVision(config)# [no] management-vlan <vid | vlan-name>
```

Only one management VLAN can be active in the switch. The `no` form of the command disables the management VLAN and returns the switch to its default management operation: note that this does not delete the VLAN.

Note

If you configure a management VLAN on a switch by using a remote connection (like SSH or Telnet) through a port that is not in the management VLAN, you lose management contact with the switch when you log off your remote session or execute `write memory` and reboot the switch. In other words, changing the management VLAN will not affect current remote access connections to the switch.

Changing the Primary VLAN

The primary VLAN is used for switch management features, as discussed earlier in this chapter. In the default VLAN configuration, the port-based default VLAN (DEFAULT_VLAN) is the primary VLAN. However, you can reassign the primary VLAN to any port-based, static VLAN on the switch:

```
ProVision(config)# primary-vlan <vid | vlan-name>
```

Reassignment must be to an existing, port-based, static VLAN. (The switch will not reassign the primary VLAN function to a protocol VLAN.) If you reassign the primary VLAN to a non-default VLAN, you cannot later delete that VLAN from the switch until you again reassign the primary VLAN to another port-based, static VLAN.

Untagged Ports in a VLAN

An untagged port in a VLAN is commonly referred to as an *access port*. An access port has connected devices that understand normal 802.3 Ethernet frames only—they do not understand 802.1Q tagging.

On a ProVision switch, a port can be an untagged member of only one VLAN. If a port was allowed to be an untagged member of more than one VLAN, the switch would be unable to determine the VLAN membership of a packet entering from a client computer. Furthermore, a port must be a member, either tagged or untagged, of at least one VLAN. At default settings, each port is an untagged member of VLAN 1. It is removed from VLAN 1 when it is defined as an untagged member of another VLAN.

To assign a port as an untagged port to a VLAN, use either of the following two configurations:

```
ProVision(config)# vlan <vid | vlan-name> untag <port-list>
```

Or

```
ProVision(config)# vlan <vid | vlan-name>
ProVision(vlan-id)# untag <port-list>
```

Here is an example that associates ports A1–A6 as untagged ports to VLAN 20 and that associates ports A22, A24, and B1–B5 as untagged ports to VLAN 30:

```
ProVision(config)# vlan 20
ProVision(vlan-20)# untag a1-a6
ProVision(vlan-20)# exit
ProVision(config)# vlan 30
ProVision(vlan-30)# untag a22,a24,b1-b5
```

For a given VLAN, the port IDs do not have to be contiguous. In the case of a switch with multiple modules, the VLAN can span modules.

You could also configure the above example in this way:

```
ProVision(config)# vlan 20 untagged a1-a6
ProVision(config)# vlan 30 untagged a22,a24,b1-b5
```

Tagged Ports in a VLAN

The switch requires VLAN tagging on a given port if more than one VLAN of the same type uses the port. When a port belongs to two or more VLANs of the same type, they remain as separate broadcast domains and cannot receive traffic from each other without routing. The switch requires VLAN tagging on a given port if the port will be receiving inbound, tagged VLAN traffic that should be forwarded. Even if the port belongs to only one VLAN, it forwards inbound tagged traffic only if it is a tagged member of that VLAN.

If the only authorized, inbound VLAN traffic on a port arrives untagged, the port must be an untagged member of that VLAN. This is the case in which the port is connected to a non-802.1Q–compliant device or is assigned to only one VLAN.

Since the purpose of VLAN tagging is to allow multiple VLANs on the same port, any port that has only one VLAN assigned to it can be configured as untagged (the default) if the authorized inbound traffic for that port arrives untagged. Any port with two or more VLANs of the same type can have one such VLAN assigned as untagged. All other VLANs of the same type must be configured as tagged. A given VLAN must have the same VID on all 802.1Q-compliant devices in which the VLAN occurs. Also, the ports connecting two 802.1Q devices should have identical VLAN configurations.

VLAN Tagging

Examine Figure 6-11. If port 7 on 802.1Q-compliant Switch X is assigned to only the red VLAN, the assignment can remain untagged because the port will forward traffic only for the red VLAN. However, if both the red and green VLANs are assigned to port 7, at least one of those VLAN assignments must be tagged so that red VLAN traffic can be distinguished from green VLAN traffic.

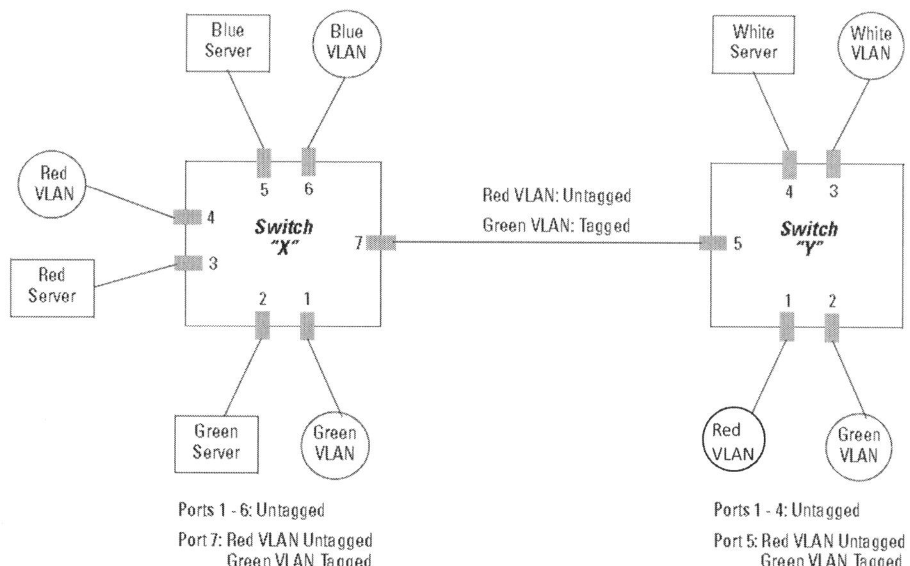

Figure 6-11. Example of a VLAN configuration on ProVision switches

Here is the information pertinent to Switch X:

- VLANs assigned to ports X1–X6 can all be untagged because there is only one VLAN assignment per port. Red VLAN traffic will go out only the red ports; green VLAN traffic will go out only the green ports, and so on. Devices connected to these ports do not have to be 802.1Q-compliant.
- However, because both the red VLAN and the green VLAN are assigned to port X7, at least one of the VLANs must be tagged for this port.

Here is the information pertinent to Switch Y:

- VLANs assigned to ports Y1–Y4 can all be untagged because there is only one VLAN assignment per port. Devices connected to these ports do not have to be 802.1Q-compliant.
- Because both the red VLAN and the green VLAN are assigned to port Y5, at least one of the VLANs must be tagged for this port.

The ports on the link between the two switches must be configured the same for the 802.1Q settings. As shown in Figure 6-11, the red VLAN must be untagged on port X7 and Y5 and the green VLAN must be tagged on port X7 and Y5 (or vice versa). Please note that the VLAN configurations of ports X7 and Y5 must match; you could have easily reversed which VLANs were tagged versus untagged or made both the green and red VLANs tagged for these ports.

Tagging VLANs on a port is commonly done for switch-to-switch connections. To assign ports as tagged ports to a VLAN, use one of the two following configurations:

```
ProVision(config)# vlan <vid | vlan-name> tag <port-list>
```

Or

```
ProVision(config)# vlan <vid | vlan-name>
ProVision(vlan-id)# tagged <port-list>
```

Note

You cannot use the `no` command to remove a port from a VLAN—a port must always belong to a VLAN and cannot be orphaned. Use the `untagged` and `tagged` commands to move a port from one VLAN to another.

VLAN Configuration Example

Let us look at the example shown previously in Figure 6-11. Here is Switch X's configuration:

```
SwitchX(config)# vlan 20
SwitchX(vlan-20)# name Red
SwitchX(vlan-20)# untagged a3-a6
SwitchX(vlan-20)# tagged a7
SwitchX(vlan-20)# exit
SwitchX(config)# vlan 30
SwitchX(vlan-30)# name Green
SwitchX(vlan-30)# untagged a1-a2
SwitchX(vlan-30)# tagged a7
```

Here is Switch Y's configuration:

```
SwitchY(config)# vlan 20
SwitchY(vlan-20)# name Red
SwitchY(vlan-20)# untagged a1
SwitchY(vlan-20)# tagged a5
SwitchY(vlan-20)# exit
SwitchY(config)# vlan 30
SwitchY(vlan-30)# name Green
SwitchY(vlan-30)# untagged a2
SwitchX(vlan-30)# tagged a5
SwitchY(vlan-20)# exit
SwitchY(config)# vlan 40
SwitchY(vlan-40)# name White
SwitchY(vlan-40)# untagged a3-a4
```

Note

To move a port from one VLAN and to another, go into the new VLAN and use the `tagged` or `untagged` command to assign it to the new VLAN. If you are in a VLAN context and use the `no tagged` or `no untagged` commands, the associated ports are placed into the default VLAN.

VLAN Verification

This section focuses on verifying the configuration of your VLANs on ProVision switches with various `show` commands. Here is a list of the most common commands to verify your configuration:

- `show vlans`—When issued without any command options, it shows all VLANs on the switch.
- `show vlans <vlan-id>`—This command shows the port membership for a single VLAN.
- `show vlans port <port-id> detail`—This command shows the VLAN membership of a single port, and the detail option shows tagged and untagged membership.
- `show ip`—This command shows IP interfaces configured on switch, if routing is enabled and if a default gateway is defined.

To see a list of all VLANs defined on the switch, use the `show vlans` command. Here is an example:

```
ProVision# show vlans

 Status and Counters - VLAN Information

  Maximum VLANs to support : 256

  Primary VLAN : DEFAULT_VLAN

  Management VLAN :


  VLAN ID Name                 | Status     Voice Jumbo

  ------- -------------------- + ---------- ----- -----

  1       DEFAULT_VLAN         | Port-based No    No

  30      VLAN30               | Port-based No    No

  40      VLAN40               | Port-based No    No
```

In the above example, the default and primary VLAN are the same (1).

Optionally, you can qualify the output by specifying a VID, like this:

```
ProVision# show vlans 30

 Status and Counters - VLAN Information - VLAN 30

  VLAN ID : 30

  Name : VLAN30

  Status : Port-based

  Voice : No

  Jumbo : No


  Port Information Mode     Unknown VLAN Status

  ---------------- -------- ------------ ----------

  1                Untagged Learn        Up

  21               Tagged   Learn        Up
```

In this example, port 1 is untagged and port 21 is tagged in VLAN 30.

To see a port's VLAN, use this command:

```
ProVision# show vlans port <port-list> [detail]
```

You can list a single port or a group of ports. Here is an example of this command:

```
ProVision# show vlans port 1

 Status and Counters - VLAN Information - for ports 1

  VLAN ID Name                 | Status     Voice Jumbo

  ------- -------------------- + ---------- ----- -----

  30      VLAN30               | Port-based No    No
```

In this example, you can see that port 1 is in VLAN 30. Adding the `detail` parameter includes information about whether the port is tagged or untagged:

```
ProVision# show vlans port 1 detail

 Status and Counters - VLAN Information - for ports 1

  VLAN ID Name                 | Status     Voice Jumbo Mode

  ------- -------------------- + ---------- ----- ----- --------

  30      VLAN30               | Port-based No    No    Untagged
```

VLAN Configuration on Comware Switches

The remainder of this section focuses on implementing VLANs on the Comware switches. This includes creating VLANs, assigning access ports to VLANs, creating trunks and hybrid ports, and assigning IP addresses to VLAN interfaces on the switches.

Creating VLANs

On Comware switches, the default VLAN is VLAN 1, and the ports default to access ports. With these settings, the port accepts frames that do not contain an 802.1Q tag and that have a source IP address in VLAN 1. Creating VLANs on the Comware switches is similar to creating VLANs on the ProVision switches using VLAN contexts. Here is the syntax for creating a VLAN:

```
[Comware] vlan <vid>
[Comware-<vlan-name>] description <description>
[Comware-<vlan-name>] name <vlan-name>
```

The VID is the number of the VLAN. If you do not assign a name to a VLAN, the default name is the word "VLAN" followed by the VID. You can create a maximum of 4,094 VLANs (VLAN 4,095 is reserved, by the 802.1Q standard).

Optionally, you can create a range of VLANs using the following syntax:

```
[Comware] vlan <vid> to <vid>
```

Here is a simple example of creating VLANs on SW-A switch (shown previously in Figure 6-10):

```
[SW-A] vlan 100
[SW-A-vlan100] description For Users PCs
[SW-A-vlan100] name Users
[SW-A-vlan100] quit
[SW-A] vlan 200
[SW-A-vlan200] description Voice VLAN
[SW-A-vlan200] name IP-Phones
```

Configuring Access Ports

By default, all ports on the Comware switches are access ports. Access ports belong to a single VLAN and are untagged. If a port was configured as a trunk or hybrid port and you want to set it back to an access port, use the following configuration:

```
[Comware] interface <interface-type> <interface-number>
[Comware-<interface-id>] port link-type access
```

Note

To change the link type of a port from trunk to hybrid or vice versa, you must first set the link type to access.

By default, all ports belong to the default VLAN, which is VLAN 1. To move a port to a different VLAN, you can either reference the port in the VLAN subcommand mode or you can reference the VLAN in the interface subcommand mode. Here is the syntax for the former method:

```
[Comware] vlan <vid>
[Comware-<vlan-name>] port <interface-list>
[Comware-<vlan-name>] port <beginning-interface> to <ending-interface>
```

You can list out the interfaces, separated by commas, or specify a range of interfaces. Here is a simple example based on the network shown in Figure 6-10:

```
[SW-A] vlan 100
[SW-A-vlan100] port gigabitethernet 1/0/2
```

Here is the syntax for associating an interface to a VLAN when in the Interface subcommand mode:

```
[Comware] interface <interface-type> <interface-number>
[Comware-<interface-id>] port access vlan <vid>
```

Optionally, instead of individually configuring each interface with the same VLAN ID, you could create a port group, discussed in "Chapter 3: Basic Setup." Here is an example based on SW-A switch in Figure 6-10:

```
[SW-A] port-group manual edge-1
[SW-A-port-group-manual-edge-1] group-member g1/0/1
[SW-A-port-group-manual-edge-1] port link-type access
[SW-A-port-group-manual-edge-1] port access vlan 100
```

Note

Like with ProVision, the default port type is an access port on Comware switches, and therefore the `port link-type access` command is not necessary, by default.

Configuring Trunks

To configure a trunk port, like a switch-to-switch link that carries traffic from multiple VLANs, use the following syntax:

```
[Comware] interface <interface-type> <interface-number>
[Comware-<interface-id>] port link type trunk
```

Each trunk port has only one default VLAN. Frames transmitted in this VLAN are untagged; they do not include the 802.1Q field. The default VLAN on Comware switches is VLAN 1. The untagged VLAN on a trunk is commonly called a *Port VLAN ID*. To change the PVID on a trunk, use the following configuration:

```
[Comware] interface <interface-type> <interface-number>
[Comware-<interface-id>] port link type trunk
[Comware-<interface-id>] port trunk pvid vlan <vid>
```

The untagged VLAN on connected trunk ports must match.

Trunk ports support only one untagged VLAN—the default VLAN. The other VLANs supported on the trunk port must be tagged. By default, the only traffic allowed on the trunk is the PVID. To allow other VLANs on the trunk, like tagged frames, you must use one of the following two interface commands:

```
[Comware] interface <interface-type> <interface-number>
[Comware-<interface-id>] port trunk permit vlan <vlan-list>
[Comware-<interface-id>] port trunk permit vlan all
```

The former command on the interface specifies which VLANs to add to the trunk. The second command allows all existing or newly created VLANs on the trunk. Connected trunk ports must support the same VLANs, or traffic will be dropped. When configuring VLANs on Comware switches, keep these guidelines in mind:

- An access port can support only one untagged VLAN.
- A trunk port can support one untagged VLAN (the default VLAN).
- The default VLAN and permitted VLANs on directly connected trunk ports must match.
- A VLAN must be created on a switch before you add it as a permitted VLAN on a trunk port.

Note

For trunks, by default, only VLAN 1 (untagged) is allowed. All other VLANs must be added. The administrator can either use the `all` parameter, to allow all VLANs, or specify any currently existing VLAN. VLANs can be added individually, as a range, or as a list. The `port trunk permit vlan <vlan-list>` command adds tagged VLANs to a trunk. It does not define the specific VLANs (or replace the existing ones).

Here is an example configuration from the Distrib1 switch in Figure 6-10:

```
[Distrib1] interface g1/0/1
[Distrib1-GigabitEthernet1/0/1] port link-type trunk
[Distrib1-GigabitEthernet1/0/1] port trunk permit vlan all
[Distrib1-GigabitEthernet1/0/1] quit
[Distrib1] interface g1/0/2
[Distrib1-GigabitEthernet1/0/2] port link-type trunk
[Distrib1-GigabitEthernet1/0/2] port trunk permit vlan all
```

Optionally, you can use port groups to set up trunks. Here is an example of the Distrib1 switch in Figure 6-10:

```
[Distrib1] port-group manual uplink-1
[Distrib1-port-group-manual-uplink-1] group-member g1/0/1 to g1/0/2
[Distrib1-port-group-manual-uplink-1] port link-type trunk
[Distrib1-port-group-manual-uplink-1] port trunk permit vlan 100 200
```

Configuring Hybrid Ports

Hybrid ports can be assigned to multiple VLANs as tagged or untagged: one VLAN can be untagged, and one or more VLANs can be tagged. In Figure 6-10, SW-A's g1/0/3 interface is an example of a hybrid interface. To designate a port as a hybrid port and to specify the VLANs associated with the port, use the following command:

```
[Comware] interface <interface-type> <interface-number>
[Comware-<interface-id>] port link-type hybrid
[Comware-<interface-id>] port hybrid vlan <vid-list> {tagged | untagged}
```

First, you have to specify that the port is a hybrid port; second, you need to specify the VLANs allowed on the port—remember that only one VLAN can be untagged on a hybrid port.

Here is an example of SW-A's configuration in Figure 6-10, assuming that the VoIP phone understands tagging:

```
[SW-A-GigabitEthernet1/0/3] port link-type hybrid
[SW-A-GigabitEthernet1/0/3] port hybrid pvid vlan 100
[SW-A-GigabitEthernet1/0/3] undo port hybrid vlan 1
[SW-A-GigabitEthernet1/0/3] port hybrid vlan 100 untagged
[SW-A-GigabitEthernet1/0/3] port hybrid vlan 200 tagged
```

In this example, the assumption is that the phone supports tagging and is in VLAN 200, and the PC is in VLAN 100 (this becomes the PVID and is untagged). If you wanted to implement two untagged VLANs on the interface because the phone didn't support 802.1Q tagging, you would need to implement a dynamic VLAN membership method on the switch, like MAC address-based or 802.1X-based user credentials, as two examples.

VLAN Verification

To see the ports assigned to VLANs, use this command:

```
[Comware] display vlan <vid>
```

Here is an example from SW-A switch in Figure 6-10:

```
[SW-A] display vlan 100
VLAN ID: 100
  VLAN Type: static
  Route interface: not configured
  Description: For Users PCs
  Name: Users
  Untagged Ports:
  GigabitEthernet1/0/1 GigabitEthernet1/0/2
```

You can also use the `display vlan all` command to see the port assignments for all VLANs.

To verify your trunk configuration, use the `display port trunk` command. Here is an example from the SW-A switch in Figure 6-10:

```
[SW-A] display port trunk
Interface            PVID  VLAN passing
GE1/0/23             1     1, 100, 200
GE1/0/24             1     1, 100, 200
```

Here is another example in which the PVID is changed from 1 to 99 on a trunk and VLAN 1 is removed from the trunk, since it is no longer used:

```
[Comware] port trunk PVID 99
[Comware] undo port trunk permit vlan 1
[Comware] display port trunk
Interface        PVID        VLAN passing
GE1/0/23         99          99, 100, 200
GE1/0/24         99          99, 100, 200
```

To verify your hybrid port configuration, use the `display port hybrid` command. Here is an example from the SW-A switch in Figure 6-10:

```
[SW-A] display port hybrid
Interface              PVID  VLAN passing
GE1/0/3                100   Tagged  :200
                             Untagged:100
```

Notice that the PVID is the untagged VLAN.

VLANs and Basic IP Routing

An Comware and ProVision Layer 3 switch can route traffic between multiple, port-based VLANs if:

- Routing is enabled.
- IP addresses are assigned to the VLANs on the switch.

With routing disabled, all routing between VLANs must be through an external router. Routing is discussed in "Chapter 11: IP Routing Overview" and in "Chapter 12: OSPF Operation and Configuration."

Note

Routing is disabled, by default, on ProVision switches but enabled, by default, on Comware switches.

Older versions of Comware did not have the DHCP client enabled for VLAN 1; however newer versions of code has this feature enabled, by default.

IP Configuration on ProVision

If a ProVision switch needs to communicate, via IP, to devices within a VLAN, the switch needs to have an IP address assigned to it for the respective VLAN. There are two ways this can be done: from global configuration mode or from the specific VLAN context. Here is the syntax for the former:

```
ProVision(config)# vlan <vid | vlan-name>
                  ip address <ip-address>/<subnet-bits>
```

Here is the syntax for the latter:

```
ProVision(config)# vlan <vid | vlan-name>
ProVision(vlan-id)# ip address <ip-address>/<subnet-bits>
```

Note that all devices in the VLAN must have an IP address from the same subnet. These commands were discussed in "Chapter 3: Basic Setup."

Here is an example of configuring an IP address on the switch for VLAN 10:

```
ProVision(config)# vlan 10 ip address 10.1.10.1/24
```

IP routing is *disabled*, by default, on ProVision switches. Enabling requires the following command:

```
ProVision(config)# ip routing
```

With this command, the ProVision switch can only route packets between VLANs on the local switch. Remote routing requires static and/or dynamic routing to be configured (discussed in "Chapter 11: IP Routing Overview," and "Chapter 12: OSPF Operation and Configuration").

To view the switch's IP addressing information for all the configured VLANs, use the `show ip` command. Here is an example:

```
ProVision# show ip

Internet (IP) Service

IP Routing : Enabled

Default TTL : 64

VLAN          : IP Config     IP Address     Subnet Mask

------------- + ------------- -------------- ----------------

DEFAULT_VLAN : Manual         10.1.1.1       255.255.255.0

VLAN10       : Manual         10.1.10.1      255.255.255.0

VLAN20       : Manual         10.1.20.1      255.255.255.0
```

IP Configuration on Comware

To assign an IP address to a Comware VLAN, perform the following:

```
[Comware] interface vlan-interface <vid>

[Comware-Vlan-interface1] ip address <ip-address> <subnet-mask-bits>
```

Notice that you create a logical Layer 3 interface that corresponds to the VLAN. This command was discussed in "Chapter 3: Basic Setup."

Note that routing is automatically enabled on Comware switches and that no special command is needed to perform routing between directly connected VLANs on the same switch.

To quickly verify your IP configuration, use the `display brief interface` command. Here is an example from the network shown previously in Figure 6-10:

```
[Comware] display brief interface
 The brief information of interface(s) under route mode:
  Interface      Link      Protocol-link   Protocol type   Main IP
  NULL0          UP        UP(spoofing)    NULL            --
  Vlan1          UP        UP              ETHERNET        10.10.1.1
  Vlan100        UP        UP              ETHERNET        10.10.100.1
  Vlan200        UP        UP              ETHERNET        10.10.200.1

 The brief information of interface(s) under bridge mode:
  Interface          Link     Speed         Duplex    Link-type  PVID
  GE1/0/1            UP       1G(a)         full(a)   trunk      1
  GE1/0/2            UP       1G(a)         full(a)   access     100
  GE1/0/3            UP       1G(a)         full(a)   hybrid     100
<-output omitted->
```

If you only want to see the status of the Layer 3 interfaces from the above output, use the `display ip interface brief` command.

Learning Check

The following questions help you measure your understanding of the material presented in this chapter. Read all of the choices carefully, since there may be more than one correct answer. Choose all correct answers for each question.

Questions

1. Match the following terms to the switch (Comware or ProVision) that uses them (regarding VLANs).
   a. Untagged
   b. Access
   c. Trunk
   d. Hybrid
   e. Tagged
2. What kind of Comware port is commonly used when a switch port has both a PC and a VoIP phone connected to it?
   a. Tagged
   b. Untagged
   c. Access
   d. Hybrid
3. What is the maximum number of VLANs that 802.1Q supports?
   a. 512
   b. 1,023
   c. 1,024
   d. 2,047
   e. 2,048
   f. 4,094
   g. 4,096

4. Which ProVision or Comware command(s) will create VLAN 10?

5. Which ProVision command(s) will assign port 11 as an untagged member of VLAN 10?

6. Which Comware command(s) will assign port g1/0/1 as a trunk port in which only VLANs 10 and 11 (plus the default VLAN) are allowed on the trunk?

Answers

1. ☑ ProVision: **A** (tagged) and **E (untagged)**; and Comware: **B (access)**, **C (trunk)**, and **D (hybrid)** are referred to regarding VLAN use.

2. ☑ **D** is correct. A PC and a VoIP phone are commonly connected to a hybrid port.

   ☒ **A** and **B** are incorrect because these are ProVision port types. **C** is incorrect because an access port only supports one VLAN.

3. ☑ **F** is correct. 802.1Q supports a maximum of 4,094 VLANs.

   ☒ **A** through **E** and **G** are incorrect because the maximum number of VLANs supported by 802.1Q is 4,094.

4. ☑ `vlan 10` is the command which will create VLAN 10.

5. ☑ `vlan 10 untagged 11` is the ProVision command which will assign port 11 as an untagged member of VLAN 10.

6. ☑
   ```
   interface g1/0/1
         port link-type trunk
         port trunk permit vlan 10,11
   ```
   (or `10-11`)

   is the Comware configuration which will assign port g1/0/1 as a trunk port in which only VLANs 10 and 11 (plus the default VLAN) are allowed on the trunk.

7 IP Services

EXAM OBJECTIVES

In this chapter, you learn to:

- ✓ Define and recognize the purpose and interaction of common TCP/UDP-based upper layer applications.
- ✓ Identify and describe available tool sets for managing HP networking products.
- ✓ Perform installation and configuration.
- ✓ Manage network assets using HP tools.
- ✓ Use general troubleshooting tools.
- ✓ Perform network management.
- ✓ Review and take action on alerts and log files.
- ✓ Verify network performance parameters.

ASSUMED KNOWLEDGE

This chapter assumes that you are familiar with the general operation and use of the following IP services:

- Dynamic Host Configuration Protocol (DHCP) for clients and servers
- Network Time Protocol (NTP)
- Syslog
- Domain Name Service (DNS)

INTRODUCTION

This chapter introduces common IP services supported by HP switches: DHCP, NTP, logging and syslog, and DNS. It is assumed that you are somewhat familiar with these different services, including their operation and basic usage, and therefore the chapter focuses on the configuration of these IP services on HP ProVision and HP Comware switches.

This chapter covers the following topics:

- Implementing DHCP server on Comware and DHCP relay on HP switches
- Implementing secure NTP on HP switches
- Understanding and configuring basic logging options on HP switches
- Implementing DNS on HP switches to resolve names to addresses

DHCP Services

The Dynamic Host Configuration Protocol allows devices to acquire their addressing information dynamically. Originally defined in RFC 2131 and updated in RFC 2939, DHCP is actually based on the Bootstrap Protocol (BootP). It is built on a client/server model and defines two components:

- **Server**—Delivering host configuration information
- **Client**—Requesting and acquiring host configuration information

DHCP provides the following advantages:

- It reduces the amount of configuration on devices.
- It reduces likelihood of configuration errors on devices acquiring address information.
- It gives you more administrative control by centralizing IP addressing information and management.

Most networks today employ DHCP because it is easy to implement and manage. Imagine that you work for a company which gets purchased by another company and you must re-address your network, which contains 2,000 devices. If you previously configured the IP addresses on these machines manually, you now must manually change each device's configuration. However, if you were using DHCP, you have to change the configuration on only the DHCP servers, and, when the clients either reboot or must renew their addressing information, they acquire the addressing information from the new addressing scheme.

Here are some drawbacks of using DHCP:

- If a client does not acquire an address because of a network outage between the client and server, it cannot access network resources.
- DHCP servers are susceptible to attacks, causing legitimate clients not to receive addresses.
- It is much more difficult to filter a user's traffic if they acquire addresses dynamically instead of always having the same address.
- Managing network resources (servers, switches, firewalls, and routers, for example) becomes more difficult.

As mentioned, DHCP contains two types of devices: servers and clients. Comware switches support both functions, whereas ProVision switches can only be clients. Servers are responsible for assigning addressing information to clients, and clients request addressing information from servers.

DHCP supports the following mechanisms for IP address allocation:

- **Static allocation**—The network administrator assigns an IP address to a client, like a WWW server, and DHCP conveys the assigned address to the client.
- **Automatic allocation**—DHCP assigns a permanent IP address to a client.
- **Dynamic allocation**—DHCP assigns an IP address to a client for a limited period of time, which is called a *lease*. Most DHCP clients obtain their addresses in this way.

Note

Comware switches can be DHCP servers *and* clients, whereas ProVision switches can only be DHCP clients. Both sets of switches support DHCP relay services.

DHCP Options

DHCP uses the same message format as Bootp, but DHCP uses the Option field to carry information for dynamic address allocation and to provide additional configuration information to clients. DHCP uses the Option field in DHCP messages to carry control information and network configuration parameters, implementing dynamic address allocation and providing more network configuration information for clients.

Common DHCP options include the following:

- **Option 3**—Router option. It specifies the gateway address to be assigned to the client.
- **Option 6**—DNS server option. It specifies the DNS server IP address to be assigned to the client.
- **Option 33**—Static route option. It specifies a list of classful static routes (the destination addresses in these static routes are classful) that a client should add to its routing table. If Option 121 exists, Option 33 is ignored.
- **Option 51**—IP address lease option. It identifies for how long the leased addressing information is valid.
- **Option 53**—DHCP message type option. It identifies the type of the DHCP message (DHCPDISCOVER, DHCPOFFER, DHCPREQUEST, DHCPDECLINE, DHCPACK, DHCPNAK, or DHCPRELEASE).
- **Option 60**—Vendor class identifier option. It is used by a DHCP client to identify its vendor and by a DHCP server to distinguish DHCP clients by vendor class and to assign specific IP addresses for the DHCP clients (for example, Wireless Access Points assigned controller details).

- **Option 66**—TFTP server name option. It specifies a TFTP server to be assigned to the client.
- **Option 67**—Boot file name option. It specifies the boot file name to be assigned to the client.
- **Option 121**—Classless route option. It specifies a list of classless static routes (the destination addresses in these static routes are classless) that the requesting client should add to its routing table.
- **Option 150**—TFTP server IP address option. It specifies the TFTP server IP address to be assigned to the client.

For more information about DHCP options, see RFC 2132.

DHCP Server

The following sections focus on using DHCP servers. You will be introduced to how DHCP operates and how to set up and verify a Comware switch as a DHCP server (ProVision switches currently do not support this feature).

DHCP Server Process

When acquiring addressing information, a DHCP client goes through four steps (see Figure 7-1):

1. A client generates a DHCPDISCOVER local broadcast to discover which the DHCP servers are on the LAN segment.
2. All DHCP servers on the segment can respond to the client with a DHCPOFFER unicast message, which offers IP addressing information to the client. If a client receives messages from multiple servers, it chooses one (typically the first one). DHCPOFFER server messages include the following information: IP address of the client, subnet mask of the segment, IP address of the default gateway, DNS domain name, DNS server address or addresses, WINS server address or addresses, and the TFTP server address or addresses. Note that this is not an all-encompassing list.
3. Upon choosing one of the offers, the client responds to the corresponding server with a DHCPREQUEST message, telling the server that it wants to use the addressing information that the server sent. If only one server is available and the server's information conflicts with the client's configuration, the client responds with a DHCPDECLINE message.
4. The DHCP server responds with a DHCPACK, which is an acknowledgment to the client indicating that it received the DHCPREQUEST message and that the client accepted the addressing information. The server can also respond with a DHCPNACK, which tells the client that the offer is no longer valid and that the client should request addressing information again. This can happen if the client is tardy in responding with a DHCPREQUEST message after the server generated the DHCPOFFER message.

When a client shuts down gracefully, it can generate a DHCPRELEASE message, telling the server it no longer needs its assigned IP address. Most DHCP configurations involve a lease time, which specifies the time period for which the client is allowed to use the address. Upon reaching this time limit, the client must renew its lease with the current server or get new IP addressing information.

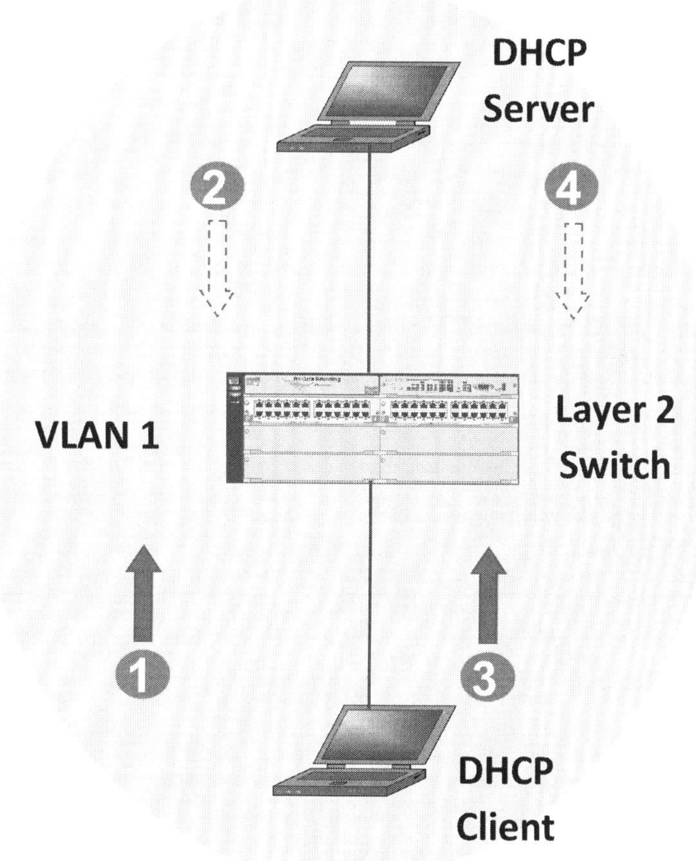

Figure 7-1. DHCP server process

Note

If a server does not respond to the client, the client's TCP/IP protocol stack automatically picks an IP address from the range of this Class B network: 169.254.0.1–169.254.255.254, based on the RFC. This process is referred to as *Automatic Private IP Addressing* (APIP). However, only Microsoft's Windows operating systems perform APIP; other operating systems, such as ProVision or Comware, or Linux, will not enable the NIC if it cannot obtain IP addressing for the NIC.

DHCP Server Configuration

The DHCP server is well suited to networks where:

- Manual configuration and centralized management are difficult to implement.
- Many hosts need to acquire IP addresses dynamically. This may be because the number of hosts exceeds the number of assignable IP addresses, so it is impossible to assign a fixed IP address to each host. For example, an ISP has a limited number of host addresses.
- A few hosts need fixed IP addresses.

DHCP address pools include common and extended address pools:

- **Common address pool**—Supports both static binding and dynamic allocation.
- **Extended address pool**—Supports only dynamic allocation.

Note that this book only focuses on dynamic allocation of addresses.

The DHCP server observes the following principles to select an address pool when assigning an IP address to a client:

1. If there is an address pool in which an IP address is statically bound to the MAC address or ID of the client, the DHCP server selects this address pool and assign the statically bound IP address to the client.
2. If the receiving interface has an extended address pool referenced, the DHCP server assigns an IP address from this address pool. If no IP address is available in the address pool, the DHCP server fails to assign an address to the client.
3. Otherwise, the DHCP server selects the smallest common address pool that contains the IP address of the receiving interface (if the client and the server reside on the same subnet) or the smallest common address pool that contains the IP address specified in the address field of the client's request (if a DHCP relay agent is in between). If no IP address is available in the address pool, the DHCP server fails to assign an address to the client because it cannot assign an IP address from the parent address pool to the client. For example, two common address pools, 1.1.1.0/24 and 1.1.1.0/25, are configured on the DHCP server. If the IP address of the interface receiving DHCP requests is 1.1.1.1/25, the DHCP server selects IP addresses for clients from address pool 1.1.1.0/25. If no IP address is available in the address pool, the DHCP server fails to assign addresses to clients. If the IP address of the interface receiving DHCP request is 1.1.1.130/24, the DHCP server selects IP addresses for clients from the 1.1.1.0/24 address.

For dynamic address allocation, you must configure a DHCP address pool, specify one and only one address range for the pool, and specify the lease duration. A DHCP address pool can have only one lease duration. To avoid address conflicts, configure the DHCP server to exclude IP addresses used by the gateway and other devices with statically assigned addresses from dynamic allocation.

Follow these steps to configure dynamic address allocation for a common address pool:

- In common address pool view, repeatedly using the `network` command overwrites the previous configuration.
- After you exclude IP addresses from automatic allocation, by using the `dhcp server forbidden-ip` command, neither a common address pool nor an extended address pool can assign these IP addresses through dynamic address allocation.
- Using the `dhcp server forbidden-ip` command repeatedly can exclude multiple IP address ranges from allocation.

Here are the commands to configure a Comware switch as a DHCP server:

```
[Comware] dhcp server ip-pool <dhcp-id>
[Comware-dhcp-pool-<dhcp-id>] network <network-id> {<mask-length> |
                                  mask <subnet-mask>}
[Comware-dhcp-pool-<dhcp-id>] expired {day <days> [hour <hours>
                                  [minute <minutes>
                                  [second <seconds]]] | unlimited}
[Comware-dhcp-pool-<dhcp-id>] domain-name <domain-name>
[Comware-dhcp-pool-<dhcp-id>] dns-list <dns-server-IP-1>
                                  [...<dns-server-IP-8>
[Comware-dhcp-pool-<dhcp-id>] gateway-list <gateway-IP-1>
                                  [...<gateway-IP-8>
[Comware-dhcp-pool-<dhcp-id>] quit
[Comware] dhcp server forbidden-ip <low-IP> [<high-IP>]
[Comware] dhcp server ping packets <number-of-packets>
[Comware] dhcp server ping timeout <milliseconds>
[Comware] interface <interface-id>
[Comware-<interface-id>] dhcp select server global-pool
[Comware-<interface-id>] dhcp server apply ip-pool <dhcp-id>
[Comware-<interface-id>] quit
[Comware] dhcp enable
```

Table 7-1 describes the commands used to set up a server on a Comware switch.

Table 7-1. Comware DHCP server commands

Command	Description
`dhcp server ip-pool`	Creates an IP pool. The DHCP ID can be any value, including a number. (This is required.)
`network`	Defines the network number that the DHCP server uses to assign addresses from (excluding the first and last address in the subnet). (This is required.)
`expired`	Specifies the lease length of the addressing information assigned to the client. (This is optional. It defaults to one day.)
`domain-name`	Assigns a domain name the client should use. (This is optional.)
`dns-list`	Assigns up to eight DNS servers to the client. (This is optional, but highly recommended.)
`gateway-list`	Assigns up to eight default gateways to the client. (This is optional, but highly recommended.)
`dhcp server forbidden-ip`	Specifies IP addresses that the server should never assign to clients from the address pool (like the DHCP server's address itself or the default gateway in that subnet, for example). (This is optional.)
`dhcp server ping packets`	Specifies the number of pings the DHCP server should perform for the addresses that will be sent to the client to verify that the address is not currently being used. (This is optional.)
`dhcp server ping timeout`	Specifies the time, in milliseconds, that the DHCP server should wait when testing an address. (This is optional.)
`dhcp select server global-pool`	Enables DHCP on the interface. (This is enabled, by default.)
`dhcp server apply ip-pool`	Specifies a specific IP address pool to use on an interface. (This is optional.)
`dhcp enable`	Enables DHCP. (This is required.)

Note

There are many more options available to you when configuring the DHCP server feature on Comware switches; however, these options are beyond the scope of this book.

DHCP Server Configuration Example

Examine the following simple DHCP server configuration on a Comware switch:

```
[Comware] dhcp server ip-pool 1
[Comware-dhcp-pool-<dhcp-id>] network 10.1.1.0 24
[Comware-dhcp-pool-<dhcp-id>] expired day 1
[Comware-dhcp-pool-<dhcp-id>] domain-name hp.com
[Comware-dhcp-pool-<dhcp-id>] dns-list 10.1.1.11
[Comware-dhcp-pool-<dhcp-id>] gateway-list 10.1.1.1
[Comware-dhcp-pool-<dhcp-id>] quit
[Comware] dhcp server forbidden-ip 10.1.1.1 10.1.1.15
[Comware] dhcp server ping packets 2
[Comware] dhcp server ping timeout 750
[Comware] dhcp enable
```

The pool of addresses is 10.1.1.0/24 (network), where 10.1.1.1-10.1.1.15 cannot be used from the pool (`dhcp server forbidden-ip`). The DNS server is 10.1.1.11 (`dns-list`), and the default gateway is 10.1.1.1 (`gateway-list`). Before assigning an address from the pool to a requesting client, the server pings the address in question twice, with a timeout of 750 milliseconds for each test (`dhcp server ping`). Last, do not forget to enable the DHCP server function with the `dhcp enable` command. Without this command, the switch will not function as a DHCP server.

Note

The `dhcp enable` command is required for the DHCP server or DHCP relay functions to work.

DHCP Server Verification

There are many display commands you can use to verify the operation of the DHCP server on your Comware switch. The most common ones are:

- `display dhcp server free-ip`—This is a list of addresses currently not assigned to clients and available in the pools.
- `display dhcp server ip-in-use`—This displays the IP-to-MAC address bindings of addresses assigned to clients.
- `display dhcp server statistics`—This displays general statistics concerning requests and assignments of addresses.

Here is an example of the second command, listing all available pools:

```
<Comware> display dhcp server ip-in-use all

Pool utilization: 0.41%

 IP address    Client-identifier/ Lease expiration      Type

               Hardware address

 10.1.1.16     0050 5697-0187     May  6 2000 13:19:10  Auto:COMMITTED

 --- total 1 entry ---
```

DHCP Relay

DHCP is commonly used to assign addresses to user devices. DHCP clients (users) use a local broadcast to obtain addressing information; however, the problem with this situation is that the DHCP server is not commonly found on the same network subnet (broadcast domain), as shown in Figure 7-2. The HP switches support a DHCP relay feature, sometimes referred to as *IP helper*. A DHCP local broadcast request is changed to a DHCP unicast request and forwarded directly to a segment that contains a DHCP server. More specifically, the routing switch takes the broadcast from the client, changes it to a unicast, which is a source IP address from the client's VLAN, and routes the request to the destination DHCP server. This section discusses the operation and configuration of DHCP relay on the HP switches.

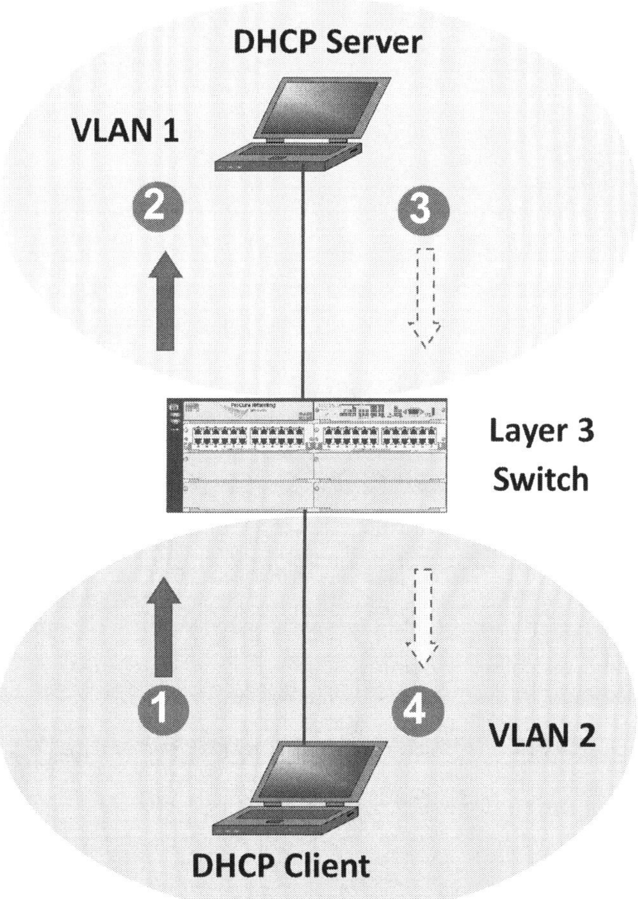

Figure 7-2. DHCP relay process

Note

The DHCP relay feature is disabled, by default, on HP switches and must be configured on a per-VLAN or per-interface basis. Likewise, IP routing must be enabled for the HP switches for DHCP relay to function. With ProVision, IP routing is disabled by default, but with Comware, it is enabled by default.

DHCP Relay Process

Figure 7-2 displays the process that occurs when DHCP relay is enabled. Here is a breakdown of this process:

1. Clients generate a DHCP broadcast address request.
2. Layer 3 switch routes a unicast packet to the DHCP server, based on the configured IP helper (relay) address, in which the source IP address is the Layer 3 switch and information indicating the network scope that should be used by the DHCP server.
3. DHCP server responds with a unicast packet back to the Layer 3 switch.
4. Layer 3 switch relays the DHCP server request to the DHCP client.

DHCP Relay Configuration for HP ProVision

For the DHCP relay feature to work, you must enable IP routing with the `ip routing` command. Without this, the DHCP relay will fail. Here is the syntax:

```
ProVision(config)# ip routing
```

The DHCP relay feature is disabled, by default, and must be configured on a per-VLAN basis, using the following command:

```
ProVision(config)# vlan <vlan-id> ip helper-address
                        <dhcp-server-ip-address>
```

Or

```
ProVision(config)# vlan <vlan-id>
ProVision(vlan-id)# ip helper-address <dhcp-server-ip-address>
```

If the DHCP server is more than one network hop away, you need to configure a static route or a dynamic routing protocol (see “Chapter 11: IP Routing Overview” and “Chapter 12: OSPF Operation and Configuration,”) so that the switch can forward the DHCP relay request. In all cases, the DHCP server must be reachable by the DHCP relay agent. Basically, the request sent to the server includes the network number defined by the IP address associated with the user VLAN.

To view the IP helper addresses you assigned, you can use the `show ip helper-address` command:

```
ProVision# show ip helper-address vlan 1
 IP Helper Addresses
  IP Helper Address
  ----------------
 10.28.227.97
 10.29.227.53
```

To view information about the operation of DHCP relay on the HP ProVision switches, use the `show dhcp-relay` command:

```
ProVision# show dhcp-relay
Status and Counters - DHCP Relay Agent
DHCP Relay Agent Enabled        : Yes
DHCP Request Hop Count Increment: Disabled
Option 82 Handle Policy         : Replace
Remote ID                       : MAC Address
Client Requests       Server Responses
Valid     Dropped      Valid    Dropped
-------- ---------    -------- --------
1425         2         1425       0
```

DHCP Relay Configuration for HP Comware

Here are the commands to enable DHCP relay on a HP Comware switch:

```
[Comware] dhcp enable
[Comware] dhcp relay server-group <group-id> ip <server-IP>
[Comware] interface <interface-id>
[Comware-<interface-id>] dhcp relay server-select <group-id>
[Comware-<interface-id>] dhcp relay select
```

Just as with a DHCP server configuration on a Comware switch, you need to enable the DHCP services with the `dhcp enable` command. Once enabled, you define the DHCP servers with the `dhcp relay server-group` command, assigning an ID to the server. This ID value groups servers together in the same group for redundancy and then is referenced on the interface where the clients are located with the `dhcp relay server-select` command.

By executing the `dhcp relay server-group` command repeatedly, you can specify up to eight DHCP server addresses for each DHCP server group. The `dhcp select relay` command then enables the operation on the switch's Layer 3/VLAN interfaces.

Please note that there are many more options that you can configure for DHCP relay, but they are beyond the scope of this book.

Here are some of the `display` commands which can be used to verify the configuration and operation of DHCP relay on Comware switches:

- `display dhcp relay`—Display information about DHCP server groups correlated to a specified or all interfaces.
- `display dhcp relay server-group`—Display information about the configuration of a specific or of all DHCP server groups.
- `display dhcp relay statistics`—Display packet statistics on relay agent.
- `display dhcp relay security`—Display the IP-to-MAC address bindings (the IP addresses assigned by the servers to the clients).

Let us look at an example to illustrate the configuration of DHCP relay on Comware switches. As shown in Figure 7-3, DHCP clients reside on network 10.10.1.0/24. The IP address of the DHCP server (Switch B) is 10.1.1.1/24. Because the DHCP clients reside on a different network with the DHCP server, a DHCP relay agent is deployed to forward messages between DHCP clients and the DHCP server. VLAN-interface 1 on the DHCP relay agent (Switch A) connects to the network where DHCP clients reside. The IP address of VLAN-interface 1 is 10.10.1.1/24, and the IP address of VLAN-interface 2 is 10.1.1.2/24.

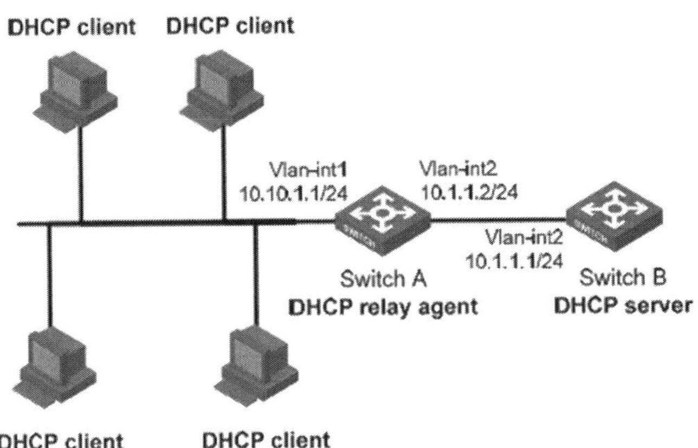

Figure 7-3. Comware DHCP relay example

Here is Switch A's configuration, with embedded comments:

```
[SwitchA] dhcp enable
#  Add DHCP server 10.1.1.1 into DHCP server group 1.
[SwitchA] dhcp relay server-group 1 ip 10.1.1.1
# Enable the DHCP relay agent on VLAN-interface 1.
[SwitchA] interface vlan-interface 1
```

```
[SwitchA-Vlan-interface1] dhcp select relay
# Correlate VLAN-interface 1 to DHCP server group 1.
[SwitchA-Vlan-interface1] dhcp relay server-select 1
```

NTP

Defined in RFC 1305, the Network Time Protocol synchronizes timekeeping among distributed time servers and clients. NTP runs over the User Datagram Protocol, using UDP port 123. The purpose of using NTP is to keep consistent timekeeping among all clock-dependent devices within a network so that the devices can provide diverse applications based on a consistent time. For a local system that runs NTP, its time can be synchronized by other reference sources and can be used as a reference source to synchronize other clocks.

Keeping time synchronized manually among all the devices within a network by changing the system clock on each station does not scale well because this can become a huge amount of work and the clock precision can vary between devices. NTP, however, allows quick clock synchronization within the entire network, and it ensures high clock precision.

It is beneficial to use NTP to keep time consistent across all devices within the network because:

- When analyzing the log and debugging information collected from different devices in network management, time must be used as reference basis.
- To implement certain functions, such as scheduled restart of all devices within the network, a consistent time minimizes downtime.
- When certificates are used for authentication, the time of the device must be reasonably correct so that the device can validate the beginning and ending dates on another device's certificate.
- When multiple systems process a complex event in cooperation, these systems must use that same reference clock to ensure the correct execution sequence.
- For incremental backup between a backup server and clients, timekeeping must be synchronized between the backup server and all the clients.

Advantages of NTP include the following:

- NTP uses a stratum to describe the clock precision and is able to synchronize time among all devices within the network.
- NTP supports access control and MD5 authentication. MD5 is used to digitally sign and verify a message to ensure that it is coming from a trusted source and was not tampered with between the source and destination.
- NTP can unicast, multicast, or broadcast protocol messages.

Note

Clock stratum determines the accuracy of a server, which ranges from 1 to 16. The stratum of a reference clock ranges from 1 to 15. The clock accuracy decreases as the stratum number increases. A stratum 16 clock is in the unsynchronized state and cannot serve as a reference clock. The local clock of a switch cannot operate as a reference clock. It can serve as an NTP server only after being synchronized.

NTP Operational Modes

Devices that run NTP can implement clock synchronization in one of the following modes:

- Client/server mode
- Symmetric peers mode
- Broadcast mode
- Multicast mode

You can select operational modes of NTP as needed:

- If the IP address of the NTP server or peer is unknown to the NTP clients and many devices in the network need to be synchronized, adopt the broadcast or multicast mode.
- If the IP address of the NTP server or peer is known, use the more precise and reliable client/server or symmetric peers mode.

The following sections introduce the four different operational modes.

Warning

Do not use the Internet, since these messages are typically not digitally signed and therefore cannot be verified as correct. It is not hard to set up an internal time source: any Windows or Unix computer can serve as a time source with NTP server software installed and a supported global positioning system (GPS) attached. Remember that a GPS gets its signal from a satellite, so you will have to plan this when determining which server to use. (Sometimes this can pose a problem when a server is in a data center.)

Client/Server Mode

When working in client/server mode, a client sends a clock synchronization message to servers (see Figure 7-4), with the Mode field in the message set to 3 (client mode). Upon receiving the message, the servers automatically work in server mode and send a reply, with the Mode field in the messages set to 4 (server mode). Upon receiving the replies from the servers, the client performs clock filtering and selection, and it synchronizes its local clock to that of the optimal reference source. In client/server mode, a client can be synchronized to a server but not vice versa.

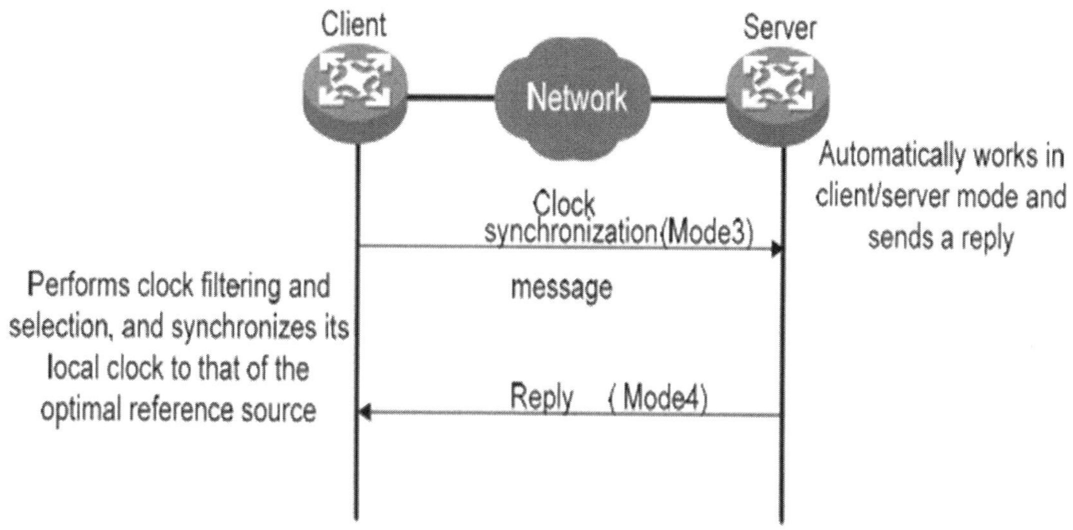

Figure 7-4. NTP client/server mode

Symmetric Peers Mode

In symmetric peers mode (see Figure 7-5), devices that work in symmetric active mode and symmetric passive mode exchange NTP messages with the Mode field 3 (client mode) and 4 (server mode). Then, the device that works in symmetric active mode periodically sends clock synchronization messages, with the Mode field in the messages set to 1 (symmetric active); the device that receives the messages automatically enters symmetric passive mode and sends a reply, with the Mode field in the message set to 2 (symmetric passive). By exchanging messages, the symmetric peers mode is established between the two devices. Then, the two devices can synchronize or be synchronized by each other. If the clocks of both devices have been synchronized, the device which has the local clock with the lower stratum level synchronizes the clock of the other device.

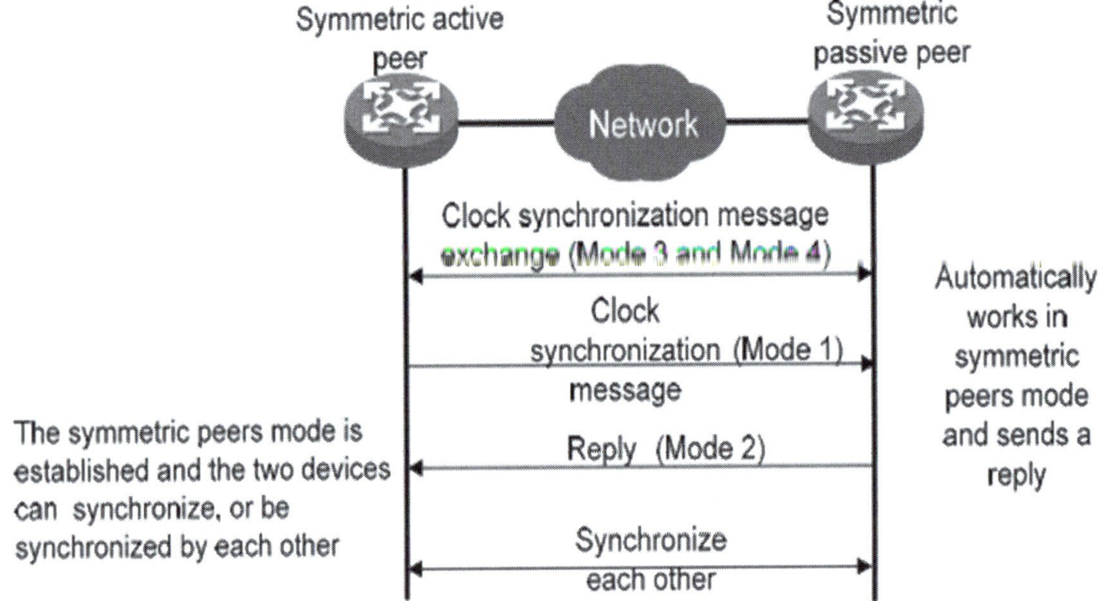

Figure 7-5. NTP symmetric peers mode

Broadcast Mode

In broadcast mode (see Figure 7-6), a server periodically sends clock synchronization messages to broadcast address 255.255.255.255, with the Mode field in the messages set to 5 (broadcast mode). Clients listen to the broadcast messages from servers. When a client receives the first broadcast message, the client and the server start to exchange messages, with the Mode field set to 3 (client mode) and 4 (server mode) to calculate the network delay between the client and the server. Then, the client enters the broadcast client mode, continues listening to broadcast messages, and synchronizes its local clock, based on the received broadcast messages.

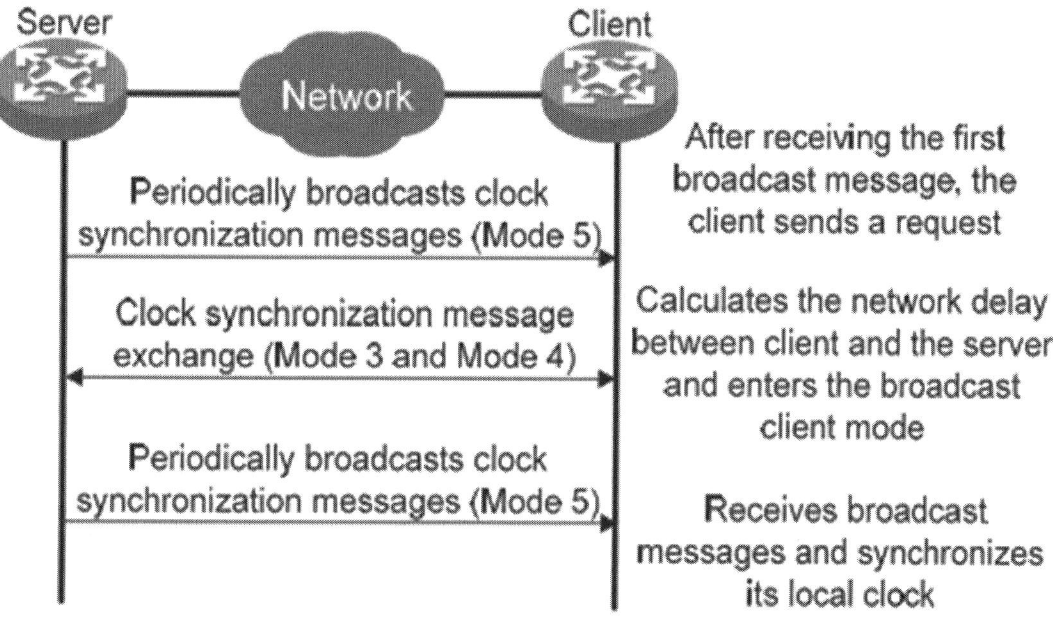

Figure 7-6. NTP broadcast mode

Multicast Mode

In multicast mode, shown in Figure 7-7, a server periodically sends clock synchronization messages to the user-configured multicast address, or, if no multicast address is configured, to the default NTP multicast address 224.0.1.1, with the Mode field in the messages set to 5 (multicast mode). Clients listen to the multicast messages from servers. When a client receives the first multicast message, the client and the server start to exchange messages, with the Mode field set to 3 (client mode) and 4 (server mode) to calculate the network delay between client and the server. Then, the client enters multicast client mode, continues listening to multicast messages, and synchronizes its local clock based on the received multicast messages.

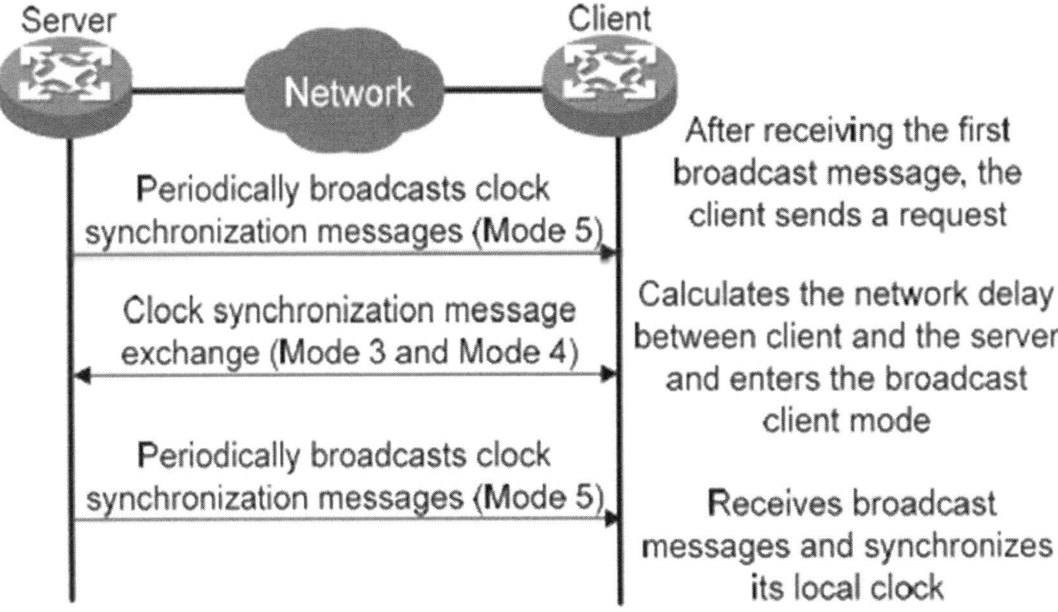

Figure 7-7. NTP multicast mode

Note

The Comware switches support all four modes. ProVision switches support the broadcast and unicast (client/server) methods. This book only focuses on the client/server implementation.

Manual Time Configuration

To manually set the system date and time on ProVision switches, use the `time` command from the command line interface. You can verify the clock settings using the `show time` command. For example:

```
ProVision(config)# time 18:45:29 9/30/2013

ProVision# show time

*18:45:29 UTC Fri September 30 2013
```

To set the time zone on ProVision switches, use the following command:

```
ProVision(config)# time timezone <-720 - 840> time
                   daylight-time-rule {none |alaska |
                   continental-us-and-canada |
                   middle-europe-and-portugal |
                   southern-hemisphere |
                   western-europe | <user-defined>}
```

On Comware switches, use the `clock datetime` command to set the current time and date of the device. The current time and date of the device must be set in an environment that requires the acquisition of absolute time. You may choose not to provide seconds when inputting the time parameters. Here is an example configuration:

```
# Set the current system time to 14:10:20 08/01/2012.
<Comware> clock datetime 14:10:20 8/1/2012
# Set the current system time to 00:06:00 01/01/2013.
<Comware> clock datetime 0:6 2013/1/1
```

For Comware switches, use the following command to configure the time zone offset information:

```
[Comware] clock timezone <time-zone-name> {add | minus} <hours>
```

NTP Configuration and Verification

The following sections cover the configuration of ProVision and Comware switches using NTP, along with the verification of the operation of NTP client running on the switches. Please note that this book only covers the unicast client configuration on the HP switches.

HP highly recommends that you have the NTP server digitally sign its time messages and have the NTP clients verify the signatures using the MD5 function (this is supported as of NTPv3). Here are situations and results that can occur, depending on whether you use digital signatures:

- If the keys on the client and server do not match, the client ignores the server's time messages.
- If the server is configured for authentication but the client is not, the client accepts the time messages.
- If the server is not configured for authentication and the client is, the client ignores the server's time messages.

Note

SNTP and NTP describe exactly the same packet format. The differences can be found in the way that a client deals with the information in these packets to synchronize the local time. An NTP server or client reaches a very high level of accuracy and avoids abrupt time adjustments as much as possible, by using different mathematical and statistical methods and smooth clock speed adjustments, whereas SNTP can only be recommended for simple applications in which the requirements for accuracy and reliability are not too demanding. ProVision switches support SNTP, and Comware devices support NTP.

SNTP Configuration for ProVision

Here are the commands to configure SNTP on ProVision switches:

```
ProVision(config)# timesync sntp

ProVision(config)# sntp unicast

ProVision(config)# sntp server priority <priority> <ip-address>
                        [key-id <key-id>]

ProVision(config)# sntp authentication

ProVision(config)# sntp authentication key-id <key-id> authentication
                        mode md5 key-value <key-string> [trusted]

ProVision(config)# sntp authentication key-id <key-id> trusted
```

The `timesync sntp` command specifies the use of SNTP for time synchronization, and the `sntp unicast` command configures the SNTP mode for unicast operation.

For unicast operation, you must also specify the IP address of at least one SNTP server. The switch allows up to three unicast servers. You can use the menu interface or the CLI to configure one server or to replace an existing unicast server with another. To add a second or third server, you must use the CLI. The `sntp server` command specifies the SNTP server, where the `priority` parameter specifies the order in which the configured SNTP servers are polled for the time; allowable values are 1 through 3.

Note

Deleting an SNTP server when only one is configured disables SNTP unicast operation.

Enabling SNTP authentication allows network devices, such as HP switches, to validate the SNTP messages received from an NTP or SNTP server before updating the network time. SNTP authentication is optional but highly recommended. When authentication is implemented, NTP or SNTP servers and clients must be configured with the same set of authentication keys so that the servers can authenticate the messages that they send and clients (HP switches) can validate the received messages before updating the time. This feature provides support for SNTP client authentication on HP switches, which addresses security considerations when deploying SNTP in a network.

The following must be configured to enable SNTP client authentication on the switch:

- The timesync mode must be SNTP (`timesync sntp`).
- SNTP must be in unicast or broadcast mode (`sntp unicast`).
- The MD5 authentication mode must be selected (`sntp authentication key-id`).
- An SNTP authentication key-identifier (`<key-id>`) must be configured on the switch, and a value (`<key-value>`) must be provided for the authentication key in the `sntp authentication key-id` command. A maximum of eight sets of `<key-id>` and `<key-value>` can be configured on the switch.
- Among the keys that have been configured, one key or a set of keys must be configured as trusted (`sntp authentication key-id`). Only trusted keys are used for SNTP authentication.
- If the SNTP server requires authentication, one of the trusted keys has to be associated with the SNTP server.
- SNTP client authentication must be enabled on the HP switch (`sntp authentication`). If client authentication is disabled, packets are processed without authentication.

All of the above steps are necessary to enable authentication on the client.

Note

SNTP or NTP server functions are not supported on ProVision or Comware switches.

If any of the SNTP parameters on the SNTP server are changed, the parameters have to be changed on all the SNTP clients in the network, as well. Otherwise, the authentication check fails on the clients, and the SNTP packets are dropped.

Note

After you enable the NTP authentication feature for the client, make sure that you configure for the client an authentication key that is the same as on the server and specify that the authentication key is trusted. Otherwise, the client cannot synchronize to the server.

Here is a configuration of SNTP with MD5 authentication:

```
ProVision(config)# timesync sntp
ProVision(config)# sntp unicast
ProVision(config)# sntp server priority 1 10.1.1.11 key-id 100
ProVision(config)# sntp authentication
ProVision(config)# sntp authentication key-id 100 authentication mode md5
                          key-value youcantseeme
ProVision(config)# sntp authentication key-id 100 trusted
```

Note that the server must use a key-id of *100* and an MD5 key of *youcantseeme*.

SNTP Verification for ProVision

The `show sntp` command displays SNTP configuration information, including any SNTP authentication keys that have been configured on the switch. Here is an example:

```
ProVision# show sntp
 SNTP Configuration
  SNTP Authentication : Enabled
  Time Sync Mode: Sntp
  SNTP Mode : Unicast
  Poll Interval (sec) [720] : 720
  Priority SNTP Server Address                  Protocol Version KeyId
  -------- ---------------------------------    ---------------- ----
  1        10.10.10.2                           3                55
  2        10.10.10.3                           3                55
```

To display all the SNTP authentication keys that have been configured on the switch, enter the `show sntp authentication` command. Here is an example:

```
ProVision# show sntp authentication
  SNTP Authentication Information
  SNTP Authentication : Enabled
  Key-ID  Auth Mode  Trusted
  ------- ---------- -------
  55      MD5        Yes
  10      MD5        No
```

To display the statistical information for each SNTP server, enter the `show sntp statistics` command. The number of SNTP packets that have failed authentication is displayed for each SNTP server address. Here is an example:

```
ProVision# show sntp statistics

SNTP Statistics

  Received Packets   : 0

  Sent Packets       : 3

  Dropped Packets    : 0

  SNTP Server Address                                  Auth Failed Pkts

  ---------------------------------------              ---------------

  10.10.10.1                                                  0
```

NTP Configuration for Comware

Here are the commands to configure a Comware switch as an SNTP unicast client:

```
[Comware] ntp-service unicast-server {<ip-address> | <server-name>}
               [authentication-keyid <keyid> | priority]
[Comware] ntp-service authentication enable
[Comware] ntp-service authentication-keyid <keyid>
               authentication-mode md5 <keystring>
[Comware] ntp-service reliable authentication-keyid <keyid>
```

The `ntp-service unicast-server` command specifies the NTP server that should be used. The `priority` parameter specifies that it should be the preferred server. Optionally, you can configure the key-id if you are implementing MD5 authentication. If so, you need to enable authentication (`ntp-service authentication enable`), define the key (`ntp-service authentication-keyid`), and define the key as trusted (`ntp-service reliable authentication-keyid`).

Here is an example of NTP client configuration with MD5 authentication of NTP server messages:

```
[Comware] ntp-service unicast-server 10.1.1.11 authentication-keyid 100
[Comware] ntp-service authentication enable
[Comware] ntp-service authentication-keyid 100 authentication-mode
               md5 youcantseeme
[Comware] ntp-service reliable authentication-keyid 100
```

NTP Verification for Comware

Here are the commands you can use to verify and troubleshoot NTP operation on the Comware switches:

- `display ntp-service status`—Display information about NTP service status.
- `display ntp-service sessions`—Display information about NTP sessions.
- `display ntp-service trace`—Display the brief information about the NTP servers from the local device back to the primary reference source.

Here is a client/server example that illustrates time synchronization on a Comware switch. Without NTP configured, the status of NTP would look like this (not currently synchronized):

```
<Comware> display ntp-service status
 Clock status: unsynchronized
 Clock stratum: 16
 Reference clock ID: none
 Nominal frequency: 64.0000 Hz
 Actual frequency: 64.0000 Hz
 Clock precision: 2^7
 Clock offset: 0.0000 ms
 Root delay: 0.00 ms
 Root dispersion: 0.00 ms
 Peer dispersion: 0.00 ms
 Reference time: 00:00:00.000 UTC Jan 1 1900 (00000000.00000000)
Notice the reference time in the above output.
Next, an NTP server is defined on the switch:
 [Comware] ntp-service unicast-server 10.1.1.11
```

After waiting a few minutes for synchronization to occur, display the status:

```
[Comware] display ntp-service status
 Clock status: synchronized
 Clock stratum: 3
 Reference clock ID: 10.1.1.11
 Nominal frequency: 64.0000 Hz
 Actual frequency: 64.0000 Hz
 Clock precision: 2^7
 Clock offset: 0.0000 ms
 Root delay: 31.00 ms
 Root dispersion: 1.05 ms
 Peer dispersion: 7.81 ms
 Reference time: 14:53:27.371 UTC Feb 2 2013 (C6D94F67.5EF9DB22)
```

The output shows that the Comware switch has been synchronized to the NTP server, and the clock stratum level of the switch is 3, while that of the server is 2.

Note

The clock status should eventually say "synchronized," indicating that the time offset of this device's time and the NTP server's time is within an acceptable margin. Depending on the vendor and the vendor's device, synchronization might happen immediately (the device matches the time it receives from the server, factoring in the delay from the server to the client) or the time might be adjusted over a period of time (slowly adjusting the clock so as to not create any issues in the network that are based on time). ProVision switches immediately adjust their local time to match the time received from the NTP server; Comware switches, however, slowly drift their time to match what was received from the NTP server.

Here is the information about the session between the two devices:

```
<Comware> display ntp-service sessions
     source    reference   stra  reach  poll  now  offset  delay disper
*****************************************************************
[12345] 10.1.1.11 127.127.1.0  2    63    64    3   -75.5    31.0  16.5
note: 1 source(master),2 source(peer),3 selected,4 candidate,5
configured
Total associations :  1
```

Logging

Use these troubleshooting approaches to diagnose switch problems:

- Check the HP Networking website for software updates that may have solved your problem: www.hp.com/networking/support.
- Check the switch LEDs for indications of proper switch operation:
  - Each switch port has a Link LED that should light whenever an active network device is connected to the port.
  - Problems with the switch hardware and software are indicated by flashing the Fault and other switch LEDs. Refer to the *Installation Guide* shipped with the switch for a description of the LED behavior and for information on using the LEDs for troubleshooting.
- Check the network topology. Refer to the *Installation Guide* shipped with the switch for topology information.
- Check cables for damage, correct type, and proper connections. You should also use a cable tester to check your cables for compliance to the relevant IEEE 802.3 specification. Refer to the *Installation Guide* shipped with the switch for correct cable types and connector pin-outs.
- Use Intelligent Management Center to help isolate problems and recommend solutions.
- Use the Port Utilization Graph and Alert Log in the Web Agent included in the ProVision switch to help isolate problems. These tools are available through the Web Agent:
  - Alert Log
  - Port Status and Port Counters screens
  - Diagnostic tools (link test, ping test, and configuration file browser)
- For help isolating problems, use the easy-to-access switch console built into the switch or Telnet to the switch console. Refer to "Chapter 3: Basic Setup," for operating information on the menu and CLI interfaces included in the console. These tools are available through the ProVision switch console:
  - Status and counters screens
  - Event Log or local log file
  - Diagnostics tools (link test, ping test, configuration file browser, and advanced user commands)

This section of the chapter focuses on an introduction to the logging features of the HP switches.

ProVision Event Log

This chapter focuses on the Event Log and logging features of the ProVision switches. The Event Log records operating events in single- or double-line entries and serves as a tool to isolate and troubleshoot problems. Starting in software release K.13.xx, the maximum number of entries supported in the Event Log is increased from 1,000 to 2,000 entries. Entries are listed in chronological order, from the oldest to the most recent. After the log has received 2,000 entries, it discards the oldest message each time a new message is received. The Event Log window contains 14 log entry lines. You can scroll through it to view any part of the log.

The Event Log is erased if power to the switch is interrupted.

The contents of the Event Log are not erased if you:

- Reboot the switch by choosing the Reboot Switch option from the menu interface.
- Enter the `reload` command from the CLI.
- You enter the `boot system` command.

You can view the Event Log from the character-based menu or from the CLI with the `show logging` command.

Event Log Messages

As shown in Figure 7-8, each Event Log entry is composed of six or seven fields, depending on whether numbering is turned on.

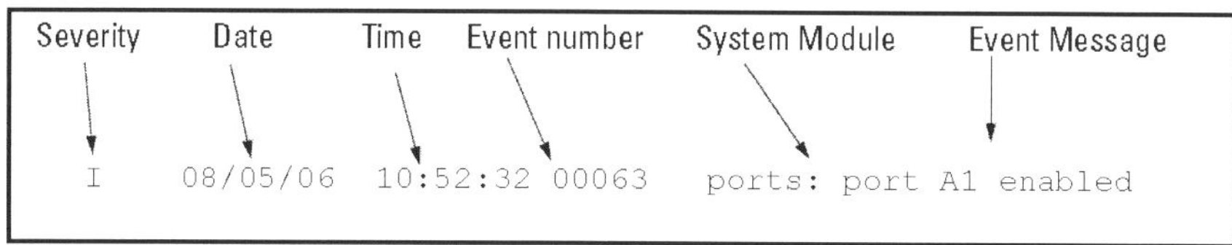

Figure 7-8. ProVision Event Log message example

Here is an explanation of the fields found in a log entry:

- **Severity** is one of the following codes (from highest to lowest severity):
  - **M** (major) indicates that a fatal switch error has occurred.
  - **E** (error) indicates that an error condition occurred on the switch.
  - **W** (warning) indicates that a switch service has behaved unexpectedly.
  - **I** (information) provides information on normal switch operation.
  - **D** (debug) is reserved for HP internal diagnostic information.

- **Date** is the date (in the format mm/dd/yy) when an entry is recorded in the log.
- **Time** is the time (in the format hh:mm:ss) when an entry is recorded in the log.
- **Event Number** is the number assigned to an event. You can turn event numbering on or off with the `[no] log-number` command.
- **System Module** is the internal module (such as "ports:" for port manager) that generated a log entry. If VLANs are configured, a VLAN name also appears for an event that is specific to an individual VLAN. There are a few dozen system modules available. See the *Management and Configuration Guide* for the ProVision switches to see the defined modules.
- **Management Module** (8200 zl switches) is either the active management module, represented by AM1 or AM2, or the standby management module, represented by SM1 or SM2.
- **Event Message** is a brief description of the operating event.

Event Log Menu

To display the Event Log from the main menu, select Event Log. Figure 7-9 shows a sample Event Log display. The log status line below the recorded entries states the total number of events stored in the Event Log and notes which logged events are currently displayed. To scroll to other entries in the Event Log (either preceding or following the currently visible portion), press the keys indicated at the bottom of the display (Back, Next page, Prev page, or End) or the keys described in Table 7-2.

Table 7-2. Event Log control keys

Key	Action
`[N]`	Advances the display by one page (next page)
`[P]`	Rolls back the display by one page (previous page)
`[v]`	Advances display by one event (down one line)
`[^]`	Rolls back the display by one event (up one line)
`[E]`	Advances to the end of the log
`[H]`	Displays help for the Event Log

```
120.226.97.181:2034 - Tera Term VT
File Edit Setup Control Window Help
ProVision-2                                                    19-Dec-2000  21:58:10
=========================- CONSOLE - MANAGER MODE -============================
I 12/16/00 01:56:19 00070 chassis: Fan OK: Fan: 3  Failures: 0
I 12/16/00 01:56:19 00070 chassis: Fan OK: Fan: 4  Failures: 0
I 12/16/00 01:56:30 00061 system: ----------------------------------------
I 12/16/00 01:56:30 00063 system: Member 1 went down:  12/16/00 01:55:28
M 12/16/00 01:56:30 00064 system: Operator cold reboot from CONSOLE session.
I 12/16/00 01:56:30 02759 chassis: Savepower LED timer is OFF.
I 12/16/00 01:56:30 02751 chassis: LEDs for Ports 1-26 configured ON.
I 12/16/00 01:56:30 02682 OOBM: OOBM - Enabled globally.
I 12/16/00 01:56:30 00092 dhcp: Enabling Auto Image Config Download via DHCP and
            turning off auto-tftp if enabled
D 12/16/00 01:56:30 00080 dhcp: entity enabled
I 12/16/00 01:56:31 00433 ssh: Ssh server enabled
I 12/16/00 01:56:31 00690 udpf: DHCP relay agent feature enabled
I 12/16/00 01:56:31 02637 srcip: TACACS admin policy is 'outgoing interface'
I 12/16/00 01:56:31 02638 srcip: TACACS oper policy is 'outgoing interface'
----  Log events stored in memory 1-8354.  Log events on screen 8255-8268.

 Actions->   Back     Next page     Prev page     End     Help

Return to previous screen.
Use up/down arrow to scroll one line, left/right arrow keys to
change action selection, and <Enter> to execute action.
```

Figure 7-9. ProVision Event Log menu

Note

One advantage of the Event Log in the menu is that it displays log messages in real time.

Event Log CLI

To display messages recorded in the Event Log from the CLI, enter the `show logging` command. Here is an example:

```
ProVision# show logging

 Keys:   W=Warning   I=Information

         M=Major     D=Debug E=Error

----  Event Log listing: Events Since Boot  ----

I 04/18/11 16:46:53 00061 system: ----------------------------------

I 04/18/11 16:46:53 00063 system: System went down:  04/18/11
16:44:46

M 04/18/11 16:46:53 00064 system: Operator cold reboot from CONSOLE
session.

I 04/18/11 16:46:53 02759 chassis: Savepower LED timer is OFF.

I 04/18/11 16:46:53 02753 chassis: Ports 1-24 configured to normal
power mode
```

```
I 04/18/11 16:46:53 00092 dhcp: Enabling Auto Image Config Download
via DHCP and turning off auto-tftp if enabled

I 04/18/11 16:46:53 00690 udpf: DHCP relay agent feature enabled

I 04/18/11 16:46:53 02637 srcip: TACACS admin policy is 'outgoing
interface'

I 04/18/11 16:46:53 02638 srcip: TACACS oper policy is 'outgoing
interface'

I 04/18/11 16:46:53 02637 srcip: RADIUS admin policy is 'outgoing
interface'

-- MORE --, next page: Space, next line: Enter, quit: Control-C
```

Keyword searches are supported. By default, the `show logging` command displays the log messages recorded since the last reboot, in chronological order.

Here is the full syntax of the command:

```
ProVision# show logging [-a, -b, -r, -s, -t, -m, -p, -w, -i, -d]
                        [<option-str>]
```

Here is an explanation of the parameters for this command:

- `-a` displays all recorded log messages, including those before the last reboot.
- `-b` displays log events as the time (instead of in a date/time format) since the last reboot.
- `-r` displays all recorded log messages, with the most recent entries listed first (reverse order).
- `-s` displays the active management module (AM) and standby management module (SM) log events.
- `-t` displays the log events with a granularity of 10 milliseconds.
- `-m` displays only major log events.
- `-p` displays only performance log events.
- `-w` displays only warning log events.
- `-i` displays only informational log events.
- `-d` displays only debug log events.
- `<option-str>` displays all Event Log entries that contain the specified text. Use an `<option-str>` value with `-a` or `-r` to further filter `show logging` command output.

For example, to display all Event Log messages that have "system" in the message text or module name, enter the following command:

```
ProVision# show logging -a system
```

To display all Event Log messages recorded since the last reboot that have the word "system" in the message text or module name, enter:

```
ProVision# show logging system
```

Note

Use the `clear logging` command to hide, but not erase, Event Log entries displayed in `show logging` command output. Only new entries generated after you enter the command are displayed. To redisplay all hidden entries, including Event Log entries recorded prior to the last reboot, enter the `show logging -a` command.

Syslog Server

To use syslog messaging, you must configure an external device as the logging destination by using the logging commands:

```
ProVision(config)# logging <ip-addr>
ProVision(config)# logging facility <facility-number>
ProVision(config)# logging severity <severity-level>
ProVision(config)# logging system-module <system-module>
```

Minimally, you need to specify the IP address of the logging server. The ProVision and Comware switches can only log to one syslog server at a time. The remaining configurations are optional. The facility feature is commonly used on Unix syslog server systems to categorize the messages for reporting. It is an optional configuration. The default severity level is to send messages from all five severity categories to the syslog server. You can control this with the `logging severity` command. The `system-module` parameter sends Event Log messages from the specified system module to the configured syslog server; the severity filter is also applied to the system module messages you select. The default setting is to send Event Log messages from all system modules.

Note

The facility feature is not commonly used on Windows servers. It is more common on Unix syslog server implementations. In the old days of syslog, the facility was used to sort incoming log messages to the correct syslog server file; today, syslog server products can look at the syslog message to appropriately sort it and place it into the correct syslog server file. The most common method of organizing syslog files is to separate them by the IP address of the syslog client.

Here is an example that sends all Event Log message from the informational severity level and higher to the 10.1.1.11 syslog server:

```
ProVision(config)# logging 10.1.1.11
ProVision(config)# logging severity info
```

Comware Information Center

Comware's logging functionality works differently from that of ProVision switches. This section introduces the Information Center, which controls the logging process on the switches. Please note that this is an introduction to the topic and not an in-depth discussion. For more information on Information Center, see the Comware switches' *Management and Monitoring Guide*.

Acting as the system information hub, the Information Center classifies and manages system information, offering a powerful support for network administrators and developers in monitoring network performance and diagnosing network problems.

The following describes the working process of Information Center:

- Receives the log, trap, and debugging information generated by each module
- Outputs the information to different information channels, according to the user-defined output rules
- Outputs the information to different destinations, based on the information channel-to-destination associations

To sum up, Information Center assigns the log, trap, and debugging information to the 10 information channels, according to the eight severity levels, and then outputs the information to different destinations.

The system information of the Information Center falls into the following types:

- Log
- Trap
- Debug

The system supports 10 channels (see Table 7-3). Channels 0 through 6 are configured with channel names and output rules and are associated with output destinations, by default. The channel names, output rules, and associations between the channels and output destinations can be changed through commands. Besides, you can configure channels 7, 8, and 9 without changing the default configuration of channels 0 through 6.

Table 7-3. Information channels and output destinations

Information Channel Number	Default Channel Name	Default Output Destination	Description
0	`console`	Console	Receives log, trap, and debugging information
1	`monitor`	Monitor terminal	Receives log, trap, and debugging information, facilitating remote maintenance
2	`loghost`	Syslog server	Receives log, trap, and debugging information and information stored in files for future retrieval
3	`trapbuffer`	Trap buffer	Receives trap information stored in a buffer inside the switch
4	`logbuffer`	Log buffer	Receives log and debugging information stored in a buffer inside the switch
5	`snmpagent`	SNMP module	Receives SNMP trap information sent to an SNMP management station
6	`channel6`	Web interface	Receives log information
7	`channel7`	Not specified	Receives log, trap, and debugging information
8	`channel8`	Not specified	Receives log, trap, and debugging information
9	`channel9`	Log file	Receives log, trap, and debugging information and is stored in a file on the switch's flash memory

Note

By default, the Information Center is enabled. An enabled Information Center affects the system performance to some degree due to information classification and output. Such impact becomes more obvious when there is an enormous amount of information waiting for processing. The CPU of the device has to process the messages, and the terminal line (user interface) must process each character one at a time, which is a very slow process, and this can seriously impact the performance of the device. Therefore, the severity level for messages sent to terminal sessions should be higher (lower number), and the severity level for messages sent to a syslog server can be lower (higher number).

Information Center Severity Levels

The information is classified into eight levels, by severity, as shown in Table 7-4. The severity levels in the descending order are *emergency*, *alert*, *critical*, *error*, *warning*, *notice*, *informational*, and *debug*. When the system information is output by level, the information with severity level higher than or equal to the specified level is output. For example, if you configure the output rule to severity level *informational*, logging with severity level *emergency* through *informational* is output.

Table 7-4. Comware information center severity levels

Severity	Severity Value	Description	Corresponding Keyword Command
Emergency	0	The system is unusable	`emergencies`
Alert	1	Action must be taken immediately	`alerts`
Critical	2	Critical conditions	`critical`
Error	3	Error conditions	`errors`
Warning	4	Warning conditions	`warnings`
Notice	5	Normal but significant condition	`notifications`
Informational	6	Informational messages	`informational`
Debug	7	Debug-level messages	`debugging`

Information Center Configuration

Here are the basic commands to tune the Comware Information Center:

```
[Comware] info-center enable

[Comware] info-center synchronous

[Comware] info-center source <module-name>
               channel {loghost | logbuffer | console | monitor ...}
               [{debug | log | trap} level <severity>]

[Comware] info-center loghost <ip-address> [facility <facility>]
```

The Information Center is enabled, by default. Therefore, the use of the `info-center enable` command is not necessary unless you want to disable logging globally on the switch.

Synchronous information means that, if the user's input is interrupted by system output, such as log, trap, or debugging information, after completing system output, the system displays a command line prompt. The prompt will be in command editing mode, or a [Y/N] string in interaction mode—and your input so far. This allows an administrator to issue commands, even when the switch is creating a large number of error messages. It is highly recommended to issue the `info-center synchronous` command on every Comware switch. Please note that:

- If system information, such as log information, is output before you input any information under the current command line prompt, the system does not display the command line prompt after the system information output.
- If system information is output when you are inputting some interactive information (non Y/N confirmation information), after the system information output, the system does not display the command line prompt but your previous input in a new line.

The `info-center source` command controls which logging information (modules, which are similar to the system modules in ProVision logging) is sent to which destination (like the console or a syslog server) and filtered based on the severity level defined.

The default output rules define the source modules allowed to output information to each output destination, the output information type, and the output information level, as shown in Table 7-5, which indicates that, by default, and in terms of all modules:

- All log information is allowed to be output to the web interface and log file; log information with severity level equal to or higher than *informational* is allowed to be output to the log host, console, monitor terminal, and log buffer; log information is not allowed to be output to the trap buffer or the SNMP module.
- All trap information is allowed to be output to the console, monitor terminal, log host, web interface, and log file; trap information with severity level equal to or higher than *informational* is allowed to be output to the trap buffer and SNMP module; trap information is not allowed to be output to the log buffer.
- All debugging information is allowed to be output to the console and monitor terminal; debugging information is not allowed to be output to the log host, trap buffer, log buffer, SNMP module, web interface, or log file.

Table 7-5. Default output rules for different output destinations

Output Destination	Log	Log Severity	Log Enabled/ Disabled	Trap Severity	Trap Enabled/ Disabled	Debug Enabled/ Disabled
Console	Enabled	Info	Enabled	Debug	Enabled	Debug
Monitor terminal	Enabled	Info	Enabled	Debug	Enabled	Debug
Log host	Enabled	Info	Enabled	Debug	Disabled	Debug
Trap buffer	Disabled	Info	Enabled	Debug	Disabled	Debug
Log buffer	Enabled	Info	Disabled	Debug	Disabled	Debug
SNMP module	Disabled	Debug	Enabled	Info	Disabled	Debug
Web interface	Enabled	Debug	Enabled	Debug	Disabled	Debug
Log file	Enabled	Debug	Enabled	Debug	Disabled	Debug

The `info-center loghost` command specifies the IP address of a syslog server to use.

Here is a configuration example that forwards all log messages at the *informational* level and higher to a syslog server:

```
[Comware] info-center enable
[Comware] info-center source default channel loghost log informational
[Comware] info-center loghost 10.1.1.1
```

Note

This book only covers the very basics of tuning the Information Center. There are a lot more options that you can use to tune the way that logging is done on your Comware devices. This book only focuses on configuring logging to a syslog server, even though logging to other output destinations can be performed (and they are similar in their configuration). For example, there are options that, when logging messages are stored in a log file in the Comware device's flash, you can automate the copying of the file to an external TFTP or FTP server periodically, but that syslog is a more common method of saving the log messages. The Comware *Network Management and Configuration Guide* covers the configuration and tuning of the Information Center over 25 pages and provides a detailed analysis of this feature.

Information Center Verification

The `display channel` command displays information of the channel with a specified number (0 to 9) or the channel name (see Table 7-3 for the channel names).

```
Comware# display channel [<channel-number> | <channel-name>]
```

Here is an example of the use of this command:

```
<Comware> display channel 0
channel number:0, channel name:console
MODU_ID  NAME     ENABLE LOG_LEVEL ENABLE TRAP_LEVEL    ENABLE
DEBUG_LEVEL
ffff0000 default  Y      warnings  Y      debugging     Y
debugging
```

The above information indicates to output log information with the severity from 0 to 4, trap information with the severity from 0 to 7, and debugging information with the severity from 0 to 7 to the console. The information source modules are all modules (default).

Use the `display info-center` command to display the information of each output destination. Here is an example of the use of this command:

```
<Comware> display info-center
Information Center : enabled
Log host:
    1.1.1.1, port number : 514, host facility : local2,
    channel number : 8, channel name : channel8
Console:
    channel number : 0, channel name : console
Monitor:
    channel number : 1, channel name : monitor
SNMP Agent:
    channel number : 5, channel name : snmpagent
Log buffer:
    enabled,max buffer size 1024, current buffer size 512,
    current messages 512, dropped messages 0, overwritten messages 740
    channel number : 4, channel name : logbuffer
Trap buffer:
    enabled,max buffer size 1024, current buffer size 256,
    current messages 216, dropped messages 0, overwritten messages 0
    channel number : 3, channel name : trapbuffer
syslog:
    channel number:6, channel name:channel6
Information timestamp setting:
    log - date, trap - date, debug - date,
    loghost - date
```

Use the `display logbuffer` command to display the state of the log buffer and the log information recorded. Absence of the size argument indicates that all log information recorded in the log buffer is displayed. The full syntax of the command is as follows:

```
<Comware> display logbuffer [reverse] [summary] [level <severity> |
            size <buffersize> ] * [ | {begin | exclude | include}
            <regular-expression>]
```

The following describes the parameters you can use with this command:

- `size <buffersize>`—Displays specified number of the latest log messages in the log buffer, where buffersize represents the number of the latest log messages to be displayed in the log buffer, in the range of 1 to 1,024.
- `|`—Filters command output by specifying a regular expression. For more information about regular expressions, see Basic System Configuration in the *Fundamentals Configuration Guide* for Comware switches.
- `begin`—Displays the first line that matches the specified regular expression and all lines that follow.
- `exclude`—Displays the lines that do not match the specified regular expression.
- `include`—Displays all lines that match the specified regular expression.
- `<regular-expression>`—Specifies a regular expression, which is a case-sensitive string of 1 to 256 characters. This argument is case-sensitive and can include spaces.

Here is a simple example of the use of this command:

```
<Comware> display logbuffer
Logging buffer configuration and contents:enabled
Allowed max buffer size : 1024
Actual buffer size : 512
Channel number : 4 , Channel name : logbuffer
Dropped messages : 0
Overwritten messages : 718
Current messages : 512

%Jun 17 15:57:09:578 2006 Sysname IC/7/SYS_RESTART:
System restarted -
<-output omitted->
```

The following example summarizes what is in the log buffer:

```
<Comware> display logbuffer summary
EMERG ALERT  CRIT ERROR  WARN NOTIF  INFO DEBUG
    0     0     0     0    22     0     1     0
```

DNS

The Domain Name System resolver feature lets you use a host name to perform `Telnet`, `ping`, `traceroute`, and other commands. You can also define a DNS domain on the device and thereby recognize all hosts within that domain.

Note
Not all CLI commands support DNS names, but basic testing tools, like `ping`, `traceroute`, and others, support it.

ProVision DNS Support

Here are the commands to configure and verify DNS on a ProVision switch:

```
ProVision(config)# ip dns domain-name <domain-name>
ProVision(config)# ip dns server-address <ip-address>
ProVision# show ip
ProVision# show ip dns
```

After you define a domain name, the device automatically appends the appropriate domain to the host and forwards it to the domain name server. To define a default domain name on a ProVision switch, use the `ip dns domain-name` command. For example, if the domain "newyork.com" is defined on a device and you want to initiate a ping to host "nyc01" on that domain, you need to reference only the host name in the command instead of the host name and its domain name. For example, you could enter either of the following commands to initiate the ping:

```
ProVision# ping nyc01
```

Or

```
ProVision# ping nyc01.newyork.com
```

You can define up to four DNS servers for each DNS entry with the `ip dns server-address` command on ProVision switches. The first entry serves as the primary default address. If a query to the primary address fails to be resolved after three attempts, the next gateway address is queried (also up to three times). This process continues for each defined gateway address until the query is resolved. The order in which the default gateway addresses are polled is the same as the order in which you enter them. You can use the `show ip` or `show ip dns` commands to view the configured DNS servers.

Suppose you want to define the domain name of newyork.com on a routing switch and then define four possible default DNS gateway addresses. To do so, enter the following commands:

```
ProVision(config)# ip dns domain-name newyork.com
ProVision(config)# ip dns server-address 209.157.22.199 205.96.7.15
                   208.95.7.25 201.98.7.15
```

In this example, the first IP address in the `ip dns server-address` command becomes the primary DNS server address and all others are secondary addresses. Because IP address 201.98.7.15 is the last address listed, it is also the last address consulted to resolve a query.

Comware DNS Support

Here are the commands to configure name resolution:

```
[Comware] ip host <host-name> <ip-address>
[Comware] dns resolve
[Comware] dns domain <domain-name>
[Comware] dns server <ip-address>
-or-
[Comware] interface <interface-id>
[Comware-<interface-id>] dns server <ip-address>
```

Comware supports a dynamic resolution feature similar to that of ProVision, with two differences. First, to use a DNS, unlike ProVision, you first have to enable DNS lookups with the `dns resolve` command. Second, you can define static DNS resolutions locally on the Comware devices with the `ip host` command. This configuration has precedence over any dynamic DNS information. Otherwise, to define a domain name, use the `dns domain` command, and, to define a DNS server, use the `dns server` command. Use the `display dns server` command to view the configured DNS servers on a Comware device.

Learning Check

The following questions help you measure your understanding of the material presented in this chapter. Read all of the choices carefully, since there may be more than one correct answer. Choose all correct answers for each question.

Questions

1. Which ProVision command enables DHCP relay for a VLAN?
   a. `ip relay`
   b. `ip helper-address`
   c. `dhcp-relay`
   d. `relay-address`
2. Which function does NTP use to authenticate NTP messages from NTP time servers?
   a. DES
   b. SHA
   c. MD5
   d. RSA
3. When is the Event Log erased on a ProVision switch?
   a. When rebooting the switch by choosing the Reboot Switch option from the menu interface
   b. When the switch is powered off
   c. When entering the `boot system` command from the CLI.
   d. When entering the `reload` command from the CLI
4. Which Comware command enables DHCP services globally?
5. List the five severity levels for messages on the ProVision switches.

6. How many channels does the Comware Information Center support?
   a. 4
   b. 5
   c. 6
   d. 9
   e. 10
   f. 12

Answers

1. ☑ **B** is correct. The `ip helper-address` command configures DHCP relay on an ProVision switch.

   ☒ **A** and **D** are incorrect because they are nonexistent commands. **C** is used to configure DHCP relay on a Comware switch.

2. ☑ **C** is correct. MD5 is the function used to create and verify digital signatures for NTP.

   ☒ **A** is incorrect because it is an encryption algorithm, not a digital signature function. **B** and **D** are digital signature functions, but they are not used by NTP.

3. ☑ **B** is correct. The ProVision Event Log is erased if the switch is powered off .

   ☒ **A, C,** and **D** are incorrect because they do not erase the Event Log.

4. ☑ `dhcp enable` is the Comware command to enable DHCP services globally.

5. ☑ Major, error, warning, informational, and debug are the five severity levels for messages on ProVision switches.

6. ☑ **E** is correct. There are 10 channels supported by the Comware Information Center.

   ☒ **A**, **B**, **C**, **D**, and **F** are incorrect because these are not the number of channels supported.

8 Introducing Spanning Tree

EXAM OBJECTIVES

In this chapter, you learn to:

✓ Describe and contrast the most common Ethernet concepts.

✓ Describe the concept, benefits, and types of redundancy, and apply redundancy types.

✓ Identify, describe, and explain VLANs.

ASSUMED KNOWLEDGE

This chapter assumes that you are familiar with the basic concepts of Ethernet and Ethernet switching, including the following topics:

- Understanding the main functions of a bridge or switch with regard to learning MAC addresses and forwarding traffic
- Understanding the purpose and implementation of VLANs
- Having a basic understanding of loop protection methods and a rudimentary introduction to Spanning Tree Protocol (STP)

INTRODUCTION

This chapter introduces spanning tree and the various standards that implement it. Networks deliver critical services to users. Failure of a network link may make the network unavailable to users, resulting in lost time or revenue. To protect a network against these failures, you can install redundant links. Redundant links allow the network to redirect traffic around a failed link to ensure uninterrupted data transmission across the network. Simply adding redundant physical links, however, is not the best way to avoid link failures. The addition of redundant links will create network loops, resulting in broadcast storms and rendering the network inaccessible. To function properly, an Ethernet network must have only one active pathway between two devices.

HP ProVision and HP Comware switches support the industry-standard Spanning Tree Protocol, which recognizes and manages redundant links. Both series of switches support other technologies for managing redundant links, as well, like link aggregation, which is discussed in "Chapter 10: Link Aggregation." This chapter begins by providing a brief review and introduction of STP, Rapid STP (RSTP), per-VLAN STP (PVST), and Multiple STP (MSTP). "Chapter 9: MSTP Configuration," focuses on configuring MSTP and STP security features on the ProVision and Comware switches.

This chapter focuses on an overview of the following topics:

- 802.1D
- RSTP
- PVST+
- MSTP

Layer 2 Loop Issues

As you can see in Figure 8-1, a redundant design was implemented: two links exist between Segment-1 and Segment-2. This redundancy commonly introduces Layer 2 loops into a network design, which can create these Layer 2 problems:

- Multiple frame copies
- Broadcast storms
- Mislearning MAC addresses

The following sections discuss these problems, using the simple example in Figure 8-1 to illustrate the issues these problems create.

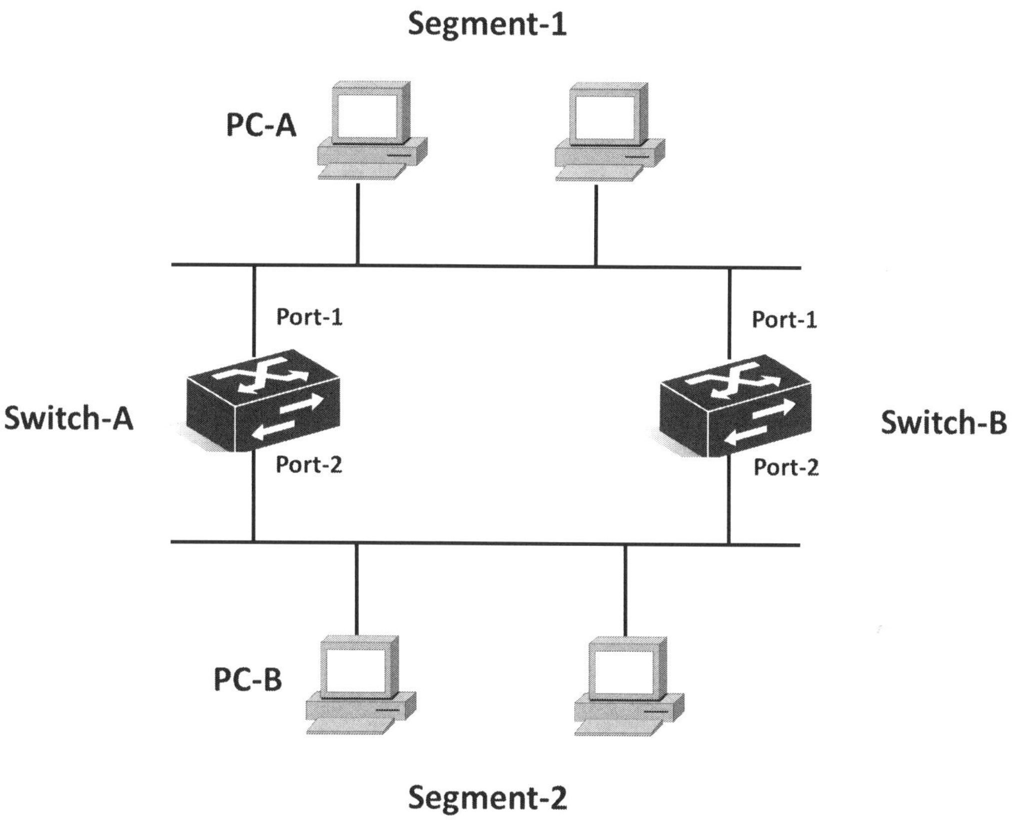

Figure 8-1. Layer 2 loop issues

Multiple Frame Copies and Broadcast Storms

By default, a switch floods three kinds of frames: broadcast, multicast, and unknown destination unicast frames. In the case of broadcast and multicast traffic, this can create serious performance issues with a Layer 2 network that has loops. For example, imagine that PC-A, in Figure 8-1, performs an ARP for PC-B's MAC address: ARP uses a broadcast mechanism to learn the MAC address that corresponds to a device's IP address. In Figure 8-1, both switches receive this frame and flood it to Segment-2, since the frame is a broadcast.

The first problem that this creates is that, although PC-A generates one frame, Segment-2, along with PC-B, sees two frames. PC-B sees these as two distinct ARPs and replies twice. In addition, depending on the application receiving the traffic, PC-B might see multiple copies of the same frame as an error and reset its connection to the source of the transmissions, creating connectivity issues.

The bigger issue here is that both switches, on their Segment-2 ports, would again see the flooded ARP request and would flood it back to Segment-1. Basically these broadcasts would continue to be flooded between the two segments, affecting all devices. Devices are affected, since their network interface cards (NICs) would be processing all of these broadcasts; as more devices generate ARPs and other types of broadcast frames, the bandwidth is eventually completely consumed by these broadcasts. In this scenario, the network will crash and the devices will run out of CPU cycles to process the broadcasts!

Multicasts are only processed by NICs in which the user has an application running that needs to see the specific multicast traffic: it notifies the NIC about the multicast address or addresses to listen for and process. So a flood of multicasts will not affect the CPU cycles of devices not running multicast. However, multicasts still affect everyone's bandwidth, since switches flood this kind of traffic. And, if the multicasts are part of a high-speed video stream, this quickly consumes all the available bandwidth.

Mislearning MAC Addresses

The third issue caused by Layer 2 loops is that the switches mislearn the location of devices (based on their MAC addresses). Going back to Figure 8-1, assume that PC-A's MAC address is 0000.01AA.AAAA. When PC-A generates an ARP for PC-B's MAC address, both Switch-A and Switch-B receive the ARP request and perform their learning function, associating PC-A's MAC address with their respective Port-1. They then flood the frame to Segment-2. Again, both switches see the broadcast and perform their learning function, associating PC-A with their respective Port-2. In this situation, both switches assume that PC-A moved from Segment-1 to Segment-2. Both switches then flood the frame to Segment-1, where they again perform their learning function, and they again think that PC-A moved from Segment-2 back to Segment-1. This flip-flopping happens over and over as the two broadcasts circle around and around between the two segments.

One problem this can create is that, if the timing is right and PC-B sends an ARP reply back to PC-A, both switches might have PC-A's MAC address associated with their respective Port-2. If this was true, both would assume that PC-A was on Segment-2 and would drop and not forward the frame. Therefore, PC-A would not get the reply to its ARP request and then could not communicate with PC-B. Of course, PC-A could perform the ARP request again, but this would just make the problem worse, since now, instead of two broadcasts circling around the loop, it would double to four!

Note

Probably the first indication that you have a Layer 2 loop in the network is that the computing devices (PCs, servers, printers, switches, and routers, among other devices) have very slow performance. After a large number of broadcasts are built up within the loop, these computing devices must use their CPU (not Application Specific Integrated Circuits [ASICs]) to process broadcasts. If you look at the CPU utilization on a device, you will see that it is running very high.

After you notice a high CPU utilization, take a look at the MAC address table on a switch. If you see flip-flopping MAC addresses (the address constantly changes between two interfaces), you are almost guaranteed to have a loop.

IEEE 802.1D

The remainder of this chapter introduces some solutions to the problems discussed with Figure 8-1, using loop avoidance solutions. These solutions are commonly used when you have two or more switches in a Layer 2 network. All three implementations use a spanning tree algorithm to create a network that avoids loops, and they are based on standard and proprietary protocols. These protocols include:

- IEEE 802.1D STP
- Rapid STP
- Per-VLAN STP
- Multiple STP

This section focuses on the original standard for implementing Layer 2 loop avoidance.

IEEE Overview

The main function of STP is to logically remove Layer 2 loops from your topology. DEC, now a part of HP, originally developed STP. (Radia Perlman, noted for her many contributions to networking standards, was primarily involved with the development of STP.) The Institute of Electrical and Electronics Engineers (IEEE) enhanced the initial implementation of STP, creating the 802.1D standard. The two different implementations of STP, *DEC* and *802.1D*, are not compatible with each other—you need to make sure that all of your devices support either one or the other.

Note

HP switches do not support the original DEC implementation of STP.

STP, as defined in IEEE's 802.1D standard, enables administrators to build redundancy into switched networks. When STP is enabled, the switches elect a switch to be the root bridge (the central point of the STP network), detect redundant links, calculate the lowest-cost path (or preferred path) to the root, and block all other redundant links. The ports that provide the lowest-cost path through the network are put in a forwarding state, and all other (redundant) ports are placed in a blocking state. A blocked port is not used to forward traffic. If a link in the preferred network path fails, STP changes the state of a blocked link from *blocking* to *forwarding* to enable connectivity. This section briefly reviews the STP technology and various implementations.

Bridge Protocol Data Units

For STP to function, the switches need to share information about themselves and their connections. What they share are Bridge Protocol Data Units (BPDUs), which are sent out as multicast frames to which only other Layer 2 switches or bridges are listening. Switches use BPDUs to learn the topology of the network: what switch is connected to other switches, and whether any Layer 2 loops are present in this topology.

If any loops are found, the switches logically disable a port or ports in the topology to remove the loops. Note that they do not actually shut down the ports, but they place the port or ports in a special disabled state for user traffic. (This is discussed in the "Port States" section.) After completing the port disabling process, only one path is available from any device to any other device in the Layer 2 network.

If any changes occur in the Layer 2 network, such as when a link goes down, a new link is added, a new switch is added, or a switch fails, the switches share this information, causing the STP algorithm to be re-executed, and a new loop-free topology is then created.

By default, BPDUs are sent out every two seconds. This helps speed up convergence. *Convergence* is the amount of time it takes to deal with changes and to recreate a loop-free network.

Faster convergence means your network recovers from changes more quickly. Setting the BPDU advertisement time to two seconds allows changes to be quickly shared with all of the other switches in the network, reducing the amount of disruption any change causes.

BPDUs contain a lot of information to help the switches determine the topology and any loops that result from the topology. For instance, each bridge has a unique identifier, called a *bridge* or *switch ID*. This is typically the priority of the switch and the MAC address of the switch itself. When switches advertise a BPDU, they place their switch ID in the BPDU so that a receiving switch can tell which switch is sending topology information.

Note

In the IEEE standards for STP, all BPDUs must be *untagged* on links.

The following sections cover the steps that occur while STP is being executed in a Layer 2 network.

Convergence

The process of detecting redundant links and calculating a preferred network path is called convergence. The first step in the convergence process is to elect a root bridge, which serves as the central point (or *root*) of the STP network. The root bridge is also responsible for notifying other switches of any network changes. To elect the root bridge, the switches exchange Bridge Priority Data Units.

BPDUs contain each switch's bridge ID and some other information. The bridge ID includes a user-configurable bridge priority value and the device's MAC address. The switch with the lowest bridge ID is elected as the root bridge. The switch with the second-lowest bridge ID is the backup or secondary root bridge. If the root bridge fails, the secondary root bridge assumes the role of root bridge.

Root Election

Spanning Tree Protocol describes the process that is used to find and remove loops from a Layer 2 network. The STP algorithm, similar to link state routing protocols, such as Open Shortest Path First (OSPF), ensures that no loops are created. Of course, STP deals with Layer 2 loops, and OSPF deals with Layer 3 loops. Link state routing protocols are discussed in "Chapter 11: IP Routing Overview," and "Chapter 12: OSPF Operation and Configuration."

Basically, a spanning tree is an inverted tree. At the top of the tree is the root, or what is referred to in STP as the *root bridge* or *switch*. From the root switch, branches (physical Ethernet connections) extend and connect to other switches, and branches from these switches connect to other switches, and so on.

The physical topology of the network shown in Figure 8-2 demonstrates a physical Layer 2 network that needs a Spanning Tree Protocol to remove loops. When STP is run, a logical tree structure is built, like that shown in Figure 8-3. As you can see from Figure 8-3, Switch-A is the root switch and is at the top of the tree. Underneath it are two branches connecting to Switch-B and Switch-C. These two switches are connected to Switch-E, creating a loop. Switch-B is also connected to Switch-D. At this point, STP is not converged and a loop still exists.

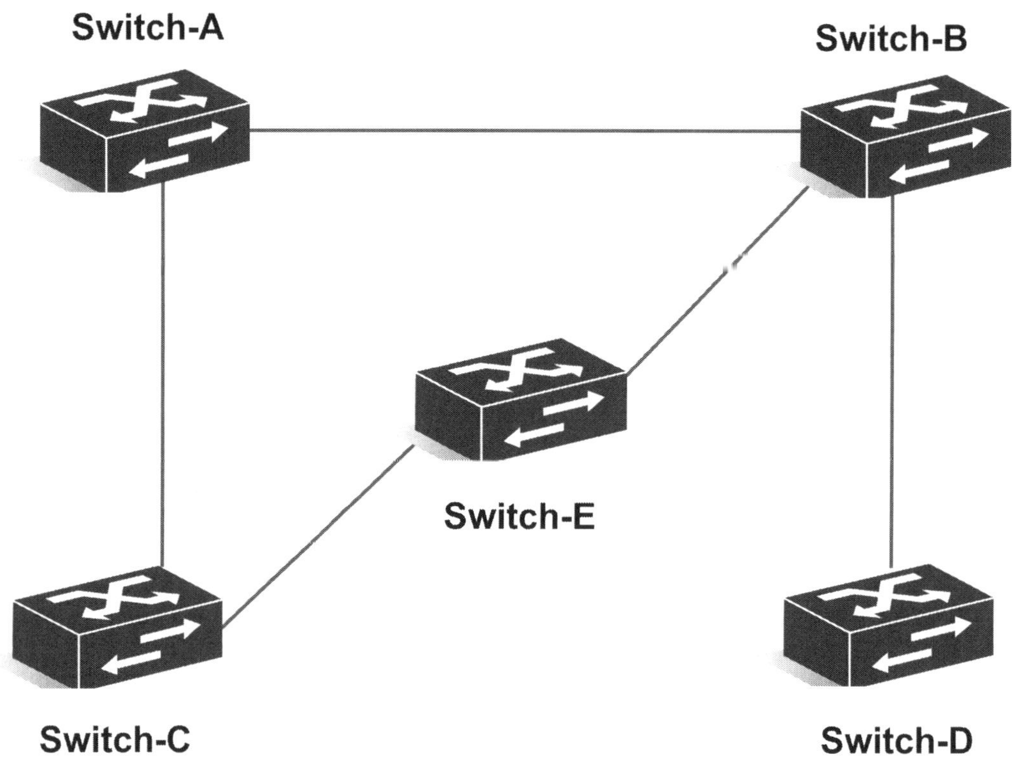

Figure 8-2. Physical Layer 2 looped topology

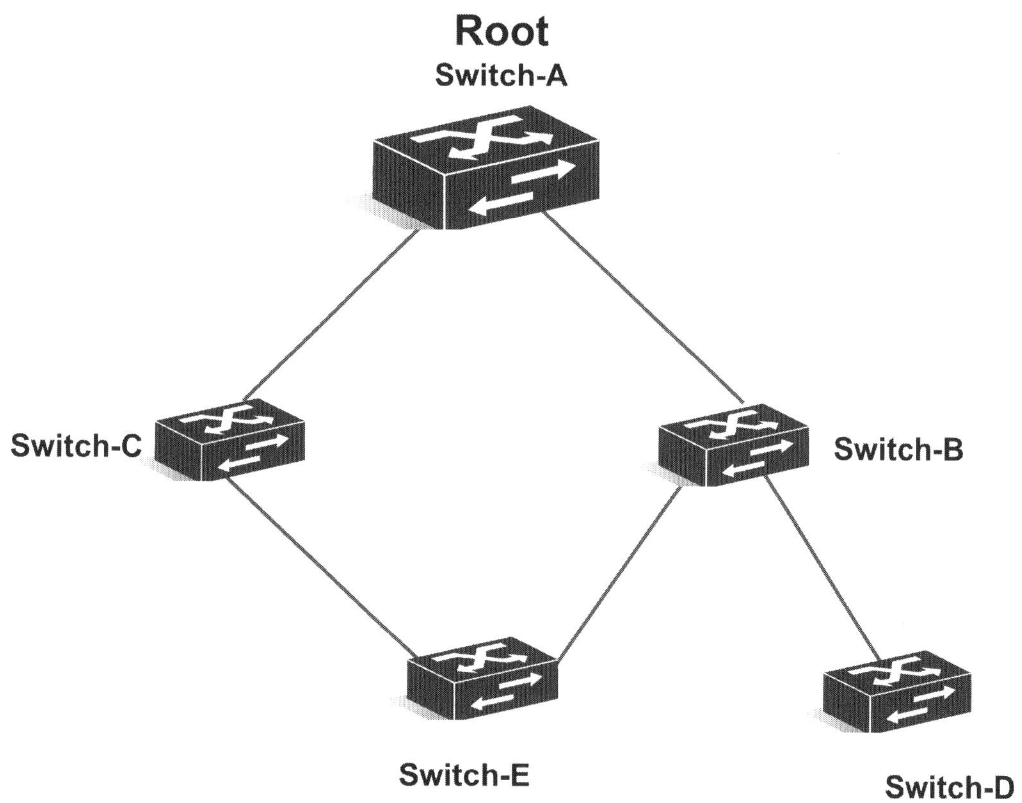

Figure 8-3. Logical Layer 2 STP topology

As STP runs, the switches determine which port of the four—Switch-A, Switch-B, Switch-C, and Switch-E—are logically disabled to remove the loop. This ensures that, from one device to any other device in the network, only one path is used to connect the devices.

Electing the Root Switch

The first step in STP is to elect the root switch. BPDUs are used for the election process. A switch puts its switch ID into the BPDU. The switch ID is used to elect the root switch. The switch with the lowest switch ID is chosen as root. The switch ID is made up of two components:

- The switch's priority, which defaults to 32,768 on HP switches (2 bytes in length)
- The switch's MAC address (6 bytes in length)

With HP's switches, the default priority is 32,768, which is defined by IEEE 802.1D. Assuming that all of your switches are HP switches and you do not change the default priority, the switch with the lowest MAC address is chosen as the root switch. You can override the election process by changing the priority value assigned to a switch. If you want one switch to be the root, assign it a priority value that is lower than 32,768. Through the sharing of the BPDUs, the switches figure out which switch has the lowest switch ID, and that switch is chosen as the root switch. Note that this election process is taking place almost simultaneously on each switch and that each switch comes up with the same result. In other words, the switch that has the lowest switch ID advertises to other switches that it has the lowest ID value, and any other switch is a non-root switch.

The election process of the root switch takes place each time a topology change occurs in the network, such as the root switch failing or the addition of a new switch. All the other switches in the Layer 2 topology expect to see BPDUs from the root switch within the maximum age time, which defaults to 20 seconds. If the switches do not see a BPDU message from the root switch within this period, they assume that the root switch has failed and they begin the election process to choose a new one.

Examining an Example Root Selection Process

To help you get more familiar with the workings of 802.1D STP, take a look at an example of STP in action. Use the network shown in Figure 8-4 as a starting point, and assume that these switches are running 802.1D STP. Assume that there is only one VLAN and that all switches have the default 802.1D bridge/switch priority. The ports on each switch are labeled with a letter and a number. The letter is the port designator, and the number is the cost of the port as a BPDU enters the port.

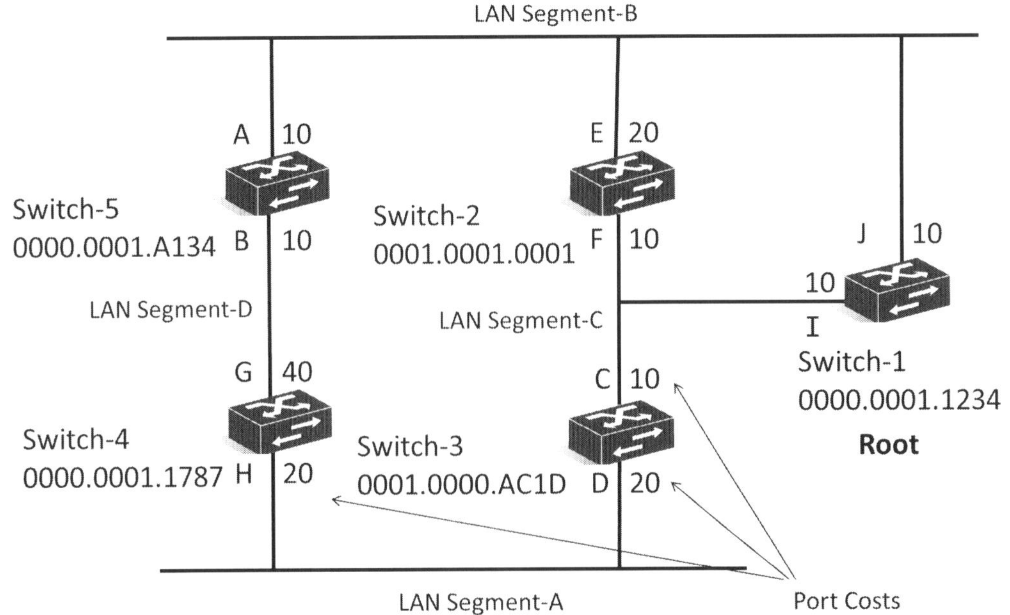

Figure 8-4. Example root switch election process

The first thing that occurs, after all of these switches are booted up, is the election of the root switch. The switches share BPDUs with one another to elect the root. In this example, all of the switches are using the default priority (32,768). Remember that the switch with the lowest switch ID is elected as root. Since all of the switches have the same priority, the switch with the lowest MAC address, which is Switch-1, is chosen as the root switch. This is illustrated in Figure 8-4.

Note

The network topology in Figure 8-4 is using non-standard port costs to make the topology a bit more complicated. Also, the numbers for each port in Figure 8-4 are port costs—not path costs!

Root Port Selection

After the root switch is elected, every other switch in the network needs to choose a single port, on itself, that it will use to reach the root. This port is called the *root port*. For some switches, this is very easy if they only have one port they can use to access the switched topology. However, other switches, such as Switch-2, Switch-3, and Switch-4 in Figure 8-5, might have two or more ports that they can use to reach the root switch. If multiple port choices are available, an intelligent method needs to be used to choose the best port. With STP, a few factors are taken into consideration when choosing a root port. It is important to note that the root switch itself will never have a root port—it is the root, so it does not need a port to reach itself!

Note

Each non-root switch must choose a *single* local port, called the root port, which is used to reach the root switch.

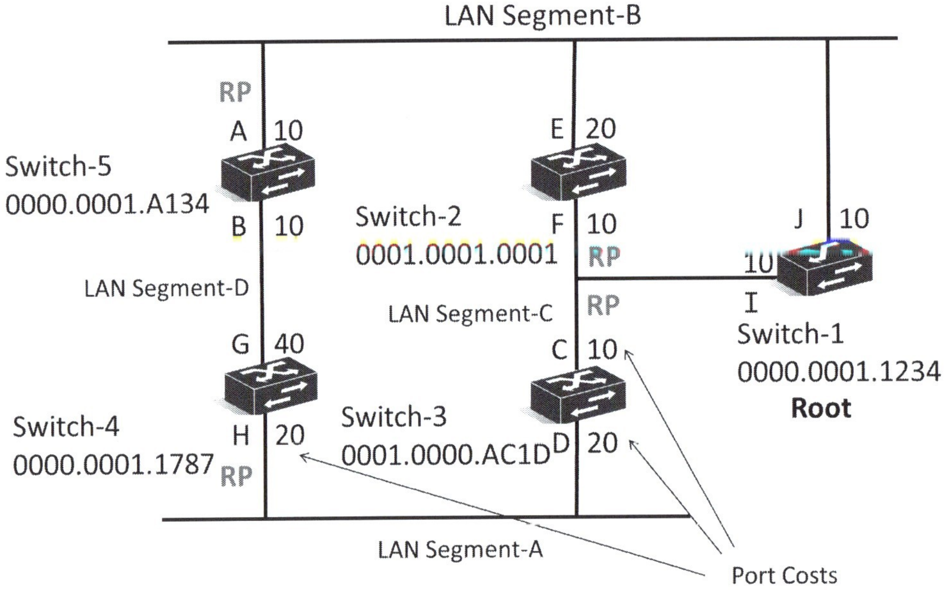

Figure 8-5. Each non-root switch chooses a single root port

Port Costs and Priorities

First, each port is assigned a cost, called a *port cost*. Lower cost ports are preferred. The cost is an inverse reflection of the bandwidth of the port. A higher bandwidth leads to a lower cost. Two sets of costs exist for 802.1D's implementation of STP—one for the old (1998) method of calculation and one for the new (2004) method, as is shown in Table 8-1. The new method was adopted by RSTP and MSTP. RSTP and MSTP are enhancements to the 802.1D standard. Switches always prefer lower cost ports over higher cost ones. Each port also has a priority assigned to it, called a *port priority value*, which defaults to 128. Again, switches prefer a lower priority value over a higher one.

Table 8-1: Default port costs

Connection Type	RSTP/MSTP	802.1D
10 Gbps	2,000	-
1 Gbps	20,000	4
100 Mbps	200,000	10
10 Mbps	2,000,000	100

One of the main reasons for replacing the old cost method (802.1D) with a newer one is the inherent weakness in the algorithm used to calculate the port cost: 1,000 divided by the port speed. The assumption was that no port would have a speed greater than 1 Gbps (1,000 Mbps). Ten Gbps Ethernet is common in today's corporate networks, and faster links are available. With the original 802.1D port cost method, 1 Gbps and 10 Gbps links were treated as having the same speed.

Eventually, 802.1D's port costs were changed so that 1 Gbps was assigned a port cost of 4 and 10 Gbps was assigned a port cost of 2. By the time this change was made, RSTP and MSTP had basically supplanted the use of 802.1D.

Note

Because the maximum value for the path cost allowed by 802.1D STP is 65,535, devices running that version of spanning tree cannot be configured to match the values defined by MSTP on 10 Mbps and 100 Mbps ports. In LANs where there is a mix of devices running 802.1D STP, RSTP, and/or MSTP, reconfigure the devices so that the path costs match for ports with the same network speeds.

Path Costs

Path costs are calculated from the root switch. A *path cost* is basically the accumulated port costs from the root switch to other switches in the topology. When the root switch advertises BPDUs out of its interfaces, the default path cost value in the BPDU frame is 0. When a connected switch receives this BPDU, it increments the path cost by the cost of its local incoming port. If the port was a Fast Ethernet port on a switch running MSTP, the path cost would be figured like this: 0 (the root's path cost) + 200,000 (the switch's port cost) = 200,000. This switch, when it advertises BPDUs to switches behind it, includes the updated path cost. As the BPDUs propagate further and further from the root switch, the accumulated path cost values become higher and higher.

Root Port Selection Process

If a switch has two or more choices of paths to reach the root, it needs to choose one path and therefore have one root port. A switch goes through the following STP steps when choosing a root port:

1. Choose the path with the lowest accumulated path cost to the root, when it has a choice between two or more paths to reach the root.
2. If multiple paths to the root are available with the same accumulated path cost, the switch chooses the neighboring switch (that the switch would go through to reach the root) with the lowest switch ID value.
3. If multiple paths all go through the same neighboring switch, it chooses the local port with the lowest priority value (that is, two or more connections to the same neighboring switch).
4. If the priority values are the same between the ports, it chooses the physically lowest numbered port on the switch. For example, on a Comware 5800, that would be interface Gigabit 1/0/1 and, on a ProVision 5400, which would be port 1.

After going through this selection process, the switch has one—and only one—port that becomes its root port.

Root Port Selection Example

After the root switch is elected, each non-root switch must choose one of its ports that it will use to reach the root, called the root port. Figure 8-5 lists example port costs, which are different for some of the interfaces, ranging from 10 to 40. Normally most of the interfaces would be the same speed, and, therefore, the same cost, but, to make the example more interesting, some of the port costs have been changed. Let us take this one switch at a time so that you can see the decision process in detail:

- **Switch-1**—The root switch has no root ports. You will recall that all ports on the root switch are designated ports.
- **Switch-2**—Has two ports to use to reach the root: E and F. When Switch-1 generates its BPDUs on ports I and J, the original path cost is set to 0. As these BPDUs are received by other switches, the receiving switch increments the path cost by the cost of the port on which the BPDU was received. As the BPDU comes into port E, Switch-2 increments the path cost to 20 and for port F, 10. The first check that Switch-2 makes is to compare the path costs. Port F has the best path cost and, therefore, is chosen as the root port, which is shown as "RP" in Figure 8-5.
- **Switch-3**—Also has two paths to reach the root—via ports C and D. Port C's accumulated path cost is 10, and D's accumulated cost is 70. Therefore, port C is chosen as the root port.

- **Switch-4**—Also has two ports to use to access the root—H and G. Port H has an accumulated path cost of 30, and G has an accumulated cost of 50, causing Switch-4 to choose port H as the root port.
- **Switch-5**—Two ports, A and B, have accumulated path costs of 10 and 40, respectively, causing Switch-5 to choose Port A as the root port.

Note that all of the switches in the network are simultaneously running STP. Each switch independently determines the same root switch. In addition, each switch determines which of their ports should be the root port. This is also true for choosing a designated port on a segment (discussed in the next section).

Figure 8-5 shows the updated STP topology for our network, where RP represents the root ports for the LAN segments.

Designated Port Selection

You now know that each switch has a single root port that it uses to reach the root switch. In addition to each switch having a root port, each segment also has a single port that it uses to reach the root, and this port is called a *designated port*. For example, imagine that a segment has two switches connected to it. Either one or the other switch will forward traffic from this segment to root switch. The port on the forwarding switch is the designated port.

Designated Port Selection Process

The third step in running STP is to elect a designated port on a single switch for each segment in the network. The chosen switch (and its port) should have the best path to the root switch. Here are the steps to determine which port on which switch is chosen as the designated port for a particular LAN segment.

1. The connected switch on the segment with the lowest accumulated path cost to the root switch is used.
2. If there is a tie in accumulated path costs between two switches, the switch with the lowest switch ID is chosen.
3. If it happens that it is the same switch, but with two separate connections to the LAN segment, the switch port with the lowest priority is chosen.
4. If there is still a tie (the priorities of the ports on this switch are the same), the physically lowest numbered port is chosen.

After going through these steps for each segment, each segment has a single designated port on a connected switch that it will use to reach the root switch. Sometimes, the switch that contains the designated port is called a *designated switch*. This term is misleading, though, since it is a port on the switch that is responsible for forwarding traffic. A switch may be connected to two segments, but it might be the designated switch for only one of those segments; another switch may provide the designated port for the second segment.

Interestingly enough, every active port on the root switch is a designated port. This makes sense because the cost of the attached network segments to reach the root is 0, the lowest accumulated cost value. In other words, each of these LAN segments is directly attached to the root switch, so, in reality, it costs nothing for the segment to reach the root switch.

Designated Port Selection Example

After the root ports are chosen, each switch figures out, on a segment-by-segment basis, whether its port that is connected to the segment should be a designated port. Remember that the designated port on a segment is responsible for moving traffic back and forth between the segment and the root switch. The segments themselves, of course, are completely unaware of this process of choosing a designated port—the switches figure this out.

When choosing a designated port, the first thing that is examined is the accumulated path cost for the switch (connected to the segment) to reach the root. For two switches connected to the same segment, the switch with the lowest accumulated path cost is the designated switch for that segment, and its port connected to that segment becomes a designated port.

Going back to our network example in Figure 8-6, let us start with the easiest segments: B and C. For Switch-1, the accumulated path cost for LAN Segment-B is 0, Switch-2 is 20, and Switch-5 is 10. Since the root switch (Switch-1) has the lowest accumulated path cost, its local port (J) becomes the designated port for LAN Segment-B. This process is also true for LAN Segment-C: the root switch has the lowest accumulated path cost (0), making port I on Switch-1 the designated port for LAN Segment-C.

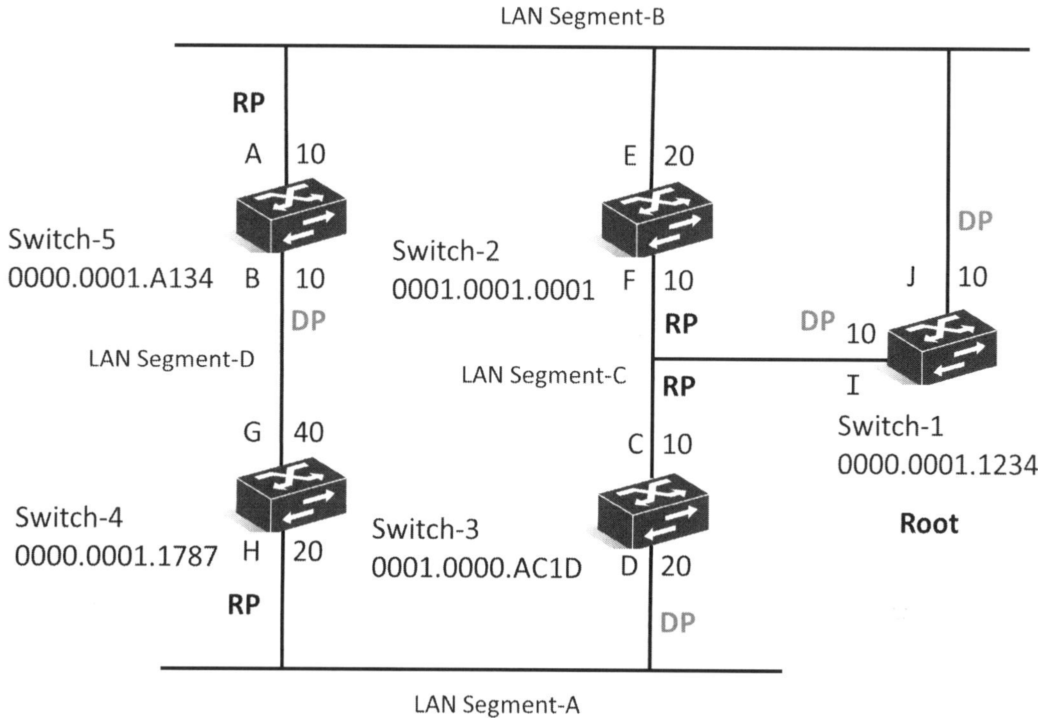

Figure 8-6. Each network segment needs a designated port on a connected switch to reach the root.

LAN Segment-A has two choices: Switch-3's D port and Switch-4's H port. Switch-3 has the lower accumulated path cost (10 versus Switch-4's 50). Therefore, Switch-3's D port becomes the designated port for LAN Segment-A.

LAN Segment-D also has two choices for a designated port: Switch-5's B port and Switch-4's G port. Switch-5 has an accumulated path cost of 10, and Switch-4 has a cost of 30. Therefore, Switch-5's B port becomes the designated port for LAN Segment-D.

Figure 8-6 shows the updated STP topology for our network, where DP represents the designated ports for the LAN segments.

Non-Root and Non-Designated Ports

After the designated ports are chosen, the switches move their root and designated ports through the various states: blocking, listening, learning, and forwarding, whereas any other ports remain in a blocked state. Port states are discussed in an upcoming section entitled "802.1D Port States and Convergence". Figure 8-7 shows the ports in a blocking state, designated by BLK. Remember that, on Switch-2, only Port F (the root port) is in a forwarding state; Port E remains in a blocking state. In this example, two ports are left in a blocking state: Switch-2's E port and Switch-4's G port.

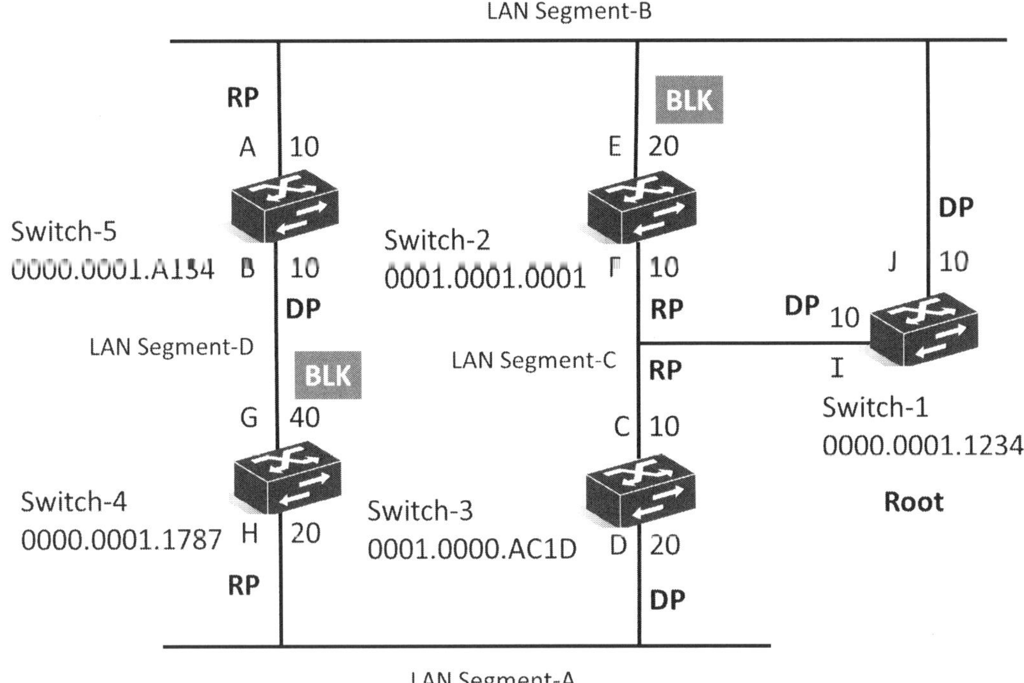

Figure 8-7. Blocking non-root and non-designated ports

STP Activity

Figure 8-8 has a simple switch topology. Assume the following:

- The cost of all links is 4 (port cost).
- All the switches have the default priority (32,768) except for switch S0, which has a priority of 0.
- All switches have a MAC address that is equal to their switch number. For example, S4 has a MAC address of 0000.0000.0004.

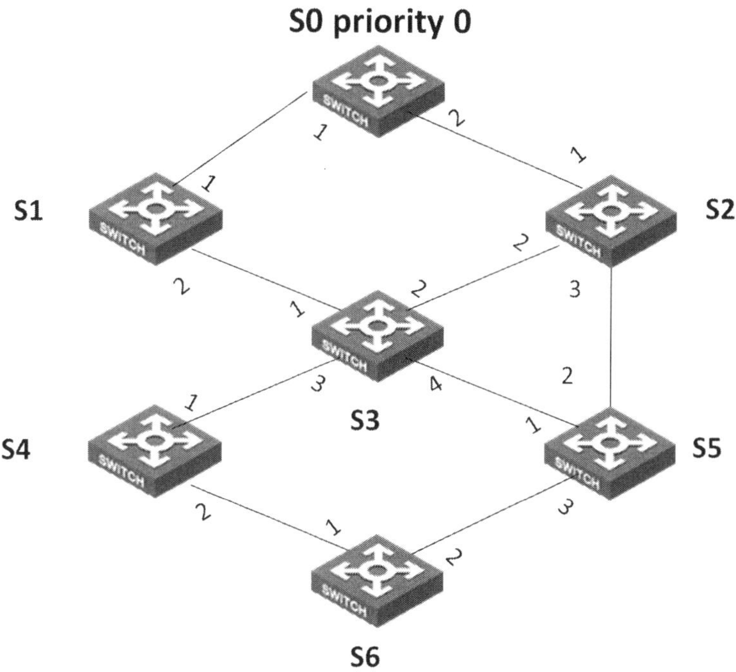

Figure 8-8. STP activity

The following two sections have the questions and answers for this activity.

STP Questions

Here are the questions for the activity:

- Which is the root switch?
- On all of the other switches, which of their ports is the root port?
- On all segments, which port is the designated port?
- Which ports that remain will be placed in a blocked state to remove any Layer 2 loops?

STP Answers

Figure 8-9 lists the answers to the activity from the previous section. RP indicates a root port, DP indicates a designated port, and BLK indicates a blocked port.

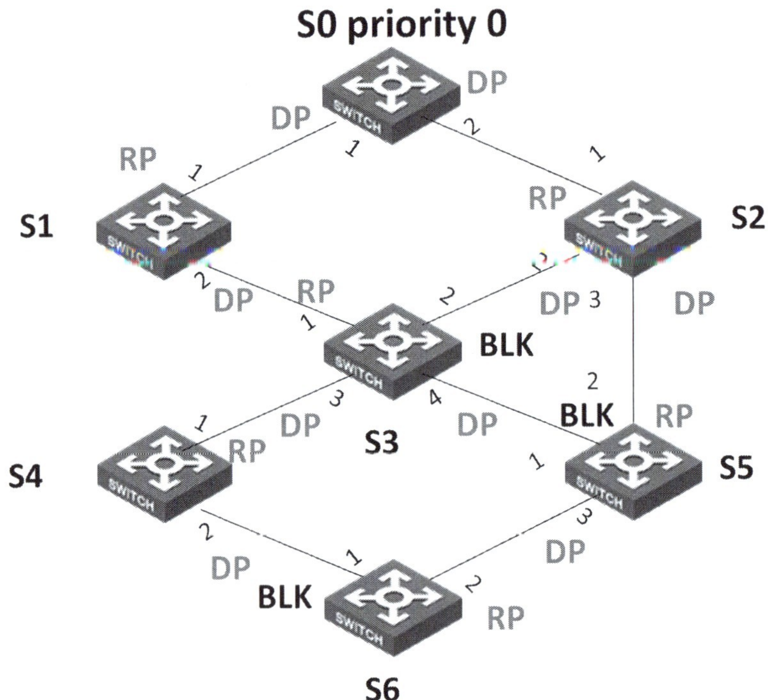

Figure 8-9. STP activity answers

802.1D Port States and Convergence

A port can be in one of five states when it is participating in STP:

- Blocking
- Listening
- Learning
- Forwarding
- Disabled

Of the five states, only the first four are used when the algorithm is running. The following sections cover these port states for STP.

Blocking

Ports go into a blocking state under one of three conditions:

- During election of a root switch (for instance, when you turn on all of the switches in a network)
- When a switch receives a BPDU on a port that indicates a better path to the root switch than the port that the switch is currently using to reach the root
- If a port is not a root port or a designated port

A port in a blocking state remains there for 20 seconds, by default (the maximum age timer). During this state, the port is listening to and processing only BPDUs on its interfaces. Any other frames that the switch receives on a blocked port are dropped. In a blocking state, the switch is attempting to figure out which port is going to be the root port, which ports on the switch need to be designated ports, and which ports will remain in a blocking state to break up any loops.

Listening

After the 20 second timer expires, a root port or a designated port moves to a *listening state*. Any other port remains in a blocking state. During the listening state, the port is still listening for BPDUs and is double-checking the Layer 2 topology. Again, the only traffic that is being processed on a port in this state consists of BPDUs; all other traffic is dropped. A port will stay in this state for the length of the forward delay timer. The default for this value is 15 seconds.

Learning

From a listening state, a root and designated ports move into a *learning state*. During the learning state, the port is still listening for and processing BPDUs on the port; however, unlike while in the listening state, the port begins to process user frames. When processing user frames, the switch is examining the source addresses in the frames and updating its MAC or port address table, but the switch is still not forwarding these frames out of the destination ports. Ports stay in this state for the length of the forward delay time (which defaults to 15 seconds).

Forwarding

Finally, after the forward delay timer expires, ports that were in a learning state are placed in a *forwarding state*. In a forwarding state, the port will process BPDUs, update its MAC address table with frames that it receives, and forward user traffic through the port.

Disabled

The *disabled state* is a special port state. A port in a disabled state is not participating in STP. This could be because the port has been manually shut down by an administrator, manually removed from STP, disabled because of security issues, or rendered nonfunctional because of a lack of a physical layer signal (such as an unplugged patch cable).

Layer 2 Convergence

As discussed in the last section, STP goes through a staged process, which slows down convergence. For switches, convergence occurs after STP has completed the following steps: a root switch is elected root and designated ports are chosen; the root and designated ports are placed in a forwarding state; and all other ports are placed in a blocking state.

Note

If a new root is elected, all ports must start in a blocking state; however, if there is just a topology change, like a newly added switch that is not the root, or a segment comes up or goes down, ports can skip the blocking state. Any port change on the switch, like a PC connection, by default, causes STP to recalculate. This can create havoc early in the workday, when employees come in and turn on their PCs in a staggered process, or in the evening, when they shut down their PCs before going home.

If a port has to go through all four states, convergence takes 50 seconds—20 seconds in blocking, 15 seconds in listening, and 15 seconds in learning. If a port does not have to go through the blocking state but starts at a listening state, convergence takes only 30 seconds. This typically occurs when the root port is still valid, but another topology change has occurred. Remember that, during this time period (until the port reaches a forwarding state), no user traffic is forwarded through the port. So, if a user was performing a Telnet session, and STP was being recalculated, the Telnet session, from the user's perspective, would appear stalled or the connection would appear lost. Obviously, a user will notice this type of disruption.

Note

STP convergence has occurred when all root and designated ports are in a forwarding state and all other ports are in a blocking state.

Rapid STP

The 802.1D standard was designed back when waiting for 30 to 50 seconds for Layer 2 convergence was not a problem. However, in today's networks, this can cause serious performance problems for networks that use real-time applications, such as Voice over IP (VoIP) or video. To overcome these issues, Cisco developed proprietary bridging features called PortFast, UplinkFast, and BackboneFast. The problem with these features, however, is that they are proprietary to Cisco.

Note

Cisco came up with some other proprietary STP protocols, like PortFast and UplinkFast, that IEEE "copied" and somewhat incorporated into RSTP: Portfast is the same as an RSTP edge port, and alternate and backup ports are derivative of UplinkFast. Cisco developed these technologies because of customer needs and a lack of a standard at the time (mid-1990s).

RSTP is an IEEE standard, defined in 802.1w, which is interoperable with 802.1D and is an extension to it. With RSTP, there are only three port states:

- Discarding
- Learning
- Forwarding

A port in a discarding state is basically the grouping of 802.1D's blocking, listening, and disabled states. Figure 8-10 compares the port states used in 802.1D and RSTP (and MSTP). The following sections cover some of the enhancements included in RSTP.

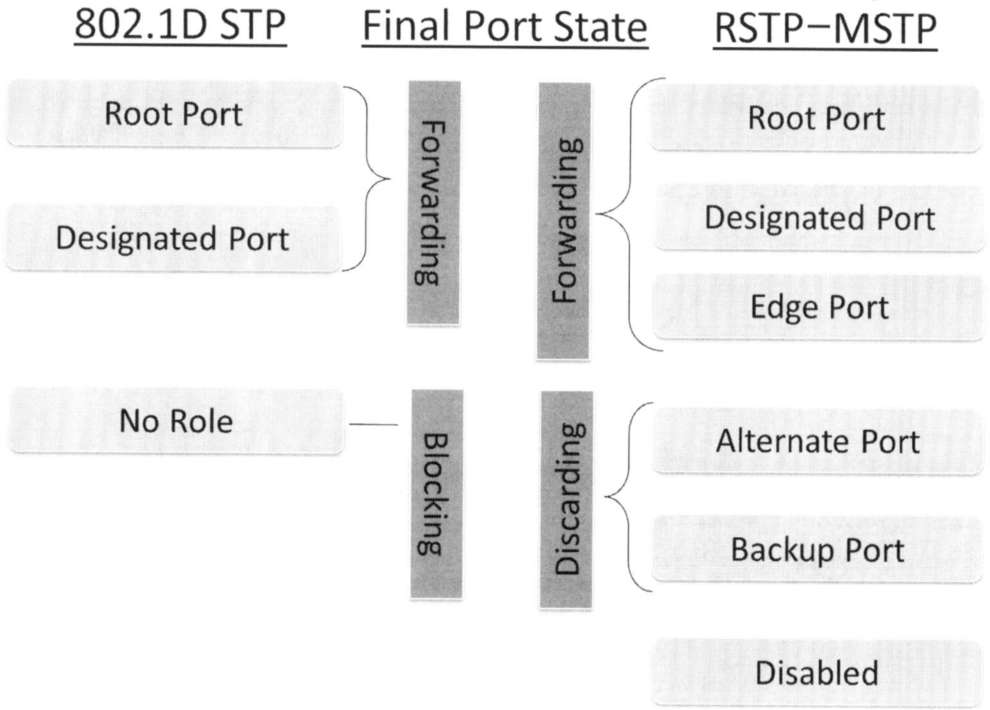

Figure 8-10. STP port state comparisons

Note

As of 2004, 802.1w had been incorporated into the 802.1D standard.

RSTP Additional Port Roles

With RSTP, there is still a root switch and there are still root and designated ports, performing the same roles as those in 802.1D. However, RSTP adds three additional port types: alternate ports, backup ports, and edge ports. The first two ports are similar to those in a blocking state in 802.1D. An *alternate port* is a port that has an alternative path or paths to the root but is currently in a discarding state. A *backup port* is a port on a segment that could be used to reach the root switch, but an active port is already designated for the segment. The best way to look at this is that an alternate port is a secondary, unused root port, and a backup port is a secondary, unused designated port.

An *edge port* connects to a non-STP device—any changes in STP do not affect the forwarding on an edge port, and any changes on the edge port do not affect the STP topology. Edge ports are typically not used between switches since this might create a loop. However, if you had a very small network, like two switches, and a single link between the two switches, you could mark those ports as edge ports. Edge ports are typically used when connecting non-switch devices to a switch, like a PC or laptop, wireless access point (AP), router, firewall, printer, or server, among other devices.

Given these new port roles, RSTP calculates the final spanning tree topology the same way as 802.1D. Some of the nomenclature was changed and extended, and this is used to enhance convergence times, as you will see in the "RSTP Convergence Features" section.

RSTP BPDUs

The 802.1w (RSTP) standard introduced a change with BPDUs. Some additional flags were added to the BPDUs so that switches could share information about the role of the BPDU source port. This can help a neighboring switch converge faster when changes occur in the network.

In 802.1D, if a switch did not see a root BPDU within the maximum age time (20 seconds), STP would run, a new root switch would be elected, and a new loop-free topology would be created. This is a time-consuming process. With 802.1w, if any BPDU is not received in three expected hello periods (a total of six seconds), STP information can be aged out instantly and the switch considers that its neighbor is lost and that actions should be taken. This is different from 802.1D, where the switch had to miss the BPDUs from the root. In this case, if the switch misses three consecutive hellos from a neighbor, actions are immediately taken.

RSTP Convergence Features

The 802.1w standard includes new convergence features that are very similar to Cisco's proprietary UplinkFast and BackboneFast features. The first feature, like Cisco's BackboneFast, allows a switch to accept inferior BPDUs.

Figure 8-11 helps to illustrate the inferior BPDU feature. In this example, the root bridge is Switch-A. Both of the ports on Switch-B and Switch-C directly connected to the root are root ports. For the segment between Switch-B and Switch-C, Switch-B provides the designated port and Switch-C provides a backup port (a secondary way of reaching the root for the segment, and, therefore, a secondary designated port). In addition, Switch-B knows that its designated port is also an alternative port (a secondary way for the switch to reach the root, and, therefore, a secondary root port), via Switch-C from Switch-C's BPDUs.

Following the example in Figure 8-11, the link between the root and Switch-B fails. Switch-B can detect this by either missing three hellos from the root port or by detecting a physical layer failure. If you were running 802.1D, Switch-B would see an inferior root BPDU (worse cost value) coming via Switch-C, and, therefore, all ports would have to go through a blocking, listening, and learning states, which would take 50 seconds, by default, to converge. With the inferior BPDU feature, assuming that Switch-B knows that Switch-C has an alternate port for their directly connected segment, Switch-B can notify Switch-C to take its alternate port and change it to a designated port, and Switch-B will change its designated port to a root port. This process takes only a few seconds or less.

The second convergence feature introduced in 802.1w is rapid transition. *Rapid transition* includes two new components: edge ports and link types. An edge port is a port connected to a non-Layer 2 device, such as a PC, server, or router. RSTP with rapid transition of edge ports to a forwarding state is the same as Cisco's proprietary PortFast. Changes in the state of these ports does not affect RSTP to cause a recalculation, and changes in other port types keeps these ports in a forwarding state.

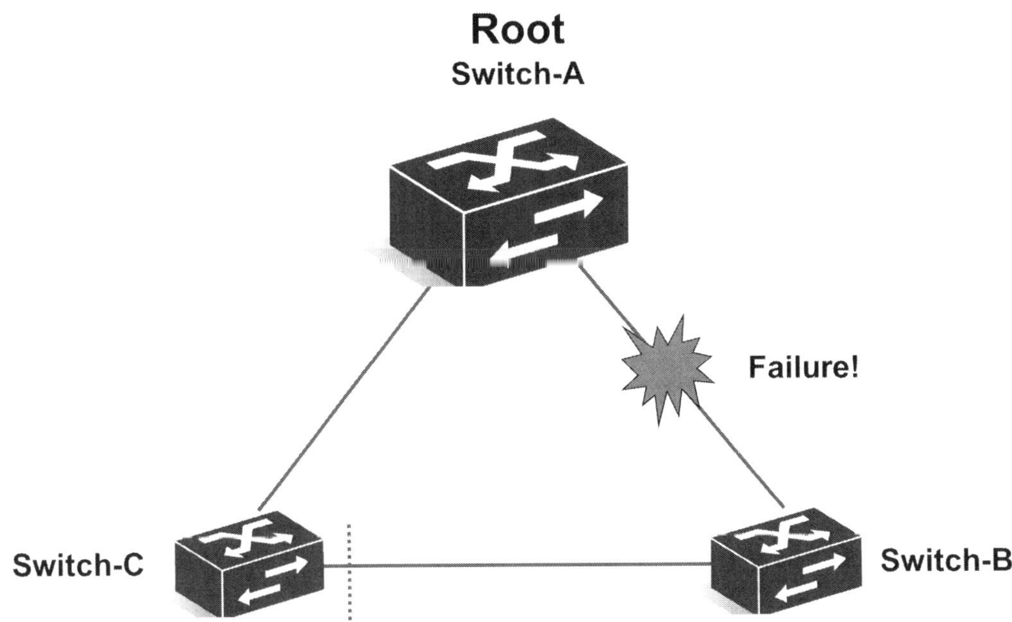

Figure 8-11. Accepting inferior BPDUs

Rapid transition can take place in RSTP only for edge ports and links that are point to point. The link type is automatically determined in terms of the duplexing of the connection. Switches make the assumption that, if the port is configured for full-duplex between the two switches, the port can rapidly transition to a different state without having to wait for any timers to expire. If they are half-duplex, this feature will not work by default, but you can manually enable it for point-to-point half-duplex switch links.

Let us take a look at an example of rapid transition of point-to-point links by using the topology in Figure 8-12. In this example, the link between Switch-A (the root) and Switch-C fails. When this happens, Switch-C can no longer reach Switch-A on its root port. However, looking at the BPDUs which it has been receiving from Switch-A and Switch-B, Switch-C knows that the root is reachable via Switch-B and that Switch-B provides the designated port (which is in a forwarding state) for the segment between Switch-B and Switch-C. Switch-C, knowing this, changes the state of the backup port to a root port and places it immediately into a forwarding state, notifying Switch-B of the change. If the failure of the segment between the root and Switch-C is a physical link failure, this update can take less than a second, instead of six seconds from three missed consecutive hello BPDUs.

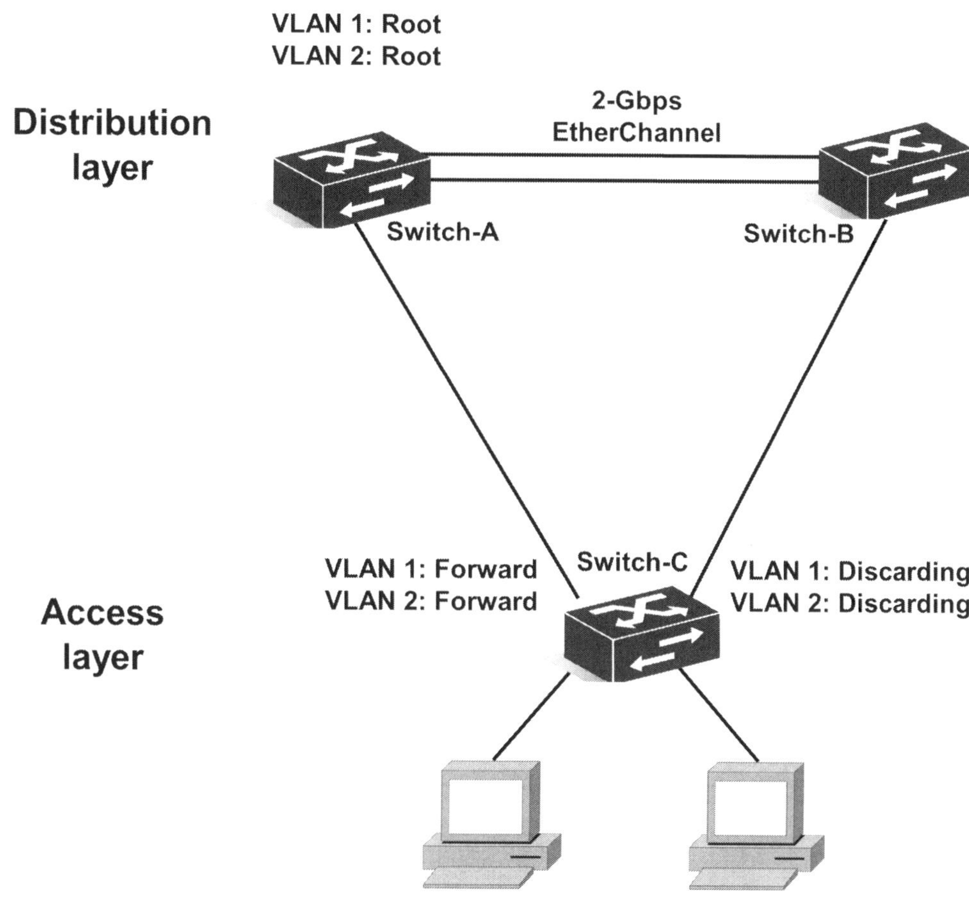

Figure 8-12. Rapid transition example

Combining STP or RSTP and VLANs

The implementation of STP or RSTP can disrupt VLAN configurations because both protocols block redundant physical links without evaluating connections between virtual broadcast domains. Consequently, network designers must implement spanning tree with great care to ensure that they do not isolate VLAN hosts from other members of their VLANS or from their default gateways.

Furthermore, because BPDUs are always untagged, VLAN configurations can disrupt communication between switches in a spanning tree because:

- Both STP and RSTP specify a single spanning tree that resolves loops.
- Redundant links between switches are blocked: network designers must ensure that VLANs are not isolated.
- BPDUs are sent untagged: VLAN configurations can disrupt communication between switches in a spanning tree.

Examine the network in Figure 8-13, which illustrates the interplay between STP and VLANs. To ensure availability, the four switches have been configured with redundant links and spanning tree enabled to ensure failover if one of the links fails. However, as shown in Figure 8-13 this topology includes multiple paths between hosts that are in the same VLAN but are connected to separate edge switches.

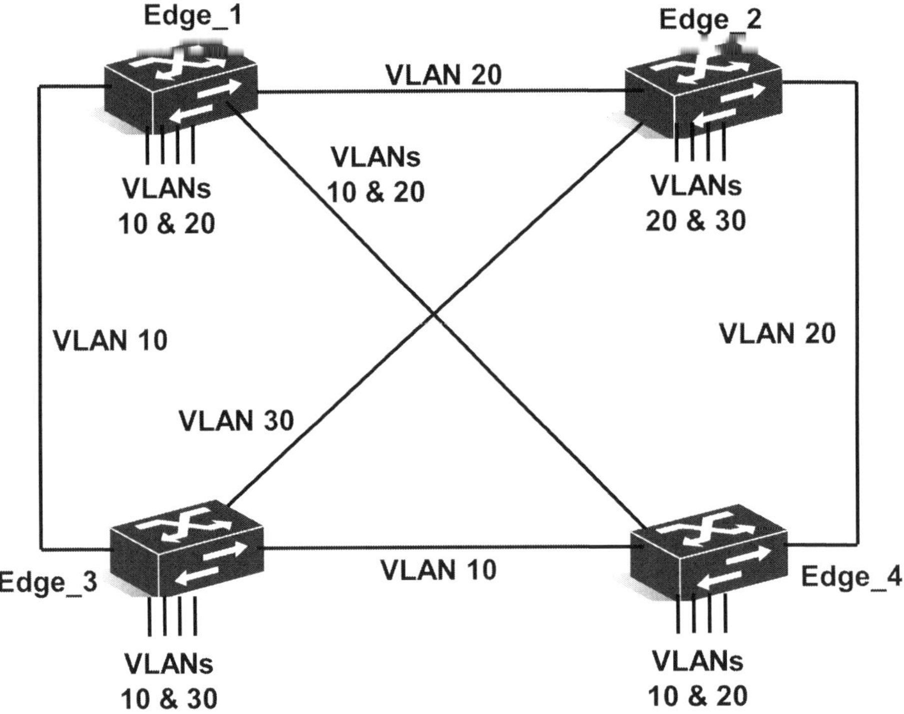

Figure 8-13. Spanning tree and VLANs

At first glance, it may seem possible to resolve the potential conflicts between STP and VLANs by simply assigning ports as tagged members of only the VLANs that are shared by the switches. For example, because VLAN 20 is the only VLAN that Edge_4 and Edge_2 have in common, we could attempt to resolve conflicts by assigning their common link as a tagged member of VLAN 20. However, as the next few pages demonstrate, this is not a satisfactory solution.

Assigning all VLANs to all redundant links ensures that no hosts are isolated from other hosts in their VLANs. Certainly, the failure of one of the edge switches would result in loss of connectivity for its directly connected hosts, but this would not affect other switches because of the redundant connections between the switches.

RSTP Port States and Roles

Figure 8-14 shows an example network. SW1 is the root switch. The bridge IDs (BID) are shown as listed. RP indicates a root port, DP indicates a designated port, Alt indicates an alternate port, BP indicates a backup port, and EP indicates an edge port. One detail to note is the connection on SW3. Obviously, you would never purposefully connect one port on a switch to a different port on the same switch. However, this kind of connection could occur if SW3 had dual connections to a dumb (non-STP-aware) switch or to a hub.

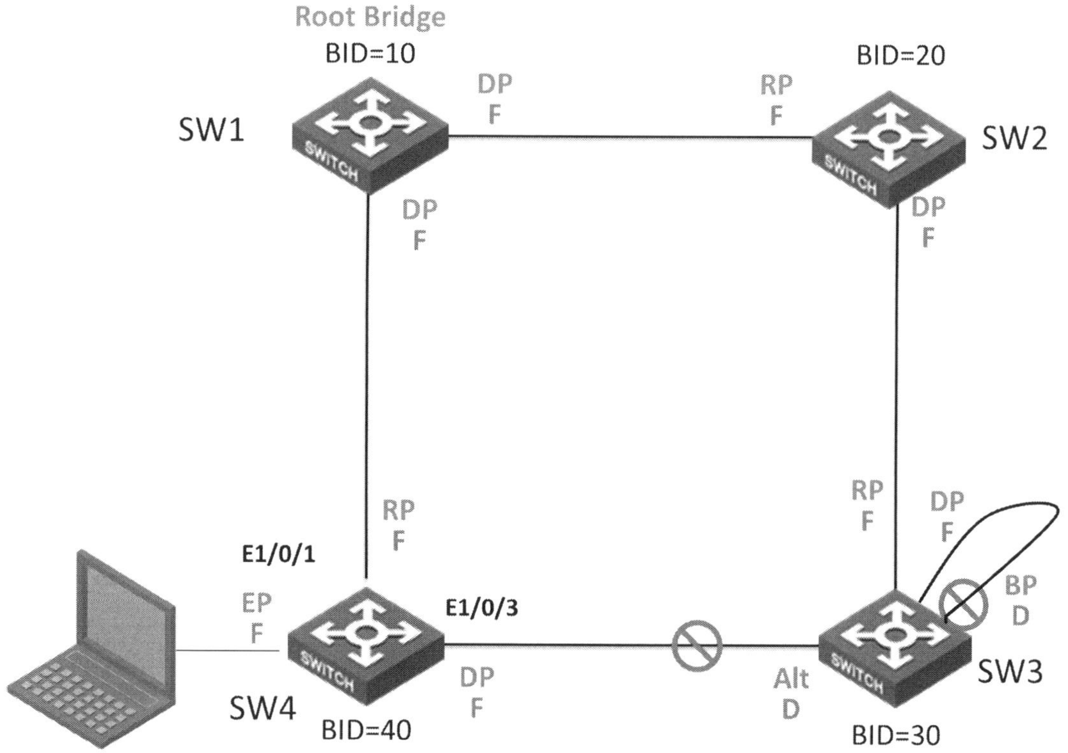

Figure 8-14. RSTP port states and roles example

Note

The loop connection on SW3 is probably not a physical loop but a logical one. Those two ports on SW3 might be connected to a hub or to a dumb Layer 2 switch that lacks STP capabilities. However, perhaps because of a cabling error, this could be a physical loop.

Problems with 802.1D and RSTP

STP does not guarantee an optimized loop-free network. For instance, take a look at the network shown in Figure 8-15. In this example, the network has two VLANs and the root switch is Switch-A. The right-side port on Switch-C is placed in a blocking/discarding state to remove any loops. If you look at this configuration for VLAN 2, it definitely is not optimized. For instance, if VLAN 2 devices on Switch-C want to access a remote VLAN, they must use their default gateway of Switch-B; however, their traffic must first traverse Switch-A before reaching Switch-B, which is an extra Layer 2 hop in the network.

In addition, even though redundancy exists, half of the uplink bandwidth from Switch-C to the upper two switches is lost because the port between Switch-C and Switch-B is placed in a blocked/discarded state.

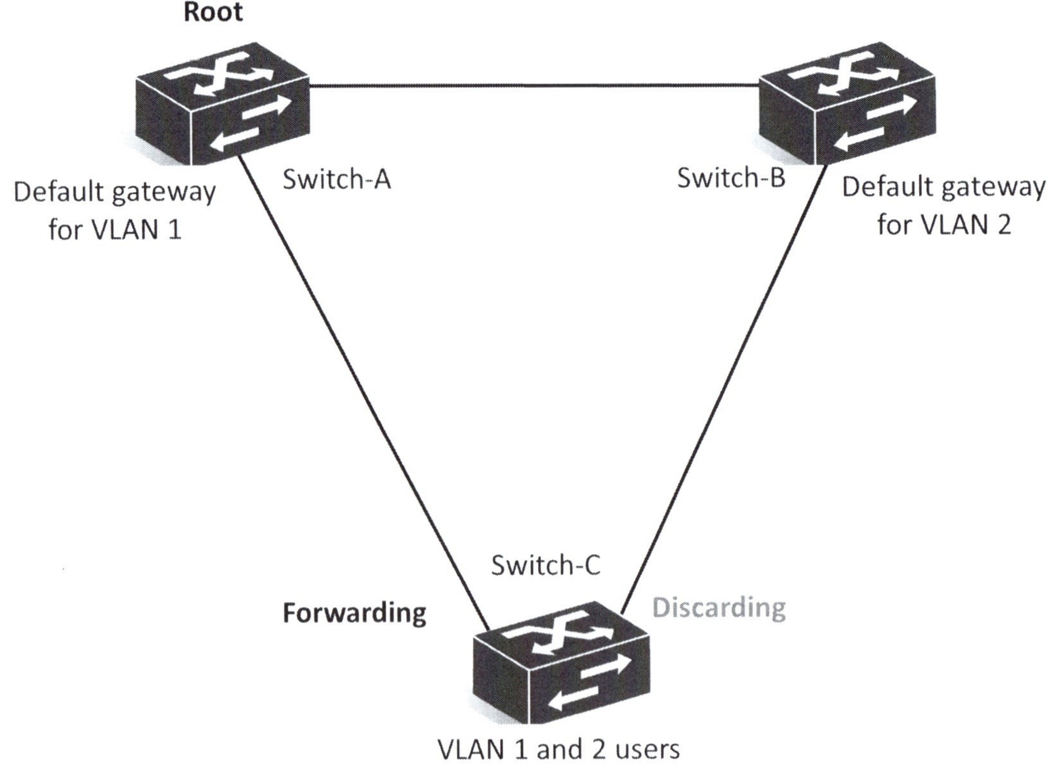

Figure 8-15. Problems with 802.1D and RSTP

When one instance of STP is running, this is referred to as a *Common Spanning Tree* (CST). Cisco also supports a process called *Per-VLAN Spanning Tree Plus* (PVST+) to overcome the deficiencies of 802.1D and RSTP. PVST+ was originally a Cisco-proprietary protocol developed to perform load-sharing of VLANs on multiple uplinks from access layer switches to distribution layer switches. With PVST+, each VLAN has its own instance of STP, with its own root switch, its own set of priorities, and its own set of BPDUs.

In PVST+, the switch or bridge ID has been enhanced. In 802.1D switch priority, extended system ID, and MAC address comprise switch or bridge ID. In PVST+, the switch or bridge ID has an additional field—the extended system ID that carries the VLAN ID (VID) for the instance of STP.

With the addition of this field, it is possible to have different priorities on switches in different VLANs. Therefore, you have the capability of having multiple root switches—one per VLAN. Each VLAN in PVST+, by default, develops its own loop-free topology (see Figure 8-16).

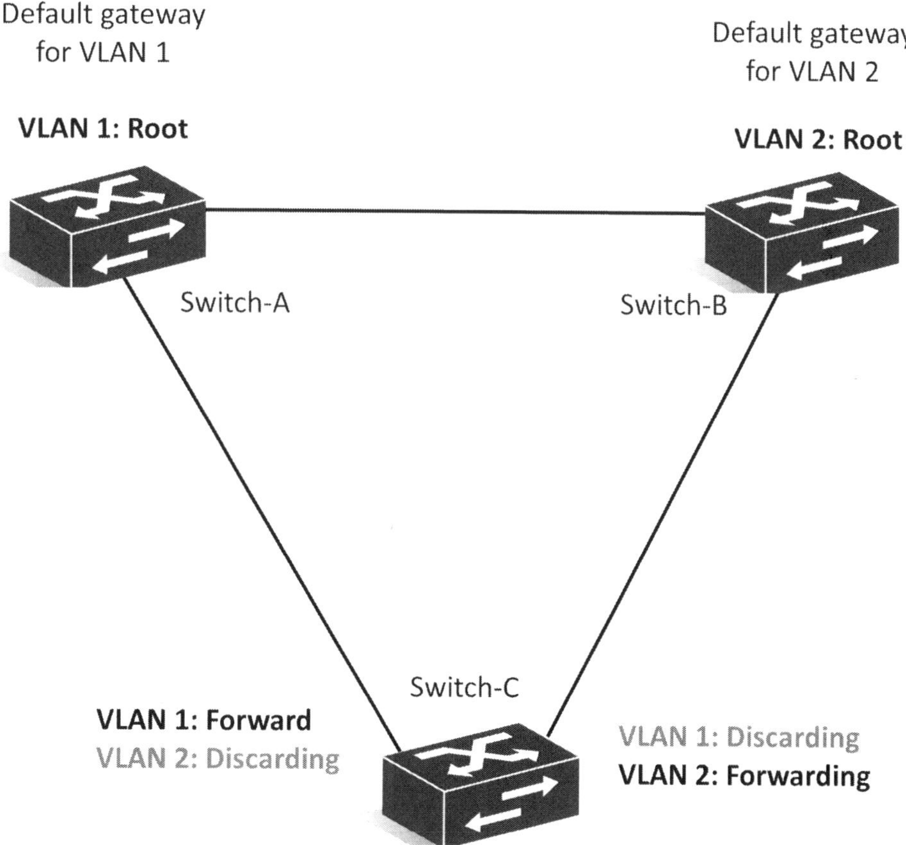

Figure 8-16. PVST+ overview

Of course, PVST+, just like CST, does not create an optimized loop-free network; however, you can make STP changes in each VLAN to optimize traffic patterns for each separate VLAN. It is highly recommended that you tune STP for each VLAN to optimize it. Also, PVST+ is more stable. If STP changes are occurring in one VLAN, they do not affect other instances of STP for other VLANs.

Note

PVST+ is *not* load balancing. Instead, PVST+ load shares—both uplinks are used, but the traffic is typically not balanced based on the loads occurring in the various VLANs.

If an uplink fails, the remaining uplink must be able to maintain the current load level. Therefore, a single uplink must be able to support the traffic for all VLANs. Given this design in Layer 2, load-sharing is typically not that important, but, obviously, redundancy is. Load-sharing becomes more important when you have three or more uplinks and have oversubscribed a single uplink—in this situation, load-sharing is a must if you do not want to create congestion problems.

The downside of PVST+ is that, since each VLAN has its own instance of STP, more overhead is involved—more BPDUs and STP tables are required on each switch. Plus, it makes no sense to use PVST+ unless you tune it for your network, which means more work and monitoring on your part.

Note

Recently, support for PVST+ was added to ProVision and Comware switches. An in-depth discussion of this topic is beyond the scope of this book, but it is covered at the HP Accredited Solutions Expert (ASE) level in the Interoperability course.

MSTP

The 802.1D and 802.1w STPs operate without regard to a network's VLAN configuration, and they maintain one common spanning tree throughout a bridged network. Therefore, these protocols map one loop-free, logical topology on a given physical topology. The 802.1s Multiple Spanning Tree Protocol uses VLAN-to-instance mappings to create multiple spanning trees in a network, and this significantly improves network resource utilization while maintaining a loop-free environment, similar to Cisco's proprietary PVST+ but without its overhead.

Released in 2002, 802.1s (MSTP) is an amendment to the 802.1Q-1998 standard. 802.1s provides an extension to STP and RSTP, allowing the protocol to use separate spanning trees for groups of VLANs. 802.1s was later merged into 802.1Q-2003.

MSTP Instances and Regions

Although the per-VLAN spanning tree approach adopted by some vendors overcomes the network utilization problems inherent in using STP or RSTP, using a per-VLAN technology with multiple VLANs can overload the switch's CPU. MSTP on the switches covered in this guide complies with the IEEE 802.1s standard, and it extends STP and RSTP functionality to map multiple independent spanning tree instances onto a physical topology.

With MSTP, each spanning tree instance can include one or more VLANs and applies a separate, per-instance forwarding topology. Therefore, where a port belongs to multiple VLANs, it may be dynamically blocked in one spanning tree instance but forwarded in another. This achieves load-sharing across the network while keeping the switch's CPU load at a moderate level (by aggregating multiple VLANs in a single spanning tree instance). MSTP provides fault tolerance through rapid, automatic reconfiguration if there is a failure in a network's physical topology.

With MSTP-capable switches, you can create a number of MST regions containing different spanning tree instances. This requires the configuration of multiple of MSTP-capable switches. However, it is not necessary to do this. You can just enable MSTP on an MSTP-capable switch and a spanning tree instance is created automatically. This instance always exists, by default, when spanning tree is enabled and is the spanning tree instance that communicates with STP and RSTP environments. The MSTP configuration commands operate exactly like RSTP commands, and MSTP is backward-compatible with the RSTP-enabled and STP-enabled switches in your network.

MSTP Structure

MSTP maps active, separate paths through different spanning tree instances and between MST regions. Each MST region comprises one or more MSTP switches. Note that MSTP recognizes an STP or RSTP LAN as a distinct spanning tree region. Table 8-2 defines some of the terms used in MSTP.

Table 8-2: MSTP terms

Term	Definition
Common and internal spanning tree (CIST)	The CIST identifies the regions in a network and administers the CIST root bridge for the network, the root bridge for each region, and the root bridge for each spanning tree instance in each region.
Common spanning tree	The CST administers the connectivity among the MST regions, STP LANs, and RSTP LANs in a bridged network.
MST Region	An MST region comprises the VLANs configured on physically connected MSTP switches. All switches in a given region must be configured with the same VLANs, the same multiple spanning tree instances (MSTIs), and the same MST configuration identifiers.
Internal spanning tree (IST)	The IST administers the topology within a given MST region. When you configure a switch for MSTP operation, the switch automatically includes all of the static VLANs configured on the switch in a single, active spanning tree topology (instance) within the IST. This is termed the *IST instance.* Any VLANs you subsequently configure on the switch are added to this IST instance. To create separate forwarding paths within a region, group specific VLANs into different MSTIs.

Note

IST occurs *within* a single region for all VLANs not assigned to a particular instance. CST occurs *across* the entire switched network that might involve multiple regions, RSTP, and/or 8021.D. However, given this distinction, many networking vendors treat the two—CST and IST—the same, from a configuration perspective (tuning IST tunes CST in the same manner), which leads to confusion between the two terms.

An MST network comprises separate spanning tree instances existing in an MST region. (There can be multiple regions in a network.) Each instance defines a single forwarding topology for an exclusive set of VLANs. By contrast, an STP or RSTP network has only one spanning tree instance for the entire network, and it includes all VLANs in the network. (An STP or RSTP network operates as a single-instance network.) A region can include two types of STP instances:

- **Internal spanning tree instance**—The default spanning tree instance in any MST region. It provides the root switch for the region and comprises all VLANs configured on the switches in the region that are not specifically assigned to MSTIs. Within a region, the IST instance provides a loop-free forwarding path for all VLANs associated with it. VLANs that are not associated with an MSTI are, by default, associated with the IST instance. Note that the switch automatically places dynamic VLANs (resulting from Generic Attribute Registration Protocol [GARP] VLAN Registration Protocol [GVRP] operation) in the IST instance. Dynamic VLANs cannot exist in an MSTI (described below). GVRP is an open standard that allows you to create VLANs on one switch and have them dynamically added to neighbor switches. (GVRP is not covered in this book.)
- **Multiple spanning tree instance**—This type of configurable spanning tree instance comprises all static VLANs that you specifically assign to it, and it must include at least one VLAN. The VLAN(s) you assign to an MSTI must initially exist in the IST instance of the same MST region. When you assign a static VLAN to an MSTI, the switch removes the VLAN from the IST instance. (Therefore, you can assign a VLAN to only one MSTI in a given region.) All VLANs in an MSTI operate as part of the same single spanning tree topology. (The switch does not allow dynamic VLANs in an MSTI.)

Note

When you enable MSTP on the switch, the default MSTP spanning tree configuration settings comply with the values recommended in the IEEE 802.1s MSTP standard. Note that inappropriate changes to these settings can result in severely degraded network performance. For this reason, HP strongly recommends that changing these default settings be reserved only for experienced network administrators who have a strong understanding of the IEEE 802.1D/w/s standards and operation.

MSTP Operation

All MSTP switches in a given region must be configured with the same instance-to-VLAN mappings and VLAN-to-instance assignments (see Figure 8-17). A VLAN can belong to only one instance within any region. Within a region:

- All of the VLANs belonging to a given instance compose a single, active spanning tree topology for that instance.
- Each instance operates independently of other instances.

Between regions there is a single, active spanning tree topology. (See Figure 8-18 for an example.)

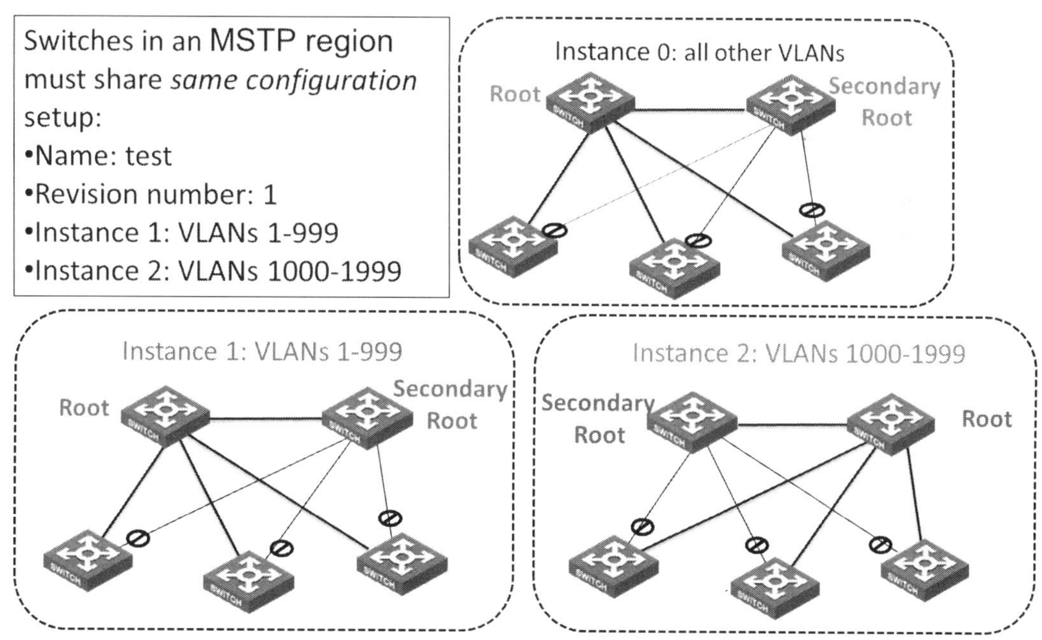

Figure 8-17. Operation of MSTP

Assigning different groups of VLANs to different instances ensures that those VLAN groups use independent forwarding paths. Although allowing only one active path through a given instance, MSTP retains any redundant physical paths in the instance to serve as backup (blocked) paths in case that the existing active path fails. Therefore, if an active path in an instance fails, MSTP automatically activates (unblocks) an available backup to serve as the new active path through the instance for as long as the original active path is down. Note also that a given port may simultaneously operate in different states (forwarding or blocking) for different spanning tree instances within the same region. This depends on the VLAN memberships to which the port is assigned for the Comware switches. For example, if a port belongs to VLAN 1 in the IST instance of a region and it belongs to VLAN 4 in MSTI "x" in the same region, the port may apply different states to traffic for these two different instances.

Here is a quick comparison between MSTP and PVST+, using Figure 8-17 on MSTP to illustrate the differences:

- **MSTP:**
  - One set of BPDUs for all instances
  - Three spanning trees (one per instance)
  - Three roots (one per instance)
- **PVST+:**
  - 1,999+ sets of BPDUs (one per VLAN)
  - 1,999+ sets of spanning trees (one per VLAN)
  - 1,999+ roots (one per VLAN)

Within a region, traffic routed between VLANs in separate instances can take only one physical path. To ensure that traffic in all VLANs within a region can travel between regions, all of the boundary ports for each region should belong to all VLANs configured in the region. Otherwise, traffic from some areas within a region could be blocked from moving to other areas within a region.

All MSTP switches (in addition to STP and RSTP switches) in a network use untagged BPDUs to exchange information from which to build multiple, active topologies in the individual instances within a region and between regions. From this information:

- The MSTP switches in each LAN segment determine a designated bridge and designated port or trunk for the segment.
- The MSTP switches belonging to a particular instance determine the root bridge and root port or trunk for the instance.
- For the IST instance within a region, the MSTP switches linking that region to other regions (or to STP or RSTP switches) determine the IST root bridge and the IST root port or trunk for the region. (For any MSTI in a region, the regional root may be a different switch that is not necessarily connected to another region.)
- The MSTP switches block redundant links within each LAN segment, across all instances, and between regions to prevent any traffic loops.

As a result, each individual instance (spanning tree) within a region determines its regional root bridge, designated bridges, and designated ports or trunks.

Spanning Tree between Different MSTP Regions

The IST instance and any MST instances in a region exist only within that region. Where a link crosses a boundary between regions (or between a region and a legacy STP or RSTP switch), traffic is forwarded or blocked as determined by the CST. The CST ensures that there is only one active path between any two regions, or between a region and a switch running STP and RSTP. (See Figure 8-18 for an example.)

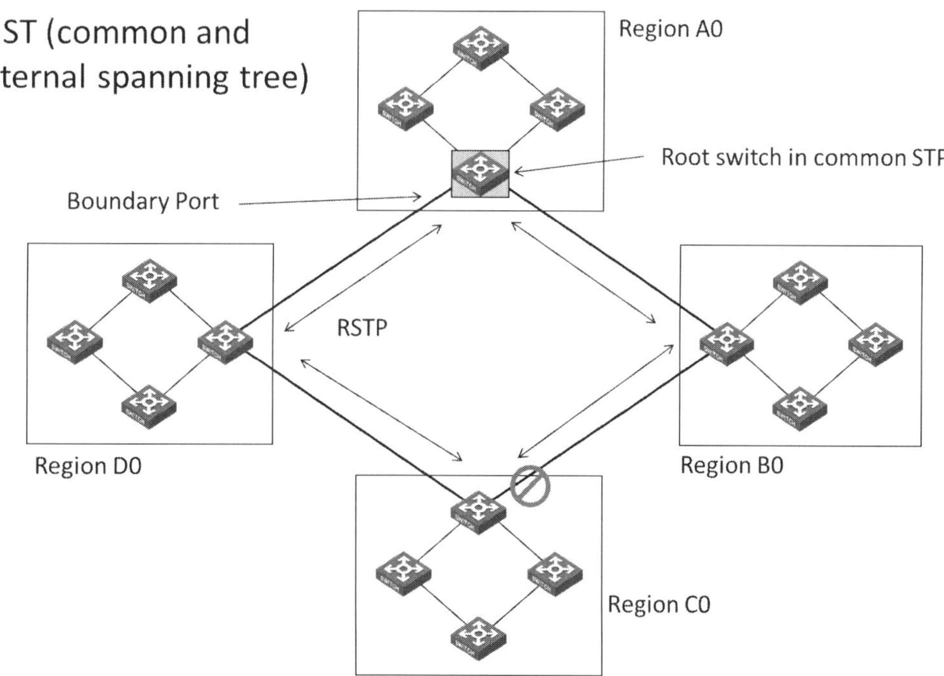

Figure 8-18. Spanning tree between different MSTP regions

Note

Some vendors do not allow you to tune IST and CST separately—they use the same parameters. Therefore, many network administrators become confused between what is IST and what is CST. They are two distinct processes within MSTP.

As indicated in the preceding sections, within a given MST instance, a single spanning tree is configured for all VLANs included in that instance. This means that, if redundant physical links exist in separate VLANs within the same instance, MSTP blocks all but one of those links. However, you can prevent the bandwidth loss caused by blocked redundant links for different VLANs in an instance by using a port trunk

Note

All switches in a region should be configured with the VLANs used in that region, and all ports linking MSTP switches together should be members of all VLANs in the region. Otherwise, the path to the root for a given VLAN will be broken if MSTP selects a spanning tree through a link that does not include that VLAN.

Because MSTP implements the same basic principles as the earlier spanning tree protocols, it is completely interoperable and compatible with STP and RSTP. IEEE 802.1s MSTP includes RSTP functionality and is designed to be compatible with both IEEE 802.1D and 802.1w Spanning Tree Protocols. Using the default configuration values, your switches interoperate effectively with RSTP and STP devices. MSTP automatically detects when the switch ports are connected to non-MSTP devices in the spanning tree and communicates with those devices using 802.1D or 802.1w STP BPDU packets, as appropriate.

To enable effective interoperation with STP (802.1D) configured devices, however, you may need to adjust the default configuration values. Here are two such examples:

- The rapid state transitions employed by MSTP may result in an increase in the rates of frame duplication and mis-ordering in the switched LAN. To allow the switch to support applications and protocols that may be sensitive to frame duplication and mis-ordering, you can disable rapid transitions by setting the Force Protocol Version parameter to STP-compatible. The value of this parameter applies to all ports on the switch.
- One of the benefits of MSTP is the implementation of a larger range of port path costs, and this accommodates higher network speeds. However, it can create some incompatibility between devices running the older 802.1D STP. For example, on ProVision switches, you can adjust to this incompatibility by implementing the global spanning tree legacy path cost command.

Note

The example shown in Figure 8-18 is unlikely in a campus network. Typically, different regions are separated by a routing process, and, if there are any Layer 3 loops between the regions, it would be a routing protocol, like OSPF, that would deal with the problem. However, data center networks are actually expanding their Layer 2 topologies, making Figure 8-21 more likely in a data center location.

MSTP Misconfiguration Issues

All information in the region configuration must match for the MSTP configuration to be successful. Even the region name, which is case-sensitive, must match. Notice in Figure 8-19, however, that there is a mismatch between the bottom switch on the left and the rest of the switches in the network. In most situations, this will not cause a Layer 2 loop because the basic BPDU structure used by STP, RSTP, and MSTP is the same. The two different regions treat the link as an RSTP link—therefore, no loop. However, the down side of this is that you have effectively lost any load-sharing from the access to the distribution layer (if the bottom switches had a second connection to the secondary root in Figure 8-19).

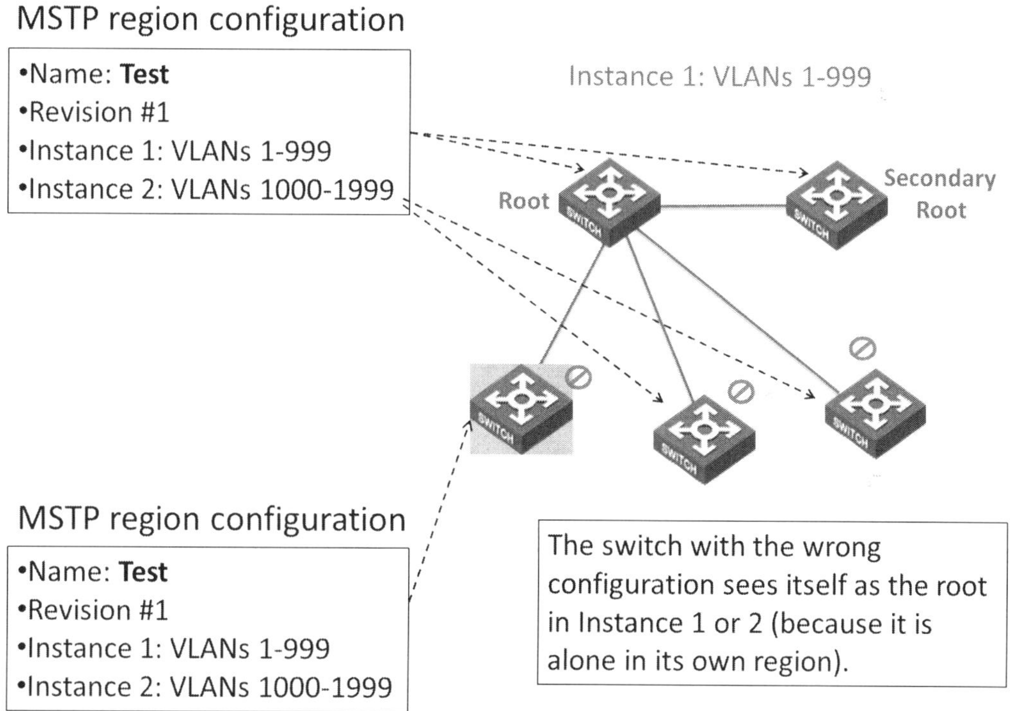

Figure 8-19. Example of an MSTP misconfiguration

MSTP Activities

The following sections introduce you to some activities to better understand the operation and troubleshooting of MSTP.

MSTP Activity 1

Given the topology shown in Figure 8-20 and given that all of the switches have the same region configuration for MSTP, what would happen if you added a currently non-existing VLAN, say VLAN 14, to Switch-D but not to the other switches?

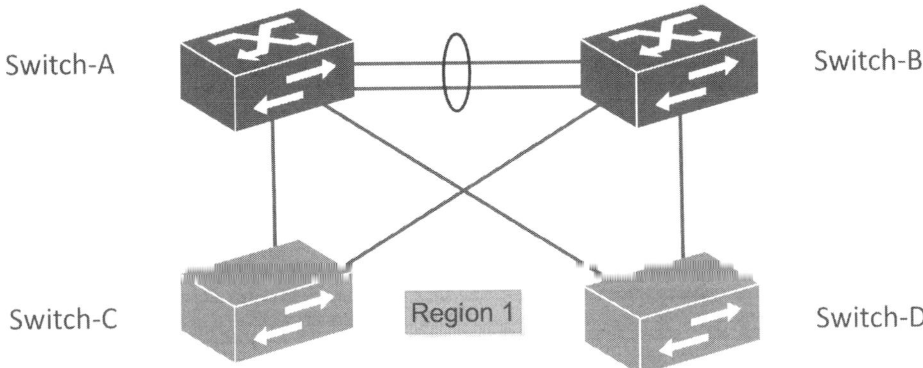

All switches have this configuration:

- Configuration name = “Region1”
- Revision #= 1
- Instance 1 = VLANs 1, 12
- Instance 2 = VLANs 11, 13
- IST instance = VLANs 2-10, 14-4094

Figure 8-20. MSTP Activity 1

Given that the region configuration did not change, MSTP does not see a change. This is an important aspect of MSTP: it is *not* aware of the actual VLAN topology in your network (which switches and ports have a particular VLAN active). Whether or not VLAN 14 exists does not impact MSTP. MSTP is not aware of which VLANs exist (or do not exist) on switches or of which ports on a switch are assigned to a VLAN. If the VLAN is defined in the region configuration, and you add the VLAN to the switch, it does not cause disruption to MSTP.

MSTP Activity 2

See Figure 8-21 for a second MSTP activity. In this activity, all of the switches originally had the same MSTP region configuration. Then, on Switch-D, the VLAN-to-instance mapping was changed, where VLAN 14 was moved from the IST (instance 0) instance to instance 2. Is there a loop in the network? Do you still have redundancy?

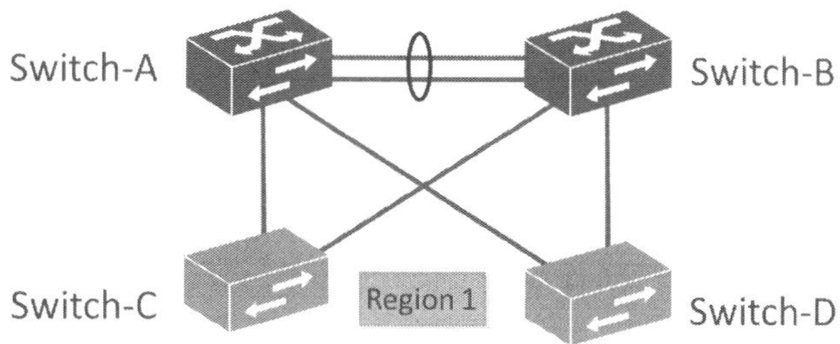

Switch-A, Switch-B, Switch-C:

- Configuration name = "Region1"
- Revision # = 1
- Instance 1 = VLANs 1, 12
- Instance 2 = VLANs 11, 13
- IST instance = VLANs 2-10, 14-4094

Switch-D:

- Configuration name = "Region1"
- Revision # = 1
- Instance 1 = VLANs 1, 12
- Instance 2 = VLANs 11, 13, 14
- IST instance = VLANs 2-10, 15-4094

Figure 8-21. MSTP Activity 2

Because the region information is different between the switches, the link connection from Switch-D to the other switches is treated as an RSTP connection (it affects MSTP). Therefore, there are no loops, but only one of the two uplinks (to Switch-A or to Switch-B) is active and the other is in a discarding state. So you still have redundancy, but you have lost the load-sharing feature.

MSTP Activity 3

This third activity with MSTP is trickier. There are two regions shown in Figure 8-22; the top region and the bottom region. The links between all the switches are multi-VLAN ports (where VLANs are tagged on the switch-to-switch links), with two exceptions:

- VLAN 100 is untagged (access port) between the two regions.
- VLAN 200 is untagged (access port) between the two regions.

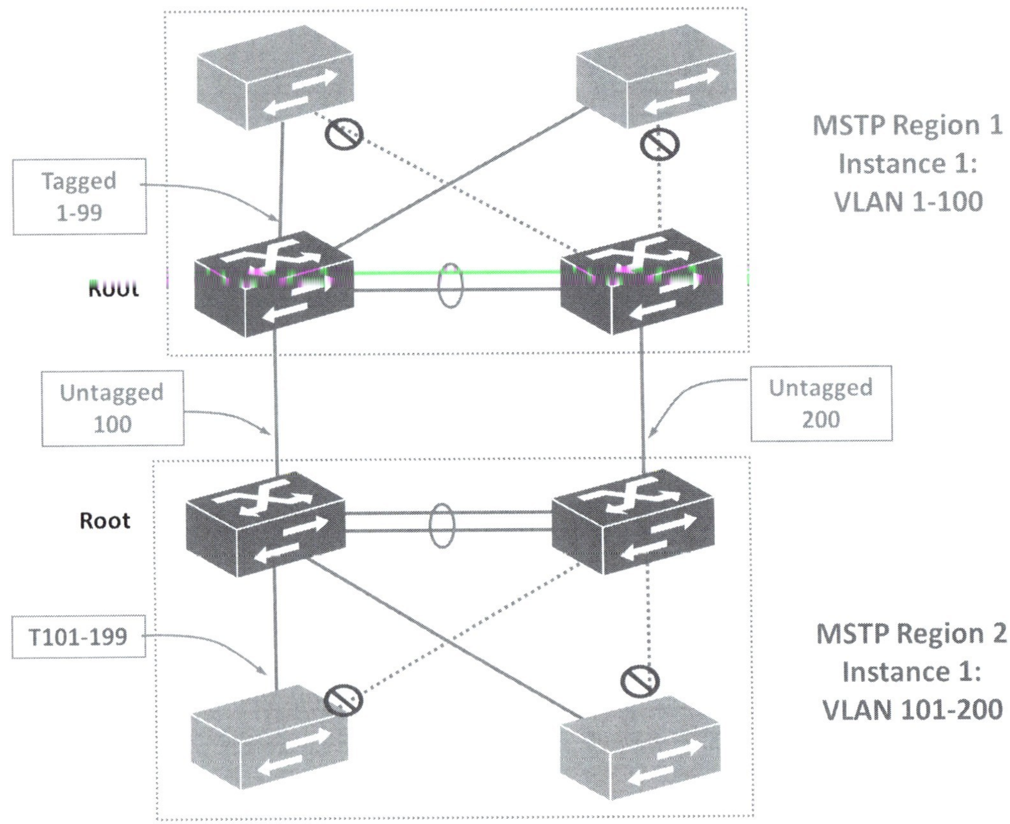

Figure 8-22. MSTP Activity 3

Is MSTP active between the two regions? Yes. By default, MSTP/RSTP/802.1D sends out BPDUs on all untagged VLAN ports.

Are the untagged links (VLANs 100 and 200) between the two regions blocked, and why or why not? No. For Region 1, VLAN 100 is in instance 1 and VLAN 200 in IST (instance 0); for Region 2, VLAN 100 is in IST and VLAN 200 in instance 1. There is at least one issue creating the two separate regions. Because the region configuration between the two regions is different, basic RSTP processing occurs. Therefore, one of the ports connecting the two switches in either VLAN 100 or VLAN 200 is placed in discarding state. So redundancy still exists, but the load-sharing ability of MSTP is lost.

What is the solution to keep both links up between the two regions? In this example, you would want to have a Layer 3 routing protocol running between the two switches to connect the two regions; however, remember that MSTP is still running also. To let the Layer 3 routing protocol deal with the Layer 3 loop, you need to do one of the following:

- Disable STP between the two regions.
- Filter the STP BPDUs between the two regions.

All the solutions will work, and one is not necessarily better than another. It really is personal preference as to which of the three you choose. Just remember that, after you effectively stop the two regions from seeing each other at Layer 2, you still have a loop between the them, where you need a Layer 3 routing protocol, like OSPF, to deal with the problem.

MSTP Activity 4

This fourth activity illustrates some of the issues with using MSTP (or even PVST+, for that matter). There is one region shown in Figure 8-23, and the region information is correctly configured on all the switches.

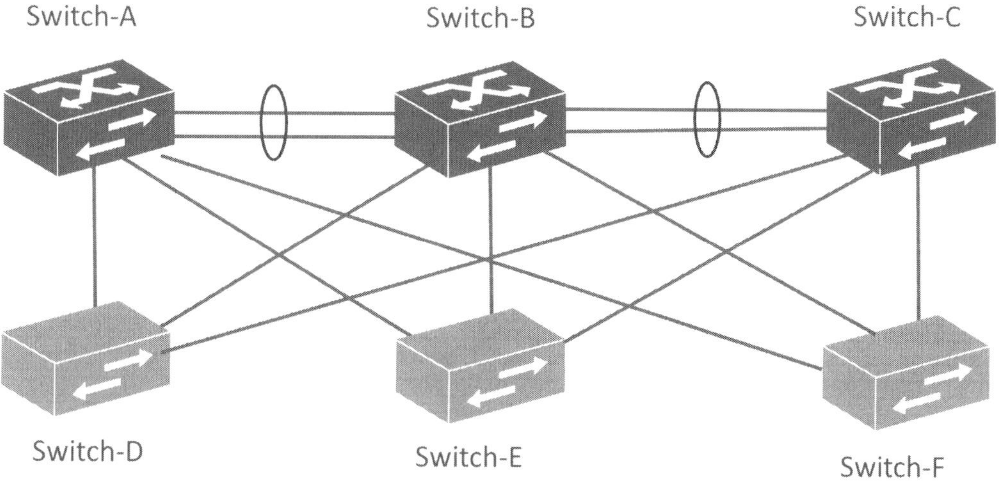

Figure 8-23. MSTP Activity 4

How many MSTP instances, in addition to the IST (instance 0), do you need to have effective load-sharing? To implement effective load-sharing, you need to have a separate instance for each distribution/aggregation switch, and split the VLANs appropriately. Then, each distribution layer switch would be the root for their respective instance. As you can see from this scenario, the more distribution layer switches you have, the more configuration you need to perform to utilize the bandwidth on the access layer switches' uplinks.

MSTP Activity 5

This fifth activity illustrates some of the issues with using MSTP versus PVST+. There is one region shown in Figure 8-24, and the region information is correctly configured on all the switches. Assume all switches have the same port cost.

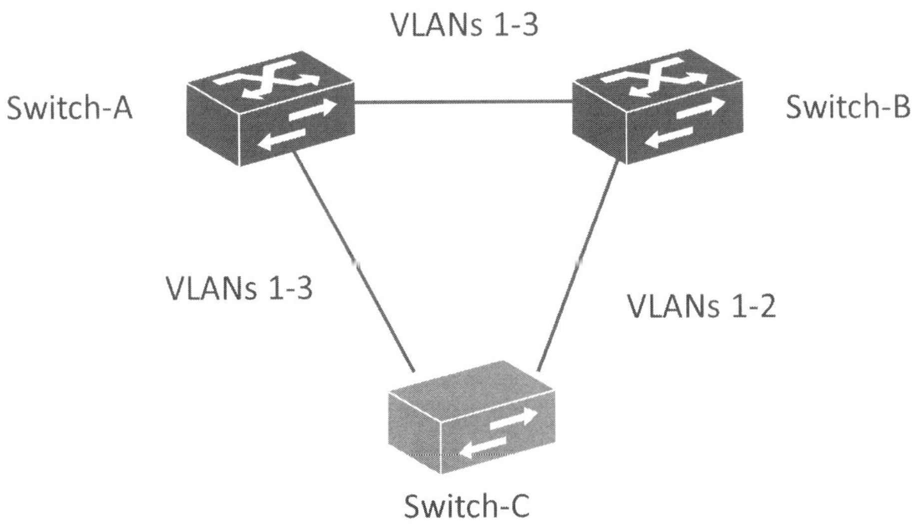

Figure 8-24. MSTP Activity 5

If Switch-A were the root, would this affect traffic for VLAN 3 on Switch-C for MSTP? for PVST? If Switch-A were the root, one of the two ports on the uplink between Switch-C and Switch-B would be placed in a discarding state. In this situation, the Switch-C to Switch-A link would be active, where all three VLANs are allowed on the multi-VLAN link. Therefore, whether this was MSTP or PVST+, traffic would flow correctly.

If Switch-B were the root, would this affect traffic for VLAN 3 on Switch-C for MSTP? For PVST? In this situation, one of the two ports between Switch-A and Switch-C would be placed in a discarding state to remove the Layer 2 loop; therefore, the uplink between Switch-C and Switch-B would be used. If you were using MSTP, for VLANs 1 and 2, this presents no problem, but it breaks traffic flows for VLAN 3 since VLAN 3 does not exist on the multi-VLAN link between the two switches. If you were using PVST+, PVST+ sends BPDUs in VLAN 3 and would know that the only possible link to use would be the Switch-C to Switch-A link, and, therefore, PVST would forward on that link instead. Recall that PVST+ sends out untagged and tagged BPDUs, but MSTP only sends out untagged BPDUs.

Learning Check

The following questions help you measure your understanding of the material presented in this chapter. Read all of the choices carefully, since there may be more than one correct answer. Choose all correct answers for each question.

Questions

1. The root switch in STP is elected using which of the following criteria?
   a. Lowest MAC address
   b. Highest MAC address
   c. Lowest priority
   d. Highest priority
   e. Lowest bridge ID
   f. Highest bridge ID
2. Place the following in the correct order when choosing a root port on a switch:
   a. The port with the lowest priority value
   b. The port with the lowest port number
   c. The path with the lowest accumulated costs
   d. The neighboring switch with the lowest priority
3. Which RSTP port role designates the second-best root port?
   a. Root port
   b. Backup port
   c. Designated port
   d. Alternate port
4. Which MSTP port role designates the second-best designated port?
   a. Root port
   b. Backup port
   c. Designated port
   d. Alternate port
5. How many MSTP instances would you need to implement effective load-sharing if you had three distribution layer switches and three access layer switches?

Answers

1. ☑ **E** is correct. The lowest bridge ID is used to elect the root switch.

   ☒ **A**, **B**, **C**, and **D** are incorrect because the priority and MAC address are used. **F** is incorrect because it is the lowest bridge ID.

2. ☑ **C**, **D**, **A**, and **B** is the correct order in which a root port is chosen on a switch.

3. ☑ **D** is correct. An alternate port is a secondary root port.

   ☒ **A** and **C** are incorrect because these are forwarding ports, not secondary ports. **B** is incorrect because this is a secondary designated port.

4. ☑ **B** is correct. A backup port is a secondary designated port.

   ☒ **A** and **C** are incorrect because these are forwarding ports, not secondary ports. **D** is incorrect because this is a secondary root port.

5. ☑ You would need four STP instances to implement effective load-sharing—three instances for VLAN load-sharing (one instance for each distribution layer switch), plus the IST.

9 MSTP Configuration

EXAM OBJECTIVES

In this chapter, you learn to:

- ✓ Describe and explain basic network security.
- ✓ Describe the concept, benefits, and types of redundancy and to apply redundancy types.
- ✓ Perform installation and configuration of devices.
- ✓ Validate the installed solution.
- ✓ Optimize small-to-medium-sized wireless, switched, and routed network infrastructures for small to mid-sized business (SMB) and commercial customers.
- ✓ Troubleshoot wireless, switched, and routed networks.
- ✓ Apply troubleshooting methodologies.
- ✓ Use general troubleshooting tools.
- ✓ Verify network performance and parameters.

ASSUMED KNOWLEDGE

This chapter assumes that you have read "Chapter 8: Introducing Spanning Tree," and that you have a basic understanding of Spanning Tree Protocols (STPs), especially Multiple STP (MSTP) and its components, including:

- Regions
- Per-instance load sharing
- Internal spanning tree (IST)
- Common spanning tree (CST)

INTRODUCTION

The last chapter introduced you to Spanning Tree Protocols. Now that you have an understanding of STP, RSTP, and MSTP, you will learn how to apply it. You have been exposed to reasons for setting bridge and port priorities and will now apply this knowledge by configuring Layer 2 networks such that all VLAN traffic is forwarded appropriately on an STP-enabled network by implementing load-sharing on the uplinks.

The first part of this chapter focuses on the configuration and verification of MSTP on the HP ProVision and HP Comware switches. The HP switches also support 802.1D, RSTP, and per-VLAN STP (PVST), but these configurations are beyond the scope of this book. The last part of the chapter focuses on STP security measures you can implement on HP switches to provide a more stable STP network.

MSTP Defaults

By default, STP is *disabled* on ProVision and Comware switches. When STP is enabled, Comware and ProVision switches default to MSTP. Also, when STP is enabled, the switch ports of newer ProVision switches are, by default, auto-edge ports. They listen for STP frames for three seconds, and, if they do not receive any, they function as edge ports. (Remember that, in an STP network, ports that connect to endpoints, such as workstations and printers, are called *edge ports.*) If the auto-edge ports do receive STP frames, they can start functioning as STP-enabled ports. You may want to adjust port settings for STP based on how the port is being used. On Comware switches, you must configure ports that connect to endpoints as edge ports. By default, Comware switch ports are not configured as edge ports.

Here is a summary:

- STP is disabled, by default, on both ProVision and Comware switches.
- When STP is enabled:
  - Both ProVision and Comware switches default to MSTP mode.
- ProVision switch ports are automatically configured as auto-edge ports unless they receive STP Bridge Protocol Data Units (BPDU) frames within three seconds.
  - Comware switch ports are configured as non-edge ports, by default.

Note

In the factory default configuration on HP switches (ProVision and Comware), spanning tree operation is off. Also the switch retains its currently configured spanning tree parameter settings when disabled. Therefore, if you disable spanning tree and then, later, re-enable it, the parameter settings will be the same as before spanning tree was disabled. The switch also includes a "Pending" feature that enables you to exchange MSTP configurations with a single command.

Table 9-1 shows the default port costs for the two switches. Notice that, in the default settings, ProVision and Comware use a *different* cost structure! It is highly recommended to match all switches to the same cost structure. For Comware, executing the following command causes it to use the open-standard RSTP/MSTP cost structure, which is what ProVision uses, by default:

```
[Comware] stp pathcost-standard dot1t
```

The Accredited Solutions Expert (ASE) network-level courses discuss issues when cost structures between switches do not match, but that is beyond the scope of this book.

Table 9-1. HP default port costs

Connection Type	ProVision	Comware
10 Gbps	2,000	2
1 Gbps	20,000	20
100 Mbps	200,000	200
10 Mbps	2,000,000	2,000

MSTP Configuration for HP ProVision

You learned from "Chapter 8: Introducing Spanning Tree," that MSTP allows you to create multiple instances of STP and to assign specific VLANs to each instance. As you may recall, each instance converges independently of other instances defined on the network. As a result, each instance can have a different root bridge and can block different redundant links.

A group of switches that collectively defines the same multiple instances is called an *MSTP region.* Within the same region, each switch must have the following configuration attributes in common:

- Configuration name
- Configuration revision number
- Associations between VLANs and MSTP instances

When configuring MSTP on your network, you should be aware that each switch can belong to only one MSTP region. In addition to using BPDUs to exchange bridge IDs and port IDs, switches use BPDUs to communicate their configuration attributes. If a neighbor's configuration attributes match its own, the switch knows that the neighbor is in the same MSTP region.

Note

All HP switches use their MAC addresses as the region name, by default. Therefore, if you enable MSTP on HP switches without defining the region information, the region information between the switches will not match. In this situation, the equivalent of RSTP is running between the switches.

MSTP Instances and the Internal Spanning Tree

When MSTP is enabled, all of the VLANs configured on the switch belong to the IST, which is the default STP instance within the MSTP region. These VLANs are in the IST until they are configured to be part of an MSTP instance.

When you configure an MSTP instance and assign a VLAN to it, the VLAN is moved from the IST to the instance. At least one VLAN must remain in the IST to ensure connectivity in case of a configuration error. Typically, this is the default VLAN. In addition, the MST region's IST enables the MSTP switches to interoperate with RSTP and STP switches. The CST comprises the ISTs of every MSTP region and the single spanning tree (SST) domains that the STP and RSTP switches form. From the point of view of the CST, an MST region appears like a single RSTP switch. The region uses the ID for the IST root bridge for the CST root bridge election. As in RSTP, the switch in the entire CST with the lowest ID is elected as root. If this switch is outside the MST region, the MST region also has a regional root, or *designated bridge*, which provides the lowest path cost to the CST root.

As shown in Figure 9-1, MST region boundary ports are enabled or blocked, just as they would be on a single RSTP switch with multiple connections to a root switch. In this way, the CST creates a single, loop-free path between all of the IST instances and all of the SST domains.

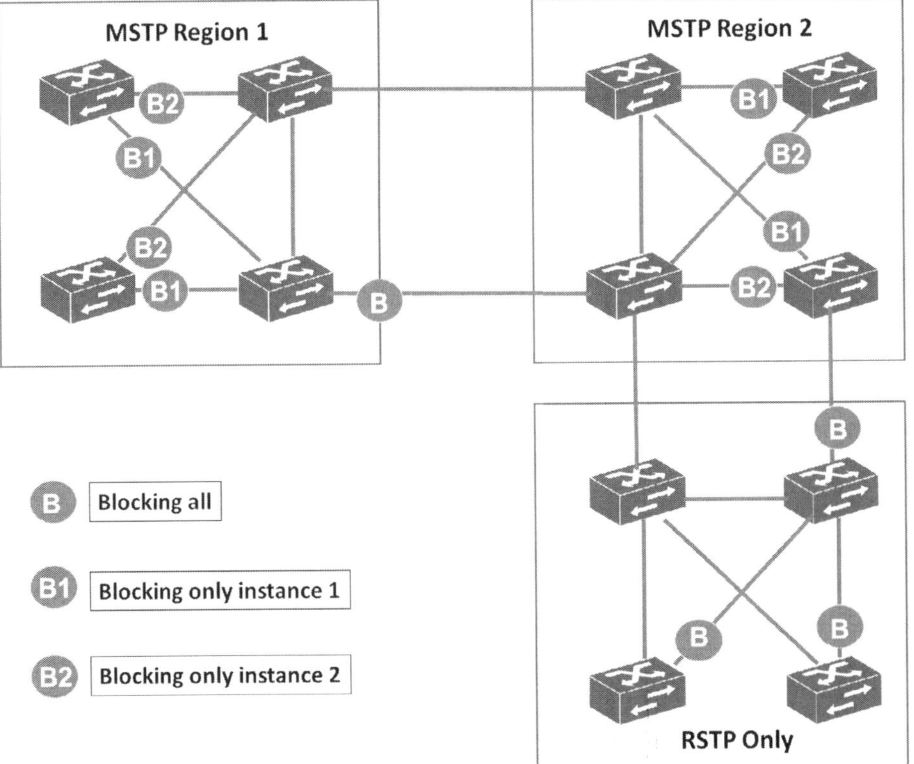

Figure 9-1. MSTP and CST

MSTP Configuration Basics

When configuring MSTP, you complete nearly the same configuration steps for both Comware and ProVision switches (although the actual commands you enter on each switch series differ).

1. Enter the commands for enabling STP as described earlier. By default, both Comware and ProVision switches use MSTP, so you do not have to configure the STP version or mode.
2. Configure MSTP regions parameters on each switch. For example, you must configure parameters, such as region name, and you must assign VLANs to MSTP instances.
3. Configure parameters to select the root port. On ProVision switches, you configure a bridge priority for each instance. On Comware switches, you specify a root (and optionally a secondary root) for each instance.
4. Configure port parameters. As you may recall, when you enable STP, ProVision switch ports are configured as auto-edge ports, by default, unless they receive STP frames within three seconds. By default, Comware switch ports are not configured as edge ports. You need to adjust these settings based on how the port is being used.

Basic ProVision Configuration Commands

You must first enable MSTP, since spanning tree is disabled, by default:

```
ProVision(config)# spanning tree
```

MSTP is the default implementation of STP enabled with the configuration of the above command.

To define an MSTP region for the switch (assign it a name and revision number), use the following commands:

```
ProVision(config)# spanning tree config-name <region-name>

ProVision(config)# spanning tree config-revision <region-number>

To associate user VLANs with MST instances, use following command:

ProVision(config)# spanning tree instance <instance-number>
                   vlan <vid-list>
```

Instance number 0 is for IST—by default, all VLANs belong to this instance. The revision number defaults to 1 if you do not configure the `config-revision parameter`. Normally, you would create two additional instances, 1 and 2, and then associate the VLANs to them accordingly.

Bridge priority may be defined for each MSTP instance to affect which switch becomes the root switch for the instance. Here is the command:

```
ProVision(config)# spanning tree instance <instance-number>
                   priority <multiplier-number>
```

The priority number is a multiplier setting which can have a value from 0 to 15.This setting multiplied by 4,096 generates the actual priority value used by and between the switches. The lower the number, the more likely the switch will become the root, where 0 is the lowest. For example, a configured multiplier number of 2 would result in a priority of 8,192.

By default, Provision ports auto-detect edge/non-edge status. To force a port to be an edge port, use the following command:

```
ProVision(config)# spanning tree <port-or-port-list> admin-edge-port
```

Note

ProVision switches support a little-known feature, similar to Comware's `active region-configuration` command. On ProVision switches, the `spanning-tree pending {config-name | config-revision | instance}` command creates a temporary configuration that is not immediately activated. So you can make all of your MSTP changes once and then execute the `spanning-tree pending apply` command to activate them, which means that MSTP is only recalculated *once* instead of on the change of each individual MSTP parameter. Use the `show spanning-tree pending` command to verify your changes. Use the `spanning-tree pending reset` command to reset the parameters back to the currently running MSTP parameters.

ProVision Configuration Example

To help illustrate the configuration of MSTP on a ProVision switch, examine the network in Figure 9-2, which shows three views of the same network. The top-level switches are the distribution switches, where L_Distrib is the left distribution switch and the R_Distrib is the right distribution switch. To define an MST region identity for the L_Distrib switch, use the following configuration (this is the same configuration applied to the R_Distrib switch):

```
L_Distrib(config)# spanning tree config-name test
L_Distrib(config)# spanning tree config-revision 1
```

Next, associate the user VLANs with the two MST instances:

```
L_Distrib(config)# spanning tree instance 1 vlan 1-999
L_Distrib(config)# spanning tree instance 2 vlan 1000-1999
```

The R_Distrib switch has the same configuration for the VLANs:

```
R_Distrib(config)# spanning tree config-name test
R_Distrib(config)# spanning tree config-revision 1
R_Distrib(config)# spanning tree instance 1 vlan 1-999
R_Distrib(config)# spanning tree instance 2 vlan 1000-1999
```

Now, to load-share the instances so that the access layer switches use the L_Distrib switch for VLANs 1–999 and the R_Distrib switch for VLANs 1,000–1,999, you need to set the bridge priorities appropriately, where the bridge priority can be defined for each MSTP instance.

Here is the configuration for the L_Distrib switch, where it is the root for instance 1 and the backup root for instance 2:

```
L_Distrib(config)# spanning tree instance 1 priority 1
L_Distrib(config)# spanning tree instance 2 priority 2
```

Here is the configuration for the R_Distrib switch, where the roles are reversed for the two instances:

```
R_Distrib(config)# spanning tree instance 2 priority 1
R_Distrib(config)# spanning tree instance 1 priority 2
```

The above configuration has accomplished the task of load-sharing the VLANs on the uplinks from the access layer switches to the distribution layer switches, where half of the VLANs are using the uplink to the L_Distrib switch and the other half are using the uplink to the R_Distrib switch.

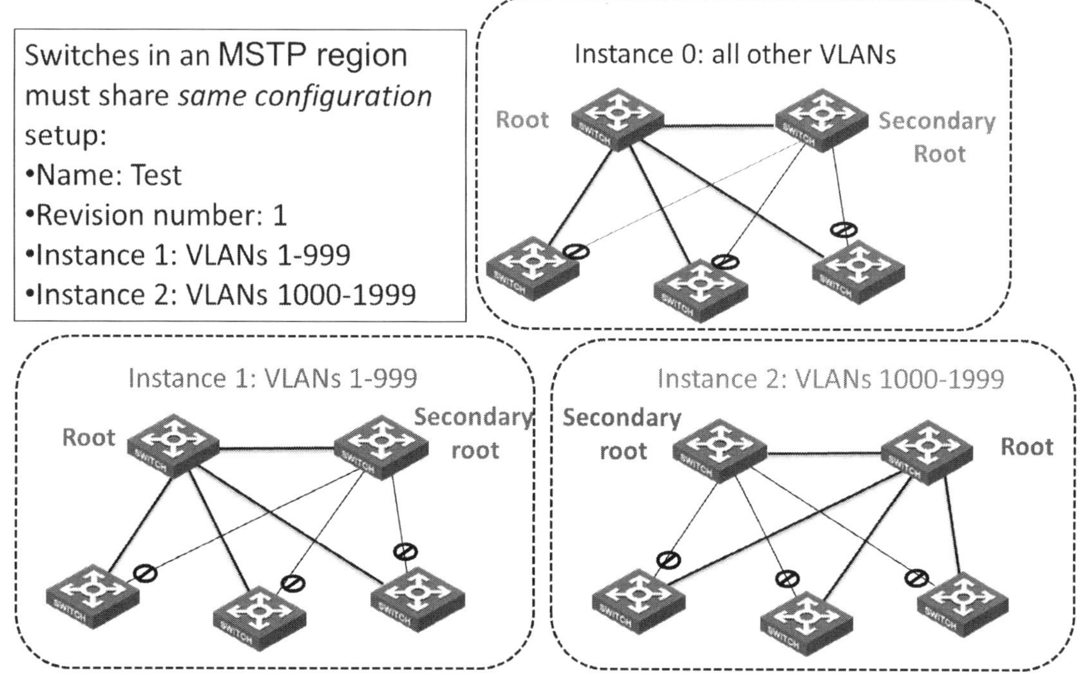

Figure 9-2. ProVision MSTP configuration example

ProVision Verification

To verify the MSTP region configuration, use the `show spanning-tree mst-config` command. Here is an example:

```
ProVision(config)# show spanning-tree mst-config
 MST Configuration Identifier Information
  MST Configuration Name : hp
  MST Configuration Revision : 1
  MST Configuration Digest : 0xE821CCEE7501115289B37C79A72E07C9
  IST Mapped VLANs : 1-9,11-19,21-29,31-39,41-4094
  Instance ID Mapped VLANs
  ----------- -------------------------------------------------
  1           10,30
  2           20,40
```

In this example, only four VLANs are mapped to instance 1 and 2 (10 and 30, and 20 and 40, respectively); all other VLANs are in the IST.

After you have set up and tuned STP/RSTP/MSTP, use the `show spanning tree` command to troubleshoot problems and to create a network map with the following information:

- Blocked and forwarding ports
- Root and designated ports
- Root priorities
- Port costs

Use the above information, and look for reasons why the actual topology might differ from the expected topology.

Here is an example where the switch is the root switch:

```
ProVision# show spanning-tree
Multiple spanning tree (MST) Information
  STP Enabled   : Yes
  Force Version : MSTP-operation
  IST Mapped VLANs : 1-4094
  Switch MAC Address : 0017a4-742700
  Switch Priority    : 4096
```

```
  Max Age   : 20
  Max Hops : 20
  Forward Delay : 15
  Topology Change Count  : 13
  Time Since Last Change : 2 mins
  CST Root MAC Address : 0017a4-742700
  CST Root Priority    : 4096
  CST Root Path Cost   : 0
  CST Root Port        : This switch is root
 Port Type      Cost      Priority State      : Designated Bridge
 ---- --------- --------- -------- ---------- + -----------------
 Trk1   100/1000T 20000     128      Forwarding : 0017a4-742700
 Trk2   100/1000T 20000     128      Forwarding : 0017a4-742700
```

Here is an example where the switch is not the root switch:

```
ProVision# show spanning tree
<-output omitted->
  IST Mapped VLANs : 1-4094
  Switch MAC Address : 0019bb-aea640
  Switch Priority    : 8192
  Max Age   : 20
  Max Hops : 20
  Forward Delay : 15
  Topology Change Count  : 10
  Time Since Last Change : 8 mins
  CST Root MAC Address : 0017a4-742700
  CST Root Priority    : 4096
  CST Root Path Cost   : 20000
  CST Root Port        : Trk1
  <-output omitted->
  Port Type      Cost      Priority State      : Designated Bridge
 ---- --------- --------- -------- ---------- + -----------------
```

```
23    100/1000T 20000     128       Blocking   : 001635-b65040
24    100/1000T 20000     128       Forwarding : 0019bb-aea640
Trk1  100/1000T 20000     128       Forwarding : 0017a4-742700
```

Notice that the switch's MAC address and the CST Root MAC address are different. Also notice that port 23 is blocking. These are two things to look for to determine whether a switch is or is not the root switch. On a root switch, the MAC addresses would be the same and none of the ports would be in a blocking state.

MSTP Configuration for HP Comware

Now that you know how to configure MSTP on ProVision switches, read this section to examine the same process on HP Comware switches. The syntax of the commands is different, but the tasks you perform are the same.

Basic Comware Configuration Commands

Here are the basic commands to enable and configure MSTP on the Comware switches:

```
[Comware] stp enable
[Comware] stp region-configuration
[Comware-mst-region] region-name <name>
[Comware-mst-region] revision-level <number>
[Comware-mst-region] instance <instance-id> vlan <vlan-list>
[Comware-mst-region] check region-configuration
[Comware-mst-region] active region-configuration
```

The `stp enable` command enables STP on the switch, defaulting to MSTP mode. The `stp region-configuration` command enters the subview to configure the MSTP parameters for the region. You must assign the region a name (which is case-sensitive), a revision number, and the mappings of VLANs to the MSTP instances. If you omit the region name, it defaults to the MAC address of the switch. If you omit the revision number, it defaults to 0. By default, there is one instance (instance 0), and all VLANs are associated with this instance. The `check region-configuration` command displays the MST region configurations that are not yet activated on the switch.

The configuration of MST region–related parameters, especially the VLAN-to-instance mapping table, causes MSTP to launch a new spanning tree calculation process, which may result in network topology instability. To reduce the possibility of topology instability caused by configuration, MSTP will not immediately launch a new spanning tree calculation process when processing MST region–related configurations. Instead, such configurations take effect only after you activate the

MST region–related parameters using the `active region-configuration` command or when you enable MSTP using the `stp enable` command (in a case where MSTP is not enabled).

Note

Any time that you make changes to the MSTP region configuration, they are not activated in the running configuration until you execute the `active region-configuration` command.

MSTP Root Bridge Selection

MSTP, by default, determines the root bridge of a spanning tree instance through the normal MSTP calculation. Alternatively, you can specify the current device as the root bridge or a secondary root bridge, using the commands available in Comware. Here are some items you need to be aware of in selecting the root bridge for an instance or instances:

- A device has independent roles in different MSTIs. It can act as the root bridge or a secondary root bridge of one MSTI while being the root bridge or a secondary root bridge of another MSTI. However, the same device cannot be the root bridge *and* be a secondary root bridge in the same MSTI at the same time.
- There is only one root bridge in a spanning tree instance. If two or more devices have been designated to be root bridges of the same spanning tree instance, MSTP selects the device with the lowest MAC address as the root bridge.
- When the root bridge of an instance fails or is shut down, a secondary root bridge takes over the role of the primary root bridge. If you have specified multiple secondary root bridges for an instance (with the same priority), when the root bridge fails, MSTP selects the secondary root bridge with the lowest MAC address as the new root bridge.

To affect which switch is the primary or secondary root bridge for an instance, use the following global system view command on the Comware switches:

```
[Comware] stp instance <instance-id> root {primary | secondary}
```

This command assigns the priority of 0 or 4,096, depending on whether you used the primary or secondary parameters, respectively.

You can also use the following command to assign a specific priority:

```
[Comware] stp [instance <instance-id>] priority <priority>
```

If you do not specify an instance, it defaults to 0.

Note

Without configuring any priorities for any instances, the priorities for all of the instances default to 32,768.

Configuring Ports as Edge Ports

If a port directly connects to a non-bridge/switch device, this port is regarded as an edge port. However, this is not the default—all of the ports on the Comware switches default to non-edge and participate in STP. If you define a port as an edge port, when a network topology change occurs, an edge port will not cause a temporary loop. Because a device does not know whether a port is directly connected to a non-bridge/switch device, you need to manually configure the port to be an edge port. After that, this port can transition rapidly from the blocked state to the forwarding state, without delay.

Any physical, port group, or bridge aggregation (BAGG) interface can be configured as an edge port. For physical or BAGG interfaces, use the following command:

```
[Comware] interface <interface-id>
[Comware-<interface-id> stp edged-port enable
```

Comware Configuration Example

The configurations shown below are based on the network topology we saw in Figure 9-2, which was also used in the ProVision example configuration. Here is the configuration performed on *both* distribution layer switches:

```
[Distrib] stp enable
[Distrib] stp region-configuration
[Distrib-mst-region] region-name test
[Distrib-mst-region] revision-level 1
[Distrib-mst-region] instance 1 vlan 1-999
[Distrib-mst-region] instance 2 vlan 1000-1999
[Distrib-mst-region] active region-configuration
```

Here is the configuration configured on the left distribution switch to implement load-sharing:

```
L_Distrib(config)# spanning tree instance 0 priority 1
L_Distrib(config)# spanning tree instance 1 priority 1
L_Distrib(config)# spanning tree instance 2 priority 2
```

Here is the configuration configured on the right distribution switch to implement load-sharing:

```
[L_Distrib] stp instance 0 priority 4096
[L_Distrib] stp instance 1 priority 4096
[L_Distrib] stp instance 2 priority 8192
```

Comware Verification

To verify the MSTP region configuration, use the `display stp region-configuration` command. The network shown in Figure 9-2 is used when covering this and future `display` commands in this section. Here is an example of any of the switches from Figure 9-2:

```
[Comware] display stp region-configuration
 Oper configuration
   Format selector    :0
   Region name        :test
   Revision level     :1

   Instance   Vlans Mapped
      0       2000 to 4094
      1       1 to 999
      2       1000 to 1999
```

In the above configuration, the region name is "test," the revision number is "1," and there are three instances (0, 1, and 2) with VLANs mapped to each.

To view the operation on STP in an instance, use the `display stp instance` command. If you do not qualify the command with an instance, all instances are displayed. Here is an example of the top-left switch (L_Distrib in the following configuration) in Figure 9-2:

```
[L_Distrib] display stp instance 1
-------[MSTI 1 Global Info]-------
MSTI Bridge ID       :0.001c-c5bc-2b11
MSTI RegRoot/IRPC    :0.001c-c5bc-2b11 / 0
MSTI RootPortId      :0.0
MSTI Root Type       :PRIMARY root
Master Bridge        :0.001c-c5bc-2b11
Cost to Master       :0
TC received          :4
[L_Distrib] display stp instance 2
-------[MSTI 2 Global Info]-------
```

```
MSTI Bridge ID        :4096.001c-c4bc-2bcc
MSTI RegRoot/IRPC     :4096.001c-c4bc-2bcc / 0
MSTI RootPortId       :0.2
MSTI Root Type        :SECONDARY root
Master Bridge         :0.001c-c5bc-2b11
Cost to Master        :20000
TC received           :0
```

In the above example, L_Distrib is the root for instance 1 (notice that the MSTI bridge ID has a priority of 0, followed by the MAC address of the switch). However, in instance 2, its bridge ID is 4096.001c-c4bc-2bcc, with a priority of 4,096, and it is the secondary (backup) root bridge.

To display the STP status of the ports of a switch (which state the port is in), use the `display stp brief` command. Here is an example of an access layer switch from any of the access layer switches shown in the bottom of Figure 9-2:

```
[Access] display stp brief
 MSTID      Port                       Role  STP State     Protection
   0        GigabitEthernet1/0/1       ROOT  FORWARDING    NONE
   0        GigabitEthernet1/0/2       ALTE  DISCARDING    NONE
   1        GigabitEthernet1/0/1       ROOT  FORWARDING    NONE
   1        GigabitEthernet1/0/2       ALTE  DISCARDING    NONE
   2        GigabitEthernet1/0/1       ALTE  DISCARDING    NONE
   2        GigabitEthernet1/0/2       ROOT  FORWARDING    NONE
```

In this example, G1/0/1 is connected to L_Distrib and G1/0/2 is connected to R_Distrib. Notice the load-sharing which occurs in the three instances: G1/0/1 is in a forwarding state for instances 0 and 1, and G1/0/2 is in a forwarding state for instance 2.

Note

If this were the root switch, all active ports would be marked as designated ports and would be in a forwarding state.

STP Protection Features

The ProVision and Comware switches support additional STP protection features. Some of these features ensure that access layer switches do not become root bridges or that a rogue switch is not accidentally plugged in to the network and creates inadvertent Layer 2 loops. This section briefly covers three STP security features:

- Root guard
- BPDU guard
- Loop guard (Comware) and loop protection (ProVision)

Figure 9-3 shows where these features are typically configured.

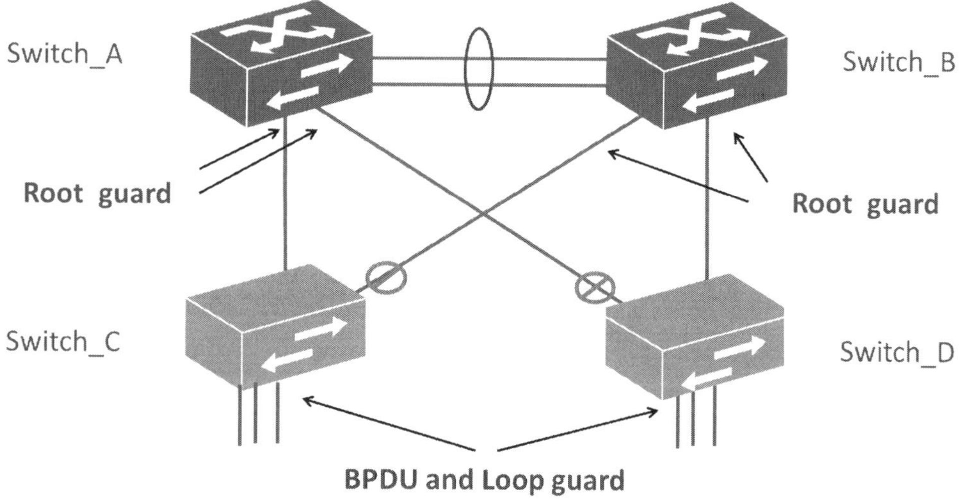

Figure 9-3. Enhanced STP features and where they are configured

Note

The terms *guard* and *protection* are interchangeable. Typically, you will see the term "guard" used with the H ProVision switches and "protection" with the Comware switches. Both terms are used in the documentation for both sets of switches. These features are not part of a standard, but most vendors in the industry implement very similar, if not the same, features.

Root Protection/Root Guard

The root bridge and secondary root bridge of a spanning tree should be located in the same MST region. Especially for the common and internal spanning tree (CIST), the root bridge and secondary root bridge are generally put in a high-bandwidth core region during network design. However, due to possible configuration errors or malicious attacks in the network, the legal root bridge may receive a configuration BPDU with a lower priority value. In this case, the current legal root bridge will be superseded by another device, causing an undesired change of the network topology. Therefore, the traffic that should go over high-speed links is switched to low-speed links, resulting in network congestion.

To prevent this situation from happening, MSTP provides the root guard function. If the root guard function is enabled on a port of a root bridge, this port will keep playing the role of designated port on all MSTIs. After this port receives a configuration BPDU with a lower priority value from an MSTI, it immediately sets that port to the listening state in the MSTI without forwarding the packet (this is equivalent to disconnecting the link connected with this port in the MSTI). If the port receives no BPDUs with a higher priority within twice the forwarding delay, it reverts to its original state. Figure 9-4 illustrates this process.

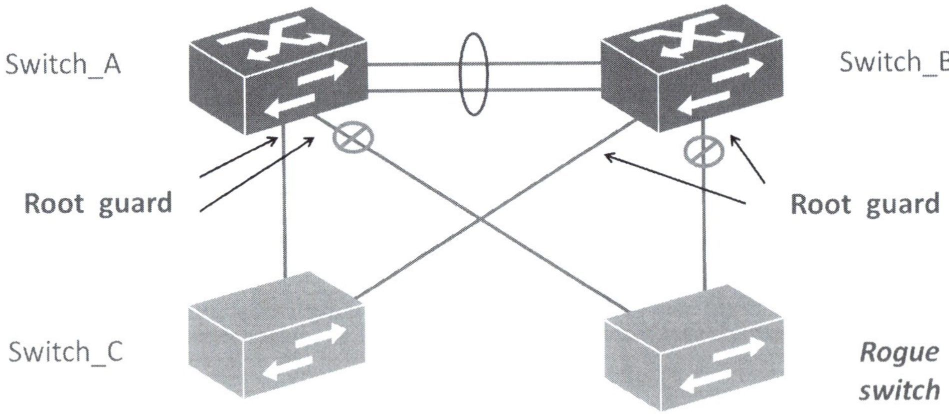

Figure 9-4. Root protection/root guard feature

BPDU Protection/Root Guard

For access layer devices, the access ports generally connect directly with user terminals (such as PCs) or file servers. In this case, the access ports are configured as edge ports to allow rapid transition when changes occur in spanning tree. When these ports receive configuration BPDUs, the system automatically sets these ports as non-edge ports and starts a new spanning tree calculation process. This causes a change of network topology. Under normal conditions, these ports should not receive configuration BPDUs. However, if someone creates BPDUs maliciously to attack the devices or if a rogue switch is connected to a user (edge port), the network becomes unstable.

MSTP provides the BPDU guard function to protect the system against such attacks (see Figure 9-5). With the BPDU guard function enabled on the devices, when edge ports receive configuration BPDUs, MSTP closes these ports and generates a log message that these ports have been closed by MSTP. The closed ports are reactivated by the device after a detection interval.

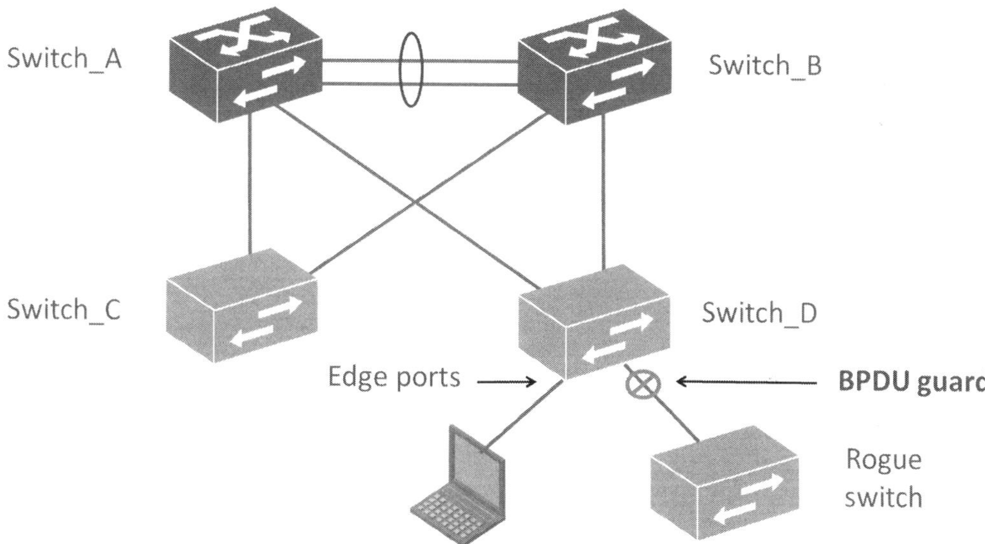

Figure 9-5. BPDU protection/root guard feature

Loop Protection/Loop Guard

By continuing to receive BPDUs from the upstream device, a device can maintain the state of the root port and blocked ports. However, due to link congestion or unidirectional link failures, these ports may fail to receive BPDUs from the upstream devices. In this case, the device reselects the port roles: the ports in the forwarding state that failed to receive upstream BPDUs become designated ports, and the blocked ports transition to the forwarding state, resulting in loops in the switched network. The loop guard function can suppress the occurrence of such loops (see Figure 9-6).

The initial state of a loop guard–enabled port is discarding in every MSTI. When the port receives BPDUs, its state transitions normally; otherwise, it stays in the discarding state, avoiding the occurrence of loops.

Note

Among loop guard, root guard, and edge port settings, only one function (whichever is configured as the first) can take effect on a port at one time.

Warning
The loop guard feature on Comware and the loop protection feature on HP ProVision are not compatible with each other—they do not understand each other's messages.

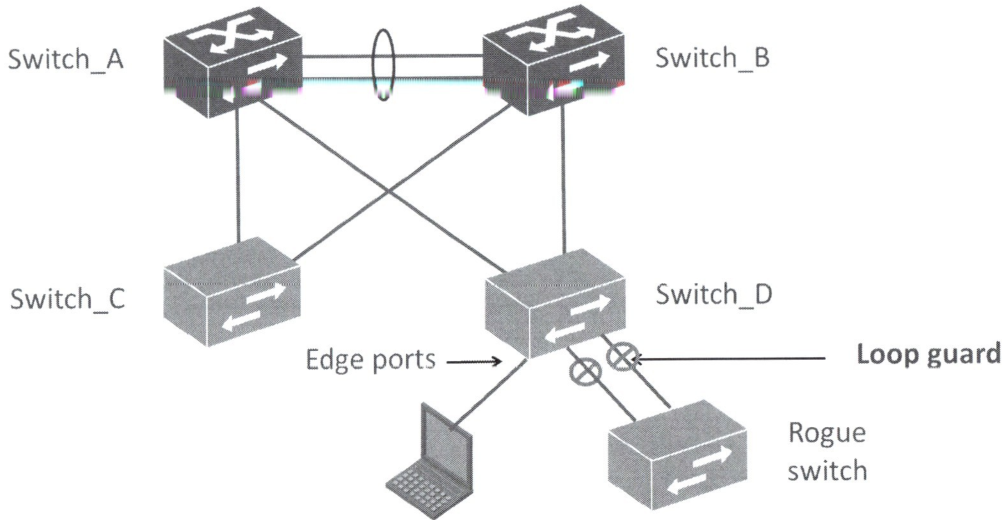

Figure 9-6. Loop protection/loop guard feature

STP Security Configuration for ProVision

The root guard feature on ProVision switches is typically configured on distribution layer switches (not access layer switches) on their downlink connections to the access switches. Root guard is enabled on interfaces:

```
ProVision(config)# spanning-tree <port-or-port-list> root-guard
```

BPDU guard is typically enabled on access layer switches on edge ports:

```
ProVision(config)# spanning-tree <port-or-port-list> bpdu-protection
```

When there is a violation, the port is disabled for a period of time, which you can tune:

```
ProVision(config)# spanning-tree bpdu-protection-timeout <seconds>
```

Loop protection can be enabled on any interface of a ProVision switch: edge and non-edge ports. However, it is typically enabled on edge ports of access layer switches:

```
ProVision(config)# loop-protect <port-or-port-list>
                   receiver-action send-disable
```

Optionally, you can change the disable timer when a violation occurs:

```
ProVision(config)# loop-protect disable-timer <seconds>
```

STP Security Configuration for Comware

Root guard is configured on the distribution/aggregation layer switches to ensure that no switch on a downlink connection becomes the root:

```
[Comware] interface <interface-id>
[Comware-<interface-id>] stp root-protection
```

Note that the `stp root-protection` command is configured on an interface-by-interface basis on all the of links connected to the access layer switches.

BPDU guard is globally enabled in the system view with the following command:

```
[Comware] stp bpdu-protection
```

This command enables the BPDU guard feature on all ports that are configured as edge ports.

To prevent loops created by cabling and other types of physical layer errors on edge ports, implement the loop guard feature with the following configuration:

```
[Comware] interface <interface-id>
[Comware-<interface-id>] stp loop-protection
```

Note

Among loop guard, root guard, and edge port settings, only one function (whichever is configured as the first) can take effect on a port at one time.

Learning Check

The following questions help you measure your understanding of the material presented in this chapter. Read all of the choices carefully, since there may be more than one correct answer. Choose all correct answers for each question.

Questions

1. Which of the following is the default STP configuration on HP switches?
   a. Spanning tree is disabled.
   b. 802.1D is enabled.
   c. RSTP is enabled.
   d. MSTP is enabled.
2. What is the Comware command that enables the switch to use the 802.1t port cost structure for STP?
3. What is the ProVision command to enable MSTP?
4. What is the Comware command that places any MSTP changes you make into immediate effect?
5. You have configured the following command on a ProVision switch: `spanning-tree instance 1 priority 2`. What is the resulting priority of the switch for the instance?
6. Which STP security feature is typically configured on edge ports and disables a port if a connected switch is detected?

Answers

1. ☑ **A** is correct. STP is disabled on both the ProVision and Comware switches, by default.
   ☒ **B**, **C**, and **D** are incorrect because STP is *disabled*, by default.

2. ☑ `stp pathcost-standard dot1t` is the Comware command that enables the switch to use the 802.1t port cost structure for STP.

3. ☑ `spanning tree` is the ProVision command to enable MSTP.

4. ☑ `active region-configuration` is the Comware command that places any MSTP changes you make into immediate effect.

5. ☑ 8,192 is the resulting priority of the ProVision switch after you configure the `spanning-tree instance 1 priority 2` command.

6. ☑ BPDU Guard/Protection is the STP security feature which is typically configured on edge ports and disables a port if a connected switch is detected.

10 Link Aggregation

EXAM OBJECTIVES

In this chapter, you learn to:

- ✓ Describe and apply the most common Ethernet concepts.
- ✓ Describe the concepts, benefits, and types of redundancy, and apply redundancy types.
- ✓ Describe and explain link aggregation.
- ✓ Perform installation and configuration of devices.
- ✓ Validate the installed solution.
- ✓ Optimize small-to-medium-sized wireless, switches, and routed network infrastructures.
- ✓ Apply troubleshooting methodology.
- ✓ Use general troubleshooting tools.
- ✓ Verify network performance parameters.

ASSUMED KNOWLEDGE

This chapter assumes that you are familiar with the following topics:

- Implementation and benefits of VLANs
- Operation and limitations of Multiple Spanning Tree Protocol (MSTP)
- Operation and limitations of per-VLAN Spanning Tree Plus (PVST+)

If you are not familiar with these topics, please re-read "Chapter 6: VLANs" and "Chapter 8: Introducing Spanning Tree."

INTRODUCTION

This chapter introduces the topic of *link aggregation*—taking multiple physical links between devices and treating them as one logical link. Link aggregation was introduced to deal with some of the limitations and issues of Spanning Tree Protocols.

This chapter focuses on the following topics:

- Reviewing problems with STP and load-sharing with STP
- Introducing link aggregation
- Comparing and contrasting the different link aggregation types
- Configuring and verifying link aggregation on HP ProVision and HP Comware switches

Problems with STP and Load-Sharing

It is common to need higher bandwidth speeds for certain kinds of connections in your network, such as connections from the access layer to the distribution layer, between distribution layer switches, between distribution and core layer switches, and between certain servers or routers and their connected switches. For example, in Figure 10-1, you can see dual Layer 2 connections between the two switches. The problem with this type of design, however, is that it creates a Layer 2 loop. And, with 802.1D or Rapid Spanning Tree Protocol (RSTP) running, the Spanning Tree Protocol ensures that only one path is active between two devices, limiting you to the bandwidth of one of possibly multiple connections.

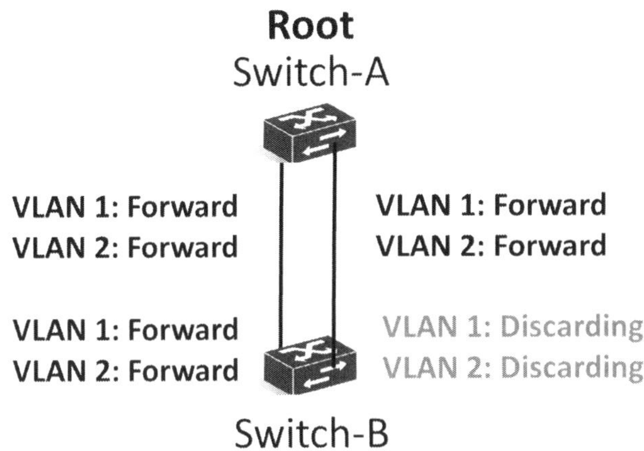

Figure 10-1. Problems with 802.1D (pre-2004) and RSTP

In addition to this problem, in a more complex network, Spanning Tree Protocols, by default, do not guarantee an optimal topology, as was discussed in the previous chapter. Protocols like MSTP or PVST+ can be used to help optimize the topology.

Problems with PVST+ and MSTP

Protocols like MSTP and PVST+ solve one of the problems that 802.1D and RSTP have in a network: they allow you to use all the links in your network but ensure that no loops exist for a particular VLAN or VLANs. Figure 10-2 illustrates this solution, where one link is forwarding for VLAN 1 and the other is blocking; the reverse is true for the other redundant link. However, these two protocols perform a process called *load-sharing*—not *load-balancing*. With load-sharing, traffic for the two VLANs is traversing the two links; however, it is almost guaranteed to be not balanced. In other words, 50 percent of the traffic is not going down each link. So, if VLAN 1 has an excessive amount of traffic and VLAN 2 has very little traffic, this could impact the traffic on the two links. In addition, traffic utilization is not constant: it changes on a minute-by-minute, hour-by-hour, and day-by-day basis. So what is true right now for VLAN 1's utilization on its currently active link could be different in five minutes.

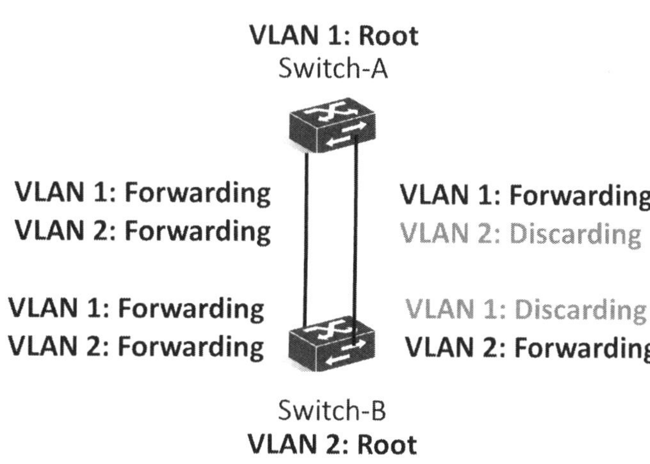

Figure 10-2. Problems with PVST+ and MSTP

And, as you learned from the previous chapter, configuring and tuning protocols like MSTP is not a simple process.

PVST+ and MSTP Problem Activity

Examine the topology in Figure 10-2, and answer the following questions:

- Assume that the switches are running MSTP in a single region, where VLAN 1 is in instance 1 and VLAN 2 is in instance 2. Answer the following questions for MSTP and PVST+:
  - How many root switches are there? For MSTP, there are three root switches: one for IST, one for instance 1, and one for instance 2. For PVST+, there are two root switches.
  - How many sets of Bridge Protocol Data Units (BPDUs) are there? For MSTP, there is one set of BPDUs. For PVST+, there is one set of BPDUs per VLAN, so there are two sets.
  - How many STP topologies are there? For MSTP, there are three topologies: IST, instance 1, and instance 2. For PVST+, there are two topologies: one per VLAN.
- With either MSTP or PVST+, given the topology in Figure 10-2 and the forwarding and discarding states of the ports, if someone in VLAN 1 or 2 generates a broadcast or multicast, which links between the switches would be affected? Even though the secondary link is used, it is not used effectively: if a broadcast or multicast occurs in either VLAN, like VLAN 1, it is transported across both switch-to-switch links. However, on the second link, it would be dropped on the ingress switch. Therefore, the more broadcasts and multicasts that exist, the less throughput you have on the second link.
- What would happen if you changed the port priorities on Switch-A so that VLAN 2 is discarding on the left-side port? You would still have the same problem as previously discussed.
- Is the solution using either MSTP or PVST+ an effective load-sharing solution, and why or why not? Usually not, since traffic patterns in the two VLANs are probably not constant but are constantly fluctuating. And, if there is a lot of multicast and/or broadcast traffic, it is affecting both links.

Link Aggregation Overview

Link aggregation is a Layer 2 solution that allows you to aggregate multiple Layer 2 Ethernet-based connections between directly connected devices, as shown in Figure 10-3. Basically, an aggregated link bundles together multiple Ethernet ports between devices, providing what appears to be single logical interface. From STP's perspective, it sees the aggregated link as a single logical connection between the connected devices, which means that you can actually use all of the individual connections, simultaneously, in the channel you have created.

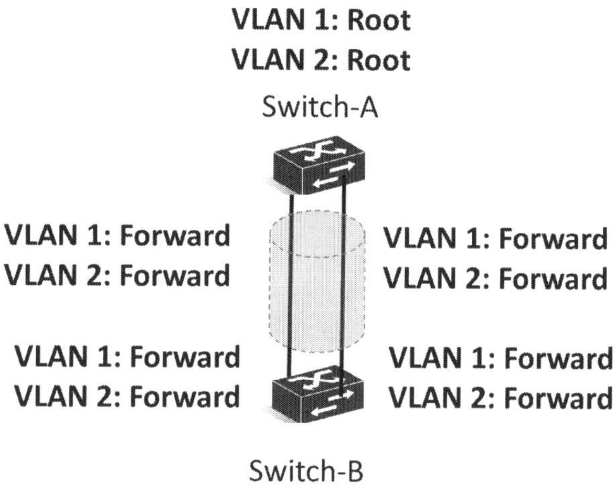

VLAN 1: Root
VLAN 2: Root
Switch-A

VLAN 1: Forward
VLAN 2: Forward

VLAN 1: Forward
VLAN 2: Forward

VLAN 1: Forward
VLAN 2: Forward

VLAN 1: Forward
VLAN 2: Forward

Switch-B

Figure 10-3. Link aggregation as a solution

Aggregated links provide these advantages:

- **Redundancy**—If one connection in the channel fails, you can use other connections in the aggregated link.
- **More bandwidth**—Each connection can be used simultaneously to send Ethernet frames.
- **Simplified management and configuration**—Configuration is done on the logical interface—not on each individual connection in the channel.
- **Better load-sharing**—Load-sharing is typically done based on MAC addresses—source, destination, or a hash of the source and destination MAC address—providing much better load-sharing than does PVST+ or MSTP.

Note

Link aggregation assumes that the aggregated link is between two devices. Therefore, if an access switch has two uplinks to two different distribution layer switches, link aggregation cannot be employed, by default. (The exception to this is the proprietary Distributed Trunking feature on ProVision switches, discussed in a later chapter.) You will see, in "Chapter 13: HP Intelligent Resilient Framework," how Comware switches can get around this issue by using the Intelligent Resilient Framework (IRF) technology. The two physical switches can appear as one logical switch to another device connecting to them. Comware switches refer to this as *distributed link aggregation*.

Terms and Devices

Different vendors use different terms to describe link aggregation, or aggregated links. For example, Cisco refers to link aggregation connections as *EtherChannels* or *port channels*. With HP, two terms are used, depending on which product set you are dealing with. ProVision switches use the term *trunking* or *port trunking* to describe an aggregated link. Remember from "Chapter 6: VLANS," that Comware also uses the term *trunk*, but a Comware trunk refers to a port transporting multiple tagged VLAN frames.

Comware devices use the terms *bridge aggregation* or *route aggregation* when referring to link aggregation. Bridge aggregation refers to aggregating multiple Layer 2 links, which is often done between most networking devices. These are commonly called *BAGG* (for **b**ridge **agg**regation) interfaces on Comware devices. Route aggregation is done on routed links between devices. Typically this is done on Comware routers, but you can turn a Comware switch interface into a routed link (which is beyond the scope of this book) and perform link aggregation on the routed interfaces. These are usually called *RAGG* (for **r**oute **agg**regation) interfaces on Comware routed links.

Note

This book uses the generic terms of "link aggregation" or "aggregated link" when referring to ProVision trunking or Comware bridge/route aggregation.

Link aggregation is supported on many different types of devices. Obviously, many network devices support this feature, like switches, routers, and firewalls, among others. However, some PC and most server-based network interface cards (NICs) also support this technology. On PCs or servers, this feature is commonly referred to as *NIC teaming*. Originally, NIC teaming referred to an active and a standby link between a server and the network (typically two different switches). However, most NIC teaming solutions today support link aggregation, as well.

Interface Requirements

Interfaces in an aggregated link must typically be configured identically, according to the IEEE 802.1AX (formerly 802.3ad) standard on link aggregation: speed, duplexing, and VLAN settings (in the same VLAN, if they are access ports, or the same VLAN trunk/tagging properties) must be the same. The implementation and protocol chosen to establish the connection will effect what actually has to match between the two devices (to be discussed in more depth later in the chapter).

When setting up an aggregated link, you can use up to eight interfaces bundled together, depending on the switch model:

- Up to eight active Fast Ethernet connections, providing up to 800 Mbps
- Up to eight active Gigabit Ethernet connections, providing up to 8 Gbps
- Up to eight active 10 Gigabit Ethernet connections, providing up to 80 Gbps

As faster links become available in the market, like 100 Gbps links, you will also be able to aggregate these. The total number of aggregate link connections which may be configured is dependent on the particular switch model and OS version.

Load-Sharing Options

How load-sharing is performed depends on the link aggregation protocol used. The different protocols, like the Link Aggregation Control Protocol (LACP) and distributed trunking, are discussed later in the chapter. The most common one, however, is the LACP. This is the preferred approach when connecting different switches together, since it guarantees that both sides of the link use the same load-sharing algorithm.

As to what is used to perform the load-sharing, most networking devices will use the MAC addresses seen in the Ethernet frames. However, some vendor products, like the ProVision and Comware devices, provide many more options, like IP addresses and ports. Table 10-1 is a comparison of the load-sharing algorithms supported by ProVision and Comware.

Table 10.1. Load-sharing algorithms supported by HP

Option	ProVision	Comware
Source MAC address only	No	Yes
Destination MAC address only	No	Yes
Source and destination MAC address (default)	Yes	Yes
Source IP address only	No	Yes
Destination IP address only	No	Yes
Source and destination IP address	Yes	Yes
Source IP address and source port number	Yes	Yes
Destination IP address and destination port number	Yes	Yes

Note

Both ProVision and Comware, by default, use a hash of the source and destination MAC addresses when doing load-balancing for link aggregation. Also, the load-sharing process is local to a switch. In other words, you can implement different load-sharing solutions on the two devices that are connected together. In addition, even when doing the same type of load-sharing on two connected devices, traffic that travels across one link is not guaranteed to return on that link—it depends on the information that is being hashed, in addition to the load-sharing algorithm implemented on the local switch.

LACP Load-Sharing

The Link Aggregation Control Protocol provides guidelines for how conversations are managed on an aggregated link. A *conversation* is a one-way communication between a source device and a destination device. For example, when a workstation sends an Ethernet frame to a server, a conversation begins. All subsequent frames from the same workstation to the same server are part of that conversation.

According to the IEEE 802.1AX standard for LACP, an LACP-enabled device should transmit all of the frames in a given conversation over the same physical link within the aggregated link, to avoid out-of-order packet delivery. If it is necessary to move a conversation (because a physical link is unavailable, for example), the LACP-enabled device must ensure that all frames already transmitted in that conversation have been successfully received by the destination device.

Link Distribution Process

As was just discussed, the HP switches define conversations according to source MAC address and destination MAC address, by default. For example, when a workstation sends a frame to a server, this frame and all subsequent frames sent from the workstation to the server constitute a conversation. The server's response to the workstation is a different conversation because the source and destination addresses are different.

Each switch builds a table of conversations and assigns each conversation to a link. Any traffic in the same conversation is forwarded over the same link. (Note that this would mean that all of an endpoint's routed traffic is forwarded over the same link because it is all destined to the same MAC address.) When traffic for a new conversation arrives, that conversation can be assigned to the same link or to another link. Neither switch is aware of the other switch's table and cannot take this into account when making link assignments. Therefore, the return traffic for a conversation might be sent over a different link.

Note

ProVision switches define conversations for routed traffic a bit differently. They use the last five bits of the source IP address and of the destination IP address to define the conversation.

Load Distribution with Multiple Conversations

Most users presume that they will see precisely even traffic distribution across all physical links. In a real-world network, some conversations consume more bandwidth than others. Even a distribution where all physical links are carrying precisely the same number of conversations will sometimes report significant differences in traffic flow across the links. In a test environment with a relatively small number of source/destination pairs, the differences in traffic distribution can be quite pronounced. In a real-world network, larger numbers of conversations each carrying variable bandwidth tend to result in port utilizations approaching, but never reaching, a theoretically even distribution.

Layer 2 load-sharing must occur at a high rate of speed, utilizing comparatively simple algorithms. If we utilized more complicated algorithms to balance the load (without risking out-of-order packet delivery), there would be so much latency due to protocol overhead that the speed and bandwidth benefits of aggregation would be lost. Operation at less than theoretically "perfect" distribution across physical links is not an error, flaw, or accident but is, instead, a consequence of deliberate design decisions made to optimize the balance between low latency packet delivery and efficient traffic distribution.

When an aggregated link carries only one or two conversations, random chance might distribute the traffic unevenly. With HP switches, load distribution is more balanced when multiple conversations are transmitted over the aggregated link. The distribution evens out because, as more conversations are transmitted, it becomes more likely that a similar number of conversations are assigned to each link. In addition, the more links that are in the aggregated link, the more likely it is that different conversations are assigned to different links. Finally, even if conversations are distributed evenly across the links, one link might have higher utilization than another because some conversations consume more bandwidth, so achieving true load-balancing is typically impossible but is a much better solution than using MSTP or PVST+.

Load-Sharing Process Examples

Figures 10-4 and 10-5 illustrate two examples of load-sharing. Figure 10-4 demonstrates when the source MAC address is used to determine which link should be used in the aggregated link. The switch looks at the user's source MAC address to make this determination, and all traffic for that user is transferred across the same link. In Figure 10-4, all of User 1's traffic is transmitted across the top link, and all of User 2's traffic is transmitted across the bottom link. The problem with this approach is that, if a user is doing something bandwidth-intensive, all that traffic must traverse one link.

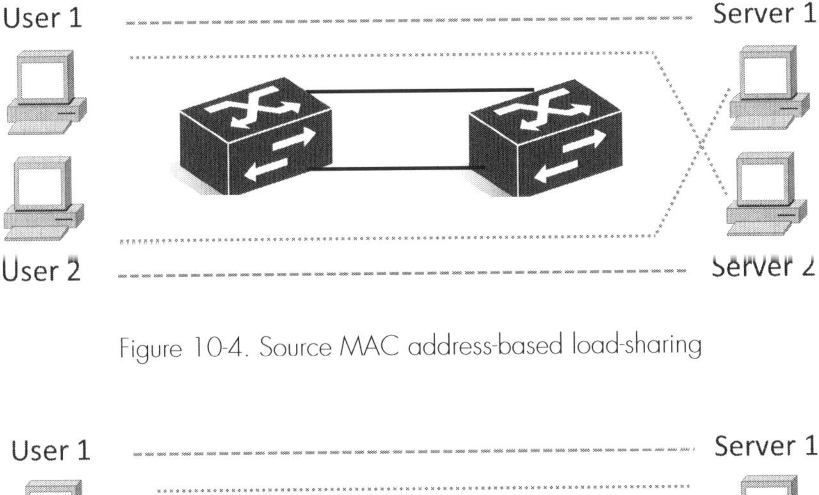

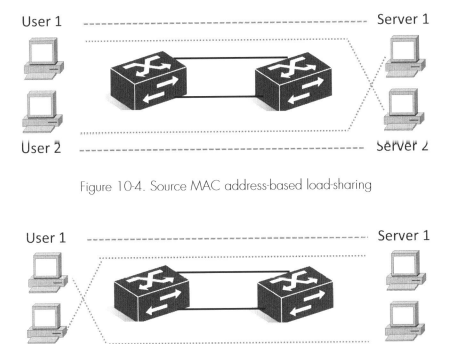

Figure 10-4. Source MAC address-based load-sharing

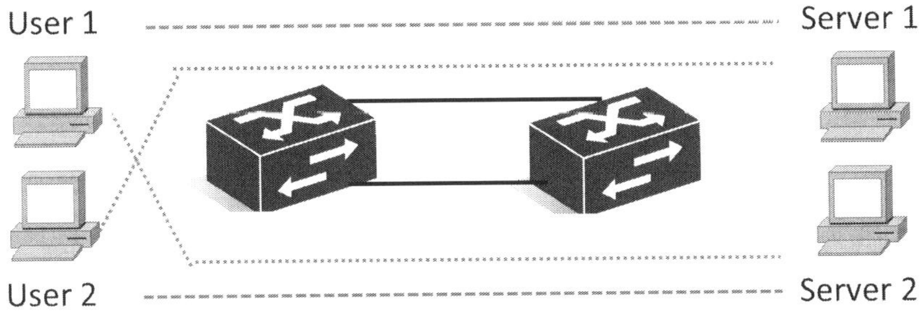

Figure 10-5. Destination MAC address-based load-sharing

Figure 10-5 illustrates load-sharing using the destination MAC address in an Ethernet frame. In this instance, which user is sending traffic does not matter—what matters is the destination they are trying to reach. For example, if either User 1 or User 2 sends traffic to Server 1, that traffic would traverse the top link. The main problem with this solution is that, if one server is heavily utilized, all traffic sent to that server would traverse one link.

Compared to the two solutions discussed in Figures 10-4 and 10-5, load-sharing based on a hash of the source and destination MAC address provides a much more even distribution of the traffic, as is illustrated in Figure 10-6. The more source and destination MAC address combinations in use, the better the distribution of the traffic becomes.

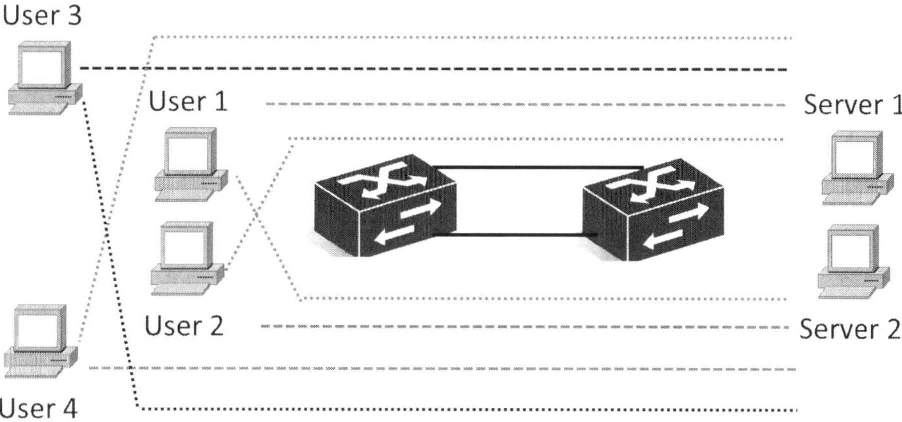

Figure 10-6. Source and destination MAC address-based load-sharing

Load-Sharing Activity

Assume that there is only one user and one web server between the two switches shown in Figure 10-7. Both switches are configured for link aggregation. The application the user accesses on the web server is web-based. Based on this topology, answer these questions:

- What load-sharing algorithm should be used on the switch connected to the user?
- What load-sharing algorithm should be used on the switch connected to the web server?

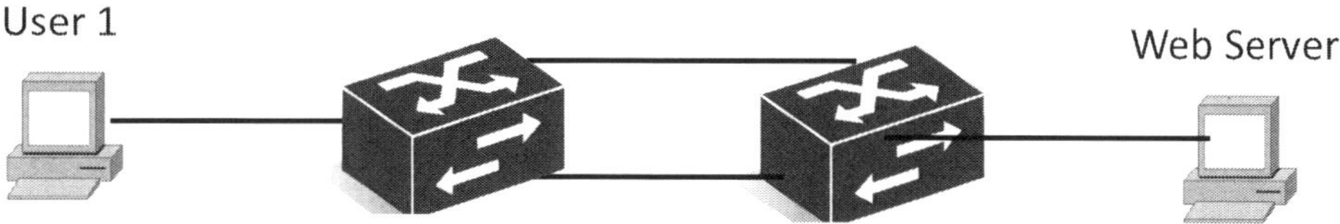

Figure 10-7. Load-sharing activity

To pick the most efficient algorithm, you must be familiar with how web applications work. A webpage is made up of many elements, and downloading each element requires a separate TCP connection, where the source ports of all these connections will be unique and the destination port is 80. Therefore, the user switch should use a load-sharing algorithm of source port. If there were multiple users, the best solution would be source IP and source port.

The web server is responding to all of the users' connections, where the source IP and source port are the web server itself (in the packet responses). It is the destination ports that are unique. Therefore, the server switch should use a load-sharing algorithm of destination port. If there were multiple users, the best solution would be destination IP and destination port.

Types of Link Aggregation

Link aggregation connections can be formed manually (statically) or dynamically. The following sections discuss both approaches to link aggregation.

Manual Link Aggregation

A static aggregated link is configured and maintained manually by you, the administrator. It recognizes only those ports that you configure as part of the link. When formed statically, it is up to you, the administrator, to define the ports that will be part of the bundle of aggregated links on two connected devices; no special messages are exchanged between the switches concerning the bundled link. One advantage of the manual approach is that it is very simple to configure. However, the downside of this approach is that you can only configure eight physical interfaces in the aggregation link—if one fails, you have just lost one-eighth of your bandwidth.

Dynamic Link Aggregation

A dynamic aggregated link is automatically established and maintained by a common protocol between the two networking devices. Not many protocols exist: Cisco has a proprietary protocol, called the Port Aggregation Protocol (PAgP), but it is only supported on Cisco switches. The most common protocol used is IEEE's Link Aggregation Control Protocol, defined in 802.1AX (formerly 802.3ad). It supports standby physical links, which provide additional failover if a functioning physical link within the aggregated link becomes unavailable. Standby physical links are typically not counted in the maximum allowed number of physical links for an aggregated link. This allows you to set up an aggregated link with the maximum number of physical links allowed by the switch (a number that varies from switch to switch) and to designate standby links, thereby providing maximum bandwidth with redundancy.

One advantage of LACP is that you can have backup or standby links, so, if an active link fails, a standby link can take over and you do not lose any bandwidth. Also, LACP verifies that the ports in common between the two switches are basically configured the same, removing the likelihood of a misconfigured aggregated link. The main disadvantage of LACP, or any protocol, is that it is more complex to configure and typically harder to troubleshoot when two devices do not successfully establish an aggregated link. Another disadvantage of dynamic LACP is that the established trunk joins only one VLAN (the untagged VLAN). Most aggregated links of any consequence are also links on which you wish to carry traffic from multiple VLANS. This cannot be done on dynamic LACP links without also implementing a complicated GARP VLAN Registration Protocol (GVRP) configuration which can open security holes. In practice, network administrators almost always prefer static LACP configurations.

Note

Not all operating systems support LACP. For example, VMware ESX/ESXi 4.0, 4.1, and 5.0 only support static link aggregation (no LACP). LACP support was added in 5.1.

LACP was defined for dynamic link negotiation of an aggregated connection. Switches use LACP data units (LACPDUs) to exchange information and to establish a dynamic aggregated link. These LACPDUs include information such as:

- **System identifier**—The system identifier has two parts: the LACP system priority and the switch's MAC address.
- **LACP system priority**—The system priority determines which switch will select the ports that are active in the aggregated link. Smaller numbers have a higher priority.
- **Port priority**—The port priority is used in the process of determining which ports are active in the aggregated link. Smaller numbers have a higher priority.

Exchanging LACPDUs allows devices to determine whether the links can be aggregated. For example, the devices can determine whether all of the links are the same media type and speed. LACPDUs also allow the devices to manage the logical aggregated link, including adding or removing physical links and handling failovers.

LACP Operational Modes

An LACP port can operate in one of two states:

- **Active**—*Active ports* transmit LACPDUs to advertise that they can create aggregated links.
- **Passive**—*Passive ports* listen for LACPDUs. If passive ports receive an LACPDU from an active port, they respond with their own LACPDU.

For an aggregated link to be established, both sides need to be in an active state or one side is in an active state and the other in a passive state. If both sides are in a passive state, neither will initiate the exchange process.

Static LACP is where both sides are basically in active mode: they both send LACPDUs to each other. Both ProVision and Comware switches support this mode. However, for some strange reason, Comware refers to this as *dynamic LACP*, which is confusing, since there is a dynamic LACP mode which is different from what Comware is implementing. With static LACP, you must specify the interfaces that are included in the aggregated link.

In dynamic LACP, one or both sides actively sends LACPDUs—one side can be in a passive mode, waiting for the active side to initiate the process. Unlike static LACP, you only need to enable dynamic LACP on an interface and the connected devices determine which interface or interfaces can be included for link aggregation. ProVision switches support this mode; however, Comware switches do not.

Note

Remember that, when you see the term "dynamic LACP" being referred to on Comware switches, it is actually the static LACP operational mode!

Distributed Trunking

In addition to supporting static and dynamic aggregated links, some ProVision switches support *distributed trunking*, which is designed to provide high availability and load-sharing for server-to-switch connections, as shown in Figure 10-8. (Support for switch-to-switch distributed trunking was added in K.15.05.0001 code.) With distributed port trunking, two or more links that are distributed across two switches form a trunk group. The grouped links appear to the downstream device as if they are from a single device.

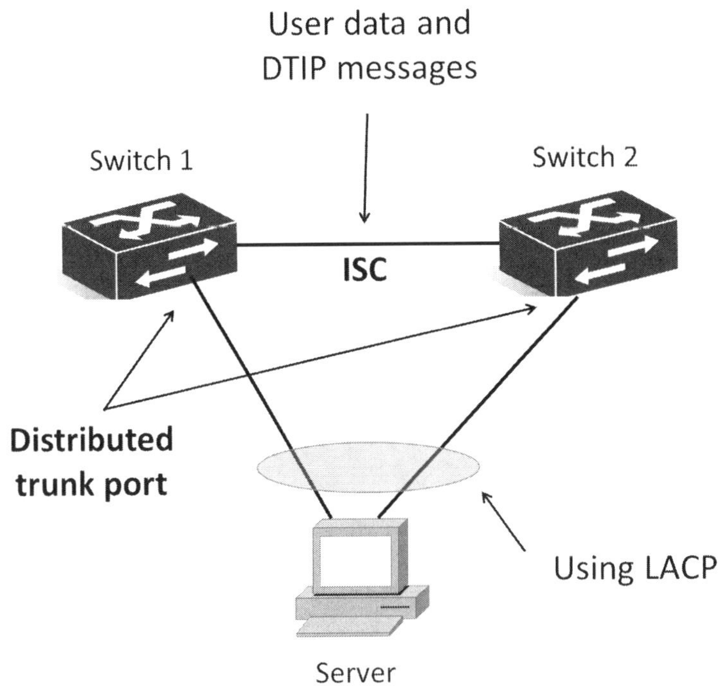

Figure 10-8. Distributed trunking on ProVision switches

In the absence of an industry standard to support this type of trunking, HP created a proprietary protocol, called the *Distributed Trunking Interconnect Protocol* (DTIP). Using this protocol, the switches exchange information over the ISC (Inter-Switch Connect port). This allows them to present the appearance of a single switch. To form an aggregated link with the switches, the server must support the industry-standard LACP and must be configured to use static mode.

Note

The ProVision switches that support distributed trunking are the 6200yl-24GmGBIC switch and the 3500, 3800, 5400zl, 6600, and 8200zl switch series. All of these switches run the same software and support distributed trunking with software version K.14 and above.

Distributed trunking provides resiliency. If one of the switches in the port trunking implementation becomes unavailable, the server continues to transmit and receive data through the other switch. Port trunking can also increase bandwidth because the server connects to two switches, and both of these connections are active—that is, the server can transmit and receive data on both connections.

Note

Many companies configure a server with two or more network adapters and run "teaming" software to eliminate a single point of failure. The teaming software can also improve throughput performance by allowing the server to use both NICs to transmit data to network clients.

Link Aggregation Configuration and Verification

The following sections cover the configuration of link aggregation on ProVision and Comware switches. This includes the configuration and verification of static (manual) and dynamic link aggregation using LACP.

Preparation for Configuration

When you add a port to a link aggregation group, that port can have one of two states:

- **Selected**—A *selected port* forwards traffic for the link aggregation group.
- **Unselected**—An *unselected port* cannot forward traffic for the link aggregation group.

A Comware switch uses certain criteria for determining a port's state, depending on whether the link aggregation group is static or dynamic. These criteria will be explained later in the chapter.

Some configuration settings affect a port's aggregation state (whether it is selected or unselected). Note that, for the purposes of aggregation, some configuration settings are grouped into *classes*, as shown in Table 10-2. HP recommends that all ports in an aggregated link be configured with the same port and class-two configuration settings (such as port type, default VLAN, and permitted VLANs).

Table 10-2: Configuration settings and link aggregation effects

Configuration	Example settings	Affects aggregation state?
Port	Port speed (rate)	Yes
	Duplex mode	
	Link status (Up or Down)	
	Flow control (ProVision)	
Class one	GVRP VLANs	No
	MSTP settings	
Class two	Port type: trunk, hybrid, or access	Yes
	Default VLAN (Port VLAN Identifier [PVID]) for the port	
	Permitted VLANs for hybrid and trunk ports	

After you add ports to a link aggregation group, all class-two configurations made to a link aggregation group are automatically synchronized to all its member ports. These configurations are retained on the member ports after they are removed from the link aggregation group.

For each link aggregation group, HP switches select a reference port. The process for selecting this reference port varies, depending on whether the link aggregation group is manual (static) or dynamic (LACP). The reference port is then used in the process of determining a port's aggregation state. The aggregation state is either selected or unselected; selected ports forward traffic, and unselected ports do not. For example, the switch compares the port attributes and class-two configurations of other member ports to those of the reference port. The ports that match can be selected (if they meet other criteria, as well).

HP ProVision Trunking

Now that you have a basic understanding of link aggregation and LACP, read the following section, which discusses the configuration and verification of static and dynamic link aggregation on the HP switches, starting with the HP ProVision switches.

Static Trunk Configuration

This section introduces the process for configuring static aggregated links on the ProVision switches. When first creating a trunk, HP recommends that you configure the trunk on the switch before connecting the cables. If you connect the cables first, you might create network loops (if STP is disabled).

When you configure static aggregated links on ProVision switches, you use the `trunk` command:

```
ProVision(config)# trunk <port-list> <trunk-name> {lacp | trunk}
```

Follow the `trunk` command with the ports that will be aggregated, the name for the trunk group, and the type of trunk. The name of the trunk is a fixed label name from the following list: `trk1`, `trk2`, and so on. Notice that you specify manual trunking with the trunk parameter.

Here is a configuration example:

```
ProVision(config)# trunk 21-22 trk1 trunk
```

In this example, ports 21 and 22 are defined as `trk1` using manual aggregation.

Note

Creating a `trk` interface and associating physical interfaces to it automatically causes the ProVision switch to erase the VLAN configurations for the included physical interfaces.

Creating an aggregated link has implications for VLAN configuration. Because aggregated ports are combined to form a single logical port, they cannot be configured individually for VLAN membership. When an aggregated link is configured, it automatically becomes an untagged member of the switch's default VLAN. You can specify it as a tagged or untagged member of a VLAN or VLANs using the configuration discussed in "Chapter 6: VLANs." Here is an example based on the previous sample configuration for `trk1`:

```
ProVision(config)# vlan 10 tagged trk1
```

Note

To avoid creating a loop, the trunk configuration for static aggregation must be completed on both switches in the trunk before the redundant links are connected.

ProVision Load-Sharing

Trunk load-sharing using Layer 4 ports allows the use of TCP/UDP source and destination port number for trunk load-sharing. This is in addition to the current use of source and destination IP address and MAC addresses. Configuration of Layer 4 load-sharing applies to all trunks on the switch. Only non-fragmented packets have their TCP/UDP port number used by load-sharing. This ensures that all frames associated with a fragmented IP packet are sent through the same trunk on the same physical link.

The priority for using Layer 4 packets when this feature is enabled is as follows:

1. If the packet protocol is an IP packet and has Layer 4 port information, use Layer 4.
2. If the packet protocol is an IP packet and does not have Layer 4 information, use Layer 3 information.
3. If the packet is not an IP packet, use Layer 2 information.

Enter the following command with the `L4-based` option to enable load-sharing on Layer 4 information, when it is present.

```
ProVision(config)# trunk-load-balance {L3-based | L4-based}
```

When the `L4-based` option is configured, it enables load-sharing based on Layer 4 information, if it is present, in the packet. If Layer 4 information is not present, Layer 3 information is used, if it is present. If Layer 3 information is not present, Layer 2 information is used.

Dynamic Link Aggregation

When you configure static LACP aggregated links on ProVision switches, you use the trunk command with the `lacp` parameter:

```
ProVision(config)# trunk <port-list> <trunk-name> {lacp | trunk}
```

Follow the `trunk` command with the ports that will be aggregated, the name for the trunk group, and the type of trunk. The name of the trunk is a fixed label name from the following list: `trk1`, `trk2`, and so on.

Here is a configuration example:

```
ProVision(config)# trunk 21-22 trk1 lacp
```

To define the LACP operational mode on ProVision switches, you use the `interface` command:

```
ProVision(config)# interface <port-list> lacp [{active | passive}]
ProVision(config)# interface <port-list> lacp key <key-id>
```

Remember the difference between active and passive ports:

- `active`—An *active port* advertises its ability to create dynamic aggregates links.
- `passive`—A *passive port* responds to an active port's request to create an aggregated link.

The default is `active` if you do not configure the option. The `key` parameter is used to control which physical interfaces comprise an ProVision trunk—interfaces configured with the same key will attempt to bond with same remote peer.

Here is an example where interfaces a1 and b7 are set up with dynamic link aggregation using LACP:

```
ProVision(config)# interface a1,b7 lacp active
ProVision(config)# interface a1,b7 lacp key 100
```

Note

Interestingly, you do not actually have to configure the `trunk` command when setting up dynamic LACP: you only need to configure the `interface lacp` command. However, using the `trunk` command allows you to control which interfaces can be used between two devices.

You cannot manually assign a dynamic aggregated link to a VLAN. Instead, you must use GARP VLAN Registration Protocol to allow the aggregated link to carry traffic from multiple VLANs. A discussion of GVRP is beyond the scope of this book. Because many administrators prefer not to use GVRP, dynamic LACP is not common on the ProVision switches—either manual or static LACP is used.

Note

LACP requires full-duplex (FDx) links of the same media type (10/100Base-T or 100FX, among others) and the same speed, and it enforces speed and duplex conformance across a trunk group. For most installations, ProVision recommends that you leave the port mode settings at Auto (the default). LACP also operates with Auto-10, Auto-100, and Auto-1000 (if negotiation selects FDx), and 10FDx, 100FDx, and 1000FDx settings.

Link Aggregation Verification

To verify which ports you have assigned as trunks and the trunk group that they belong to, use the `show trunk` command. Here is an example:

```
ProVision# show trunk

 Load Balancing

  Port | Name                          Type      | Group Type
  ---- + ----------------------------- --------- + ----- -----
  21   | Router                        100/1000T | Trk1  LACP
  22   | Router                        100/1000T | Trk1  LACP
```

Use the `show lacp` command to verify the LACP operation on the switch's ports. Here is an example of a switch using static LACP:

```
ProVision# show lacp

                            LACP

   PORT   LACP      TRUNK     PORT      LACP      LACP
   NUMB   ENABLED   GROUP     STATUS    PARTNER   STATUS
   ----   -------   -------   -------   -------   ------
```

```
1       Active    Trk1    Up        Yes      Success
2       Active    Trk1    Up        Yes      Success
3       Active    Trk1    Up        Yes      Success
4       Active    Trk1    Up        Yes      Success
5       Active    Trk1    Blocked   Yes      Failure
6       Active    Trk1    Blocked   Yes      Failure
7       Active    7       Down      No       Failure
8       Active    8       Down      No       Failure
```

If one of the other ports becomes disabled, a blocked port will replace it. (Port status becomes "Up.") When the other port becomes active again, the replacement port goes back to blocked. (Port status is "Blocked.") It can take a few seconds for the switch to refresh the current status of the ports.

Here is an example of setting up dynamic LACP with its verification:

```
ProVision(config)# interface 23-24 lacp key 100
ProVision(config)# interface 23-24 lacp active
Provision(config)# show lacp
                              LACP
      LACP     Trunk   Port               LACP     Admin   Oper
Port  Enabled  Group   Status  Partner    Status   Key     Key
----  ------   ------  ------  -------    -------  -----   -----
23    Active   Dyn2    Up      Yes        Success  100     100
24    Active   Dyn2    Up      Yes        Success  100     100
```

Notice that, in the above output, the logical trunk (interface) "Dyn2" was automatically created and that the two interfaces were successfully negotiated with the remote peer and added to the trunk. With static LACP, ports are statically assigned to the link aggregation. However, with dynamic LACP, the ports are assigned if LACP negotiation is successful, resulting in the different designation for the logical interface, DynX, where "X" is the logical port number.

For troubleshooting, you can examine the LACP messages in the Event Log. From the command-line interface (CLI), qualify the logging output by referencing `lacp`, like this:

```
ProVision# show log lacp
Keys: W=Warning I=Information
M=Major D=Debug
Event Log listing: Events Since Boot
---- ----
```

```
I 01/01/90 00:00:09 lacp: Passive Dynamic LACP enabled on all ports
I 01/01/90 00:00:22 lacp: Port 1 is blocked - negotiation
I 01/01/90 00:00:22 lacp: Port 2 is blocked - negotiation
I 01/01/90 00:00:22 lacp: Port 5 is blocked - negotiation
I 01/01/90 00:00:22 lacp: Port 6 is blocked - negotiation
I 01/01/90 00:00:22 lacp: Port 13 is blocked - negotiation
I 01/01/90 00:00:22 lacp: Port 17 is blocked - negotiation
I 01/01/90 00:00:26 lacp: Port 13 is moved to trunk Trk1
I 01/01/90 00:00:26 lacp: Port 17 is moved to trunk Trk1
I 01/01/90 00:00:27 lacp: Dynamic LACP trunk Trk1 is now on-line
I 01/01/90 00:00:28 lacp: Port 1 is moved to trunk Trk1
I 01/01/90 00:00:29 lacp: Port 2 is moved to trunk Trk1
I 01/01/90 00:00:30 lacp: Port 5 is moved to trunk Trk1
```

To verify the load-balancing performed by the ProVision switch, you can use the `show interface display` command, which provides a dynamic display of port activity (information is automatically updated every five seconds). Use the `clear statistics` command to reset the statistics to 0s:

```
ProVision# clear statistics <int-id or list>
ProVision# clear statistics global
```

The two trunk group options (LACP and trunk) on ProVision switches use source address/destination address (SA/DA) pairs for distributing outbound traffic over trunked links. SA/DA causes the switch to distribute outbound traffic to the links within the trunk group on the basis of source/destination address pairs. That is, the switch sends traffic from the same source address to the same destination address through the same trunked link, and it sends traffic from the same source address to a different destination address through a different link, depending on the rotation of path assignments among the links in the trunk.

Likewise, the switch distributes traffic for the same destination address but from different source addresses through different links. Because the amount of traffic coming from or going to various nodes in a network can vary widely, it is possible for one link in a trunk group to be fully utilized while others in the same trunk have unused bandwidth capacity, even though the address assignments are evenly distributed across the links in a trunk. In actual networking environments, this is rarely a problem. However, if it becomes a problem, you can use the HP Intelligent Management Center (IMC) network management software to quickly and easily identify the sources of heavy traffic (top talkers) and make adjustments to improve performance. IMC is discussed in "Chapter 15: HP Intelligent Management Center." Broadcasts, multicasts, and floods from different source addresses are distributed evenly across the links.

As links are added or deleted, the switch redistributes traffic across the trunk group. For example, in Figure 10-9 (a three-port trunk), traffic could be assigned as shown in Table 10-3. The `show interface display` command is a quick way of seeing the traffic utilization on the links to verify the load-balancing of the trunk or trunks.

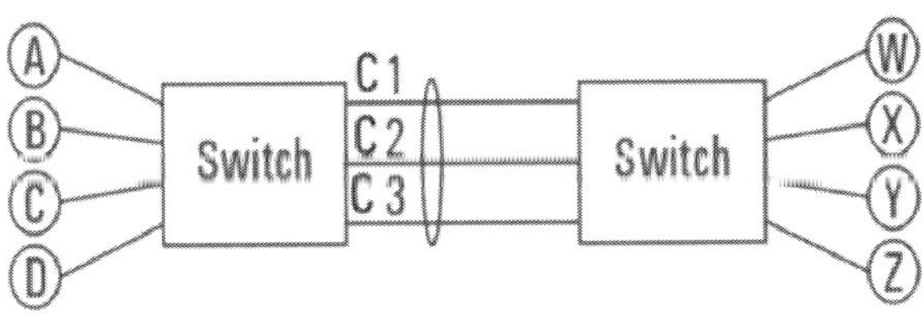

Figure 10-9. ProVision traffic distribution example

Table 10.3. ProVision traffic distribution example

Source	Destination	Switch Link
Node A	Node W	1
Node B	Node X	2
Node C	Node Y	3
Node D	Node Z	1
Node A	Node Y	2
Node B	Node W	3

HP Comware Bridge Aggregation

On the HP Comware products (switches and routers), link aggregation is used to bundle more than one link between two Comware devices in such a way that it works as a single logical interface. Link aggregation is designed to increase bandwidth by implementing load-sharing among the member ports in an aggregation group.

The Comware link aggregation feature supports two categories:

- **Static aggregation**—No LACP protocol runs between the switches (manual configuration).
- **Dynamic LACP aggregation**—LACP BPDUs are exchanged between connected devices. According to the LACP standard, this is the static LACP operational mode

The following sections discuss the configuration and verification of link aggregation on Comware switches.

Manual Link Aggregation Configuration

To create a static link aggregation group on the Comware switches, you must be at the system view command level. Enter the following command to create the logical interface, called a BAGG, and assign it a number:

```
[Comware] interface bridge-aggregation <number>
[Comware-<interface-id>] description <text>
```

The default mode for aggregated links is static (manual), so you do not have to configure this setting.

Next, you must move to a port interface view to add the port to the link aggregation group. Access the port interface view and assign it to your new logical bridge group interface, using the following configuration:

```
[Comware] interface <interface-id>
[Comware-<interface-id>] port link-aggregation group <number>
```

Repeat the last command for each port interface that is a part of the link aggregation group.

Here is an example configuration:

```
[Comware] interface bridge-aggregation 1
[Comware-Bridge-Aggregation1] description Connection-to-Distribution-1
[Comware-Bridge-Aggregation1] quit
[Comware] interface g1/0/1
[Comware-GigabitEthernet1/0/1] port link-aggregation group 1
[Comware-GigabitEthernet1/0/1] quit
[Comware] interface g1/0/2
[Comware-GigabitEthernet1/0/2] port link-aggregation group 1
```

For static link aggregation groups, a Comware switch selects a reference port from member ports that:

- Are in the "Up" state.
- Have the same class-two configurations as the aggregate interface.

A Comware switch uses the following selection criteria in the order listed:

- Full-duplex, high-speed links
- Full-duplex, low-speed links

If two ports have the same duplex mode and speed, the switch selects the port with the lower port number.

After the switch selects a reference port, it determines the aggregation state of each member port in the static link aggregation group. To make this determination, the switch uses criteria such as:

- Does the port support the reference port's line speed and duplex mode?
  - **Yes**—The switch considers the next criterion.
  - **No**—The port's state is set to "Unselected."
- Is the port Up or Down?
  - **Up**—The switch considers the next criterion.
  - **Down**—The port's state is set to "Unselected."
- Do the port attributes and class-two configuration match those of the reference port?
  - **Yes**—The switch considers the next criterion.
  - **No**—The port's state is set to "Unselected."
- Has the link aggregation group reached the maximum number of links?
  - **Yes**—The port's link is set to "Unselected."
  - **No**—The port's link is set to "Selected."

The ports with a "Selected" state forward traffic for the logical aggregate interface. The ports with an "Unselected" state do not. (They can be used as backup links in case the "Selected" links become unavailable.)

You can configure the link aggregation group just as you would any port on the Comware switches—whether it is dynamic or static. For example, you can make a link aggregation group a trunk port and add permitted VLANs, as shown here:

```
[Comware] interface bridge-aggregation 1
[Comware-Bridge-Aggregation1] description Connection-to-Distribution-1
[Comware-Bridge-Aggregation1] port link-type trunk
[Comware-Bridge-Aggregation1] port trunk permit vlan 100 200
```

After you configure a command on a Layer 2 aggregate interface, the system starts applying the configuration to the aggregate interface and its aggregation member ports. If the system fails to do that on the aggregate interface, it stops applying the configuration to the aggregation member ports. If it fails to do that on an aggregation member port, it simply skips the port and moves to the next port.

Note

After you have created the BAGG interface, all other configurations, like port type (access, hybrid, trunk) and VLANs associated to it, among other considerations, are done on the BAGG interface—not on the physical interfaces that comprise the BAGG.

Dynamic Link Aggregation Configuration

As with a static aggregate interface, you must first create a link aggregation group and assign it a number when configuring dynamic link aggregation (static LACP). Unlike a static link aggregation interface, however, you must specify the mode as dynamic (static LACP). Here is the syntax to accomplish this:

```
[Comware] interface bridge-aggregation <number>
[Comware-<interface-id>] description <text>
[Comware-<interface-id>] link-aggregation mode dynamic
```

You then add ports, just as you would for a static aggregate interface, by first accessing the port interface and then adding the port to the aggregation group:

```
[Comware] interface <interface-name> <interface-number>
[Comware-<interface-id>] port link-aggregation group <number>
```

Here is a simple example configuration of defining a static LACP BAGG on a Comware switch:

```
[Sw-A] interface bridge-aggregation 2
[Sw-A-Bridge-Aggregation2] description Static LACP to Dist-2 Switch
[Sw-A-Bridge-Aggregation2] link-aggregation mode dynamic
[Sw-A-Bridge-Aggregation2] quit
[Sw-A] interface g1/0/3
[SW-A-GigabitEthernet1/0/3] port link-aggregation group 2
[SW-A-GigabitEthernet1/0/3] quit
[SW-A] interface g1/0/4
[SW-A-GigabitEthernet1/0/4] port link-aggregation group 2
[Sw-A] interface bridge-aggregation 2
[Sw-A-Bridge-Aggregation2] port link-type trunk
[Sw-A-Bridge-Aggregation2] port trunk permit vlan 100 200
```

In this example, ports 3 and 4 are part of the aggregated link, and the aggregated link is a VLAN trunk (tagged port).

Note

Remember that when you configure a BAGG, you create the BAGG, assign the interfaces to it, and then configure the BAGG properties, like VLAN information.

To select a reference port for a dynamic aggregate interface, the local switch negotiates with the remote switch. The negotiation is a two-step process:

- Select the switch on which the reference port will reside.
- Select the reference port.

To select which switch hosts the reference port, the two switches compare their LACP system priority. The switch with the lower priority number is selected. If the switches have the same LACP priority, the selected switch is the one with the lowest MAC address. The selected switch then determines the reference port, based on which port in its link aggregation group has the lowest LACP port priority. If two ports have the same port priority, the port with the lowest port number is selected.

In the reference port selection process, the two switches that are forming a dynamic aggregated link identify which switch has the lower LACP system priority. This switch determines the aggregation state, selected or unselected, for member ports on both switches. The switch uses the same criteria for dynamic link aggregation groups as it did for static groups. In addition to these criteria, it checks whether the port attributes and class-two configurations of each member port match those on its peer port.

Table 10-4 compares the advantages and disadvantages of static and dynamic link aggregation on the Comware switches and routers.

Table 10-4. Comware link aggregation comparison

Type	Advantages	Disadvantages
Static (manual)	Aggregation is stable. A port's aggregation state is not affected by other ports within the group.	You must manually manage the aggregation state. The switch cannot change the aggregation state of a port to match its peer's aggregation state.
Dynamic (static LACP)	Connected switches automatically maintain link aggregation.	Depending on the network environment, aggregation can be unstable.

Load-Sharing Configuration

Unlike ProVision switches, the Comware devices provide flexibility in how traffic is distributed across the physical links in the link aggregation group. You can configure load-sharing in two ways: globally or per link aggregation group.

For the global setting, you can configure the switch to load-balance, based on one of the following:

- Source IP address
- Destination IP address
- Source MAC address
- Destination MAC address

- Or you can specify two criteria:
  - Source IP address and destination IP address
  - Source IP address and source port number
  - Destination IP address and destination port number

For each link aggregation group, you can configure the switch to load-balance, based on one of the following:

- Source IP address
- Destination IP address
- Source MAC address
- Destination MAC address
- Or you can specify two criteria
  - Source IP address and destination IP address
  - Destination MAC address and a source MAC address

Note
By default, the load-sharing mode is performed on source and destination MAC addresses of bridged frames or on source IP addresses and destination IP addresses of routed packets. This is the recommended setting by HP.

To change the load-sharing mode on the global level and in the bridge aggregation configuration context, use the following configuration:

```
[Comware] link-aggregation load-sharing mode <mode>
```

Or

```
[Comware] interface bridge-aggregation <interface-id>
[Comware-<interface-id>] link-aggregation load-sharing mode <mode>
```

Notice that the command is the same for the global or interface configuration, but some of the parameters are different.

Link Aggregation Verification

To verify the configuration of link aggregation on your Comware switches, use the `display link-aggregation summary` command. Here is an example:

```
<Comware> display link-aggregation summary
Aggregation Interface Type:
```

```
BAGG -- Bridge-Aggregation, RAGG -- Route-Aggregation
Aggregation Mode: S -- Static, D -- Dynamic
Loadsharing Type: Shar -- Loadsharing, NonS -- Non-Loadsharing
Actor System ID: 0x8000, 000f-e267-6c6a
AGG          AGG     Partner ID               Select   Unselect
Share
Interface    Mode                             Ports    Ports      Type
--------------------------------------------------------------------
BAGG1        S      none                      2        0          Shar
BAGG2        D      0x8000, 000f-e267-57ad    2        0          Shar
```

In this example, two BAGG interfaces have been configured, where the first is a static configuration and the second is a dynamic configuration.

Unfortunately, the command on the previous page does not display the ports included in the aggregated connection nor the status of the link aggregation. To see this information, use the following command:

```
<Comware> display link-aggregation verbose [bridge-aggregation <number>]
```

You can also qualify the output and display a single interface instead of all the interfaces. Here is an example of the above command:

```
[Comware] display link-aggregation verbose bridge-aggregation 2
Loadsharing Type: Shar -- Loadsharing, NonS -- Non-Loadsharing
Port Status: S -- Selected, U -- Unselected
Flags: A -- LACP_Activity, B -- LACP_Timeout, C -- Aggregation,
         D -- Synchronization, E -- Collecting, F -- Distributing,
         G -- Defaulted, H -- Expired
Aggregation Interface: Bridge-Aggregation2Aggregation Mode: Dynamic
Loadsharing Type: Shar
System ID: 0x8000, 000f-e267-6c6a
Local:
    Port       Status   Priority   Oper-Key   Flag
   ----------------------------------------------------------------
   GE1/0/3      S        32768       2         {ACDEF}
   GE1/0/4      S        32768       2         {ACDEF}
```

```
Remote:
    Actor    Partner  Priority  Oper-Key  SystemID              Flag
   ----------------------------------------------------------------
    GE1/0/3   32      32768      2        0x8000, 000f-e267-57ad {ACDEF}
    GE1/0/4   26      32768      2        0x8000, 000f-e267-57ad {ACDEF}
```

You can see the status of the links, indicated by the Flag column, for both the local and remote sides of the aggregated link.

Note

If the flags specify ACDEF, this indicates that the link is functioning and load-sharing. If they are denoted by anything else, there is a problem. There are various `debug` commands you can use to further troubleshoot the problem. (ProVision does not currently support `debug` commands for link aggregation.)

Learning Check

The following questions help you measure your understanding of the material presented in this chapter. Read all of the choices carefully, since there may be more than one correct answer. Choose all correct answers for each question.

Questions

1. Which proprietary HP solution on the ProVision switches allows for load-sharing across multiple switch connections to a server?
   a. Distributed trunking
   b. Dynamic trunking
   c. LACP
   d. Static trunking

2. Which ProVision switch configuration includes interfaces as an aggregated static link?
   a. `trunk <port-list>`
   b. `interface <port-list>`
   c. `interface bridge-aggregation <number>`
   d. `port trunk`

3. What ProVision switch command establishes an aggregated link between ports A1 and A2 as the first trunk using static LACP?

4. What Comware switch configuration creates a bridge aggregation group with an ID of 1, using static LACP, and includes both ports G1/0/1 and G1/0/2?

5. On a Comware switch, which of the following ports would have preference as the reference port in link aggregation in a static LACP configuration?
   a. 10 GbE port operating in half-duplex mode
   b. 1 GB port operating in full-duplex mode
   c. 1 GB port operating in half-duplex mode
   d. 100 Mbps port operating in full-duplex mode

6. What is the default load-sharing mode on ProVision and Comware switches for link aggregation?

Answers

1. ☑ **A** is correct. Distributed trunking, proprietary to the ProVision switches, allows for load-balancing between a server (or switch) and two ProVision switches.

   ☒ **B** and **D** are incorrect because they are general terms related to link aggregation. **C** is incorrect because it is an open standard.

2. ☑ **A** is correct. Use the `trunk` command to configure static link aggregation on ProVision switches.

   ☒ **B** is incorrect because the `interface` command is used to establish dynamic LACP. **C** is incorrect because this command configures link aggregation on Comware switches. **D** is incorrect because this is a non-existent command.

3. ☑ `trunk a1-a2 trk1 lacp` is the ProVision switch command that establishes an aggregated link between ports A1 and A2 as the first trunk using static LACP.

4. ☑

```
interface bridge-aggregation 1
    link-aggregation mode dynamic
    quit
  interface g1/0/1
    port link-aggregation group 1
    quit
  interface g1/0/2
    port link-aggregation group 1
```

   is the Comware switch configuration that creates a bridge aggregation group with an ID of 1, using static LACP, and includes both ports G1/0/1 and G1/0/2.

5. ☑ **B** is correct. 1 GB would be preferred.

   ☒ **A** and **C** are incorrect because half-duplex is not supported by LACP. **D** is incorrect because Gigabit Ethernet is preferred over Fast Ethernet.

6. ☑ Source and destination MAC addresses is the default load-sharing algorithm used by both Comware and ProVision switches.

11 IP Routing Overview

EXAM OBJECTIVES

In this chapter, you learn to:

- ✓ Explain Layer 3 routing concepts and apply Layer 3 protocols.
- ✓ Perform installation and configuration of devices.
- ✓ Verify Layer 3 routing protocol convergence and scalability.
- ✓ Apply troubleshooting methodology.
- ✓ Perform troubleshooting methodology on wired networks.

ASSUMED KNOWLEDGE

This chapter assumes that you have a good understanding of IP addressing, including the following topics:

- IP subnetting
- VLANs (covered in "Chapter 6: VLANs")

If you are not familiar with these topics, access the HP video tutorials, covered in "Chapter 1: Introduction," for a review.

INTRODUCTION

This chapter introduces IP routing on the HP ProVision and HP Comware switches. Many of the ProVision switches support routing, even though it is disabled by default, and the vast majority of Comware switches support routing.

Layer 2 switches make switching decisions based on destination MAC addresses. However, to move traffic between different subnets (VLANs), a networking device has to look at the destination Layer 3 address, like an IP address, to make a forwarding decision. Routing is done by every device in the network, from a user's PC or server, to a Layer 3 switch, and to a traditional router.

On Ethernet networks, the routing device finds the destination IP address in the header of the IP packet, which is encapsulated in the Ethernet frame. After determining a packet's destination IP address, the device must know the route, or pathway, to the destination network. The networking device must know the next hop in the route—the next device that will forward the packet to its final destination. This next hop is also called the *gateway*. ProVision switches, Comware switches, and Comware routers can perform the routing function between VLANs and/or subnets.

This chapter provides an overview of routing and routing protocols. Here are the topics covered in this chapter:

- VLANs and routing
- Static routing
- Dynamic routing with Routing Information Protocol (RIP)

Dynamic routing with OSPF is covered in "Chapter 12: OSPF Operation and Configuration."

Types of Routing

Layer 3 switches and routers typically support two types of routes, as shown in Figure 11-1.

- **Direct routes are for local networks**—Networks that are directly connected to the Layer 3 device. Layer 3 devices can route at Layer 3 between devices in different directly connected networks without a routing protocol.
- **Indirect routes are for remote networks**—Networks that are not directly connected to the switch. A routing protocol or static routing configuration is needed to learn and choose the best paths for indirect routes.

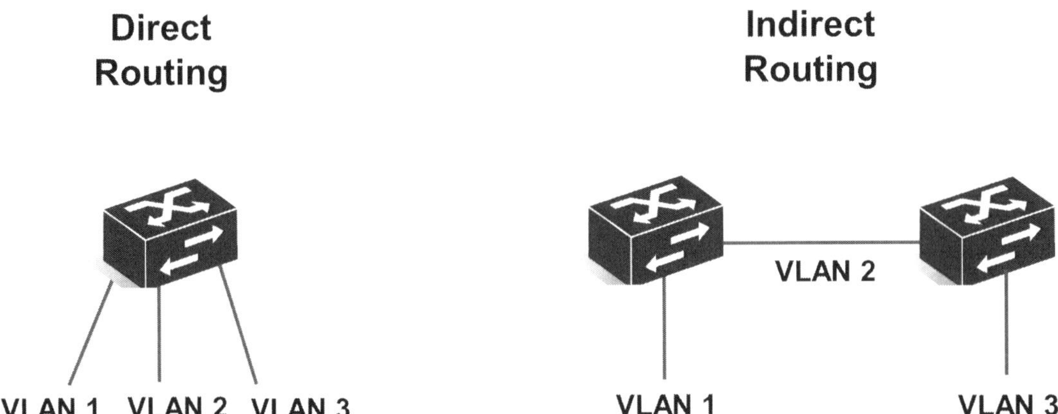

Figure 11-1. Types of routes

Layer 3 switches and routers learn direct routes through their local interfaces, which can be physical ports, VLANs, or aggregated links. Layer 3 switches and routers recognize all local routes as soon as IP routing is enabled and an IP address is configured for the VLAN or subnet associated with an interface. These local routes are commonly referred to as *directly connected*, *local*, or *connected routes*.

For example, Figure 11-2 shows a network in which Switch C has been assigned the IP address 10.1.10.1/24 for VLAN 10. IP routing has been enabled on the switch to allow it to function as a Layer 3 switch. The Switch C interface that is associated with VLAN 10 is connected to Switch A (which also supports the 10.1.10.0 network). Also notice that Switch C is connected to VLAN 20 and VLAN 30. If Switch C has IP addresses for both of these VLANs, Switch C would have three direct routes and could route between these directly connected VLANs. However, notice that Switch D is connected only to VLAN 30 and, therefore, would need to use another Layer 3 device, like Switch C, to route traffic to remote VLANs and subnets.

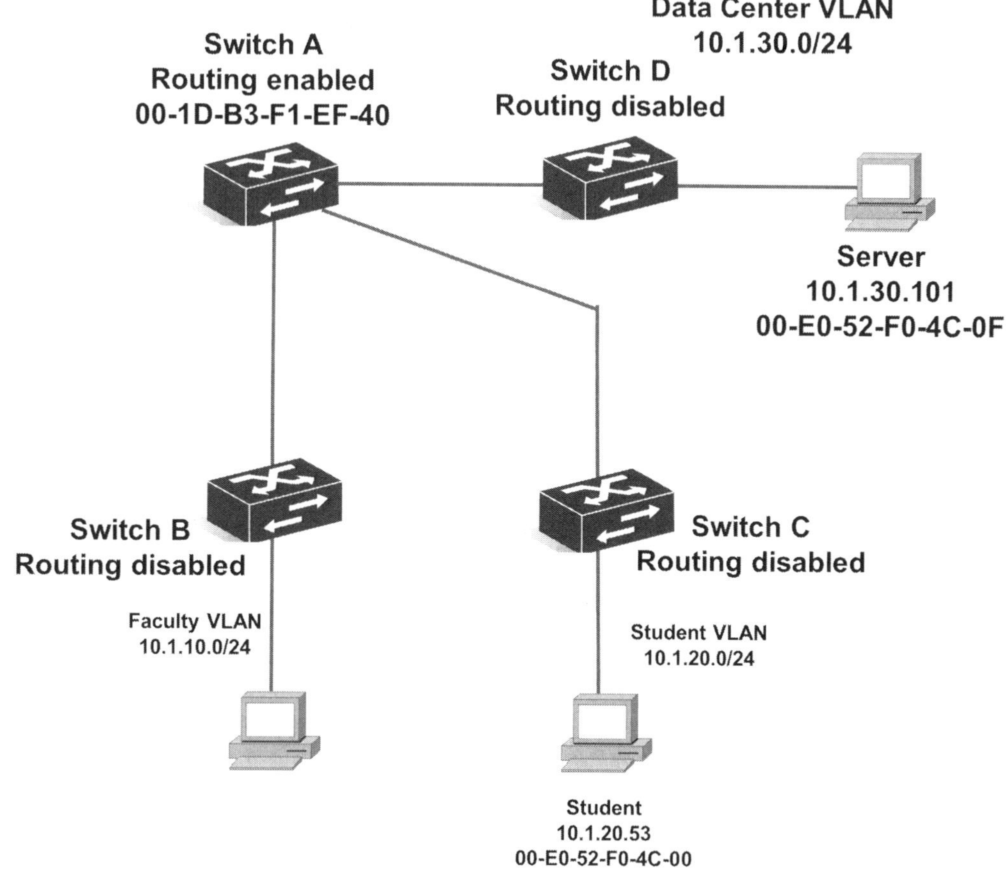

Figure 11-2. Example routing network

Indirect Routing

An indirect route enables a Layer 3 device to communicate with "non-local" destinations, using one or more intermediate hops. As per the previous section, Switch D (Figure 11-2) needs indirect routing information to help it determine which Layer 3 device to use to forward IP packets to remote subnets or VLANs.

There are three types of indirect routes:

- A *static route* must be entered by a network administrator and is a route to a specific remote network.
- A *default route* is a special type of indirect route that tells the Layer 3 switch how to forward a packet when it does not know a specific route to the destination address. Typically, default routes are implemented on a networking device as a special type of static route.
- A *dynamic route* is learned through Layer 3 routing protocols, such as RIP or OSPF. This chapter briefly covers RIP. OSPF is introduced in this book, but a more in-depth discussion of OSPF is covered in HP's Accredited Solutions Expert (ASE) courses for networking.

These routes are placed in a local routing table, which is used to make decisions on how to forward Layer 3 packets. (Routing tables are discussed later in the chapter.)

Interior Gateway Protocols and Exterior Gateway Protocols

Dynamic routing protocols are used for more complex network topologies. Routers communicate with each other to discover available routes and the best paths to destinations. Routing information is exchanged with neighbor routers to learn the existing topology and to learn about changes that occur in the networking topology. The dynamic routes are placed in a routing table, and the routing table is constantly updated to ensure that the best route to each destination is listed and used.

There are two general types of dynamic routing protocols:

- Interior Gateway Protocol (IGP)
- Exterior Gateway Protocol (EGP)

An IGP routing protocol facilitates the exchange of routing information among routers under the same organizational control—within the same autonomous system. An *autonomous system* is a group of devices under the same administrative control, like a company's networking devices. Examples of IGP routing protocols include static, RIP, and OSPF.

An EGP routing protocol facilitates exchange of routing information among routers in different autonomous systems. Border Gateway Protocol v4 (BGP4) is an example of an EGP and is commonly used by Internet service providers (ISPs) to route traffic on the Internet backbone. The most common EGP is a default static route.

Distance Vector and Link State Protocols

Two types of standard interior gateway protocols are commonly used in IP networks:

- Distance vector protocols
- Link state protocols

Routers use *distance vector protocols* to integrate information into their route tables and to resend the resulting entries, as modified from their own perspectives. Sometimes this is referred to as *routing by rumor*, since the networking device basically trusts the routing information shared by its neighbors to reach remote destinations—it is not receiving the routing information directly from the source of the route. Distance vector protocols tend to be very simple and have little overhead but do not scale to a large size. The RIP is an example of a distance vector protocol.

Routers use *link state protocols* to establish neighbor relationships with adjacent routers. Routers generate updates based on local information and send the updates to neighbors, which then flood these updates to all of their neighbors. Because of this process, link state protocols are commonly referred to as *routing by propaganda*, since all destination routers are receiving the routing information by the source. Ideally, within a few seconds, every router in an administratively defined area has identical information. Each router builds a logical tree that traces out the shortest path to each advertised destination, using itself as the root. As a result, every router has a consistent picture of the network from its own perspective. The OSPF and the Intermediate System to Intermediate System (IS-IS) protocols are examples of link state protocols.

Note

Make sure you understand the difference between routing by rumor and routing by propaganda. With distance vector protocols, you typically only know how to reach a remote network by using the next-hop neighbor. With link state protocols, you typically understand who actually originated a route and the actual links used to reach the destination (a more complete view of the network).

Table 11-1 provides a simple comparison between the RIP and OSPF routing protocols.

Table 11-1. RIP and OSPF comparison

	RIP	OSPF
Updates	Periodic updates are sent every 30 seconds as a broadcast or multicast.	Triggered updates are sent as multicasts when changes occur.
Neighbor relationships	Neighbors are learned via the periodically advertised routing updates.	A defined process is used to establish a neighbor relationship. After it is formed, routes can be shared.
Route decisions	Best paths are chosen based on the number of hops away the router is from the network.	Best paths are chosen based on cost, which is an inverse of the bandwidth of the interfaces involved; in other words, faster paths are preferred over slower paths.
Convergence	Converges slowly	Converges quickly
Advantages	Has low overhead and is simple to configure.	Converges very fast and provides a loop-free topology.
Disadvantages	Converges slowly because of measures needed to deal with routing loops, like hold-down timers; also is susceptible to routing loops.	Complex to configure and has more overhead (CPU and memory).

Although RIP and other distance vector protocols are easier to configure than link state protocols, the distance vector protocols have many disadvantages. Probably the biggest disadvantage is that changes in the routing topology often propagate slowly because information in a router's table is acquired from other routers that may be as many as 15 hops away, and, since RIP is susceptible to routing loops (in addition to all distance vector protocols), care must be taken to ensure that a chosen route is not part of a routing loop (which slows down convergence).

OSPF, like other link state protocols, avoids the convergence issues of RIP by not relying on "secondhand" information. A router sends an advertisement when it recognizes a link state change. Along with the topology change, the update contains the attributes of all of the router's currently active links. The router sends the advertisement to its immediate neighbors, which are required by the protocol to immediately flood the advertisement to all of their neighbors.

Unlike RIP or other distance vector protocol routers, OSPF or other link state protocol routers do not increment the costs as they flood updates. In fact, an OSPF router is not permitted to make any changes to advertisements it receives on one network before sending it out onto another network. As a result, all of the routers in the OSPF "area" have a consistent picture of the connections between all routers and networks in the area. Each router builds a tree based on "firsthand" information that traces the shortest path between itself and every router and network in the area. When a link state changes, the router recalculates the tree, based on the new information. Ideally, less than a second or a handful of seconds pass between the time the router advertises its new state and the time when all of the routers have found an alternate path, if one exists.

Note

At its heart, BGP is a distance vector protocol. However, many of its enhanced features fall outside of the typical category of distance vector protocols. Sometimes, BGP is referred to as a *hybrid routing protocol*, borrowing features from link state protocols.

Information Required for Routing

All IP devices need to store routes (direct and indirect) in a local table, called a *routing table*, to help with their Layer 3 forwarding decisions. The content of a routing table will differ based on an edge device, like a PC or server, from one found in a networking device, like a Layer 3 switch or router.

At a minimum, Layer 3 switches and routers require the following information about each IP route:

- **Destination network**—This is the network number and subnet mask of the destination network.
- **Gateway**—This is the next-hop address the packet needs to be forwarded to in order to route the packet to the destination.
- **Route prioritization methods**—This is used to prefer one route over another route.

There are two types of route prioritization methods: internal and external. An *internal prioritization* method is chosen within a route type (a best path). Internal prioritization is commonly referred to as a *routing metric*, where each routing protocol has its own path selection structure. For example, if RIP has learned of two ways to reach the same destination, you want to make sure that your Layer 3 device is using the best path of the two learned options. In this case, the internal prioritization method used is based on the routing protocol implemented. For example, RIP uses an internal prioritization method by using the number of hops to the destination, whereas OSPF uses the least-cost path (the fastest path) to reach the destination.

External prioritization is used when two different routing protocols know about the same destination: a method is needed to determine which routing protocol has the better path to the destination. For example, specifying the same preference for different routes to the same destination can allow for load-sharing, and specifying different preferences for these routes enables route backup. Different vendors use different terms. For example, in the Comware products, the term *preference* or *precedence* is commonly used; with the ProVision products and with Cisco, the term *administrative distance* is used.

The routing table on each networking device is displayed differently, depending on the vendor's implementation. With the Comware and ProVision products, you can see that the display of these tables is similar. Here is an example of a routing table on a ProVision switch:

```
IP Route Entries

Destination    Gateway      VLAN Type       Sub-Type Metric Dist.
-------------- ------------ ---- ---------- -------- ------ -----
10.1.2.0/24    DEFAULT_VLAN 1    connected                1  0
10.1.10.0/24   VLAN10       10   connected                1  0
10.1.20.0/24   VLAN20       20   connected                1  0
10.1.30.0/24   10.1.30.1    30   static                   1  0
127.0.0.0/8    reject            static                   0  0
127.0.0.1/32   lo0               connected                1  0
```

The ProVision Layer 3 switches display the following information in their routing tables:

- Destination network address and subnet mask (networking bits)
- Gateway (or next hop address)
- Local VLAN used to reach the remote destination
- Type of route (and possibly a sub-type)
- Metric of the route (internal prioritization)
- Administrative distance of the route (external prioritization)

Routing tables are discussed in more depth later in the chapter.

Note

Load-sharing is done per-connection—traffic for each unique connection always traverses the same link when load-sharing traffic across multiple equal-cost paths.

Routing Protocol Prioritization

Different routing protocols may find different routes to the same destination. However, not all of those routes are optimal. In fact, at a particular moment, only one protocol is selected by a Layer 3 device to provide the current optimal route to the destination. For the purpose of route selection, each routing protocol (including static routes) is assigned a preference. The routing protocol with the lowest preference value is preferred for finding the best route. Table 11-2 lists some routing protocols and the default priorities for routes found by them—the smaller the preference value, the more preferred the routing protocol. The BGP support is new with the ProVision switches. IS-IS is only supported by the Comware products but is not commonly used throughout networks in the world.

Table 11-2. Routing protocol prioritization (external)

Routing Protocol	ProVision	Comware
Direct (connected)	0	0
Static	1	60
IS-IS	N/A	15
External BGP (eBGP)	20	255
OSPF (internal)	110	10
OSPF (external)	110	150
RIP	120	100
Internal BGP (iBGP)	200	255

The priority for a direct route is always 0, which you cannot change. Any other type of route can have its priority manually configured—256 represents a route from the least trustworthy source. Each static route can be configured with a different priority, where the default is 60 on Comware but 1 on ProVision. Notice that OSPF routes are preferred over static routes by default on Comware, but the opposite is true of ProVision switches!

Note

Route prioritization guidelines on ProVision switches are consistent with those found on Cisco products, but Comware devices have their own, distinct prioritization scheme. Remember that you can always change the priorities for static routes or the dynamic routing protocols.

Packet-Forwarding Activity

Examine the network shown in Figure 11-3. All of the switches are Comware switches. In this example, a student wants to access a database server in the data center. Switch A has routing disabled but is connected to two VLANS—10 and 20. Switch B also has routing disabled and is connected to the same two VLANs. Switch D is connected to VLAN 30 and has routing disabled. Switches A, B, and D cannot route between VLANs because routing is disabled, but Switch C has routing enabled and is connected to all three VLANs. Therefore, any traffic that needs to travel between VLANs must be forwarded to Switch C to be routed.

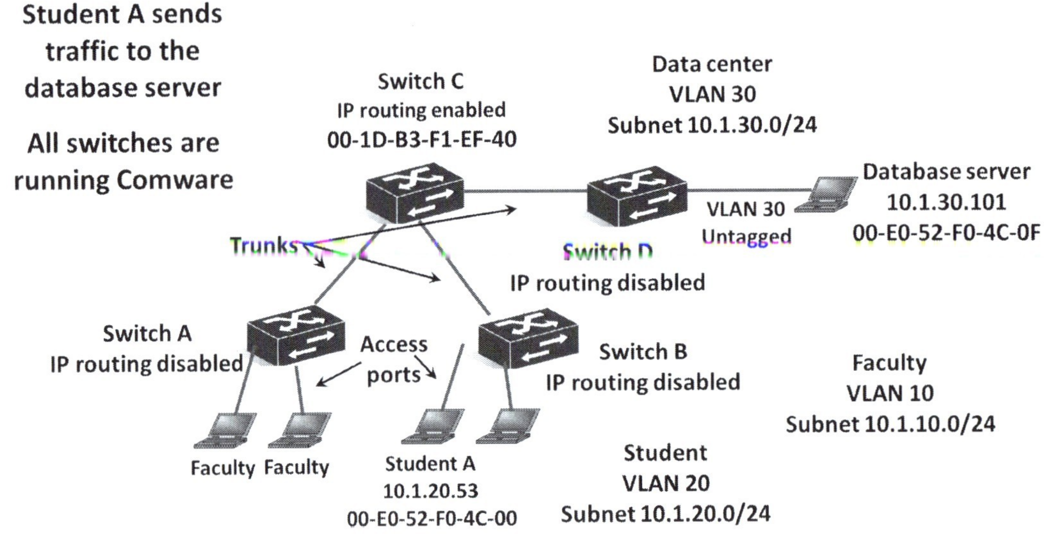

Figure 11-3. Packet-forwarding network topology activity

The following network activity is based on this network topology, with Student A in VLAN 20 accessing the database server in VLAN 30. Switches A, B, and D are Layer 2 switches (routing is disabled). The connections between the switches are trunks (multi-VLAN links).

Activity Explanation

Based on the topology in Figure 11-3 and the scenario explained in the previous section, complete the table below, detailing each segment of the traffic's flow from Student A to the database server. For each segment, you need to define;

- Whether the frame will be tagged using 802.1Q.
- The VLAN associated with the frame at this step.
- The source and destination MAC addresses currently on the packet.
- An explanation for your answer.

Table 11-3. Activity table

Step	Ports in Route	Tagged? and VLAN?	Source MAC Address	Destination MAC Address	Reason
1	Student A to Switch B				
2	Switch B to Switch C				
3	Switch C to Switch D				
4	Switch D to Server				

Activity Answer

The following section describes the answer, in detail, for Table 11-4.

Table 11-4. Answer to the packet-forwarding activity table (from Figure 11-3)

Step	Ports in Route	Tagged? and VLAN?	Source MAC Address	Destination MAC Address	Reason
1	Student A to Switch B	Untagged 20	Student A	Switch C	The workstation does not support 802.1Q, so it sends an untagged frame.
2	Switch B to Switch C	Tagged 20	Student A	Switch C	The port carries traffic for multiple VLANs. The switch adds the 802.1Q field with VLAN ID 20.
3	Switch C to Switch D	Tagged 30	Switch C	Server	The port carries traffic for multiple VLANs. To route the traffic to its final destination, Switch C replaces the Ethernet header with a new one, using the database servers traffic for multiple VLANs. To route the traffic to its final destination, Switch C replaces the Ethernet header
4	Switch D to Server	Untagged 30	Switch C	Server	The database server does not support 802.1Q, so its port must be untagged. Therefore, Switch D removes the 802.1Q tag before sending the frame to the server.

Basic Traffic Flow

To access this server, the student's workstation addresses an IP packet to the database server. The workstation must then encapsulate the IP packet in an Ethernet frame, but, to do so, the workstation must supply a destination MAC address in the Ethernet header. Because the workstation cannot discover the database server's MAC address—the database server is in VLAN 30 and, therefore, would not receive an Address Resolution Protocol (ARP) request from the workstation. It uses the MAC address of its default gateway, Switch C, as the destination for the Ethernet header. The Ethernet frame has a destination MAC address of the 00-1D-B3-F1-EF-40 router interface on Switch C. The destination IP address is 10.1.30.101, the database server's IP address.

The student's workstation sends the Ethernet frame to its directly connected switch, Switch B, which is operating as a Layer 2 switch because IP routing on the switch is not enabled. The switch checks its forwarding (MAC address) table for the destination MAC address in the Ethernet frame (see Table 11-5). Notice that B17 is a multi-VLAN port to Switch C—Switch B will use port B17 to forward the packet to Switch C, which uses the IP addresses 10.1.10.1 and 10.1.20.1 for VLANs 10 and 20, respectively.

Table 11-5. Switch B's MAC address table

IP Address	VLAN	MAC Address	Type	Port	IP Address
10.1.20.15	20	001aa0-1f8deb	Dynamic	B15	10.1.20.15
10.1.20.1	20	001db3-f1ef40	Dynamic	B17	10.1.20.1
10.1.20.101	20	001ec3-10e80b	Dynamic	B19	10.1.20.101
10.1.10.34	10	001ac9-f5d4bf	Dynamic	A10	10.1.10.34
10.1.10.1	10	001db3-f1ef40	Dynamic	B17	10.1.10.1

When Switch C receives the Ethernet frame, it recognizes its own MAC address in the Ethernet header and determines that it must user Layer 3 information to make a forwarding decision. It removes the Ethernet header and uses its routing table, shown in Table 11-6, to find a match for the IP packet.

Table 11-6. Switch C's IP routing table

Destination	Gateway	VLAN	Type	Metric	Distance
10.1.2.0/24	DEFAULT_VLAN	1	Connected	1	0
10.1.10.0/24	VLAN10	10	Connected	1	0
10.1.20.0/24	VLAN20	20	Connected	1	0
10.1.30./24	VLAN30	30	Connected	1	0
127.0.0.0/8	Reject		Static	0	0
127.0.0.1/32	lo0		Connected	1	0

Switch C has a direct route, or a directly connected route, to the destination 10.1.30.0/24. The switch now checks its ARP cache table to see if it has an entry for the destination IP address. If not, Switch C uses ARP to determine the MAC address for the destination IP address.

Switch C creates a new Ethernet header for the IP packet, using the database server's MAC address as the destination address. The switch then forwards the frame to the next hop—Switch D. Switch D receives the frame, checks its MAC address table, and forwards the traffic to the database server's switch port.

VLAN Tagging

Now that you understand how traffic is routed between VLANs, let us see how the HP switches handle VLAN tagging for that traffic. Using the same scenario of tracing an IP packet from a workstation in VLAN 20 to a database server in VLAN 30, you will see how the switches along the route employ 802.1Q tagging.

Table 11-7. VLAN tagging example

Step	Ports in the Route	Tagged?	Reason
1	Workstation switch port (Switch B)	Untagged	The workstation does not support 802.1Q, so it sends an untagged frame.
2	Switch B uplink (to Switch C)	Tagged VLAN 20	The port carries traffic for multiple VLANs. The switch adds the 802.1Q field with VLAN ID 20.
3	Switch C uplink (from Switch B)	Tagged VLAN 20	The port carries traffic for multiple VLANs and receives the frame from Switch B. The uplink port must have the same VLAN settings as the directly connected switch.
4	Switch C uplink (to Switch D)	Tagged VLAN 30	The port carries traffic for multiple VLANs. To route the traffic to its final destination, Switch C replaces the Ethernet header with a new one, using the database server's MAC address as the destination. Switch C also adds the 802.1Q field with VLAN ID 30 and forwards it to Switch D.
5	Switch D uplink (from Switch C)	Tagged VLAN 30	The port carries traffic for multiple VLANs. The switch receives the tagged frame from Switch C. The uplink port must have the same VLAN settings as the directly connected switch, Switch C.
6	Database server switch port (Switch D)	Untagged	The database server does not support 802.1Q, so its port must be untagged. Therefore, Switch D removes the 802.1Q tag before sending the frame to the server.

In the example shown in Figure 11-3, the switches are forwarding traffic from multiple VLANs. The uplink ports (switch-to-switch links) are access ports (untagged) that are members of their specified VLANs. The sending student workstation and destination database server do not support 802.1Q. Table 11-7 shows a more detailed process of what a packet would go through when a workstation in VLAN 20 connected to Switch B tries to access the database server in VLAN 30 connected to Switch D.

Static Route Configuration

The only routing configuration topic covered in this chapter is the configuration of static routes on ProVision and Comware switches. "Chapter 12: OSPF Operation and Configuration" covers the operation, configuration, and verification of OSPF on HP switches. The next two sections discuss the configuration of static routes on ProVision and Comware switches.

HP ProVision Static Routes

Before you can set up routing on your HP ProVision switch, you must first set up IP addressing for your VLAN interfaces. On the routing switches, IP addresses are associated with individual VLANs. By default, there is a single VLAN (Default_VLAN) on the routing switch. In that configuration, a single IP address serves as the management access address for the entire device. If routing is enabled on the routing switch, the IP address on the single VLAN also acts as the routing interface.

Each IP address on a routing switch must be in a different subnet. You can have only one VLAN interface that is in a given subnet. For example, you can configure IP addresses 192.168.1.1/24 and 192.168.2.1/24 on the same routing switch, but you cannot configure 192.168.1.1/24 and 192.168.1.2/24 on the same routing switch in different VLANs.

Note

You can configure multiple IP addresses on the same VLAN. The number of IP addresses you can configure on an individual VLAN interface is 32. This is sometimes referred to as *sub-addressing* or *secondary addressing*.

IP Address Assignment Review

Recall from "Chapter 3: Basic Setup," that you can assign an IP address to the switch in this VLAN by using the following configuration:

```
ProVision(config)# vlan <vid>
ProVision(vlan-<vid>)# ip address <ip-address>/<subnet-mask>
```

Or

```
ProVision(config)# vlan <vid> ip address <ip-address>/<subnet-mask>
```

If your switch is a Layer 3 switch, it can have multiple IP addresses—one for each VLAN—where the switch is the default gateway for each VLAN (VLANs were discussed in "Chapter 6: VLANs").

Note

After you create a VLAN and assign an IP address to it, the network number for the VLAN appears as a (directly) connected route in the routing table of the ProVision switch.

Basic IP Routing Configuration

If your switch needs to contact other devices in remote VLANs or subnets when routing is disabled, you need to configure a default gateway on your switch, using the following command:

```
ProVision(config)# ip default-gateway <ip-address>
```

To enable routing on your ProVision switch, use the following command:

```
ProVision(config)# ip routing
```

Note

ProVision routing switches, like the 8200, are in Layer 2 mode, by default. Routing is disabled. When in Layer 2 mode, you can use the `ip default-gateway` command to define an exit point for the management subnet. After routing is configured, the `ip default-gateway` command is ignored on the ProVision switch. This command is only used when the switch is operating as a Layer 2 switch. However, HP highly recommends that you remove this command after you have enabled routing on the ProVision switch.

ProVision Static Route Syntax

As was discussed earlier in the chapter, you can use different forms of indirect routing to help your switch learn remote destination networks. For smaller networks, static routing is the most commonly used method.

When you configure a static IP route, you must specify the following parameters:

- The IP address and network mask for the route's destination network or host.
- The route's path, which can be one of the following:
    - The IP address of a next-hop router.
    - A *null interface*—The routing switch drops traffic forwarded to the null interface. (This is a logical interface used by the router to drop traffic to undesirable destinations.)

You can configure the following types of static IP routes:

- **Standard**—The *static route* consists of a destination network address or host, a corresponding network mask, and the IP address of the next-hop IP address.
- **Null**—The *null route* consists of the destination network address or host, a corresponding network mask, and either the `reject` or `blackhole` keyword. Typically, the null route is configured as a backup route for discarding traffic if the primary route is unavailable. By default, when IP routing is enabled, a route for the 127.0.0.0/8 network is created to the null interface. Traffic to this interface is rejected (dropped). This route is for all traffic to the "loop-back" network, with the single exception of traffic to the host address of the switch's loopback interface (127.0.0.1/32).

To configure a static route on your ProVision switches, use the following syntax:

```
ProVision(config)# ip route <dest-ip-addr>/<mask-length>
                   <next-hop-ip-addr> | vlan <vlan-id> | reject |
                   blackhole> [metric <metric>] [distance <1-255>]
```

The next-hop can be a gateway IP address, a VLAN, or the keyword `reject` or `blackhole`. The `blackhole` parameter specifies a null route where IP traffic for the specified destination is discarded and no ICMP error notification is returned to the sender. The `reject` parameter specifies a null route where IP traffic for the specified destination is discarded and an ICMP error notification is returned to the sender.

Note

A gateway IP address does not have to be directly reachable on one of the local subnets. If the gateway address is not directly reachable, the route is added to the routing table as soon as a route to the gateway address is learned.

The `metric` parameter specifies an integer value that is associated with the route. It is used to compare a static route to routes in the IP route table from other sources to the same destination.

The routing switch also applies default values for the route's administrative distance. In the case of static routes, this is the value that the routing switch uses to compare a static route to routes from other route sources to the same destination before placing a route in the IP route table. A lower value will be chosen over a higher value. The default administrative distance for static IP routes is 1, but it can be configured to any value between 1 and 255. The fixed administrative distance values ensure that the routing switch always prefers static IP routes over routes from other sources to the same destination. With the default administrative distance, the switch prefers static routes over routes learned from a dynamic routing protocol, like RIP.

IP static routes remain in the IP route table as long as the IP interface to the next-hop router is up. If the next-hop interface goes down, the software removes the static route from the IP route table. If the next-hop interface comes up again, the software adds the route back to the route table. This feature allows the routing switch to adjust to changes in network topology. The routing switch does not continue trying to use routes on unreachable paths but instead uses routes only when their paths are reachable.

Note

To configure a default route, use a destination network and mask of 0.0.0.0/0.

Here is an example that illustrates the configuration of static routes:

```
ProVision(config)# ip route 10.10.40.0/24 10.10.10.1
ProVision(config)# ip route 0.0.0.0/0 10.10.10.2
```

The first command creates a static route to the 10.10.40.0/24 network with a next-hop gateway of 10.10.10.1. The second command creates a default route with a next-hop gateway of 10.10.10.2.

Routing Verification

After you have set up IP addressing on your switch, you can set up IP routing. By default, routing is disabled on the ProVision switches, as can be seen from the `show ip` command:

```
ProVision# show ip

 Internet (IP) Service

  IP Routing        : Disabled

  Default Gateway : 15.255.120.1

  Default TTL       : 64

  Arp Age           : 1000

  Domain Suffix    :

  DNS server        :

VLAN          | IP Config  IP Address      Subnet Mask     Proxy ARP

-------------+ ---------- --------------- --------------- ---------

DEFAULT_VLAN | Manual     15.255.111.13   255.255.248.0   No
```

To see the routing table on your ProVision switch, use the `show ip route` command. This command displays all of the direct and indirect routes in the routing table. You can also qualify the output by specifying the protocol you wish to examine. For example, if you want to view only the static routes in the routing table, use this command:

```
ProVision# show ip route static

                          IP Route Entries

Destination       Gateway     VLAN  Type     Sub-Type  Metric Dist.

---------------- ----------- ---- -------- --------- ------ ----

10.10.20.177/32  reject            static                1     1

10.10.40.0/24    VLAN10      10    static                1     1

10.10.50.128/27  VLAN10      10    static                1     1

10.11.30.0/24    blackhole         static                1     1

127.0.0.0/8      reject            static                0     0
```

Notice the `reject` route at the bottom of the display—this is for the loopback on the switch. The `blackhole` route drops all traffic sent to 10.11.30.0/24, with no Internet Control Message Protocol (ICMP) message sent back to the source specifying the reason why the IP packets are being dropped. `Blackhole` routing is commonly used to drop traffic for security reasons.

Note

If there is more than one match in the routing table for a specified destination address, the routing device always chooses the most specific match (the one with the most number of matching bits in the subnet mask).

From a user or network administrator's perspective, you could use the `ping` command discussed in "Chapter 3: Basic Setup," to test Layer 3 connectivity in the network. The problem with `ping`, however, is that it does not tell you what hops (Layer 3 devices) the packet takes to reach the destination.

The `traceroute` command enables you to trace the route from the switch to a host address. This command outputs information for each (router) hop between the switch and the destination address. Table 11-8 shows some optional parameters you can use to qualify the `traceroute` command.

```
ProVision# traceroute {<ip-address> | <hostname>}
```

Table 11-8. ProVision `traceroute` parameters

Parameter	Description
`minttl` <1-255>	For the current instance of `traceroute`, this changes the minimum number of hops allowed for each probe packet sent along the route. If `minttl` is greater than the actual number of hops, the output includes only the hops at and above the `minttl` threshold. (The hops below the threshold are not listed.) If `minttl` matches the actual number of hops, only that hop is shown in the output. If `minttl` is less than the actual number of hops, all hops are listed. For any instance of `traceroute`, if you want a `minttl` value other than the default, you must specify that value. (Default: 1)
`maxttl <1-255>`	For the current instance of `traceroute`, this changes the maximum number of hops allowed for each probe packet sent along the route. If the destination address is further from the switch than `maxttl` allows, `traceroute` lists the IP addresses for all hops it detects up to the `maxttl` limit. For any instance of `traceroute`, if you want a `maxttl` value other than the default, you must specify that value. (Default: 30)
`timeout <1-120>`	For the current instance of `traceroute`, this changes the timeout period that the switch waits for each probe of a hop in the route. For any instance of `traceroute`, if you want a `timeout` value other than the default, you must specify that value. (Default: 5 seconds)

Parameter	Description
probes <1-5>	For the current instance of traceroute, this changes the number of queries that the switch sends for each hop in the route. For any instance of traceroute, if you want a probes value other than the default, you must specify that value. (Default: 3)
source {<ip-addr> | <vlan-id>}	This parameter defines the source IP address or VLAN. The source IP address must be owned by the router. If a VLAN is specified, the IP address associated with the specified VLAN is used.

Note

To halt an ongoing traceroute search, press the Ctrl+C keys.

Use Table 11-9 to help troubleshoot problems in your network.

Table 11-9. Commands used for basic troubleshooting

Check	Commands
Can A reach B?	Use ping commands.
If B is in same subnet, check VLAN membership.	Use show arp, show mac, and show vlan commands in the local subnet.
If B is in a different subnet, check routing.	Use traceroute, show ip, and show ip route commands.
If B is in a different subnet, check hops to the destination.	Use show arp, show mac, and show vlan commands in subsequent and remote subnets.

Note

Comware networking products also support traceroute; however, the syntax of the command is not covered in this book. You can easily use Comware's context-sensitive help, though, to figure out the available parameters.

HP Comware Static Routes

Before you can set up routing on your HP Comware switch or router, you must first set up IP addressing for your VLAN (switch) and physical (router) interfaces. Recall from "Chapter 3: Basic Setup," that you can assign an IP address to the switch in this VLAN by using the following configuration:

```
[Comware] interface <interface-type> <interface-ID>
[Comware-<int-view>] ip address <ip-address> <subnet-mask-bits>
```

Here is an example of the configuration of a Comware router interface's IP address:

```
[Router] interface GigabitEthernet 0/0
[Router-GigabitGigabitEthernet0/0] ip address 10.1.1.1 24
```

Here is the configuration of an IP address for VLAN 1 on a Comware Layer 3 switch:

```
[Switch] interface vlan-interface 1
[Switch-Vlan-interface1] ip address 10.10.1.1 24
```

Static Route Syntax

Static routes are added manually to the device by the network administrator; they are not added or learned by any routing protocol. As was mentioned earlier in this chapter, static routes are commonly used in smaller networks or for manual control of smaller sections within larger networks.

Static routes are added to the Comware products by using the following syntax:

```
[Comware] ip route-static <destination-network> <mask>
          <next-hop-ip-address> [preference <preference>]
          [description <description>]
```

When creating a static route, you must enter the destination network, the destination subnet mask, and the next-hop IP address or gateway. You can also change the preference or assign a description to the static route. To set up a blackhole route, use the term `null0` for the next-hop address.

If you want to change the default preference of all static routes on the Comware product, use this command:

```
[Comware] ip route-static default-preference <0-255>
```

Note

IP routing is enabled by default on the Comware products—no special command needs to be entered to enable it.

Here is a configuration example using static routes:

```
[Comware] ip route-static 10.1.2.0 255.255.255.0 10.1.6.1
[Comware] ip route-static 0.0.0.0 0.0.0.0 10.1.6.2
[Comware] ip route-static 10.6.22.0 255.255.255.0 10.6.21.2
          description To Chicago Branch
```

In the above example, to go to the network segment 10.1.2.0/24, the router should send the traffic to the next-hop address of 10.1.6.1. The second static route is a default route with a gateway address of 10.1.6.2. The last static route has a description associated with it.

To change the preference of a given static route, use the preference parameter, like this:

```
[Comware] ip route-static 10.6.22.0 24 10.6.21.2 preference 1
```

IP Routing Verification

To examine the routing table of a Comware device, use the `display ip routing-table` command. Here is an example with connected (direct) and static routes:

```
[Comware] display ip routing-table

Routing Tables: Public

Destinations : 7 Routes : 7

Destination/Mask Proto   Pre Cost NextHop  Interface

0.0.0.0/0        Static  60  0    1.1.4.2  Vlan500

1.1.2.0/24       Direct  0   0    1.1.2.3  Vlan300

1.1.4.0/30       Direct  0   0    1.1.4.1  Vlan500

<-output omitted->
```

In this example, there is one static route, a default route, which has a default preference of 60.

RIP Overview

RIP is an IP route exchange protocol that uses a *distance vector* (a number representing distance) to measure the metric of a given route. These updates, which include a copy of a neighbor's routing table, are sent out every 30 seconds, by default. The frequency of these updates can be modified. The metric is a distance vector because the metric often is equivalent to the number of router hops between the Layer 3 routing device and the destination network.

A Layer 3 routing device can receive multiple paths to a destination. The software evaluates the paths, selects the best path, and saves the path in the IP route table as the route to the destination. The routing table for RIP stores only the best route to a destination. The best path is defined as the destination path with the fewest hops. If information is received that indicates another route as the best path to a given destination, that route becomes the new route and replaces the previously stored entry. This information is then relayed to all other IP/RIP routers.

RIP Layer 3 routing devices modify a route's metric by adding to it upon receipt from a neighboring RIP router. To bias the selection of a route for a given destination, the administrative distance or preference in a Comware switch can be modified to a higher metric, making a given route less likely to be used than other, lower-cost routes. An RIP route can have a maximum hop count of 15. Any destination with a higher cost is considered unreachable. The low maximum hop count prevents endless loops in the network.

Note

An overview of RIP is discussed in this book, but, because RIP is rarely used in modern networks, its configuration is not covered. However, an overview of OSPF and a single area configuration are covered in the next chapter.

RIPv1 Versus RIPv2

HP supports the following RIP implementations:

- Version 1 (the default on Comware devices)
- Version 1 compatible with version 2
- Version 2 (the default on ProVision switches)

Table 11-10 provides a brief comparison of RIPv1 and RIPv2.

Table 11-10. RIPv1 and RIPv2 comparison

Routing Information	RIPv1	RIPv2
Updates	Periodic only	Periodic by default, with triggered updates when topology changes occur
Routing advertisements	Broadcasts	Multicasts
Route authentication	None	Yes, with either clear-text passwords or MD5 digital signatures
Route entry	Contains only network numbers	Contains network numbers and subnet masks and, therefore, supports Variable Length Subnet Masking (VLSM) and Classless Interdomain Routing (CIDR); allows support for route summarization

Routing Loops

All distance vector protocols, including RIP, are susceptible to routing loops. A routing loop is where routers in the network have a misunderstanding of the topology and, therefore, packets sent to a particular destination or destinations are not routed correctly but are stuck in a loop in the network.

For example, in Figure 11-4, without any loop prevention mechanisms employed, SwB could see SwA as a path to Network A. However, if SwB's link to Network A were to fail and if SwB were to route to SwA to reach Network A, a loop would occur.

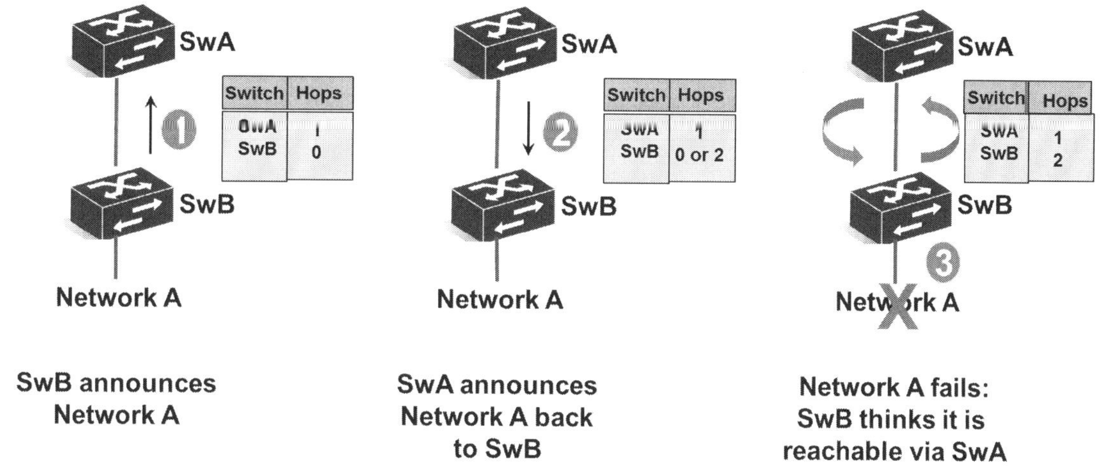

Figure 11-4. Brief illustration of routing loops

Routing Loop Solutions for Distance Vector Protocols

RIP includes a number of features that help stabilize its performance in the wake of rapidly changing network conditions, like:

- Split horizon.
- Poisoned routes.
- Poison reverse routing updates.
- Hop-count limits.
- Hold-down timers.

A maximum of 15 hops is supported by IP/RIP. Any destination that is greater than 15 hops away is considered unreachable. Although limited to smaller networks, it prevents endless loops in the network.

Split horizon is designed to prevent routing loops from being generated by adjacent routers. This feature is of particular value when a router's path to a given router is via another router. Split horizon allows a routing broadcast to be modified so that routers with intermediate routers in their path to a destination router are not seen as a path to the destination router by the intermediate router. Split horizon is used to deal with small routing loops in a network.

Poison reverse updates are used to prevent larger loops within the network by setting the metric (hop count) of neighboring routes to infinity. In RIP's case, the metric of the failed route is set to 16 (unreachable, since the maximum hop count is 15). This type of route is commonly called a *poisoned route*. This solution prevents multi-hop loops, or larger loops.

To ensure all networking devices understand that the downed network is not reachable, a *hold-down timer* instructs routers to delay (hold down) action upon update messages received from routes believed inactive. The period of time is generally longer than the time required to update the entire network of a routing change (typically at least three times larger than the periodic update interval). In RIP's case, the period timer is 30 seconds, but the hold-down timer is 240 seconds, by default. The use of the hold-down timer basically freezes the poisoned route in the routing table and allows all other routers to receive this update via periodic announcements. After the hold-down timer expires, an alternative path for the destination can be installed in the routing table. This safeguard prevents a removed or bad route from being reinstated in error. The only time the hold-down timer rule is broken is if there is an alternative path advertised with the same or better metric than the original route. Otherwise, paths with higher hop count metrics are looked upon as suspicious, since they might be part of a multi-hop loop.

RIP Update Example

When RIP is enabled for an interface or network, the router prepares an update that advertises the address ranges in its route table. In many cases, each address range in the table represents a network (a single broadcast domain). However, this is not always the case. Sometimes, the entries represent an address range that includes many networks, known as a *summarized network*.

Examine the network shown in Figure 11-5. In this example, Router_1 in Group 1 advertises all of its connected networks except the network associated with the interface through which the router sends the update. The RIP update is being sent over the interface 10.0.200.11/24. Accordingly, network 10.0.200.0/24 is omitted from the update, since this and the core router are directly connected to this network.

Network	Metric
10.1.2.0/24	1
10.1.20.0/24	2
10.2.10.0/24	16
10.3.10/0/24	16

Network	Gateway	Type	Metric
10.1.2.0/24	10.1.200.11	RIP	2
10.1.20.0/24	10.1.200.11	RIP	3
10.2.10.0/24	10.1.200.11	RIP	16
10.3.10/0/24	10.1.200.11	RIP	16

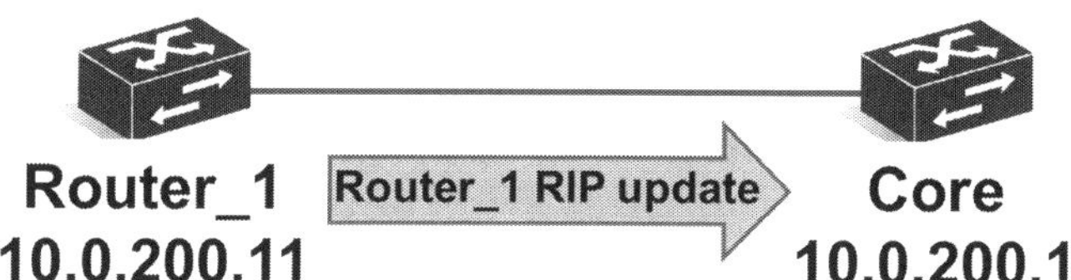

Figure 11-5. RIP update example

By default, this update occurs every 30 seconds. When this interval expires, the router sends updates over all of its RIP-enabled interfaces. The metric associated with each of the advertised networks is 1 for directly connected networks and 2 or more for remote networks. Although Router_1 internally associates a metric of 0 with its locally connected networks, it advertises these networks with a cost of 1. In some vendor implementations, the cost used internally will be 1. However, the external cost reported is the same.

By default, the ProVision and Comware products implement poison reverse. This technology prevents routing loops by enabling RIP routers to distinguish legitimate redundant routes from routes that have been learned from immediate neighbors. Before sending an update over an interface, a router using poison reverse examines the next-hop address for each entry in its route table. If an update is being directed to the source for a particular route, the update is sent with a metric of 16, which is considered infinity for RIP. In this way, the poison reverse technology informs the neighbor that it cannot reach the network in question through the local router.

For example, Router_1 in Group 1 sends periodic updates over interface 10.0.200.0/24. Networks learned over that interface have metric of 16:

- Core adds networks in 10.1.0.0/16 to its route table.
- Core and Router_1 learn 10.2.0.0/16 and 10.3.0.0/16 from other peers.

An alternative to poison reverse for preventing routing loops is *split horizon*, which forbids a router from advertising a route to the neighbor from which it was learned. In general, poison reverse is preferred in multi-path networks because it offers faster convergence times.

Learning Check

The following questions help you measure your understanding of the material presented in this chapter. Read all of the choices carefully, since there may be more than one correct answer. Choose all correct answers for each question.

Questions

1. Examine the Comware routing protocol prioritizations. Place the following in order, from lowest preference number to the highest preference number.
   a. Static
   b. RIP
   c. Internal OSPF
   d. BGP

2. Which ProVision switch command defines a static route to 10.1.1.0/24 with a next-hop address of 10.2.2.2?

3. Which RIP routing loop solution prevents advertising a route out an interface from which it was received?

4. Which ProVision term is used to choose between a network that was discovered by two routing protocols, but where only one is placed in the routing table?
   a. Precedence
   b. Preference
   c. Administrative distance
   d. Metric

5. What is the default administrative distance of a ProVision static route?

6. What metric is assigned to a RIP route to poison it?

Answers

1. ☑ Based on the default preferences/precedents defined in Comware, the choice between routing protocols is ranked as follows: **internal OSPF**, **static**, **RIP**, and **BGP**.

2. ☑ `ip route 10.1.1.0/24 10.2.2.2` is the ProVision switch command that defines a static route to 10.1.1.0/24 with a next-hop address of 10.2.2.2.

3. ☑ Split horizon prevents a route from being advertised out an interface from which it was learned.

4. ☑ **C** is correct. Administrative distance is used by ProVision switches to weight (rank) different routing protocols.

   ☒ **A** and **B** are incorrect because these are Comware terms. And **D** is incorrect because metric is used to select routes within a routing protocol—not between routing protocols.

5. ☑ The default administrative distance of an ProVision route is 1.

6. ☑ RIP assigns a hop count of 1 to poison a route.

12 OSPF Operation and Configuration

EXAM OBJECTIVES

In this chapter, you learn to:

- ✓ Explain Layer 3 routing concepts and apply Layer 3 protocols.
- ✓ Perform installation and configuration of devices.
- ✓ Verify Layer 3 routing protocol convergence and scalability.
- ✓ Apply troubleshooting methodology.
- ✓ Use general troubleshooting tools.
- ✓ Perform troubleshooting methodology on wired networks.
- ✓ Verify network performance parameters.

ASSUMED KNOWLEDGE

This chapter assumes that you have a good understanding of IP addressing and basic routing, including the following topics:

- IP subnetting
- Routing basics (covered in "Chapter 11: IP Routing Overview")
- VLANs (covered in "Chapter 6: VLANs")
- Variable-length subnet masking (VLSM)
- Classless interdomain routing (CIDR)

INTRODUCTION

The Open Shortest Path First (OSPF) routing protocol, as an Interior Gateway Protocol (IGP), functions between routing devices within the same domain, or *autonomous system* (AS), which is generally defined as a group of networked devices under the control of the same entity. It enables the routing devices to exchange information with each other about the IP subnets within the AS to discover routes between them. This chapter introduces the operation and configuration of OSPF in a single area on HP ProVision and HP Comware products.

This chapter focuses on the following topics:

- OSPF terms
- Designated and backup designated routers
- Adjacencies
- OSPF configuration for a single area

OSPF Overview

The OSPF protocol is a link state protocol that handles routing for IP traffic. Version 2 of OSPF, which is explained in RFC 2328, is an open standard, such as Routing Information Protocol (RIP) v1 and RIPv2. As a link-state protocol, OSPF functions differently from a distance-vector protocol, such as RIP. Rather than advertise routes to each other, OSPF routers advertise the links that they support. Specifically, they advertise links on which OSPF is enabled.

OSPF routers forward their link state advertisements (LSAs) throughout the OSPF domain until all routers have received all LSAs. These LSAs give the routers the information they need to construct a topology of the OSPF domain. With the complete picture, the routers can select the best path to each network.

OSPF was created in the mid-1980s to overcome many of the deficiencies and scalability problems that RIP had in large enterprise networks. Because it is based on an open standard, OSPF is very popular in many corporate networks today and has many advantages, including:

- It runs on most routers, since it is based on an open standard.
- It uses the SPF algorithm, developed by Edsger Dijkstra, to provide a loop-free topology.
- It provides fast convergence with triggered, incremental updates via link state update (LSU) advertisements.
- It is a classless protocol and allows for a hierarchical design with VLSM and route summarization (CIDR).
- It has an intelligent metric (cost), which is the inverse of the bandwidth of an interface.

Given its advantages, OSPF does have its share of disadvantages:

- It requires more memory to hold the *adjacency* (list of OSPF neighbors), *topology* (a link state database containing all of the routers and their routes/links), and routing tables.
- It requires extra CPU processing to run the SPF algorithm, which is especially true when you first turn on your routers and they are initially building the adjacency and topology tables.
- For large networks, it requires careful design to break up the networks into appropriate hierarchical designs by separating routers into different areas.
- It is more complex to configure and more difficult to troubleshoot than distance vector protocols.

Knowing the advantages and disadvantages of any routing protocol is useful when it comes to picking a protocol. Typically, OSPF is used in large enterprise networks that have either a mixed routing vendor environment or a policy that requires an open standard for a routing protocol. Using OSPF gives a company flexibility when it needs to replace any of its existing routers.

OSPF Terms

There are many terms used in OSPF to describe routers, locations, and routing information. Here are some common ones:

- Router ID
- Area
- Area border router (ABR)
- Autonomous system boundary router (ASBR)
- Designated router (DR)
- Backup designated router (BDR)
- Adjacencies
- Link state advertisements (LSAs)
- Link state database (LSDB)

The following sections will introduce you to these terms.

Router ID

For any LSA, the advertising router includes its *router ID*, which is a consistent IP address that identifies that router. It is recommended that you assign a router ID to the OSPF process to ensure a consistent ID on each router in the OSPF domain. If you do not configure a router ID, the HP routing switch selects a router ID, as follows:

1. It uses the global router ID.
2. If the global router ID is not configured, it uses the highest IP address on a loopback interface.
3. If a loopback interface is not configured, it uses the highest IP address on any VLAN or routed physical interface.

The IP address remains the router ID regardless of whether that interface is up. However, a new router ID is selected if the interface is removed or if its IP address is changed. Most vendors (for example, Comware and Cisco) use these three steps in choosing a router ID. ProVision uses a slightly different process, described in the configuration section of this chapter ("Single Area OSPF Configuration").

Note

Since the router ID is a 32-bit number, any valid number would suffice for a router ID, including 0.0.0.0 and 255.255.255.255. Some administrators use the first octet to represent the OSPF area number the device is associated with.

OSPF Messages and LSAs

OSPF uses messages to communicate information between OSPF routers. The messages are used to discover neighboring OSPF routers, build adjacencies with these routers, share routing information with each other (LSAs), and detect dead neighbors (previously discovered neighbors that are no longer reachable after the dead interval timer that has expired). There are many different LSA types, some of which are discussed later in the chapter. LSAs concerning routing information are stored in an LSDB.

Areas

To provide scalability for very large networks, OSPF supports two important concepts: autonomous systems and areas. Within an AS, areas are used to provide hierarchical routing. An *area* is a group of contiguous networks. Basically, areas are used to control when and how much routing information is shared across your network. In flat network designs, such as those that use IP RIP, if a change occurs on one router (perhaps a flapping route problem), it affects every router in the entire network. With a correctly designed hierarchical network, these changes can be contained within a single area.

OSPF implements a two-layer hierarchy: the backbone and areas off the backbone, as shown in Figure 12-1. This network includes a backbone and three areas connected to the backbone. Each area is given a unique number that is 32 bits in length. The area number can be represented by a single decimal number, such as 1, or in a dotted decimal format, such as 0.0.0.1. Area 0 is a special area and represents the top-level hierarchy of the OSPF network, commonly called the *backbone.* Through a correct IP addressing design, you should be able to summarize routing information between areas. By summarizing your routing information (perhaps one summarized route for each area), you reduce the amount of information that routers need to know about. For instance, each area in Figure 12-1 is assigned a separate Class A subnet network number. Through summarization on the border routers between areas, other areas would not need to see all the Class A subnets—only the summarized network numbers for each respective area (the range of addresses representing the areas themselves: 10.0.0.0/16 for Area 0, 10.1.0.0/16 for Area 1, and 10.2.0.0/16 for Area 2).

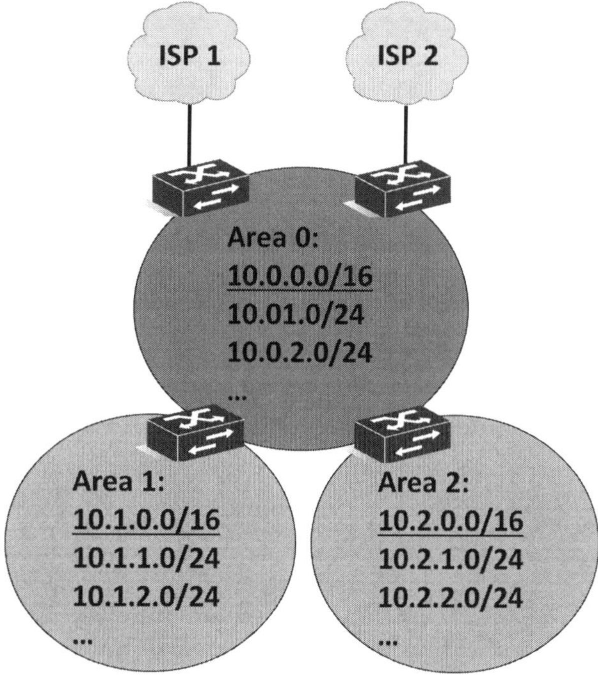

Figure 12-1. OSPF and areas

Area 2, for instance, does not need to see all of the subnets of Area 1's 10.1.0.0/16 network number, since only one path exists out of Area 2 to the backbone. Area 2, however, needs to see all of its own internal subnets to create optimized routing tables to reach its own internal networks within Area 2. Therefore, in a correctly designed OSPF network, each area should contain specific routes only for its own areas, plus summarized routes to reach other areas. By performing this summarization, the routers have a smaller topology database (they know only about links in their own area and the summarized routes) and their routing tables are smaller (they know only about their own area's routes and the summarized routes). Through a correct hierarchical design, you can scale OSPF to very large sizes.

ABRs

Area border routers have interfaces in at least two areas, one of which is Area 0. Area 0 is the backbone area, and OSPF design requires all areas to connect to this backbone (physically or logically). As a member of multiple areas, the ABR maintains multiple LSDBs, one for each area. In the example shown in Figure 12-2, ABR A receives LSAs from other routing devices within Area 1 (called *internal routers*), synchronizing its Area 1 LSDB with theirs. LSA Type 1 and LSA Type 2 are routes internal to an area (this is discussed in more depth later in the chapter (see the "LSAs and the Link State Database" section). When routes need to be shared between areas, ABRs change the original LSA Type (1 or 2) to a 3. The "3" indicates that the route is from a different area than the router receiving the update. Thus, an internal router knows that it must go to the ABR to reach the destination network.

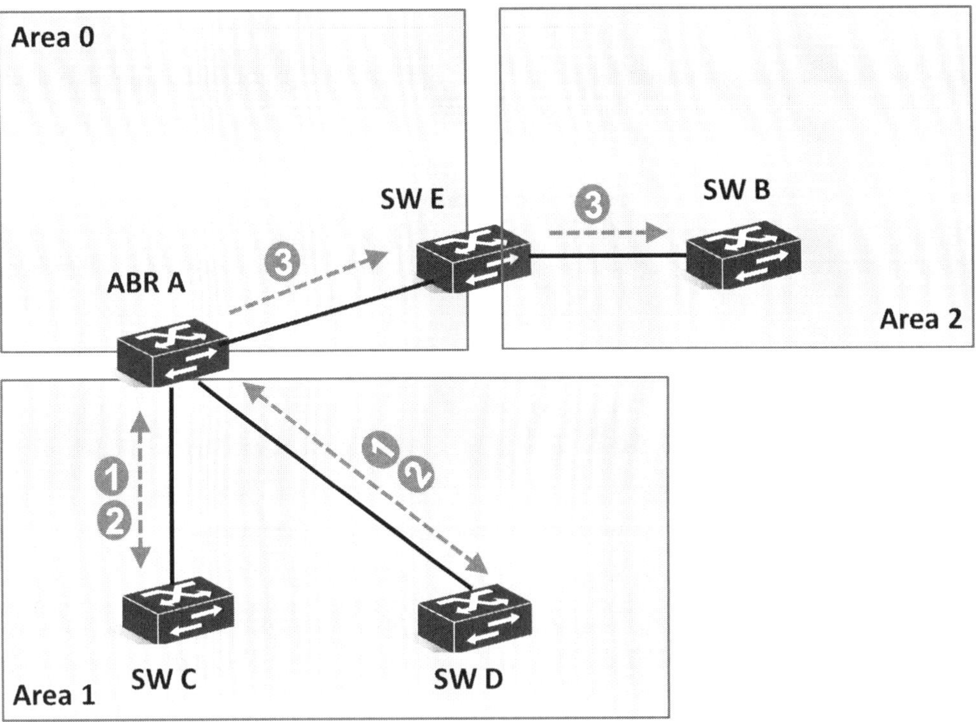

Figure 12-2. Network utilizing ABRs

ABRs control routes between areas. They can advertise the original route, summarize routes for an area and advertise a single route, advertise a default route, or even filter routes. A more in-depth discussion on ABRs and their abilities is discussed at the Accredited Solutions Expert (ASE) networking-level courses.

ASBRs

In some environments, an OSPF domain needs to learn about networks that connect to non-OSPF routers. In Figure 12-1, two routing switches connect to the Internet via two different ISPs using Border Gateway Protocol (BGP). The ISPs use BGP to send routes to the core routing switch. The other routing switches in the campus LAN need to learn about this route so that they can forward Internet-destined traffic correctly. You do not want to simply add static default routes on the routing switches because these routes would not reflect the current situation if one of the ISPs experiences problems. Instead, the core switches need to advertise their default routes using OSPF. Then, if one of the switches no longer receives the default route, it can stop advertising it.

This environment requires ASBRs. OSPF defines an *autonomous system boundary router* as a router that advertises external routes. A route is considered *external* when it is learned by a method or protocol other than the current OSPF process and is then redistributed or imported into the current OSPF process. In this example, both core switches must act as ASBRs. These external routes could be from another protocol, like BGP or a different OSPF network, static or default routes, or even directly connected external routes.

OSPF Area and Router Activity

Given the topology in Figure 12-3:

- Which area is the backbone?
- Which routers are ASBRs?
- Which routers are ABRs?

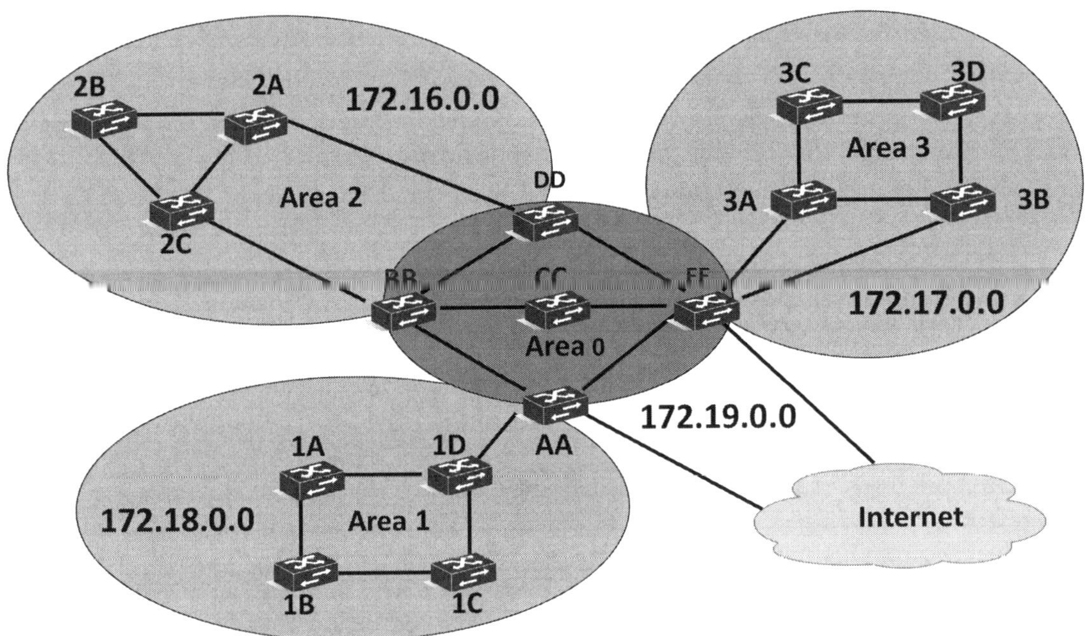

Figure 12-3. Find the OSPF components.

Here are the answers for the activity:

- Which area is the backbone? **0**
- Which routers are ASBRs? **AA** and **EE**
- Which routers are ABRs? **AA**, **BB**, **DD**, and **EE**. Note that a router can perform more than one role, like AA and EE, which are both ASBRs and ABRs.

DRs and BDRs

This book focuses on implementing OSPF in Ethernet LANs. OSPF defines *Ethernet* as a broadcast network, which supports multiple routers. If all of the routers must exchange LSAs with each other, OSPF can begin to generate a great deal of traffic. To minimize the LSAs, the routers do not achieve adjacency with each neighbor; instead, the routers in the Ethernet network elect a Designated Router (DR) and Backup Designated Router (BDR) and achieve adjacency with them. The DR, which is adjacent to all routers, can forward LSAs between them.

If the DR fails, the network needs a new one. To prevent a lengthy process of reelecting the DR and of that DR achieving adjacency with each router in the network, the OSPF routers in the network elect a BDR at the same time as they elect the DR. All routers in the network achieve adjacency with the BDRs, as well.

To ensure smooth operation, all routers in the broadcast network must achieve adjacency with two routers: DR and BDR. If the DR fails, the BDR can take over without a lengthy period during which a new DR is elected and that DR achieves adjacency with other routers.

Note

Only broadcast links support DRs and BDRs, like Ethernet. In WAN networks that use virtual circuits (VCs) for connections, a point-to-point connection is established. On this type of link, no DR or BDR is necessary. A point-to-point connection supports only two devices, whether it is a dedicated serial link or a virtual circuit. By default, Ethernet is treated as a broadcast domain even if the two OSPF devices are directly connected together.

Also, ProVision does not support point-to-point links. Even if there are only two ProVision switches in a VLAN, the VLAN is still treated as a broadcast domain in which one switch is the DR and the other switch is the BDR.

DR/BDR Election Process

Here is the process used for determining which routers become the DR and BDR:

- The first router that is active on the link becomes the DR.
- The second router that is active on the link becomes the BDR.
- Link/interface priority is used for a re-election, if the DR/BDR fails.
- Default priority is 1.
- Highest priority is elected. If a tie, the highest router ID (not IP address on the interface) is elected.
- A priority of 0 prevents a router from becoming a DR or BDR.

There must always be a DR and/or BDR on a broadcast segment. The DR and BDR are not necessary on point-to-point links—only multipoint or broadcast links, like Ethernet. When the first router's link to a broadcast segment goes active and there are no other OSPF routers active on the segment, the new router becomes the DR. Then, the second router to become active on the link becomes the BDR. Any other routers that become active on the broadcast segment later are referred to as *designated router others*, or DROTHERs.

To influence the election process of the DR and BDR, you must set the DR priority highest on the desired DR and next highest on the desired BDR. To ensure that the desired DR is actually elected, enable OSPF on that device first. Then, enable OSPF on the BDR and, finally, do so on the other routing devices.

The OSPF router with the highest priority becomes the DR for the segment when an election takes place. If there is a tie, the router with the highest router ID (not IP address on the segment) becomes the DR. By default, all routers have a priority of 1 (priorities can range from 0 to 255—it is an 8-bit value). If the DR fails, the BDR is promoted to DR and another router is elected as the BDR.

After the DR and BDR roles are established, there is no preemption. So, for example, if a new router becomes active with a higher priority, it will not preempt the DR or BDR—the priorities would only be used if two routers go active on a link at the same time or if the current DR and/or BDR failed and a new router needed to be elected.

In a WAN that uses a hub-and-spoke topology with virtual circuits, like Multi-Protocol Label Switching (MPLS) or Frame Relay, all the devices might be in the same subnet, but only the hub (typically the corporate office) has full connectivity to the spokes (branch offices). The branch offices typically do not have virtual circuits to each other. In this example, the hub must be the DR and the spokes are never the DR/BDR, so their priority should be set to 0 on those interfaces.

Note

You should generally configure the switches that offer the highest performance as the DR and BDR. Set the DR priority highest on the desired DR and next highest on the desired BDR. To ensure that the desired DR is actually elected, enable OSPF on that device first. Then, enable OSPF on the BDR and, finally, do so on the other routing devices. The main purpose of the DR and BDR is to offload the updating process. This was very important in the early 1990s, when OSPF was introduced and processing power and memory on devices was minimal. Today, it is not as much of a concern.

DR/BDR Activity

In this activity, answer the following questions concerning Figure 12-4, assuming that all routers become active on the link at the same time:

- Which routing switch is the DR?
- Which routing switch is the BDR?
- Which routing switches are the DROTHERs?

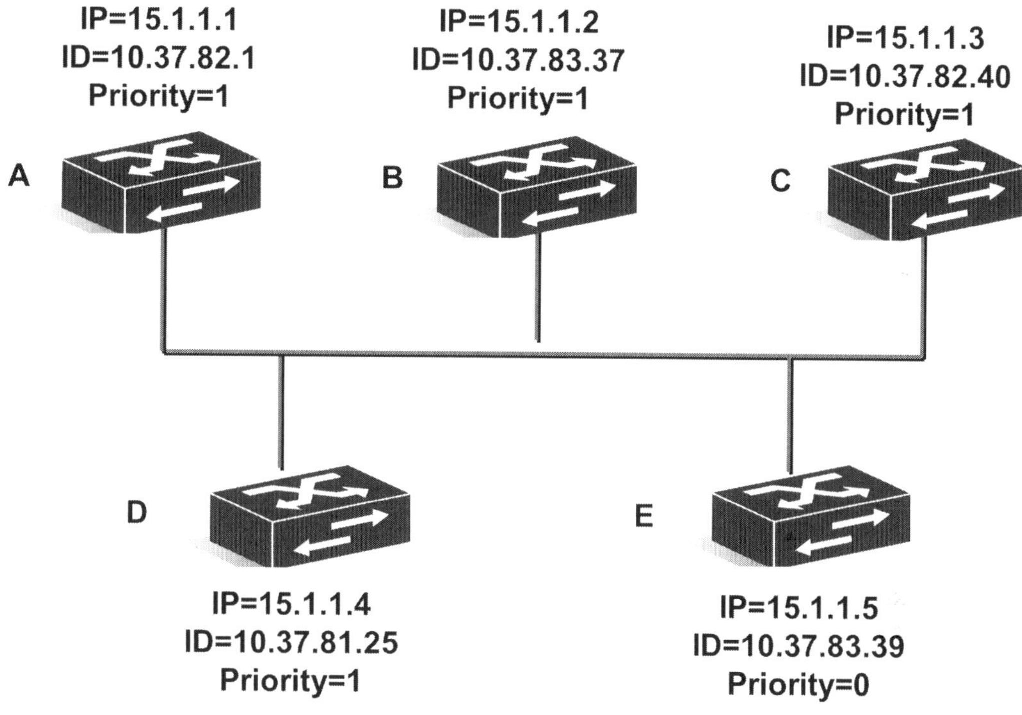

Figure 12-4. Which switches are the DR and BDR?

The answers to the questions for Figure 12-4 are as follows:

- Which is the DR? **B**
- Which is the BDR? **C**
- Which are the DROTHERs? **A**, **D**, and **E**

Note that routing switch E, even though it has a higher router ID than the other routing switches, does not participate in the election since its priority is 0.

DR/BDR Example

Figure 12-5 illustrates four routing switches that connect together on a common subnet, in addition to showing their neighbor and adjacency relationships. With only four routing devices, you do not see significantly fewer adjacency relationships than neighbor ones. In a network with more routers, however, the effects would soon accumulate.

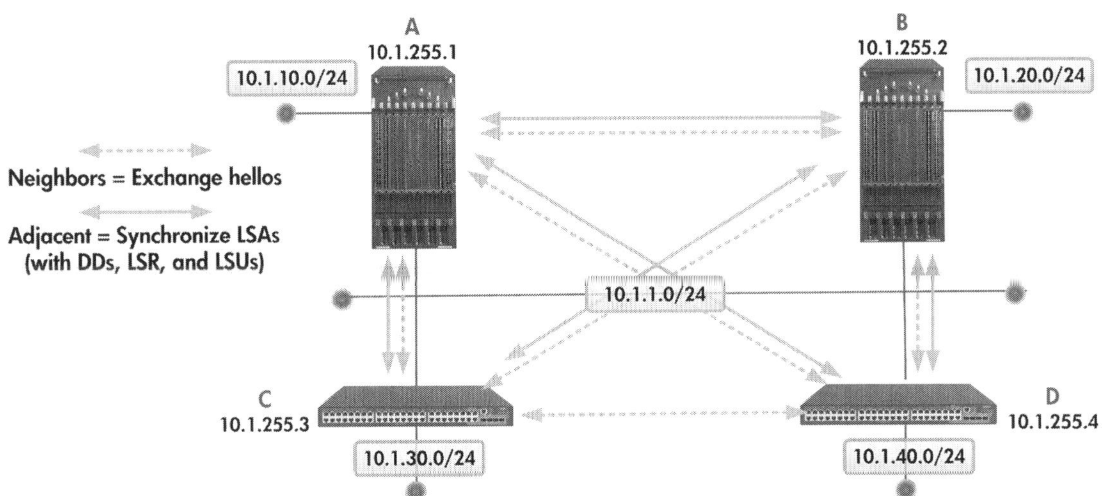

Figure 12-5. Example DRs and BDRs

Here is the neighbor relationship on Switch A (the syntax of this command is discussed later in the chapter in the "Verifying OSPF on Comware" section):

```
<Comware> display ospf peer
                    OSPF Process 1 with Router ID 10.1.255.3
                          Neighbor Brief Information
 Area: 0.0.0.0
 Router ID       Address      Pri Dead-Time  Interface     State
 10.1.255.1      10.1.1.1      1    37         Vlan1       Full/DR
 10.1.255.2      10.1.1.2      1    36         Vlan1       Full/BDR
 10.1.255.4      10.1.1.4      1    37         Vlan1       2-Way/DROther
```

The two-way/DROTHER status in Figure 12-5 indicates that C and D (10.1.1.4) are neighbors but not fully adjacent (this is discussed in the next section, "Forming Adjacencies"). The DROTHER role indicates that the routing device is an OSPF router *other than* the DR or BDR. In this example, both D and C have the DROTHER role. Two DROTHER routers in a network do not achieve full adjacency. After the appropriate routers have achieved adjacency, these routing switches do not exchange LSAs directly; they both achieve adjacency with the network's DR and BDR. Therefore, their LSDBs become synchronized.

Forming Adjacencies

OSPF routers forward their link state advertisements throughout the OSPF domain until all routers have received all LSAs. These LSAs give the routers the information they need to construct a topology of the OSPF domain. With the complete picture, the routers can select the best path to each network.

An OSPF router learns about its OSPF neighbors and builds its adjacency and topology tables by sharing LSAs, which exist in different types. When learning about the neighbors to whom a router is connected, in addition to keeping tabs on known neighbors, OSPF routers generate LSA hello messages every 10 seconds. The default hello timer of 10 seconds and the dead interval timer of 40 seconds can be adjusted; however, the timers must be the same on all the OSPF neighbors on the same segment. When a neighbor is discovered and an adjacency is formed with the neighbor, a router expects to see hello messages from the neighbor. If a neighbor's hello is not seen within the dead interval time, the neighbor is declared *dead*. When this occurs, the router advertises this information, via an LSA message, to other neighboring OSPF routers.

Whereas RIP accepts routing updates from just about any other RIP router (unless RIPv2 with authentication is configured), OSPF has some rules concerning if and how routing information should be shared. First, before a router accepts any routing information from another OSPF router, the routers must build an adjacency between them, on their connected interfaces. When this adjacency is built, the two routers (on the connected interfaces) are called *neighbors*, indicating a special relationship between the two. For two routers to become neighbors, the following must match on each router:

- The area number
- The network or subnet number
- The hello and dead interval timers on their connected interfaces
- The OSPF authentication password (optional), if it is configured
- The area type: normal, stub, or not-so-stubby (NSSA) (Area types are discussed in the ASE level networking courses.)
- The link type (broadcast or point-to-point)
- Maximum transmission unit (MTU) sizes on the connected interfaces

If these items do not match, the routers will not form an adjacency and will ignore each other's routing information. The OSPF routers use a special type of message, called a *hello message*, to discover new neighbors and to detect dead ones. By default, the hello interval is 10 seconds and the dead interval is 40 seconds. This must match on every OSPF router on the same segment.

Adjacency Process for All Routers

Let us assume that you turned on all of your routers simultaneously on a segment. In this case, all the OSPF routers will go through three states, called the *exchange process*, in determining whether they will become neighbors:

1. **Down state**—The routers have not exchanged any OSPF information with any other router.
2. **Init state**—A destination router has received a new router's hello and adds it to its neighbor list (assuming that values in the preceding bullet points match). Note that communication is only unidirectional at this point.
3. **Two-way state**—The new router receives a unidirectional reply (from the destination router) to its initial hello packet and adds the destination router to its neighbor database.

After the routers have entered a two-way state, they are considered neighbors. At this point, an election process takes place to elect the DR and the BDR on the segment. (On a segment with pre-existing OSPF routers, the election process would not be necessary since the identity of the DR and BDR would have been learned from the initial hello packets.)

Additional Adjacency Steps with the DR/BDR

An OSPF router will not form full adjacencies to just any router. A full adjacency allows the routers involved to actually share routing information. Instead, a client/server design is implemented in OSPF on each broadcast segment. For each multi-access broadcast segment, such as Ethernet, there is a DR and a BDR, in addition to other OSPF routers, called *DROTHERs*. As an example, if you have 10 VLANs in your switched area, you will have 10 DRs and 10 BDRs. The one exception would be on a WAN point-to-point link.

When an OSPF router comes up, it forms full adjacencies with the DR and the BDR on each multi-access segment to which it is connected—if it is connected to three segments, it forms three sets of adjacencies. Any exchange of routing information is between these DR/BDR routers and the other OSPF neighbors on a segment (and vice versa). An OSPF router talks to a DR using the IP multicast address of 224.0.0.6. The DR and the BDR talk to all OSPF routers using the 224.0.0.5 multicast IP address.

After electing the DR/BDR pair, the routers continue to generate hellos to maintain communication. This is called the *exstart state*, in which the OSPF routers are ready to share link state information (the actual routes). The process the routers go through is called an *exchange protocol*, and it is outlined here:

1. **Exstart state**—The DR and BDR form adjacencies with the other OSPF routers on the segment. Then, within each adjacency, the router with the highest router ID becomes the master and starts the exchange process first (shares its link state information). Note that the DR is not necessarily the master for the exchange process. The remaining router in the adjacency will be the slave.

2. **Exchange state**—The master starts sharing link state information first with the slave. These are called *database description packets* (DBDs or DDPs). The DBDs contain the link state type, the ID of the advertising router, the cost of the advertised link, and the sequence number of the link. The slave responds back with an LSACK—an acknowledgment to the DBD from the master. The slave then compares the DBD's information with its own.
3. **Loading state**—If the master has more up-to-date information than the slave, the slave responds to the master's original DBD with a link state request (LSR). The master then sends a link state update with the detailed information of the links to the slave. The slave then incorporates this into its local link state database. Again, the slave generates an LSACK to the master to acknowledge the fact that it received the LSU. If a slave has more up-to-date information, it repeats the exchange and loading states.
4. **Full state**—After the master and the slave are synchronized, they are considered to be in a full state.

Note that these steps are in addition to the three mentioned in the previous section. To summarize these four steps, OSPF routers share a type of LSA message to disclose information about available routes—basically, an LSA update message contains a link and a state, in addition to other information. A *link* is the router interface on which the update was generated (a connected route). The *state* is a description of this interface, including the IP address configured on it, along with the relationship that this router has with its neighboring router. However, OSPF routers will not share this information with just any OSPF router—just between themselves and the DR/BDR on a segment. DROTHER routers never share routing information with each other directly.

Note

OSPF routers will not share information with each other unless an adjacency is first established.

OSPF Updates

OSPF uses incremental updates after entering a full state. This means that, whenever changes take place, only the change is shared with the DR, which then shares this information with other routers on the segment. Figure 12-6 shows an example of this. In this example, Network Z, connected to router C, goes down. Router C sends a multicast to the DR and the BDR (with a destination multicast address of 224.0.0.6), telling them about this change. After the DR and the BDR incorporate the change internally, the DR then tells the other routes on the segment (via a multicast message sent to 224.0.0.5, which is all OSPF routers) about the change concerning Network Z. Any router receiving the update then shares this update to the DRs of other segments to which they are connected.

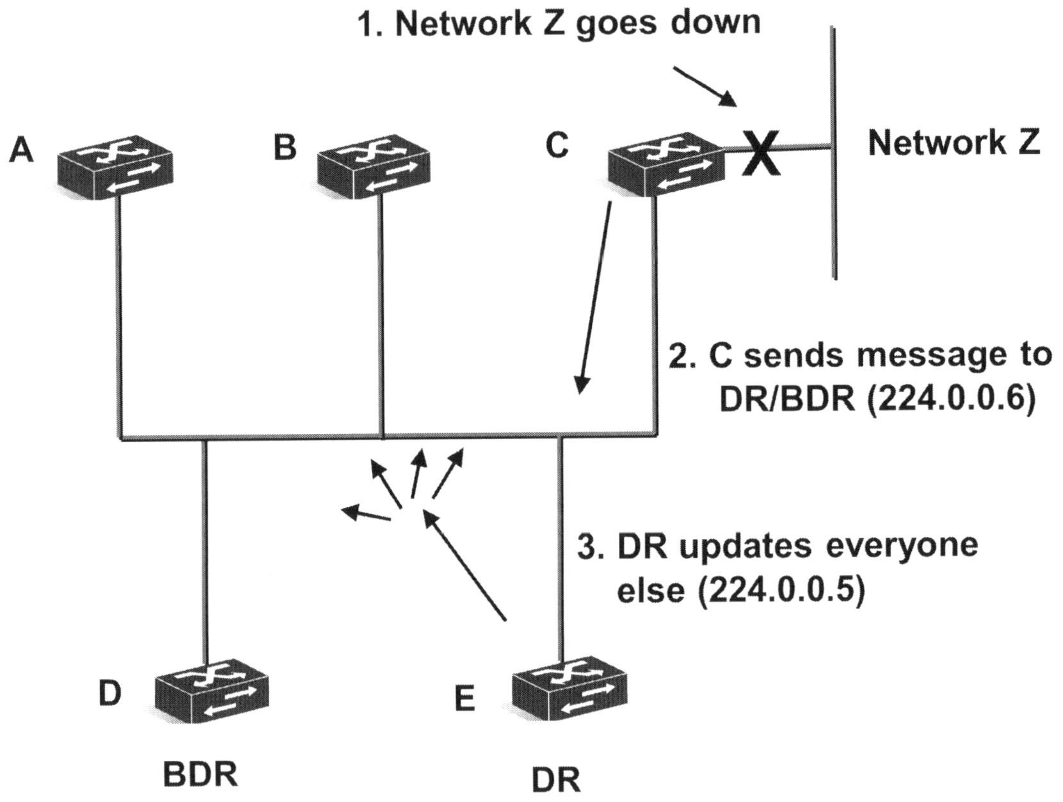

Figure 12-6. OSPF and routing updates

Note that the communications between OSPF routers is connection-oriented, even though multicasts are used. For example, if a router tells a DR about a change, the DR acknowledges this new piece of information with the source of the communication. Likewise, when the DR shares this information with the other routers on the segment, the DR expects acknowledgments from each of these neighbors. Remember that, when an OSPF router exchanges updates with another, the process requires an acknowledgment. This ensures that a router or routers have received the update.

The exception to the incremental update process is that the DR floods its database every 30 minutes to ensure that all of the routers on the segment have the most up-to-date link state information. It does this with a multicast destination address of 224.0.0.5 (all OSPF routers on the segment).

Note

The multicast address of 224.0.0.5 is used when a router needs to interact with all OSPF routers, but 224.0.0.6 is only used when a router needs to interact with the DR and BDR.

LSAs and the Link State Database

After every OSPF router has achieved adjacency with at least one neighbor in its network, all connected OSPF routers will have identical LSDBs. The LSDB helps the routers to generate an accurate picture of the current network topology. Here is a summary of the more common OSPF LSA types:

- **Type 1**—Generated by a DROTHER to be send to the DR/BDR (router LSA)
- **Type 2**—Update from the DR on a segment (network LSA)
- **Type 3**—Generated by an ABR when sending a route into a different area
- **Type 4**—Announces an available ASBR
- **Type 5**—Generated by an ASBR announcing external routes

Although OSPF defines nine types of LSAs, Type 1 and Type 2 LSAs provide all of the information required for a simple single-area OSPF configuration, and, in this book, you focus on those types. Type 3 LSAs are generated by an ABR. Inside an area, if you see a Type 3 LSA, this indicates that the destination network is outside the local area and the traffic must be routed to an ABR to reach it. Type 4 and Type 5 LSAs involve ASBRs and their routers. Type 4 indicates a reachable ASBR, and Type 5 refers to the external routes imported into the OSPF network. LSA Types 3, 4, and 5 are discussed in much more depth at the ASE-level networking courses.

Every OSPF router generates Type 1 LSAs, which advertise the router's own links. Type 2 LSAs are generated by the DR to update everyone from received routing information. Type 1 and Type 2 LSAs are further categorized into two sub-types in an Ethernet network:

- Stub network
- Transit network

A *stub network* is a network on which the router has no neighbors. The router advertises these networks as stub networks. The network address for the stub link is defined as the link ID, and the network mask is defined as the link data.

A link with two or more OSPF routers that have formed an adjacency is referred to as a *transit network*. For these networks, the link ID is the DR (or the other end of the connection, in the case of some types of networks). The link data is the routing switch's own IP address on the network.

Another important component of the LSA is its metric, which indicates the cost associated with the link. How the OSPF routing devices use the cost to select routes is examined later.

The transit link Type 1 LSAs only display the advertising device's IP address and, for broadcast and non-broadcast multi-access (NBMA) networks, the DR's IP address. In this case, a Type 2 LSA is required to indicate all of the routers connected to that network. The DR generates this LSA. Therefore, if you see a Type 2 LSA, you know that it originated from a DR.

If you understand the relationships between the LSAs, topology, and routes, you can better troubleshoot your network. For example, if your switch is not routing traffic to a specific destination as expected, you can look for LSAs to that network. You can then interpret those LSAs, looking for the advertising router or comparing costs. Or, if the LSAs do not exist, you can look for missing neighbor relationships. Alternatively, you can examine the network (Type 2) LSAs and check whether a network lists all expected routers. If a router is missing, perhaps it is down or its OSPF settings are incorrect.

Shortest Path First Calculation

Each OSPF routing device transforms the shared LSDB into its own shortest path tree, which indicates the best path from that routing device to each network. Each LSA associates a cost with the advertised link, and this cost plays the vital role in selecting shortest paths. This cost is basically an inverse of the bandwidth of a link—faster links have lower costs.

For example, Router D has two paths to 10.1.10.0/24:

- Router A (10.1.1.17) to 10.1.10.0/24 = 10 + 100 = 110
- Router B (10.1.1.9) to Router A (10.1.1.1) to 10.1.10.0/24 = 10 + 1 + 100 = 111

Router D selects the first path because the cost is lower. It converts it to a route with Router A, 10.1.1.17, as the next hop.

Single Area OSPF Configuration

With the background knowledge discussed in the previous sections, you can effectively deploy a basic OSPF system that uses a single area. Before implementing OSPF, you should assess the current environment and ensure that the IP addressing is as you desire and that IP routing is enabled. HP also recommends that you configure loopback interfaces for the ProVision and Comware routing switches to use for their router IDs, but this is optional. (The router ID should be an active interface IP address.) At that point, you can configure OSPF—a fairly straightforward process for a single-area domain.

Configuring OSPF in a single-area design involves three required steps:

1. Create an OSPF process, and assign the router ID.
2. Create the area.
3. Associate networks to OSPF areas.

Optionally, you can adjust the bandwidth reference and define passive or silent interfaces—these are optional steps, but they are highly recommended. The following sections explore these configuration steps in more depth.

OSPF and HP Comware

The following sections discuss the configuration and verification of OSPF in a single area on HP Comware switches.

Configuring OSPF on Comware

This section focuses on the basic commands to configure OSPF on Comware switches.

Creating the OSPF Process

Comware routing switches support multiple OSPF processes, each of which isolates routing information from the others. The process ID is purely locally significant. You could assign a different process ID to various devices in your domain, although using the same process ID helps you to track the configuration.

On the Comware routing switches, the same command creates the OSPF process and assigns the router ID:

```
[Comware] ospf <process-ID> [router-id <router-id>]
```

As explained earlier, it is recommended that you statically assign a router ID or create a loopback interface to enhance stability. If using a loopback interface, you might then explicitly set the router ID to the loopback interface address to avoid misconfigurations.

Note

If you originally forget to hardcode the router ID, it will not be used unless you reset the OSPF process with the `reset ospf process` command or reboot the Comware device.

Creating OSPF Areas

In this single-area configuration, you must set the same area on all routing devices (otherwise, neighbors cannot establish adjacency). It can be a good idea to use Area 0. Later, if you decide that you need to segment the domain, you can segment areas off of the existing Area 0.

```
[Comware-ospf-<id>] area <area-id>
```

The area is a 32-bit number and can be entered as a decimal number or in dotted decimal format. For Area 0, you can enter either of the following:

```
[Comware-ospf-<id>] area 0
[Comware-ospf-<id>] area 0.0.0.0
```

Associating Networks to OSPF Areas

The network command enables OSPF on interfaces with IP addresses within the specified network:

```
[Comware-ospf-<id>-area-<id>] network <network-id> <wildcard-mask>
```

You must assign a wildcard mask to match on the range of addresses on the Comware devices interfaces that will belong to the area. To include all interfaces in the area, use a network number and wildcard mask of 0.0.0.0 255.255.255.255. To include a single interface in an area, you can specify the IP address of the interface with an inverted host mask of 10.1.1.1 0.0.0.0. To include a specific subnet in an area, specify the subnet and the inverted subnet mask of 10.1.1.0 0.0.0.255.

Note
To convert a subnet mask to a wildcard mask, subtract the subnet mask from 255.255.255.255. This results in its corresponding wildcard mask. For example, if you have a subnet mask of 255.255.255.252, the resulting wildcard mask would be 0.0.0.3.

On an HP switch, the Layer 3 interface can be a VLAN interface or a physical interface that is configured in routing mode. (The examples in this chapter use VLAN interfaces.) You can also specify a network address that includes the network addresses for several interfaces within it. The second option enables you to configure your system more quickly—as long as you are sure that you want OSPF to run on each network and you do not plan to divide networks into different areas later. The first option gives you more precise control.

The Comware routing switch performs the following after a network is defined:

- Discover neighbors and achieve adjacencies on that network (as described earlier).
- Advertise that network in Type 1 LSAs (and possibly in Type 2).

Preferring a Link

If a network includes 10G, Gigabit, and 100 Mbps Ethernet connections, you want to ensure that traffic flows on high-speed links in preference to lower-speed links. As you learned earlier, OSPF selects the route with the lowest cost. To prefer a specific link, assign that link a lower cost than the costs of non-preferred high-speed links. You must, therefore, understand how the Comware routing switches assign OSPF costs by default. OSPFv2 calculates an interface's cost by dividing the reference bandwidth by the interface's bandwidth. The default reference bandwidth is 100 Mbps (see Table 12-1). An interface's bandwidth depends on the type of interface.

The higher-end modular Comware routing switches support some modules with routed Ethernet interfaces. You can set an IP address directly on the interface, which acts at Layer 3. In this case, the bandwidth is taken directly from the interface's bandwidth. In other cases, the Ethernet interfaces only act at Layer 2. You can make the link imitate a routed link by making the interface an access port in a VLAN reserved for it. You then configure the IP address and OSPF settings on the

VLAN interface. A Comware routing switch always sets the bandwidth of a VLAN interface to 100 Mbps. Therefore, in a default configuration, the Comware (and ProVision) routing switch assigns cost 1, the lowest possible cost, to all VLAN interfaces, as in Table 12-1 (cost values are rounded up so you never have a cost less than 1).

Table 12-1. Default costs on Comware devices

Interface	Default cost = default reference bandwidth (100 Mbps) / interface bandwidth
VLAN	100 Mbps / default bandwidth (100 Mbps) = 1
Fast Ethernet	100 Mbps / 100 Mbps = 1
Gigabit Ethernet	100 Mbps / 1,000 Mbps = 1 (rounded up)
Ten Gigabit Ethernet	100 Mbps / 10,000 Mbps = 1 (rounded up)

Adjusting Costs

You can manually set a cost on the VLAN interfaces that consist of high-speed Ethernet links. However, at this point, all VLAN interfaces already have the lowest possible cost, so you cannot distinguish the higher-speed links. Therefore, you must first raise the reference bandwidth. It is recommended that you match the reference bandwidth to the speed of the highest speed OSPF interface in the system. In this example, VLAN 2 consists of a single 10G link, so you can consider that VLAN interface as providing 10G. You set the reference bandwidth to 10,000 Mbps. Note that you should make the change on every OSPF routing device in the system, even on those that do not have a high-speed interface themselves. Otherwise, the costs will not be consistent, leading to incoherent route selection.

The `bandwidth-reference` command is used to affect the cost computed when deriving OSPF metrics:

```
[Comware] ospf <process-id>

[Comware-ospf-<id>] bandwidth-reference <reference>
```

By default, if you do not change it, switches assume 10G and 1G interfaces have the same cost value, which, obviously, is undesirable. The default is 100 Mbps to calculate the cost for an interface, where "100" is the default reference—you need to change the default reference so that the Layer 3 device can perceive the difference between 100G, 10G, 1G, and Fast Ethernet interfaces.

After you adjust the reference bandwidth, the costs for the VLAN interfaces adjust accordingly. With a reference bandwidth of 10,000 Mbps, the default VLAN interface cost becomes 100. If your switches feature any routed physical interfaces, the OSPF cost also adjusts automatically.

However, if you want to adjust the cost on VLAN interfaces that consist of high-speed Ethernet links, you must complete an additional step. You cannot alter the bandwidth reported by the VLAN, which always remains 100 Mbps. Therefore, the formula always calculates the same cost for VLAN interfaces. You can, however, override the cost calculated by the formula by manually setting the cost on the VLAN interface. Enter this command:

```
[Comware] interface <interface-id>
[Comware-Vlan-interface<id>] ospf cost <1-65535>
```

Remember that you must set the same cost for the VLAN on all OSPF routing devices that connect to that VLAN. (Interface costs should match on both sides of the link.)

Note

The bandwidth reference affects the costs calculated globally. Make sure you include situations where you might be using aggregated links, like four 10Gbps links in a bridge aggregation link. The problem with the bandwidth reference is that, when it calculates the cost, it does not look at the current speed of the port but at the physically highest speed of the port, and, therefore, the second method of individually assigning the cost on a per-VLAN (switch) or per-interface (router) basis is the preferred approach.

Preventing Unnecessary OSPF Traffic

Some OSPF domains might feature stub networks that include only one OSPF router. In the example shown in Figure 12-7, each OSPF routing switch connects to one network of this network type (VLAN 10, VLAN 20, VLAN 30, or VLAN 40). You should generally suppress OSPF traffic on VLANs of this type to minimize overhead and, perhaps, to prevent your routing switch from establishing adjacency with an unauthorized device. However, you cannot simply remove the stub network from the OSPF configuration because the routing switch would then cease advertising its link to the network.

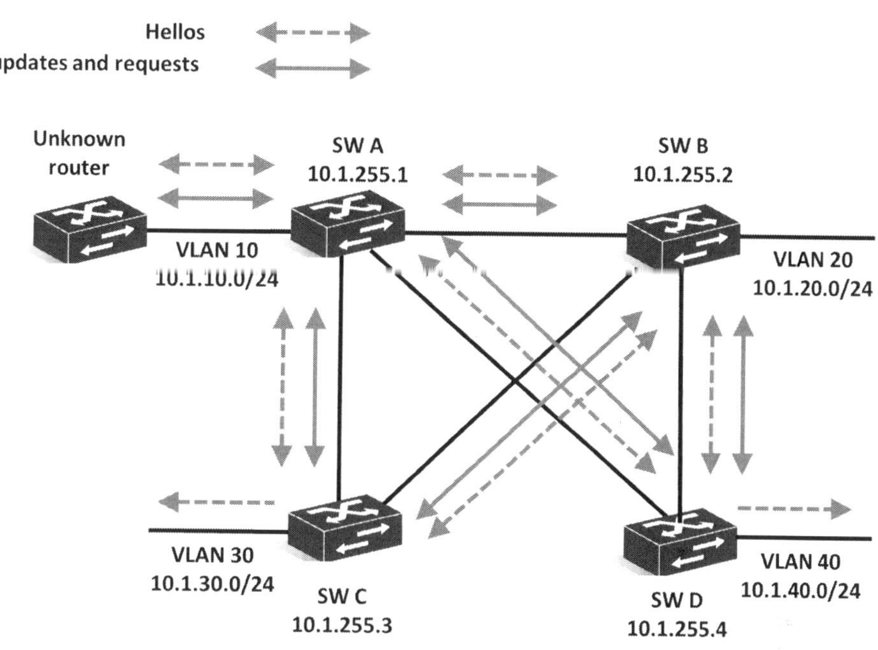

Figure 12-7. Preventing unnecessary OSPF traffic

You can configure the stub network interface as a silent interface (sometimes called a *passive interface*), as shown in Figure 12-8. This type of interface runs OSPF. However, it blocks all OSPF traffic, including incoming and outgoing hellos. Therefore, even if an OSPF device does exist on the network, the Comware routing switch with the silent interface does not establish a neighbor relationship of any kind with it. The network connected to the silent interface, however, remains visible to OSPF, and the routing switch includes it in Type 1 and Type 2 LSAs when advertised out other links.

Here is the configuration to define a silent interface:

```
[Comware] ospf <process-id>
[Comware-ospf-<ID>] silent-interface <interface-id>
```

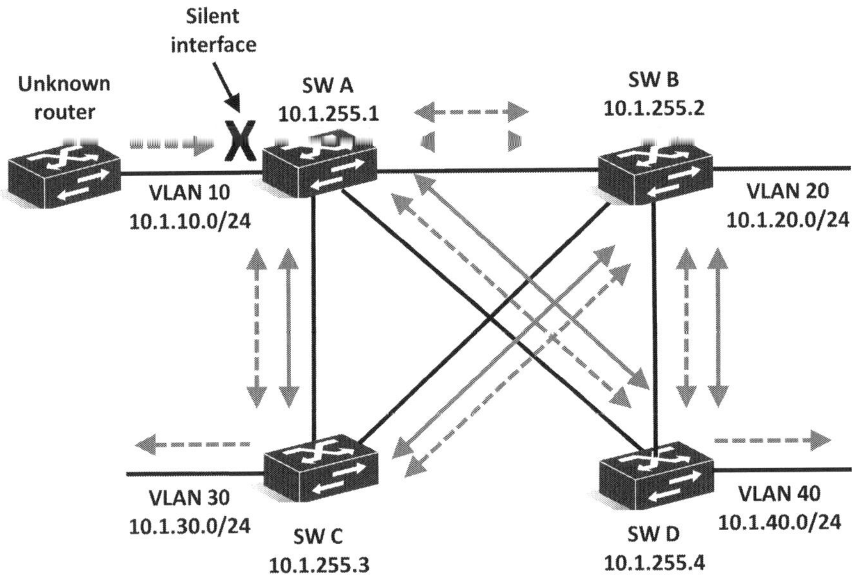

Figure 12-8. Using silent interfaces (preferred)

Note

Silent or passive interfaces are used on stub networks where we do not want the routing switch to listen to LSAs on the link (because there should not be any OSPF routers) but still want to advertise the network of that link to OSPF routers on other links.

Loopback Interfaces

Loopback interfaces are logical interfaces that are always up. The HP switches (Comware and ProVision) support loopback interfaces—the number supported on a device depends on the product. For example, ProVision switches support a maximum of eight loopback interfaces per switch. Typically, only one is necessary.

Creating a loopback interface is as simple as configuring any other interface—you just need to specify a unique number. From there, treat it as any other interface. With Comware, the IP address assigned to it must use a 32-bit mask. In other words, you cannot do subnetting of networks for loop interfaces.

Here is the syntax to create a loopback interface:

```
[Comware] interface loopback <loopback-number>
[Comware-<interface-id> ip address <ip-address> 255.255.255.255
```

As you can see from the syntax, this is very similar to configuring a loopback interface on a ProVision switch, with the exception of how the subnetting information is identified.

Comware Configuration Example

Here is an example OSPF configuration on a Comware switch:

```
[Comware] interface vlan 1
[Comware-vlan-1] ip address 10.1.1.1 255.255.255.0
[Comware-vlan-1] quit
[Comware] interface vlan 2
[Comware-vlan-1] ip address 10.1.2.1 255.255.255.0
[Comware-vlan-1] quit
[Comware] interface loopback 1
[Comware-vlan-1] ip address 1.1.1.1 255.255.255.255
[Comware-vlan-1] quit
[Comware] ospf 1 router-id 1.1.1.1
[Comware-ospf-1] area 0
[Comware-ospf-1-area-0.0.0.0] network 0.0.0.0 255.255.255.255
```

-or-

```
[Comware-ospf-1-area-0.0.0.0] network 1.1.1.1 0.0.0.0
[Comware-ospf-1-area-0.0.0.0] network 10.1.1.0 0.0.0.255
[Comware-ospf-1-area-0.0.0.0] network 10.1.2.0 0.0.0.255
```

Notice that the loopback address and the router ID are the same values.

Note

HP highly recommends that a loopback address be the device's router ID and that it is able to be pinged. To ping it, you must include it in the OSPF routing process.

Also notice, at the bottom of the above configuration, the two different ways of including interfaces in Area 0: the first, in the above configuration, includes IP addresses of all interfaces in a single command; the second includes the addresses of the three interfaces with three separate `network` commands. Either approach works in this example. Also, remember to use wildcard, not subnet masks, when matching on a range of IP addresses to include in an area.

Verifying OSPF on Comware

The `display ospf peer` command displays the OSPF neighbor table:

```
[Comware] display ospf peer
OSPF Process 1 with Router ID 10.0.0.31
                        Neighbor Brief Information

 Area: 0.0.0.0
 Router ID     Address        Pri  Dead-Time  Interface    State
 10.0.0.21     10.1.220.1     1    36         Vlan220      Full/DR
 10.0.0.41     10.1.220.2     1    33         Vlan220      Full/DROther
```

Neighbors are listed based on their router IDs, followed by their IP addresses. Note the State column on the right side for the two neighbors, indicating the state with the neighbor and the role the neighbor plays on the segment.

The `display ospf interface` command displays, by area, each of the IP addresses participating in OSPF on the Comware device, the role it is playing on that particular interface, and the DR and BDR associated with that interface:

```
[Comware] display ospf interface

         OSPF Process 1 with Router ID 10.0.0.31
                 Interfaces

 Area: 0.0.0.0
 IP Address     Type      State  Cost  Pri  DR            BDR
 10.1.220.3     Broadcast BDR    1     1    10.1.220.1    10.1.220.3
```

The `display ospf lsdb` command displays the link state database, sometimes referred to as a *topology table*, on a Comware device:

```
[Comware] display ospf lsdb

         OSPF Process 1 with Router ID 10.0.0.31
                 Link State Database

                         Area: 0.0.0.0
```

```
Type      LinkState ID   AdvRouter     Age   Len   Sequence  Metric
Router     10.0.0.41     10.0.0.41     1732  36    8000001F       0
Router     10.0.0.31     10.0.0.31     1402  36    80000027       0
Router     10.0.0.21     10.0.0.21      871  36    80000024       0
Network    10.1.220.1    10.0.0.21      751  36    80000022       0
```

Notice the Type column, which indicates the type of LSA. “Router” indicates an LSA Type 1 and “Network” indicates an LSA Type 2.

The `display ospf routing-table` command displays the routing information that OSPF has learned about the reachable networks:

```
<Comware> display ospf routing-table
Destination     Cost  Type   NextHop   AdvRouter   Area
10.2.128.0/18    30   Intra  10.1.1.5  10.1.255.1  0.0.0.0
10.2.0.0/18     110   Intra  10.1.1.5  10.1.255.1  0.0.0.0
10.2.64.0/18    130   Intra  10.1.1.13 10.1.255.2  0.0.0.0
10.2.192.0/18    40   Intra  10.1.1.13 10.1.255.2  0.0.0.0
<-output omitted->
Total Nets: 50
Intra Area: 50 Inter Area: 0 ASE: 0 NSSA: 0
```

“Intra,” in the type column, indicates a route within this area. “Inter” indicates a route in a different area.

The `display ip routing` command displays the IP routing table on a Comware device:

```
<Comware> display ip routing-table
Destination/Mask  Proto  Pre  Cost  NextHop    Interface
10.2.0.0/18       OSPF   10   110   10.1.1.5   Vlan3
10.2.64.0/18      OSPF   10   130   10.1.1.13  Vlan5
10.2.128.0/17     OSPF   10   30    10.1.1.5   Vlan3
10.2.192.0/17     OSPF   10   40    10.1.1.13  Vlan5
```

Notice the Proto column, indicating from where the route was learned. The Pre column refers to the routing protocol preference or precedence. (ProVision refers to this as the *administrative distance*.)

OSPF and HP ProVision

The following sections discuss the configuration and verification of OSPF in a single area on HP ProVision switches.

Configuring OSPF on ProVision

To create an OSPF process and assign a router ID on a ProVision switch, use the following configuration:

```
ProVision(config)# ip router-id <router-id>
ProVision(config)# router ospf
ProVision(config)# router ospf enable
```

Before enabling OSPF on a ProVision switch, it is advisable to statically define a router ID with the `ip router-id` command. If no router ID is configured, the switch assigns one automatically. On the ProVision switches, the choice of ID depends on other configuration items. Five possible cases are:

- **A single loopback interface and multiple VLANs with addresses**—The loopback interface is used as the router ID.
- **A single loopback interface with multiple IP addresses**—The lowest loopback IP address is used as the router ID.
- **Multiple loopback interfaces with multiple IP addresses**—The lowest loopback number and lowest loopback IP address are used as the router ID.
- **Multiple VLANs with a single IP Address in each VLAN**—The IP address of the VLAN that becomes active first is used as a router ID. Typically, on ProVision switches, the lowest number VLAN becomes active first. Consequently, if an address is defined in VLAN 1, it becomes the router ID. If VLAN 1 is down, the switch uses the next lowest number VLAN.
- **Multiple VLANs with multiple IP addresses in each VLAN**—The lowest IP address of the first active VLAN is used as a router ID. In most cases, this is a default VLAN IP address.

As you can see from the examples, the ProVision switches do not use the same procedure in choosing a router ID as the Comware devices and most other networking vendors.

After the ID is defined, two separate commands are required to enable OSPF globally on the ProVision switches. In the first, you simply enable OSPF by issuing the `router ospf` command. In newer versions of KA15 code, the `router ospf enable` command allows you to enable or disable OSPF without losing your configuration

You must define at least one area with the `area` command. By default, OSPF is disabled and must be enabled. To create the OSPF areas, use the following configuration:

```
ProVision(config)# router ospf
ProVision(ospf)# area <area-number>
```

To associate networks to the areas, use the following configuration:

```
ProVision(config)# vlan <vid>
ProVision(vlan-<vid>)# ip ospf [area <area-id>]
```

To form adjacencies, which are fundamental to OSPF operation, two OSPF routers must agree on an area ID, among other items described earlier in the chapter. If you omit the area number, it defaults to Area 0, the backbone.

Unlike Comware switches, there is no global command to change the bandwidth reference. Instead, it must be done on a VLAN-by-VLAN basis with the `ip ospf cost` command:

```
ProVision(config)# vlan <vid>
ProVision(vlan-<vid>)# ip ospf cost <cost-value>
```

On the ProVision switches, configuration of OSPF at the global and interface level is dynamic. Enabling OSPF on an interface may cause the router to:

- Begin sending hello packets through this interface in an effort to establish adjacencies.
- Include the network address range associated with this interface in its router LSA.

To minimize OSPF processing overhead, interfaces with no neighboring routers may be defined as *passive* or *silent*. The routing device does not send hello messages over a passive interface, which means it can never form an adjacency and it never sends link state updates over this type of interface. To define an interface as passive (stub link), use the following configuration:

```
ProVision(config)# vlan <vid>
ProVision(vlan-<vid>)# ip ospf passive
```

To create a loopback interface, use the following configuration:

```
ProVision(config)# interface loopback <loopback-number>
ProVision(lo-<loopback-number>) ip address <ip-address>
```

It is highly recommended to configure an IP address on the loopback interface—the same as the switch's router ID.

ProVision Configuration Example

Here is an example OSPF configuration for a ProVision switch:

```
ProVision(config)# ip router-id 10.1.0.3
ProVision(config)# router ospf
ProVision(ospf)# area 0
ProVision(ospf)# exit
ProVision(config)# vlan 10
ProVision(vlan-10)# ip ospf area 0
ProVision(vlan-10)# ip ospf passive
ProVision(vlan-10)# exit
ProVision(config)# vlan 30
ProVision(vlan-30)# ip ospf area 0
ProVision(vlan-30)# ip ospf passive
ProVision(vlan-30)# exit
ProVision(config)# interface loopback 0
ProVision(lo-0)# ip address 10.1.0.3
ProVision(lo-0)# ip ospf all
```

Note that the configuration for the loopback interface must include an argument specifying which IP addresses are included in OSPF advertisements. In the example shown above, `all` indicates that all addresses are included.

Verifying OSPF on ProVision

The ProVision `show ip ospf` command shows the basic configuration and operation of OSPF on the switch:

```
ProVision# show ip ospf

 OSPF Configuration Information

  OSPF protocol  : enabled
  Router ID      : 10.10.10.1
```

```
Currently defined areas:

                               Stub              Stub            Stub
 Area ID           Type    Default Cost      Summary LSA     Metric Type
 ---------------   ------  -------------     ------------    --------------
 backbone          normal  1                 send            ospf metric
```

With this command, you can see the router's ID and the OSPF areas defined.

After assigning each IP interface to an OSPF area, you can verify the status of configured OSPF interfaces by issuing the `show ip ospf interface` command:

```
ProVision# show ip ospf interface

OSPF Interface Status

 IP Address   Status    Area ID    State  Auth-type  Cost  Pri  Passive
 ----------   -------   --------   -----  ---------  ----  ---  -------
 10.1.0.3     enabled   backbone    LOOP  none        1     1    no
 10.1.10.1    enabled   backbone    DR    none        1     1    yes
 10.1.30.1    enabled   backbone    DR    none        1     1    yes
 10.1.65.2    enabled   backbone    DR    none        1     1    no
 10.1.67.2    enabled   backbone    DR    none        1     1    no
```

In this example, only the backbone area is defined and all interfaces are associated with the backbone area. All of these interfaces were configured with default settings for authentication type, cost, and priority. OSPF interfaces 10.1.10.1/24 and 10.1.30.1/2 ProVision# **show ip ospf neighbor**

```
OSPF Neighbor Information

 Router ID   Pri  IP Address   NbIfState  State  Rxmt QLen  Events
 ---------   ---  ----------   ---------  -----  ---------  ------
 10.1.0.1    1     10.1.65.1    BDR        FULL    0
 10.1.0.3    1     10.1.65.3               2WAY    0           5
```

Use the OSPF neighbor table to troubleshoot routing problems that may arise from the failure to form an adjacency.

All routers within an OSPF area hold a common set of LSAs in their link state databases. This is due to mandatory flooding that is enabled by router adjacency. To view header information for the LSAs in the switch's link state database, issue the command `show ip ospf link-state`:

```
ProVision# show ip ospf link-state

 OSPF Link State Database for Area 0.0.0.0

                                  Advertising
  LSA Type  Link State ID   Router ID    Age   Sequence #  Checksum
  -------  --------------  ----------   ---   ----------  ----------
  Router    10.0.0.1       10.0.0.1     153   0x8000000a  0x00008d26
  Router    10.1.0.1       10.1.0.1     91    0x80000010  0x00009e72
  Router    10.1.0.2       10.1.0.2     1742  0x8000000f  0x0000010d
  Router    10.1.0.3       10.1.0.3     998   0x8000000a  0x00004a14
  Router    10.1.0.4       10.1.0.4     1069  0x8000000a  0x00006ff4
  Network   10.0.100.100   10.0.0.1     1798  0x80000003  0x0000a76a
  Network   10.1.64.2      10.1.0.2     962   0x80000003  0x0000c1ff
  Network   10.1.65.2      10.1.0.3     998   0x80000003  0x0000ba04
  Network   10.1.66.2      10.1.0.4     1074  0x80000003  0x0000a337
  Network   10.1.67.2      10.1.0.3     998   0x80000003  0x0000b209
  Network   10.1.68.2      10.1.0.4     1074  0x80000003  0x00007f5a
```

Every LSA is uniquely identified by four items:

- LSA type
- Link state ID
- Advertising router
- Sequence number, which increments each time a new instance of the LSA is originated

The age is the number of seconds that the LSA has been in the database. When the router receives a new instance of an LSA, the age value is reset to 0. The LSA continues to age for as long as it is in the database. If an LSA's age reaches 3,600, the router purges it from the database. Every router is responsible for regenerating the LSAs for which it has origination responsibilities once every 30 minutes.

If you see an LSA with an age greater than 1,800, it is likely an obsolete entry that has not been refreshed due to some configuration change on one of the routers. When the router runs its SPF algorithm, it does not use entries with an age greater than 1,800. Even in a small intranet, the volume of entries in the link state database can make it difficult to locate specific LSAs. Use help at the command-line interface (CLI) to see additional filtering options. You can filter by LSA type or by advertising router among other items.

Use the `show ip route` command to view the IP routing table that the ProVision switch will use to route IP packets:

```
ProVision# show ip route

                          IP Route Entries

  Destination    Gateway     VLAN  Type    Sub-Type   Metric   Dist.
  -----------    ----------  ----  -----   ---------  -------  ----
  <-output omitted->
  10.1.20.0/24   10.1.65.1   65    ospf    IntraArea  120      110
  10.1.40.0/24   10.1.67.1   67    ospf    IntraArea  120      110
  10.1.64.0/24   10.1.65.1   65    ospf    IntraArea  20       110
```

Notice that the Type column indicates the type of route (OSPF, in this instance) and that the Sub-Type column indicates the kind of OSPF route (internal routes to an area, in this instance).

Learning Check

The following questions help you measure your understanding of the material presented in this chapter. Read of all the choices carefully, since there may be more than one correct answer. Choose all correct answers for each question.

Questions

1. Which of the following is not a characteristic of OSPF?
   a. Triggered updates are sent as multicasts when changes occur.
   b. It converges very fast and provides a loop-free topology.
   c. Neighbors are learned via the periodically advertised routing updates.
   d. Faster paths are preferred over slower paths.
2. Place the following OSPF states in the correct order to reflect an OSPF router forming a full adjacency with the DR or BDR:
   a. Init
   b. Full
   c. Down
   d. Exstart
   e. Two-way
   f. Exchange
   g. Loading
3. Which Comware commands only place the IP address of 10.1.1.1/24 for the VLAN 2 interface in Area 0 of OSPF process 1?
4. On a ProVision switch, under which configuration mode do you place an interface or interfaces in a specific area?
   a. Router
   b. OSPF
   c. Interface
   d. VLAN

5. Which ProVision feature causes adjacencies to fail within a VLAN configured for an OSPF area?

6. What is the recommendation for the IP address on a loopback interface when an HP switch has OSPF configured?

Answers

1. ☑ **C**. Periodic announcements is a characteristic of a distance vector protocol.

   ☒ Answers **A**, **B**, and **D** are incorrect because they are characteristics of OSPF.

2. ☑ **Down**, **Init**, **Two-Way**, **Exstart**, **Exchange**, **Loading**, **Full**

3. ☑
   ```
   ospf 1
      area 0
      network 10.1.1.1 255.255.255.255
   ```
   are the Comware commands which place the IP address of 10.1.1.1/24 for the VLAN 2 interface in Area 0 of OSPF process 1.

4. ☑ **D** is correct. Areas are specified in the VLAN context of the ProVision switches.

   ☒ **A**, **B**, and **C** are incorrect because they are not options for enabling OSPF on a link.

5. ☑ Passive interface is the ProVision feature which causes adjacencies to fail within a VLAN configured for an OSPF area.

6. ☑ The IP address should be a routable address and should be included in OSPF. Therefore, the router ID can be used for testing connectivity.

13 HP Intelligent Resilient Framework

EXAM OBJECTIVES

In this chapter, you learn to:

- ✓ Describe the concept, benefits, and types of redundancy and to apply redundancy types.
- ✓ Perform installation and configuration of devices.
- ✓ Validate the installed solution.
- ✓ Optimize small-to-medium-sized wireless, switched, and routed network infrastructures.
- ✓ Apply troubleshooting methodology.
- ✓ Use general troubleshooting tools.
- ✓ Verify network performance and parameters.

ASSUMED KNOWLEDGE

This chapter assumes that you are familiar with the general operation and use of the following topics:

- Spanning Tree Protocols (STPs) (See "Chapter 8: Introducing Spanning Tree" and "Chapter 9: MSTP Configuration.")
- Manual and Link Aggregation Control Protocol (LACP) link aggregation (See "Chapter 10: Link Aggregation.")

INTRODUCTION

This chapter introduces the HP Intelligent Resilient Framework (IRF) technology that is currently supported on the HP Comware switching product line. IRF is an HP proprietary solution that provides fast failover, scalability, manageability, and high availability by creating a large IRF virtual device from multiple physical. IRF virtualization technology takes advantage of the augmented processing power, interaction, unified management, and uninterrupted maintenance of multiple switches. This chapter assumes that you are new to the IRF technology, and it provides an introduction to its operation and configuration. The topics covered in this chapter include:

- Understanding the technologies and concepts involving IRF.
- Understanding the advantages that IRF provides.
- Describing a split stack and how the multi-active detection (MAD) protocol deals with this problem.
- Configuring a simple IRF topology.
- Verifying and troubleshooting an IRF topology.

IRF Technologies and Concepts

IRF is a software virtualization technology developed by H3C/3Com, which was purchased by HP in 2010 and is part of the Comware switch products. (The HP ProVision switches do not support this feature.) IRF allows you to connect multiple devices through physical IRF ports to combine them into a logical device after necessary configurations. With this virtual device, you can manage and maintain multiple devices.

Traditional stacking allows you to manage multiple switches through a single IP address, but each switch in the stack continues to operate independently. As a result, traditional stacking simplifies management but provides few additional benefits. IRF goes beyond basic stacking by combining two or more Comware switches into one virtual switch (see Figure 13-1). It not only simplifies management but also streamlines operations, facilitates expansion, increases performance, and decreases costs. You can easily deploy IRF at any location in your network: the core layer, distribution layers, or access layers.

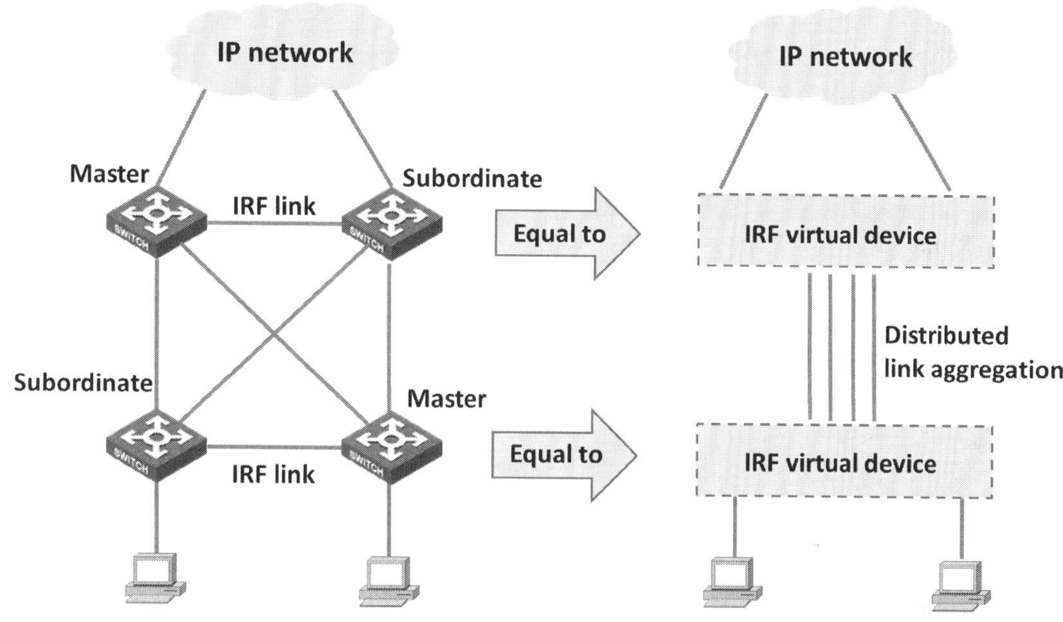

Figure 13-1. IRF virtualization

Note

IRF virtualizes two to nine physical switches as one logical switch. With proper configuration, STP would no longer be necessary on the right side of Figure 13-1, assuming distributed link aggregation was configured between the two IRF virtual devices, commonly referred to as *topologies* or *domains*.

Traditional Network Issues

Within a web of interlinked switches, STP is used to detect and prevent *loops*—a highly undesirable, sometimes disastrous situation that can occur when there are multiple active paths to the same switch. To eliminate loops, STP and its more modern variants, such as Rapid Spanning Tree Protocol (RSTP) and Multiple Spanning Tree Protocol (MSTP), are designed to allow only one active path from one switch to another, regardless of how many actual connections might exist in the network. If the active path fails, the protocol automatically selects a backup connection and makes that the active path.

STP is widely used and is fairly effective at making a network resilient, that is, dealing with a sudden failure of a link between switches. In a network that is operating normally, when a link or switch goes down, STP automatically chooses a backup path and the network reconverges. After a short period, the network operates normally again. But for modern, high-speed, mission-critical networks, this approach may not be the best solution. Here are some of the issues when using the STP technology in Layer 2 networks.

- **Slow network convergence**—The reconvergence time for STP can be several seconds—a lifetime, by modern computing standards. When a garden-variety laptop computer can execute millions of instructions in the blink of an eye, a multisecond network hiccup will have end users cursing the spinning hourglass on their monitors. And a financial transaction that executes in milliseconds cannot wait several seconds for an outdated network protocol to do its job.
- **Management complexity**—Even though MSTP and RSTP converge more quickly than the original STP, all of these protocols can be devilishly difficult to configure properly, especially in a large network. You must manage the switches individually, and you need to set up spanning tree instances on each switch in turn, making sure that the parameters for one switch match those of its neighbor. Additionally, troubleshooting spanning-tree-related issues is no easy task, usually requiring a great deal of time to locate the root cause of the failure.
- **Poor performance**—Because it blocks all parallel paths except the one it has selected as active, even when the network is operating normally, STP actually reduces the effective bandwidth. In fact, half (or more) of the available system bandwidth can be squandered in a backup role, off limits to data traffic. This is not a very good use of the network equipment investment.
- **Too many tradeoffs**—Even choosing which STP to use is difficult. For example, you need to handle traffic forwarding over redundant links: should you implement MSTP, which is highly efficient but complex, or should you use STP or RSTP, which is less efficient but easier to configure?

IRF Advantages

Fortunately, HP networking offers a better way: the Intelligent Resilient Framework. It is an innovative technology that can actually give you a network that is fully resilient yet simpler to set up and manage, faster to converge, and easier to scale.

IRF technology extends network control over multiple active switches. Management of a group of IRF-enabled switches is consolidated around a single management IP address, which vastly simplifies network configuration and operations. You can combine as many as nine Comware switches to create an ultra-resilient virtual switching fabric comprising hundreds or even thousands of 1-GbE or 10-GbE switch ports.

One IRF member operates as the primary system switch, maintaining the control plane and updating forwarding and routing tables for the other devices. If the primary switch fails, IRF instantly selects a new primary, preventing service interruption, and helps deliver network, application, and business continuity for business-critical applications. Within the IRF domain, network control protocols operate as a cohesive whole to streamline processing, improve performance, and simplify network operation. So routing protocols calculate routes based on the single logical domain rather than the multiple switches it represents. Moreover, edge or aggregation switches that are dual homed to IRF-enabled core or data center switches "see" the associated switches as a single entity, eliminating the need for slow convergence technologies, like STP. And administrators have fewer layers to worry about, along with fewer devices, interfaces, links, and protocols to configure and manage.

IRF combines two or more Comware switches (depending on the model) into one virtual switch, providing the following advantages:

- **Simplified design and operations**—With IRF, you no longer need to laboriously connect to, configure, and manage switches individually. You perform a configuration on the primary switch, and that configuration is distributed to all associated switches automatically, considerably simplifying network setup, operation, and maintenance. And, although all Comware switches can be provisioned via the command line, adding HP Intelligent Management Center (IMC) makes management even easier. IMC lets you see and control the entire network from a single console by consolidating management of multiple, discrete devices into a single, easy-to-manage, virtual switch that operates at every layer of the network.
- **Flatter topology**—IRF makes possible a simplified, higher performing, more resilient, and flatter network design. In fact, thanks to IRF and Comware switches, enterprise networks can be designed with fewer devices and fewer networking layers—a big improvement over the low performance, high cost, and crippling latency of conventional multitier legacy solutions, which often rely on a variety of different operating systems and complex resiliency protocols.
- **Higher efficiency**—IRF's loop-free, non-blocking architecture keeps all links active, enabling highly efficient and high-bandwidth connectivity throughout the switching plane. Simply stated, you get all the bandwidth you are paying for.
- **Scalable performance**—IRF and LACP, used together, can further boost performance by bundling several parallel links between switches and servers, allowing scalable "on-demand" performance and capacity to support critical business applications.
- **Faster failover**—Should a network failure occur, IRF can deliver rapid recovery and network reconvergence in less than 10 milliseconds—much faster than the several seconds required for STP.
- **Distributed high availability and resiliency**—For high availability, the IRF fabric can be configured for full N+1 redundancy, and mission-critical virtualization capabilities, such as live migration and application mobility, are available across the IRF domain and extend across the Layer 2 WAN infrastructure.
- **Geographic resiliency**—Within an IRF domain, the geographic location of switches does not matter. Switches can be extended horizontally, and they continue to function as a single logical unit—whether they are installed locally, distributed regionally, or even situated at distant sites. Moreover, employing IRF can enhance disaster recovery by linking installations up to 70 kilometers apart and giving them the same fast failover as if they were sitting side by side within the data center. Such location independence is extremely important to support the global on-demand application access and dynamic traffic flows of today's technology-oriented businesses.
- **In-Service-Software-Upgrade (ISSU)**—IRF delivers a network-based ISSU capability that allows an individual IRF-enabled switch to be taken offline for servicing or software upgrades, without affecting traffic going to other switches in the IRF domain.

Note

ISSU is beyond the scope of this book but is covered in the Accredited Solutions Expert–level (ASE-level) networking courses.

Figure 13-2 demonstrates how IRF is used to increase port density. Figure 13-3 shows how IRF is used to increase bandwidth between the access and aggregation layers.

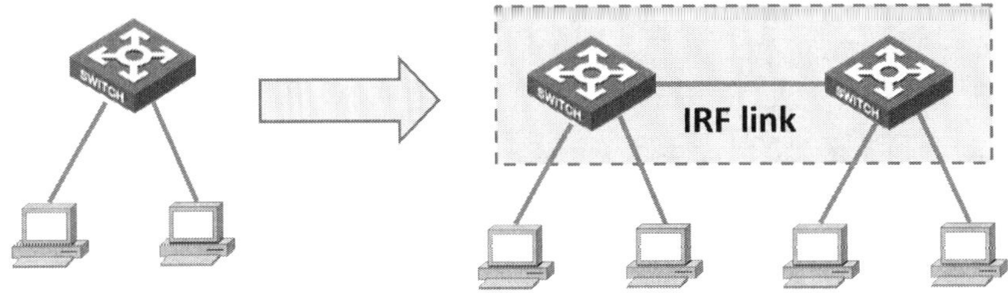

Figure 13-2. IRF example that increases port density

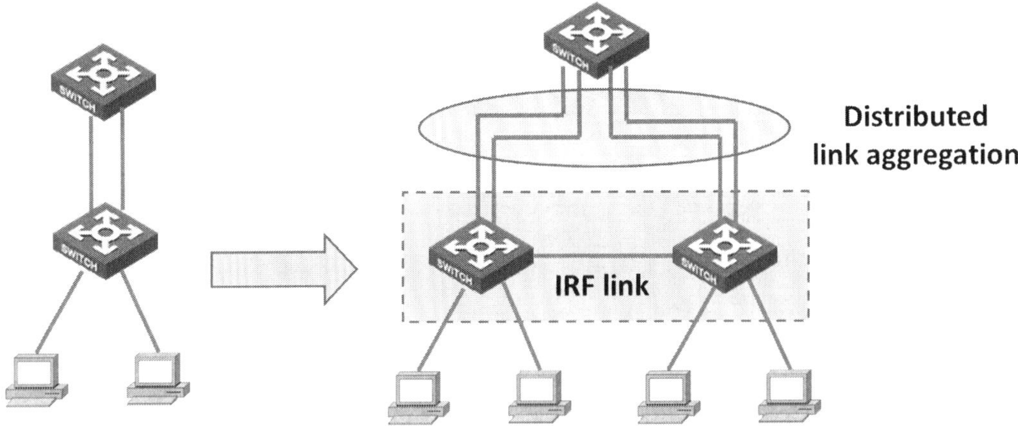

Figure 13-3. IRF example that increases bandwidth

With IRF, you can simplify the network design at both Layer 2 and Layer 3, while simultaneously simplifying network operations. In "Chapter 8: Introducing Spanning Tree" and "Chapter 9: MSTP Configuration," you learned how to build a resilient network using MSTP.

Instead of implementing a complicated spanning tree topology for Layer 2 redundancy, however, you can use IRF, which provides both device and link redundancy. See Figure 13-4 as an example. When you connect the virtual switch to the network, you can use link aggregations, which efficiently load-balance traffic across themselves for full utilization of the bandwidth. If necessary, you can expand the uplink bandwidth by simply adding another link to the link aggregation group.

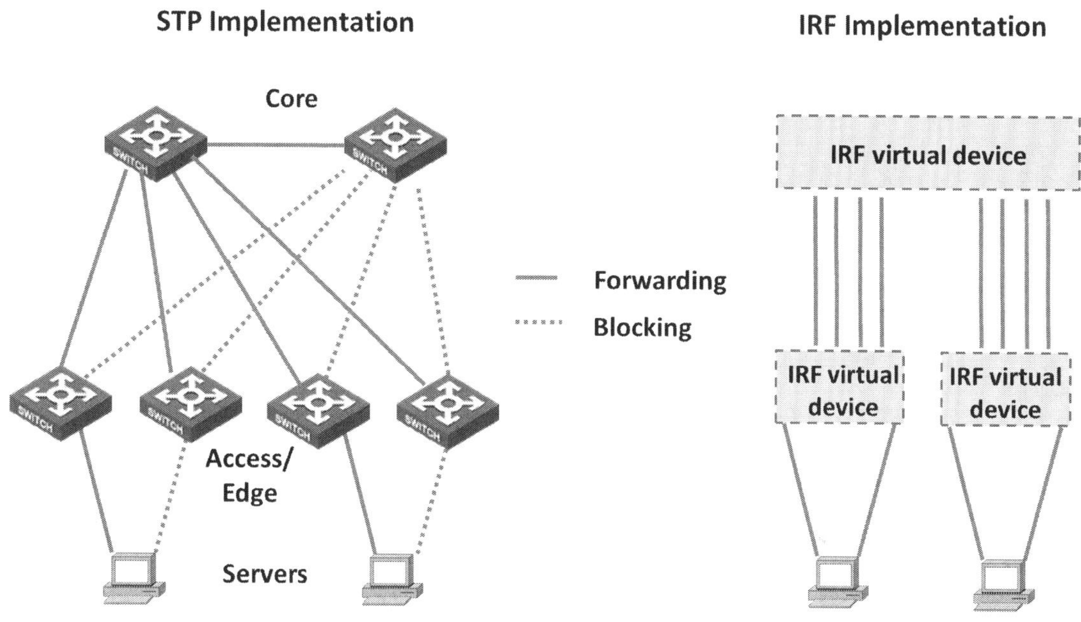

Figure 13-4. Simplified network design

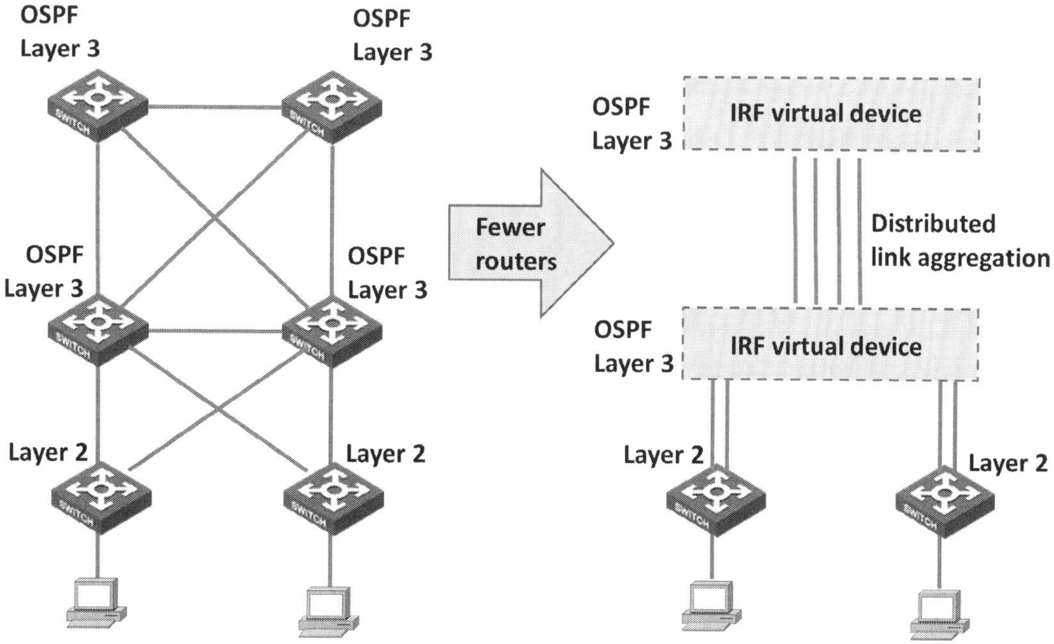

Figure 13-5. Simplified network operations

IRF also allows you to simplify the network design at Layer 3 (see Figure 13-5). The IRF virtual device acts as a single router with a single IP address per interface. For example, the IRF device can act as a redundant default gateway without Virtual Router Redundancy Protocol (VRRP), and routing protocols calculate the routes of the IRF virtual device instead of calculating the routes of each member. This design eliminates numerous protocol packet exchanges among the members, simplifies network operations, and shortens the convergence time.

In addition, without IRF, routing switches with redundant routes between themselves would need to use equal-cost multipath (ECMP) routing to load balance traffic. But with IRF, you can simply create a link aggregation between the IRF virtual devices and run the desired routing protocol.

IRF provides both link and node redundancy. You can aggregate members' IRF links and the links between the IRF virtual device and its upper or lower layer devices. In addition, the IRF virtual device includes multiple member devices that operate in 1:N redundancy: if the master fails, the IRF virtual device immediately elects a new master to prevent service interruption. As Table 13-1 shows, failover is extremely fast—less than two milliseconds.

Table 13-1. High level of reliability

Scenario	Failover Time
Link aggregation: port removal/insertion	2 ms/0.7 ms
Link aggregation: board removal/insertion	2 ms/1 ms
Chassis off/on	2 ms/0.14 ms
Software upgrade	2 ms

Whether you manage the IRF system from the command line interface (CLI) or use a management platform, such as IMC, you can manage the IRF system as a single device. You can connect to the IRF device's management interfaces through any member's AUX port or through Telnet, SSH, HTTP, or HTTPS to the IRF device's IP address. Configurations are performed on the master and distributed to all associated switches, greatly simplifying network setup, operation, and maintenance.

As you learned earlier, the various management planes automatically communicate with each other, so any configuration changes apply transparently across the system. In addition, IRF systems are scalable. You can increase the bandwidth and processing capability of an IRF virtual device simply by adding member devices. Each member device has its own CPU, and they independently process and forward protocol packets.

IRF Activity

In this activity, you will look at an existing network and create an IRF design to solve the problem in the scenario.

Before IRF

Figure 13-6 illustrates a network before IRF was implemented. In this example, two different MSTP regions exist in the same network, which must be maintained and tuned separately. For the load-sharing with MSTP, the VRRP was implemented for default gateway redundancy and tuned to match the MSTP topology. VRRP is briefly introduced in "Chapter 16: Basic Network Design Concepts." A more in-depth discussion is covered in the ASE-level networking courses.

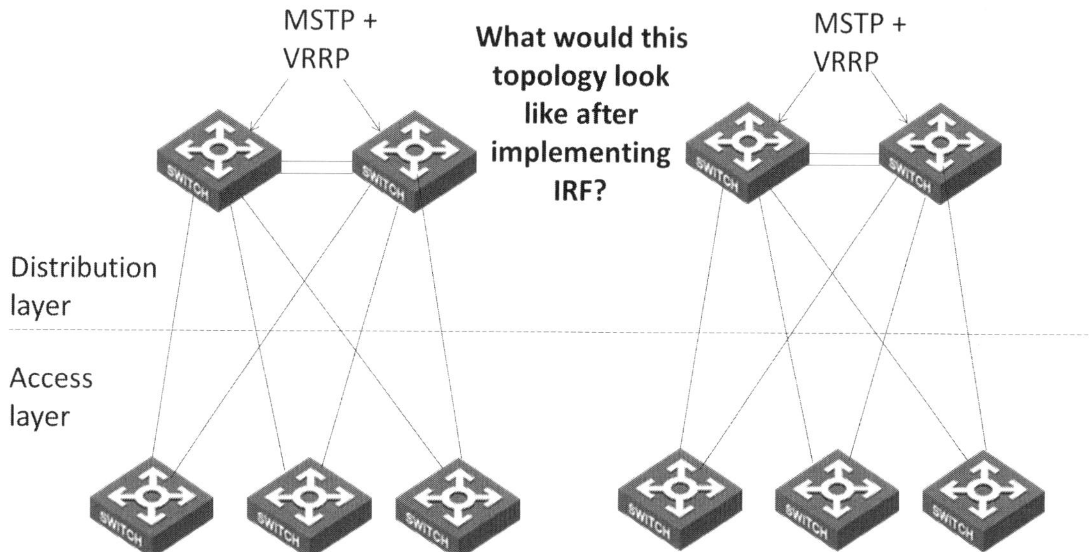

Figure 13-6. A network before IRF implementation

After IRF

Figure 13-7 illustrates a conversion of the network shown in Figure 13-6. In Figure 13-7, the four distribution layer switches are formed into a single IRF topology (*single virtual switch*). The access layer switches see the IRF topology as a single switch, so distributed link aggregation can be configured. Logically, an access layer switch's connection to the IRF topology appears as a single link. Therefore, protocols like MSTP and VRRP are no longer necessary.

It is important to understand that distributed link aggregation is *not* distributed trunking, which is proprietary to the ProVision switches. With distributed trunking, you are still dealing with two physical switches from a configuration and management perspective, which is not true of IRF.

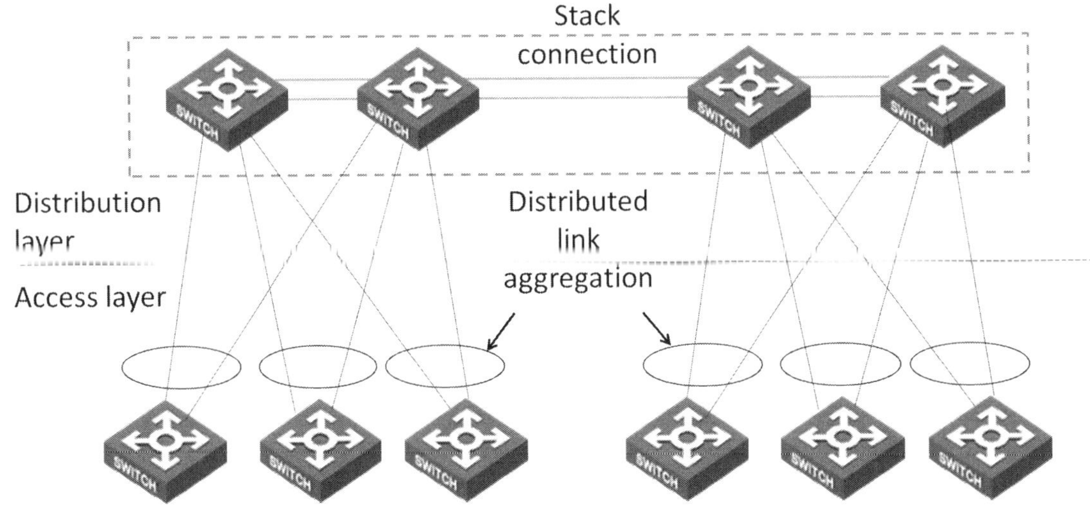

Figure 13-7. A network after IRF implementation

Note

The answer shown in Figure 13-7 is just one example. You could have easily applied IRF to the access layer, as well.

IRF Versus STP

Upon examining Table 13-2, you can see that IRF is a better alternative for redundancy, load-balancing, and network simplification than spanning tree.

Table 13-2. IRF and STP comparison

	IRF	STP
Rapid failover	Yes (sub 10 ms)	No (often measured in seconds)
Design simplification—common across data center/campus core/edge	Yes (virtualizes up to nine switches, common across layers/devices)	No (switch-by-switch configuration)
Support for Layer 2/3, Multi-Protocol Label Switching (MPLS), IPv6 protocols	Yes	Layer 2 only
Performance	Very high	Low
Geographic resiliency	Yes (supported across 70 kilometers)	No
Overall administration effort and cost	Low	No extra cost

Supported HP Comware Products

Most of the HP Comware switches support IRF capabilities. Table 13-3 gives an overview of the higher-end switches. IRF requires a 10 GE interface (or faster) connection between the switches. The amount of bandwidth that can be used between the switches (stack) depends on the switch model: these are the physical links between two respective IRF members and are referred to as an *IRF port* or *stack port*. (This is the Stack Bandwidth column in Table 13-3.) Likewise, each switch model has a limited number of switches that can be included in the IRF stack. (This is the Stack Number column in Table 13-3). Currently, each model must be mated with the same model: the exceptions are the 5800 and 5820 and the 5900 and 5920, which can be mixed in a stack.

10GE links (or faster) are required for the IRF links. There are exceptions, like the 5120 SI switch, but it has a restricted feature list when it comes to implementing IRF. The stack bandwidth is the extension of the backplane between the switches: this is the logical IRF port made up of one or more physical 10 GE links (or faster). Based on forwarding decisions, traffic might not exit this switch but might have to be forwarded to another member before leaving the IRF topology. Therefore, the amount of bandwidth between the switches is *critical*. (Forwarding of traffic is discussed later in the chapter in the "IRF Topology and Forwarding Traffic" section.)

Table 13-3. IRF product example

Switch	Stack Interface	Stack Bandwidth	Stack Number	Stack with Different Model
3100	1GE	2x1GE	4	No
3600	1GE	2x1GE	4	No
5120-SI	1GE	2x1GE	4	No
5120-EI	10GE	2x10GE	4	No
5500-SI	10GE	2x10GE	4	No
5500-EI	10GE	2x10GE	9	No
5500-HI	10GE	3x10GE	9	No
5800	10GE	4x10GE	9	Yes with 5820
5820	10GE	4x10GE	9	Yes with 5800
5830	10GE	4-8x10GE	4	No
6125	10GE	2-4xGE	10	No
5900AF	10GE	4x10GE	4	Yes with 5920
5920AF	10GE	4x10GE	4	Yes with 5900
7500	10GE	8x10GE	2-4	No
9500	10GE	8x10GE	4	No
10500	10GE	12x10GE	4	No
12500	10GE	12x10GE	4	No

Note

There are many important restrictions and requirements when choosing switches for an IRF topology. Even within some switching models, you might have restrictions (for example, the 5830AF-48G and the 5830AF-96G cannot be in the same IRF topology). Or, as another example, the 12500 switches originally supported two members in a topology but can now support four. A third example is where the 5120 SI supports IRF links of 1 Gbps, but all the other Comware switches require at least a 10 Gbps link. Therefore, you should always examine HP's website when doing any planning about choosing switches for an IRF solution.

Also, HP uses a mixture of terms when referring to IRF configurations. The terms *topology* and *domain* refer to a set of switches in the same IRF group. The terms *IRF port* or *stack port* refer to the link or links between the IRF members.

IRF Operation

This section introduces the terms used in IRF, the election process of the master for the IRF topology, how IRF operates, and how IRF forwards traffic.

IRF Analogy

Before you can begin to understand IRF operations, you must first understand the operation of the switches that comprise the IRF system. HP switches divide functions across the following planes:

- Management (MGMT)
- Centralized control (CTRL)
- Forwarding (FWD)

Each switch has a centralized *management plane*. When you access the switch to manage or configure it, you interact with this plane, whether you access the switch through a console, Telnet, Secure Shell (SSH), File Transfer Protocol (FTP), or Simple Network Management Protocol (SNMP) session. The centralized control plane also handles the file system, including configuration files. Finally, it manages the hardware, monitoring its temperature, power, fan, and modules.

The *centralized control plane* runs the protocols (Layer 2 and Layer 3), builds the routing table, and handles Quality of Service (QoS) and Access Control Lists (ACLs).

The *forwarding plane* contains the switch fabric that receives and transmits traffic. The forwarding plane's schedulers and packet processors manage the traffic flow, using copies of the forwarding and routing tables that were built in the control plane. In other words, the forwarding plane handles the bulk of traffic flow (as directed by the management and control planes). The forwarding plane is hardware-based (rather than software-based) because of speed requirements.

Note

The IRF topology operates like a traditional chassis-based modular switch. The master performs the control/management plane functions, and all the switches in the topology are like line cards: they perform data functions by forwarding users' frames.

Chassis-Based Switches

A *chassis-based switch architecture* includes two main processing units (MPUs), each of which contains a management plane, control plane, and forwarding plane (see Figure 13-8). One of the MPUs is active, and the other is in standby mode. The switch can load-balance traffic through its standby MPU's forwarding plane.

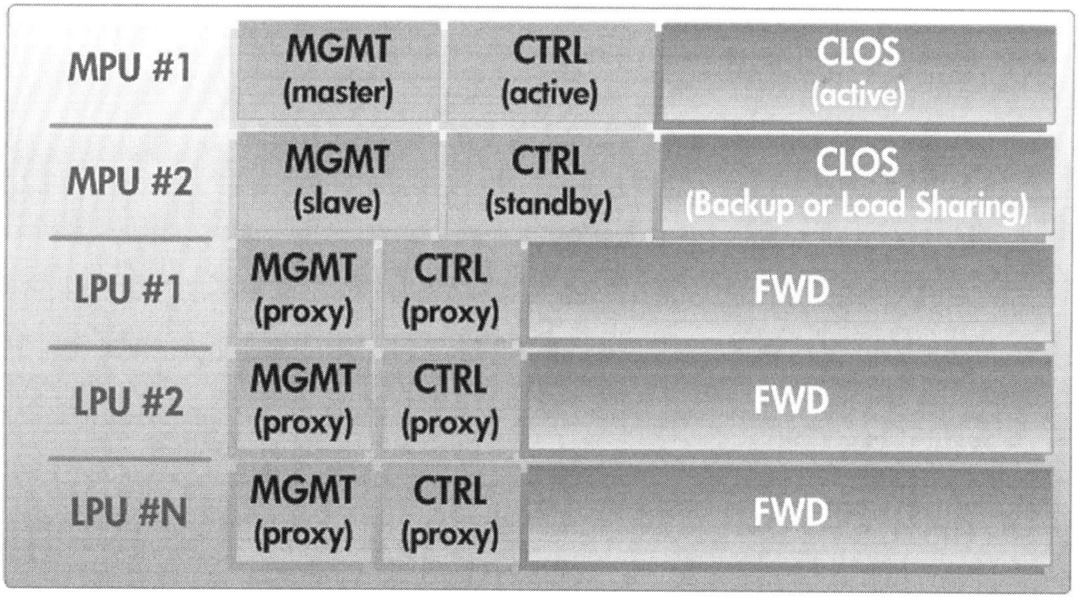

Figure 13-8. Traditional modular switch architecture

On a chassis-based switch, each interface module has its own line processing unit (LPU) with its own management, control, and forwarding planes. The LPU's management and control planes simply proxy information from the single active MPU, making this information immediately available to the local forwarding plane. With so many forwarding planes, this switch is much more scalable than a stackable switch with its single forwarding plane.

Note

In Figure 13-8, *CLOS* refers to the switching mechanism deployed, developed by Charles Clos. A CLOS solution is required when the physical circuit switching needs exceed the capacity of the largest feasible single crossbar switch. The key advantage of CLOS networks is that the number of cross-points (which make up each crossbar switch) required can be much fewer than were the entire switching system implemented with one large crossbar switch. HP's 12500 switches is an example of a switch deploying a CLOS architecture. Most smaller modular switches in the industry employ a crossbar matrix switching fabric.

Chassis-Based Switches with IRF

The architecture of an IRF system, which can have up to nine stackable switches (depending on the switch models used), is very similar to the chassis-based switch architecture. The master's management and control planes are active, like the chassis-based switch's active MPU. The other members in the IRF system can be compared to interface modules with their own proxy management and control planes and active forwarding planes. Within an IRF system, however, one member's management and control planes can take over as the active planes, if necessary.

When an IRF system is composed of chassis-based switches, you can think of it as a single chassis to which you have added more interface boards and more standby MPUs (see Figure 13-9). IRF supports up to four chassis-based switches per IRF topology and up to nine fixed configuration switches per IRF topology. You can now understand how the IRF system provides the simple, efficient operation of a single virtual chassis-based switch but with the reliability of distributed hardware in different switch chassis.

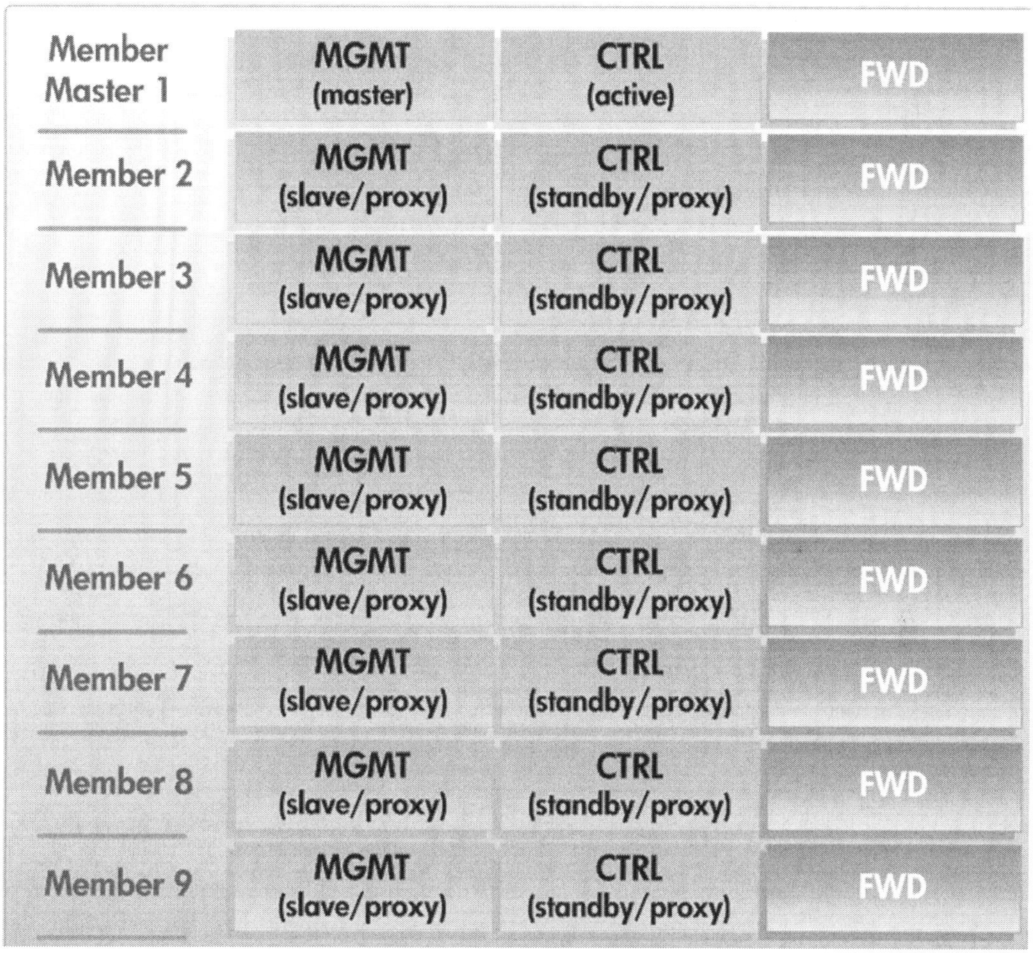

Member			
Member Master 1	MGMT (master)	CTRL (active)	FWD
Member 2	MGMT (slave/proxy)	CTRL (standby/proxy)	FWD
Member 3	MGMT (slave/proxy)	CTRL (standby/proxy)	FWD
Member 4	MGMT (slave/proxy)	CTRL (standby/proxy)	FWD
Member 5	MGMT (slave/proxy)	CTRL (standby/proxy)	FWD
Member 6	MGMT (slave/proxy)	CTRL (standby/proxy)	FWD
Member 7	MGMT (slave/proxy)	CTRL (standby/proxy)	FWD
Member 8	MGMT (slave/proxy)	CTRL (standby/proxy)	FWD
Member 9	MGMT (slave/proxy)	CTRL (standby/proxy)	FWD

Figure 13-9. IRF topology

IRF Topologies

When you implement an IRF stack, you must decide how the members, or *switches*, will be connected. The two connection choices are a daisy chain or a ring connection, as shown in Figure 13-10.

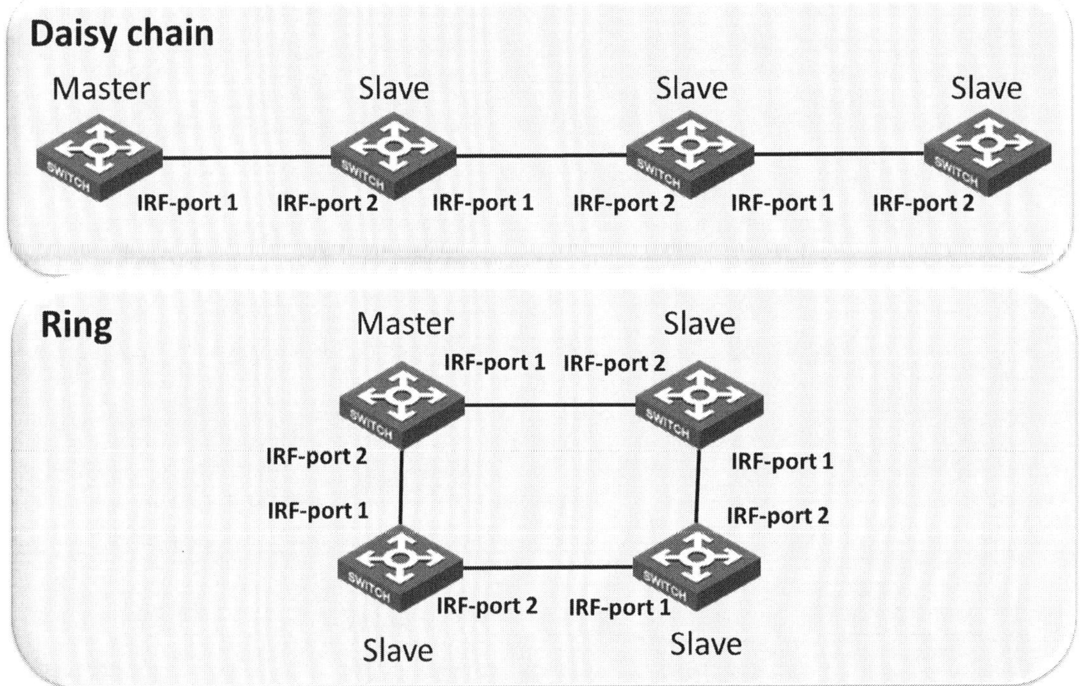

Figure 13-10. IRF connections

In a *daisy chain* connection, each switch is connected to at least one other switch, essentially forming a line. This topology is typically used when the switches in the IRF stack are separately located. The daisy chain configuration can be less reliable than the alternative ring connection, because a failed link in the chain results in the IRF stack separating into two independent virtual switches.

In a *ring connection*, each switch is connected to exactly two other switches, forming a ring. Because each switch connects to two others, this topology is more reliable than the daisy chain and provides better fault tolerance. If a link in the ring fails, the topology becomes a daisy chain and the productivity of the IRF stack is not affected.

The switches in an IRF stack communicate through logical ports, called *IRF ports*, which are bound to the actual physical ports that connect the switches. As shown in Figure 13-10, IRF ports are numbered IRF-port 1 and IRF-port 2.

Note

A Comware IRF configuration rule requires that IRF-port 1 on one member be connected to IRF-port 2 on a second member. Connecting port 1 to port 1 or port 2 to port 2 causes the IRF topology to fail. Logical IRF ports extend a logical backplane between the switches. This is not a bridge aggregation group, even though the Comware software load-balances traffic if there are multiple physical links comprising the IRF port.

As a recommendation, if you only have two switches in an IRF stack, you should configure them in a daisy chain topology to take advantage of the stack bandwidth of the two switches. If you set up two IRF ports between two daisy-chained members, you have just lost half of your bandwidth between the switches. However, if you have more than two switches in an IRF topology, you should configure them in a ring topology to reduce the likelihood of a split-stack condition.

IRF Components

When implementing an IRF system, you should be aware of a few requirements. First, generally speaking, all the members in an IRF system must be the same switch model. There is one exception: because the 5800 and 5820 switches use the same Comware code, they can be used in one IRF system. However, you cannot configure an IRF topology that involves different Comware models (for example a 7503 switch and a 5800 switch).

Second, the members in an IRF system must be connected by 10 GbE ports (or ports capable of higher speeds, like 40 GbE or 100 GbE). Finally, the members must be running compatible switch software. By default, the auto-upgrade feature is enabled. When a switch is added into an IRF system, the new member compares its software version with that of the master. If the versions are not consistent, the new member automatically downloads the boot file from the master, reboots with the new boot file, and joins the IRF system. (If the downloaded boot file and the local boot file have duplicate file names, the local file is overwritten.)

If the auto-upgrade feature is disabled, the new member cannot upgrade its boot file if it is not using compatible software. In this case, the new member or the member with a low priority does not boot normally and you need to update the switch's software and add the device to the IRF system again. If auto-upgrade is disabled, you can enable it again by entering:

```
[Comware] irf auto-update enable
```

Topology Collection

Each member exchanges hello packets with the directly connected neighbors to collect topology of the IRF virtual device. The IRF hello packets carry the topology information, including IRF port connection states, member IDs, priorities, and bridge MAC addresses. Each member records its known topology information locally. At the startup of a member switch, the member switch records the topology information of the local device. When an IRF port of a member becomes `UP`, the member switch sends its known topology information from this port periodically. Upon receiving the topology information from the directly connected neighbor, the member switch updates the local topology information. Topology collection lasts until all members have obtained the complete topology information (known as *topology convergence*). The IRF virtual device then enters the next stage: role election.

After you connect the members of an IRF stack and configure the IRF settings, the members exchange hello packets with their directly connected IRF neighbors. These packets provide topology information:

- **IRF port connection states**—The port states are `UP`, `DOWN`, or `DISABLED`.
- **Domain ID**—If you need to restrict which switches form a stack, you can assign a domain identifier.
- **Member IDs**—Each member of the IRF stack must have a unique ID.
- **Priorities**—You can configure a priority for the IRF members. This setting is one of the factors considered in the election of the master (a process explained in the "Electing a Master" section). The master is the switch that runs, manages, and maintains the stack.
- **Bridge MAC addresses**—Each switch has its own system MAC address and this is shared across the topology; however, one these system MAC addresses is chosen to represent the IRF topology when using protocols like STP BPDUs or LACP messages. This topology MAC address will remain the same even if a new master is elected.

If topology changes are made late to the IRF stack, members exchange hello packets to communicate these changes.

Logical IRF Ports

The switches in an IRF system communicate through logical ports, called *IRF ports*. You assign the actual physical ports that connect the switches in the IRF system to these logical IRF ports. You can assign one physical port to an IRF port, or you can assign multiple physical ports to provide redundancy and to increase bandwidth.

After you bind a physical port to an IRF port, a limited number of commands are available from the port interface. For example, you can shut down the port, configure a description, and enter flow-control commands. However, other commands, such as VLAN settings, are no longer available.

As shown in the Figure 13-10, IRF ports are numbered as IRF-port 1 and IRF-port 2. When setting up an IRF system, you *must* connect IRF port 1 on one switch to IRF port 2 on the directly connected switch. If you connect the IRF port 1 on one switch to the IRF port 1 on another switch, the switches cannot form an IRF system.

When configuring IRF ports, keep in mind the following:

- 5800 switches with more than 48 ports have two ASICs. IRF ports must be composed of ports that are all on the same ASIC: either 10 GbE (or higher) ports in the front panel or 10 GbE (or higher) ports when implementing a ring topology. in the same module.
- In modular switches, HP Networking recommends that you bind physical ports in different modules to the same IRF ports when implementing a ring topology. This setup enhances the IRF system's failover capabilities because, if one module fails, the remaining modules provide the IRF connection.

Note

The logical IRF port connections are sometimes referred to as a *stack cable*; however, this term can be misleading since many switching products support "stacking" and connecting those switches with stack cables. IRF is *not* your traditional stacking technology.

IRF Domain

If you have multiple IRF systems on the same network, you should configure an IRF domain ID for each one. In the example network shown in Figure 13-11, one IRF system is assigned the domain ID of 10, and the second IRF system is assigned the domain ID of 20. This prevents either IRF system from interfering with the other.

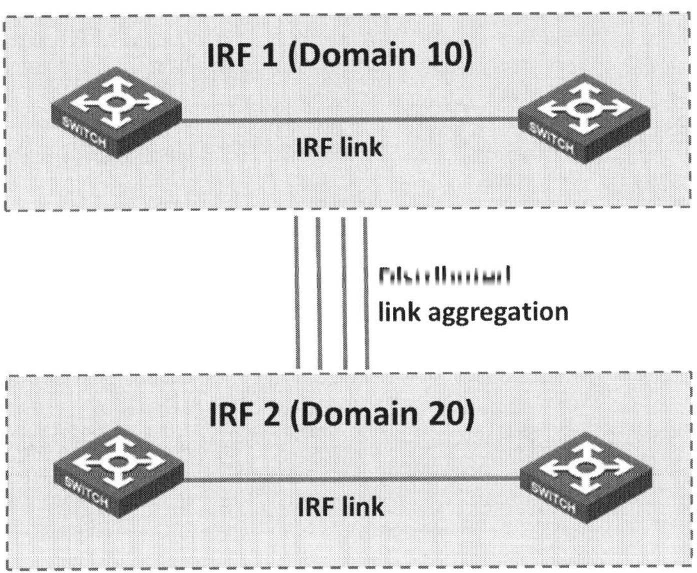

Figure 13-11. IRF domain

IRF Member IDs

The IRF system uses member IDs to uniquely identify and manage the members (see Figure 13-12). If member IDs are not unique, the IRF system cannot be established. Further, a switch that has the same member ID as an existing member cannot join the IRF system.

Note

The 5120 and 5500 Switches support dynamic member ID allocation. If two members have the same ID, one changes its member ID automatically.

By default, each switch is assigned member ID 1. You should change this setting for all members except the master. You can assign members an ID number from 1 to 10. When you change this ID, you must reboot the switch for the change to take effect. This member ID remains in effect until you manually change it again and reboot the switch. The member ID is saved to the switch's ASIC and survives a return to factory default settings.

Member IDs are used in interface names to identify the interfaces on each member:

- For a stackable switch that supports IRF, the interface is named `GigabitEthernet X/0/1`, with X being the device's member ID.
- For a chassis-based switch that supports IRF, the member ID is inserted before the interface name: `X/1/0/1`, with X being the member ID.

Member IDs are also used in file management. To access the file system on stackable switches in an IRF system:

- On the master, use the name of the storage device as you would if a switch operated in stand-alone mode.
- On slaves, use the path *slot#*flash:/test.cfg. Replace the slot # with the member ID. To access the file system on chassis-based switches in an IRF system, use the path *chassis#slot#*flash:/test.cfg. Replace the chassis# with the member ID, and replace the slot# with the module number.

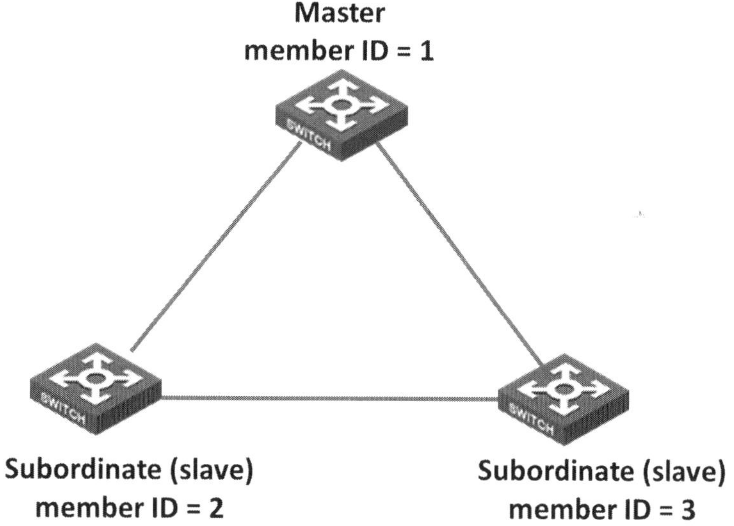

Figure 13-12. Member IDs in an IRF topology

IRF Resiliency

An IRF stack provides redundancy on several levels.

- **N:1**—The IRF stack protects against switch failure. If the master fails, the slaves immediately elect another master.
- **Protocol information**—Within the IRF stack, *protocol information* is backed up to each member. You have already seen that the stack members synchronize and save routing tables locally. This feature, called *resilient distributed routing*, protects against a single port routing failure.

- **Link**—With IRF, you can create an aggregation port group and add physical Ethernet ports on different members to this group. If an aggregated link port fails, the stack can automatically distribute the traffic to other ports in that aggregated link. This distributed link aggregation technology provides link backup, increasing network reliability.
- **IRF port**—IRF uses an aggregation technology to implement IRF port redundancy, as well. You can bind multiple physical ports to the virtual IRF ports. The traffic is then load-balanced across the physical ports, increasing bandwidth and performance. If a link fails, the IRF stack is not affected, thus increasing the device reliability.

When you implement an IRF system, one of the switches is elected as the *master*, which manages and maintains the system. (You will learn more about the election process later in the "Electing a Master" section.) The other members act as *slaves*, which process services and function as backups. If the master fails, one of the slaves is elected master and assumes responsibility for managing the IRF system. This can be seen in Figure 13-13.

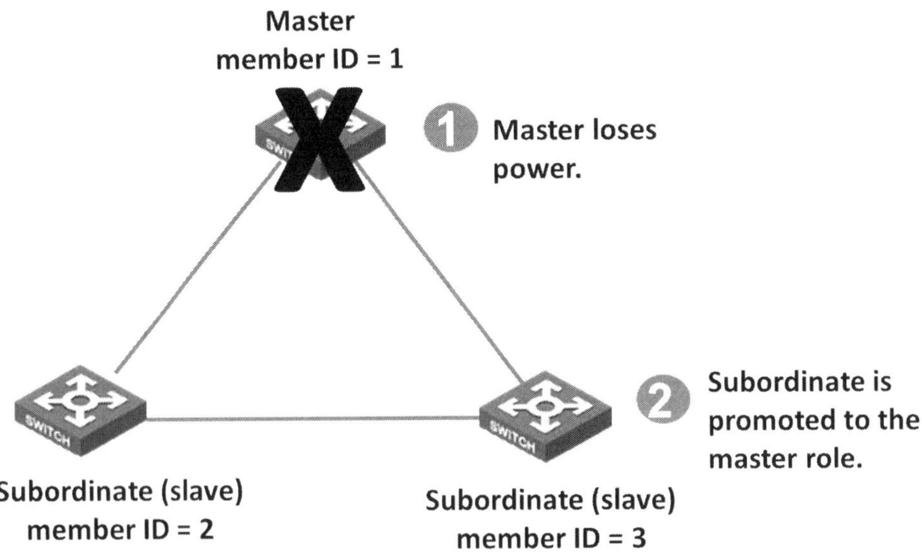

Figure 13-13. Resilience of IRF when failures occur

Electing a Master

In an IRF system, every unit is called an *IRF member*. One of the IRF members plays the role of the master, and all the others play a slave role. The IRF master is the unit in which the control and management planes are active, and the IRF slaves are the units where the control and management planes are in standby.

When a new IRF stack is formed or topology changes occur in an existing stack, the members undergo an election process to identify a master. The IRF stack members use the following rules to determine which switch will be the master:

1. The current master wins.
2. The member with a higher priority wins.
3. The member with the longest system uptime wins.
4. The member with the lowest bridge MAC address wins.

The other members of the stack function as slaves. In addition to executing tasks as directed by the master, each slave is a backup for the master. If the master fails, the remaining stack members immediately elect a new master to prevent service interruption.

After role election, an IRF is established. The operation of the IRF depends on whether the switches are fixed-port (5820 models and smaller) or are chassis-type (7500 models and higher) switches. An IRF that combines box-type devices operates like a chassis-type distributed device. The master operates as the active main board (AMB) of the IRF, and the slaves operate as the standby main boards (SMBs). This is similar to a line card in a traditional modular switch.

An IRF virtualized by chassis-type distributed devices also operates like a chassis-type distributed device. It has more standby main boards and interface boards. The active main board of the master is the active main board of the IRF; the standby main boards of the master and the active main board and standby main boards of the slaves are the standby main boards of the IRF.

If two IRF systems are running (each one with its own master) and an IRF link is established between them, an IRF merge process starts. The most important part of this process is the election of the new master:

1. First, during the boot process, a device will not compete with the active master. So the active master wins and the inserted device becomes a slave. This is the difference between a device insertion and an IRF merge.
2. Second, if there are two or more active masters (because a connection failure caused a stack to split), the member with the highest priority wins.
3. Third, if there are two master candidates with the same priority, the one that has been up for the longest time wins. The granularity of this comparison is 10 minutes. If the uptime difference is less than 10 minutes, none wins.
4. Finally, if all of the previous rules do not allow election of the master, the device with the lowest bridge MAC address wins.

Note

An IRF merge causes automatic device reboot of IRF members whose original master loses the election process.

After role election, an IRF is established. All member devices operate as a virtual device on the network, and all resources on the member devices are processed and managed by this virtual device.

An IRF uses member IDs to uniquely identify and manage member devices. If a member wants to join an IRF but its member ID is the same as an existing one, the device cannot join the IRF. You can use the following methods to ensure the uniqueness of member IDs:

- Before establishing an IRF, plan and configure member IDs for IRF members.
- Use the member ID collision processing mechanism.

In an IRF, if a member becomes down or the IRF link is down, its neighbor broadcasts the information to all the other members immediately. The member devices that receive the message determine whether it is the master or a slave that is down, according to the local IRF topology information table. If the master is down, a new election is triggered and the local IRF topology is updated. If a slave is down, the local IRF topology is updated to ensure fast convergence of the IRF topology.

Switch Configuration Files

IRF uses a strict configuration file synchronization mechanism to ensure that switches in an IRF virtual device can work as a single switch on the network and to ensure that after the master fails, the other switches can operate normally. When a slave starts up, it automatically determines the master, synchronizes the master's configuration file, and executes the configuration file. If all switches in an IRF virtual device start up simultaneously, the slaves synchronize the master's initial configuration file and execute it.

When the IRF virtual device operates normally, all of your configurations are recorded into the current configuration file of the master and synchronized to each switch in the IRF virtual device. When you save the current configuration file of the master as the initial configuration file by using the save command, all slaves execute the same saving operation to make the initial configuration files of all switches consistent. Through real-time synchronization, all switches in the IRF virtual device keep the same configuration file. If the master fails, all of the other switches can execute various functions according to the same configuration file.

The configuration file can be divided into two parts: global configuration and port configuration. When a slave applies these two kinds of configurations obtained from the master, it deals with them in different ways.

- **Global configuration**—All slaves exactly execute the current global configuration obtained from the master—that is, all members of the IRF virtual device apply the same global configuration.
- **Port configuration**—When a slave applies the port configuration obtained from the master, it cares about the configuration related to its own port. For example, the slave with the member ID of 3 only cares about the configuration related to the `GigabitEthernet 3/0/x` port on the master. If there is a configuration related to its own port, it applies the configuration; if not, no matter which configuration has been made to the port before the slave joins the IRF virtual device, the slave functions by using a null configuration.

Note

Most commands are replicated from the master to the slaves in the IRF topology. For example, if you execute the `save` command on the master to save the configuration file, this command is replicated to all of the slave switches, as well. Not all commands are replicated, like most control/management commands. For example, if you executed a `ping` on the master, since this is a management plane function, it would only be executed on the master.

IRF Topology and Forwarding Traffic

After the master is elected, the IRF stack functions as one virtual switch, allowing protocols to operate as if the stack is, in reality, one device. For example, all members forward routing protocol packets to the master, which calculates routes as if for a single virtual switch and distributes the routing table to each member. Therefore, the IRF stack members do not exchange numerous protocol packets with each other, thereby simplifying network operation. In addition, if the master fails, the new master takes over seamlessly and each device does not recalculate routing tables.

While the IRF functions as a single virtual switch, it uses a distributed forwarding and routing model. The members in the IRF stack synchronize forwarding and routing tables, but each member in the stack forwards frames or routes packets independently.

When a member receives a frame to be forwarded, it finds the outbound interface (and next hop) by searching its Layer 2/Layer 3 forwarding table. The member then forwards the packet to the outbound interface, which can be on the local device or on another member device.

In a modular switch, the main processing board distributes forwarding tables to each interface module. Interface modules encapsulate Ethernet headers with special inner headers that indicate the frame's source interface and outbound interface according to the table. Similarly, in an IRF stack—a virtual modular switch—the master distributes forwarding tables to each member. Using this table, a member encapsulates an Ethernet frame with an IRF header that indicates the proper outbound interface without further processing by other members.

Switching at Layer 2

Each member in the IRF system learns MAC addresses, which it forwards to the active management plane (see Figure 13-14). The active management plane on the master, in turn, distributes the learned MAC addresses. Each member can then handle traffic immediately, no matter where the traffic arrives, and traffic flooding is minimized.

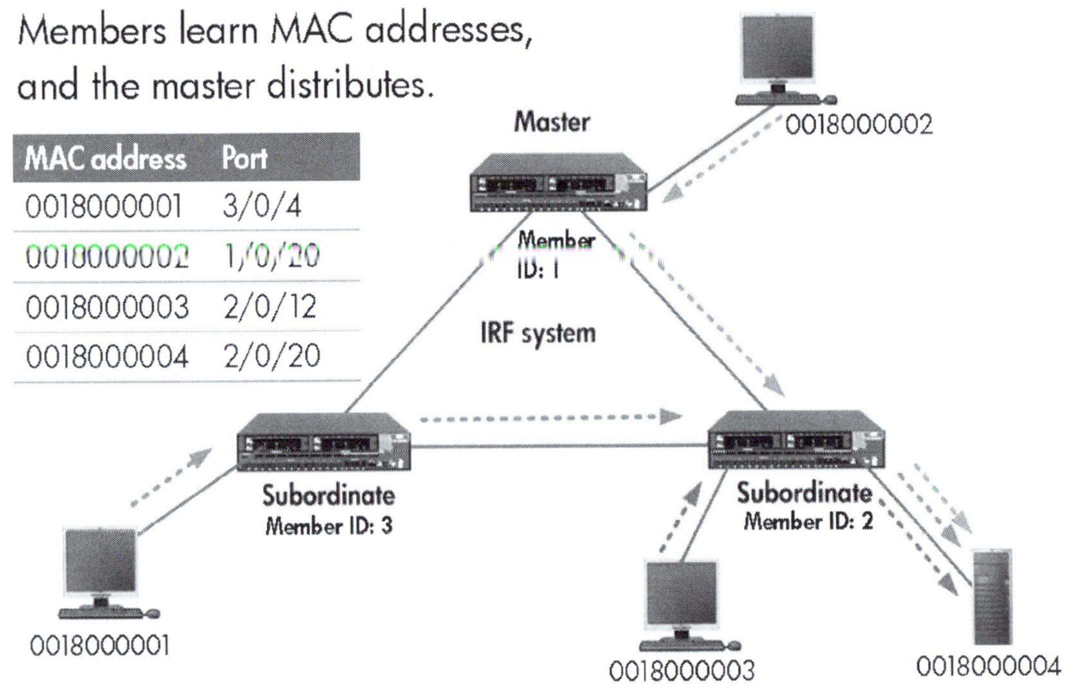

Figure 13-14. Forwarding traffic in an IRF topology

When a member device receives a frame to be forwarded at Layer 2, it finds the outbound interface of the frame by searching its Layer 2 forwarding table and then forwards the packet to the outbound interface, which might be on the local member or on another member device. If the outbound interface is on another member, the frame is forwarded within the IRF system—a process that is not detected by devices outside of the IRF system.

Note that, in Figure 13-14, each IRF member has a unique member ID, which affects how its ports are numbered. The ports for member 3 are numbered starting with a "3," such as 3/0/4. The ports for member 2 are numbered starting with a "2" (2/0/12 and 2/0/20).

When the master receives a frame from the workstation with the MAC address 0018000002 and determines that the source MAC address is 0018000004, it checks the IRF system's Layer 2 forwarding table. The master then forwards the frame to the slave with member ID 2. This slave can then forward the frame to its final destination.

Routing at Layer 3

When a member receives packets to route at Layer 3, it scans its Layer 3 routing table to identify the forwarding egress port and the next hop, and then it sends the packets to the appropriate egress port, which, again, might be on the local member or another member in the IRF system. Because the IRF system functions as a single virtual device, forwarding the packet to a port on any member is an internal action, which is not noticeable to outside devices. For Layer 3 packets, the hop number increases only by one, no matter how many IRF members handle the packets as they are forwarded through the IRF system. To the outside network, the packets travel one hop—as if one device routed the packets.

Split Stacks and the MAD Protocol

If an IRF link failure occurs and members in an IRF system cannot communicate, it can cause an *IRF split stack* (see Figure 13-15). Two separate IRF systems are formed. Each system elects a master and uses the IP addresses and configuration settings assigned to the original IRF system. You can immediately see the issues that such a split stack would cause. Address collisions occur, creating chaos on the network.

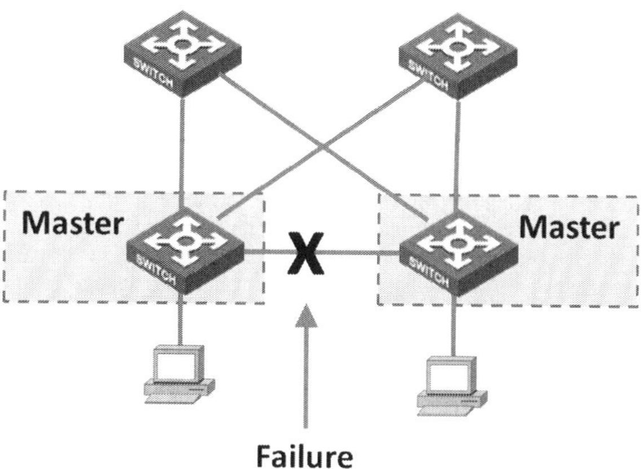

Figure 13-15. Split stack condition in IRF

Note

All of the physical interfaces comprising the logical IRF port would have to fail for the IRF link to fail.

Multi-Active Detection

As described earlier, IRF link failures may cause an integral IRF system to split into two or more IRFs operating with the same global configuration. Because these IRFs look the same to other devices in the network, problems, such as route flapping and STP calculation, result. To offset the risk, the MAD mechanism detects the presence of multiple identical IRFs split from an IRF system and handles the problem to make the network operate normally. The MAD mechanism provides the following functions:

- **Detection**—Enabled in an IRF system, the MAD mechanism periodically detects the IRF system for multiple active IRFs with the same global configuration. This is done with the LACP, the Bidirectional Forwarding Detection (BFD) protocol, or gratuitous ARP.
- **Collision-handling**—If multiple identical active IRFs are detected, the MAD mechanism keeps only the one with the lowest master ID (the active ID) to operate normally. The state of all the other IRFs will be set to recovery and all the ports in them will be shut down, except for the IRF ports and ports manually directed not to do so.
- **Failure recovery**—When the IRF port fails, the IRF devices try to automatically repair the failed IRF port. If the repair fails, the administrator needs to manually repair the physical problem. After a failed IRF link is recovered, the member devices in the recovery state reboot to join the active IRF and all disabled ports come up to forward traffic.

IRF includes a mechanism, called MAD, to quickly discover IRF split stacks. You can implement three types of MAD:

- LACP MAD
- BFD MAD
- ARP MAD

MAD mitigates the effect of the split stack on the network. It first prevents address conflicts by permitting only one IRF system to be active. After this problem is resolved, MAD tries to re-establish the failed link and to re-establish the IRF system.

In summary, MAD:

- Detects multiple active IRF systems with the same global configuration.
- Prevents address conflicts by allowing one active IRF system to function and placing the other in recovery state (disabling it).
- Initiates failure recovery.

The rest of this section looks at the MAD process in more depth.

Note

The part of the topology that is placed in a recovery state basically shuts down all its data interfaces (not the IRF ports and not the MAD ports, but you have to specifically exempt the latter). Therefore, external devices only see one master and whichever slaves are associated with it. After the problem has been fixed, the switches that were in a recovery state automatically reboot and rejoins the stack.

Detecting a Split Stack with Comware LACPDUs

To use LACP to detect IRF split stacks, you must use an aggregated link between the IRF members and a non-member Comware switch. After you configure IRF members to use LACP MAD, they send extended LACP data units (LACPDUs) that non-member IRF Comware switches can interpret (see Figure 13-16). The extended LACPDUs include a type length value (TLV) that indicates the active ID of an IRF system. The active ID matches the member ID of the master, making it unique to the IRF system.

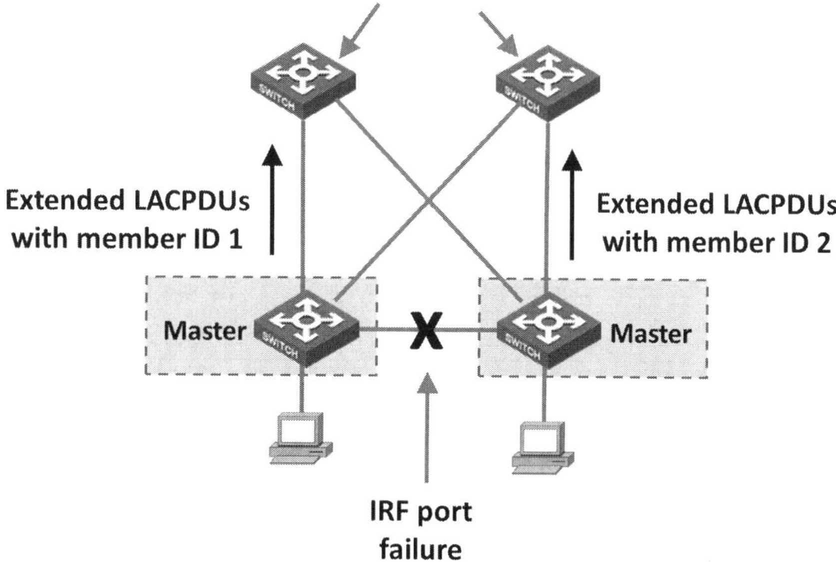

Figure 13-16. Detecting a split stack with Comware LACPDUs

When the IRF system is operating normally, all members in the IRF system send the same active ID in their extended LACPDUs. If the IRF system splits, however, the separated members send extended LACPDUs that have different active IDs. This indicates that a problem has occurred and triggers MAD to take action to prevent address conflicts.

Note

Comware LACPDUs that implement MAD are not normal LACP data units—only other Comware switches understand these extended messages. Therefore, the MAD LACP solution should only be used when the connecting switches are Comware switches (whether they are in a stand-alone configuration, as shown in Figure 13-16, or in a separate IRF domain). In Figure 13-16, if the top two switches were ProVision switches, they would discard the Comware-based LACPDUs because they would not understand them. In this instance, if the IRF link failed, the IRF members would not see each other on the uplinks and then you would have more than one master in the topology—with the same configuration and addressing. This would create all kinds of problems for your network.

Detecting a Split Stack with BFD

To implement BFD MAD, you must connect the IRF members with another link that is dedicated for BFD (see Figure 13-17). You must also configure an IP address for this interface, and, on all members, the IP addresses must be in the same subnet and VLAN (which cannot be VLAN 1). This MAD address identifies the IRF member during BFD MAD detection. The BFD interface should be dedicated for detecting multi-active IRF systems; no other services should be provided through this interface.

When the IRF system operates normally, only the MAD IP address of the master is active. If the IRF system splits, however, the MAD IP addresses of both masters in the separate IRF systems become active. This triggers MAD to take action to avoid address conflicts caused by the split stack.

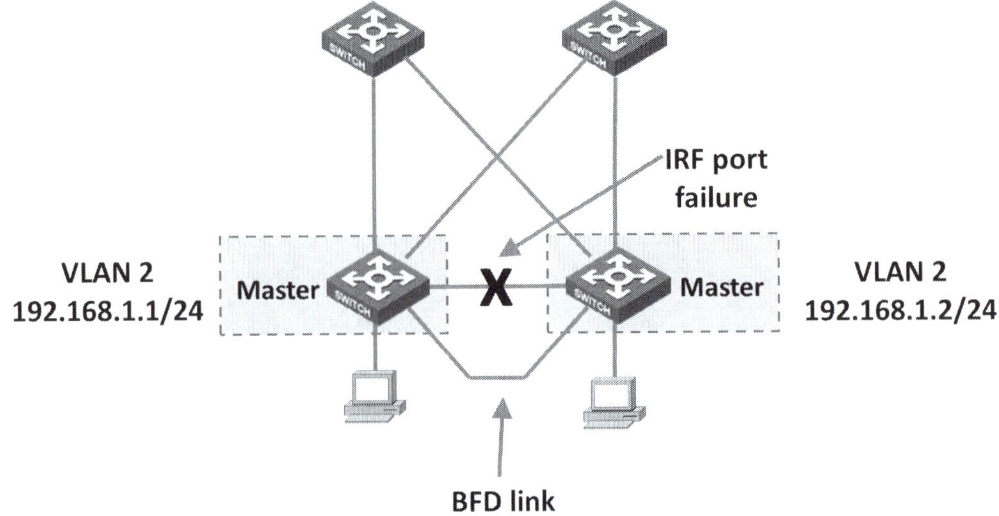

Figure 13-17. Detecting a split stack with BFD

Detecting a Split Stack with ARP

ARP MAD detects multi-active collisions by sending extended gratuitous ARP packets that convey the active IDs of IRF virtual devices.

You can set up ARP MAD links between neighbor IRF member switches, or, more commonly, between each IRF member switch and an intermediate switch. In the latter case, you must also enable MSTP on the IRF virtual device and the intermediate switch. As Figure 3-18 illustrates:

- If the IRF virtual device is operating normally, MSTP blocks the redundant link between the intermediate switch and the IRF virtual device. The gratuitous ARP packets sent by one member switch cannot reach the other.
- When the IRF virtual device splits, MSTP unblocks the redundant link and the two IRF virtual devices can receive gratuitous ARP packets from each other. These gratuitous packets carry the same IP address but different MAC addresses, resulting in collisions. Then, the separated IRF virtual devices compare their active IDs. The virtual device with higher active ID changes to the recovery state and shuts down all physical ports except the IRF ports. The IRF virtual device with lower active ID remains in the active state and forwards traffic.

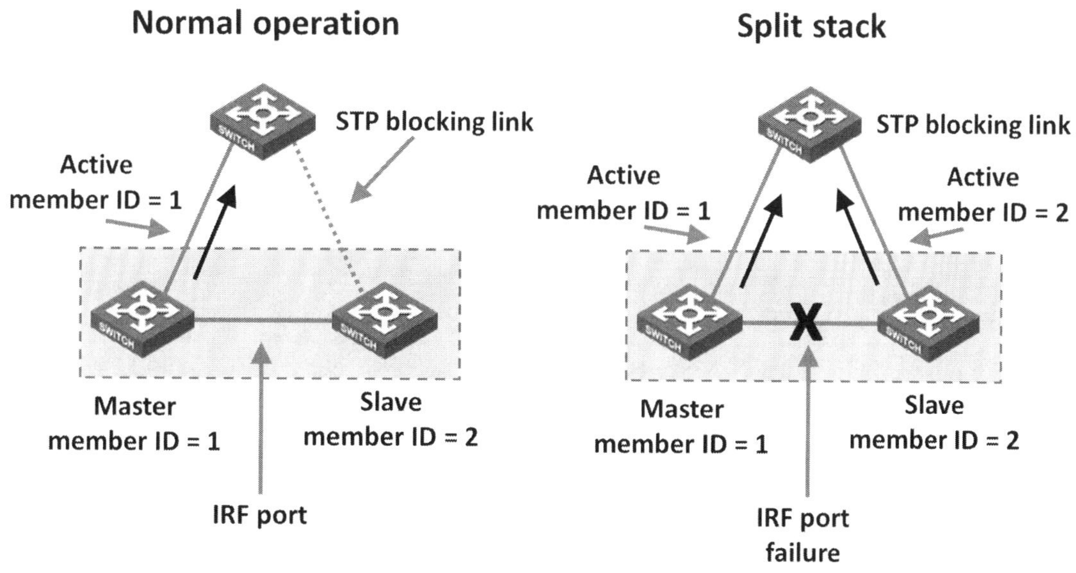

Figure 3-18. Detecting a split stack with ARP MAD

Note

Configure the IRF virtual device to update its bridge MAC address as soon as the master switch leaves, so ARP MAD can promptly detect IRF partition events.

Table 13-4 compares the three implementations of MAD.

Table 13-4. MAD implementations

MAD Implementation	Advantages	Disadvantages
LACP MAD	• Very fast detection speed • Suitable for link aggregation scenarios • Requires no dedicated physical ports	• Requires an intermediate switch which must support the Comware extended LACPDUs
BFD MAP	• Fast detection speed • Suitable for various network scenarios • No special requirements for intermediate devices	• Requires dedicated physical ports and Layer 3 interfaces, which cannot be used to transmit user traffic
ARP MAD	• No special requirements for intermediate devices • Requires no dedicated physical ports if the detection is through an intermediate switch	• Slower detection speed than the other two implementations • Requires dedicated Layer 3 interfaces on the switches for IP addressing (separate VLAN interface)

Preventing Addressing Conflicts and Stack Recovery

When MAD detects the split stack, it initiates an election between the two IRF systems. Specifically, MAD determines which of the two IRF systems has the master with the smaller member ID. For example, suppose one IRF system has a master with a member ID of 1, and the other system has a master with a member ID of 4. In this example, the system that has a master with the member ID of 1 wins the election. MAD allows this system to operate normally, using the IP addresses and the other configuration settings assigned to the original IRF system.

MAD then places the other IRF system into a recovery state, which shuts down all of its ports except the IRF ones. This action prevents the second IRF system from using the IP addresses configured for the original IRF system, thereby eliminating address conflicts on the network.

Note

You can manually exclude a port from MAD. You might do this when the connecting device uses the port for a purpose such as a management connection.

You most clearly see the benefits of MAD (and IRF) when you design the topology properly. Whenever possible, devices have multiple link-aggregated connections to different chassis within the IRF system. Therefore, when one IRF member is shut down by MAD, the connecting devices seamlessly fail over to the other links in their link aggregation group—just as they fail over seamlessly if one of the IRF members fails.

After placing one device in recovery mode, MAD tries to automatically repair the failed IRF links. If the repair operation fails, however, you need to manually repair the failed links. When the link is recovered, the IRF system that is in recovery state automatically reboots and then the IRF virtual devices, both in active state and in recovery state, automatically merge into one—just as they were before the IRF split stack occurred.

Typically, recovery occurs automatically in this way. You would only need to implement recovery manually with the MAD `restore` command in the rare event that MAD places one IRF device in recovery mode and the active device then fails. In that case, executing MAD `restore` activates the IRF device shut down by MAD recovery.

In summary, MAD prevents addressing conflicts by:

- Initiating an election between the two IRF systems.
- Placing the IRF system that loses the election in recovery mode.
- Trying to repair the link.

After the link is repaired, the IRF system in recovery mode reboots. The reconnected members then re-establish the IRF system.

Note

HP networking recommends that you use both LACP *and* BFD for MAD. Remember that, with LACP, you must be connecting the IRF members to a Comware switch. If you are not connecting the IRF system to another Comware switch, you must use either MAD BFD or MAD ARP. MAD works best when the IRF system has been properly designed—that is, whenever possible, devices have multiple link-aggregated connections to a different chassis within the IRF system. Therefore, when one IRF member is shut down by MAD, the connecting devices fail over to the other links in their link aggregation group.

Basic IRF Configuration

This section introduces a basic approach to configuring an IRF topology. The ASE-level networking courses go into a more detailed approach, with a few solutions you can use to approach the IRF implementation. Also, the configuration of MAD is beyond the scope of this book but is covered in the ASE-level networking courses.

Assigning a Domain ID

To differentiate IRF virtual devices, each IRF virtual device (topology) is assigned a domain ID. If there is a MAD detection link between two IRF virtual devices, the devices send MAD detection packets to each other through the detection link. In this case, the system statuses and operations of both IRF virtual devices are affected. To solve this problem, specify different domain IDs for the two IRF virtual devices.

After assigning a domain ID to an IRF virtual device, the extended LACPDUs sent by the member switches carry the IRF domain information to distinguish the LACP detection packets from different IRF virtual devices. If LACP MAD detection is applied for multiple IRF virtual devices and LACP MAD detection links exist among the IRF virtual devices, assign different domain IDs for the IRF virtual devices. If there is no LACP MAD detection link among IRF virtual devices, or if BFD MAD detection is applied, you do not need to assign domain IDs to them.

To assign a domain name, use the following command:

```
[Comware] irf domain <domain-id>
```

By default, the domain ID of an IRF virtual device is 0.

Assigning a Member ID

An IRF virtual device uses member IDs to uniquely identify its physical switch members. A lot of information and configurations relate to member IDs, such as port (physical or logical) numbers, configurations on ports, and member priorities.

After you change the member ID of a switch:

- If you do not reboot the switch, the original member ID still takes effect, and all physical resources are identified by the original member ID. In the configuration file, only the IRF port numbers, configurations on IRF ports, and priority of the device change with the member ID; other configurations do not change.
- If you save the current configuration and reboot the switch, the new member ID takes effect and all physical resources are identified by the new member ID. In the configuration file, only the IRF port numbers, configurations on IRF ports, and priority of the device still take effect.

For a switch that is already in an IRF virtual device, you can use configuration discussed in this section to modify the member ID of the switch and this modification is effective after the switch reboot.

Note

The IRF master commonly has a member ID of 1 (common practice in implementing IRF), and the master typically has a configured priority higher than the other switches in the topology.

IRF Initial Configuration Process

For a switch that is not in an IRF virtual device, set its member ID by following the steps in the following sections to enable IRF in a new topology:

Step 1: Convert to IRF mode for only chassis-based switches.

Plan the member IDs in advance. You can view the member IDs of an IRF and find an unused ID for the new switch.

```
[Comware] chassis convert mode irf
```

Note

In newer versions of code, the `chassis convert` command must be executed after renumbering the member ID. Also, this command is not necessary on the 10500s.

Step 2: Configure the domain ID (optional).

Log in to the switch to be added into the IRF virtual device, and change its domain ID to match that of the other Comware switches in the same IRF topology.

```
[Comware] irf domain <domain-id>
```

Step 3: Configure the member ID.

Configure the member ID on each switch in the topology, making sure that the member IDs are unique throughout the domain.

```
[Comware] irf member <current-member-id> renumber <new-member-id>
```

Each device in the IRF needs a different member ID. Member IDs are numbers from 1 to 10. Use number 1 for the master, and then use consecutive numbers for the other switches (slaves). After assigning a member ID to each of the switches, reboot them. (This is necessary every time you change a switch's member ID.)

Warning

Member ID change takes effect at the reboot of the switch. Member IDs are used to identify members of an IRF virtual device. Therefore, modifying a member ID may cause device configuration change or even loss. Please modify member IDs with caution. For example, suppose three members (of the same switch model) with the member IDs of 1, 2, and 3 are connected to an IRF, and suppose that each member has several ports. Change the member ID of switch 2 to 3, change that of switch 3 to 2, reboot both switches, and add them into the IRF virtual device again. Then, switch 2 will use the original port configurations of switch 3, and switch 3 will use those of switch 2.

Step 4: Configure the priority (optional).

The IRF priority is a value used, when two IRF stacks merge, to decide which active master remains the master and which one becomes a slave. IRF priority values range from 1 to 32, with 1 being the default and 32 the maximum priority. The greater the priority value, the higher the priority. A member with a higher priority is more likely to be a master. For example, assign the designated master a priority of 32.

To assign an IRF priority to your switch, use the following command:

```
[Comware] irf member <member-id> priority {1-32}
```

Note

The priority setting takes effect immediately after configuration. No switch reboot is required.

Configuring the IRF Ports

IRF ports are logical. IRF can be enabled on a switch only after the IRF ports are configured. (In other words, the IRF ports are bound to physical IRF ports.) After connecting the cables and binding physical IRF ports to an IRF port with the `DIS` (disabled) or `DOWN` (link failure) link state, which you display with the `display irf topology` command (discussed in the "IRF Verification and Troubleshooting" section), you need to activate configurations on all IRF ports on the switches to establish the IRF virtual device. After the activation, the states of all IRF ports transit to `UP`, and the master election is held among IRF members. The switches which do not win the election automatically reboot and then join the IRF virtual device as slaves.

The configuration of the IRF ports involves multiple steps, detailed in the following sections:

Step 5a: Disable the physical IRF interface(s).

Your first step is to enter the physical interface or interfaces to be used as the logical IRF link and to disable these interfaces:

```
[Comware] interface <physical-interface-id>
[Comware-<interface-id>] shutdown
[Comware-<interface-id>] quit
```

Remember that 10 Gigabit Ethernet (or faster) interfaces are required in your IRF link.

Note

Before binding a physical IRF port to an IRF port or canceling one of these bindings, you must manually disable the physical IRF port (that is, execute the shutdown command on the port), as described in the previous section.

Step 5b: Create the logical IRF interface.

Next, you need to create the logical IRF port (interface), which is accomplished with the following configuration:

```
[Comware] irf-port <member-id/1-or-2>
[Comware-irf-port<port-id>] port group interface <interface-id>
[Comware-irf-port<port-id>] quit
```

The `<member-id/1-or-2>` parameter specifies the IRF port number, where member-id represents the ID of the IRF member switch (from the `irf member <current-member-id> renumber <new-member-id>` command) and the port number argument specifies the port number. The value can be 1 or 2. The port number is important in that port 1 on one physical switch must connect to port 2 on the next physical switch. (Refer to Figure 13-10.) In both the daisy chain and ring topologies, notice that the IRF port numbers are not the same between two switches. For example, in the daisy chain figure, the master is using IRF-port 1, where its connected slave is using IRF-port 2.

By default, an IRF port is not bound to any physical IRF port. To realize IRF link redundancy and load-sharing and to increase the bandwidth and reliability of IRF links, bind one IRF port to multiple physical IRF ports by repeatedly executing the `port group interface` command. The number you specify depends on the Comware switch model. When the upper limit is reached, the execution of this command fails.

Note

You can bind from 1 to 12 physical ports to an IRF port, depending on the switch model (see Table 13-3). They must be located on the *same* expansion interface module (line card). Please note that the logical IRF port is for IRF management communications between the switches, not for data communications.

Step 5c: Re-enable the physical IRF interface(s).

After you have finished assigning the physical interfaces to the logical IRF port, you manually bring up the physical interfaces with the `undo shutdown` command:

```
[Comware] interface <physical-interface-id>
[Comware-<interface-id>] undo shutdown
[Comware-<interface-id>] quit
```

After you have re-enabled the physical interfaces that are part of the logical IRF interface, save your configuration with the `save` command.

Step 5d: Activate the IRF port configuration.

The last step required on non-chassis (box-type) switches is to save your configuration and then activate the IRF port configuration.

```
[Comware] save
[Comware] irf-port-configuration active
```

For chassis-based switches, like the 7500s and higher, this configuration is not necessary. Optionally, you could just reboot the switch.

Completing the IRF Configuration Process

After you have performed the previous configuration steps, complete the IRF setup by performing the steps in the following sections.

Step 6: Save configuration of all devices, and turn them off.

Non-chassis devices automatically reboot; however chassis devices request a reboot.

Step 7: Connect the IRF links to build the IRF fabric.

Remember that IRF-port 1 of one device must be connected to IRF-port 2 of the next device.

Step 8: Turn on the unit configured to be master.

Wait until the boot process is complete before turning on the next device, to guarantee that this unit becomes the master.

Step 9: Repeat the process for each of the other members/slaves (turn on and wait).

The process of turning on a device connected through IRF ports to a running IRF is called *device insertion*. During the boot process, the device is neither a master nor a slave, and the last step of the process is to look (sending IRF hello packets) for a running IRF master by sending messages through its IRF ports. If an IRF master device is found, the inserted device becomes a slave. This is why a device needs its IRF ports bound to physical ports and those ports properly connected before being ready for insertion.

In some product families, like the 5800 and 5820 models, when a device is inserted in the IRF, the master verifies that the inserted device has the same software version, and, if not, it downloads its own application file onto it. This happens even if the new device's software is newer than the master's. Likewise, the configuration files are compared and, if the slave's differs from the master's, the master downloads its own configuration file onto the slave. And finally, if a slave has updated either the application or the configuration file, it reboots the new member.

IRF Configuration Example

Here is a simple example of setting up IRF on a slave member, where its member ID is 3:

```
[Comware] irf member 1 renumber 3
[Comware] interface ten-gigabitethernet 3/0/1
[Comware-Ten-GigabitEthernet1/0/1] shutdown
[Comware-Ten-GigabitEthernet1/0/1] quit
[Comware] irf-port 3/1
[Comware-irf-port3/1] port group interface ten-gigabitethernet 3/0/1
[Comware-irf-port3/1] quit
[Comware] interface ten-gigabitethernet 3/0/1
[Comware-Ten-GigabitEthernet1/0/1] undo shutdown
[Comware-Ten-GigabitEthernet1/0/1] quit
```

Notice that the IRF port ID is 3/1, where 3 is the member ID of the switch.

Note

It is always recommended that you save your configuration and reboot before adding a slave to an existing topology. In other words, you typically should not use the `irf-port-configuration active` command to add a new member to an IRF topology.

IRF Verification and Troubleshooting

Now that you have configured IRF, there are various `display` commands you can use to verify the configuration and operation of IRF on your switch and newly formed stack. The following sections cover the `display` commands used to verify and troubleshoot your IRF configuration.

Viewing the IRF Members

Use the `display irf` command to display information about the IRF virtual device and the entire virtual stack:

```
<Comware> display irf
Switch  Role    Priority  CPU-Mac         Description
  *+1   Master    2       0023-8929-4f83    -----
    2   Slave     1       0023-8980-54ad    -----
--------------------------------------------------
* indicates the device is the master.
+ indicates the device through which the user logs in.
The Bridge MAC of the IRF is: 0023-8929-4f70
Auto upgrade    :     no
Mac persistent :     6 min
Domain ID:      0
```

The above command displays information about all switches that have joined or are joining this IRF virtual device.

Note

Even though all the switches have different local MAC addresses, there is one MAC address used to represent the IRF topology (stack). If the current master fails, the newly elected master processes control and management plane traffic involving this MAC address, making it transparent that a failure even occurred to the devices connected to the IRF topology.

Viewing the IRF Port Connections

Use the `display irf configuration` command to display the member IDs and port connections of all IRF member switches:

```
<Comware> display irf configuration
MemberID NewID IRF-Port1                IRF-Port2
   1       1    disable                  Ten-GigabitEthernet1/1/2
   2       2    Ten-GigabitEthernet2/2/1 disable
```

The above command displays the member ID, priority, IRF port state, and port information.

Viewing the IRF Topology Status

Use the `display irf topology` command to display topology management information for the IRF virtual device. Here is an example:

```
<Comware> display irf topology
   Topology Info
-------------------------------------------------------------------
   IRF-Port1    IRF-Port2
Switch    Link  neighbor    Link  neighbor    Belong To
1  DIS    --    UP    2     0023-8929-4f83
2  UP     1     DIS   --    0023-8929-4f83
```

Notice that the display is broken into two columns, one for each IRF port on the switch (if there is more than one). If you see `DOWN` as a state, there is problem with the activated IRF port. The above is an example of a daisy chain topology. `DIS` indicates that the associated logical IRF port is not used (or configured) on the switch.

Learning Check

The following questions help you measure your understanding of the material presented in this chapter. Read all of the choices carefully, since there may be more than one correct answer. Choose all correct answers for each question.

Questions

1. Minimally, which speed interface is needed to form an IRF link to a connected switch?
   a. 10 Mbps
   b. 100 Mbps
   c. 1 Gbps
   d. 10 Gbps

2. Choose only the applicable options from the following list, and then name the order in which the master is elected in an IRF topology.
   a. The member with the highest priority
   b. The member with the lowest priority
   c. The member with the longest system uptime
   d. The member with the highest MAC address
   e. The member with the lowest MAC address

3. Which mechanism detects the presence of multiple identical IRFs split from an IRF system and handles the problem to make the network operate normally?
   a. LACP
   b. MAD
   c. MSTP
   d. VRRP

4. Before you can create the logical IRF interface, which task must you perform first?
   a. Shut down the physical interfaces that will be used for the logical IRF interface.
   b. Reboot the switch.
   c. Disconnect all cables from the switches.
   d. Assign a member ID to the switch.

5. Which of the following commands creates a logical IRF interface?

   a.
   ```
   irf-port <member-id/port-number>
         port group interface <interface-id>
   ```

   b.
   ```
   interface irf-port <member-id/port-number>
         port group interface <interface-id>
   ```

   c.
   ```
   interface bridge <member-id/port-number>
         port group interface <interface-id>
   ```

   d.
   ```
   interface irf-port <member-id/port-number>
         member-interface <interface-id>
   ```

6. What is the 5800 series command used to activate the IRF port configuration (without having to reboot the switch)?

Answers

1. ☑ **D** is correct. With very few exceptions, you need to use 10 Gbps or faster links for the physical interfaces comprising an IRF port.

   ☒ **A** and **B** are not supported by IRF. **C** is supported by IRF but only on low-end switches.

2. ☑ Use **A** (the member with the highest priority), **C** (the member with the longest system uptime), and **E** (the member with the lowest MAC address), in that order, for the election process.

   ☒ **B** and **D** are incorrect because they are not used for the election process.

3. ☑ **B** is correct. MAD is used to detect a split stack.

   ☒ **A** is incorrect because Comware extended LACPDUs are used—not the open standard LACP data units. **C** and **D** are not supported by MAD.

4. ☑ **A** is correct. You must shut down the physical interfaces before including them in the logical IRF port.

   ☒ **B**, **C**, and **D** are incorrect because they are not necessary when setting up the IRF port.

5. ☑ **A** is correct. The `irf-port` and `port group interface` commands are used to create a logical IRF interface.

   ☒ **B** is incorrect because you do not create a logical interface with the `interface` command. **C** is incorrect because the IRF port is not a bridge aggregation group. **D** is incorrect because the `member-interface` command is nonexistent.

6. ☑ `irf-port-configuration active` is the 5800 series command used to activate the IRF port configuration (without having to reboot the switch).

14 Mobility and Wireless

EXAM OBJECTIVES

In this chapter, you learn to:

- ✓ Describe and apply the most common data link (Layer 2) protocols.
- ✓ Describe, identify, and explain wireless technologies.
- ✓ Identify and explain products and features in the HP Networking product line.
- ✓ Compare and contrast HP Networking solutions and features.
- ✓ Identify which HP Networking products should be positioned, given various customer environments and infrastructure needs.
- ✓ Perform installation and configuration of devices.

ASSUMED KNOWLEDGE

This chapter assumes that you have some basic knowledge of wireless networking technologies. You should be familiar with following concepts before proceeding with this chapter:

- VLANs (See "Chapter 6: VLANs.")
- Dynamic Host Configuration Protocol (DHCP) (See "Chapter 7: IP Services.")

INTRODUCTION

This chapter introduces you to wireless networks, focusing on those used in LANs for small-office environments. The first half of the chapter introduces you to the technologies used in wireless, and the latter part introduces basic configuration tasks on an HP wireless Multi-Service Mobility (MSM) access point (AP).

This chapter focuses on the following topics:

- Understanding the IEEE 802.11 standards
- Comparing the wireless network types
- Differentiating between the different wireless security solutions
- Understanding how Power over Ethernet (PoE) works and configuring it on HP ProVision and HP Comware switches
- Accessing and configuring HP's MSM APs

802.11 Standards

This section provides a brief introduction to some of the terms used in wireless and the 802.11 wireless standards, the technology used, and the standards themselves.

Wireless Terms

Wireless networks are based on a set of standards developed by the IEEE. Together, these standards are collectively called the *802.11 standard*, or simply 802.11. Specific subsets within that standard are indicated by lowercase letters—such as a, b, g, and n—after the 11. This chapter focuses on the subsets listed here: 802.11a, 802.11b, 802.11g, and 802.11n.

Note

IEEE 802.11ac is not discussed in this book: at the time of this book's development, the standard was still in the draft state and HP did not have any products available that implemented it.

The IEEE published the original 802.11 standard in 1997. An addition to the 802.3 family of standards which define the functions of wired LANs, 802.11 defined the physical and data link layers of wireless networks. In other words, the original 802.11 standard adapted the well-understood LAN standard for a network that uses radio waves as its physical medium.

- The physical layer controls the physical medium, defining the electrical and mechanical specifications for the network connections. For a wireless network, the physical medium consists of the radio waves.
- The data link layer describes the procedures (called *protocols*) that control data transfer across the physical infrastructure at Layer 1.

The 802.11 standard defines the behavior of devices, such as APs and wireless stations, on a wireless network. For example, it defines the physical properties, like modulation schemes, radio frequency bands, channels, and transmission speeds, which the APs and wireless stations use to establish the wireless network and to transmit data.

Physical Wireless Properties

To fully understand the 802.11 standards, you should understand the basic physical properties they define:

- A *modulation scheme* is used to encode data onto a radio wave.
- A *radio frequency band* is a range of frequencies in the spectrum of electromagnetic waves (see Figure 14-1).
- *Transmission speeds* are the rates at which data can be sent over the radio medium.
- A *channel* is a narrow band of contiguous wireless frequencies that has been assigned a number.

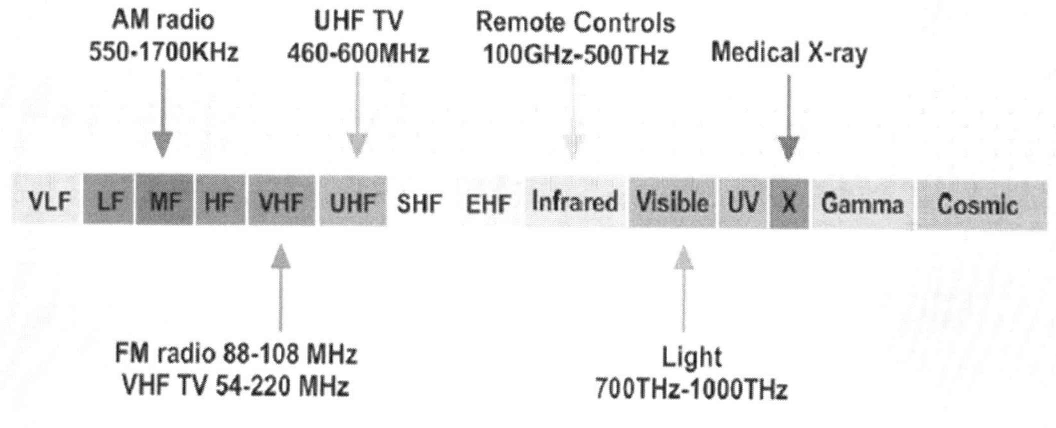

Figure 14-1. Frequency bands

RF Bands and Channels

Typically, a *radio frequency* (RF) band is a range of frequencies that is defined or reserved for a particular use (see Figure 14-2). For wireless networking devices, the 802.11 standard defines two frequency bands—2.4 GHz and 5 GHz—which are in the super high frequency (SHF) band. Other devices, such as cordless phones, can also operate in the SHF band. Such devices can cause interference for wireless networking devices operating in the same vicinity.

Within the 2.4 GHz and 5 GHz frequency bands, the 802.11 standard defines channels. As mentioned, each channel is a band of contiguous frequencies that is designated as a single unit for transmission and assigned a number. (You learn more about channels later in this chapter.)

Modulation Schemes

In addition to defining frequency bands and channels, the 802.11 standard defines several modulation schemes. For the purposes of this book, it is not necessary to know the exact details of each modulation scheme, but you should know that wireless networking devices use these modulation schemes to encode data so that they can be physically transmitted over radio waves. Over time, the IEEE has developed modulation schemes that can encode more data in the same radio wave, thereby increasing possible transmission speeds.

Note
Wireless modulation schemes should not be confused with encryption methods. Without additional security measures, data transmitted over radio waves is not encrypted. Such data is accessible to anyone with compatible equipment.

802.11 Standards

This section introduces you to the IEEE 802.11 wireless standards. These currently include:

- 802.11b
- 802.11a
- 802.11g
- 802.11n
- 802.11ac (currently in a draft state)

Note
Even though 802.11ac is in a draft state, devices are shipping from manufacturers with a pre-standard implementation of 802.11ac.

802.11b

Now that you understand the types of physical properties that are defined in the 802.11 standard, let us take a look at specific subsets within that standard, starting with 802.11b, the first widely adopted wireless standard.

Adopted in 1999 by the IEEE, 802.11b operates in the 2.4 GHz range. Within its RF band, the 802.11b standard defined 14 channels. Many vendors offered 802.11b APs and wireless network interface cards (NICs), and the products were inexpensive. However, network interference from devices, such as microwave ovens and some cordless and wireless phones, left users wanting better performance from their wireless networks.

802.11a

Although, as the name implies, work began on 802.11a first, it took longer to complete and was adopted after 802.11b. 802.11a not only increased transmission speeds substantially but also provided support for more channels. However, the higher speeds came at the cost of range: to achieve the highest transmission speeds, 802.11a devices must be 25 to 50 percent closer together than 802.11b devices.

Also, 802.11a uses a different RF band (5 GHz) than 802.11b uses. As a result, 802.11a is not backward compatible with 802.11b. The 5 GHz band is tightly regulated, so vendors must ensure that their devices comply with these regulations. The tighter regulations mean that this RF band is less crowded than the 2.4 GHz band used by 802.11b and, therefore, less prone to interference.

802.11g

802.11g was the next revision adopted. This standard matches the speed of 802.11a but is compatible with 802.11b. That is, you can configure APs operating at 802.11g speeds to also provide access for 802.11b devices. As you would expect, 802.11g supports the same channels as 802.11b.

When an AP supports both 802.11g and 802.11b stations, it makes some adjustments that reduce the throughput for 802.11g stations. Throughput should not be confused with transmission speed. *Transmission speed* is the AP's actual signaling rate as it transmits data. *Throughput*, on the other hand, measures what devices actually receive. Many factors affect throughput on wireless networks. For example, all stations must share the radio and take turns transmitting data, and the AP must send broadcast and management frames at the speed that all stations in the wireless cell support.

Note

To guarantee higher throughput for 802.11g stations, you can configure 802.11g devices to ignore 802.11b equipment in the vicinity.

802.11n

Users are demanding more from their wireless networks, especially higher speeds to support applications such as videoconferencing. In fact, many users would like the more convenient wireless access to replace their wired connection altogether.

Adopted in 2009, 802.11n meets these demands. It increases transmission speeds, improves reliability, and extends the operating distance of wireless networks. Operating in both the 2.4 GHz and 5 GHz bands, 802.11n is backward compatible with 802.11a/b/g.

One reason 802.11n can achieve such high throughput is its multiple input multiple output (MIMO) design. Devices that support MIMO use multiple transceivers, each of which sends part of the data stream. Each transmission can take a different path to the receiver. Devices that receive the data stream also have multiple transceivers, which combine the multiple transmissions into a single data stream. Multiple data streams transmitted simultaneously effectively multiply the bandwidth.

Wireless Channels

802.11 divides each of the bands into channels. This division is similar to how radio and TV broadcast bands are subdivided but with greater channel width and overlap in wireless networking. For example, the 2.4000–2.4835 GHz band is divided into 13 channels, each with a 22 MHz width but spaced only five MHz apart, with channel 1 centered on 2.412 GHz and channel 13 on 2.472 GHz—to which Japan adds a fourteenth channel (12 MHz above channel 13). This section introduces how channels are used in the IEEE 802.11 standards.

802.11b/g Channels

802.11b and 802.11g standards identify 83.5 MHz of bandwidth in the 2.4 GHz spectrum for use with wireless protocols. This bandwidth is divided into 14 channels, beginning at 2.412 GHz. Thirteen of the 14 channels are spaced five MHz apart (see Figure 14-2). That is, the center frequency of channel 1 is 2.412 GHz, the center frequency of channel 2 is 2.417 GHz, and so forth. Channel 14, designed specifically for Japan, has its center frequency at 2.484 GHz. Of the 14 channels, Europe, Latin America, and Asia Pacific support 1 through 13; North America only allows channels up to 11; and Japan supports all 14.

It is important that you understand the spectral placement of 802.11b/g channels because signals spread up to 22 MHz from the center frequency. Because channels are spaced only five MHz apart, they overlap up to five channels on each side. For example, if you look at channel 4 in Figure 14-2, you can see it overlaps with channels 1, 2, 3, 5, and 6.

Dividing the spectrum into channels allows wireless APs in the same area to operate without interfering with each other: radios are simply tuned to transmit on frequencies that do not overlap one another at the boundaries. Because different regulatory agencies permit different channels, the non-overlapping channels you can use varies based on your country. Wireless designers in North America typically work with channels 1, 6, and 11 to avoid interference from overlapping channels. Designers in other regions can also use those three channels or channels 1, 7, and 13.

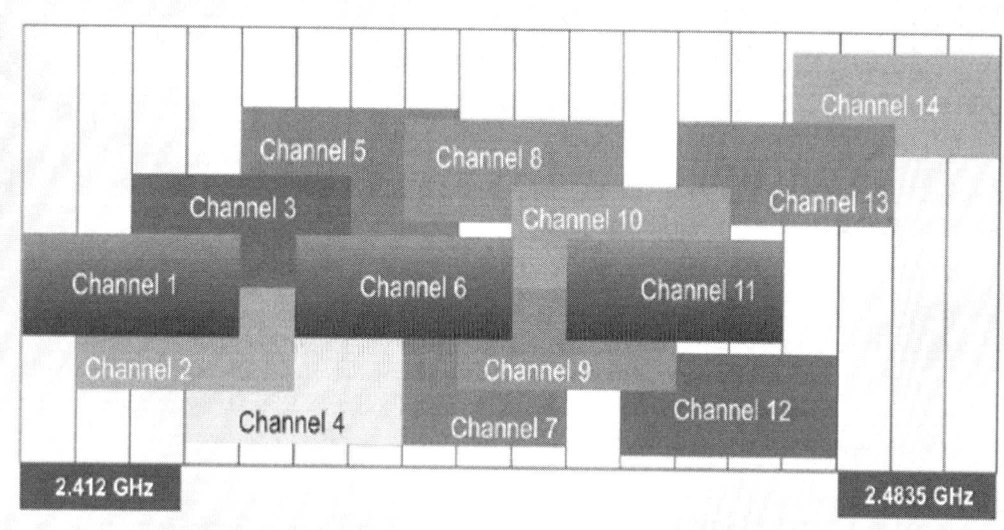

Figure 14-2 802.11b/g channels

Note

As long as you use non-overlapping channels, you can place your APs in close proximity to each other without worrying about interference.

802.11a Channels

The 802.11a standard provides more non-overlapping channels and more channels overall than 802.11b/g. 802.11a channels are spaced every 20 MHz because a single 802.11a standard encompasses four channel numbers. For example, the center frequency of channel 36 is 20 MHz below the center frequency of channel 40 (5.20 GHz). The 5 GHz frequency band is more tightly regulated than the 2.4 GHz band. The allowed channels vary, depending on the country where you are implementing the wireless network.

Channel Boundaries

The 802.11b and 802.11g standards dictate that, at 11 MHz above and below any one of the center frequencies in the 2.4 GHz band, the signal should be one one-thousandth the strength (30 dB lower) of the signal at the center frequency. Similarly, although the 802.11a channel boundaries lie 20 MHz above and below the center frequency, the signal is significant only over a 20 MHz range around the center frequency.

Like with the 802.11b and 802.11g standards, the 802.11a allowed channels vary depending on regulatory domain. For the 802.11a, b, and g standards, the Federal Communications Commission (FCC) regulates wireless networks in the United States, and, in Europe, the European Telecommunications Standards Institute (ETSI) defines allowed sets of channels. Local regulatory bodies adopt one of these sets and may add some local exceptions or restrictions.

802.11n Channel Bonding

When operating in the 2.4 GHz band, 802.11n supports the same channels as 802.11b/g. Likewise, when operating in the 5 GHz band, 802.11n supports the same channels as 802.11a. However, 802.11n provides an important enhancement: using channel bonding, 802.11n can combine two adjacent 20 MHz channels into a single 40 MHz channel. Bandwidth is more than doubled because the guard band between the two 20 MHz channels can be removed when they are bonded. (The guard band is used to prevent interference between channels.)

Channel bonding is typically used in the 5 GHz frequency band because it has more non-overlapping channels. Because the 2.4 GHz frequency band has only three non-overlapping 20 MHz channels, bonding two 20 MHz channels leaves only one non-overlapping channel.

Comparison of the Wireless Standards

Table 14-1 provides a quick comparison of the 802.11a/b/g/n standards, including transmission rates, RF band, year ratified, and some of the main advantages and disadvantages of each.

Table 14-1. 802.11 wireless comparison

Standard	Transmission speed	RF band	Advantages	Disadvantages
802.11a	6–54 Mbps	5 GHz	Less crowded RF band; more non-overlapping channels	More regulated; not backward compatible with 802.11b; shorter range to attain maximum data speeds
802.11b	1–11 Mbps	2.4 GHz	Inexpensive equipment	Slow transmission speeds; more crowded RF band; fewer non-overlapping channels
802.11g	6–54 Mbps	2.4 GHz	Inexpensive equipment; backward compatible with 802.11b	More crowded RF band; fewer non-overlapping channels
802.11n	Up to 600 Mbps	2.4 and 5 GHz	Highest transmission speeds; supports both RF bands; increased range	More expensive equipment

Note

HP MSM products, when properly configured for 802.11n, support up to 900 Mbps using MIMO.

Wireless Concerns and Data Rates

When you design a wireless network solution, one of the first decisions you must make is to determine which 802.11 standard or standards the network will support. To make this decision, you must consider the following:

- **Usage**—As you have learned, different standards provide different amounts of bandwidth per AP radio. Therefore, you must consider how many users will typically access each radio and the types of applications which these users will run. For example, if users are accessing video applications or using Voice over IP (VoIP), they need a lot of bandwidth.
- **Equipment**—The wireless stations, in addition to the wireless AP, must support the standard that you select. In some environments, you can choose the equipment; in others you must work with the equipment that users bring (most stations now support at least 802.11a/b/g/n).
- **Frequency band**—Sometimes the 5 GHz frequency band used by 802.11a and 802.11n exhibits less interference than the 2.4 GHz band used by 802.11b/g and 802.11n. However, the 5 GHz band is also more highly regulated by governments. A site survey can help you select the best frequency for your environment.

The next two sections focus on data rate and signal strength and data rate versus actual throughput. In other words, there are many items that affect the actual throughput of your data, so becoming familiar with these issues can help you best maximize your throughput.

Data Rate and Signal Strength

To design a wireless network, you must understand data rates and signal strength. Each AP advertises two types of data rates:

- **Basic rates**—Used to transmit 802.11 management frames, multicast frames, and broadcast frames
- **Supported rates**—Used for a station's unicast traffic

Although the station must support the AP's basic rates, during the association process, the station and the AP will select a data rate for their transmissions. Because this data rate is based on the Received Signal Strength (RSS) (the strength of the signal over the background noise when the signal reaches the receiver) of their transmissions, the selected data rate depends on factors that affect the RSS. These factors include:

- **Attenuation** (due to the distance between the station and the AP)—As a radio wave is propagated through space, the strength of the signal fades. Therefore, even though the AP uses a constant transmit power, the farther the station is from the , the more the RSS at the station decreases.
- **Obstacles**—Obstacles, such as shelves and walls (particularly metal, concrete, and brick walls), can weaken the signal significantly. Obstacles can either absorb (attenuate) or reflect the signal. Reflections can act as noise, causing a signal to interfere with itself. When obstacles intervene between a station and its AP, the data rate can be low even when the station is relatively close to the AP.
- **Interference**—Other devices operating on the same channel as (or a channel close to) your devices cause interference or background noise. Because RSS is the signal strength over background noise, high interference decreases the RSS and data rate. In effect, the AP's range is decreased.

Data Rate Versus Actual Throughput

Although a station's selected data rate determines the speed at which it sends and receives data, the station's actual throughput is considerably less for several reasons.

- **Shared medium**—A single AP radio might support many stations. However, only one device can transmit at a time. Therefore, the total bandwidth is effectively divided between the stations. In addition, collisions and methods for avoiding collisions cut into the time available for actual data transmission.
- **Overhead**—All devices connected to an AP radio must be able to receive certain transmissions, including management frames, control frames, broadcast frames, and multicast frames. Therefore, these frames are always transmitted at a lower data rate, called the *basic rate*, which all stations are required to support to connect to the AP.
- **Management frames**—These are dictated by the 802.11 standard that helps stations and APs establish and maintain connections (for example, authentication, association, and disassociation frames).
- **Control frames**—This type of frame is dictated by the 802.11 standard that help stations and APs avoid collisions (for example, Request to Send [RTS] and Clear to Send [CTS] frames).
- **Broadcast frames**—Broadcast frames are sent to every device connected to the AP.
- **Multicast frames**—These are sent to devices that have joined a particular multicast group.

Wireless Network Types

Wireless networks are implemented using one of three network types:

- Ad hoc mode
- In-cell relay mode
- Infrastructure mode

The following sections discuss the three wireless modes.

Ad Hoc Mode

An ad hoc network includes two or more stations (devices) that communicate directly with each other using wireless transmissions. Each station in an ad hoc network receives every 802.11 frame transmitted. To avoid collisions and to prevent the loss of data, stations use Carrier Sense Multiple Access with Collision Avoidance (CSMA/CA).

CSMA/CA reduces collisions because stations "listen" for other transmissions before they attempt to start transmitting data. If another station is sending data, the listening station waits. If there are no transmissions, the listening station starts to send its own data.

Ad hoc networks are sometimes referred to as *Independent Basic Service Sets* (IBSSs) because they do not require a connection to a wired network or an AP. Inexpensive and easy to establish, such networks are used most often for exchanging files in small meeting areas when access to the wired network is not necessary or possible.

In-Cell Relay Mode

In-cell relay mode is used to connect two or more network segments over a wireless connection. The segments can be different segments of a LAN or unconnected wireless networks. For example, if a company's IT department wants to connect the LANs in two buildings, they could use two APs, operating in in-cell relay mode, rather than trying to run cable for a wired connection between the buildings. This mode is also called *wireless bridging*, *Wireless Distribution System* (WDS), or *local mesh*.

Infrastructure Mode

The most common implementation for wireless networks is the infrastructure mode. In this mode, an AP establishes the wireless network and handles all communications from wireless stations that associate with it. The AP also controls the data rates for the network and, depending on the wireless LAN (WLAN) architecture used, enforces security settings and other settings, such as quality of service (QoS). WLAN architectures determine which type of wireless devices establish and manage the wireless network and where wireless data is bridged onto the wired network.

In addition to connecting wireless stations to each other, the AP is connected to a wired network. As the interface between the wired and the wireless networks, the AP receives wireless traffic from stations and forwards it on to the wired network. Likewise, the AP receives and forwards traffic that is being sent from the wired network to the wireless stations.

Infrastructure Mode: BSS

This and the next section focus on guidelines for the infrastructure mode because it is the mode that you will encounter most often. In this mode, an AP and the station or stations connected to it compose a Basic Service Set (BSS), shown in Figure 14-3. Each BSS has a unique, 48-bit identifier, called the BSSID, which is usually the media access control (MAC) address of the AP's radios. Every frame transmitted to and from the stations in a BSS contains the BSSID in the frame header, identifying the frame as belonging to a particular AP's coverage area. Thus, the BSSID distinguishes one BSS from others and increases efficiency by allowing the access AP and stations to ignore frames not belonging to their BSS. When a new station joins the BSS, it appends the AP's BSSID to all frames as the receiver address in the 802.11 header.

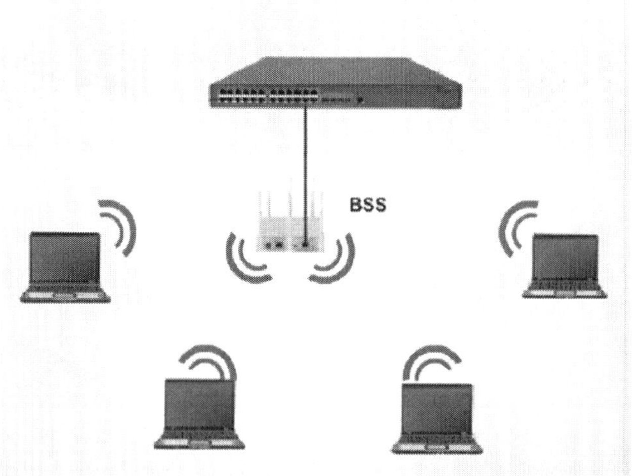

Figure 14-3. BSS infrastructure mode

Infrastructure Mode: ESS

Two or more BSSs compose an Extended Service Set (ESS), as shown in Figure 14-4. Like the BSS, each ESS has a unique 48-bit identifier. The Extended Service Set Identifier (ESSID) is commonly called the SSID, or network name. To access a wireless network, users select this SSID in their wireless client utility. The SSID is included in the 802.11 header of every frame transmitted on a wireless network. Note that, in Figure 14-10, the BSSs are visually separated, but, typically, the BSSs overlap to allow users to roam without losing their wireless connection.

An ESS can also be called a WLAN. A WLAN defines a broadcast domain. That is, everyone who accesses the WLAN receives all of the broadcast frames. The WLAN also defines various settings for the ESS, such as the SSID and security options.

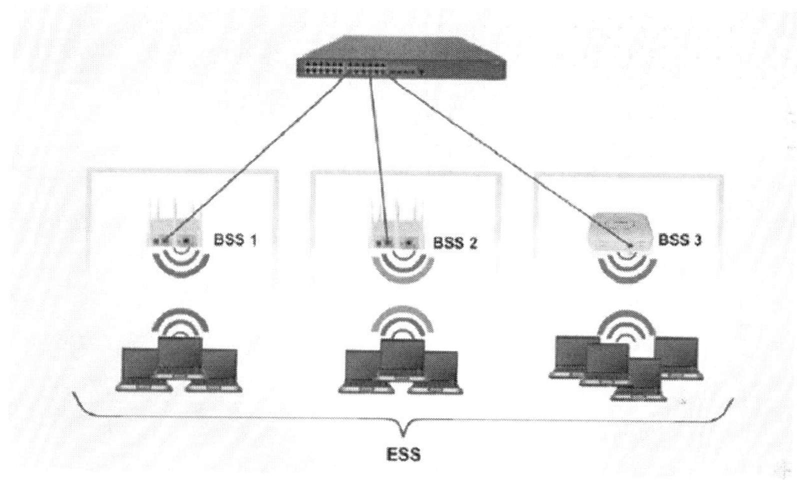

Figure 14-4. ESS infrastructure mode

WLANs on wireless networks can be compared to VLANs on Ethernet networks: they divide users into different groups, steering each user toward the appropriate resources and access levels. Just as VLANs on a switch effectively transform the switch into several virtual switches, WLANs on an AP effectively divide the AP into several virtual APs, each providing a separate network connection to a group of mobile users. IT managers can exercise a great deal of control over wireless access through carefully planned WLAN options.

Note

To allow a user to roam seamlessly between APs (transparent that a handoff from one AP to another has taken place), the user's SSID and IP addressing information (VLAN) must remain the same across multiple APs. Therefore, routing at the access layer (discussed in "Chapter11: IP Routing Overview" and "Chapter 12: OSPF Operation and Configuration") breaks roaming. To solve this problem, you can either make sure that the APs are all connected via a Layer 2 network or, when routing at the access layer, set up the APs in controlled mode (discussed later in the chapter) and have the APs tunnel the traffic to a wireless access controller. In this sense, the wireless access controller is acting as a virtual switch interconnecting the APs. An in-depth discussion of tunneling is beyond the scope of this book.

AP Implementation Types

There are three basic types of APs:

- Thin
- Fit
- Fat

Thin APs establish the wireless network and forward all traffic to a wireless controller for further processing. The controller provides all the intelligence for the wireless network.

Intelligent, or *fit*, APs establish the wireless network but can perform other functions, as dictated by the controller and the WLAN architecture used. Fit APs still require the interaction of a wireless controller but provide intelligence that the thin APs lack.

Stand-alone APs are also referred to as *autonomous* or *fat* APs. Stand-alone APs can operate without any direction from a wireless controller. They are more common in smaller networks where there are a small number of APs that need to be managed; in larger networks, it is easier to deploy thin or fit APs where the intelligence is centralized on the wireless controller or controllers and is therefore easier to manage.

Note

The main advantage of fat APs is that, if you only have a few APs, it is more cost-effective to use a fat implementation than to buy wireless access controllers to implement a solution. The big advantage of a thin/fit AP is that most of the policies are centralized, allowing you to quickly deploy many APs with minimal configuration. One problem with a wireless access controllers implementation, besides cost, is throughput, since most wireless access controllers only support Gigabit Ethernet interfaces and wireless speeds are becoming faster and faster.

Open Versus Closed

The 802.11 standard specifies two types of systems:

- Open
- Closed

In an *open* system, such as a public hotspot, 'APs send beacon frames to advertise the SSID at regular intervals. Because anyone with a wireless device can join the WLAN, open systems are typically used for public networks.

In a *closed* system, APs do not advertise the SSID (although it is still included in plaintext in the header of every frame transmitted within the WLAN). A closed system is intended to limit access to users who know the SSID. If an AP supports only closed system WLANs, stations within range may detect its radio signal, but their client utilities will not display any available wireless networks.

To join a network, users must manually configure their wireless configuration utility with the correct SSID. In practice, however, a closed system does not provide much security. Applications that can discover the SSIDs in closed systems are readily available.

Active and Passive Scanning

To determine which APs are in range and which WLANs they support, a station uses a process called *scanning*. A station can scan for APs in two ways:

- **Active scanning**—In *active scanning* (also called *probing*), stations send probe request frames on a particular channel. APs that are within range and operating on that channel respond with a probe response frame. This response frame contains information about the APs SSIDs (for open systems), capabilities, data rates, and more.
- **Passive scanning**—In *passive scanning*, stations "listen" for beacon frames from APs within range. APs broadcast beacons at regular intervals.

These management frames contain:

- Radio settings
- Capabilities
- SSID
- Time stamps
- Other data

Stations can listen for beacon frames on all supported channels. This type of passive scanning is called *sweeping*. If multiple APs are within range, the station chooses which one to associate with, based on signal strength. At the same time, the station builds a table to keep track of SSIDs and other connection data. If the station changes location, it can more quickly reconnect to another AP that supports the correct SSID using the data compiled in the table.

Wireless Security

When a station performs a scan (active or passive) and finds an AP within range, it can begin the process of joining a WLAN, as outlined in the 802.11 standard. This process includes two main parts:

- 802.11 authentication
- 802.11 association

Open-system authentication allows any station to be validated by the AP. A station first sends an authentication request frame, which contains its MAC address and a value that indicates that it is using open-system authentication.

The AP sends an authentication response frame that contains the result of the request, which is typically successful authentication. Although the station is authenticated, it is not yet associated. It cannot send data onto the wireless network.

Shared-Key Authentication

With 802.11 shared-key authentication, each device must first prove to the AP that it has the correct key and should be granted network access. The device then uses this key to encrypt data it transmits and to decrypt data it receives. Likewise, the AP uses the same key to encrypt and decrypt data.

Shared-key authentication was first implemented using Wired Equivalent Privacy (WEP) as an encryption algorithm. The steps of shared-key authentication are as follows:

1. The station sends an authentication request frame containing the station's MAC address and a value indicating shared-key authentication.
2. The AP issues a response frame containing challenge text—a 128-byte, randomly generated data stream.
3. Using the key it should already possess, the station encrypts the challenge text from the AP and sends it back.
4. Using the same key, the AP decrypts the challenge text received from the station.

If the decrypted challenge text matches the challenge text that was sent in the second frame, the authentication is successful. The final frame in the exchange indicates authentication success or failure.

Shared-key authentication (which is also called *static WEP*) is seldom used because it opens a security hole. Because the AP sends the challenge in plaintext and the station encrypts it, a hacker can obtain a segment of plaintext and the equivalent cipher text. Then, the hacker can reverse engineer the key stream, gain access, and even crack the key. (This is very easy with today's technology.) Almost all wireless networks now use 802.11 open authentication and then enforce another form of authentication after the station has completed the 802.11 association.

As you learn in the following sections, you have several options for implementing supplemental authentication.

802.11 Association

If the 802.11 authentication (whether open system or shared key) is successful, the station sends an association request frame to the AP, which can accept or reject the request. If it accepts the association, the AP assigns an association ID to the station and allocates RAM and other resources to the connection. The AP registers the station on the network so that frames destined for the new station are sent to the correct AP for processing.

If no supplemental authentication is in place, the station is now authenticated and associated and it is part of the network. The station is allowed to transmit data frames, and the AP begins to process frames for it. The association remains active until it is terminated by either party. Stations cannot associate with more than one AP at a time. They can, however, roam and re-associate to a new AP in the same WLAN.

To completely secure wireless transmissions, you need to implement a security option that provides the following:

- **Authentication**—Ensures that only authorized users access the network.
- **Data privacy**—Ensures that only the intended recipient can read the data, preventing other users from reading it.
- **Data integrity**—Protects data from being tampered with before it reaches the intended device.

WEP Overview

The 802.11 standard's first attempt to secure wireless transmissions was WEP. To make wireless security equal to that of a wired network, WEP was designed to provide authentication, data privacy, and data integrity. With WEP, all stations encrypt 802.11 frames with a secret key using the RC-4 encryption algorithm before transmitting them to the AP. The AP uses the same key to decrypt the frame. Similarly, the AP encrypts all traffic destined to the station with the key.

In controller-based wireless solutions, stations may make associations with the AP or the controller, depending on the implementation. If the association is made with the controller rather than the AP, the controller encrypts and decrypts traffic.

WEP has two methods of authentication:

- **WEP key**—Also known as *static WEP*, in which a secret key shared by all stations associated with the AP acts as de facto authentication. (If the AP receives a frame it cannot decrypt, it simply drops that frame.)
- **802.1X**—Also known as *dynamic WEP*, in which users authenticate individually to a network Remote Authentication Dial-In User Service (RADIUS) server and receive individual secret keys. A RADIUS server can store and manage user and device information in a central database. It uses this information to approve or deny users' access to the network and resources on that network. (You learn more about 802.1X and other security measures used with it later in this chapter.)

Although WEP's weaknesses are well-known, it does encrypt the wireless data. This makes it a more secure option than MAC authentication (MAC-Auth) (discussed in the next section), which enforces authentication only. Static WEP also controls which users can send and receive data (because these users must have the key). Dynamic WEP provides user-based authentication and less-easily cracked keys (because each user has his or her own).

The WEP algorithm, however, has severe limitations. Applications that crack WEP are readily available on the Internet, and hackers need only a small sample of data to successfully use these applications to infiltrate a wireless network. Also, dynamic WEP is more difficult to configure because it requires a RADIUS server. In addition, it is less secure than other methods that use 802.1X.

Note

Unfortunately, WEP failed to live up to the promise of its name. It was cracked almost immediately, making it a very dubious choice for consumers and businesses.

MAC Authentication

One of the first restrictions you can place on wireless access is to filter authentication requests based on a frame's MAC address. When MAC-Auth is enabled, frames are accepted or rejected based on their MAC address.

MAC-Auth can be enabled in different ways. Some APs and controllers use allowed or blocked lists of MAC addresses. Other APs and controllers check MAC addresses against either their local database of user accounts or an external RADIUS server's database. In this case, the MAC address is typically both the username and password in the account.

MAC-Auth requires no configuration or special software on the device attempting to access the wireless network. Because all devices must include their MAC address in the access request, all devices can be controlled through MAC-Auth. In fact, many vendors support MAC-Auth because it is the only option for devices that do not have a user interface or support 802.1X. MAC-Auth can also be combined with other authentication methods, like port security and Bridge Protocol Data Units (BPDU) protection, strengthening the level of security it provides.

MAC-Auth has several disadvantages. First, this authentication method can be compromised because MAC addresses are easily spoofed. Second, tracking and entering MAC addresses can be both tedious and labor intensive. Third, this authentication method is hardware-based, not user-based. As a result, you cannot use it to grant users different levels of access.

WPA with WPA2

After WEP was compromised, the IEEE 802.11i Task Group began to create a new standard that was more secure. Because companies could not wait until the new standard was completed, however, the Wi-Fi Alliance designed Wi-Fi Protected Access (WPA) as an interim solution.

WPA meets only the first part of the 802.11i standard. It provides backward compatibility for equipment designed to support WEP while substantially strengthening security. WPA2 was created to meet the complete 802.11i standard.

Note

WEP isn't necessarily "weaker" than WPA/WPA2. The main issue with WEP is that 24 bits used to randomize the data were sent in clear text, which simplified the process of breaking the WEP encryption process. WPA/WPA2 fixed this keying issue.

Both WPA and WPA2 include encryption and authentication algorithms to provide data privacy and data integrity. However, the WPA2 algorithms are more secure (data encryption standard [DES], Triple Data Encryption Standard [3DES], and Advanced Encryption Standard [AES]). Therefore, WPA2 should be implemented if end-users' stations support it. When using WPA or WPA2, you have two authentication options:

- Pre-shared keys (PSKs)
- 802.1X

You learn more about these options in the next two sections.

WPA/WPA2 with PSK

With WPA/WPA2-pre-shared key (WPA2-PSK), all the users accessing the WLAN share the same key. Before a station can submit the pre-shared key for approval, it must first associate with the AP. After the station is associated, it submits the pre-shared key. If this key does not match the one configured for the WLAN, the station cannot transmit or receive data on the wireless network.

Like other wireless security options, WPA/WPA2-PSK has advantages and disadvantages. WPA2 provides the best data privacy and integrity measures available for wireless networks. WPA is less secure but still provides much stronger security than WEP. In addition, WPA/WPA2-PSK is easy to configure and does not require a RADIUS server (like 802.1X does).

WPA/WPA2-PSK's weakness is its authentication. Because all users share the key, it is more likely that someone will "leak" that key to an unauthorized user. In addition, this security option is not user-based. That is, you cannot grant users who access the WLAN different levels of access.

WPA/WPA2 with 802.1X

802.1X enforces user-based authentication, making sure that only authorized users are allowed to authenticate to the network. It further allows you to enforce a particular level of access for each user. For example, a user in the marketing group could receive different access rights than an executive at the same company.

802.1X requires three participants in the authentication process:

- **Supplicant**—This is the station that is requesting access to the network.
- **Authenticator**—The authenticator controls access to the network, preventing the supplicant from transmitting data onto the network until it has successfully authenticated. On a wireless network, stand-alone or fat APs operate as the authenticators. Controlled APs may operate as authenticators or may rely on the controller to perform this function: APs forward all user authentication requests to it. (However, the APs can still distribute users' data directly onto the wired network.)
- **Authentication server**—This server makes access decisions based on whether the user supplies valid authentication credentials. The authentication server is often a RADIUS server, which could be an external server, such as the Microsoft Network Policy Server (NPS), or the WLAN access controller's internal RADIUS server (if the controller includes one).

When a station associates with a WLAN that is protected by WPA/WPA2 with 802.1X, the AP or the controller immediately blocks all transmissions, except those used to authenticate the station. The exact authentication process varies, depending on the 802.1X options configured for the WLAN. What you need to know is that the authenticator—in this case, the controller—forwards the user's credentials to the RADIUS server. This server, in turn, notifies the authenticator whether the user is authorized.

If a user authenticates successfully, his or her station is allowed to transmit data onto the wireless network. Transmissions are encrypted and protected according to the WPA or WPA2 specifications.

There are advantages and disadvantages to using WPA/WPA2 with 802.1X. WPA/WPA2 with 802.1X provides the strongest security for wireless networks. 802.1X prevents anyone from transmitting or receiving any data on the network until he or she has authenticated successfully. Further, 802.1X provides user-based authentication, allowing you to grant users different levels of access. WPA2 also provides the best data privacy and integrity measures available for wireless networks. WPA is less secure but still provides much stronger security than WEP.

However, WPA/WPA2 with 802.1X has more requirements than other security options. For example, your network must include a RADIUS server that supports 802.1X options for wireless networks, and you must configure that server correctly to support the WLANs protected by 802.1X. In addition, the station must have an 802.1X supplicant, and some user setup is required for that supplicant.

Web Authentication

Web authentication, or *Web-Auth*, enables users to access the wireless network through their familiar web browser. Because no client software is required, this solution is typically used for guests and partners. Web-Auth can simply direct users to a welcome page (if no login credentials are required) or to a login page that prompts users to enter a username and password. Some solutions also allow users to pay a subscription fee and create their own accounts.

Web-Auth provides user-based authentication, and, depending on the user's credentials, the AP or controller might implement various forms of access control on the user. Web-Auth can also be combined with WEP or WPA/WPA2 to provide data privacy and integrity.

Web-Auth does not require a special client. Any station can authenticate on a WLAN that uses it as long as the user has a legitimate username and password and a web browser. Web-Auth also allows you to open parts of your network to guests by providing limited access to unauthenticated users. In addition, Web-Auth provides user-based authentication.

Web-Auth does have its disadvantages. It does not require encryption, although encryption is an option on some wireless devices. Because Web-Auth requires interaction with the user, you cannot use it to authenticate stations or devices that do not have a web browser interface.

Power over Ethernet

PoE is method of providing power over Ethernet to a connected device. This allows devices to be installed without having to have a power outlet in the same location. Power supplied to these devices typically involves a low number of watts—enough to power low-end devices like wireless APs, VoIP phones, and video cameras, among other devices. This section briefly introduces you to PoE and its use in wireless networks.

PoE Standards

IEEE has defined two PoE standards:

- 802.3af
- 802.3at

The original PoE standard, 802.3af, allows each device to receive up to 15.4 watts of power. The enhanced PoE+ standard, 802.3at, allows each device to receive up to 25.5 watts. Many devices support PoE, but some devices—such as 802.11n APs, video phones, touch-screen devices, and pan-tilt-zoom (PTZ) security cameras—might need more than 15 watts of power and require PoE+.

Infrastructure devices, like switches, can provide PoE or PoE+ to multiple devices, or you can use a specialized device, called a *PoE injector*, to power one device. HP Networking offers both E-Series and A-Series switches and WLAN access controllers that provide PoE and PoE+. The next chapter ("Chapter 15: HP Intelligent Resilient Framework") provides more detailed information on which switches, switch cards, and WLAN access controllers provide PoE and/or PoE+.

PoE Advantages

Using PoE/PoE+ to power devices has several advantages:

- PoE/PoE+ can make deployments of new devices less costly. For example, deploying devices, such as APs or IP video security cameras, is less expensive if you do not have to wire remote locations for both power and Ethernet.
- PoE/PoE+ enables you to remotely monitor and control power to devices. For example, if you need to power cycle a device to force a reboot, you can do so from the switch that is providing power.
- PoE/PoE+ provides more freedom in device placement; you are not limited to locations where an alternating current (AC) outlet is nearby.

Keep in mind that these advantages are provided by standards-based PoE/PoE+ products, such as those offered by HP.

PoE Preparation and Configuration

You might want to establish PoE connections for your APs so that you do not have to manage power supplies for devices in hard-to-access locations. Instead, the Ethernet cable provides connectivity and power. Both ends of the connection must support PoE (802.3af). All HP MSM APs support this protocol as *powered devices* (PDs)—the devices receiving power. Many ProVision and Comware switches feature PoE capable ports, which *are power-sourcing equipment* (PSE)—the components providing power. If your switch does not provide PoE, you could connect your AP to a PoE injector.

The AP automatically draws power on the cable if it has no other power source. You do not need to complete any configuration; simply connect the AP to a PSE. To configure PoE on a ProVision or Comware switch, you should:

1. Ensure that PoE is enabled on the switch port.
2. Plan the PoE power budget.
3. Set a PoE priority on the port.

Step 1: Ensure that PoE is enabled on the switch port.

This step is optional. By default, PoE is enabled on all ProVision switch ports that support PoE. The command for enabling and disabling PoE is:

```
ProVision(config)# [no] interface <port-list> power-over-ethernet
```

Or

```
[Comware] interface <interface-id>
[Comware-<interface-id>] poe enable
```

In addition, by default, the switch allocates just as much power to the port as the device draws. (The switch could also allocate a set number of watts or a set power class, which defines the number of watts. In short, establishing the PoE connection might be as simple as connecting the cable.)

Step 2: Plan the PoE power budget.

The maximum power allowed over a standard PoE connection is 15.4 watts. The ProVision APs draw 6 to 12 watts, depending on the number of radios and the radio operation modes. (802.11n generally requires more power.)

Note

Some 802.11n APs draw more than 15.4 watts, which means that they require PoE+ (802.3at) support. However, the MSM 802.11n-capable APs typically use PoE (802.3af).

You can look up (in their datasheets) how much power your APs require. Add the power demands and determine whether they exceed the amount of power provided by your switch (see the switch's datasheet). Note, however, that when a switch reaches less than 17 watts of remaining PoE power, it cannot allocate any more power to a new device even if the device draws less than 17 watts. Therefore, you need to plan for a slight amount of leeway.

You should also remember that other devices might draw power from the switch. Some switches provide enough power to fully provision every PoE port, in which case, you do not need to worry. Others switches provide only enough power for some ports. In that case, you must either disable PoE on some ports or set up prioritization such that important devices, like your APs are guaranteed the power that they need.

You can also connect many ProVision switches to an external power supply (EPS), which furnishes additional power for PoE. For example, EPSs for ProVision devices include:

- 630 redundant power supply/external power supply.
- 620 redundant power supply/external power supply.

You can also purchase HP zl power supply shelves for HP zl switches.

Note

HP switches provide up to 30 watts of power for each PoE+ port: 25.5 watts for the 802.3at standard and 4.5 watts for cable dissipation, equating to 30 watts of total power.

Step 3: Set a PoE priority on the port.

This step is optional. As mentioned above, you would only need to set a priority if you determine that the switch might not have enough power for all PoE devices that might connect to it. The ProVision devices define three priority classes: critical, high, and low. All critical ports are provisioned before any high ports, which are provisioned before any low ports. In the case of a tie (for example, devices on critical ports demand more power than is available), the lower-numbered ports are provisioned first.

The command for setting the PoE priority class is:

```
ProVision(config)# interface <port-list> power-over-ethernet
                            [critical | high | low]
```

Or

```
[Comware] interface <interface-id>
[Comware-<interface-id>] poe priority {critical | high | low}
```

Other devices also use PoE. VoIP phones often draw PoE power, as do security cameras and other video devices. You can provide PoE to these devices just as you do wireless APs. Simply plan your power budget and enable PoE on the correct ports, prioritizing power on those ports, as necessary.

Sometimes you must configure the correct power level for the port. However, many multimedia devices support Link Layer Discovery Protocol-Media Endpoint Detection (LLDP-MED), which they can use to inform LLDP-MED-capable switches of their power needs and of the types of special service that they require. PoE-capable HP Series switches support this feature.

MSM AP Configuration

The following sections introduce you to access the HP MSM APs and about placing a basic configuration on them.

Accessing an MSM AP

Generally, you complete the initial configuration of a stand-alone HP MSM device through its web browser interface. To reach this interface, you must know the AP's IP address. At factory defaults, the AP attempts to receive a DHCP address. However, if its DHCP requests time out, the address defaults to 192.168.1.1/24. There are several strategies for establishing the initial connection to the AP's web browser interface. These are shown in Figure 14-5 and discussed in the following sections.

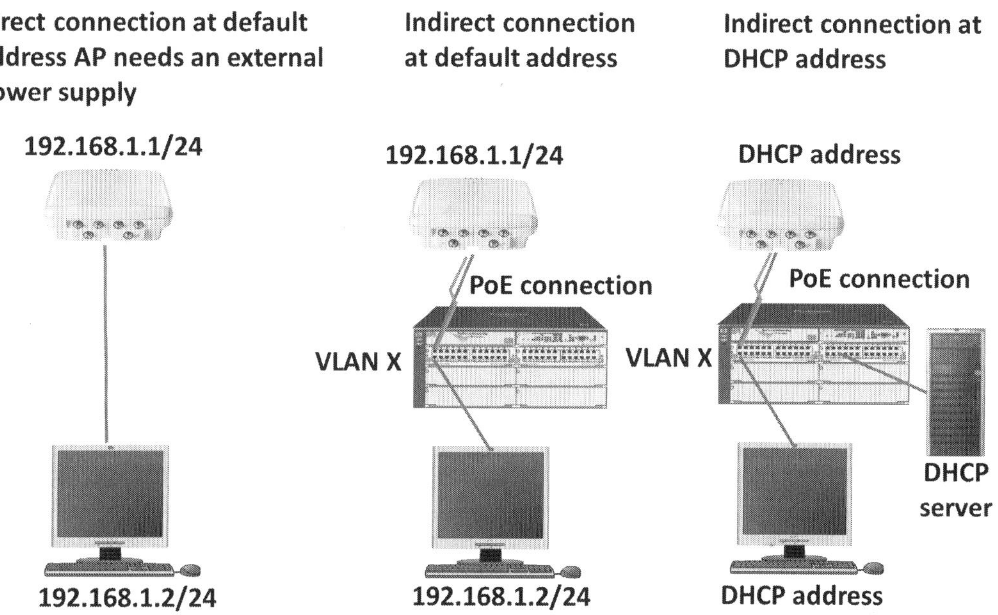

Figure 14-5. Accessing an MSM AP

Direct Connection at the Default IP Address

Connect your management station directly to the AP's Ethernet port (port 1, if it has multiple ports). Power up the AP with an external power supply, if necessary. Configure your PC's Ethernet NIC to use these IP settings:

- IP address = 192.168.1.2 (You can actually use any IP address in the 192.168.1.0/24 subnet, except 192.168.1.1.)
- Subnet mask = 255.255.255.0
- Default gateway = 192.168.1.1

Note

Some of the MSM APs support multiple Ethernet ports; however, for the initial configuration, this must be done via port 1. Also, the Ethernet ports on the MSMs support trunking (tagging VLANs); however, the default management address of the AP is sent out untagged, unless overridden in the graphical user interface (GUI) configuration.

Indirect Connection at the Default IP Address

In a variation on the previous approach, you can connect the AP to a PoE-enabled switch port. First, configure the switch port, activating PoE and making the port an untagged member of a VLAN that is not used in your system. Then, connect the AP to that port.

Make another switch port an untagged member of the same VLAN by connecting your station to that port. Then, configure your station's Ethernet NIC with an IP address in 192.168.1.0/24, as described in the previous section. After you connect to the AP and change its IP address to one that is valid in your LAN, you need to change the VLAN membership on the switch's ports.

Indirect Connection at a DHCP-Assigned IP Address

If you plan to have the AP use a DHCP-assigned IP address, you can contact the AP on that address initially. Generally, the AP should have a fixed DHCP reservation so that you always know its IP address. Contact your network's DHCP administrator, and discuss a fixed DHCP reservation. Then, connect the AP to any switch port in the correct VLAN. Connect your management station to the LAN, and ping the AP's fixed DHCP address to ensure that you can reach the AP.

In a variation on this strategy, you can have the AP receive a DHCP address without reservation. In that case, you would need access to the DHCP server so that you could find the IP address assigned to the AP. You could then change the AP's address to a static address.

Note

LLDP will not function on the AP until you accept the license agreement the first time you log in.

Logging in to an MSM AP

After you have connected the AP and your management station, open a web browser connection to the AP's IP address. You will see the screen shown in Figure 14-6. Use these default credentials to log in:

- Username = *admin*
- Password = *admin*

E-MSM460

System name: CN29D32302

Welcome to HP
E-MSM460 MultiService Access Point

Authorized access only.
This system is property of [COMPANY NAME].
Contact [EMAIL] for more information.

Current IP address: 192.168.1.1
Ethernet base MAC address: B4:B5:2F:4F:75:33
Wireless MAC address (radio 1): C8:CB:B8:F6:EF:20
Wireless MAC address (radio 2): C8:CB:B8:F6:EF:30

Uptime: 3 hours 16 minutes

Software version: 5.7.0.2-01-10750

Username: Password: Login

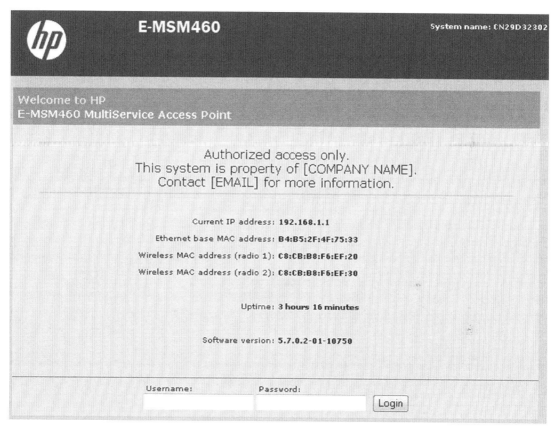

Figure 14-6. Accessing the MSM AP via a web browser

Note

It is recommended that you use Internet Explorer 7.0+ or Mozilla Firefox 2.0+ to access the AP's web browser interface, but you might be able to use other browsers, as well.

Autonomous Versus Controlled Modes

By default, HP MSM APs act as controlled devices, managed and configured by an MSM Access Controller or MSM Mobility Controller. We focus on the APs as stand-alone devices, which can provide wireless services for an SMB on their own. The HP Accredited Solutions Expert (ASE) Implementing and Troubleshooting HP Wireless Networks course goes into great detail on the available MSM controllers.

After you log in, you see the screen in Figure 14-7. To convert an MSM AP to autonomous mode, simply click the **Switch to Autonomous Mode** button shown in the figure. The AP automatically restarts itself.

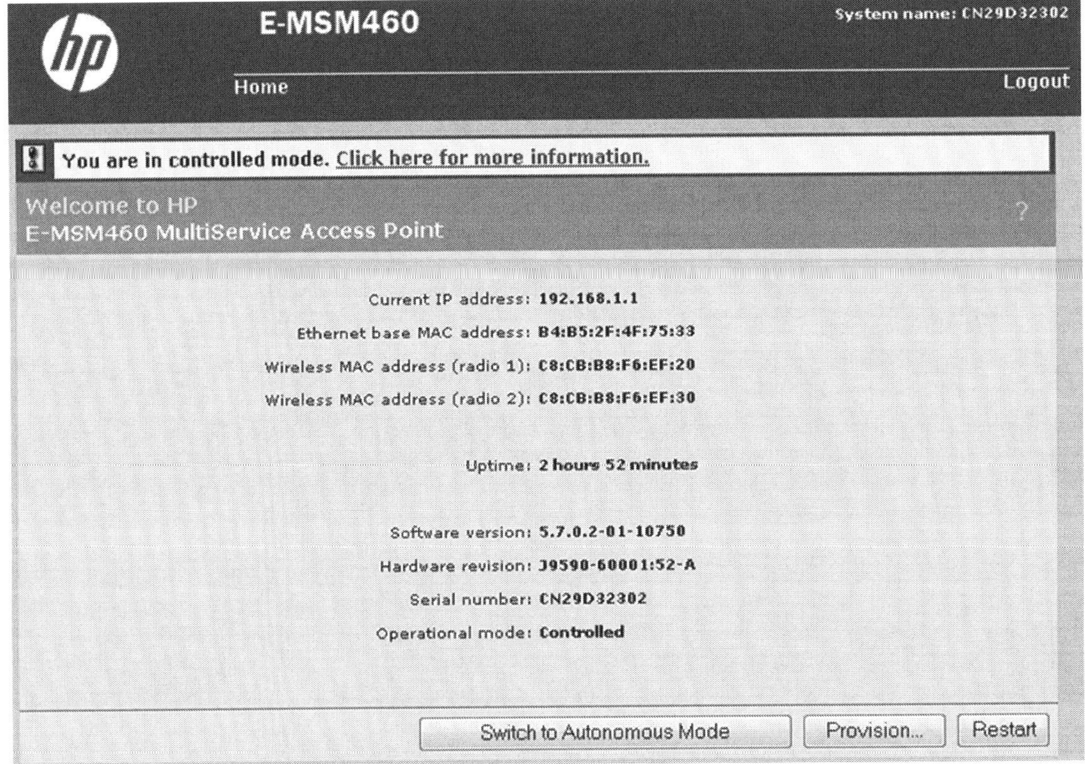

Figure 14-7. Autonomous versus controlled modes

Completing the Initialization

With your initial access to the AP, a wizard leads you through three basic steps:

- Accept a license and register the AP
- Set the AP's country code.
- Change the AP's password for the admin account.

You must select the country code for your region. This automatically configures the AP to use legal channels and transmit powers. Change the password (and username) for management access to the AP.

Changing the Management IP Address

After the wizard is finished, the home page for the AP displays. The AP's web browser interface has a navigation bar at the top (see Figure 14-8). This bar includes tabs for various configuration and management tasks. When you select a tab, the sub-tabs for that tab are displayed in a row below. Select a sub-tab to configure specific settings.

The remainder of this chapter covers how to change the IP address on the AP, configure a VLAN, and create a Virtual Service Community (VSC), plus how to perform some basic management tasks.

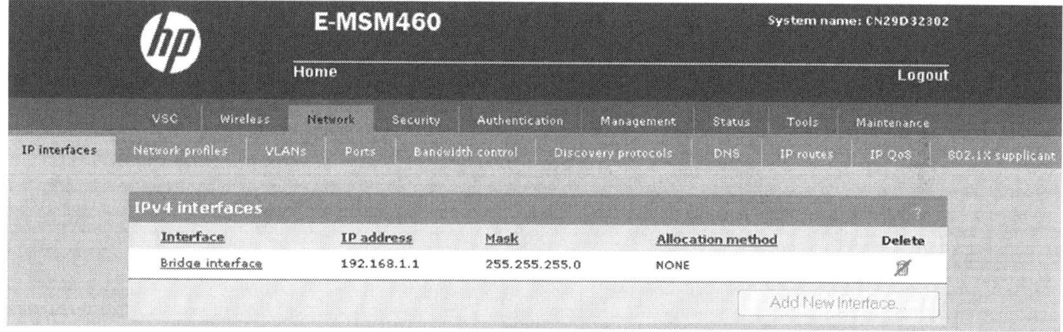

Figure 14-8. Changing the management IP address of the AP

As you learned earlier, the AP can dynamically acquire an address via DHCP or it defaults to an address of 192.168.1.1. You can override this process by assigning a static IP address to the AP. To do this:

1. In the top navigation bar, select **Network > IP Interfaces** (see Figure 14-8).
2. You see one interface listed, by default. The port on which you configure the IP address is called the *bridge interface* or *bridge port*, which is a virtual port that handles bridging traffic on the wireless radios and the AP's Ethernet port. Click the **Bridge interface** hyperlink.
3. Select **Static**, and click **Configure** (the default is DHCP if not selected, as shown in Figure 14-9).
4. Assign the static IP addressing information (see Figure 14-10).
5. In both windows, click **Save**.
6. After changing the IP address of the AP, you lose management access to the AP until you re-address or PC (if you used 192.168.1.2 as your IP address).

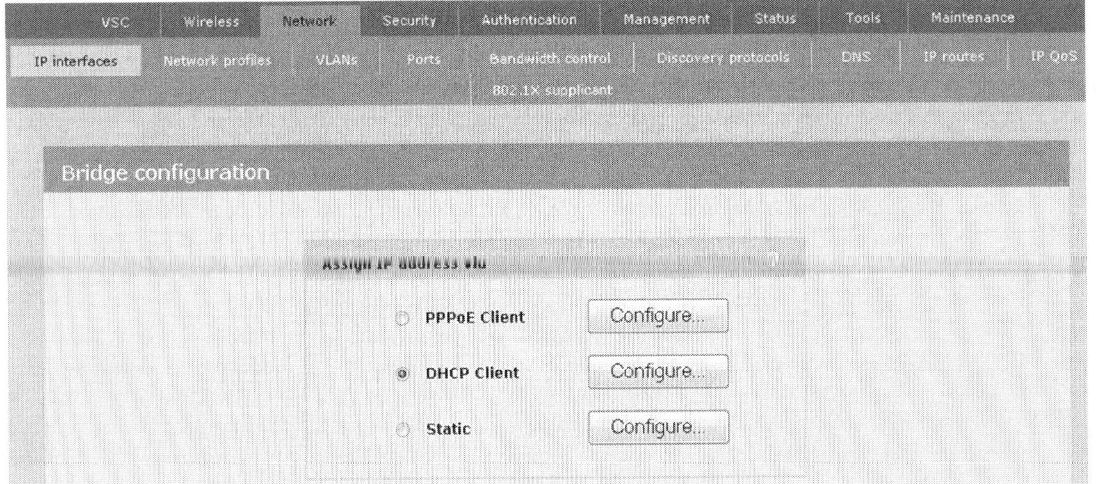

Figure 14-9. MSM IP address assignment

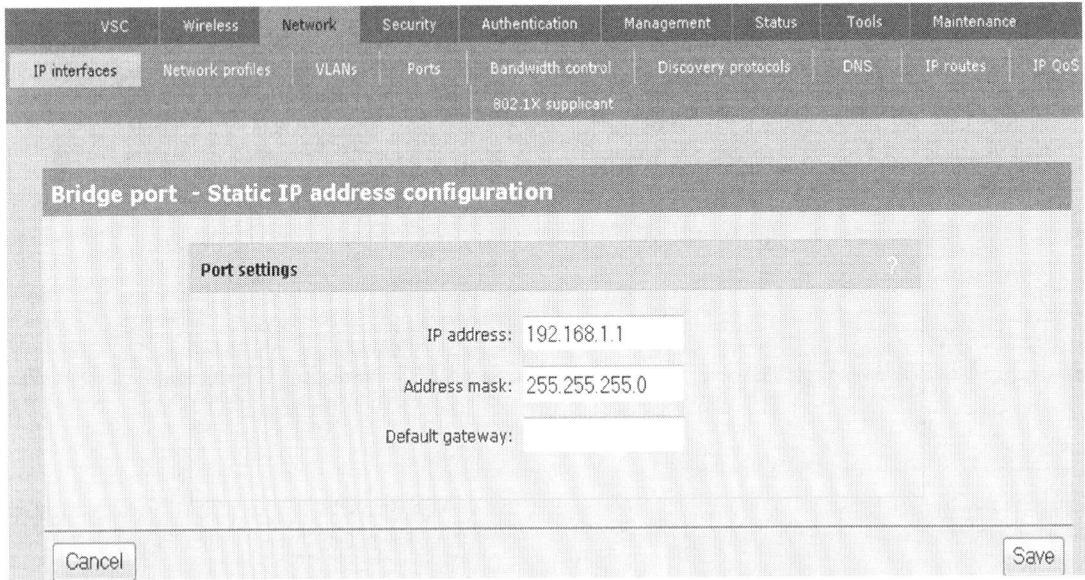

Figure 14-10. MSM static address assignment

VLAN Management

VLANs can be used to segregate your wireless traffic so that different groups of wireless users cannot connect to each other without going through a Layer 3 device, like a router, route switch, or firewall—that is, VLANs can be used to perform filtering. Follow these steps to configure VLANs:

1. Select **Network > Network profiles** (see Figure 14-11).
2. Click the **Add New Profile** button (see Figure 14-11).
3. Enter a VLAN name, select the VLAN check box, and then enter a VLAN number (see Figure 14-11).
4. Click the **Save** button.
5. Select **Network > VLANs** (see Figure 14-12).
6. Click the hyperlink of the name of the Network Profile you just created.
7. If there is more than Ethernet port, select the port on the AP (see Figure 14-12). Use the drop-down selector to select the port (defaults to **Port 1**).
8. Click the **Save** button.
9. The screen shown in Figure 14-13 now displays, and you can see your new assignment.

By default, the VLANs are tagged on the egress Ethernet port. Also by default, the MSM APs bridge the wireless traffic to the Ethernet ports.

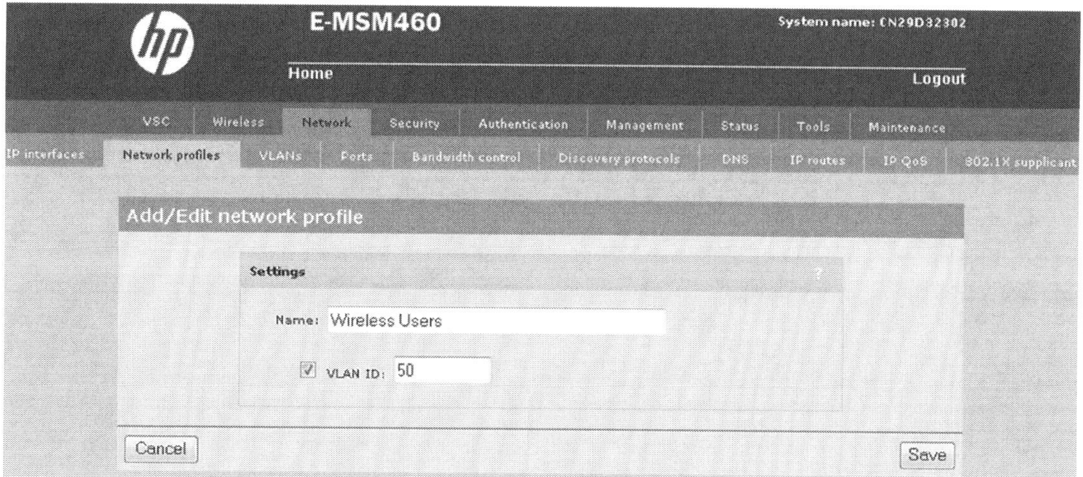

Figure 14-11. Creating VLANs on the MSM AP

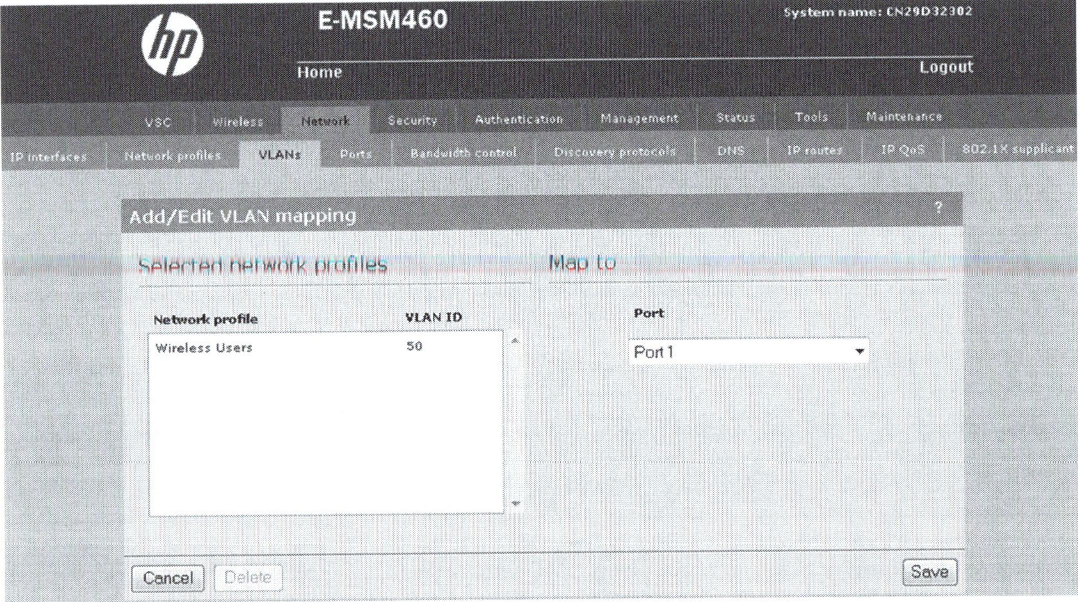

Figure 14-12. Assigning a VLAN to a port

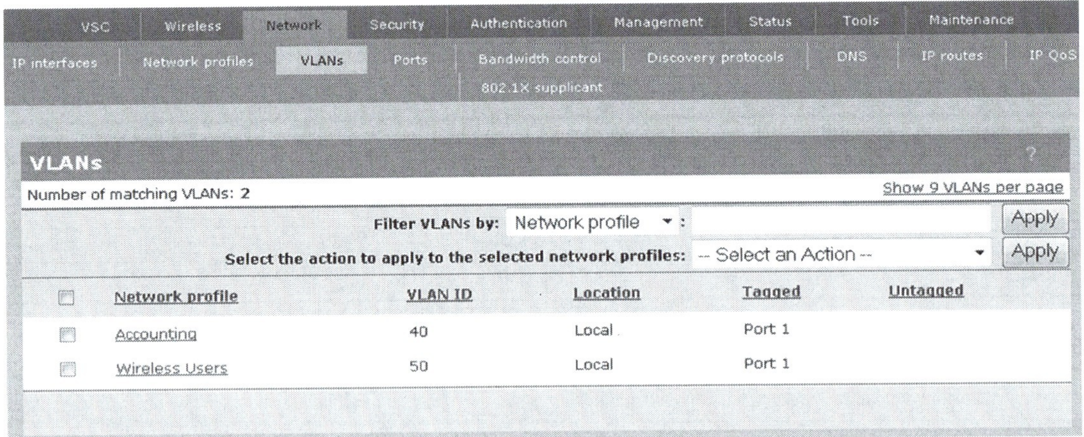

Figure 14-13. Network profile to VLAN and Ethernet port mappings

Create a Virtual Service Community

A Virtual Service Community (VSC) defines the wireless services offered by the AP. Therefore, it specifies not only WLAN settings but also the egress VLAN for wireless traffic and the filters that control the traffic. The VSC is similar to a virtual AP. Each group of users can be associated to a different VSC, which can affect their security, QoS, VLAN, and other settings within the same physical MSM AP.

Note

If a VSC is not set up, all wireless traffic is associated with one subnet, and the Ethernet port on the AP is an access port. The VLAN assigned to the access port on the connected switch is the VLAN for the wireless traffic.

To create a VSC, follow these steps:

1. In the navigation bar, click **VSC** (see Figure 14-14). A default VSC already exists. You can edit that one by clicking its name or the **Add New VSC Profile** button at the bottom of the screen.
2. The screen shown in Figure 14-15 (top portion), Figure 14-16 (middle portion), and Figure 14-17 (bottom portion) now displays. In the General section, enter a name for the VSC. If you want to run the AP in controlled mode, select the **Use HP MSM Controller** check box. Then, select the **Virtual AP** check box. Enter an SSID name and wireless restrictions. Please note that some radios only support certain 802.11 standards, like 802.11a/n or 802.11b/g/n, depending on what you purchased. The Wireless protection section allows you to set up dynamic or static WEP, WPA, or WPA2 (supports 802.1X). The Egress VLAN section allows you to specify the VLAN for the VSC. You can also set up MAC-based authentication to restrict source MAC addresses and MAC address filters (that is, restrict destination MAC addresses).
3. At the bottom of the screen (not shown), click the **Save** button to save your VSC.

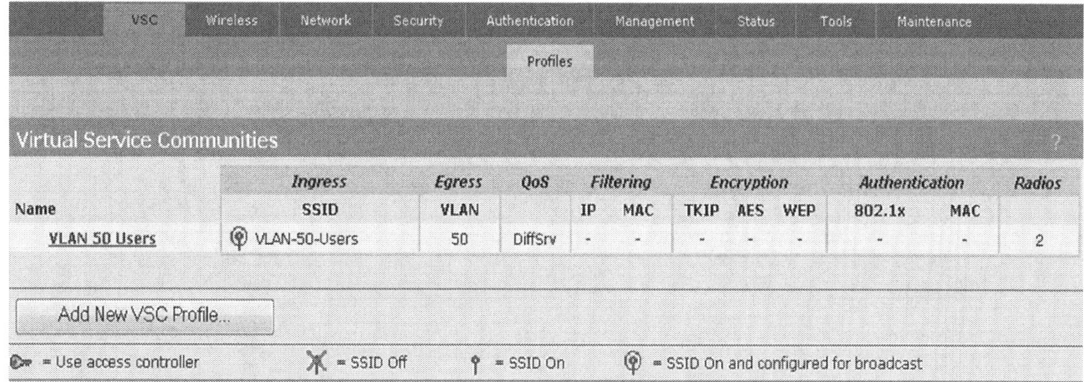

Figure 14-14. VSC profile window

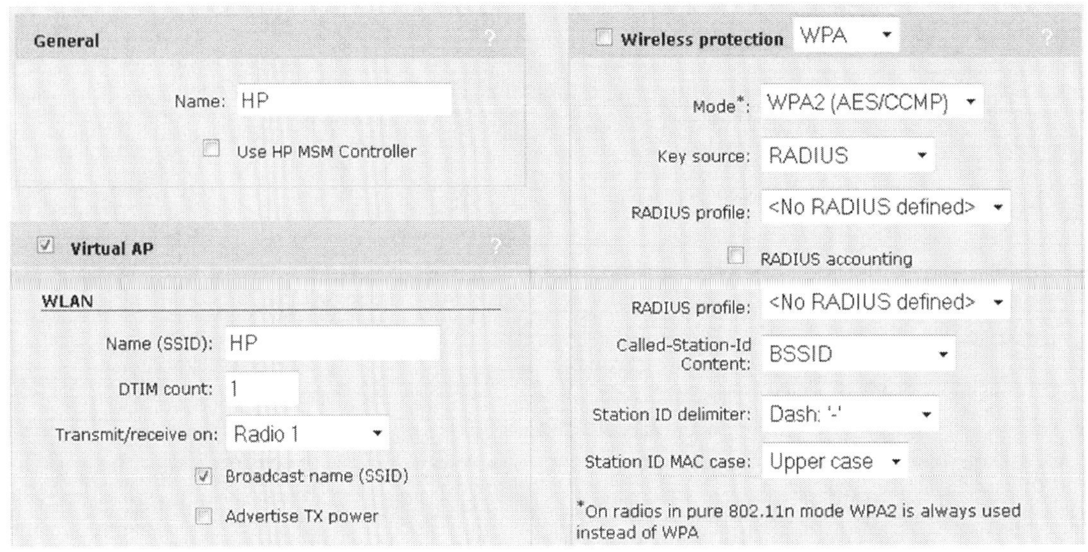

Figure 14-15. MSM virtual service parameters (top of screen)

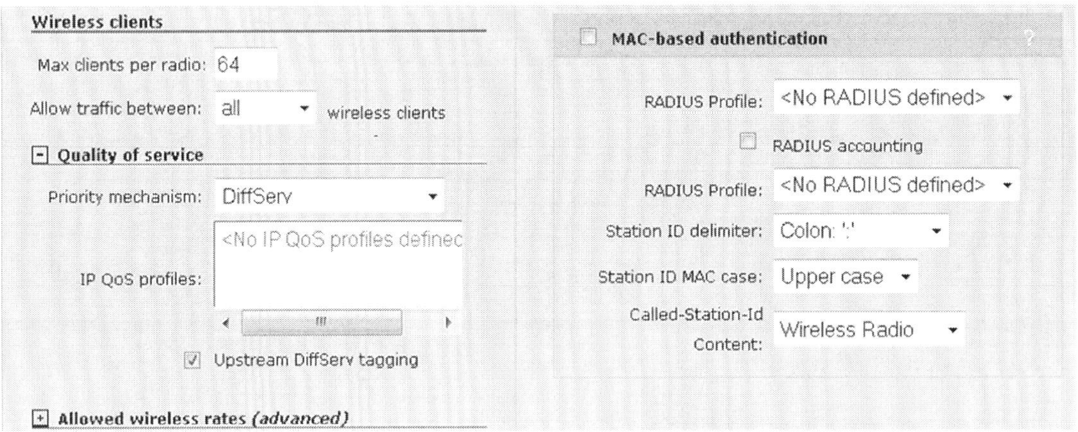

Figure 14-16. MSM virtual service parameters (middle of screen)

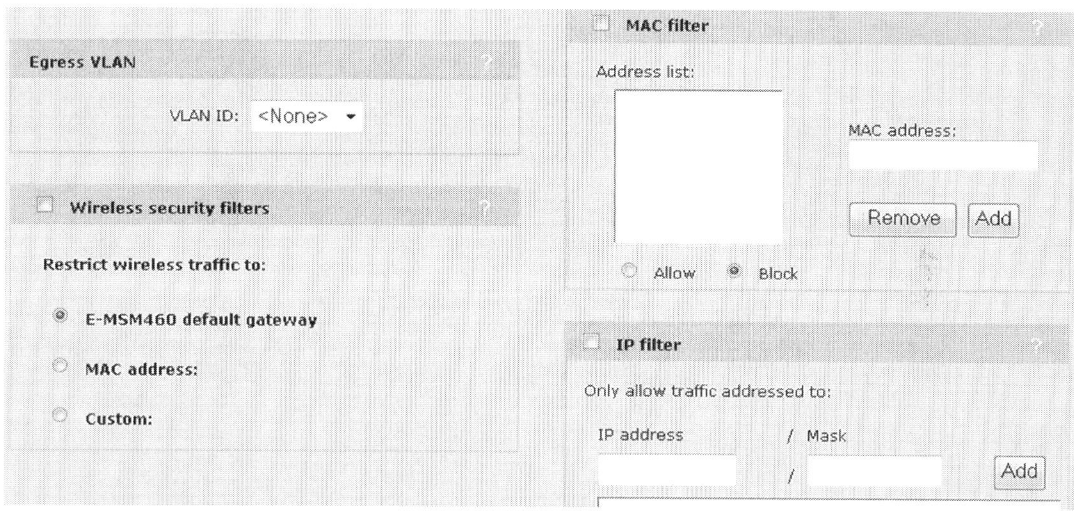

Figure 14-17. MSM virtual service parameters (bottom of screen)

Configure the Radios

MSM APs support several modes for radio operation. For this example, the only mode that you want to use is "Access point only," which enables the radio to support wireless clients. You can also configure the radio's 802.11 operation mode: 802.11n/b/g. To set up the wireless radios on the MSM AP:

1. Click **Wireless > Radios** (see Figure 14-18).
2. You see one or more radios (see Figure 14-18) that you can enable and configure. The number of radios depends on the AP. From this screen, you can, for example, select the channels used by each radio and the number of devices for each radio.
3. If you expand the advanced wireless settings, you can configure the power settings for the radios.
4. To save your changes, click the **Save** button at the bottom of the screen.

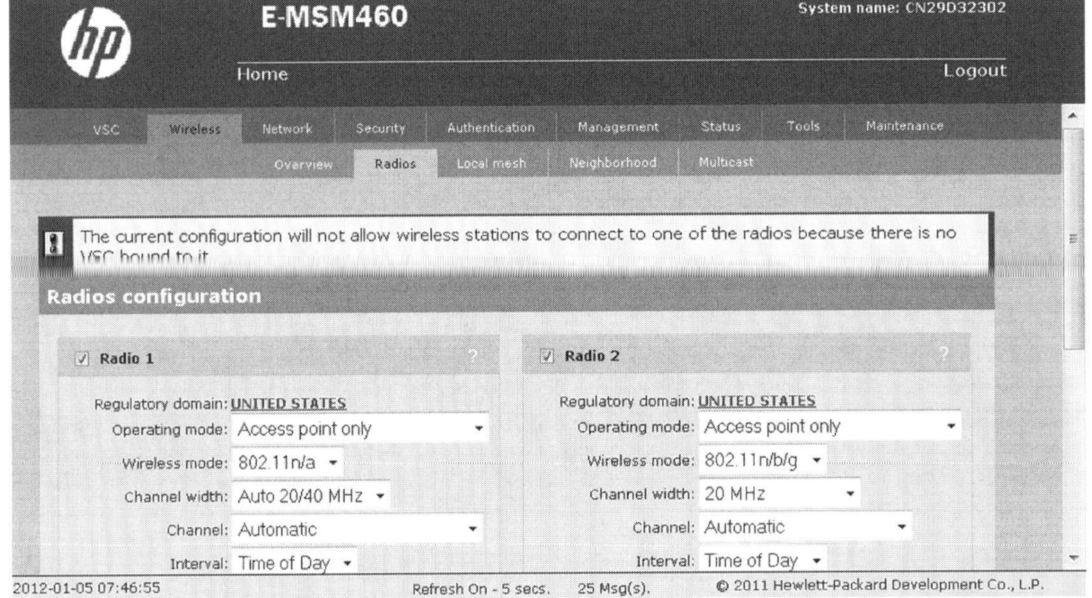

Figure 14-18. MSM radios

Verifying Connectivity

If you go to **Status > Wireless**, you can see the status of the radios in the AP, in addition to the users connected to each radio (if more than one is installed). See Figure 14-19 for an example.

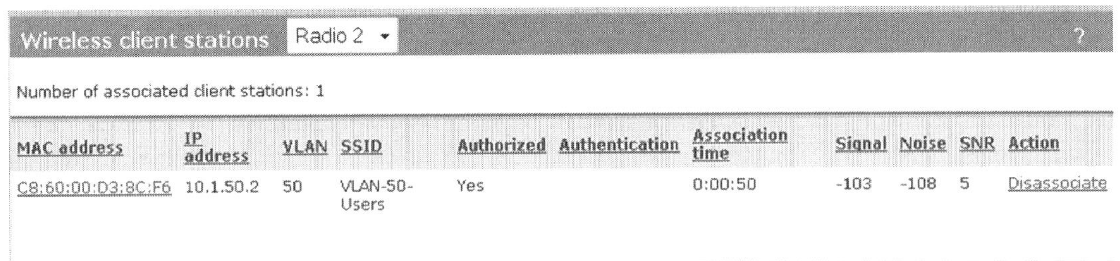

Figure 14-19. Viewing connected wireless users

Learning Check

The following questions help you measure your understanding of the material presented in this chapter. Read all of the choices carefully, since there may be more than one correct answer. Choose all correct answers for each question.

Questions

1. Match the following IEEE standards with the appropriate description. Each option can only be used once.

a. 802.11a	1. Uses the 5 GHz frequency only
b. 802.11b	2. Supports MIMO for higher throughput
c. 802.11g	3. Supports speeds up to 54 Mbps
d. 802.11n	4. Was the first IEEE wireless standard to achieve widespread adoption

2. Which of the following is true concerning PoE?
   a. 802.3ae supports up to 15.4 watts of power.
   b. 802.3af supports up to 15.4 watts of power.
   c. 802.3au supports up to 25 watts of power.
   d. 802.3av supports up to 25 watts of power.

3. Which is not a component of 802.1X?
   a. Supplicant
   b. Authenticator
   c. Authentication server
   d. WPA

4. Which of the following wireless services for an MSM AP does a VSC not include?
   a. SSID
   b. Power settings for the AP wireless radios
   c. Number of wireless clients
   d. Wireless protection, like WEP or WPA2
   e. MAC authentication

5. What is the default IP address of an MSM AP, if one cannot be obtained via DHCP?

6. Name the default username and password of an MSM access point.

Answers

1. ☑ **A** is **1** (802.11a uses the 5 Ghz frequency only); **B** is **4** (802.11b was the first IEEE wireless standard to achieve widespread adoption); **C** is **3** (802.11g supports speeds up to 54 Mbps); and **D** is **2** (802.11n supports MIMO for higher throughput).

2. ☑ **B** is correct. 802.3af supports up to 15.4 watts of power.

   ☒ **A**, **C**, and **D** are incorrect because they list the invalid IEEE standards.

3. ☑ **D** is correct. WPA is not a component of 802.1X.

   ☒ **A**, **B**, and **C** are incorrect because they are components of 802.1X

4. ☑ **B** is correct. The VSC on the MSM does not define the power settings for the wireless radios.

   ☒ **A**, **C**, **D**, and **E** are incorrect because they are configured under the VSC.

5. ☑ The default IP address of an MSM AP, if one cannot be obtained via DHCP, is **192.168.1.1/24**.

6. ☑ The default username of an MSM AP is **admin**, and the default password is **admin**.

15 HP Intelligent Management Center

EXAM OBJECTIVES

In this chapter, you learn to:

- ✓ Describe network management.
- ✓ Identify and describe available tool sets for managing HP Networking products.
- ✓ Install and configure a management and administration solution.
- ✓ Validate the installed solution.
- ✓ Manage network assets using HP tools.
- ✓ Use general troubleshooting tools.
- ✓ Perform network management (best practices).
- ✓ Review and take action on alerts and log files.
- ✓ Perform administrative tasks, including moves, adds, changes, deletions, and password resets.

ASSUMED KNOWLEDGE

This chapter assumes that you have an understanding of Simple Network Management Protocol (SNMP), discussed in "Chapter 4: Protecting Management Access." If you do not feel comfortable with your knowledge of SNMP, please revisit Chapter 4.

INTRODUCTION

In this book, you have focused on configuring and managing the HP ProVision and HP Comware devices from the command line interface (CLI), along with the HP Multi-Service Mobility (MSM) access point (AP) using the graphical user interface (GUI). Sometimes, however, you may need to use specialized tools to troubleshoot certain network devices. Or you may want to manage all of your network infrastructure devices from a single SNMP application. SNMP configuration on the

ProVision and Comware devices is discussed in "Chapter 4: Protecting Management Access." This chapter explains technologies that can help you meet these and other network requirements when deploying devices from HP and from other vendors using HP Intelligent Management Center (IMC) to manage a network.

This chapter focuses on the following topics:

- Understanding the components of IMC
- Understanding how to install IMC
- Understanding how to access IMC
- Implementing a basic configuration using IMC

HP IMC Overview

HP IMC is a centralized network management platform that allows you to manage both your physical and virtual networks. From a single interface, you can monitor and manage network traffic and devices. HP IMC supports both HP and third-party network devices. In fact, IMC 5.2 supports thousands of network devices from dozens of vendors, including Cisco.

Note

The IMC product was acquired by HP through their 3Com purchase, which also included the Comware equipment. IMC was one of the main reasons that HP was interested in purchasing 3Com.

HP IMC includes an auto discovery feature, which you can invoke to locate all of the devices on the network, categorize the network devices into types (such as switches, routers, servers, and desktops), and map them on a network topology. You can view the devices based on IP address or device type. You can also create custom views to make it easier to view and manage devices.

In addition, IMC allows you to establish baseline configurations and software images. You can compare configurations, track versions, and establish alerts if configuration changes are made. IMC also helps you manage virtual machines (VMs). It discovers VMs and virtual switches, showing their relationship to the physical network. You can also easily migrate VMs to new physical servers, and IMC automatically reconfigures the associated network policies accordingly, ensuring that the policies remain tied to VMs and virtual workloads.

Here is a summary of the features supported by IMC:

- **HP IMC**—The solution cohesively integrates fault management, element configuration, and network monitoring from a central vantage point. With support for third-party devices, IMC enables network administrators to centrally manage all network elements with a variety of automated tasks, including discovery, categorization, baseline configurations, and software images. IMC also provides configuration comparison tools, version tracking, change alerts, and more.

- **Modular architecture**—With IMC's architecture, new modules can be added to enrich a network's management capabilities. Modules for user access management, VPN management, and traffic analysis can be quickly added and can provide instant benefits. The architecture allows modules to share information and to provide collaborative policy creation and reports.
- **Virtualization management**—IMC is one of the first management tools to integrate management and monitoring of both virtual and physical networks. IMC provides insight and management of virtual networks and helps reduce migration complexity by aligning and automating network policies with virtual images. Both VMware and Hyper-V are supported.
- **Highly flexible and scalable deployment models**—IMC Standard Edition delivers an extensive set of capabilities for managing large heterogeneous networks. This self-contained solution provides scalability and high availability through a flexible distributed deployment model. With its modular design, IMC can be deployed across multiple servers to provide increased scalability and resilience.
- **Rich resource management**—IMC provides powerful network discovery and topology, including a detailed inventory of the network and highly accurate depictions of how it is configured. Supported views include Layer 2 and Layer 3, in addition to VLAN topology and the ability to create custom views, like a dashboard home page. Customization enables administrators to organize and control the network infrastructure based on their preferred organizational model.
- **Flexible, centralized reporting**—Centralized report management simplifies an organization's report administration. IMC software's flexible historical reports provide the information necessary for network trend analysis and capacity planning, and they offer predefined reports or customization options to define parameters. Reports can be viewed in a number of formats, including .pdf and .xls, and can be sent automatically via email or set to run on a particular schedule.
- **Access control list (ACL) management**—IMC simplifies the definition, deployment, and control of ACLs with effective policy-based control of network security and quality of service (QoS) across an organization's network infrastructure. ACL rule optimization helps ensure efficient use of the ACL device resources.
- **Identification and access management**—With the addition of the HP User Access Manager (UAM) add-on module, the system implements unified and centralized access management, supporting access through authentications, such as LAN, WAN, wireless LAN (WLAN), and virtual private network (VPN). It supports strong authentication using smart card, certificate, and other methods, and it supports various types of endpoint access control and identity-based network services that efficiently integrate the management of user resources and services.
- **HP Endpoint Admission Defense (EAD)**—With additional modules, IMC can be used to analyze a network endpoint's security status to locate security threats, detect security events, and carry out protective measures to reduce network vulnerabilities. EAD can determine endpoint patch level, Address Resolution Protocol (ARP) attack, abnormal traffic, and the installation and operation of illegal software. Administrators can choose enforcement policies and remediation options that are appropriate to particular endpoints.

- **HP Network Traffic Analyzer (NTA)**—With the additional NTA module, the system can also collect flow information from devices enabled for sFlow, NetFlow, and NetStream. Through traffic analysis, NTA can help identify network bottlenecks, recognize anomalous traffic, and pinpoint varying levels of bandwidth traffic for different services and applications. The correlation of traffic flows to users is available with the additional User Behavior Auditor (UBA) module.
- **Compliance Center**—The Compliance Center associates compliance policies with devices that need to be checked. The compliance check function can promptly fix configuration and security problems in the network.
- **Virtual Connect Support**—IMC supports add/remove connections for Virtual Connect Manager and displays the connect information from the device detail page.
- **HP IMC mobile application**—IMC provides a new mobile application for iPhone and Android. This allows administrators mobility by allowing them to monitor the network from anywhere.
- **Telnet/SSH proxy**—With the Telnet/SSH proxy, an administrator can use a browser to remotely access and manage devices through Telnet/SSH, without installing a Telnet/SSH tool on the PC client used to access the device. This promotes secure and controlled access to devices while providing auditing of change on any device.
- **Unified Task Management and Wizard Center**—The IMC Wizard Center is a section which services many of the configuration wizards found within IMC, such as Quick Start and third-party device configuration wizard, among others. New to this release is Unified Task Management, which is a section that hosts all tasks within IMC.
- **New traffic topology**—The traffic topology is based on the network's physical topology. It enables you to view the traffic conditions of various links.
- **Customized functions and third-party device support**—IMC basic network management platform extends device management and configuration functions. You can either extend an existing function to support third-party devices by compiling interactive scripts and Extensible Markup Language (XML) files, or you can customize a function by compiling interactive scripts, XML files, and user interface (UI) configuration files.

Note

This book focuses on IMC 5.2. There are two main implementations of IMC for larger networks: Standard and Enterprise. A third implementation, IMC Basic Software Platform, is designed for simplicity and ease of use, with single-pane-of-glass visibility to the network infrastructure, for small-to-medium-sized businesses (SMBs), and it offers many of the capabilities of the Standard and Enterprise software solutions. This book focuses on the Standard implementation.

HP IMC Add-On Modules

HP IMC has a modular architecture (see Figure 15-1), allowing you to add management capabilities, as needed. (The picture only shows some of the modules.) The IMC architecture allows these modules to share information and to integrate functionality, covered in the following sections:

- HP IMC Wireless Services Manager
- HP IMC User Behavior Auditor Software Module
- HP IMC Quality of Service Manager
- HP IMC Network Traffic Analyzer
- HP IMC Service Operation Manager
- HP IMC Multi-Protocol Label Switching (MPLS) VPN Manager
- HP IMC Endpoint Admission Defense
- HP IMC IPSec/VPN Manager
- HP IMC User Access Manager
- HP IMC P Branch Intelligent Management Software (BIMS)

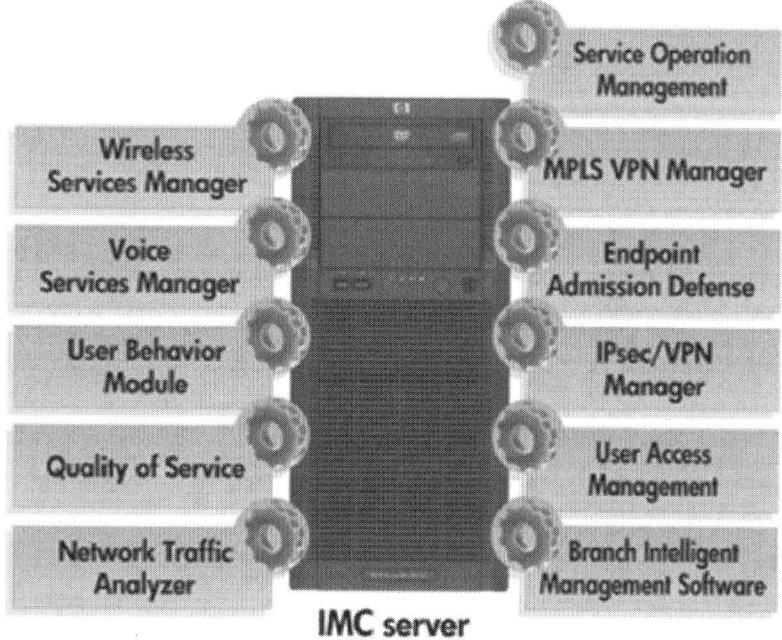

Figure 15-1. Add-on modules for IMC

HP IMC Wireless Services Manager

The Wireless Services Manager unifies the management of wired and wireless networks on the IMC platform. The Wireless Services Manager adds wireless devices to the IMC network topology and allows you to configure and apply policies to these devices. You can configure WLANs and use radio frequency (RF) heat mapping to plan and adjust wireless coverage. The Wireless Services Manager also provides WLAN intrusion detection and defense.

HP IMC User Behavior Auditor Software Module

The User Behavior Auditor module allows you to audit the online behavior of internal users so that you can detect and eliminate internal security threats. Working with User Access Manager to track users' network behavior, User Behavior auditor module provides comprehensive log collection and audit functions. It supports various log formats, such as Network Address Translation (NAT), NetStreamV5, and DIG. The User Behavior Analysis Module provides logs for you to audit security-sensitive operations and to digest information from HyperText Transfer Protocol (HTTP), File Transfer Protocol (FTP), and Simple Network Management Protocol (SNMP) packets.

HP IMC Quality of Service Manager

The Quality of Service Manager gives you greater visibility into QoS configurations and allows greater control over them. It provides real-time QoS configuration detection, traffic classification options, automatic topology discovery, and functions to ensure that bandwidth is equitably distributed between stations. To help you manage the challenges of a converged network infrastructure, the Quality of Service Manager identifies network-wide QoS configurations, unifying the management of QoS policies.

In addition, you can monitor committed access rate (CAR), generic traffic shaping (GTS), priority marking, queue scheduling, and congestion avoidance. Armed with current and past trends, you can allocate network resources more efficiently. This module also includes the Service Level Agreement (SLA) Manager, which allows you to track, manage, and optimize services for your customers. You can verify service levels by leveraging synthetic testing instrumentation (network quality analysis or NQA) in the Comware series switches and routers and from third-party vendors (Cisco's IP SLA).

HP IMC Network Traffic Analyzer

NTA is a graphical network-monitoring tool that provides real-time information about users and applications consuming network bandwidth. You can use NTA to plan, monitor, enhance, and troubleshoot networks and to identify bottlenecks and apply corrective measures for enhanced throughput.

NTA also allows you to monitor Internet egress traffic, analyzing the bandwidth usage of specific applications and monitoring the impact of non-business applications (such as network games) on user productivity. In addition, NTA can help you to protect the network against virus attacks. It provides granular, network-wide surveillance of complex, multilayer switched and routed environments and helps you rapidly identify and resolve network threats.

HP IMC Service Operation Manager

Service Operation Manager is a comprehensive system to help you manage the entire IT life cycle, by providing services, such as policy design, network operation and improvement, in addition to recovery. Service Operation Manager is a real-time configuration management database, allowing you to manage assets, make configuration changes, recognize problems, and auto-generate a knowledge base. Service Operation Manager also includes a self-service feature, which helps end users to recognize network issues and to create and track service requests. With Service Operation Manager, your organization adheres to Information Technology Infrastructure Library (ITIL) v3.0.

HP IMC MPLS VPN Manager

MPLS VPN Manager automatically discovers VPNs and allows you to monitor and audit them. You can evaluate performance and manage the allocation of resources. It also contains a traffic engineering component that helps you to monitor an entire network and to deliver service quality by distributing suitable network resources, as needed.

HP IMC Endpoint Admission Defense

EAD helps protect networks from internal threats. It can prevent devices infected with malware from spreading the infection to other devices on the network. It can also help companies ensure that devices and applications are patched so that hackers cannot exploit these vulnerabilities.

To protect network devices, companies create a posture that defines the minimum requirements that endpoints must meet before accessing the network. IMC EAD then allows users to update their endpoint so that it is compliant. Note that, although both UAM and EAD are sold separately, EAD requires UAM. The reverse is not true, however. UAM does not require EAD.

HP IMC IPSec/VPN Manager

IPSec VPN Manager allows you to manage and monitor all aspects of IPsec VPNs. It is designed to reduce the complexity of configuring IPsec VPNs, allowing you to deploy them more quickly. It provides a graphical VPN topology, VPN channel status, and other configurable monitors. It also provides real-time and historic status information and performance metrics. In addition to providing VPN management capabilities, the IPSec VPN Manager notifies you of problems and helps you resolve them.

HP IMC User Access Manager

UAM allows you to translate business policies for access controls into network configurations. From a single management interface that is integrated into the IMC platform, you can create service policies and then apply those service policies to user accounts. These policies can be enforced no matter where and how users connect—whether through local Ethernet connections, wirelessly through APs, or remotely through a VPN.

The policies can be simple or complex. For example, the policies can simply permit authenticated users to connect without any further customization of their access. Or the policies can permit or deny access based on circumstances, such as login time, location, or device. This is especially important in environments that support "bring your own device" (BYOD) in their network infrastructure. Finally, the policies can modify access in a variety of ways, such as moving a user to the correct VLAN, applying a rate limit, or assigning resources using ACLs.

HP IMC Branch Intelligent Management Software

BIMS allows you to securely manage customer premise equipment (CPE) in WANs. It is based on the TR-069 protocol, which is used to enable communications between CPE and Auto-Configuration Servers. In addition, TR-069 incorporates management functions, including software management, status and performance monitoring, and diagnostic capabilities. BIMS allows you to configure resources, services, groups, and user rights. In addition, it provides alarms for significant events.

Licensing

HP IMC requires one license for each managed node. (A *node* is any networked device, like a server, PC, switch, router, firewall, or access point, among others.) The baseline IMC Enterprise license is 200 nodes; the baseline IMC Standard license is 100 nodes. You then have the option of adding licenses in 100-node, 500-node, 1,000-node, and 5,000-node increments. You cannot buy increments of 1-node licenses, but you need to purchase sufficient licenses to cover every node that IMC will manage. Alternatively, you can purchase an unlimited node license. IMC can support more than 10,000 devices.

Note

You can download a 60-day trial license version of IMC from HP's web site (www.hp.com/networking). After the 60 days, you need a valid license for your IMC product to continue functioning.

The HP IMC Basic Software Platform, the newest edition to IMC, is next-generation network management software with unified resource and device management. IMC Basic software is designed for simplicity and ease of use, and it offers many capabilities that make it an ideal choice for SMBs with small network environments that need single-pane-of-glass visibility into their network infrastructures. IMC Basic software supports the management of HP and third-party devices and is compatible with Microsoft Windows and Linux operating systems. The software has a maximum limit of 100 nodes and supports these features for small businesses:

- Centralized deployment for small network environments
- Integrated sFlow traffic monitoring
- Low maintenance costs and total cost of ownership (TCO)
- Detailed interface performance monitoring and management
- Flexible centralized reporting

HP has an upgrade license to upgrade from their end-of-sale (EOS) product, called ProCurve Manager Plus (PCM+), to IMC Basic.

HP IMC Installation

The following sections introduce you to the installation requirements (servers and clients) for IMC and the two main deployment options.

Installation: Server Hardware Requirements

Ensure that each computer on which you install the IMC platform meets the software and hardware requirements for the number of nodes you want to manage. For example, if you are using IMC to manage 200 nodes (and, therefore, have an IMC 5.2 SP1 200-node license), the *minimum* hardware requirements are listed in Table 15-1.

Table 15-1. Deployment requirements for IMC components

Minimum Hardware	Recommended Hardware
3.0 GHz Intel Xeon or Intel Core 2 Duo processor	3.0 GHz Intel Xeon or Intel Core 2 Duo processor or equivalent
4 GB RAM	6 GB RAM
80 GB storage	100 GB storage
10/100 network interface card (NIC)	10/100 NIC

Note

The more devices you manage, the more RAM you need on the server. For example, the requirements listed in Table 15-1 support between 200 and 500 devices. For 10,000 devices, you need, at minimum, 64 GB of RAM. Likewise, the more nodes you want to support, the more cores or processors and RAM that you need.

Installation: Server Software Requirements

Here is a detailed list of the operating systems supported by the IMC server component:

- Windows Server 2003 with Service Pack 2 (SP2)
- Windows Server 2003 x64 with SP2 and KB942288
- Windows Server 2003 R2 with SP2
- Windows Server 2003 R2 x64 with SP2 with KB942288
- Windows Server 2008 with SP2
- Windows Server 2008 x64 with SP2
- Windows Server 2008 R2 with SP1
- Windows Server 2008 R2 x64 with SP1
- Windows Server 2012 with KB2836988
- Red Hat Enterprise Linux 5
- Red Hat Enterprise Linux 5 x64
- Red Hat Enterprise Linux 5.5
- Red Hat Enterprise Linux 5.5 x64
- Red Hat Enterprise Linux 6.1 x64

The operating system can be run on a physical server or as a virtual machine, where VMware Workstation, VMware ESX Server, and Windows Server 2008 R2 with Hyper-V are officially supported.

Externally supported database products include the following:

- Microsoft SQL Server 2005, 2008, and 2012
- Oracle 11g (only Linux platforms)
- MySQL Enterprise Server 5.1 and 5.5

Note

HP strongly recommends that you deploy a 64-bit operating system. Otherwise, you are restricted to less than 4 GB of RAM, which greatly limits the number of nodes you can manage in IMC.

Installation: Client Requirements

HP IMC is managed using a web-based user-interface and requires a web browser for use. You can run IMC locally on the server with a supported web browser, or you can do it from your local desktop across the network. The requirements listed in Table 15-2 are for your local desktop.

Table 15-2. Client requirements for remotely accessing IMC

Component	Requirements
Hardware	Processor: Intel Pentium 4 2.0 GHz processor
	RAM: 2 GB
	Disk: 50 GB
Operating system	Windows XP, Windows Vista, or Windows 7
Web browser	Firefox 3.6+ or Internet Explorer 8.0+
	Java 6.1.10+

Note

HP IMC does not install any "special" client software on your desktop. However, there are certain requirements you need to meet on your desktop to access and use IMC. A different operating system or browser might successfully work, but HP only officially supports those listed in this book.

Deployment Options

HP IMC supports two types of installations:

- **Centralized**—All IMC components and add-on modules are installed and deployed on the same server.
- **Distributed**—All IMC components and add-on modules are installed on the master IMC server, but some components and modules are deployed on slave servers. The master server is the management center for IMC; slave servers are responsible for specific management tasks. You access the master server to complete all management tasks, and it interacts with slave servers, as needed, to manage the network.

If you are using the IMC platform but no other add-on modules, HP recommends that you use the centralized deployment. Otherwise, use the distributed installation, which is described in more depth in the next section.

For either centralized or distributed installations, IMC requires a database to store information about managed devices and users. The IMC Standard Edition ships with SQL Server, which you can install at the same time that you install IMC. However, this embedded database supports only a small network with a limited number of network devices. For most environments, you should use a separate database rather than the embedded database. (In fact, IMC Enterprise Edition does not support the embedded database.) When you install IMC, you provide details about the database server so that IMC can save information in the database and then retrieve it, as needed.

To complete a distributed installation, keep these requirements in mind:

- Master and slave IMC servers must use the same:
    - Operating system version
    - Database server
- Java Runtime Environment 6.0 installed on master and slave servers
- The following IMC platform components must be deployed on the master server:
    - Resource Manager
    - Data Analysis Manager
    - NE Manager
    - Report Manager
    - Security Control Center

All other IMC platform components can be distributed to slave servers. However, all components must first be installed on the master server, even if they will be deployed to slave servers.

The example in Figure 15-2 shows an IMC distributed installation. The IMC server is the master. The EAD, UAM, and Wireless Services Manager modules are installed on separate servers. To manage this network, you access the IMC master server. All of the capabilities offered by IMC, EAD, UAM, and Wireless Server Manager are available (if the modules are deployed properly).

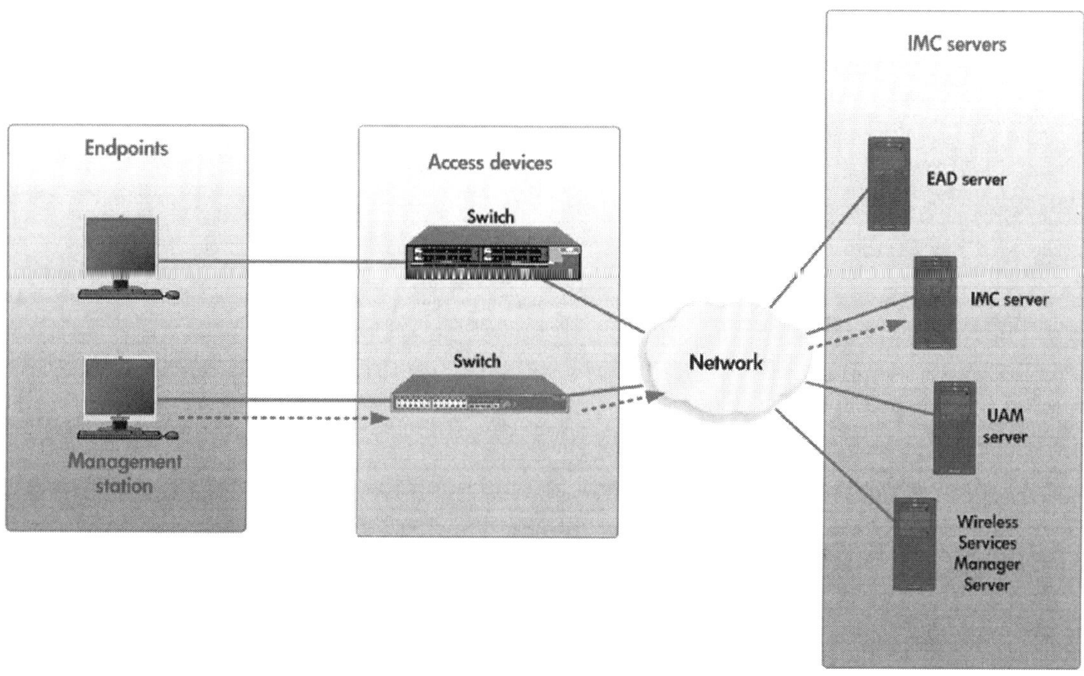

Figure 15-2. Distributed deployment option example

This example also shows a network with the access controlled through UAM, which is enforcing 802.1X authentication to ensure that only authorized users can access the network. After users are authenticated, UAM works with access devices to ensure that the users can access only the network resources they are authorized to use.

In addition, EAD is being used to scan authorized users' endpoints and to make sure that they meet the company's security policy. For example, the security policy may stipulate that endpoints must be running a certain version of antivirus software, antispyware, and hardware encryption software. The security may also require endpoints to have up-to-date patches installed.

Deployment Monitoring Agent

To help you monitor IMC and deploy the components and add-on modules, IMC includes a Deployment Monitoring Agent (DMA), shown in Figure 15-3. The agent allows you to perform tasks such as:

- Install the IMC server.
- Start and stop the IMC server.
- View the CPU usage and memory usage.
- Determine the status (starting, started, or stopped) of IMC processes.
- Deploy or delete components or add-on modules.

In addition, the DMA provides information about the server on which it is running. For example, it lists the amount of:

- Database space available and used.
- Log file space available and used.

The agent can provide details about the platform operating system and database used. For example, it might list the Windows Server 2008 R2 operating system and the Microsoft SQL Server 10.50.1600. The DMA is also used to back up the IMC install and database itself.

Note

You do not initially have to install any add-on modules—these can be added after the installation has been completed via the DMA.

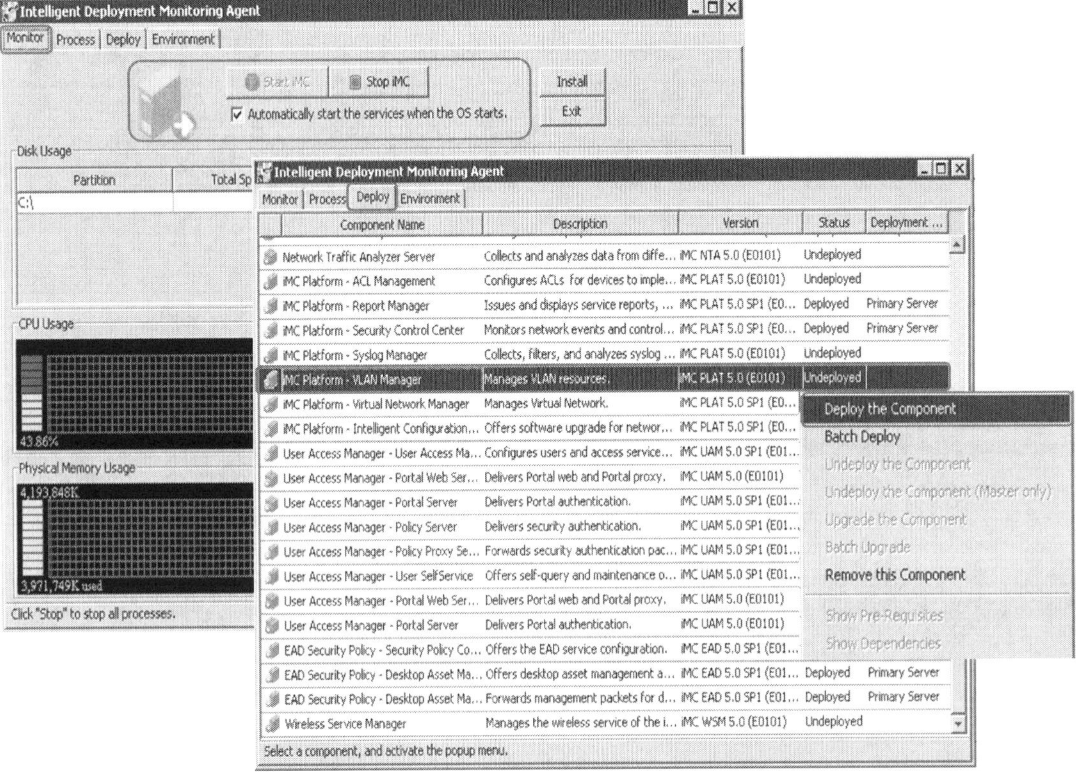

Figure 15-3. IMC Deployment Monitoring Agent

Port Usage

HP Networking recommends that you configure your firewall to control the data that can be sent to the IMC servers, thereby protecting the IMC server from attacks. Specifically, you should use the firewall to block non-service data. You should open the ports listed in Table 15-3. If you install add-on modules, check the installation guide and readme file to determine whether other ports must be opened to enable operation.

Table 15-3. IMC communications used through a firewall`

Port	Purpose
TCP 8025	TCP 8025 used for the IMC server shutdown command
TCP 9091	Monitoring port used by the IMC server
TCP 9044	Used for the command to shut down the IMC server
TCP 9055	Used for the command to shut down Deployment Monitoring Agent process
TCP 61616	HP Intelligent Resilient Framework (IRF) master-subordinate
TCP 61626	Communication to the IMC server and Deployment Monitoring Agent
UDP 161	Access network components through SNMP
UDP 162	Accept SNMP traps
TCP 22	SSH/Secure FTP (SFTP) port
TCP 20/21	FTP port
TCP 23	Telnet port
TCP 25	Simple Mail Transfer Protocol (SMTP)
ICMP	ICMP port, which the Resource Management Module uses to discover devices and to check their reliability
UDP 69	TFTP daemon
TCP 80	Used to launch the Web Management System
TCP 443	HTTPS port
TCP 514/515	IMC-specific syslog daemon
TCP/UDP 137	NetBIOS name resolution service port
TCP 8080	IMC-specific web server for HTTP
TCP 8443	IMC-specific web server for HTTPS
TCP 8800	IMC listening port
TCP 1433	SQL Server database listening port

In a distributed installation, you should also ensure that master and slave IMC servers can freely exchange IP packets.

Note

Some of the ports in Table 15-3 are used between IMC servers in a distributed implementation, but many are used to external devices, like the devices being managed by IMC. The problem with the latter is that you probably have a firewall or two between those devices and IMC and, to succeed, your firewall has to allow these ports through for communication between IMC and other devices.

In distributed deployments, an intermediate firewall might separate the IMC masters and slaves. The most common solution to this problem is to tunnel the IMC connections using Generic Route Encapsulation (GRE) or an IPsec site-to-site VPN between the locations and to "hide" these connections from the firewall. This makes the rule configuration much simpler on intermediate firewalls.

Access and Use IMC

The following sections briefly introduce how to access IMC, along with some basic navigation tasks. For more information on IMC, you can attend HP's week-long class, entitled "IMC Essentials for Network Administrators."

Accessing IMC

To remotely access IMC, enter the following URL in a supported web browser:

```
https://<<ip-address> | <hostname>>:8443/imc
```

If you are accessing IMC from the local server on which IMC is installed, enter the following URL in a supported web browser:

```
http://<<ip-address> | <hostname>>:8080/imc
```

Use a loopback IP address, local IP address, or a fully-qualified domain name. The first time you log in, enter *admin* as the username and *admin* as the password (see Figure 15-4). You should, of course, then change the default password.

Note

In newer versions of IMC, you can omit the "/imc" in the URL; however, in older versions, you must include it.

You must make sure that the IMC server has Java Runtime Environment 6.0+ installed. If you try to access the IMC login page and enter the default operator name and password but do not move beyond the login page, check the Java Runtime Environment version.

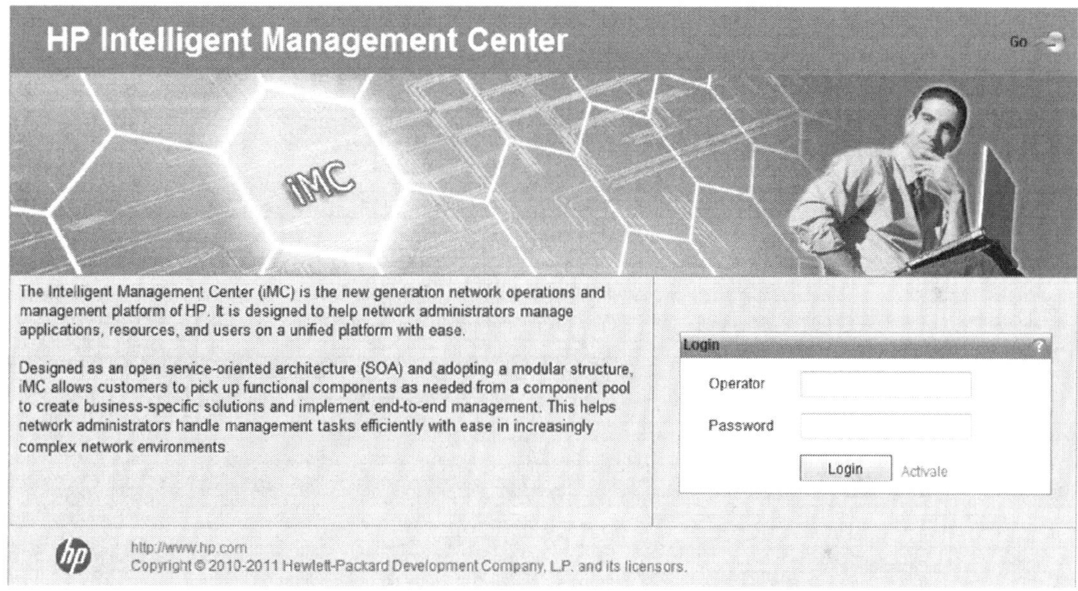

Figure 15-4. Accessing IMC

Operator Groups and Privileges

HP IMC supports different types of operator groups, allowing you to grant each operator only the rights needed to complete certain tasks. IMC provides three preconfigured operator groups (see Figure 15-5):

- **Administrator group**—Operators in this group have all rights to IMC. They can manage all users, including adding and deleting them. They can configure all network devices and view any information gathered and stored by IMC. Administrators have exclusive rights (rights that no other operator group has), including:
    - Operator management.
    - Device group management.
    - User group management.
    - Login control template management.
    - Password strategy management.
    - System parameter settings.

- **Maintainer group**—Operators in the maintainer group have rights to configure network devices and can complete most configuration tasks that IMC supports. However, they cannot perform tasks that require the exclusive rights assigned to the administrator group. In addition, operators in this group can view all information gathered and stored by IMC. This allows them to monitor key systems.
- **Viewer group**—As the name suggests, operators in the viewer group have access to information but cannot perform management tasks. This allows them to monitor systems, although they must notify a maintainer or administrator to remedy a problem.

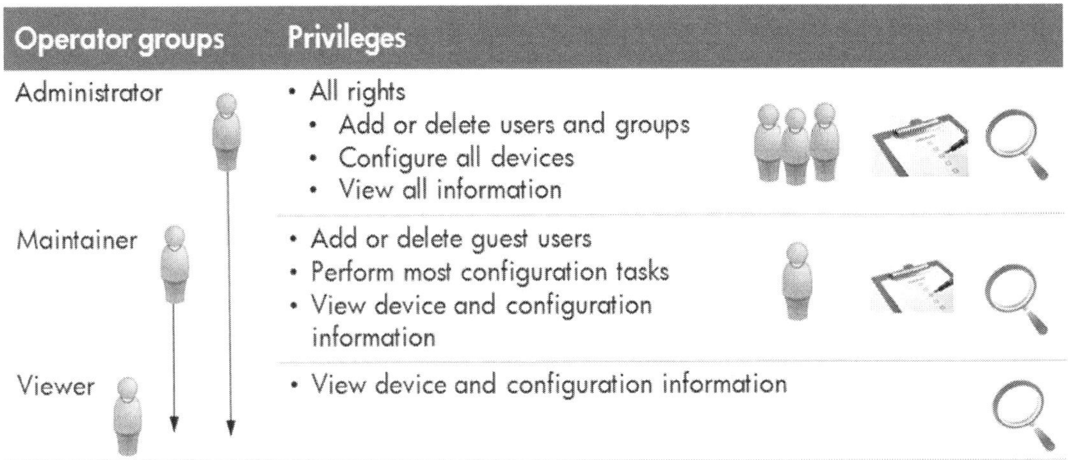

Figure 15-5. Operator groups and privileges in IMC

By default, IMC has one operator (or management user): admin is part of the administrator group. You can add operators and then assign them to one of the existing operator groups, or you can create a new operator group and customize the rights that operators in this group have. IMC gives you granular control over the rights you assign each operator group and the devices that they may access or manage. You also have several options for authenticating operators. You can configure a password in IMC, or you can authenticate users through a Remote Authentication Dial-In User Server (RADIUS) or Lightweight Directory Access Protocol (LDAP) server.

Device Discovery

The following sections cover the steps you go through in IMC to discover and import networking devices and their configurations.

Using Templates

The next several pages describe the basic steps to set IMC to discover devices that have been added to the network. The first step is to create an SNMP template with one of the following (see Figure 15-6):

- SNMPv2c community strings (read-only and read-write)
- SNMPv3 group, user, authentication, and encryption information

Normally, you use SNMPv2c to quickly import devices into IMC, since it is simpler to set up. However, after it has been imported, HP recommends that you change the devices' SNMP settings to use SNMPv3, preferably making the change in IMC and pushing it out to your networking devices. You can also set up templates for Telnet and/or SSH, which can be used by IMC to remotely log in to the networking devices to perform tasks that are not supported by the SNMP protocol.

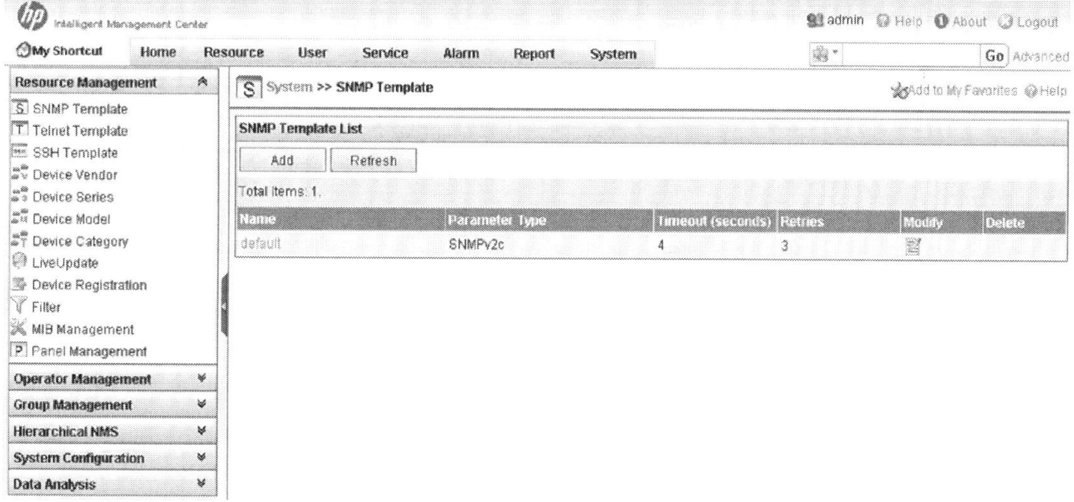

Figure 15-6. Adding an SNMP template: Step 1

For an SNMPv2c template, you need to give the template a name, specify the type (SNMPv2c), and identify the read-only and read-write community strings (see Figure 15-7). For an SNMPv3 template, you need to define the SNMPv3 group, user, authentication method (Message Digest 5 [MD5] or Secure Hash Algorithm [SHA]) and the authentication password (key), and the encryption method (Advanced Encryption Standard [AES], Data Encryption Standard [DES], or Triple DES [3DES]) and the encryption password (key).

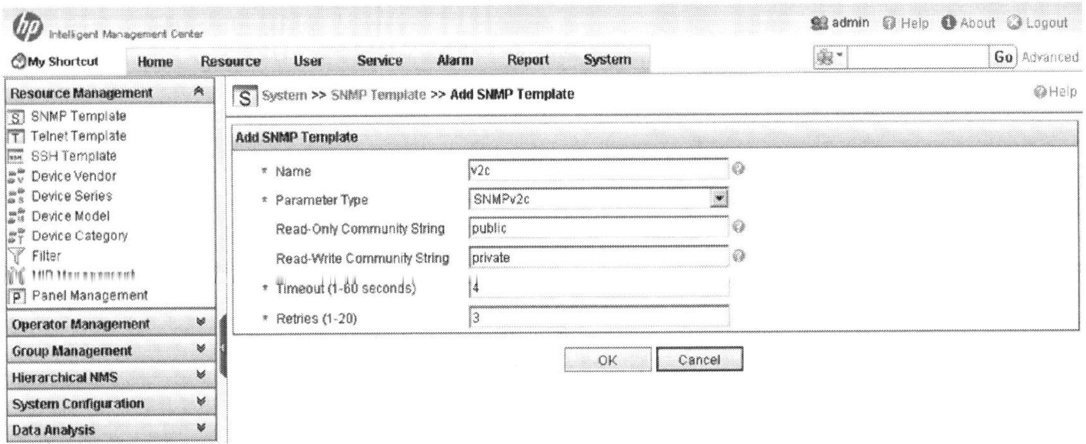

Figure 15-7. Adding an SNMP template: Step 2

Note

In most cases, you only want a very simple configuration on your networking devices—just enough so that IMC can quickly add them and start managing them. Therefore, even though you eventually want to use protocols like SSH and SNMPv3 on your networking devices, you initially configure them for SNMPv2c and Telnet, since that is a lot easier to initially set up. After you have imported the devices into IMC, you can then push your security changes to the managed devices. This ensures that what you define in IMC matches what ends up on the device. This book does not cover Telnet or SSH templates, but they are simple to configure.

Using Auto Discovery

HP IMC supports multiple modes of auto discovery, which determines how IMC searches for devices to import their configurations and settings. Here are the modes:

- **Routing-based**—IMC reads the routing table of a "seed" router and explores all of the nodes in all of the IP subnets discovered in the routing table.
  - **Pros**—Benefits include full automatic discovery of the network.
  - **Cons**—If the routing table is large, discovery could take hours or even days. Plus, if networks are missing from the routing table, these must be added manually.
  - **Recommendation**—Use when the network has very few subnets.

- **ARP-based**—IMC reads the ARP table of a "seed" device to find nodes.
  - **Pros**—The search is restricted to active devices of a local IP subnet as found on a routing switch (default gateway), so the search is quicker and typically captures most devices.
  - **Cons**—If devices are not active in IP, they are not be found in the routing table. Likewise, a distribution switch connected to many different VLANs might have a very large ARP table, which could cause the auto discovery process to take quite a long time.
  - **Recommendation**—Use for a quicker search.
- **IPSec VPN-based**—IMC scans the IP addresses on the remote end of an IPSec VPN.
  - **Pros**—The search focuses on remote devices related to IPSec VPNs.
  - **Cons**—It may be time consuming if you have a large hub-and-spoke, site-to-site topology.
  - **Recommendation**—Use if you have an IPsec site-to-site deployment.
- **Network Segment-based**—You enter specific ranges of IP addresses to reduce the scope of the IMC discovery process.
  - **Pros**—You can target the management VLAN IP subnets and specific addresses in your subnets where you are likely to have managed devices. (For example, your networking devices might be reserved to using the first 10 addresses in a subnet, so only have IMC scan the first 10 addresses instead of all of the addresses in a subnet.)
  - **Cons**—It requires more manual configuration.
  - **Recommendation**—Use with large networks or when the range of IP addresses of network devices is known. Use to decrease the discovery time.
- **Point-to-Point Protocol–based (PPP-based)**—You enter a specific seed device that uses the PPP.
  - **Pros**—You can target dialup devices and discover their remote peers.
  - **Cons**—Not many network deployments implement dialup or use the PPP (like remote access Layer 2 Tunneling Protocol [L2TP] VPNs).
  - **Recommendation**—Use with a large WAN comprised of dedicated circuits employing PPP as an encapsulation protocol.

All of these options are available if you choose the **Advanced** auto discovery (see Figure 15-8). With **Basic** auto discovery, it defaults to network segment-based. Even if you use an auto discovery process like routing-based, you can always complement it with network segment-based. In most cases, though, you control the auto discovery by using the network segment-based approach.

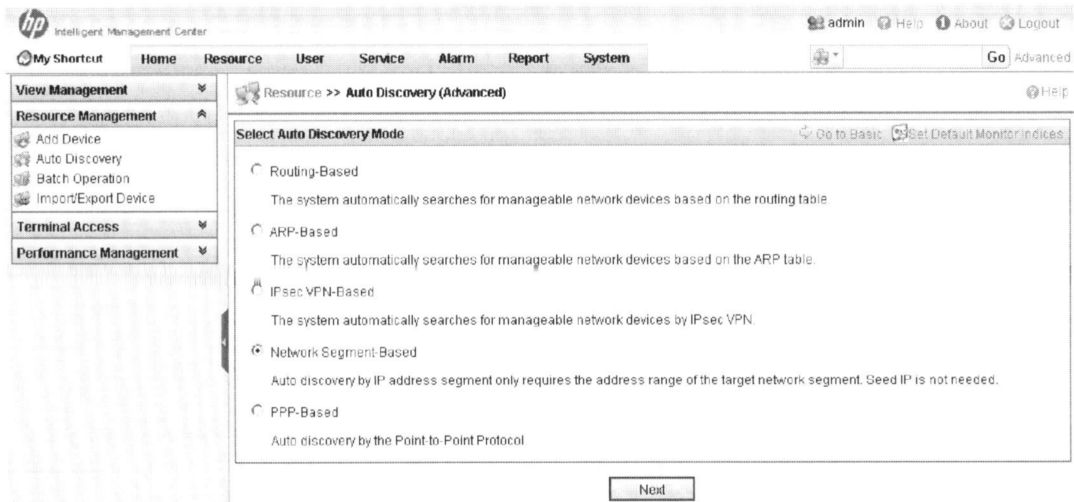

Figure 15-8. Advanced auto discovery

Figure 15-9 shows the IMC window on which you define network segment-based auto discovery. Configuration tasks for this window include:

- Configure a range of IP addresses to be discovered (required).
- If you want to use your devices' loopback interface IP address as the management address, select the check box.
- Select the **Automatically register to receive SNMP traps from supported devices** check box.
- Configure the type of remote access login: Telnet or SSH.
- Configure the SNMP parameters manually, or optionally specify the SNMP template to use (one of these to is required).
- Configure the parameters to log in via Telnet/SSH, or reference a Telnet or SSH template that has these properties defined (one of these two is required).

Please note that you either must use templates or specific configuration settings for SNMP and/or telnet/SSH during the intiial import. Templates are commonly used when importing many sets of devices with the same SNMP, telnet, and/or SSH settings.

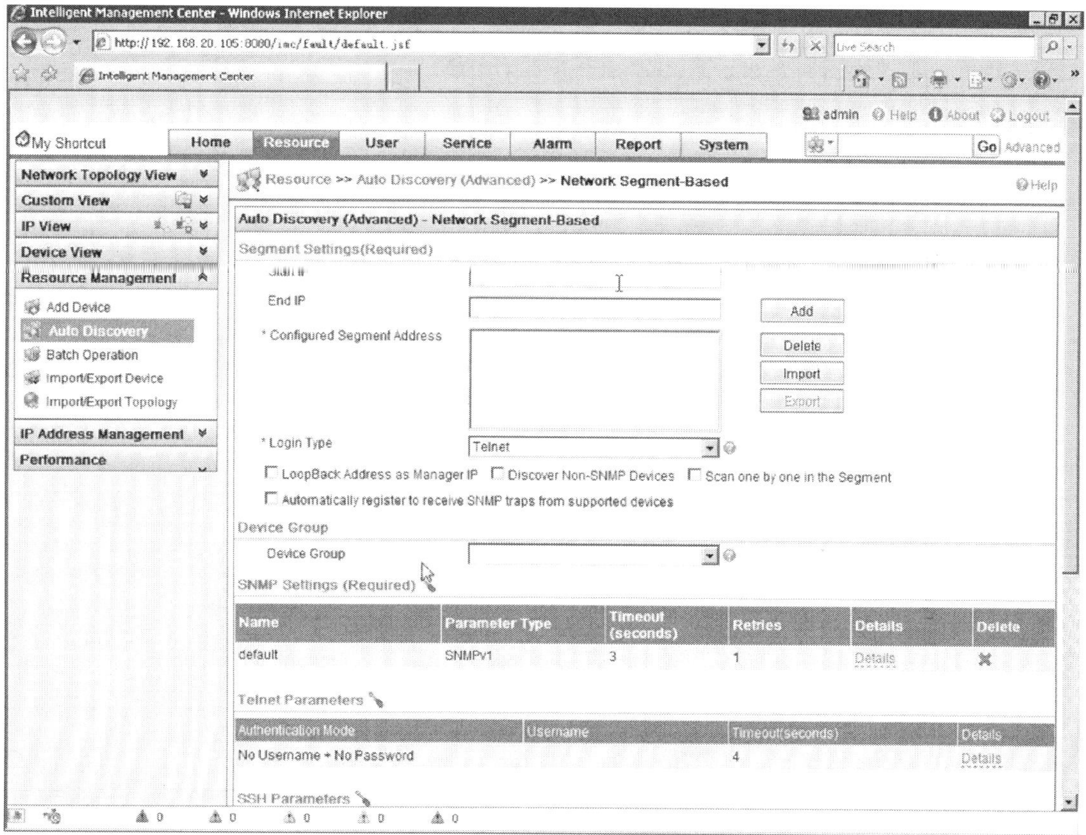

Figure 15-9. Network auto discovery approach

After you click the **Auto Discovery** button at the bottom of the page (not shown in Figure 15-9), auto discovery occurs. Optionally, you can schedule when this takes place. The type of discovery process used and the number of devices in your network affect how long the discovery process take—from minutes or hours to days. Using the network-segment approach is best, since you can slowly import devices in a large network in a controlled and manageable fashion. Figure 15-10 illustrates the discovery process as it occurs.

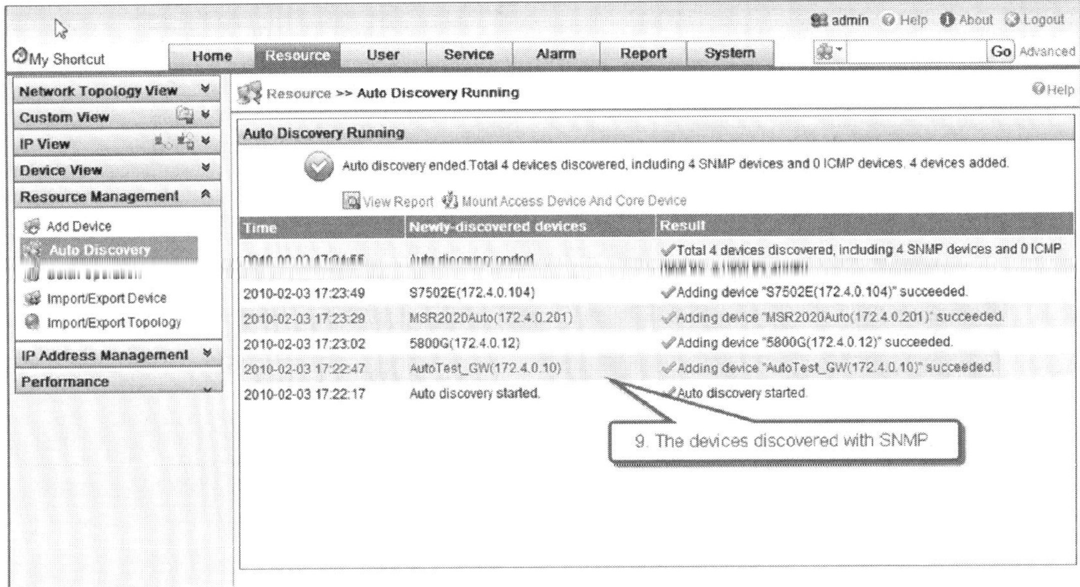

Figure 15-10. Network auto discovery status

HP Comware and HP ProVision Requirements

HP IMC is primarily an SNMP-based management product, with support for remote CLI access via Telnet and/or SSH for items that cannot be performed via SNMP. Therefore, for IMC to initially access the devices for remote management, you need to define the following on a HP Comware device:

- Define SNMP settings.
- Enable Telnet or SSH.
- Define the authentication mode and privilege level for the VTYs.

On a HP ProVision switch, you only need to define the SNMP settings: remember that, with ProVision switches, Telnet is enabled by default and no manager password is necessary.

Note

In most cases, to quickly discover and import the devices into IMC, you use SNMPv2c settings and Telnet with no authentication. This kind of configuration is simple on any networking device but is not secure. Obviously, you change this after you import the device into IMC by using IMC itself to make the changes, like disabling Telnet and enabling SSH, or changing from SNMPv2c to SNMPv3. You have IMC push these kinds of changes to the networking devices.

SNMP Activity

Here is a list of guidelines for this activity:

- You have a Comware and ProVision switch that IMC auto discovers.
- You use SNMPv2c, with a read community string of "public" and a write community string of "private."
- Telnet access is used initially for remote access, using no username or password.
- For the HP switches, make sure that the user logging in has the highest privilege level.
- Refer to "Chapter 4: Protecting Management Access," and create the necessary commands for the Comware and Provision switches.

Your goal is to refer back to Chapter 4 to create a simple configuration on a Comware and Provision switch that meets these requirements. Do not look at the next section, since it gives a sample answer. This activity is a good CLI review.

SNMP Activity Answer

Based on the requirements from the previous section, here is the configuration of the Comware switch:

```
[Comware] snmp-agent sys-info version v2c
[Comware] snmp-agent community write private
[Comware] snmp-agent community read public
[Comware] telnet server enable
[Comware] user-interface vty 0 4
[Comware-ui-vty0-4] authentication-mode none
[Comware-ui-vty0-4] user privilege level 3
```

Remember that Comware switches require that you enable Telnet or SSH and that you set up the VTYs. ProVision switches are simpler: Telnet is already enabled, and no passwords are required. Here is the configuration for a ProVision switch:

```
ProVision(config)# no snmp-server community public
ProVision(config)# snmp-server community private manager unrestricted
ProVision(config)# snmp-server community public operator unrestricted
```

Notice how simple the configuration is. Obviously, this configuration is not secure; however, the goal in using a network management tool like IMC is to make the device import process as simple and quick as possible. You would then use IMC to change the security settings, like converting the SNMP configuration from SNMPv2c to SNMPv3 and from Telnet to SSH.

Learning Check

The following questions help you measure your understanding of the material presented in this chapter. Read all of the choices carefully, since there may be more than one correct answer. Choose all correct answers for each question.

Questions

1. On which of the following operating systems can you not install IMC server?
   a. Windows 2003
   b. Windows 2008
   c. Red Hat Linux
   d. Ubuntu Linux
2. Which of the following are deployment options of IMC? (Choose two.)
   a. Distributed
   b. Hierarchical
   c. Centralized
   d. Master
   e. Tiered
   f. Slave
3. Which of the following are the default groups in IMC? (Choose three.)
   a. Administrator
   b. Maintainer
   c. Manager
   d. Operator
   e. Viewer
4. What URL would you use from your web browser if you were on the IMC server itself and wanted to access IMC locally?
5. List the default username and password that you use to log in to IMC after first installing it.
6. What is the most common auto discovery method used in IMC to import devices and their configurations?

Answers

1. ☑ **D** is correct. Ubuntu Linux is not supported by IMC.

   ☒ **A**, **B**, and **C** incorrect because they are supported by IMC .

2. ☑ **A** and **C** are correct. Distributed and centralized deployments are supported by IMC.

   ☒ **B**, **D**, **E**, and **F** incorrect because they are not deployment options for IMC.

3. ☑ **A**, **B**, and **E** are correct. Administrator, Maintainer, and Viewer are the three default groups in IMC.

   ☒ **C** and **D** incorrect because they are non-existent groups in IMC.

4. ☑ Use a URL of **http://127.0.0.1:8080/imc** to locally access IMC on the server on which it is installed.

5. ☑ Use the username *admin* and the password *admin* to initially log in to IMC.

6. ☑ The most common auto discovery method used in IMC is the **network segment-based** approach.

16 Basic Network Design Concepts

EXAM OBJECTIVES

In this chapter, you learn to:

- ✓ Describe and explain the most common layer media (Layer 1).
- ✓ Describe and explain the most common data link (Layer 2).
- ✓ Describe and explain the most common Ethernet concepts.
- ✓ Explain Layer 3 routing concepts and apply Layer 3 protocols.
- ✓ Describe the concept, benefits, and types of redundancy, and apply redundancy types.
- ✓ Identify, describe, and explain VLANs.
- ✓ Compare and contrast data center, campus LAN, and branch environments.
- ✓ Optimize small-to-medium-sized wireless, switched, and routed network infrastructures for small-to-medium-sized business (SMB) and commercial customers.

ASSUMED KNOWLEDGE

This chapter brings together a lot of the knowledge you that you have already gained from this book, focusing on the design aspects of building an SMB network. At this point, you should feel comfortable with the information discussed in these chapters:

- Chapter 6: VLANs
- Chapter 8: Introducing Spanning Tree
- Chapter 10: Link Aggregation
- Chapter 12: OSPF Operation and Configuration
- Chapter 13: HP Intelligent Resilient Framework

INTRODUCTION

This chapter introduces you to basic network design concepts. Many of the technologies seen in this chapter were discussed in previous chapters. This chapter builds on the earlier information—beyond gaining an understanding of the technologies. It looks at some of the best design guidelines and practices you should follow when deploying those technologies.

This chapter focuses on the following topics:

- Understanding the differences between the access, distribution, and core layers
- Comparing and contrasting a two-tier versus a three-tier design
- Choosing appropriate links for connections
- Implementing the appropriate redundant solution
- Understanding special IP addressing requirements
- Understanding good practices in Open Shortest Path First (OSPF) designs

Advanced design concepts are not discussed in this book; however, you can take HP's five-day Accredited Solutions Expert–level (ASE-level) Architect Certification course. Or you can read the HP Press book on best design practices, entitled *Architecting Open Standard HP Network Solutions*.

Design Model Layers

Most vendors in the industry commonly refer to a three-layer hierarchical model to help you design campus networks. HP and other vendors use this model to simplify designing, implementing, and managing large-scale networks. With traditional network designs, it was common practice to place the networking services at the center of the network and the users at the periphery. However, many things in networking have changed over the past decade, including advancements in applications, developments in graphical user interfaces (GUIs), the proliferation of multimedia applications, the explosion of the Internet, and fast-paced changes in your users' traffic patterns. The three-layer model has become the most commonly used to accommodate these rapid changes.

Three Design Layers

The hierarchical model, shown in Figure 16-1, contains three layers: core, distribution, and access. A well-designed network typically follows this topology. The following sections cover the functions of the three layers, including the devices that function at the various layers. As you will see, smaller networks do not necessarily have all three layers. However, the functions of the layers typically remain the same—whether you are designing a small, medium, large, or enterprise network.

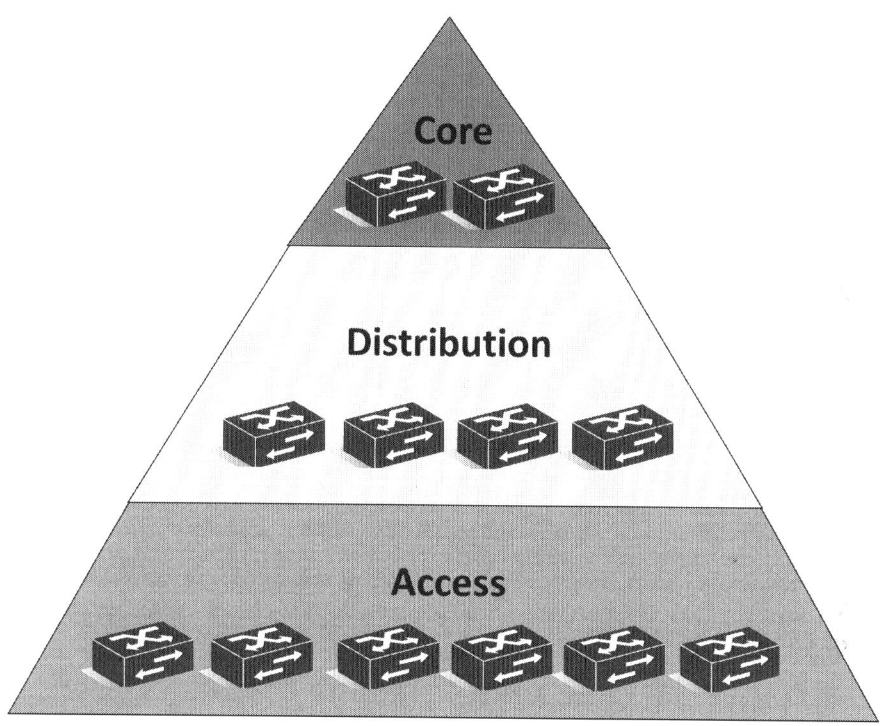

Figure 16-1. Layers found in a common design model

Core Layer

The *core layer*, as its name suggests, is the backbone of the network. It provides a high-speed connection between the different distribution layer devices. Because of the need for high-speed connections, the core consists of high-speed switches and does not, typically, perform any type of packet or frame manipulations, such as filtering or Quality of Service (QoS). Because switches are used at the core, the core is referred to as a *Layer 2 core*. However, if you are dealing with a large number of distribution layers that you need to connect to the core, the core might perform Layer 3 processing of traffic, like routing and QoS. The traffic that traverses the core is typically to access enterprise corporate resources: connections to the Internet, gateways, email servers, and corporate applications. These services are commonly found in a server farm in smaller networks or in a data center in larger networks. The server farm and data center commonly follow the same design practice, where these resources use an access or an access/distribution design.

Distribution (Aggregation) Layer

Of the three layers, the distribution layer, commonly called the *aggregation layer*, performs most of the connectivity tasks. In larger networks, routing switches or traditional routers are used at the distribution layer to connect the access layers to the core. For smaller networks, sometimes switches are used. The responsibilities of the distribution layer include the following:

- Containing broadcasts between the layers.
- Securing traffic between the layers.
- Providing a hierarchy through Layer 3 logical addressing and route summarization.
- Translating between different media types.

Routers or routing switches give you, by far, the most flexibility in enforcing your company's networking policies, since these Layer 3 devices deal with logical addresses. And, because routers and routing switches are used at the distribution layer, the implementation of most of your policies is done here.

Containing Broadcasts

One of the main functions of the distribution layer is to contain broadcast and multicast traffic that the access layer devices create. If a broadcast storm is created in one access layer, or if there is a large amount of multicast traffic from a real-time video stream, the distribution layer, by default, confines this traffic in the access layer and, therefore, prevents it from creating problems in other areas.

Providing Logical Addressing

Routers also provide for logical addressing of devices in your network. This makes it much easier to implement your networking policies, including filtering and QoS, since you control how addresses are assigned to machines. It is very difficult to do this with Layer 2 MAC addresses. Another advantage that logical addressing provides is that, again, with the correct address layout in your network, you should be able to create a highly scalable, hierarchical network. (IP addressing is not covered in this book.)

Performing Security

Another function of this layer is to enforce your security policies. Because switches are used at the core and access layers, Layer 3 security is not typically implemented at these layers, given the issues of filtering MAC addresses. Since routers deal with logical addresses, however, they make it much easier to implement your policies. Access control lists (ACLs), firewalls, and intrusion prevention systems (IPSs) are commonly used at this layer to enforce your security policies.

Connecting Different Media Types

If you have two different media types that you want to connect, a WAN T1 and Ethernet, for instance, a traditional router is the best solution. And, since routers are used at the distribution layer, this is where the media type conversion takes place.

Access Layer

The bottom layer of the three-layer hierarchical model is the *access layer*. Actually, the access layer is at the periphery of your campus network, separated from the core layer by the distribution layer. The main function of the access layer is to provide the user's initial connection to your network. Typically, this connection is provided by a switch or wireless access point. Sometimes, if the user works at a small branch office or home office, this device can also be a router or firewall. But, in most cases, the connection is typically provided by a switch. As more and more traditional Layer 2 switches support Layer 3 routing and ACL features, the access layer can be used to provide routing and security features at the edge or ingress to the network.

Two-Tier Model

The design of local area networks has evolved into a small number of logical layout models based on a single- or dual-root tree. The logical layout is conditioned by the physical layout—in other words, by the physical distribution of client workstations—a single-story building, a multistory building, or a campus—but, in general, these models apply.

In two-tier LAN models, all servers are connected directly to a switching layer called the *core layer*. This core layer can be made up of one or two interconnected switches, depending on the level of redundancy required. A second layer of switching is used to connect all clients and is called the *access layer*. The set of all access switches is sometimes called the *edge*. In the case of a single switch core (top of Figure 16-2), each access switch is directly connected to this core switch and, in the case of a core with two interconnected switches (bottom of Figure 16-2), each access switch is connected to each of them (dual-homed). Two-tier models are mostly used when designing a single building network, like in Figure 16-3.

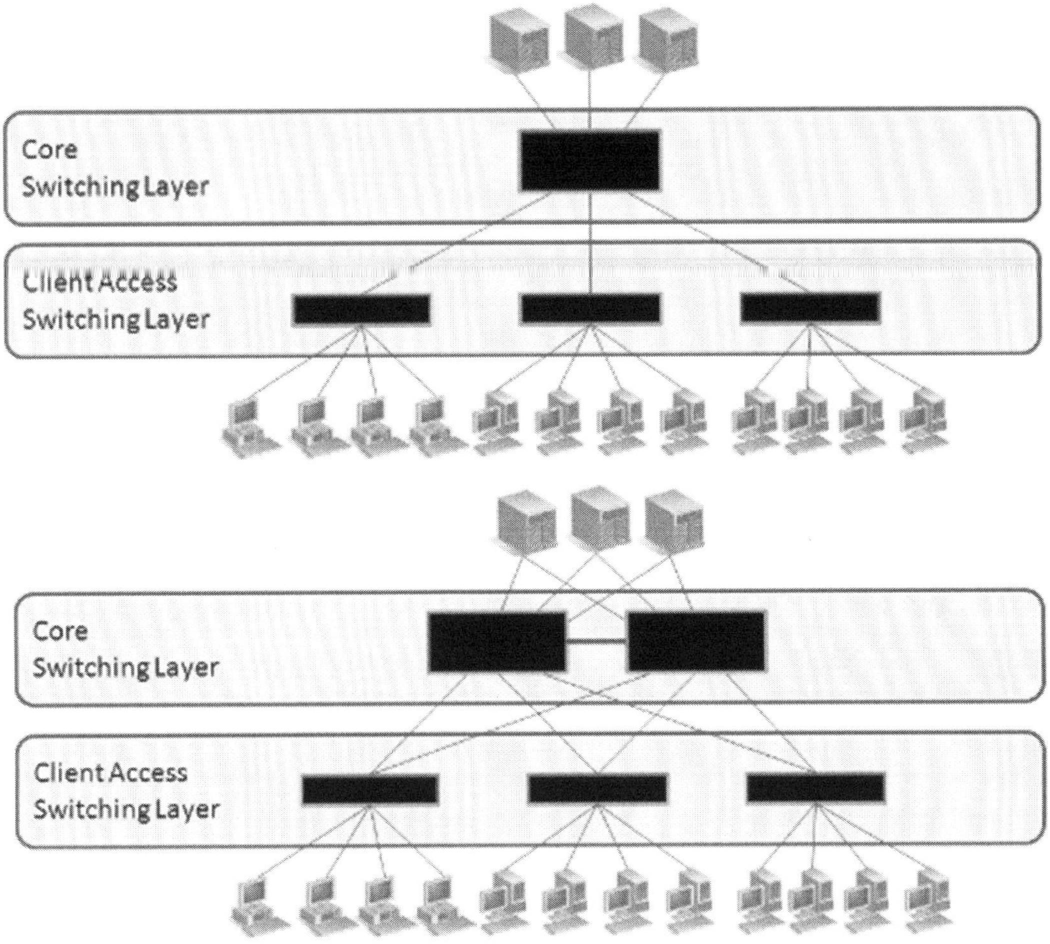

Core
Switching Layer

Client Access
Switching Layer

Core
Switching Layer

Client Access
Switching Layer

Figure 16-2. Examples of two-tier models

Figure 16-3. Example of a two-tier model

Three-Tier Model

In the case of campuses, the topology (layout model) of each building is composed of two switching layers, but all of the servers are located in a dedicated facility (server room), so an additional tier is required (see Figure 16-4). Again, the servers are connected directly to the core switching layer, and all of the clients are connected to the access switches. In between, an aggregation layer (also called a *distribution layer*) connects the edge to the core.

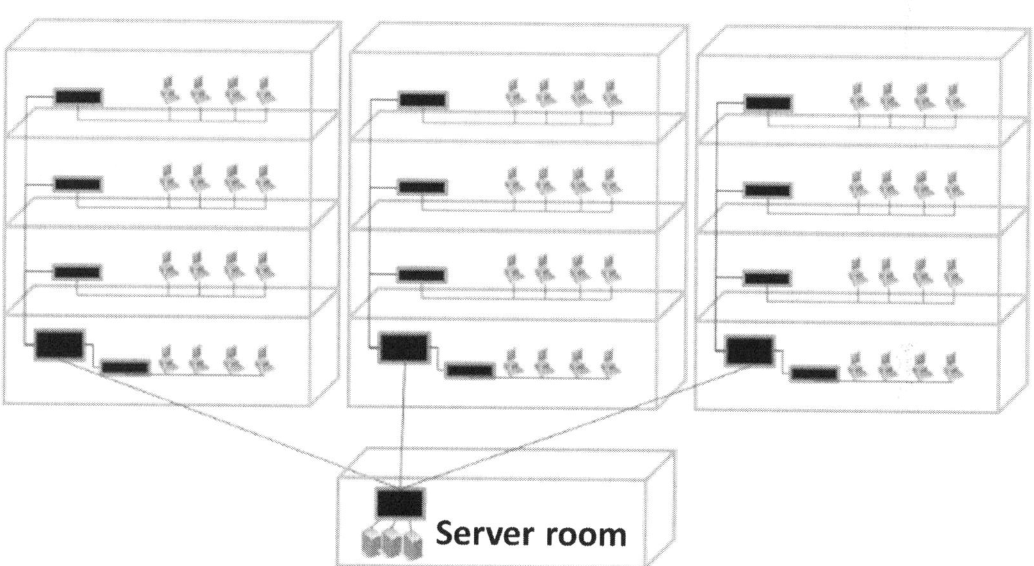

Figure 16-4. Three-tier model design

Figure 16-5 shows two implementations of three-tier designs. The one on the top is using a single root device at each layer, so no hardware redundancy is implemented. The network shown on the bottom has dual roots at each layer, allowing for hardware redundancy.

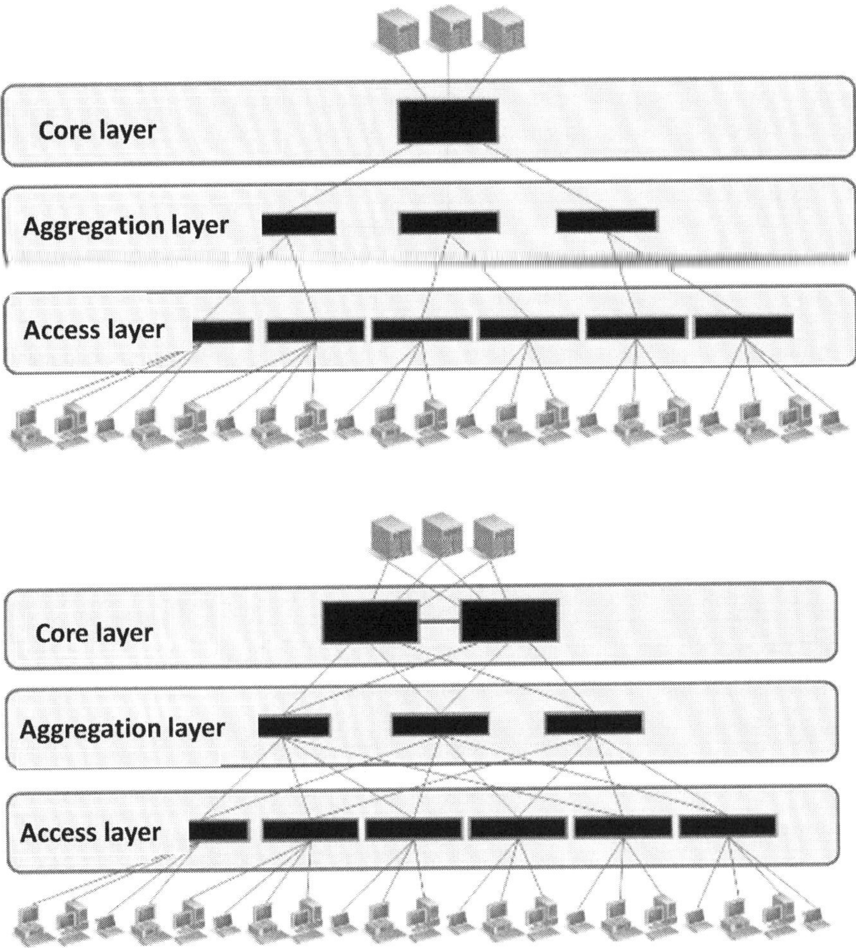

Figure 16-5. Implementations of three-tier design models

Model Comparisons

A LAN covering a campus is basically a set of interconnected devices that transport traffic:

- Between clients and servers in traditional business applications (including between internal clients and Internet services).
- Between clients in collaboration applications.

Figure 16-6 compares the two- and three-tier model designs. The left side illustrates a traditional three-tier design, and the middle and left designs leverage HP Intelligent Resilient Framework (IRF) technology.

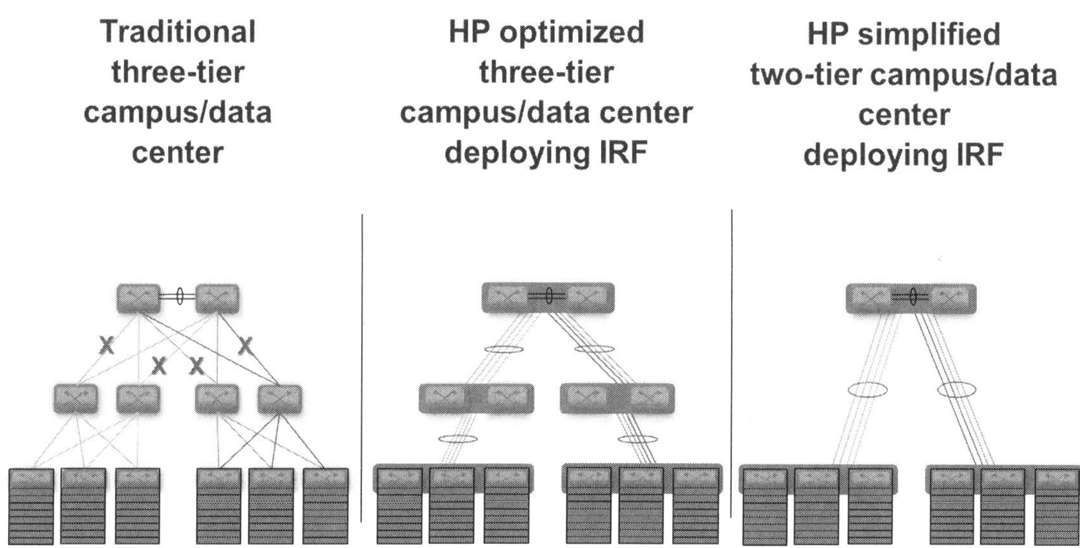

Figure 16-6. Two- and three-tier model comparison

Currently, the optimal models for a campus LAN are based on a structured, multitier approach (see Figure 16-7).

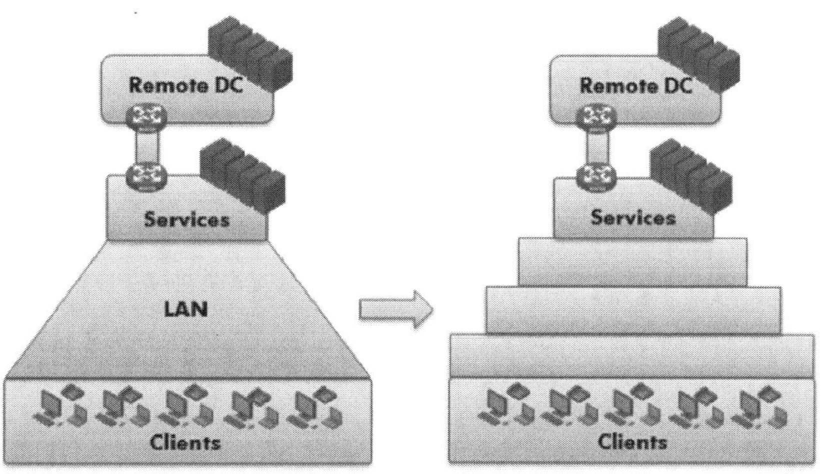

Figure 16-7. Multitiered campus network

In the simplest one-tier LAN, a single switch (or switch fabric) connects clients to servers and services. This model is usually applied to small and medium-sized branches. However, in medium-to-large campuses, one switching layer is usually not enough.

Using HP technologies, a two-tier model can be applied to most campuses (see Figure 16-8 and Figure 16-9). In a two-tier LAN, all client devices connect to the client access layer and a core layer connects the client access switches to the services. There are cases, however, especially in multibuilding campuses, in which an additional layer is required between the core and the access layers. This additional layer is called the *aggregation* or *distribution layer* (see Figure 16-8).

Note

It is important to note that, in the case of a local data center or server farm, the services part of the network can also be structured and multitiered. For example, the servers can be connected to a server access layer that is itself connected to the LAN core.

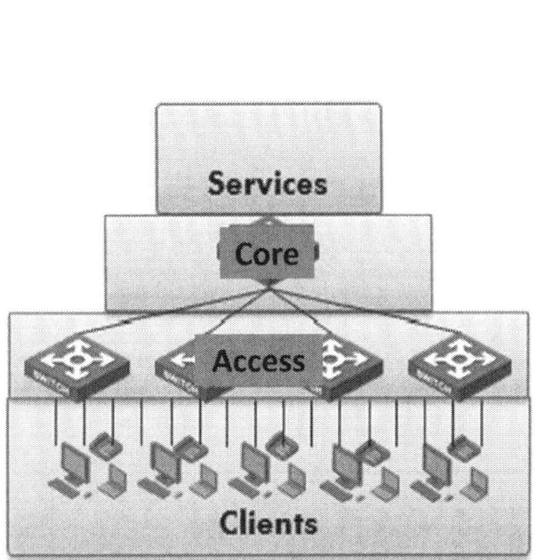

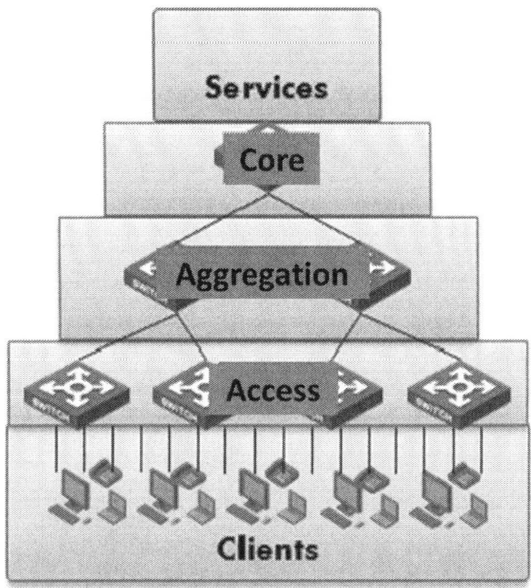

Figure 16-8. Two- and three-tier LANs

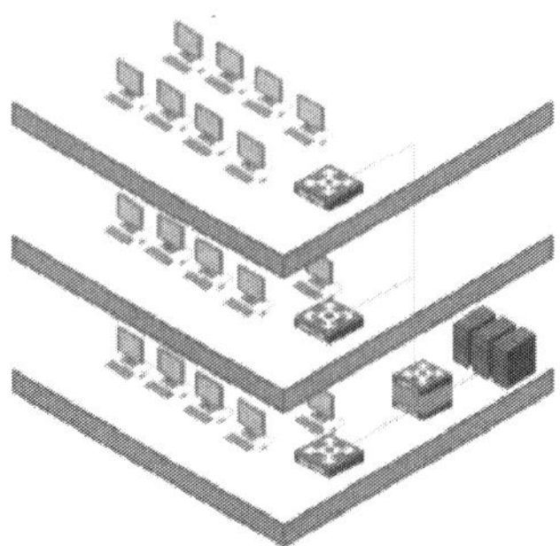

Figure 16-9. Two-tier design

However, the actual design must be analyzed on a case-by-case basis. In some cases, a single building requires (or a few remote buildings require) an aggregation switch, yet the rest of the LAN requires only two tiers. In others, the size of a building leads to adding aggregation switches. And, in some multibuilding situations, multiple fibers run between buildings. In these cases, the aggregation layer is not required, especially when the buildings have a small number of clients and, as a consequence, a small number of access switches.

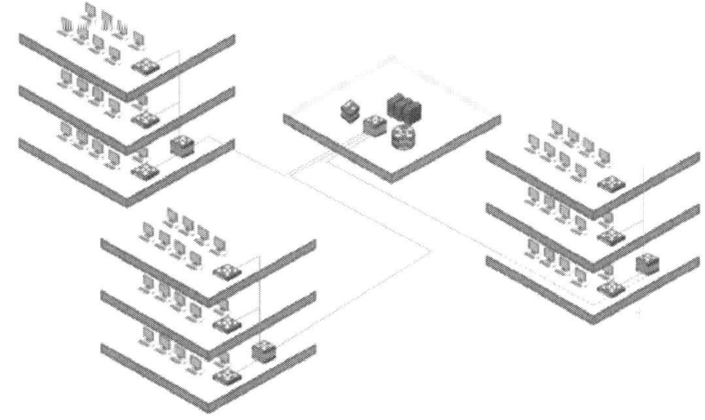

Figure 16-10. Three-tier design

Layer Requirements

The access layer is composed of switches to which the client devices are connected. Access switches connect to the next layer (core or aggregation) by means of *uplink ports*. Client devices are mostly PCs and IP phones. In many cases, WLAN access points are also connected to the access switches.

Additionally, surveillance cameras and other endpoint devices can be connected. Access switches may be required to offer some of the following features:

- A balanced relation between the number and speed of the access ports and the uplink ports
- VLANs, including MAC-based and voice VLANs for endpoint devices
- IP routing
- Internet Gateway Management Protocol (IGMP) snooping or multicast routing
- QoS boundary node features, like traffic classification, remarking, and prioritization
- Power over Ethernet (PoE) or Power over Ethernet Plus (PoE+) for IP phones, access points, and IP cameras
- Security via access control
- Link layer detection protocol (LLDP) for discovery of IP phones and other peripherals

In cases where this layer is present, most of the routing is provided here. Aggregation switches may also be used to host service modules, like WLAN controllers. Requirements for aggregation layer switches may be:

- High-speed switching and routing.
- Similar bandwidth toward the access and the core layers.
- High availability.

Specific core layer requirements are:

- High port density.
- High-speed routing and switching.
- High availability.
- Direct current power (in some cases).

Two-Tier Physical Infrastructure Models

There are three types of two-tier models:

1. Non-redundant (see Figure 16-11):
    - These are composed of a single core switch connected to all access switches.
    - If there is a need for uplink redundancy, 802.3 Link Aggregation Control Protocol (LACP) can be used.
    - Switches at the two tiers can use internal redundancy, such as redundant management, fabric, and power, providing a reasonable amount of redundancy.
2. Traditional redundant core and uplinks (see Figure 16-12):
    - Add another core switch interconnected to the first by a high-speed link.
    - Have two uplinks per access switch, creating a dual-homed access layer.
    - If there is also a service access layer, these switches are also dual-homed.
    - If there are servers directly connected to the core, they are dual-homed.
3. HP Optimized/fully redundant (see Figure 16-13):
    - Switch and link aggregation is implemented to achieve full redundancy, fault tolerance, and load-balancing with active-active links and devices.
        - Layer 2 redundancy is provided by the link aggregation groups.
        - Layer 3 redundancy is provided by the internal mechanisms of the HP ProVision Meshed Stacking or HP Comware IRF technology.

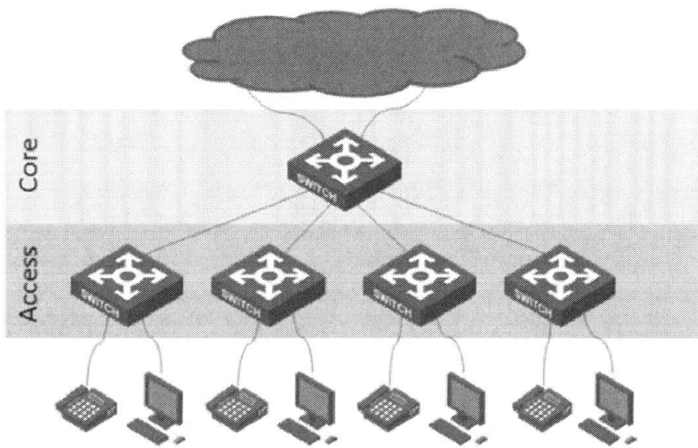

Figure 16-11. Non-redundant two-tier design

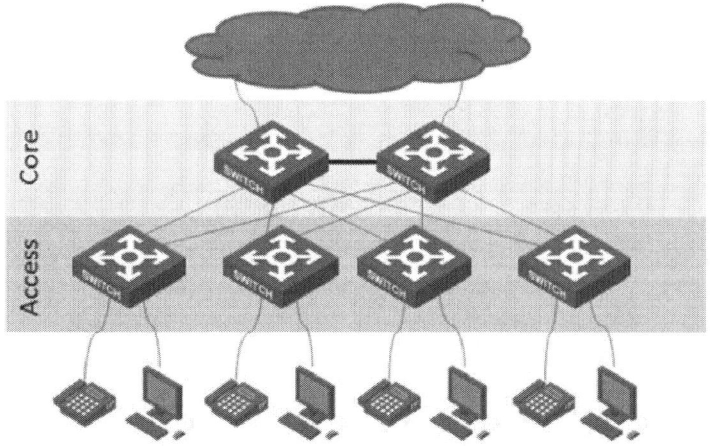

Figure 16-12. Traditional two-tier LAN with redundant core and uplinks

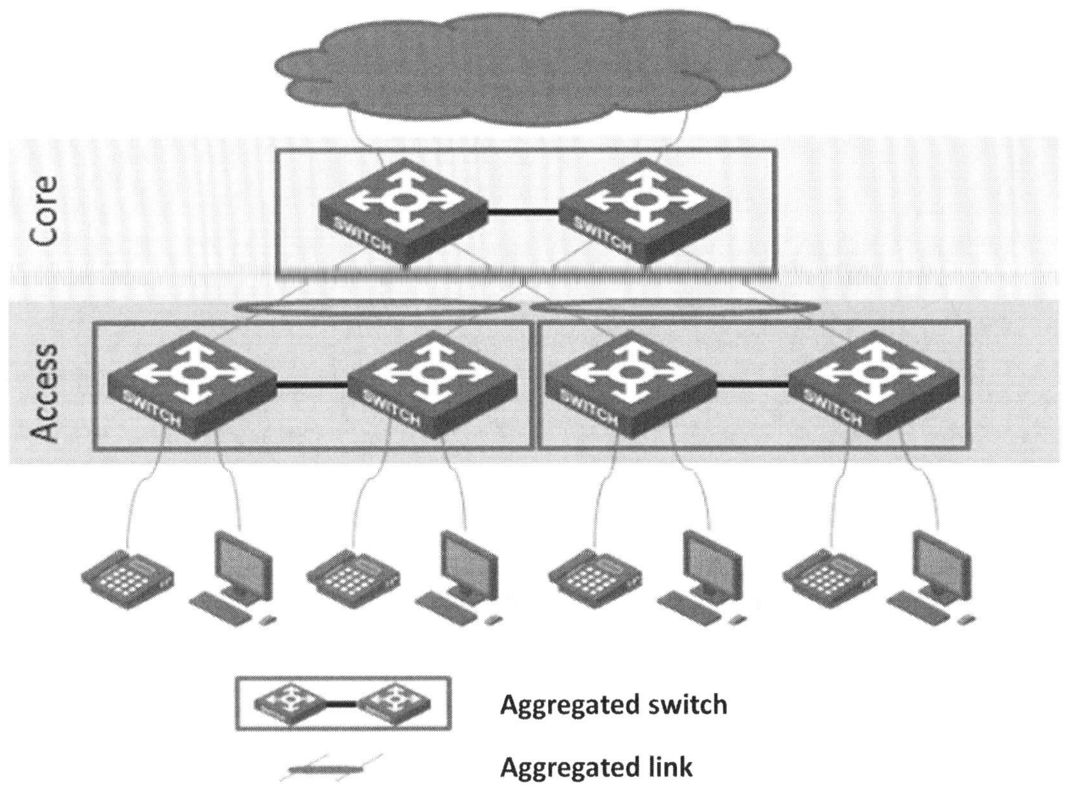

Figure 16-13. HP Optimized two-tier design

Three-Tier Physical Infrastructure Models

There are four types of three-tier models:

- Non-redundant (see Figure 16-14):
    - Switches in each layer have a single link to switches in the adjacent layers.
    - If there is a need for the inter-switch links to be redundant, 802.3 link aggregation can be used.
    - Switches in each layer can have internal redundancy, such as redundant management, fabric, and power, providing a reasonable amount of redundancy against failure.
- Redundant core and aggregation layer uplinks (see Figure 16-15):
    - Aggregation layer switches are dual-homed.

- Redundant core and aggregation layer with redundant uplinks (see Figure 16-16):
  - Pairs of aggregation switches are interconnected by high-speed links.
  - Access switches are connected to each one of the switches in the aggregation layer pair.
  - Each switch in the aggregation layer pair is connected to each core switch.
- HP Optimized/fully redundant (see Figure 16-17):
  - Switch and link aggregation is implemented to achieve full redundancy, fault tolerance, and load-balancing with active-active links and devices.
    - Layer 2 redundancy is provided by the link aggregation groups.
    - Layer 3 redundancy is provided by the internal mechanisms of the HP Meshed Stacking technology.

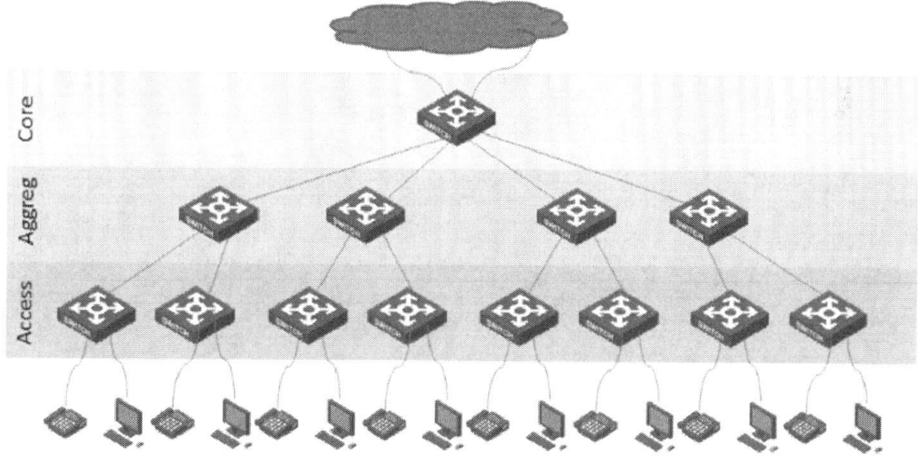

Figure 16-14. Non-redundant three-tier LAN design

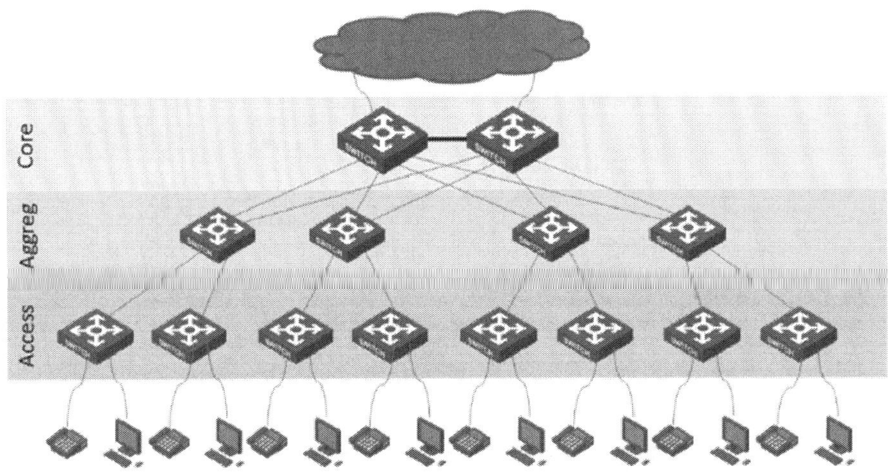

Figure 16-15. Traditional LAN design with redundant core

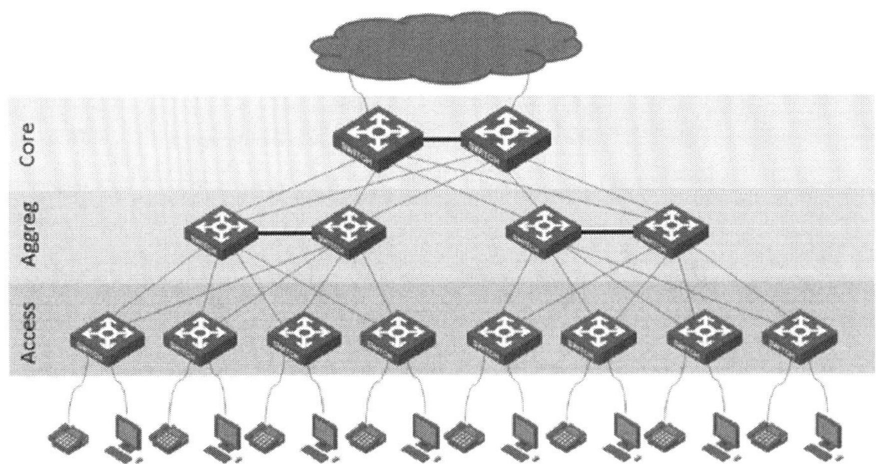

Figure 16-16. Traditional LAN design with redundant core and aggregation layer

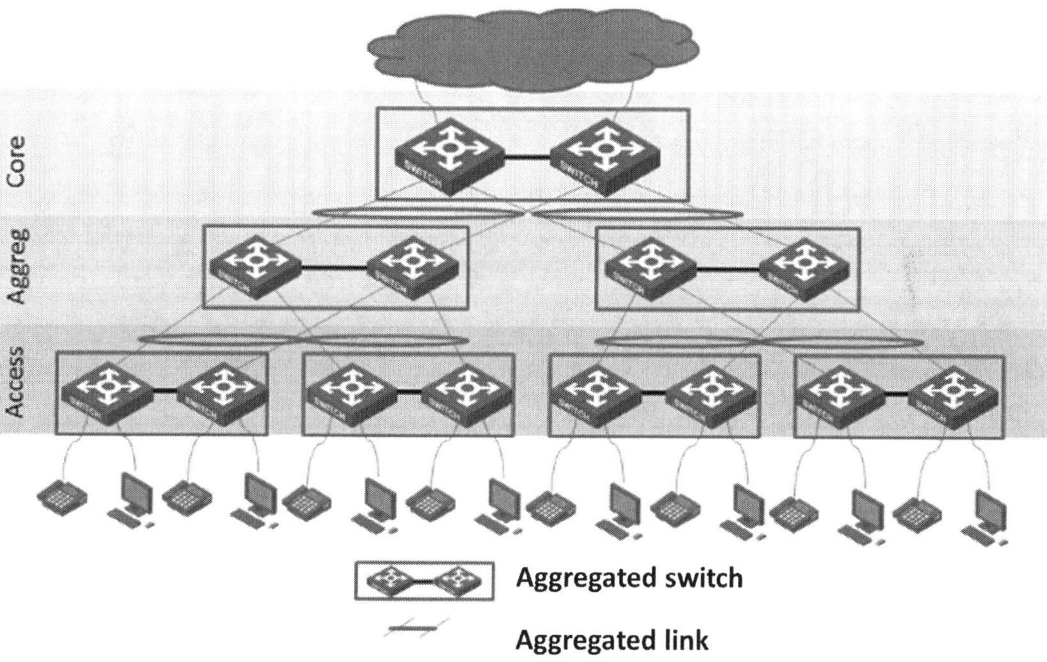

Figure 16-17. HP Optimized three-tier LAN design

Additional Layers

Actual LANs may require additional layers, especially on the server side. Before getting into the details, it is important to understand that the server area actually includes not only servers but also services: application servers, storage servers, Internet access, WANs, virtual private networks (VPNs), and more. If the number of links between the core and the services is too large, an additional server access layer and even a server aggregation layer can be required. In the case of medium-to-large data centers, this area can become especially complex and can require its own set of design criteria. (These criteria are not covered in this book.)

It is not always obvious where to connect the different services. Wireless access points, for instance, can be connected either to the aggregation switches or, most commonly, to the edge. On the other hand, WAN routers and Internet firewalls can be connected directly to the core or to an aggregation (client or server aggregation) switch.

Link Design

This step has two phases:

- **Phase 1**—Bandwidth requirements
- **Phase 2**—Length and media type, based on distances for the connections

In Phase 1, bandwidth requirements are considered and applied. In Phase 2, distances (link lengths) are added to determine the types of links (in terms of speed and media) needed for each connection. The following sections cover these topics in more detail.

Phase 1: Bandwidth Requirements

This section focuses on bandwidth requirements of the three different layers: access, distribution (aggregation), and core.

Access Layer

Since a vast majority of traffic is generated by client requests, to establish the bandwidth requirements, the edge must be considered as the starting point. Today, most client workstations (PCs and laptops) are equipped with a GbE interface. So *access* switches are typically gigabit switches. The first difficult decision must be made when choosing the *uplinks*—links that connect the access switches to the next layer (aggregation or core, depending on the number of tiers).

At first glance, if the access switch is connected to *N* gigabit clients, the bandwidth of its uplink must be N gigabits per second. But this assumes that all clients are both sending and receiving at maximum speed all the time, and that is never the case. So the necessary decision is, "What is the right oversubscription rate of the uplink?" Oversubscription normally ranges between 2:1 and 24:1 rates, but it could be higher (like 48:1) in certain situations. In most cases, a 10:1 rate is enough.

If a more refined estimate is needed, client traffic patterns must be considered. Fortunately the client traffic patterns can be estimated and measured. They depend heavily on which applications are used by the client and on the application usage pattern. For example, how often does the application need to send a request to the server, and what is the average amount of traffic generated by the request (and in which direction), and, finally, how much time does the client use each application?

To simplify this estimation, clients can be categorized and grouped in client profiles. For example, Human Resources (HR) users may have a different profile than software developers. These patterns give an average utilization percentage of the client's access links. By adding the usage percentage of all clients connected to the access switch (Sum [utilization %]), the uplink bandwidth requirement can be calculated. One benefit of using these patterns to estimate bandwidth requirements is that all manageable switches offer a per-port statistic on the link usage, mostly as a percentage of the total port's bandwidth, and these estimates can be tested and monitored.

Distribution Layer

In this layer, the oversubscription rate between the access-distribution links and the distribution-core link cannot be too large. A rate of 2:1 (but not much more) is usually acceptable. At this point, link aggregation may need to be considered and the number of aggregation switches may need to be reviewed to reduce the oversubscription rate.

Core Layer

Because of its position, oversubscription in the core is not acceptable. The rate between the sum of bandwidth of all client-side and all server-side links must be 1:1.

At the core, the question becomes, "How is the traffic distributed on the server-side?" Or, in other words, "What percentage of the total traffic goes to and comes from each server/service?" This distribution is determined by the applications. The type of links which are required also needs to be determined. Some servers may need a 10GbE link, and others would work perfectly with a gigabit link. An example of the latter would be the case of the Internet firewall connection.

Phase 2: Media and Length

After the bandwidth requirement of each link has been established, the link's length comes into play to determine the media required. Note that, in some cases, the media depends not only on the length but also on the environment. For instance, inter-building links should be fiber—not copper—to avoid weather- and electrical ground-related issues. Security is also another consideration in choosing media type. For example, fiber is not as susceptible to eavesdropping as copper media. The final result of this step is to put together all of the link types needed at each switch to decide the port configuration that each one of them needs.

Table 16-1 displays the standard distance limitations, based on the respective cable. Here is an explanation of some of the acronyms used in this table:

- **MMF**—Multi-mode fiber
- **SMF**—Single-mode fiber
- **nm**—Nanometer
- **m**—Meter
- **CWDM**—Conventional/coarse wave division multiplexing

This is not to say that every vendor's products support all of these standards, but at least you have an idea of the kinds of media you need to be looking at, based on your speed and distance requirements for a particular link.

Table 16-1. Cables and distance limitations

Standard	Media	Distance	Fiber wavelength
10Base-T	Cat-3 (2-pair)	100m	N/A
100Base-T	Cat-5 (2-pair)	100m	N/A
1000Base-T	Cat-5 (4-pair) or Cat-5e	100m	N/A
1000Base-TX	Cat-6 or Cat-7	100m	N/A
100Base-FX	62.5µm MMF	2km	1300nm
1000Base-SX	62.5µm MMF	220m	850nm
1000Base-SX	50µm MMF	500m	850nm
1000Base-LH	50µm MMF or SMF	550m-10km	1310nm
1000Base-LX	62.5µm MMF	550m	1310nm
1000Base-LX	50µm MMF	550m	1310nm
1000Base-ZX	SMF	70km	1550nm
10GBase-SR	62.5µm MMF	26-82m	850nm
10GBase-LRM	62.5µm MMF	2250m	1310nm
10GBase-LX4	62.5µm MMF	300m	1300nm CWDM
10GBase-SR	50µm OM3	300m	850nm
10GBase-LRM	50µm OM3	260m	1310nm
10GBase-LX4	50µm OM3	300m	1300nm CWDM
10GBase-LR	SMF	10-15km	1310nm
10GBase-LX4	SMF	10km	1310nm CWDM
10GBase-ER	SMF	40km	1550nm
10GBase-ZR	SMF	80-120km	1550nm
10GBase-T	Cat-5e, Cat6, Cat6a	45, 55, 100m	N/A

When designing aggregated links, in addition to bandwidth, the most important consideration is the load-sharing algorithm. The default for most switches is to apply a hashing algorithm to a combination of the source and destination MAC address. In an inter-switch link, if both switches are routing, all packets (in one direction) use the same source and the same destination MAC address. In this case, all frames will be transmitted through the same physical port and link aggregation has no effect.

To avoid this situation, many switches offer the option of changing the parameters of the hashing algorithm. Layer 3/Layer 4 load-sharing must be implemented, where available, to utilize the source and destination IP addresses or TCP/UDP port numbers to distribute load across routed physical links. This fact must be considered during the design stage and before the switches are chosen.

VLAN Design

The most common VLAN design criterion is broadcast traffic in a flat LAN, where all switches forward according to Layer 2 addresses (broadcasts travel everywhere). In other words, the whole LAN is a single broadcast domain. This is an important issue because, if a broadcast is, for example, a (very conservative) 1 percent of the total traffic, the LAN can be forwarding well over 100Mbps of broadcasts. These broadcasts congest smaller links, so WLANs, Internet firewall links, client access links, and those to servers may be overloaded. The solution is to divide the LAN into smaller and sometimes dedicated broadcast domains. This was the purpose of the IEEE 802.1Q standard.

A second reason for VLANs is security: it is simpler to control/filter traffic between VLANs than in a flat network (see the fourth and sixth rules, below).

Some basic rules can be established when designing a VLAN solution:

- The number of wired clients per VLAN must be kept below a certain number. This number depends on the applications, and it varies between 100 and 200 workstations.
- If Voice-over Internet Protocol (VoIP)/IP telephony is implemented, a dedicated voice-VLAN is recommended and all IP phones and PSTN gateways must be connected to it. This configuration prevents the need for multicast routing in the LAN.
- If possible, network printers should be in the same VLAN as their clients.
- Guest clients must be connected automatically to a guest VLAN that is isolated from the rest of the network and that only provides hospitality services. If a guest VLAN is not configured, unknown devices present a security risk unless denied access to the network.
- Wi-Fi access points need a VLAN that is not shared with wired clients and servers. In most cases, a single VLAN would work for up to a 100 APs. Today's access points (APs) can associate service set identifiers (SSIDs) to different VLANs, and wireless clients with different security clearance levels can be connected to different VLANs. For example, this feature can be combined with the fourth rule for guest client devices.
- ACLs, firewalls, IPSs, and other security devices and features can be implemented at the VLAN boundary to enforce protection.

Port-Based VLANs

Port-based VLANs are the most common VLANs. By factory default, switches are configured with a single port-based VLAN with a VLAN identifier (VID) of 1. Switch ports can be configured to support traffic from one or more VLANs. Ports supporting only one VLAN are called *access ports*, or, more accurately, they are defined as access link–type ports and the single VLAN supported is called the *default VLAN* for that port. In this case, the Port VLAN ID (PVID) would be the VID of the default VLAN. By factory default, all ports are access link–type ports and their PVID is 1.

Ports can also be configured to be trunk link–type ports. (Note that the word *trunk* has traditionally been used to refer to two different features: multi-VLAN ports and aggregated links. To avoid confusion in this document, the full denomination *trunk link–type port* is used). These ports support traffic from several VLANs, one of which must be untagged and is the default VLAN (PVID).

The general design rule for port link types is:

- Workstations are connected to access link–type ports.
- Inter-switch links are composed of trunk link–type ports, where the default VLAN is the management VLAN and it is used by the network management system to discover and maintain the network inventory and topology information.
- Servers can be connected either to access or trunk link–type ports, depending on the need.
- Finally, there can be hybrid link–type ports. These ports support several untagged and several tagged VLANs. They can be used in two situations:
    - The first is when there is a need to configure many tagged VLANs and no untagged VLANs (for example, in an inter-switch link in which the other end is connected to a switch that supports either tagged or untagged ports but not trunks—usually low-end switches).
    - The second is when there is a need to have more than one untagged VLAN.

In the second case, the hybrid port requires additional configuration for it to be able to distinguish the untagged VLAN to which each incoming frame belongs. For this purpose, special VLAN types have been defined: protocol-based VLANs, IP subnet-based VLANs, and MAC-address-based VLANs.

Note

Remember that only the Comware products support hybrid ports—this feature is not currently supported on ProVision switches. Not all of the VLAN types in the following sections are supported on the ProVision switches; however, Comware switches do support these types.

Protocol-Based VLANs

Protocol-based VLANs are only configurable in hybrid ports. A protocol-based VLAN is not, in itself, a VLAN but is a mechanism that uses the IEEE 802.3 header's Length/Type field to determine the VLAN to which the frame belongs. It is useful when Layer 3 protocols other than IPv4 are used in the workstation and are required to be directed to a certain VLAN. Examples include SNA, IPX, AppleTalk, and IPv6. Since servers are usually capable of tagging traffic, there is no need to use hybrid ports for server access.

IP Subnet-Based VLANs

IP subnet-based VLANs are only configurable in hybrid ports. An IP subnet-based VLAN is not in itself a VLAN but a mechanism that uses the source IP address and a subnet mask to determine the VLAN to which the frame belongs. It must be used with fixed IP addresses or static Dynamic Host Configuration Protocol (DHCP) entries.

MAC Address-Based VLANs

MAC address-based VLANs are only configurable in hybrid ports in Comware. MAC address-based VLAN is not in itself a VLAN but a mechanism that uses the source MAC address and a MAC mask to determine the VLAN to which the frame belongs. It can be used to assign devices, like IP surveillance cameras, IP phones, and printers to certain VLANs.

Super VLANs

As a general rule, one IP host address is used per VLAN interface. There can be cases in which the IP host addresses are scarce and optimization is required. This optimization can be achieved by implementing a *super VLAN*. (This feature is also called *VLAN aggregation*.) As shown in Figure 16-18, the super VLAN has a group of sub-VLANs and it provides a single IP interface (a gateway) to all of the hosts in its sub-VLANs. It is a Layer 3 feature.

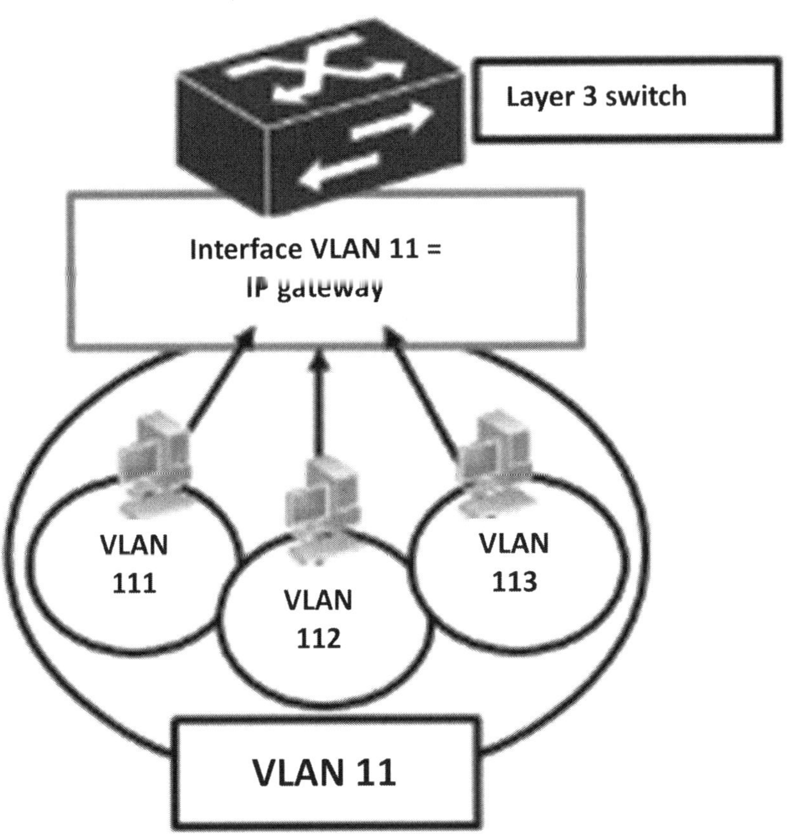

Figure 16-18. Super VLAN example

It is important to notice that, when the super VLAN feature is used, communication between the sub-VLANs is lost because ARP requests cannot travel across VLANs and there is no routing between them. If peer-to-peer communication is required (for example, for IP telephony), the local proxy ARP feature has to be enabled.

Note

On the Comware products, only the chassis-based switches, the 5800s, and the 5900s support super VLANs.

Isolate User VLANs

The main purpose of this feature is to be able to reuse VLAN IDs. It is implemented at Layer 2 switches. As shown in Figure 16-19, when configuring VLAN 20 at the Layer 2 switch, it must be declared as isolate user VLAN. VLANs 211, 212, 213 are associated to VLAN 20 as secondary VLANs. The same can be configured for VLAN 21 at the other Layer 2 switch.

This feature can be used for two reasons:

- To isolate the secondary VLANs (hence the feature's name)
- To reuse VLAN IDs

In the second case, local proxy ARP can be required to re-enable communication between secondary VLANs.

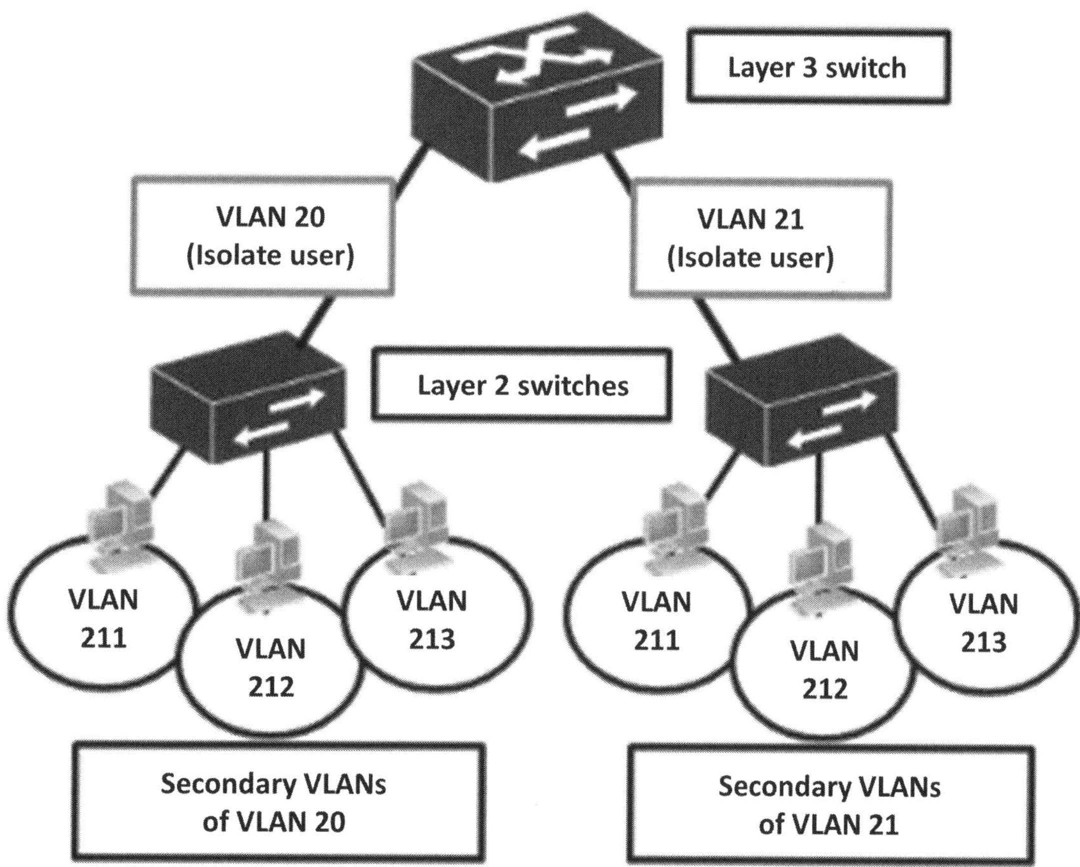

Figure 16-19. Isolate user VLAN example

802.1X-Based on VLANs

802.1X authentication is becoming more common in networks, especially with the growth of wireless networks in companies. As you learned in "Chapter 14: Mobility and Wireless," 802.1X was introduced as part of WPA to provide a better way of authenticating wireless devices. It has since been ported to LAN-based topologies that include Ethernet connections. One option with 802.1X implementations is that the user's policy defined on the authentication server can optionally have a VLAN associated to the user. Upon successfully authenticating, the server can pass back the VLAN identifier to the switch or AP to be used on the user's port. Both Comware and ProVision products support this feature.

Redundancy

The following two sections briefly introduce two redundancy options:

- **Option 1**—Traditional STP is used at Layer 2, and virtual router redundancy protocol (VRRP) is used at Layer 2.
- **Option 2**—IRF is used for Layer 2 and Layer 3.

Redundancy Option 1: MSTP or PVST+ with VRRP

LANs can be designed to be redundant independently from the number of layers (tiers) required. In the case of a two-tier LAN, access switches (and servers) have a link to each one of the core switches. (See Figure 16-20.) If one of the core switches fails, all traffic is handled by its peer and the network continues its operation. Notice that, since workstations usually have a single connection to the network, this is not true for the access switches. An access switch failure disconnects all of its attached clients from the network, unless the client is dual-connected to two switches.

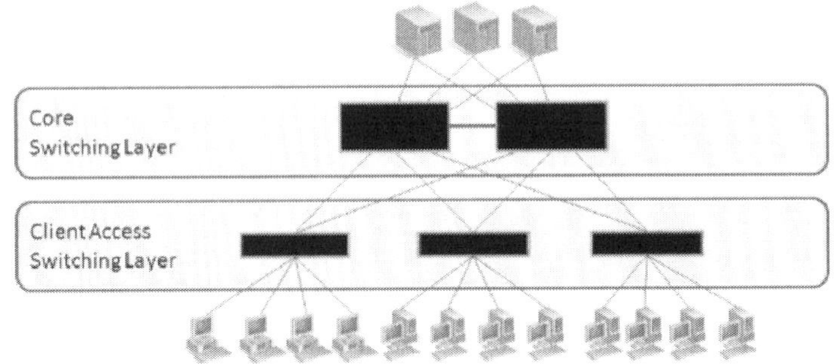

Figure 16-20. Two-tier, dual-root design

A similar, but more complex situation happens in a three-layer LAN (Figure 16-21), and all of the following considerations apply.

Many two-tier LANs are designed with:

- VLANs.
- Layer 3 switching (inter-VLAN routing) at the core.

In these cases, the combination of two protocols is necessary: Multiple Spanning Tree Protocol (MSTP) or Per VLAN Spanning Tree Plus (PVST+); and VRRP. MSTP or PVST+ provides Layer 2 redundancy and load-balancing, and VRRP provides redundant Layer 3 gateway services to the clients.

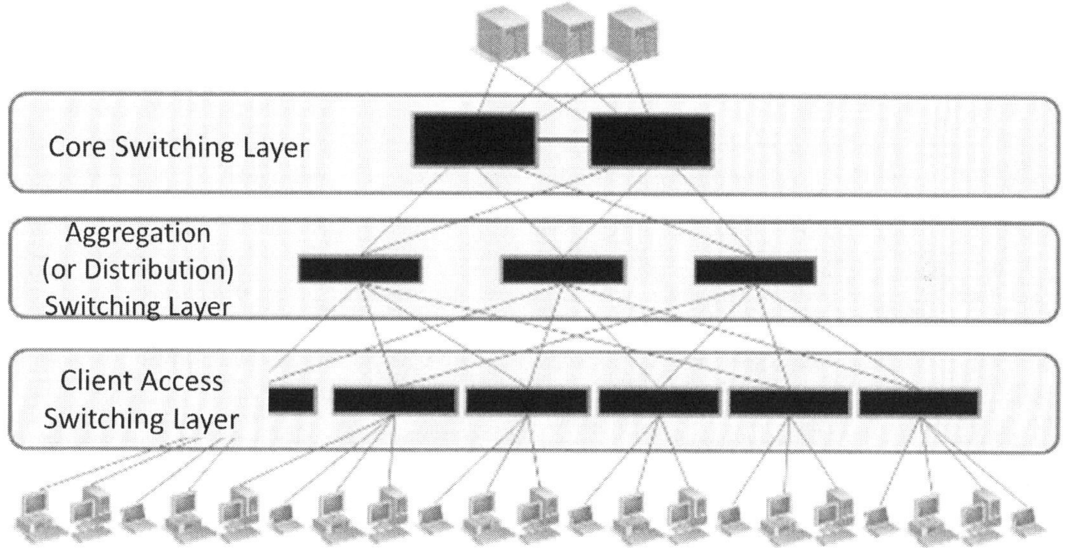

Figure 16-21. Three-tier, dual-root design

MSTP Planning

In a vast majority of scenarios, a single-region MSTP design is enough. If the scenario is complex enough to deserve a multiregion design, a Layer 3 redundancy solution should be considered. OSPF-based routing is usually the best solution to this type of scenario. In the past, a multiregion MSTP design could be necessary when routers were slow and could not handle millions of packets per second. But, since the advent of Layer 3 switching (hardware-based Layer 3 forwarding) in the late '90s, switches forward LAN traffic at the same speed in Layer 2 and Layer 3.

In a scenario like the one shown in Figure 16-22, the following MSTP design criteria can be applied:

- VLANs must be divided into two groups (VG1 and VG2). Ideally, these two VLAN sets should have a similar traffic load, for example:
    - VG1 = {VLAN 1, VLAN 10, VLAN 20, VLAN 30}
    - VG2 = {VLAN 40, VLAN 50, VLAN 60}
- If using MSTP, two MSTP instances (STI1 and STI2) are necessary to map VLAN groups:
    - VG1 <> STI1
    - VG2 <> STI2

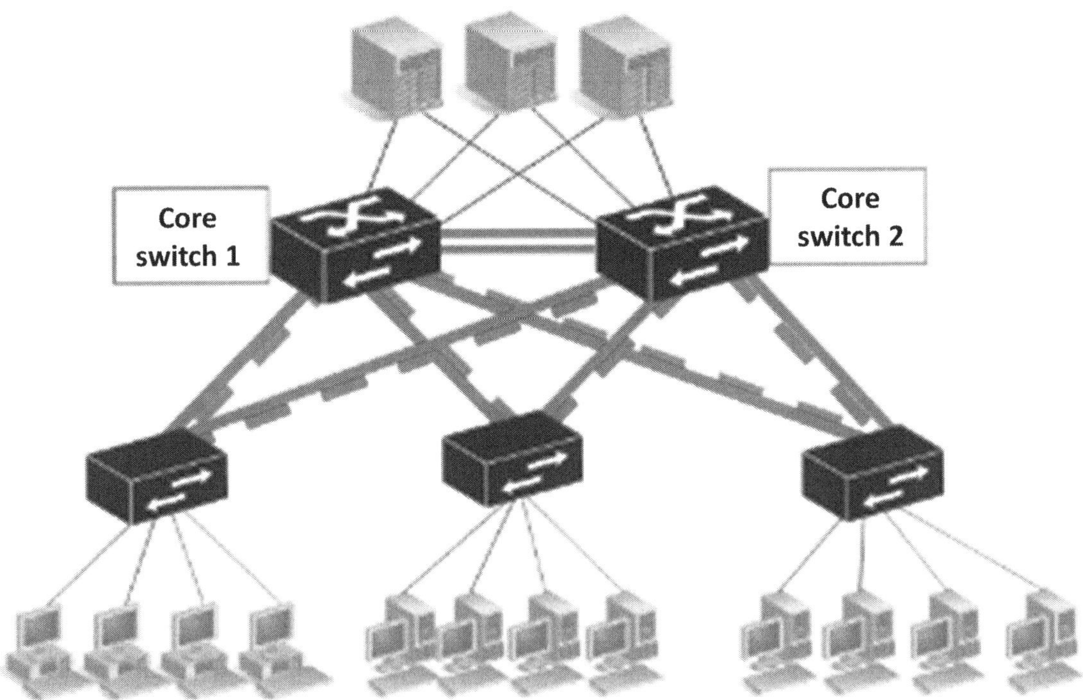

Figure 16-22. Redundancy option 1 illustration with MSTP/PVST+ and VRRP

Each core switch is the primary root for one instance or VLAN group and the secondary root for the other, as shown in Table 16-2.

Table 16-2. Spanning tree configuration for Figure 16-22

Switch	VLAN Group 1 (VG1)	VLAN Group 2 (VG2)
Core switch 1	Primary root	Secondary root
Core switch 2	Secondary root	Primary root

With this configuration, Layer 2 redundancy and load-balancing is achieved and the result is shown in Figure 16-22, with Instance 1/VLAN Group 1 depicted in red and Instance 2/VLAN Group 2 depicted in blue.

VRRP Planning

Two virtual routers must be created, VR1 and VR2, with the mapping shown in Table 16-3. It is recommended that you set up the virtual routers to track the server links (in the case of Figure 16-22) so that, if the server link fails, the traffic is redirected through the other core switch.

Clients' default gateways must be configured according to the VLAN to which they belong:

- The default gateway of clients in VG1 should point to VR1.
- The default gateway of clients in VG2 should point to VR2.

Table 16-3. VRRP configuration for Figure 16-22

Switch	VR1	VR2
Core switch 1	Master	Backup
Core switch 2	Backup	Master

Redundancy Option 2: IRF

The most important differentiator of Comware switches is IRF. IRF, as you learned in "Chapter 13: HP Intelligent Resilient Framework," allows the configuration of redundant virtual switches, called *IRF stacks* or *IRF systems*. An IRF stack is a multidevice system that behaves both from a Layer 2 and Layer 3 point of view as a single switching and routing engine. The number of switches in a stack depends on the switch model and the version of software running on the switch.

From a network design point of view, the most critical feature is distributed link aggregation (DLA). A typical multitier network with IRF would look like Figure 16-23. In this diagram, the access switches on the right are connected to an IRF-stack using two links, one of them ending at a different stack member device. In the access switch, these two links are configured as a standard link aggregation group. In the stack, a link aggregation group is also created with ports in each member (a *DLA group*).

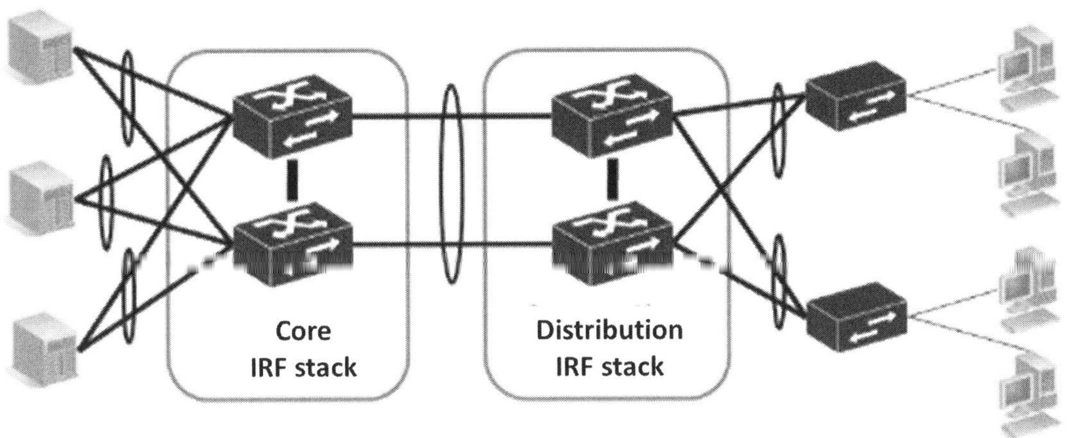

Figure 16-23. Distributed link aggregation in a three-tier LAN with IRF

Layer 2 load-balancing and redundancy are embedded in the DLA mechanism. And, because each IRF stack is a single router, Layer 3 redundancy is embedded in the IRF mechanism. So MSTP/PVST+ and VRRP are not necessary when IRF is implemented at the core and aggregation layer.

DLA includes another important feature: when a frame has been assigned the egress interface and this interface is a DLA, the distribution process first verifies whether there is a physical port in the stack member where the frame is currently buffered. In that case, other ports in the DLA are not considered. (See Figure 16-24.) This significantly reduces the intra-stack traffic.

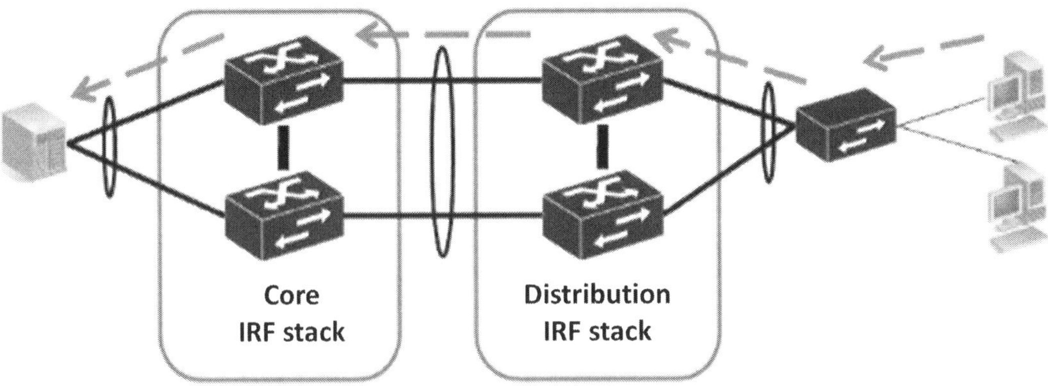

Figure 16-24. Traffic distribution in DLA

IP Addressing and Routing Design

To design a healthy and efficient IPv4 solution for the enterprise, three main aspects of planning need to be considered:

- Subnet
- An IPv4 (and/or IPv6) address
- Routing

IP Address Planning

The following are subnets and IP addresses for LAN design considerations:

- In a LAN, subnet planning is strongly related to VLAN planning. In general, VLANs and subnets overlap completely, or, said differently, a subnet is a VLAN from the point of view of Layer 3. There are only a few exceptions, such as in the case of super VLANs and isolate user VLANs.
- So, in practice, VLANs and IP subnets—including IP gateways—must be designed together, and all the VLAN design criteria defined in "Chapter 6: VLANs" also apply to subnets.
- A Class C subnet address range (with a 24-bit subnet mask) typically has enough addresses for all hosts in a VLAN. (A recommended maximum of 100-200 hosts still leaves room to add management addresses to switches or printers in the VLAN.)
- In some cases, a longer subnet mask can be used.
    - For example, a decision is made to keep the number of stations per VLANs below 100. In this case, a 25-bit mask is enough. This solution duplicates the number of subnet addresses available.
    - In another example, one VLAN per access switch, and routing at the aggregation layer. In this case, the maximum number of IP addresses required per VLAN is below 64 and a 26-bit mask can be used. Here are two examples:
- If a decision is made, below 100, a 25-bit mask is enough. This solution doubles the number of subnets available in a given range of addresses.
- Select one VLAN per access switch, and route across all layers.

The following are subnet and IP address considerations in a WAN design:

- In a WAN, subnets are also determined by the Layer 2 links. Each Layer 2 link defines a subnet.
- Unlike a LAN, there are neither clients nor servers in a Layer 2 WAN link, leaving a very small number of nodes: 2 nodes for a Point-to-Point Protocol (PPP) link and between 2 and 10 nodes in a Frame Relay network.
- So the recommended mask length for PPP links is 30 bits. Note that, in the case of Frame Relay using sub-interfaces, links are seen as point-to-point, in which case a mask length of 30 bits also applies.

Private IP Addresses

Internet Assigned Numbers Authority (IANA) has reserved the following IPv4 address ranges for private use:

- 10.0.0.0/8
- 172.16.0.0/12
- 192.168.0.0/16

These addresses cannot be used in public services (servers accessible through the Internet); they should be used for "private Internets," as stated in RFC 1918. If a private network using one of these ranges is connected to the Internet, an Internet gateway must be used to provide Network Address Translation (NAT). This feature replaces the source address of outbound packets for a valid public IPv4 address. Comware routers can implement address translation policies.

Since these addresses are *invisible* in the Internet, they can be reused, and there are millions of private networks today using subnets in one of these three ranges. The network size determines which of these three ranges should be used:

- Range 1 offers 16,777,216 addresses.
- Range 2 offers 1,048,576 addresses.
- Range 3 offers 65,536 addresses.

Small and medium-sized networks can use addresses in Range 3 and a single Class C subnet (192.168.x.0) for each VLAN.

Address Summarization

One important element to consider when planning the IPv4 addresses is the possibility of reducing the size of routing tables. Because of the IPv4 address space structure, it is possible to assign address ranges to subnets in a way that allows for using summary address spaces by applying shorter subnet masks.

- The address ranges of these subnet addresses (see Figure 16-25)—192.168.8.0/24, 192.168.9.0/24, 192.168.10.0/24 and 192.168.11.0/25—can be summarized in a single, larger address range: 192.168.8.0/22.
- If these four subnets are connected to Router B, the routing table in Router A can be reduced. Compare Tables 16-4 and 16-5, where Table 16-4 has no summarization and Table 16-5 performs summarization for Router A's routing table.

Table 16-4. Routing table without summarization

Destination	Mask length	Next hop
192.168.8.0	24	192.168.0.2
192.168.9.0	24	192.168.0.2
192.168.10.0	24	192.168.0.2
192.168.11.0	24	192.168.0.2

Table 16-5. Routing with summarization

Destination	Mask length	Next hop
192.168.8.0	22	192.168.0.2

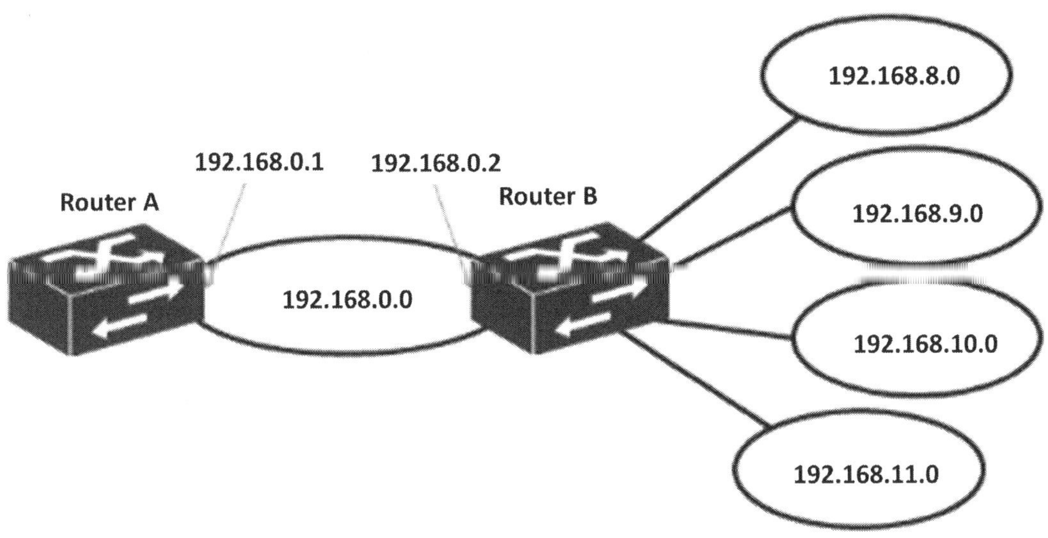

Figure 16-25. Subnet and IP address planning

Therefore, the recommendation when designing IP networks is to:

- Use contiguous address ranges for networks connected to the same device and at the same level.
- Reserve some other contiguous address ranges for future growth.

In the previous example, you could reserve the whole 192.168.8.0/21 address range (instead of 22). The result is that subnets 192.168.12.0/24, 192.168.13.0/24, 192.168.14.0/24, and 192.168.15.0/24 are reserved and can be used for VLANs connected to the right of Router B.

Note

Being able to summarize routes may not be important within a LAN, but it can become critical in a corporate network with multiple branches connected by a WAN.

Special IP Addresses

The following two sections briefly cover special IP addresses used when designing IP networks: loopback and default gateway addresses.

Loopback Address

Many IPv4 routing protocols require a router ID to be used for operations like peer/neighbor identification. When a router ID is not manually configured, the routing protocol uses the IP address of a Layer 3 interface. Because Layer 3 interfaces attached to either a port or a VLAN can go down, it is always recommended that you use a more stable interface.

The loopback interface is a virtual or logical interface—in other words, it is attached neither to a physical nor a VLAN interface. Because of that, the loopback interface is always in the `UP` state or active. This is why routing protocols, like OSPF, with a router ID that has not been configured, checks first if there is a loopback interface configured and, in that case, adopts its IPv4 address as the router ID.

Loopback addresses are also used for other purposes:

- As the device's address for management applications
- As the source address for routing protocols and other application packets: Simple Network Management Protocol (SNMP) traps, Network Time Protocol (NTP), Border Gateway Protocol (BGP), Intermediate System to Intermediate System (IS-IS), and OSPF routing updates, syslog, and more
- As the destination for `ping` and `traceroute`

Loopback address format is: an IPv4 address with a 32-bit mask. Configuring a loopback interface in every router and Layer 3 switch is recommended.

Note

Depending on the application, routes to loopback addresses may not need to be injected into the routing protocols (for example, as default router IDs). But, since they may need to be used for other applications in the future, it is recommended that they be designed in such a way as to allow them to be part of the general routing scheme.

Default Gateway Address

For subnets where clients or servers are present (Figures 16-26 and 16-27), it is important to be consistent when assigning the IPv4 address to the router(s) attached to it. Some engineers use the higher addresses in the subnet, and others prefer the lowest. If the subnet has more than one gateway, it is recommended that successive addresses, like X.Y.Z.253 and X.Y.Z.254, be assigned. If you are using VRRP, you might need a third IP address for the virtual IP address (the address that the clients use as their default gateway).

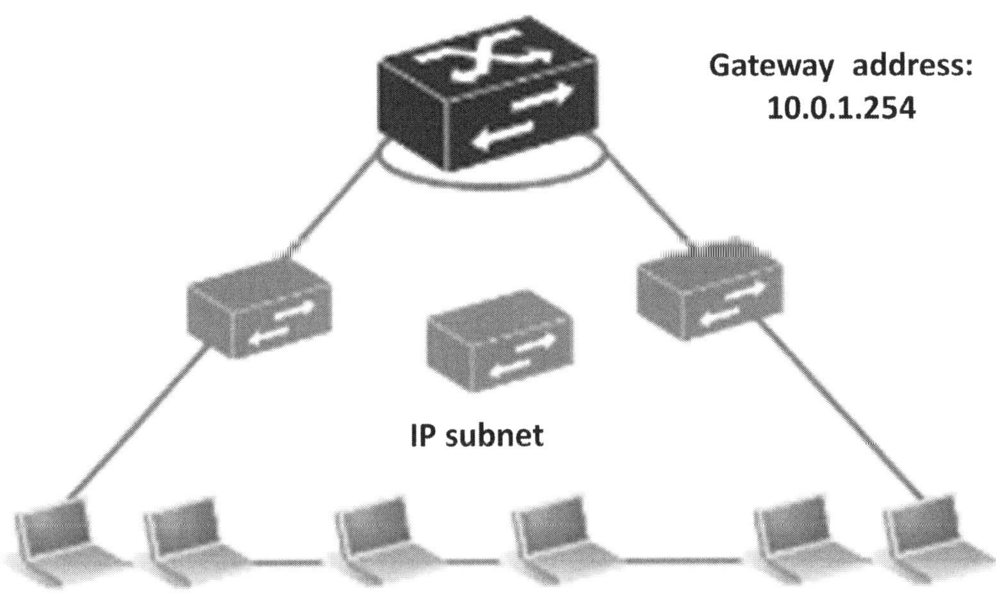

Figure 16-26. IP subnet with hosts and one gateway

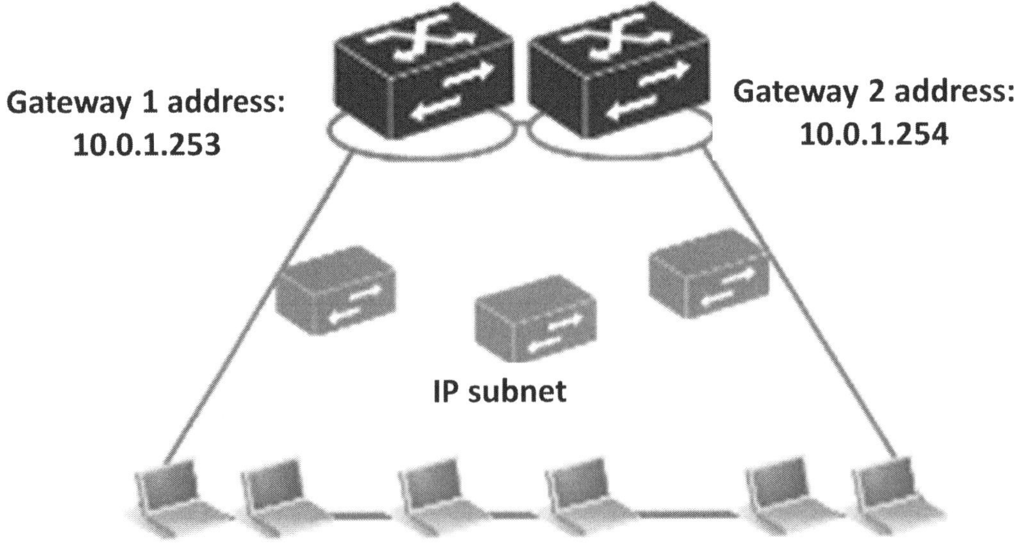

Figure 16-27. IP subnet with hosts and two gateways

Routing Design Practices

The most widely used routing protocol in private networks today is OSPF. It has proved to have the right features and to scale properly. For this section, it is assumed that OSPF is the interior gateway protocol (IGP) to be used. However, it is also accepted that other forms of routing (default and static) and other routing protocols (like RIP and BGP) can or will be present.

In the ideal design situation of a brand new network, only OSPF and default routing should be used internally and BGP should be used externally.

Network Scenarios

When planning IP routing for large networks, there are many factors to consider, so no definitive guidelines can be offered. However, most networks can be mapped into one the following scenarios:

- Centralized
- Distributed

In a *centralized* scenario, the main application of the network is to connect clients in different sites to a central data center where a large majority of the servers are located. In other words, it is a data-centric network. This scenario can have several variations. One variation is the presence of multiple regional data centers. Another is the duplication of data centers for fault tolerance and redundancy.

On the other hand, an ISP with a core business of data transportation and connectivity may require a fully *distributed* network. In this scenario, the network *is* the business.

In the rest of this section, a centralized scenario is considered. A network with the servers and a campus LAN are located at a central site, and several smaller sites are connected to this central site. The following considerations can be extended and combined for larger, more complex, scenarios.

Routing in the LAN

In a three-tier LAN, there are many options for where to route: at the core, at the distribution layer, at the edge, or everywhere. In this section, it is assumed that clients are connected to the edge and that servers are located in the core. Similar three-tier LANs can be designed for large data centers. In this case, servers would be connected to the data center edge (top of rack) and the core would be connected to the campus LAN and the WAN routers.

In general, it is recommended that the core is reserved for high-speed forwarding and that no routing is performed there. For small and medium-sized LANs (two-tier), all routing can be performed in the core without any real impact on performance. In some cases, engineers recommend routing at the edge and having every access port as a single subnet. The main reasons for this approach are to avoid the use of spanning tree or to enforce security at the edge. In this case, OSPF is deployed everywhere and used for redundancy.

A good balance between fast failure recovery and a small number of subnets is achieved by routing at the distribution/aggregation layer. In any case, the size and physical layout of the LAN and the applications deployed help to make this decision.

OSPF Design Considerations

Designing a good, scalable, manageable, and fast-converging network involves many components, most of which are beyond the scope of this book. However this section covers three of them:

- Router IDs
- Areas
- Default routes

Router IDs

As was covered in "Chapter 12: OSPF Operation and Configuration," OSPF uses router IDs to identify the routers. Since OSPF is a link state protocol, routers must be identified by their ID when building a Link State Data Base (LSDB) of all routers and networks in the area. Router IDs are four-byte identifiers that are usually represented using the same notation as IPv4 addresses. Because of that similarity, OSPF routers without a manually configured router ID use the IPv4 address from one of its Layer 3 interfaces for OSPF identification.

Because normal interfaces are dynamic, use one of the following two options for OSPF router IDs:

- Manually configure the router ID.
- Assign an IPv4 address to a loopback address, and use this as the router ID.

The advantage of using manually configured router IDs is that the ID can be planned with only the OSPF structure in mind and independently of the general IPv4 address planning. The advantage of the second or loopback option is that it allows routers to be identified with the same ID for every application: SNMP or OSPF, for example, which may result in simpler troubleshooting.

Areas

One of the main advantages of OSPF is its capacity to divide the autonomous system (AS) into many areas to provide for routing scalability. In this type of design, the following should be true concerning the backbone area:

- Area 0 routers and links should be stable.
- Links should be fast and reliable.
- The number of routers should typically not exceed 30 (this is a rule of thumb and is dependent on the number of routing devices—physical or logical, in the case of IRF—and the number of routes).

In the case of a centralized network (see Figure 16-28), this can be achieved by locating Area 0 in the central site and assigning non-backbone areas to the other sites. In some cases, a non-backbone area can span several sites within a region. Depending on the size of the central site, the backbone area will, in most cases, span the whole site.

Finally, because area border routers (ABRs) are part of the backbone and to comply with the rules listed at the beginning of this section, they should be located in the central site. If remote sites require redundant or load-balancing connections to the central site, links to two ABRs can be implemented (Figure 16-28).

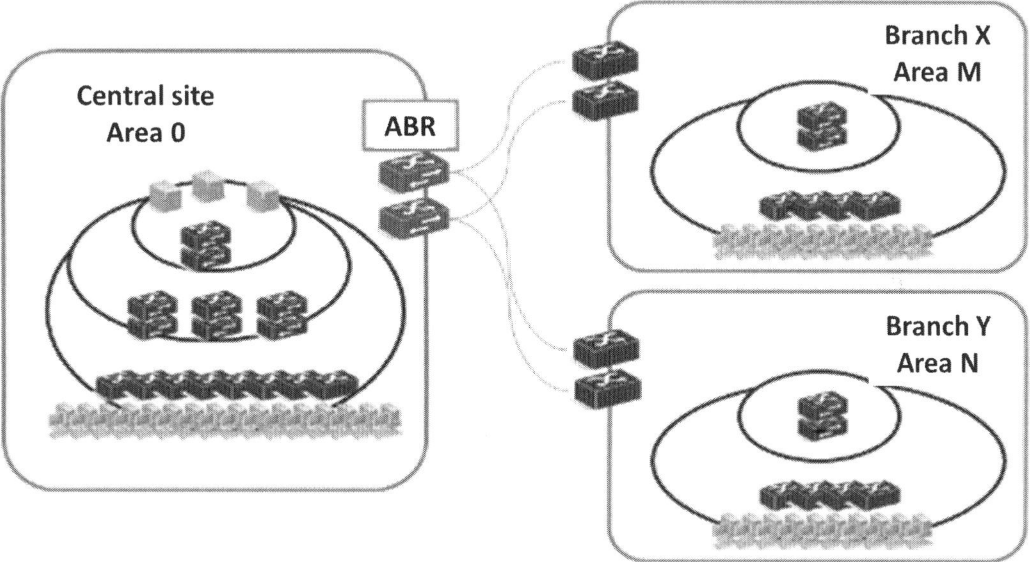

Figure 16-28. A possible area plan for a centralized corporate office

In general, it is desirable that all non-backbone areas are stub areas. This would mean that the only LSAs managed by the internal routers are types 1, 2, and/or 3.

There are two main exceptions to this practice:

- When there is the need for a virtual link to traverse the area. In this case, the only solution is to leave the area in the default configuration as the transit area.
- When there is the need for an autonomous system boundary router (ASBR) to be located in the area. This situation can happen for two reasons:
    - Another protocol is being used in the same location (for example, Routing Information Protocol [RIP]).
    - There is a direct connection to the Internet within the area. In this case, the area can be defined as a not-so-stubby area (NSSA).

Again, it is important to notice that this is one of many possible solutions and that the applications, physical distribution, available bandwidth, and WAN services may force you to look for different solutions.

Default Routes

Even in the case of a network where OSPF has been fully deployed, one or more default routes are needed.

OSPF uses two types of default routes—internal and external.

- **Internal default routes**—These are part of OSPF's inter-area mechanisms, are generated by ABRs, and are distributed within stub areas as their only route to the other areas.
- **External default routes**—These are the simplest way to connect the private network to the Internet. They are implemented at ASBRs.

Learning Check

The following questions help you measure your understanding of the material presented in this chapter. Read all of the choices carefully, since there may be more than one correct answer. Choose all correct answers for each question.

Questions

1. Which of the following is not a function of the distribution layer?
   a. Contain broadcasts.
   b. Secure traffic.
   c. Implement hierarchical Layer 3 addressing and route summarization.
   d. Translate between media types.
   e. Separate PVST regions.
2. Which media type allows Gigabit Ethernet to span over 20 kilometers?
   a. 100BaseFX
   b. 1000BaseSX
   c. 1000BaseFX
   d. 1000BaseZX
3. Which of the following is true regarding VLAN design?
   a. VoIP devices should be in the same VLAN as other devices.
   b. Network printers should be in the same VLAN as the users.
   c. Access points should be in the same area as wired devices.
   d. ACLs and firewalls are typically used for traffic within a VLAN.
4. Name the three layers of the design model.
5. Which VLAN type is supported by both Comware and ProVision switches? (Choose two.)
   a. MAC-based VLAN
   b. Super VLAN
   c. 802.1-based VLAN
   d. Isolate user VLAN
6. What are the two recommendations for configuring router IDs?

Answers

1. ☑ **E** is correct. PVST does not contain regions; however, MSTP does.

   ☒ **A**, **B**, **C**, and **D** are incorrect. They are functions of the distribution layer.

2. ☑ **D** is correct. 1000Base-ZX can span over two kilometers.

   ☒ **A**, **B**, and **C** are incorrect. They do not span up to two kilometers or more.

3. ☑ **B** is correct. Network printers should be in the same VLAN as their respective users.

   ☒ **A** is not true since VoIP devices should be in a separate VLAN or VLANs from other devices. **C** is not true because wired and wireless devices should be placed in separate VLANs. **D** is not true because ACLs and firewalls are typically used *between* VLANs, not *within* a VLAN.

4. ☑ **Core**, **distribution** (or aggregation), and **access** are the three layers of the design model.

5. ☑ **A** and **C** are correct. Comware and ProVision switches support both MAC-based VLANs and 802.1-based VLANs.

   ☒ **B** and **D** are only supported by the Comware switches.

6. ☑ OSPF router IDs should be manually configured and/or obtained from a loopback interface.

17 Practice Test

INTRODUCTION

The *HP Accredited Technical Professional (ATP) – FlexNetwork Solutions V1* certification validates your ability to configure and implement HP ProVision and HP Comware networking products, focusing on the ProVision switches and wireless Multi-Service Mobility (MSM) access points (APs) and the Comware switches in small-to-medium-sized businesses (SMBs).

The intent of this book is to set expectations about the context of the exam and to help candidates prepare for it. Recommended training to prepare for this exam can be found at the HP ExpertOne website (www.hp.com/ExpertOne) and in books like this one. It is important to note that, although training is recommended for exam preparation, successful completion of the training alone does not guarantee that you will pass the exam. In addition to training, exam items are based on knowledge gained from on-the-job experience and application and on other supplemental reference material that may be specified in this guide.

Minimum Qualifications

To achieve the *HP ATP – FlexNetwork Solutions V1* certification, you must pass the HP0-Y46, HP2-Z25 or HP2-Z26 exams. The candidate should have a thorough understanding of HP switch and access point implementations in SMBs. To pass the exam, you should have at least one year of experience in designing networks with intermediate switching, basic routing, and wireless technologies. Exams are based on an assumed level of industry-standard knowledge that may be gained from the training, hands-on experience, or other prerequisite events.

HP0-Y46 Exam Details

The following are details about the HP0-Y46 exam:

- **Exam ID:** HP0-Y46
- **Number of items:** 68
- **Item types:** Multiple choice (single-response), multiple choice (multiple-response), drag-and-drop
- **Exam time:** 115 minutes
- **Passing score:** 66%
- **Reference material:** No online or hard copy reference material is allowed at the testing site.

HP0-Y46 Testing Objectives

20% Fundamental networking architectures and technologies

- Describe and apply the most common data link (Layer 2) protocols.
- Describe and contrast the most common Ethernet concepts.
- Explain Layer 3 routing concepts, and apply Layer 3 protocols.
- Define and recognize the purpose and interaction of common TCP/UDP-based upper layer applications.
- Describe and explain basic network security.
- Describe the concept, benefits, and types of redundancy, and apply redundancy types.
- Describe and explain (apply) link aggregation.
- Identify, describe, and explain VLANs.
- Describe network management.
- Describe, identify, and explain wireless technologies.

9% Server and storage technologies and solutions

- Identify key Gen 8 features.
- Identify HP MOE features
- Identify and describe servers and features.
- Describe server infrastructure technologies.
- Describe deduplication technologies.
- Identify disk volume movement technologies.
- Describe the use of Open-Source Software.
- Describe Storage Provisioning Mgr benefits.

Note: This book does not cover this portion of the exam. To prepare for this content, HP recommends you take the *HP innovations for today's IT infrastructure* web-based training course (Course ID: 00772374) that is accessible from the exam's page in The Learning Center.

13% HP Networking solutions and offerings

- Identify components and elements of the HP Networking solutions (data center, campus LAN, and branch), and explain their roles.
- Identify and explain products and features in the HP Networking product line.
- Compare and contrast HP Networking solutions and features.
- Compare and contrast data center, campus LAN, and branch environments.

- Identify which HP Networking products should be positioned, given various customer environments and infrastructure needs. (Include the criteria needed to make such a recommendation.)
  - Identify and describe available tool sets for managing HP Networking products (command-line interface–based [CLI-based], web, Simple Network Management Protocol [SNMP], and others).

25% Solution implementation (install, configure, start up, and upgrade the network solution as per planned design)

  - Prepare equipment for installation.
  - Perform installation and configuration of devices.
  - Install and configure management and administration solution.
  - Validate the installed solution.

9% Solution enhancement (performance-tune, optimize, upgrade)

- Optimize small-to-medium-sized wireless, switched, and routed network infrastructures for SMB and commercial customers.
- Manage network assets using HP tools.
  - Verify Layer 3 routing protocol convergence and scalability (Open Shortest Path First [OSPF], Routing Information Protocol [RIP], and static routes).

12% Solution troubleshooting (perform troubleshooting procedures)

- Use general troubleshooting tools.
- Perform troubleshooting methodology on the wired networks.
- Perform troubleshooting methodology on the wireless networks.
- Perform troubleshooting methodology on the WAN networks.

12% Solution management (administrative and operational tasks)

- Perform network management (best practices).
- Review and take action on alerts and log files.
  - Perform administrative tasks (moves, adds, changes, and deletions, password resets, managed devices, authentication, authorization, and accounting [AAA], and others).
- Verify network performance and parameters.

Note: The testing objectives and percentages vary slightly for the web-based exams HP2-Z25 and HP2-Z26. Refer to the appropriate Exam Preparation Guide for details. The guides can be found at www.certificationexplorer.com.

Test Preparation Questions and Answers

The following questions help you measure your understanding of the material presented in this book. Read all of the choices carefully, since there may be more than one correct answer. Choose all correct answers for each question.

Questions

1. Which HP data center product is used on server blade solutions to connect to external Fibre Channel and Ethernet-based switches?
   a. 5830 Module
   b. Virtual Connect
   c. HP 6125XG
   d. 12500 switch

2. Match the product or component with its corresponding placement in the HP FlexNetwork architecture.

a. 6120XG	1. HP FlexBranch
b. 3800	2. HP FlexCampus
c. MSR50	3. HP FlexFabric
d. HP Intelligent Management Center (IMC)	4. HP FlexManagement

3. Which component of software-defined networking (SDN) implements and applies the actual policies for traffic flows?
   a. Application
   b. Control
   c. Infrastructure
   d. Management

4. Which interface identifier correctly specifies the second port on the second module of a ProVision 5400zl switch?
   a. 2/2
   b. A2/2
   c. B2
   d. 2/0/2

5. Which operational mode is used on Comware switches to execute the `reset` command?
   a. Manager
   b. Operator
   c. System View
   d. User View

6. Match the command with the correct operating system (ProVision or Comware).

a. `ip route-static`	1. ProVision
b. `vlan ip address`	2. Comware
c. `hostname`	
d. `disable`	
e. `interface vlan-interface`	
f. `port-group`	

7. Which button or buttons on the chassis of a ProVision switch are used to perform the password recovery process?
   a. Reset and Clear
   b. Reset
   c. Clear
   d. Delete

8. Which Comware privilege level are you taken to when you log in to the console port of a Comware router or the auxiliary port of a Comware switch?
   a. Manager
   b. Monitor
   c. System
   d. Viewer

9. Which statements are true concerning the defaults on ProVision and Comware switches? (Select three.)
   a. Telnet is disabled on ProVision switches.
   b. Telnet is enabled on Comware switches.
   c. SSH is enabled on ProVision switches.
   d. SSH is enabled on Comware switches.
   e. Web SSL is disabled on ProVision switches.
   f. Web SSL is enabled on Comware switches.

10. Which command correctly installs a new operating system from a USB drive on a ProVision switch?
   a. `upgrade usb flash KA.15.03.3004.swi primary`
   b. `copy usb flash KA.15.03.3004.swi secondary`
   c. `copy usb:/ KA.15.03.3004.swi flash:/KA.15.03.3004.swi secondary`
   d. `copy primary usb flash KA.15.03.3004.swi primary`

11. Which Comware command correctly identifies the configuration file that will be used upon the next reboot of the device?
   a. `startup saved-configuration`
   b. `startup-default`
   c. `boot system startup-config`
   d. `boot-file startup-config`

12. Which commands are used to prevent an administrator from recovering a file from the flash file system of a Comware device? (Select two.)
   a. `erase /permanent`
   b. `delete /reset`
   c. `delete /unreserved`
   d. `reset /unreserved`
   e. `reset recycle-bin`

13. Which Comware configuration correctly configures a trunk allowing only VLANs 30 and 31, along with the untagged VLAN, based on the following output?

```
[Comware] display port trunk
Interface            PVID  VLAN passing
GE1/0/23             1       1, 100, 101
```

a.
```
interface g1/0/23
  port trunk permit vlan 30 31
```

b.
```
interface g1/0/23
  undo port trunk permit vlan 100 101
  port trunk permit vlan 30 31
```

c.
```
vlan 30-31
  permit interface g1/0/23
```

d.
```
vlan 100-101
  undo permit interface g1/0/23
vlan 30-31
  permit interface g1/023
```

14. A PC is connected to the data port of a phone, and the phone is then connected to the port of a Comware switch. Neither the PC nor the phone support 802.1Q. Given this information, which port type should be configured on the Comware switch to place the two devices in different VLANs?

   a. Access
   b. Trunk
   c. Hybrid
   d. Multihost
   e. Multiple-mode
   f. Untagged

15. Examine the network topology in Figure 17-1.

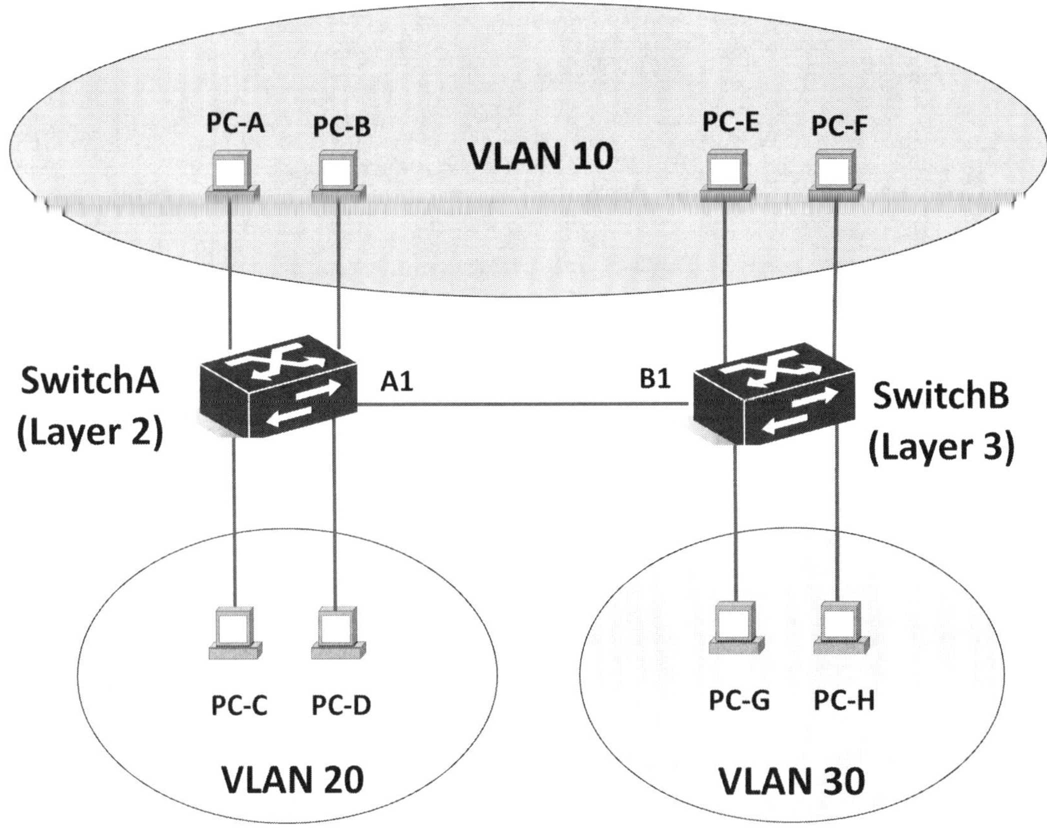

Figure 17-1. Question 15 network topology

SwitchA is a Layer 2 ProVision switch, and SwitchB is a Layer 3 ProVision switch. Based on this topology, what is the correct configuration for port B1 to ensure connectivity within VLAN 10 and inter-VLAN connectivity between all three VLANs?

a.
```
vlan 10 tagged B1
vlan 20 tagged B1
vlan 30 tagged B1
```

b.
```
vlan 10 tagged B1
vlan 20 tagged B1
```

c.
```
vlan 10 tagged B1
vlan 30 tagged B1
```

d.
```
interface B1
   port mode trunk 10 20 30
```

16. Examine the network topology in Figure 17-2.

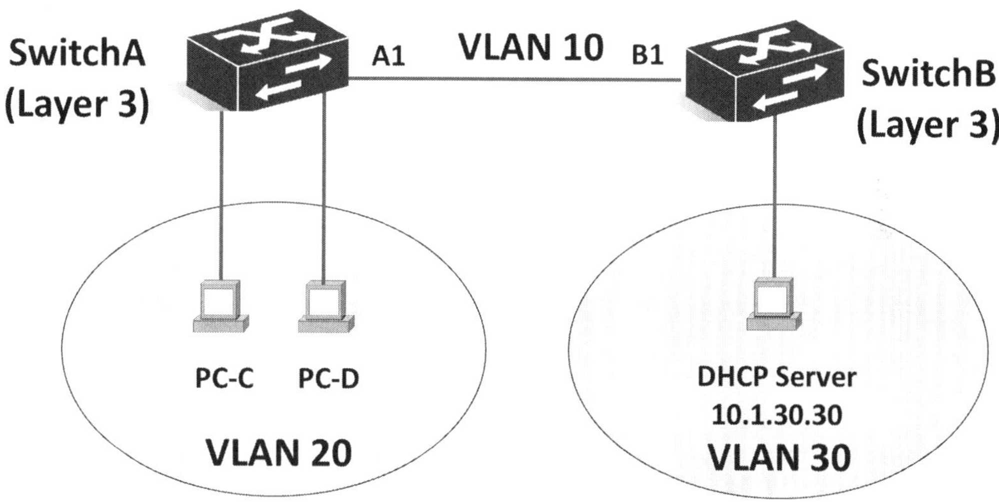

Figure 17-2. Question 16 network topology

Based on this topology, which configuration correctly sets up DHCP relay so that users in VLAN 20 can acquire addressing information from the DHCP server in VLAN 30?

a.
```
SwitchA(config)# vlan 20
SwitchA(vlan-id 20)# ip helper-vlan 30
```

b.
```
SwitchA(config)# vlan 20
SwitchA(vlan-id 20)# ip helper-address 10.1.30.30
```

c.
```
SwitchA(config)# vlan 10
SwitchA(vlan-id 10)# ip helper-address 10.1.30.30
```

d.
```
SwitchB(config)# vlan 10
SwitchB(vlan-id 10)# ip helper-address 10.1.30.30
```

17. Which of the following are logging level on a ProVision switch? (Select four.)

    a. Critical
    b. Debug
    c. Error
    d. Informational
    e. Minor
    f. Warning

18. Which Comware command causes the operating system to redisplay the command line and text input after a log message is displayed on the console?

    a. `info-center logging`
    b. `logging synchronous`
    c. `logging display`
    d. `info-center display`
    e. `info-center synchronous`

19. Examine the network topology in Figure 17-3.

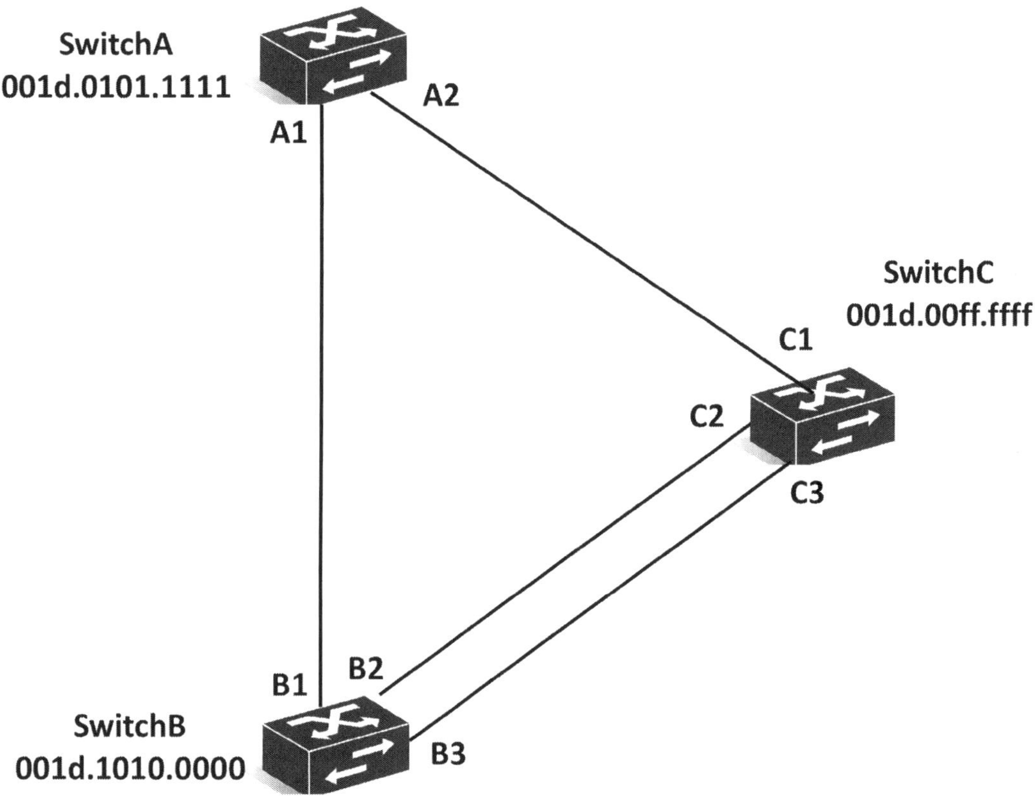

Figure 17-3. Question 19 network topology

The topology is composed of ProVision switches configured for 802.1D. All interfaces are associated with VLAN 1 only. Assume that all port costs and priorities are the same and that all switches have the same switch priority. Given this topology, which statements are correct? (Select three.)

a. SwitchA is the root.

b. Port A2 is a root port.

c. SwitchB is the root.

d. Port C2 is a root port.

e. Port B3 is in a discarding state.

f. Port A1 is a designated port.

20. Examine the network topology in Figure 17-4.

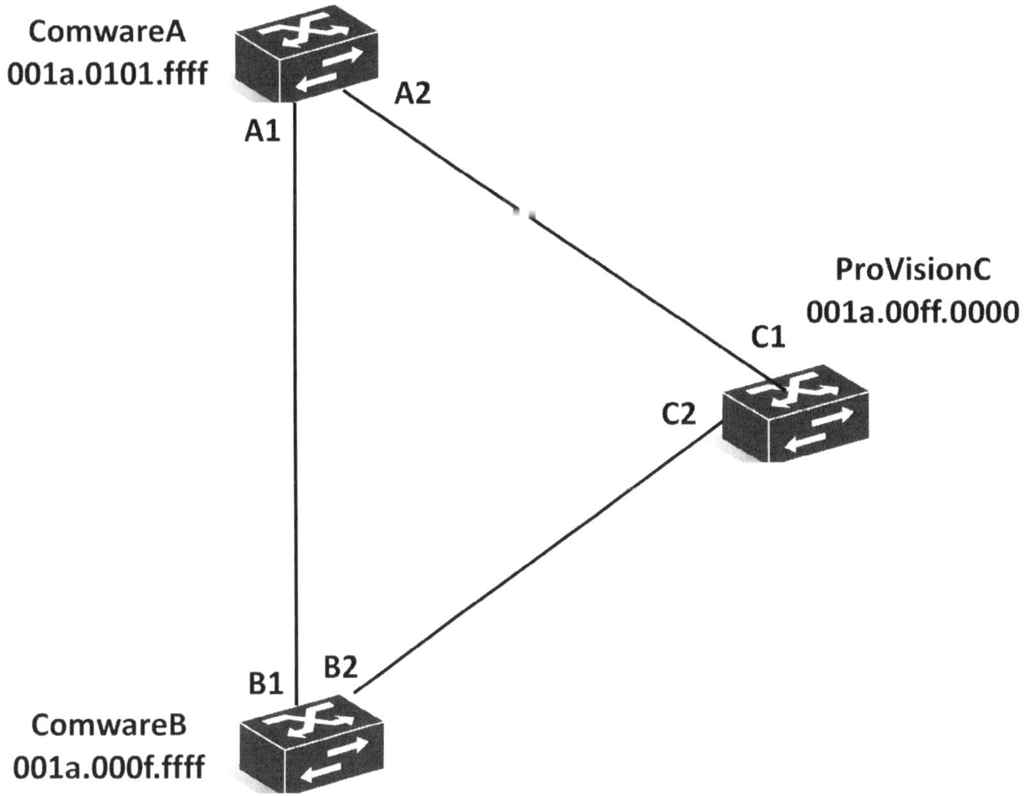

Figure 17-4. Question 20 network topology

ComwareA and ComwareB are Comware switches, and ProVisionC is a ProVision switch. All switches are at their factory default configurations with the exception of spanning tree being enabled on all three switches. Based on this information, which statements about this topology are correct? (Select two.)

a. ComwareA is the root switch.
b. ComwareB is the root switch.
c. ComwareC is the root switch.
d. Port A1 is a designated port.
e. Port A2 is a designated port.
f. Port B2 is a root port.

21. Which is a secondary root port designation for switches that support Rapid Spanning Tree Protocol (RSTP)?

    a. Backup

    b. Alternate

    c. Designated

    d. Failover

22. Examine the network topology in Figure 17-5.

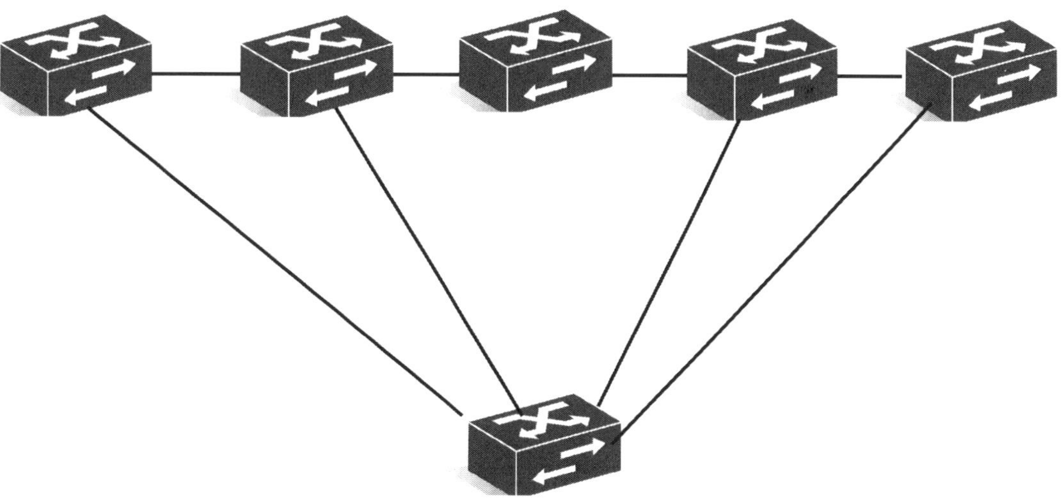

Figure 17-5. Question 22 network topology

This topology is using Multiple STP (MSTP) for spanning tree. Given this topology, how many instances would need to be created so that the access layer switch can implement load-sharing across all of its uplinks?

a. One

b. Two

c. Three

d. Four

e. Five

23. Which ProVision command would configure a ProVision switch to have an MSTP priority of 16,384 for the internal spanning tree?

    a. `spanning tree instance ist priority 4`

    b. `spanning tree instance 0 priority 4`

    c. `spanning tree instance 0 priority 16384`

    d. `spanning tree mstp instance 0 priority 16384`

24. Examine the network topology in Figure 17-6.

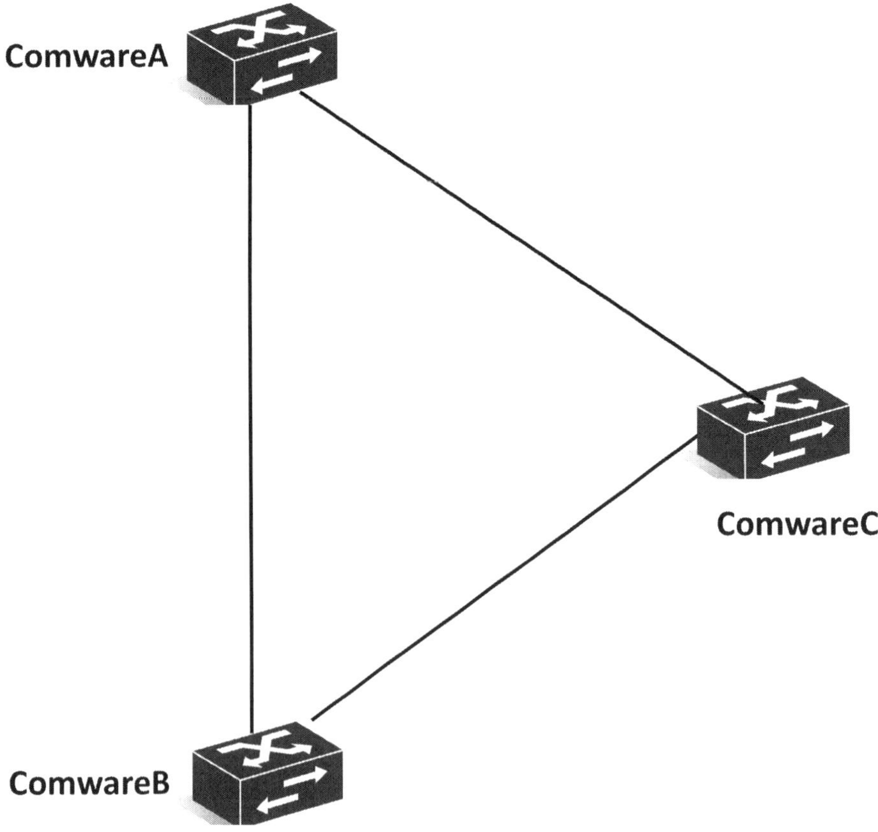

Figure 17-6. Question 24 network topology

Examine the commands executed on each switch from its factory default configuration:

```
[ComwareA] stp enable
[ComwareA] stp region-configuration
[ComwareA-mst-region] region-name HP
[ComwareA-mst-region] revision-level 1
[ComwareA-mst-region] instance 0 vlan 1,4-4094
[ComwareA-mst-region] instance 1 vlan 2
[ComwareA-mst-region] instance 2 vlan 3
[ComwareA-mst-region] active region-configuration
[ComwareA-mst-region] quit
[ComwareA] stp instance 0 root primary
[ComwareA] stp instance 1 root primary
[ComwareA] stp instance 2 root secondary

[ComwareB] stp enable
[ComwareB] stp region-configuration
[ComwareB-mst-region] region-name HP
[ComwareB-mst-region] revision-level 1
[ComwareB-mst-region] instance 0 vlan 1,4-4094
[ComwareB-mst-region] instance 1 vlan 2
[ComwareB-mst-region] instance 2 vlan 3
[ComwareB-mst-region] active region-configuration
[ComwareB-mst-region] quit
[ComwareB] stp instance 0 root secondary
[ComwareB] stp instance 1 root secondary
[ComwareB] stp instance 1 root primary

[ComwareC] stp enable
[ComwareC] stp region-configuration
[ComwareC-mst-region] region-name HP
[ComwareC-mst-region] revision-level 1
[ComwareC-mst-region] instance 0 vlan 1,4-4094
[ComwareC-mst-region] instance 1 vlan 2
[ComwareC-mst-region] instance 2 vlan 3
[ComwareC-mst-region] active region-configuration
[ComwareC-mst-region] instance 2 vlan 3-4
```

Based on the commands that were executed, which statement is true?

a. A Layer 2 loop exists.

b. ComwareC is the root switch for all three instances.

c. A spanning tree topology change will occur, with load-sharing no longer functioning on the uplinks from ComwareC.

d. No spanning tree topology change occurs, and load-sharing is functioning normally.

25. When spanning tree is enabled on a Comware switch, what is the name of the default region?

    a. The MAC address of the switch

    b. HP

    c. H3C

    d. The serial number of the switch

26. Examine the network topology in Figure 17-7.

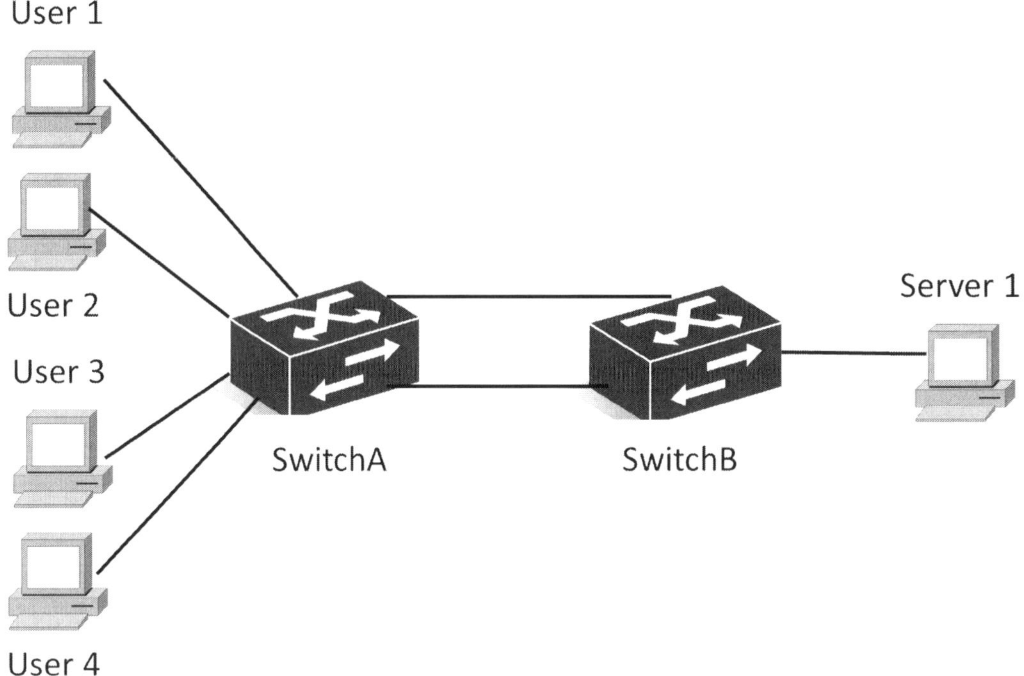

Figure 17-7. Question 26 network topology

The two ProVision switches are configured for link aggregation. Examine the output of SwitchA:

```
SwitchA# show trunk
 Load Balancing
  Port | Name                             Type       | Group  Type
  ---- + -----------------------------   ---------  + -----  -----
   1    | Router                           100/1000T  | Trk1   LACP
   2    | Router                           100/1000T  | Trk1   LACP


SwitchA# show lacp
                          LACP
   PORT   LACP      TRUNK     PORT      LACP      LACP
   NUMB   ENABLED   GROUP     STATUS    PARTNER   STATUS
   ----   -------   -------   -------   -------   ------
    1      Active   Trk1        Up      Yes       Success
    2      Active   Trk1        Up      Yes       Success


SwitchA# show interface display
               Status and Counters - Port Counters
                                                        Flow  B*
 Port    Total Bytes Total Frames Errors Rx Drops Rx  Ctrl L*
 ------- ----------- ------------ --------- --------  ---- -*
 1-Trk1       375,648       40,516         0        0   off  0
 2-Trk1             0            0         0        0   off  0
<-output omitted->
```

Based on this configuration and output, which statement is true concerning the link aggregation configuration and load-sharing operation?

a. The two switches have failed to form an aggregated link.

b. SwitchA is using destination MAC addresses for its load-sharing method, and SwitchB is using source MAC addresses for its load-sharing.

c. SwitchA is using source MAC addresses for its load-sharing method and SwitchB is using destination MAC addresses for its load-sharing.

d. SwitchA and SwitchB are using source and destination MAC addresses for their load-sharing.

27. Examine the network topology in Figure 17-8.

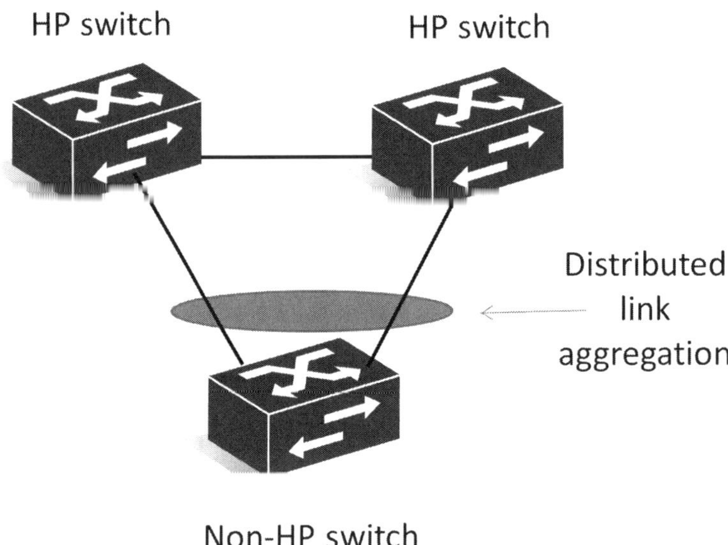

Figure 17-8. Question 27 network topology

Based on this topology, which technology should you deploy to successfully establish link aggregation from the non-HP switch to the two HP switches? (Select two.)

a. Comware using IRF

b. Comware using meshed stacking

c. ProVision using IRF

d. ProVision using distributed trunking

e. Comware using distributed trunking

28. What is the maximum number of links you can configure when deploying Link Aggregation Control Protocol (LACP) link aggregation on a single aggregate connection between two devices?

a. 4

b. 8

c. 16

d. 24

29. Which ProVision switch command configures link aggregation to a connected device?
    a. `link-aggregate`
    b. `interface bridge-aggregation`
    c. `interface trunk`
    d. `trunk`

30. When configuring a static route on a Comware switch, which parameter changes the administrative distance of the route?
    a. `preference`
    b. `distance`
    c. `administrative-distance`
    d. `precedence`

31. What mechanism does RIP employ so that routes learned from a neighbor connected to an interface are not advertised back out the same interface?
    a. Poison reverse
    b. Poison routing
    c. Split horizon
    d. Sanity updates

32. Which statement describes a characteristic of RIPv1?
    a. Broadcasts are used to advertise routes.
    b. Authentication of routing updates is optional.
    c. Variable-length subnet masking (VLSM) and classless interdomain routing (CIDR) are supported.
    d. Triggered updates are used to speed up convergence.

33. What states must OSPF routers go through when forming an adjacency with all OSPF routers on a segment? (Select three.)
    a. Down
    b. Exstart
    c. Full
    d. Init
    e. Loading
    f. Two-way

34. Which statement is true concerning OSPF?
    a. All OSPF routers send updates to 224.0.0.5.
    b. Link state advertisement (LSA) Type 1s announce stub network availability.
    c. The maximum transmission unit (MTU) sizes must match between neighbors to form an adjacency.
    d. An area may be identified by any number.

35. Examine the following OSPF configuration on a Comware switch:

```
[Comware] interface vlan 10
[Comware-vlan-1] ip address 10.1.10.1 255.255.255.0
[Comware-vlan-1] quit
[Comware] interface vlan 11
[Comware-vlan-1] ip address 10.1.11.1 255.255.255.0
[Comware-vlan-1] quit
[Comware] interface vlan 12
[Comware-vlan-1] ip address 10.1.12.1 255.255.255.0
[Comware-vlan-1] quit
[Comware] interface vlan 13
[Comware-vlan-1] ip address 10.1.13.1 255.255.255.0
[Comware-vlan-1] quit
[Comware] interface vlan 14
[Comware-vlan-1] ip address 10.1.24.1 255.255.255.0
[Comware-vlan-1] quit
[Comware] ospf 1 router-id 1.1.1.1
[Comware-ospf-1] area 0
[Comware-ospf-1-area-0.0.0.0] network 10.1.8.0 0.0.3.255
```

    Based on this information, which interfaces belong to Area 0?
    a. VLAN 10 only
    b. VLAN 10 and 11 only
    c. VLAN 10, 11, and 12 only
    d. VLAN 10, 11, 12, and 13 only
    e. VLAN 10, 11, 12, and 13

36. Which ProVision command includes a network in a specific OSPF area?
    a. `ip ospf area`
    b. `ospf area`
    c. `network`
    d. `router ospf`

37. Which HP switches can be included with different Comware switch models in the same IRF topology?

    a. 5500s

    b. 5800s

    c. 7500s

    d. 12500s

38. Four Comware switches boot up at the same time and form an HP Intelligent Resilient Framework (IRF topology). What is used to determine which switch becomes the master of the IRF topology?

    a. System uptime

    b. Lowest system MAC address

    c. Highest IP address

    d. Lowest IP address

    e. Highest system MAC address

39. Which technology cannot be used in IRF to detect a split stack?

    a. ARP

    b. BFD

    c. LACP

    d. MSTP

40. Examine the following Comware configuration:

```
<Comware> display irf topology
   Topology Info
------------------------------------------------------
   IRF-Port1   IRF-Port2
Switch   Link  neighbor    Link  neighbor    Belong To
1  DIS   --    UP    2     0023-8929-54ad
2  UP    1     DIS   --    0023-8929-4f83
```

    Based on this configuration, which statement is true?

    a. This is a daisy-chain topology.

    b. The IRF ports are misconfigured.

    c. Switch 2 is the master.

    d. Switch 1 has a higher priority in the IRF topology.

41. Which wireless mode is used to bridge traffic between two locations?
    a. Ad hoc mode
    b. In-cell relay mode
    c. Infrastructure mode
    d. Switch mode

42. Which statement concerning 802.1X is true?
    a. Requires a web browser for authentication
    b. Encrypts message transmissions
    c. Used between a supplicant and an authentication server
    d. Implements the RADIUS protocol between an authenticator and an authentication server

43. What is the default operational mode of an MSM access point?
    a. Autonomous
    b. Controlled
    c. Infrastructure
    d. Managed

44. Which IMC module can prevent devices infected with malware from spreading the infection to other devices on the network?
    a. Endpoint Admission Defense (EAD)
    b. Network Traffic Analyzer (NTA)
    c. Intrusion Prevention System (IPS)
    d. User Access Manager (UAM)

45. Which group does the admin account belong to in IMC?
    a. Administrator
    b. Maintainer
    c. Manager
    d. Operator

46. Which method is not supported for auto-discovering devices in IMC?
    a. ARP-based
    b. IPsec VPN-based
    c. LLDP-based
    d. Point-to-Point protocol-based
    e. Router-based

47. When importing devices into IMC, which item must you configure in IMC?
    a. SNMP template
    b. Telnet or SSH authentication credentials
    c. Loopback interface
    d. SNMP traps

48. Match the layer with its corresponding description.

a. Access	1. Contain broadcasts
b. Core	2. Contains wireless access points
c. Distribution	3. Performs few packet manipulations

49. Which gigabit Ethernet technology supports the longest cable hauls?
    a. 1000Base-LX
    b. 1000Base-SX
    c. 1000Base-T
    d. 1000Base-LH

50. Which VLAN types are only supported on Comware switches (not on ProVision switches)? (Select three.)
    a. 802.1X-based
    b. IP subnet-based
    c. Isolate user-based
    d. Protocol-based
    e. Super-based
    f. MAC address-based

Answers

1. ☑ **B** is correct. Designed for the HP BladeSystem C-series, Virtual Connect enables deployment of access layer solutions, including Fibre Channel over Ethernet (FCoE), in a simple and extremely flexible way, to connect blade servers to IP LANs and FC storage area networks (SANs).

   ☒ **A** and **D** are incorrect because these products are switches, not modules. **C** is incorrect because this module only provides Ethernet connections.
   For more information, see Chapter 2.

2. ☑ **A is 3**. The 6120XG and 6125XG are switch cards for the C-series blade server solutions in the FlexFabric (data center) architecture. **B is 2**. The ProVision 3800 switches are used commonly at the distribution and access layers of the FlexCampus architecture. **C is 1**. The MSR series routers are commonly used in the FlexBranch architecture. **D is 4**. IMC is HP's networking management product for the FlexManagement architecture.
   For more information, see Chapter 2.

3. ☑ **C** is correct. The infrastructure layer includes the underlying ports and forwarding hardware that move data across your network.

   ☒ **A** is incorrect because the application layer represents the actual applications in SDN. **B** is incorrect because the control layer presents an abstracted view of the infrastructure, allowing the network administrator to apply one or more policies across the network. The controller's job is to enforce these policies. A controller needs to communicate with the infrastructure but must also be able to communicate with applications. Answer **D** is incorrect because management is a nonexistent layer in SDN.
   For more information, see Chapter 2.

4. ☑ **C** is correct. The ProVision modular switches identify modules with letters and starting number ports at 1, so the correct answer is B2.

   ☒ **A** and **B** are incorrect because this is an invalid nomenclature for HP switches. **D** is incorrect because this nomenclature is used on Comware modular switches.
   For more information, see Chapter 3.

5. ☑ **D** is correct. The `reset and debug` command, along with flash file system management, can only be performed from User View on a Comware device.

   ☒ **A** and **B** are incorrect because these are ProVision privilege levels. **C** is incorrect because System View is used to make configuration changes on a Comware device.
   For more information, see Chapter 3.

6. ☑ **A is 2**. The `ip-route static` command configures a static route on a Comware device. **B is 1**. The `vlan ip address` command configures an IP address for a VLAN on a ProVision switch. **C is 1**. The `hostname` command configures the local host name on a ProVision switch. **D is 1**. The `disable` command disables an interface on a ProVision switch. **E is 2**. The `interface vlan-interface` command configures the logical VLAN interface on a Comware device. **F is 2**. The `port-group` command allows you to apply a configuration across multiple ports on a Comware device.
   For more information, see Chapter 3.

7. ☑ **C** is correct. The Clear button clears the passwords stored in the mgrinfo.txt file in the flash file system of the ProVision switches.

   ☒ **A** is incorrect because the Reset and Clear buttons, when pressed together, clear only the configuration of the switch (and reboot it), but they do not delete the mgrinfo.txt file. **B** is incorrect because the Reset button reboots the switch. **D** is incorrect because this is a nonexistent button.
   For more information, see Chapter 4.

8. ☑ **A** is correct. When you log in to the console port of a Comware router or the auxiliary port of a Comware switch, you are immediately given Manager access, which is the highest privilege level of a Comware device.

   ☒ **B**, **C**, and **D** are incorrect. Even though they are valid privilege levels, they are not the default levels of access to the Comware router console port or the Comware switch auxiliary port.
   For more information, see Chapter 4.

9. ☑ **B**, **C**, and **E** are correct. The defaults for the ProVision switches are Telnet, SSH, and clear-text web access is enabled. The defaults for Comware devices are Telnet, and clear-text web access is enabled. SSL web server functions are disabled, by default, on ProVision switches.

   ☒ **A** is incorrect because Telnet is enabled on ProVision, by default. **D** is incorrect because SSH is disabled, by default, on Comware. **F** is incorrect because only clear-text web access is enabled on Comware, by default.
   For more information, see Chapter 4.

10. ☑ **B** is correct. The correct syntax to upgrade the ProVision operating system from a USB drive is: `copy usb flash <image-name> {primary | secondary}`.

    ☒ **A** is incorrect because the `upgrade` command is a nonexistent command. **C** and **D** are incorrect because the `copy` command is used for operating system upgrades, but these examples have incorrect syntax.
    For more information, see Chapter 5.

11. ☑ **A** is correct. Use the `startup saved-configuration` command to specify a startup configuration file to be used at the next startup of a Comware device.

    ☒ **B** is incorrect because this command is used to accomplish the task on a ProVision switch. **C** and **D** are incorrect because they are invalid commands.
    For more information, see Chapter 5.

12. ☑ **C** and **E** are correct. To permanently delete a file so that it cannot be recovered, use the `delete /unreserved` command. To empty the recycle bin so that the files cannot be recovered, use the `reset recycle-bin` command.

    ☒ **A** is incorrect because this is a nonexistent command. **B** and **D** are incorrect because these are invalid parameters.
    For more information, see Chapter 5.

13. ☑ **B** is correct. The `port trunk permit vlan` command adds VLANs to the existing trunk—you must manually remove the VLANs that you don't want from the trunk.

    ☒ **A** is incorrect because this configuration adds VLANs 30 to 31 to the trunk—it does not replace them. **C** and **D** are invalid configurations and, therefore, are incorrect.
    For more information, see Chapter 6.

14. ☑ **C** is correct. A hybrid port on a Comware device allows you to support multiple tagged or untagged VLANs on the same port.

    ☒ **A** is incorrect because an access port supports only a single untagged VLAN. **B** is incorrect because a trunk supports many VLANS, but only one can be untagged. Answers **D** and **E** are incorrect because they are nonexistent port types. Answer **F** is incorrect because this is a ProVision term.
    For more information, see Chapter 6.

15. ☑ **B** is correct. Because VLAN 10 extends between the two switches, it must be included on the trunk. And, to route traffic to VLAN 20, it also must be included on the VLAN trunk.

    ☒ **A** is incorrect because VLAN 30 is local and, therefore, doesn't have to be included on the VLAN trunk. SwitchB will route traffic to/from it as necessary for the other VLANs. **C** is incorrect because VLAN 20—not 30—needs to be included on the trunk. **D** is incorrect because there is no such command as `port mode trunk` on the ProVision switches.
    For more information, see Chapter 6.

16. ☑ **B** is correct. The correct syntax requires that you specify the DHCP relay with the `ip helper-address` command for the VLAN where the users reside.

    ☒ **A** is incorrect because there is no such command as `ip helper-vlan`. **C** is incorrect because it doesn't specify the correct user VLAN. **D** is incorrect because it is configured on the wrong switch.
    For more information, see Chapter 7.

17. ☑ **B**, **C**, **D**, and **F** are correct. ProVision switch logging levels include major, error, warning, informational, and debug.

☒ **A** and **E** are not logging levels on the ProVision switches and, therefore, are incorrect answers.

For more information, see Chapter 7.

18. ☑ **E** is correct. *Synchronous information* (configured with the `info-center synchronous` command) means that, if the user's input is interrupted by system output, such as log, trap, or debugging information, after completing system output, the system displays a command line prompt. This is accomplished with the `info-center synchronous` command on Comware devices.

☒ **A** is incorrect because `logging` is an invalid parameter. **B** and **C** are incorrect because there is no `logging` command for Comware. **D** is incorrect because `display` is an invalid parameter.

For more information, see Chapter 7.

19. ☑ **B**, **E**, and **F** are correct. SwitchC is the root switch, making port A2 on SwitchA a root port. Because SwitchB has two links to the root switch (B2 and B3) and the port priorities are the same, the lowest number port (B2) becomes the root port and port B3 is placed in a discarding state. Since SwitchA and SwitchB have the same cost to the root, the tie breaker is the lowest switch ID. Since SwitchA has a lower switch ID (lower MAC address), port A1 becomes the designated port for the segment between the two switches.

☒ **A** and **C** are incorrect because SwitchC is the root. **D** is incorrect because all active ports on the root are designated ports.

For more information, see Chapter 8.

20. ☑ **B** and **E** are correct. ComwareB has the lowest switch ID (lowest MAC address) and, therefore, is the root switch. (The default priority on all HP switches is 32,768.) Comware switches use the older cost structure and, therefore, port A2 is the designated port since ComwareA has a lower cost path to the root than ProVisionC.

☒ **A** and **C** are incorrect because these switches have higher MAC addresses. **D** is incorrect because A1 is a root port. **F** is incorrect because all active ports on the root switch are designated ports.

For more information, see Chapter 8.

21. ☑ **B** is correct. The best port to reach the root is called a *root port*. Secondary ports are designated as alternate ports in RSTP.

☒ **A** is incorrect because a backup port is a secondary designated port. **C** is incorrect because a designated port is the best port a network segment can use to reach the root switch. **D** is incorrect because this is not a port type.

For more information, see Chapter 8.

22. ☑ **D** is correct. Since there are four uplinks, you need to create four instances, separating out the VLANs appropriately, and configure a corresponding switch at the distribution layer as the root and the remaining distribution layer switches as secondary roots.

☒ **A**, **B**, and **C** are incorrect because this configuration would not utilize all four uplinks. **E** is incorrect because, even though there are five distribution switches, there are only four uplinks.

For more information, see Chapter 8.

23. ☑ **B** is correct. The syntax to set the MSTP priority for an instance on ProVision switches is: `spanning tree instance <number> priority <number>`. Note that the priority is a *multiplier*—not an actual priority number. This value is then multiplied by 4,096 to derive the actual switch priority.

☒ **A** is incorrect because it is an invalid parameter. **C** is incorrect because you specify a multiplier—not an actual priority. **D** is incorrect because `mstp` is an invalid parameter.

For more information, see Chapter 9.

24. ☑ **D** is correct. Because the `active region-configuration` command was not executed on ComwareC after changing instance 2's VLAN mappings, the change does not go into effect and, therefore, no STP recalculation occurs.

☒ **A** is incorrect because MSTP is configured and operating correctly. **B** is incorrect because ComwareA and ComwareB are the root switches based on their changed priorities. **C** is incorrect because the `active region-configuration` command was not executed after the `instance 2 vlan 3-4` command on SwitchC and, therefore, the change does not go into effect.

For more information, see Chapter 9.

25. ☑ **A** is correct. All HP switches use their MAC addresses as the region name, by default. Therefore, if you enable MSTP on HP switches without defining the region information, the region information between the switches will not match. In this situation, the equivalent of RSTP is running between the switches.

☒ **B**, **C**, and **D** are incorrect because the region name defaults to the system MAC address of the switch.

For more information, see Chapter 9.

26. ☑ **B** is correct. Based on the `show lacp` command, both sides have successfully negotiated link aggregation. Since there are four users and one server, and only one link is being utilized, SwitchA is load-sharing based on destination MAC addresses and SwitchB is load-sharing based on source MAC addresses.

☒ **A** is incorrect because this contradicts the output of the `show lacp` command. **C** and **D** are incorrect because, if this was the case, traffic should be traversing both links in the aggregate connection.

For more information, see Chapter 10.

27. ☑ **A** and **D** are correct. Comware using IRF or ProVision using distributed trunking allows you to set up distributed link aggregation from a neighboring device with a link to each individual HP switch.

☒ **B**, **C**, and **E** are incorrect because the related technology is not supported on the specified switch.
For more information, see Chapter 10.

28. ☑ **C** is correct. When configuring link aggregation with LACP, you can have up to eight active links and up to eight backup links, totaling 16 links.

☒ **A**, **B**, and **D** are incorrect because they have the wrong value.
For more information, see Chapter 10.

29. ☑ **D** is correct. Use the `trunk` command to configure link aggregation on a ProVision switch.

☒ **B** is incorrect because this command is used to set up link aggregation on a Comware switch. **A** and **C** are incorrect because these are nonexistent commands on ProVision switches.
For more information, see Chapter 10.

30. ☑ **A** is correct. To configure a static route on a Comware switch, use the following syntax:

```
[Comware] ip route-static <destination-network> <mask>
          <next-hop-ip-address> [preference <preference>]
          [description <description>]
```

The `preference` parameter defines the administrative distance, which defaults to 1 if omitted.

☒ **B**, **C**, and **D** are incorrect because these are nonexistent parameters.
For more information, see Chapter 11.

31. ☑ **C** is correct. Split horizon prevents RIP from advertising a network back out the same interface it was learned on.

☒ **A** is incorrect because, when a network goes down, it is advertised with an infinite metric, notifying neighbors that it is not reachable. **B** and **D** are incorrect because these are invalid terms.
For more information, see Chapter 11.

32. ☑ **A** is correct. Broadcasts are used to advertise routes in RIPv1. RIPv2 uses multicasts.

☒ **B**, **C**, and **D** are incorrect because these are characteristics of RIPv2, not RIPv1.
For more information, see Chapter 11.

33. ☑ **A**, **D**, and **F** are correct. All OSPF routers go through three states, called the *exchange process*, to determine whether they become neighbors: down, init, and two-way.

☒ **B**, **C**, and **E** are incorrect because these states only occur when building an adjacency with a designated router (DR) or a backup designated router (BDR).
For more information, see Chapter 12.

34. ☑ **C** is correct. For two routers to become neighbors, the following must match on each router: the area number, the network or subnet number, the hello and dead interval timers on their connected interfaces, the OSPF authentication password (optional), if it is configured, the area type (normal, stub, or not-so-stubby [NSSA]—area types are discussed in the ASE level networking courses), the link type (broadcast or point-to-point), and the MTU sizes on the connected interfaces.

☒ **A** is incorrect because routing updates must be sent to the DR/BDR first via a 224.0.0.6 multicast. **B** is incorrect because an LSA 1 advertisement is any network directly connected to a router. **D** is incorrect because only the backbone can be identified by an area number of 0.
For more information, see Chapter 12.

35. ☑ **B** is correct. A wild card mask matches on a range of four addresses, starting on a power or a multiple of a power of 2, for which 8, in the third octet of the network number, qualifies. Therefore, addresses from 8 through 11 would match in the third octet, which includes 10.1.10.0/24 and 10.1.11.0/24.

☒ **A** is incorrect because it doesn't include 10.1.11.0/24. **C**, **D**, and **E** are incorrect because they include networks other than subnets 10 and 11.
For more information, see Chapter 12.

36. ☑ **A** is correct. To associate networks to the areas, use the `ip ospf area` command under the VLAN context.

☒ **B** is incorrect because the command begins with `ip`. **C** is incorrect because the `network` command is used on Comware switches for this purpose. **D** is incorrect because the `router ospf` command creates the OSPF process only.
For more information, see Chapter 12.

37. ☑ **B** is correct. The 5800s and 5820s can be included in the same IRF topology, and the 5900AF and 5920AF switches can also be intermixed in an IRF topology.

☒ **A**, **C**, and **D** cannot be mixed with other models and, therefore, are incorrect answers.
For more information, see Chapter 13.

38. ☑ **B** is correct. If all switches in an IRF topology boot up at the same time and their priorities are the same, the tie breaker is the switch with the lowest system MAC address.

☒ **A** is incorrect because the switches all booted up at the same time. **C** and **D** are incorrect because, with few exceptions, the switches have identical configurations (and the same IP addresses). Answer **E** is incorrect because it lists the highest MAC address.
For more information, see Chapter 13.

39. ☑ **D** is correct. MSTP cannot be used to detect a split stack, however, when using multi-active detection (MAD) ARP, MSTP (or some type of STP) protocol is necessary to test failures.

☒ **A**, **B**, and **C** are all protocols that can be implemented by MAD and therefore are incorrect answers.
For more information, see Chapter 13.

40. ☑ **A** is correct. Based on the CLI output "DIS", or disabled state, this is a daisy-chain topology.

☒ **B** is incorrect because the IRF ports are matched up 1 to 2. **C** and **D** are incorrect because there is not enough information to determine who the master is or who has the higher priority.
For more information, see Chapter 13.

41. ☑ **B** is correct. In-cell relay mode is used to connect two or more network segments over a wireless connection.

☒ **A** is incorrect because only two devices communicate with each other directly. **C** is incorrect because an access point is used for devices to intercommunicate with each other. **D** is incorrect because this is an invalid mode.
For more information, see Chapter 14.

42. ☑ **D** is correct. An AAA protocol like RADIUS is used between the networking device (authenticator) and the authentication (AAA) server.

☒ **A** is incorrect because 802.1X is a data link layer protocol. **B** is incorrect because not all methods of 802.1X encrypt information, and those that do typically only encrypt passwords. **C** is incorrect because 802.1X defines the operation between the supplicant and the authenticator.
For more information, see Chapter 14.

43. ☑ **B** is correct. The default operational mode of an MSM AP is controlled.

☒ **A** is incorrect because you have to change the mode to autonomous and reboot for the change to take effect. **C** and **D** are incorrect because these are non-existent modes.
For more information, see Chapter 14.

44. ☑ **A** is correct. The Endpoint Admission Defense module helps protect networks from internal threats. It can prevent devices infected with malware from spreading the infection to other devices on the network. It can also help companies ensure that devices and applications are patched, so that hackers cannot exploit these vulnerabilities.

    ☒ **B** is incorrect because the Network Traffic Analyzer module is a graphical network-monitoring tool that provides real-time information about users and applications consuming network bandwidth. You can use NTA to plan, monitor, enhance, and troubleshoot networks and to identify bottlenecks and apply corrective measures for enhanced throughput. **C** is incorrect because this is a nonexistent module. **D** is incorrect because the User Access Manager allows you to translate business policies for access controls into network configurations. From a single management interface that is integrated into the IMC platform, you can create service policies and then apply those service policies to user accounts. It functions as an AAA server.
    For more information, see Chapter 15.

45. ☑ **A** is correct. Operators in the Administrator group have all rights to IMC. They can manage all users, and they can add and delete users. They can configure all network devices and view any information gathered and stored by IMC. The default admin account is associated to this group, by default.

    ☒ **B** is incorrect because the Maintainer group has restricted access in IMC. Answers **C** and **D** are incorrect because these are ProVision privilege levels.
    For more information, see Chapter 15.

46. ☑ **C** is correct. LLDP is not a supported method for IMC auto-discovering devices.

    ☒ **A**, **B**, **D**, and **E** are valid methods of auto-discovering devices, are network-based, and, therefore, are incorrect answers.
    For more information, see Chapter 15.

47. ☑ **B** is correct. IMC needs CLI access to a device to perform management tasks that cannot be performed via SNMP. Either Telnet or SSH can be configured. You can predefine a template for this access or define the parameters during the auto-discovery or device import process.

    ☒ **A** is incorrect because you can manually define the SNMP parameters or use a template. **C** and **D** are incorrect because you can optionally specify these in IMC.
    For more information, see Chapter 15.

48. ☑ **A is 2**, **B is 3**, and **C is 1**. The bottom layer of the three-layer hierarchical model is the access layer. Actually, the access layer is at the periphery of your campus network, separated from the core layer by the distribution layer. The main function of the access layer is to provide the user's initial connection to your network. Typically, this connection is provided by a switch or wireless access point. The distribution layer, commonly called the *aggregation layer***,** performs most of the connectivity tasks. In larger networks, routing switches or traditional routers are used at the distribution layer to connect the access layers to the core. For smaller networks, sometimes switches are used. The responsibilities of the distribution layer include: contain broadcasts between the layers, secure traffic between the layers, provide a hierarchy through Layer 3 logical addressing and route summarization, and translate between different media types. The core layer, as its name suggests, is the backbone of the network. It provides a high-speed connection between the different distribution layer devices. Because of the need for high-speed connections, the core consists of high-speed switches and does not, typically, perform any type of packet or frame manipulations, such as filtering or Quality of Service (QoS).
For more information, see Chapter 16.

49. ☑ **D** is correct. 1000Base-LH supports distances up to 70km.

☒ **A** is incorrect because 1000Base-LX supports distances up to 550m. **B** is incorrect because 1000Base-SX supports distances up to 500m. **C** is incorrect because 1000Base-T supports distances up to 100m.
For more information, see Chapter 16.

50. ☑ **B**, **C**, and **E** are correct. Of HP switches, only Comware switches support IP subnet-based, isolate user-based, and super VLANs.

☒ **A**, **D**, and **F** are incorrect because both ProVision and Comware switches support these VLAN implementations.
For more information, see Chapter 16.

Glossary

AAA—There are three components to AAA: authentication, authorization, and accounting. AAA provides a uniform framework for implementing network access management. AAA usually uses a client/server model. The client runs on the network access server (NAS), and the server maintains user information centrally.

access layer—The bottom layer of the three-layer hierarchical model is the *access layer*. Actually, the access layer is at the periphery of your campus network, separated from the core layer by the distribution layer. The main function of the access layer is to provide the user's initial connection to your network. Typically, this connection is provided by a switch or wireless access point. Sometimes, if the user works at a small branch office or home office, this device can also be a router or firewall. But, in most cases, the connection is typically provided by a switch. As more and more traditional Layer 2 switches support Layer 3 routing and access control list (ACL) features, the access layer can be used to provide routing and security features at the edge or ingress to the network.

access port—An access port belongs to one VLAN, and frames are untagged. An access port belongs to only one VLAN. It is typically used to connect a terminal device unable to recognize VLAN-tagged frames or when there is no need to separate different VLAN members.

ad hoc mode—An ad hoc network includes two or more stations (devices) that communicate directly with each other using wireless transmissions. Each station in an ad hoc network receives every 802.11 frame transmitted.

administrative distance—External prioritization is used when two different routing protocols know about the same destination, and a method is needed to determine which routing protocol has the better path to the destination. For example, specifying the same preference for different routes to the same destination can allow for load-sharing, and specifying different preferences for these routes enables route backup. Different vendors use different terms. For example, in the HP Comware products, the term *preference* or *precedence* is commonly used; with the HP ProVision products and with Cisco, the term *administrative distance* is used.

aggregation layer—The aggregation layer, commonly called the *distribution layer*, performs most of the connectivity tasks. In larger networks, routing switches or traditional routers are used at the distribution layer to connect the access layers to the core. For smaller networks, sometimes switches are used. The responsibilities of the distribution layer include containing broadcasts between the layers, securing traffic between the layers, providing a hierarchy through Layer 3 logical addressing and route summarization, translating between different media types, and other functions.

alternate port—An alternate port is a spanning tree port that has an alternative path or paths to the root but is currently in a discarding state.

Area Border Router (ABR)—ABRs are Open Shortest Path First (OSPF) routers that have interfaces in at least two areas, one of which is Area 0. Area 0 is the backbone area, and OSPF design requires all areas to connect to this backbone (physically or logically). As a member of multiple areas, the ABR maintains multiple link state databases, one for each area.

authentication server—The authentication server in wireless transmissions makes access decisions based on whether the user supplies valid authentication credentials. The authentication server is often a Remote Authentication Dial-In User Server (RADIUS), which could be an external server (such as the Microsoft Network Policy Server [NPS]) or the WLAN access controller's internal RADIUS server (if the controller includes one).

authenticator—The authenticator in wireless transmissions controls access to the network, preventing the supplicant from transmitting data onto the network until it has successfully authenticated. On a wireless network, stand-alone or fat access points (APs) operate as the authenticators. Controlled APs may operate as authenticators or may rely on the controller to perform this function: APs forward all user authentication requests to it. (However, the APs can still distribute users' data directly onto the wired network.)

autonomous access point—Stand-alone APs are also referred to as *autonomous* or *fat* APs. Stand-alone APs can operate without any direction from a wireless controller. They are more common in smaller networks where there are a small number of APs that need to be managed; in larger networks, it is easier to deploy thin or fit APs where the intelligence is centralized on the wireless controller or controllers and, therefore, is easier to manage.

Autonomous System Boundary Router (ASBR)—An ASBR is a router that advertises external routes. A route is considered external when it is learned by a method or protocol other than the current OSPF process and is then redistributed or imported into the current OSPF process. In this example, both core switches must act as ASBRs. These external routes could be from another protocol, like Border Gateway Protocol (BGP) or a different OSPF network, static or default routes, or even directly connected external routes.

backup designated router (BDR)—The BDR is a secondary or backup of the designated router (DR). See *designated router*.

backup port—A backup port is a spanning tree port on a segment that could be used to reach the root switch, but an active port is already designated for the segment.

Basic Service Set (BSS)—An access point and the station or stations connected to it compose a BSS. Each BSS has a unique, 48-bit identifier, called the *BSSID*, which is usually the MAC address of the AP's radios. Every frame transmitted to and from the stations in a BSS contains the BSSID in the frame header, identifying the frame as belonging to a particular AP's coverage area. Thus, the BSSID distinguishes one BSS from others and increases efficiency by allowing the AP and stations to ignore frames not belonging to their BSS. When a new station joins the BSS, it appends the AP's BSSID to all frames as the receiver address in the 802.11 header.

BPDU protection (BPDU guard)—For access layer devices, the access ports generally connect directly with user terminals (such as PCs) or file servers. In this case, the access ports are configured as edge ports to allow rapid transition when changes occur in spanning tree. When these ports receive configuration BPDUs, the system automatically sets these ports as non-edge ports and starts a new spanning tree calculation process. This causes a change of network topology. Under normal conditions, these ports should not receive configuration BPDUs. However, if someone creates BPDUs maliciously to attack the devices or if a rogue switch is connected to a user (edge port), the network becomes unstable. Multiple STP (MSTP) provides the BPDU guard function to protect the system against such attacks. With the BPDU guard function enabled on the devices, when edge ports receive configuration BPDUs, MSTP closes these ports and generates a log message that these ports have been closed by MSTP.

Bridge Protocol Data Units—For Spanning Tree Protocol (STP) to function, the switches need to share information about themselves and their connections. What they share are BPDUs, which are sent out as multicast frames to which only other Layer 2 switches or bridges are listening. Switches use BPDUs to learn the topology of the network—what switch is connected to other switches and whether any Layer 2 loops are present in this topology.

Common Spanning Tree (CST)—The CST administers the connectivity among the MST regions, STP LANs, and Rapid STP (RSTP) LANs in a bridged network.

core layer—The core layer, as its name suggests, is the backbone of the network. It provides a high-speed connection between the different distribution layer devices. Because of the need for high-speed connections, the core consists of high-speed switches and does not, typically, perform any type of packet or frame manipulations, such as filtering or Quality of Service (QoS). Because switches are used at the core, the core is referred to as a *Layer 2 core*. However, if you are dealing with a large number of distribution layers that you need to connect to the core, the core might perform Layer 3 processing of traffic, like routing and QoS. The traffic that traverses the core is typically to access enterprise corporate resources: connections to the Internet, gateways, email servers, and corporate applications.

Deployment Monitoring Agent (DMA)—To help you monitor IMC and deploy the components and add-on modules, HP Intelligent Management Center (IMC) includes DMA. The agent allows you to perform tasks, including installing the IMC server, starting and stopping the IMC server, viewing the CPU usage and memory usage, determining the status (such as starting, started, or stopped) of IMC processes, deploying or deleting components or add-on modules, and other management tasks.

designated port—In addition to each switch having a root port, each segment also has a single port that it uses to reach the root, and this port is called a *designated port*. For example, imagine that a segment has two switches connected to it. Either one or the other switch forwards traffic from this segment to the root switch. The port on the forwarding switch is the designated port.

designated router—To minimize the link state advertisements (LSAs), OSPF routers do not achieve adjacency with each neighbor on a broadcast segment. Instead, the routers in the Ethernet network elect a DR and a BDR and achieve adjacency with them. The DR, which is adjacent to all routers, can forward LSAs between them.

distribution layer—See *aggregation layer*.

distributed trunking—Some ProVision switches support distributed trunking, which is designed to provide high availability and load-sharing for server-to-switch or switch-to-switch connections. With distributed port trunking, two or more links that are distributed across two switches form a trunk group. The grouped links appear to the downstream device as if they are from a single device. This feature is proprietary to the ProVision switches.

Dynamic Host Configuration Protocol (DHCP)—DHCP allows devices to acquire their addressing information dynamically. Originally defined in RFC 2131 and updated in RFC 2939, DHCP is actually based on the Bootstrap Protocol (Bootp).

Dynamic Host Configuration Protocol relay—DHCP clients (users) use a local broadcast to obtain addressing information; however, the problem with this situation is that the DHCP server is not commonly found on the same network subnet (broadcast domain). The HP switches support a DHCP relay feature, sometimes referred to as *IP helper*. A DHCP local broadcast request is changed to a DHCP unicast request and forwarded directly to a segment that contains a DHCP server. More specifically, the routing switch takes the broadcast from the client, changes it to a unicast, which is a source IP address from the client's VLAN, and routes the request to the destination DHCP server.

edge port—An edge port is a port connected to a non-Layer 2 device, such as a PC, server, or router. RSTP with rapid transition of edge ports to a forwarding state is the same as Cisco's proprietary PortFast. Changes in the state of these ports does not affect RSTP to cause a recalculation, and changes in other port types keeps these ports in a forwarding state.

Endpoint Admission Defense (EAD)—With EAD add-on module, IMC can be used to analyze a network endpoint's security status to locate security threats, detect security events, and carry out protective measures to reduce network vulnerabilities. EAD can determine endpoint patch level, ARP attack, abnormal traffic, and the installation and operation of illegal software. Administrators can choose enforcement policies and remediation options that are appropriate to particular endpoints.

Event Log—The ProVision Event Log records operating events in single- or double-line entries and serves as a tool to isolate and troubleshoot problems. Entries are listed in chronological order, from the oldest to the most recent. After the log has received 2,000 entries, it discards the oldest message each time a new message is received. The Event Log window contains 14 log entry lines. You can scroll through it to view any part of the log.

Extended Service Set (ESS)—Two or more BSSs compose an ESS. Like the BSS, each ESS has a unique 48-bit identifier. The Extended Service Set Identifier (ESSID) is commonly called the *SSID*, or *network name*. To access a wireless network, users select this SSID in their wireless client utility. The SSID is included in the 802.11 header of every frame transmitted on a wireless network. The BSSs are visually separated, but typically the BSSs overlap to allow users to roam without losing their wireless connection. An ESS can also be called a *wireless LAN* (WLAN). A WLAN defines a broadcast domain—that is, everyone who accesses the WLAN will receive all the broadcast frames. The WLAN also defines various settings for the ESS, such as the SSID and security options.

Exterior Gateway Protocol (EGP)—An EGP routing protocol facilitates exchange of routing information among routers in different autonomous systems. Border Gateway Protocol v4 (BGP4) is an example of an EGP and is commonly used by Internet service providers (ISPs) to route traffic on the Internet backbone. The most common EGP is a default static route.

fat access point—See *autonomous access point*.

Fibre Channel (FC)—FC is a high-speed network technology (commonly running at speeds of 2, 4, 8, and 16 gigabits) primarily used for storage networking. Basically, FC is running Small Computer System Interface (SCSI), a bus standard for connecting computers and their peripherals. FC runs SCSI directly between the server hardware and the storage area network (SAN).

Fibre Channel over Ethernet (FCoE)—FCoE is an encapsulation of Fibre Channel frames over Ethernet networks. This allows Fibre Channel to use 10 Gigabit (or higher) Ethernet networks while preserving the Fibre Channel protocol. Many data centers use Ethernet for TCP/IP networks and Fibre Channel for SANs. The main limitation of FCoE is that the devices must be in the same Layer 2 network (broadcast domain or VLAN).

fit access point—Intelligent, or fit, APs establish the wireless network but can perform other functions, as dictated by the controller and the WLAN architecture used. Fit APs still require the interaction of a wireless controller but provide intelligence that thin APs lack.

FlexBranch—The HP branch office networking solution converges infrastructure and network applications to significantly improve performance, simplify deployments, centralize management, and reduce IT costs. The branch solution is a component in the HP end-to-end enterprise network infrastructure, which optimizes the network for secure, reliable, high-performance application delivery and a foundation for converged infrastructure for the extended enterprise.

FlexCampus—The FlexCampus network is a modular building block of the FlexNetwork architecture, allowing enterprises to converge and secure wired and wireless LANs to deliver consistent, video-optimized and identity-based network access.

FlexFabric—The FlexFabric Network architecture is a blueprint for interconnected, integrated, and aligned servers, storage, software, and power and management in an end-to-end Converged Infrastructure in data center networks. The FlexFabric architecture combines advanced, standards-based platforms and advanced networking technologies to optimize performance and to reduce latency in virtualized server environments.

FlexManagement—FlexManagement combines a capability for single-pane-of-glass multivendor management with automated virtual machine orchestration and automatic synchronization of network connectivity information. It is available today in the HP IMC.

FlexNetwork architecture—FlexNetwork architecture is designed to allow IT to manage these different network segments through a single pane-of-glass management application, HP IMC. Due to the fact that FlexNetwork architecture is based on open standards, companies have the freedom to choose the best-in-class solution for their businesses. Its components include FlexFabric, FlexCampus, FlexBranch, and FlexManagement.

hold-down timers—To ensure that all networking devices understand that the downed network is not reachable, a hold-down timer instructs routers to delay (hold down) action upon update messages received from routes believed inactive. The period of time is generally longer than the time required to update the entire network of a routing change (typically at least three times larger than the periodic update interval). In Routing Information Protocol's (RIP's) case, the period timer is 30 seconds, but the hold-down timer is 240 seconds, by default. The use of the hold-down timer basically freezes the poisoned route in the routing table and allows all other routers to receive this update via periodic announcements.

hybrid port—A hybrid port belongs to multiple VLANs, where they can be untagged and tagged. This is typically used for Voice over Internet Protocol (VoIP) phones that share a switch, two or more virtual machines (VMs) sharing an interface, or two or more protocols used by a PC or server (like IPv4 and IPv6). If there is more than one untagged VLAN on a hybrid port, some method is needed for the switch to correctly identify the VLAN that should be associated with the traffic. Dynamic methods include MAC addresses, IP addresses, protocol, 802.1X credentials, and Link Layer Discovery Protocol–Media Endpoint Discovery (LLDP-MED) (voice) information. Like a trunk port, a hybrid port can carry multiple VLANs to receive and send traffic for them. Unlike a trunk port, a hybrid port allows traffic of different VLANs to pass through the same interface untagged and/or tagged. Usually, hybrid ports are configured to connect those devices for which support of VLAN tagged frames is unclear.

in-band management—With in-band management, your management communications run over network connections. You require IP connectivity to the networking device through a direct or indirect Ethernet connection. To open an in-band management session to access the network device's command-line interface (CLI), you must use terminal emulation software, such as PuTTY, that supports either Telnet or SSH. With Telnet, data is transmitted in clear text, whereas SSH encrypts the data you exchange with the switch.

in-cell relay mode—In-cell relay mode is used to connect two or more network segments over a wireless connection. The segments can be different segments of a LAN or unconnected wireless networks. For example, if a company's IT department wants to connect the LANs in two buildings, they could use two APs, operating in in-cell relay mode, rather than trying to run cable for a wired connection between the buildings. This mode is also called *wireless bridging*, *Wireless Distribution System* (WDS), or *local mesh*.

Information Center—Acting as the system information hub, the Information Center classifies and manages system information, offering a powerful support for network administrators and developers in monitoring network performance and diagnosing network problems. Information Center assigns the log, trap, and debugging information to the 10 information channels, according to the eight severity levels, and then outputs the information to different destinations.

infrastructure mode—The most common implementation for wireless networks is the infrastructure mode. In this mode, an AP establishes the wireless network and handles all communications from wireless stations that associate with it. The AP also controls the data rates for the network and, depending on the WLAN architecture used, enforces security settings and other settings, such as QoS. WLAN architectures determine which type of wireless devices establish and manage the wireless network and where wireless data is bridged onto the wired network.

Intelligent Management Center—HP IMC is a unified, single-point network management solution that provides visibility across entire networks, enabling complete management of resources, services, and users. Unifying wired, wireless, and user management leads to increased performance, enhanced security, and reduced infrastructure complexity and costs. IMC is Simple Network Management Protocol–based (SNMP-based) but does have support for other vendor products that do not primarily use SNMP, like Cisco.

Intelligent Resilient Forwarding stack port (or interface)—This is the logical interface, made up of 10Gbps (or faster) links, that extends the backplane between two Comware switches.

Intelligent Resilient Framework (IRF)—HP IRF is a technology that is currently supported on the Comware switching product line. IRF is an HP proprietary solution that provides fast failover, scalability, manageability, and high availability by creating a large IRF virtual device from multiple physical devices. IRF virtualization technology takes advantage of the augmented processing power, interaction, unified management, and uninterrupted maintenance of multiple switches.

Interior Gateway Protocol (IGP)—An IGP routing protocol facilitates the exchange of routing information among routers under the same organizational control—within the same autonomous system. An *autonomous system* is a group of devices under the same administrative control, like a company's networking devices. Examples of IGP routing protocols include static, RIP, and OSPF.

Internal Spanning Tree (IST)—The IST administers the topology within a given MST region. When you configure a switch for MSTP operation, the switch automatically includes all of the static VLANs configured on the switch in a single, active spanning tree topology (instance) within the IST. This is termed the *IST instance*. Any VLANs you subsequently configure on the switch are added to this IST instance. To create separate forwarding paths within a region, group specific VLANs into different MST instances (MSTIs).

Internet Small Computer System Interface (iSCSI)—iSCSI uses TCP, allowing two hosts to negotiate and then exchange SCSI commands using IP networks across different subnets (routed links). By doing this, iSCSI takes a popular high-performance local storage bus and emulates it over different networks, creating a SAN. Unlike some SAN protocols, iSCSI requires no dedicated cabling; it can be run over existing IP infrastructure. As a result, iSCSI is often seen as a low-cost alternative to Fibre Channel, which requires dedicated infrastructure except in its FCoE form. However, the performance of an iSCSI SAN deployment can be severely degraded if not operated on a dedicated network or subnet (LAN or VLAN).

IP helper—See *Dynamic Host Configuration Protocol relay.*

IP subnet-based VLANs—In IP subnet–based VLANs, frames are assigned to VLANs based on their source IP addresses and subnet masks. A port configured with IP subnet-based VLANs assigns a received untagged frame to a VLAN, based on the source IP address of the frame. This feature is used to assign frames from the specified network segment or IP address to a specific VLAN.

isolate user VLAN—The main purpose of the isolate user VLAN feature is to be able to reuse VLAN IDs. It is implemented at Layer 2 switches. When configuring a primary VLAN, say VLAN 20, on the Layer 2 switch, it must be declared an *isolate user VLAN*. Subordinate VLANs, say VLANs 211, 212, 213, are associated to the primary VLAN (VLAN 20) as secondary VLANs. This feature can be used for two reasons: to isolate the secondary VLANs (hence the feature's name) and to reuse VLAN IDs. In the second case, local proxy ARP can be required to re-enable communication between secondary VLANs.

link aggregation—Link aggregation is a Layer 2 solution that allows you to aggregate multiple Layer 2 Ethernet-based connections between directly connected devices. Link aggregation was introduced to deal with some of the limitations and issues of STPs. Cisco refers to link aggregation connections as *EtherChannels* or *port channels*. With HP, two terms are used, depending on which product set you are dealing with. ProVision switches use the term *trunking* or *port trunking* to describe an aggregated link. Comware devices use the term *bridge aggregation* or *route aggregation* when referring to link aggregation.

Link Aggregation Control Protocol (LACP)—LACP is an IEEE protocol (802.1AX) that negotiates with a neighboring device as to which physical links can participate in link aggregation. One advantage of LACP is that you can have up to eight active links and up to eight backup or standby links, so, if an active link fails, a standby link can take over and you do not lose any bandwidth. LACP provides guidelines for how conversations are managed on an aggregated link. A *conversation* is a one-way communication between a source device and a destination device. For example, when a workstation sends an Ethernet frame to a server, a conversation begins. All subsequent frames from the same workstation to the same server are part of that conversation.

Link Layer Discovery Protocol (LLDP)—The Internet Engineering Task Force (IETF) drafted the LLDP in IEEE 802.1AB. The protocol operates on the data link layer to exchange device information between directly connected devices. With LLDP, a device sends local device information (including its major functions, management IP address, device ID, and port ID) as type, length, and value (TLV) triplets in LLDP data units (LLDPDUs) to the directly connected devices and, at the same time, stores the device information received in LLDPDUs sent from the LLDP neighbors in a standard management information base (MIB). It allows a network management system to fast detect Layer 2 network topology change and to identify what the change is.

loop protection (loop guard)—By continuing to receive BPDUs from the upstream device, a device can maintain the state of the root port and blocked ports. However, due to link congestion or unidirectional link failures, these ports may fail to receive BPDUs from the upstream devices. In this case, the device reselects the port roles: the ports in the forwarding state that failed to receive upstream BPDUs become designated ports, and the blocked ports transition to the forwarding state, resulting in loops in the switched network. The loop guard function can suppress the occurrence of such loops.

loopback interfaces—Loopback interfaces are logical interfaces that are always up.

MAC address-based VLANs—The MAC address-based VLAN feature assigns hosts to VLANs based on their MAC addresses. With the MAC-based VLAN configured, the device processes received frames and then looks up the list of MAC-to-VLAN mappings, based on the source MAC address of the frame, for a match. Matches can be defined manually from the CLI, where you specify which MAC addresses belong to which VLAN, or you can use an authentication server to associate MAC address-to-VLAN mappings. In either approach, you can specify that a range of MAC addresses, like those for a particular vendor's VoIP phone, are assigned to the same VLAN.

Manager level—This ProVision access level allows read/write access. As a manager, you can make configuration changes and view information.

Multi-Active Detection (MAD)—As described earlier, IRF link failures may cause an integral IRF system to split into two or more IRFs operating with the same global configuration. Because these IRFs look the same to other devices in the network, problems, such as route flapping and STP calculation, result. To offset the risk, the MAD mechanism detects the presence of multiple identical IRFs split from an IRF system and handles the problem to make the network operate normally.

multiple input multiple output (MIMO)—Devices that support MIMO use multiple transceivers, each of which sends part of the data stream. Each transmission can take a different path to the receiver. Devices that receive the data stream also have multiple transceivers, which combine the multiple transmissions into a single data stream. Multiple data streams transmitted simultaneously effectively multiply the bandwidth.

Multiple Spanning Tree Protocol—The IEEE's 802.1s MSTP uses VLAN-to-instance mappings to create multiple spanning trees in a network, and this significantly improves network resource utilization while maintaining a loop-free environment, similar to Cisco's proprietary Per-VLAN Spanning Tree Plus (PVST+) but without its overhead. Released in 2002, 802.1s (MSTP) is an amendment to the 802.1Q-1998 standard. 802.1s provides an extension to STP and RSTP, allowing the protocol to use separate spanning trees for groups of VLANs. 802.1s was later merged into 802.1Q-2003.

Multiple Spanning Tree region—An MST region comprises the VLANs configured on physically connected MSTP switches. All switches in a given region must be configured with the same VLANs, the same multiple spanning tree instances, and the same MST configuration identifiers.

Network Time Protocol (NTP)—Defined in RFC 1305, NTP synchronizes timekeeping among distributed time servers and clients. NTP runs over the User Datagram Protocol (UDP), using UDP port 123. The purpose of using NTP is to maintain consistent timekeeping among all clock-dependent devices within a network so that the devices can provide diverse applications based on a consistent time.

Network Traffic Analyzer (NTA)—With the NTA add-on module for IMC, the system can also collect flow information from sFlow-, NetFlow-, and NetStream-capable devices. Through traffic analysis, NTA can help identify network bottlenecks, recognize anomalous traffic, and pinpoint varying levels of bandwidth traffic for different services and applications. The correlation of traffic flows to users is available with the additional User Behavior Analysis (UBA) module.

Open Shortest Path First—The OSPF routing protocol, as an IGP, functions between routing devices within the same domain, or autonomous system (AS), which is generally defined as a group of networked devices under the control of the same entity. It enables the routing devices to exchange information with each other about the IP subnets within the AS to discover routes between them. It is based on a link state implementation.

Operator level—This ProVision access level allows read-only access. You can only view statistics and configuration information.

out-of-band management—Out-of-band management is the most secure form of managing a networking product. With this method, you connect your management station to the switch's console port with a serial cable. This connection is dedicated to your management session, which you open using terminal emulation software, such as TeraTerm, HyperTerminal, or PuTTY.

passive interface—You can configure the stub network interface as a silent interface (sometimes called a *passive interface*). This type of interface runs OSPF. However, it blocks all OSPF traffic, including incoming and outgoing hellos. Therefore, even if an OSPF device does exist on the network, the Comware routing switch with the silent interface does not establish a neighbor relationship of any kind with it. The network connected to the silent interface, however, remains visible to OSPF, and the routing switch includes it in Type 1 and Type 2 LSAs when advertised out other links.

Per-VLAN Spanning Tree Plus—PVST+ was designed to overcome the deficiencies of 802.1D and RSTP. PVST+ was originally a Cisco-proprietary protocol developed to perform load-sharing of VLANs on multiple uplinks from access layer switches to distribution layer switches. With PVST+, each VLAN has its own instance of STP, with its own root switch, its own set of priorities, and its own set of BPDUs. In PVST+, the switch or bridge ID has been enhanced. In 802.1D, switch priority, extended system ID, and MAC address comprise switch or bridge ID. In PVST+, the switch or bridge ID has an additional field—the extended system ID that carries the VLAN ID (VID) for the instance of STP. With the addition of this field, it is possible to have different priorities on switches in different VLANs. Therefore, you are able to have multiple root switches—one per VLAN. Each VLAN in PVST+, by default, develops its own loop-free topology.

poison reverse—Poison reverse updates are used to prevent larger loops within the network by setting the metric (hop count) of neighboring routes to infinity. In RIP's case, the metric of the failed route is set to 16 (unreachable, since the maximum hop count is 15). This type of route is commonly called a *poisoned route*. This solution prevents multihop loops or larger loops.

policy-based VLANs—Policy-based VLANs are sometimes referred to as *dynamic VLAN assignment*. Policy-based VLAN assignment is probably the second-most common method of VLAN assignment, and it is typically employed in networks using 802.1X. Based on something from the user, like MAC or IP address, or login credentials from 802.1X, the switch dynamically assigns the port to a particular VLAN. In the case of 802.1X, since AAA and an AAA server are used to authenticate the user, the AAA server passes back the VLAN number to assign to the port, based on the user's profile or the group profile to which the user belongs on the AAA server.

port-based VLANs—Port-based VLANs group VLAN members by port. A port forwards traffic for a VLAN only after it is assigned to the VLAN—in other words, the port maintains the VLAN boundaries. For example, if a port was associated to VLAN 1, traffic for VLAN 2 would not be forwarded to the port. With port-based VLANs, the network administrator must manually map ports to their associated VLANs.

port groups—Some interfaces on your Comware switch may use the same set of settings. To configure these interfaces in bulk rather than one by one, you can assign them to a port group. You create port groups manually. All settings made for a port group apply to all of the member ports of the group. For example, you can configure a VLAN for multiple interfaces in bulk by assigning these interfaces to a port group. Any configuration command you make for a port group is replicated and saved for all of the interfaces within that group. Therefore, creating and using port groups reduces the number of commands you must configure if you have multiple interfaces that need to share the same properties. This is a Comware-only feature.

Port VLAN Identifier (PVID)—The PVID is the untagged VLAN assigned to the port.

Power over Ethernet—PoE is a method of providing power over Ethernet to a connected device. This allows devices to be installed without requiring a power outlet in the same location. Power supplied to these devices typically involves a low number of watts—enough to power low-end devices, like wireless APs, VoIP phones, and video cameras, among others. The original PoE standard, IEEE 802.3af, allows each device to receive up to 15.4 watts of power. The enhanced PoE+ standard, IEEE 802.3at, allows each device to receive up to 25.5 watts.

protocol-based VLANs—Protocol-based VLAN configuration applies to hybrid ports only. Inbound frames are assigned to different VLANs based on their Ethernet protocol types and encapsulation formats. The protocols that can be used for VLAN assignment include IP, IPX, and AppleTalk. The encapsulation formats include Ethernet II, 802.3 raw, 802.2 Logical Link Control (LLC), and 802.2 Sub-network Access Protocol (SNAP).

Rapid STP—RSTP is an IEEE standard, defined in 802.1w, which is interoperable with 802.1D and is an extension to it. With RSTP, there are only three port states: discarding, learning, and forwarding. With RSTP, there is still a root switch and there are still root and designated ports, performing the same roles as those in 802.1D. However, RSTP adds three additional port types: alternate ports, backup ports, and edge ports. These additional port states are intended to speed up convergence when Layer 2 topology changes occur.

Remote Authentication Dial-In User Service—RADIUS is a distributed client/server system that secures networks against unauthorized access. It is an open standards protocol that uses UDP to share information between the NAS and the security server. The only part that is encrypted between these two devices is the key (password)—all other information is sent in clear text, making this protocol susceptible to eavesdropping attacks. Radius uses UDP, and its packet format and message transfer mechanism are based on UDP. It uses UDP port 1812 for authentication and port 1813 for accounting.

rollover cable—The ProVision and Comware console cable is a rollover cable. With a rollover cable, pin 1 on one side connects to pin 8 on the other side, pin 2 to pin 7, pin 3 to pin 6, and so on. In other words, the pin-out of the remote side of the cable is reversed (rolled).

root port—After the root switch is elected in spanning tree, every other switch in the network needs to choose a single port, on itself, that it will use to reach the root. This port is called the *root port*.

root protection (root guard)—The root bridge and secondary root bridge of a spanning tree should be located in the same MST region. Especially for the common and internal spanning tree (CIST), the root bridge and secondary root bridge are generally put in a high-bandwidth core region during network design. However, due to possible configuration errors or malicious attacks in the network, the legal root bridge may receive a configuration BPDU with a lower priority value. In this case, the current legal root bridge will be superseded by another device, causing an undesired change of the network topology. To prevent this situation from happening, MSTP provides the root guard function. If the root guard function is enabled on a port of a root bridge, this port will keep playing the role of designated port on all MSTIs. After this port receives a configuration BPDU with a lower priority value from an MSTI, it immediately sets that port to the listening state in the MSTI without forwarding the packet (this is equivalent to disconnecting the link connected with this port in the MSTI).

Routing Information Protocol (RIP)—RIP is an IP route exchange protocol that uses a distance vector (a number representing distance) to measure the metric of a given route. These updates, which include a copy of a neighbor's routing table, are sent out every 30 seconds, by default. The frequency of these updates can be modified. The metric is a distance vector because the metric often is equivalent to the number of router hops between the Layer 3 routing device and the destination network. Because of slow convergence issues, RIP is not commonly used in large networks.

scheme—A Comware scheme requires the use of user names and passwords. For local authentication, a local user must be created. For RADIUS or Terminal Access Controller Access-Control System (TACACS) authentication, an AAA server configuration must be completed.

silent interface—See *passive interface*.

Simple Network Management Protocol—SNMP is an Internet-standard protocol for managing devices on IP networks. Devices that typically support SNMP include routers, switches, servers, workstations, and printers, among others. It is used mostly in network management systems to monitor network-attached devices for conditions that warrant administrative attention. SNMP is a component of the Internet Protocol Suite as defined by the IETF. An SNMP-managed network consists of three main components: managed devices—devices that are to be managed, like a switch or router; an agent—software which runs on managed devices and is responsible for the management information base (MIB); and a network management station (NMS)—software which runs on the manager.

software-defined networking (SDN)—SDN redefines the way we think about the network and removes the barriers to innovation by giving cloud providers and enterprises complete programmatic control of a dynamic, abstracted view of the network. With software-defined network technologies, IT can become more agile by orchestrating network services and automatically controlling the network according to high-level policies rather than low-level network device configurations. SDN represents a new architecture that separates the network control plane from the forwarding hardware, allowing a centralized controller (or set of controllers) to define forwarding behavior through high-level policy.

Spanning Tree Protocol—STP, as defined in IEEE's 802.1D standard, enables administrators to build redundancy into switched networks. When STP is enabled, the switches elect a switch to be the root bridge (the central point of the STP network), detect redundant links, calculate the lowest-cost path (or preferred path) to the root, and block all other redundant links. The ports that provide the lowest-cost path through the network are put in a forwarding state, and all other (redundant) ports are placed in a blocking state. A blocked port is not used to forward traffic. If a link in the preferred network path fails, STP changes the state of a blocked link from blocking (or discarding) to forwarding to enable connectivity.

split horizon—Split horizon is designed to prevent routing loops from being generated by adjacent routers. This feature is of particular value when a router's path to a given router is via another router. Split horizon allows a routing broadcast to be modified so that routers with intermediate routers in their path to a destination router are not seen as a path to the destination router by the intermediate router. Split horizon is used to deal with small routing loops in a network.

storage area network—A SAN is a dedicated network that provides access to consolidated, block-level data storage. SANs are primarily used to make storage devices, such as disk arrays and tape libraries, accessible to servers so that the devices appear like locally attached devices to the operating system.

stub network—An OSPF stub network is a network on which the router has no neighbors. The router advertises these networks as *stub networks*. The network address for the stub link is defined as the link ID, and the network mask is defined as the link data.

super VLAN—As a general rule, one IP host address is used per VLAN interface. There can be cases in which the IP host addresses are scarce and optimization is required. This optimization can be achieved by implementing a super VLAN. (This feature is also called *VLAN aggregation*.) The super VLAN has a group of sub-VLANs, and it provides a single IP interface (a gateway) to all of the hosts in its sub-VLANs. It is a Layer 3 feature. It is important to notice that, when the super VLAN feature is used, communication between the sub-VLANs is lost because ARP requests cannot travel across VLANs and there is no routing between them. If peer-to-peer communication is required (for example, for IP telephony), the local proxy ARP feature has to be enabled. Only certain Comware switches support this feature.

supplicant—The supplicant is the wireless station that is requesting access to the network.

System View—Comware's System View allows you to make changes to the switch's configuration.

Terminal Access Controller Access-Control System—TACACS is an open standard (IETF Request for Comments [RFC]) AAA protocol, but different vendors, like Cisco and HP, made their own proprietary changes to it, basically making it a closed protocol between different vendors' networking equipment.

thin access point—Thin APs establish the wireless network and forward all traffic to a wireless controller for further processing. The controller provides all the intelligence for the wireless network.

transit network—A link with two or more OSPF routers that have formed an adjacency is referred to as a *transit network*. For these networks, the link ID is the DR (or the other end of the connection, in the case of some types of networks). The link data is the routing switch's own IP address on the network.

trunk port—A trunk port supports multiple VLANs on a single physical link; VLANs are 802.1Q tagged, and the port VLAN identifier is untagged. The PVID, by default, is the default VLAN (VLAN 1). A trunk port can carry multiple VLANs to receive and send traffic for them. Except for traffic of the default VLAN, traffic sent through a trunk port will be VLAN tagged. Usually, ports connecting network devices are configured as trunk ports.

User Access Manager (UAM)—With the UAM add-on module for IMC, the system implements unified and centralized access management, supporting access through authentications, such as LAN, WAN, WLAN, and virtual private network (VPN). It supports strong authentication using smart card, certificate, and other methods, and it supports various types of endpoint access control and identity-based network services that efficiently integrate the management of user resources and services.

User View—Comware's User View allows you to view settings, perform troubleshooting (`debug` command), clear tables (`reset` command), and manage configurations and files, and move to the System View by entering `system-view`.

Virtual LAN (VLAN)—VLANs enable you to group users by logical function instead of by physical location. This helps to control bandwidth usage within your network by allowing you to group high-bandwidth users on low-traffic segments and to organize users from different LAN segments according to their need for common resources and/or their use of individual protocols. You can also improve traffic control at the edge of your network by separating traffic of different protocol types. In addition, VLANs can enhance your network security by creating separate subnets to help control in-band access to specific network resources.

Virtual Service Community (VSC)—A VSC on an MSM AP defines the wireless services offered by the AP. Therefore, it specifies not only WLAN settings but also the egress VLAN for wireless traffic and the filters that control the traffic. The VSC is similar to a virtual AP. Each group of users can be associated to a different VSC, which can affect their security, QoS, VLAN, and other settings within the same physical MSM AP.

Wired Equivalent Privacy (WEP)—The 802.11 standard's first attempt to secure wireless transmissions was WEP. To make wireless security equal to that of a wired network, WEP was designed to provide authentication, data privacy, and data integrity. With WEP, all stations encrypt 802.11 frames with a secret key using the RC-4 encryption algorithm before transmitting them to the AP. The AP uses the same key to decrypt the frame. Similarly, the AP encrypts all traffic destined to the station with the key. The WEP algorithm, however, has severe limitations. Applications that crack WEP are readily available on the Internet, and hackers need only a small sample of data to successfully use these applications to infiltrate a wireless network.

Index

Symbols

A

B

F

G

H

I

M

N

P

Q

T